Anglo-Saxon England 27

Her mon mæg giet gesion hiora swæð

ANGLO-SAXON ENGLAND
27

Edited by
MICHAEL LAPIDGE
University of Cambridge

MALCOLM GODDEN
University of Oxford

SIMON KEYNES
University of Cambridge

PETER BAKER
University of Virginia

CARL BERKHOUT
University of Arizona

MARTIN BIDDLE
University of Oxford

MARK BLACKBURN
University of Cambridge

DANIEL DONOGHUE
Harvard University

ROBERTA FRANK
University of Toronto

RICHARD GAMESON
University of Kent at Canterbury

HELMUT GNEUSS
Universität München

PATRIZIA LENDINARA
Università di Palermo

ANDY ORCHARD
University of Cambridge

FRED ROBINSON
Yale University

DONALD SCRAGG
University of Manchester

CAMBRIDGE
UNIVERSITY PRESS

Published by the Press Syndicate of the University of Cambridge
The Edinburgh Building, Cambridge CB2 2RU, United Kingdom
40 West 20th Street, New York, NY 10011-4211, USA
10 Stamford Road, Oakleigh, Melbourne 3166, Australia

© Cambridge University Press 1998

First Published 1998

Typeset by
Servis Filmsetting Ltd
Manchester

Printed in the United Kingdom by
Redwood Books Ltd
Trowbridge

ISBN 0 521 62243 3
ISSN 0263-6751

SUBSCRIPTIONS: Anglo-Saxon England (ISSN 0263-6751) is an annual journal. The subscription price including postage (excluding VAT) of volume 27 is £67 for institutions (US$115 in the USA, Canada and Mexico), £51 (US$76 in the USA, Canada and Mexico) for individuals ordering direct from the Press and certifying that the annual is for their personal use. EU subscribers (outside the UK) who are not registered for VAT should add VAT at their country's rate. VAT registered subscribers should provide their VAT registration number. Japanese prices for institutions are available from Kinokuniya Company Ltd., P.O. Box 55, Chitose, Tokyo 156, Japan. Orders, which must be accompanied by payment, may be sent to a bookseller, subscription agent, or direct to the publishers: Cambridge University Press, The Edinburgh Building, Shaftesbury Road, Cambridge CB2 2RU, UK. Orders from the USA, Canada or Mexico should be sent to Cambridge University Press, 40 West 20th Street, New York, NY 10011-4211, USA. Prices include delivery by air.

Back volumes: £67.00 (US$115.00 in the USA, Canada and Mexico) each available from Cambridge or the American Branch of Cambridge University Press.

A catalogue record of this book is available from the British Library.

Contents

Contents

*Abbreviations listed before the bibliography (pages 295–7) are used throughout the
volume without other explanation*

The editorial assistance of Clare Orchard and Peter Jackson is gratefully acknowledged.

Illustrations

ACKNOWLEDGEMENTS

By permission of the Trustees of the British Museum the design on the cover is taken from the obverse of a silver penny issued to celebrate King Alfred's occupation and fortification of London in 886.

Permission to publish photographs has been granted by the trustees of the British Library (pls. I and II) and by the Schlossmuseum, Sondershausen (pls. III and IV).

Material should be submitted to the editor most convenient regionally, with these exceptions: an article should be sent to Martin Biddle if concerned with archaeology, to Mark Blackburn if concerned with numismatics, to Daniel Donoghue if concerned with Old English metrics, to Richard Gameson if concerned with art history, to Simon Keynes if concerned with history or onomastics, and to Michael Lapidge if concerned with Anglo-Latin or palaeography. Whenever a contribution is sent from abroad it should be accompanied by international coupons to cover the cost of return postage. A potential contributor is asked to get in touch with the editor concerned as early as possible to obtain a copy of the style sheet and to have any necessary discussion. Articles must be in English.

The editors' addresses are:

Professor P. S. Baker, Department of English, University of Virginia, Charlottesville, Virginia 22903 (USA)

Professor C. T. Berkhout, Department of English, University of Arizona, Tucson, Arizona 85721 (USA)

Mr M. Biddle, Hertford College, Oxford OX1 3BW (England)

Dr M. A. S. Blackburn, Fitzwilliam Museum, Cambridge CB2 1RB (England)

Professor D. Donoghue, Department of English, Harvard University, 8 Prescott Street, Cambridge, Massachusetts 02138 (USA)

Professor R. Frank, Centre for Medieval Studies, University of Toronto, 39 Queen's Park Crescent East, Toronto, Ontario M5S 1A1 (Canada)

Dr R. Gameson, Faculty of Humanities, Rutherford College, University of Kent at Canterbury, Canterbury, Kent CT2 7NX

Professor H. Gneuss, Institut für Englische Philologie, Universität München, Schellingstrasse 3, D-80799 München (Germany)

Professor M. R. Godden, Pembroke College, Oxford OX1 1DW (England)

Dr S. D. Keynes, Trinity College, Cambridge CB2 1TQ (England)

Professor M. Lapidge, Department of Anglo-Saxon, Norse and Celtic, University of Cambridge, 9 West Road, Cambridge CB3 9DP (England)

Professor P. Lendinara, Cattedra di Filologia Germanica, Università degli Studi di Palermo, Facoltà di Magistero, Piazza Ignazio Florio 24, 90139 Palermo (Italy)

Dr A. Orchard, Emmanuel College, Cambridge CB2 3AP (England)

Professor F. C. Robinson, Department of English, Yale University, New Haven, Connecticut 06520 (USA)

Professor D. G. Scragg, Centre for Anglo-Saxon Studies, The University of Manchester, Manchester M13 9PL (England)

Record of the eighth conference of the International Society of Anglo-Saxonists, at Università di Palermo, 7–12 July 1997

I The following papers were presented on the general theme of the conference, Anglo-Saxon Studies in the Twentieth Century: Retrospect and Prospect.

A. N. Doane, 'The History and Codicology of the "Werden Glossary"'

Scott Gwara, 'Glosses to Aldhelm's Prose *De virginitate* and Glossaries from the Anglo-Saxon Golden Age, *c.* 670–800'

Kazuyoshi Yamanouchi, 'Corrections in Old English Glosses to the Third Part of the Lambeth Psalter (Ps. XCVII–CL)'

John Gray, 'Recent Teaching Resources and "Instant Anglo-Saxon" in Australia'

Jane Roberts, '"Words and Containers": a New Look at Some Old Problems'

Susan Irvine, 'Binding the Spoken to the Unspoken: *The Wanderer* and Oral Discourse'

Haruko Momma, 'Old English as Living Language: Henry Sweet and an English School of Philology'

Kees Dekker, 'Francis Junius (1591–1677): Copyist or Editor?'

Michael D. C. Drout, 'J. R. R. Tolkien's Bequest of Anglo-Saxonism'

Jonathan Wilcox, 'Anglo-Saxon Attitudes to Laughter: the Case of Abraham and Sarah in London, British Library, Cotton Claudius B. iv'

David Johnson, 'Winchester Revisited: Æthelwold, Lucifer and the Date and Provenance of MS Junius 11'

Malcolm Godden, 'The Anglo-Saxons and the Bible: Using the *Fontes Anglo-Saxonici* Database'

Andy Orchard, 'Old Sources and New Resources: Finding the Right Formula for Boniface'

Dora Faraci, 'Sources and Cultural Background: the Example of the OE *Phoenix*'

Angelika Lutz, 'Æthelweard's *Chronicon* and Old English Literature'

Paul Szarmach, 'Alfred, Alcuin and the Soul'

Ursula Lenker, 'The Gospel Lectionary in Anglo-Saxon England: Manuscript Evidence and Liturgical Practice'

Christopher A. Jones, 'Ælfric as Liturgist: the *Letter to the Monks of Eynsham*'

Éamonn Ó Carragáin, 'Northumbria Imitating Rome: Good Friday at Ruthwell in the Eighth Century'

J. R. Hall, 'Interpreting the Thorkelin Transcripts of *Beowulf*'

Patrick Wormald, '*Beowulf*: the Redating Reassessed'

Joyce Hill, 'Exemplum and Exegesis: Working with an Intertextual Tradition'

Thomas N. Hall, 'Four Anglo-Latin Sermons in London, British Library, Cotton Tiberius C.i'

Mary T. Swan, 'Lambeth Palace 487: a Manuscript on the Margins'

C. R. E. Cubitt, 'Virginity and Misogyny in Anglo-Saxon England'

Catherine E. Karkov, 'Æthelwold and the Saints: Death, Translation and the Making of History in Tenth-Century England'

John Hines, 'Old English Studies and Anglo-Saxon Archaeology'

Catherine Hills, '*Beowulf* and Brooches? Anglo-Saxon Archaeology in the Twentieth Century'

Tim Malim, 'Investigating Anglo-Saxons in Cambridgeshire, England' (read by Catherine Hills)

Stephanie Hollis, 'The Social Milieu of Bald's *Leechbook*'

Georges Whalen, 'The Monastic Memoria of Royal Benefactors in Eleventh-Century Hagiography and Cartulary Texts'

Carole Hough, 'A New Reading of Alfred, ch. 26'

Katherine O'Brien O'Keeffe, 'Body and "Self": Construing the Anglo-Saxon Subject'

Daniel P. O'Donnell, 'A New Theory of Poetic Textual Transmission'

The following media presentation was given.

Martin Foys, 'Electronic Threads: the Bayeux Tapestry and the Digital Revolution'

The following reports were given.

Patrick Conner, Joyce Hill and Nicholas Howe, Friends of 'The Dictionary of Old English' Campaign

Phillip Pulsiano, 'Anglo-Saxon Manuscripts in Microfiche Facsimile'

Paul Szarmach, 'Sources of Anglo-Saxon Literary Culture'

A round-table discussion on Anglo-Saxon Studies in the Twenty-First Century was offered by Wilhelm G. Busse, Joyce Hill, Nicholas Howe, Katherine O'Brien O'Keeffe and Ursula Schaefer.

II   General Business Meeting held at the Facoltà di Scienze della Formazione, Via Aquileia, n. 32, Università di Palermo, on 11 July 1997, at 4:15 p.m., President Patrizia Lendinara presiding.

A The President reported on behalf of the Executive Committee:

The 1997 conference of the International Society of Anglo-Saxonists

1 The Society expressed sorrow at the deaths of Peter Clemoes, James E. Cross and John C. Pope.
2 The conference was dedicated to the memory of Peter Clemoes.
3 Gratitude was expressed to Loradana Teresi, Claudia Di Sciacca, Rosanna Zaffuto and Lilla Kopar for their generous assistance in running the conference.
4 Note was made of the appointments and honours bestowed upon the following members: Hans Sauer has become the editor of *Anglia*, and has been appointed to the Chair of English Philology at Universität München; Jonathan Wilcox has become editor of the *Old English Newsletter*; Joyce Hill continues as Pro-Vice-Chancellor of Leeds University.
B The Executive Director reported on behalf of the Executive Committee:
1 Membership dues have generated revenues of $10,330.00, yielding a balance after expenditures as of 30 June 1996 of $21,585.60. Of this amount, $8,800.32 is retained in a certificate fund.
2 As of the date of the Università di Palermo meeting, the Society records 637 active members, an increase of 34 since the last meeting of the Society. Lifetime memberships, which were introduced at the last meeting of the Society, stand at 77.
3 The Eastern European dues programme will continue until such time as individual members indicate they are able to pay dues to the Society.
4 Officers of the Society. In accordance with the Society's constitution, Patrizia Lendinara completes her term as President on 31 December 1997, after which Katherine O'Brien O'Keeffe will assume the post of President. Matti Kilpiö will assume the post of First Vice-President. Phillip Pulsiano completes his term in the office of Second Vice-President, which will be assumed by Joyce Hill. Patrick Conner completes his term as Executive Director and will be succeeded by Phillip Pulsiano.
5 Membership of the Advisory Board. The term of office expires on 31 December 1997 for the following members: Michelle Brown, Mary Clayton, Matti Kilpiö and Tadao Kubouchi. The following have been appointed as members of the Advisory Board from 1 January 1998 until 31 December 2001: Hugh Magennis, Michiko Ogura, Katalin Halácsy Scholz and Elaine M. Treharne.
6 Honorary Memerships of the Society. The Honorary Membership consists of †Peter Clemoes, Rosemary Cramp, André Crepin, René Derolez, Henry Loyn, Bruce Mitchell, Shigeru Ono, †John Pope, Helmut Gneuss, Edward B. Irving and Barbara Raw. Janet Bately has now been awarded honorary membership.
7 The Officers and Advisory Board propose the following amendment to the constitution: 'Members elected to the Advisory Board are expected

3

to fulfil the duties of a board member. Advisory Board members may be removed from the board at the discretion of the Executive Committee for non-performance of duties.' Ballots will be distributed to the membership for a vote on the proposed amendment.

8 New business. The Second Vice-President proposed to examine the possibility of publishing a volume of selected papers from the conference and to report back to the membership. The proposal was approved. On behalf of the Dictionary of Old English, Nicholas Howe asked that the Society contribute funds to the project. The Executive Committee agreed to examine the treasury and make its recommendation. During open discussion, members voiced concern regarding representation of the various fields within the discipline. The Executive Committee and the Advisory Board will examine means by which representation within in the Society can be promoted.

9 The Society expressed its gratitude to Nancy Brotherton of the Department of English of West Virginia University for her help in administering ISAS.

C The First Vice-President reported on behalf of the Executive Committee:

1 Thanks were expressed to Patrizia Lendinara for hosting a successful conference.

2 The ninth conference of the Society will be held at the University of Notre Dame, 8–14 August 1999; the theme of the conference will be 'Imagined Endings: Borders, Reigns, Millennia.'

III   The conference included two day-long excursions, the first to Palermo, Monreale and Cefalù, the second to Morgantina and Piazza Armerina.

Registration forms for the ISAS conference to be held at Notre Dame University will be mailed to all paid-up members of the Society. Payment may be made by cheque or postal money order for $15.00 or £10.00 sterling (regular members) or for $10.00 or £7.00 (student and retired members) and should be sent to Professor Phillip Pulsiano, Exec. Dir., International Society of Anglo-Saxonists, Department of English, Villanova University, Villanova, Pennsylvania, USA. Payment may be made to the Executive Director by Visa or MasterCard or by personal cheque. For members outside the US, transfers in sterling may be sent to the ISAS account, Midland Bank plc, 32 Market Hill, Cambridge CB2 3NU; sorting code no. 40-16-08, account no. 21241605. Members may arrange to pay dues for more than one year. Payment forms are available from the Executive Director.[1]

[1] This record of the Palermo meeting was compiled by Phillip Pulsiano.

4

Classical rhetoric in Anglo-Saxon England

GABRIELE KNAPPE

Hwær cwom mearg? Hwær cwom mago? Hwær cwom maþþumgyfa?
Hwær cwom symbla gesetu? Hwær sindon seledreamas?

(The Wanderer 92–3)[1]

This passage from The Wanderer demonstrates some of the rhetorical techniques
which have been noted in Old English texts. Its most striking features are the
rhetorical questions and the figure of anaphora which is produced by the repetition of 'Hwær'. Another rhetorical element is the use of the theme (topos) of ubi
sunt ('where are . . .?') to lament the loss of past joys.[2] In classical antiquity, features such as these, which served to create effective discourse, were the products
of ars rhetorica. This art was distinguished from the more basic subject of ars
grammatica in that rhetoric, the 'ars . . . bene dicendi' (Quintilian, Institutio oratoria
II.xvii.37), aimed at the good production of text (for oral delivery) with the aim of
persuading the listeners to take or adopt some form of action or belief, whereas
grammar, the 'recte loquendi scientia', was responsible for correct speech and also
for the interpretation of poetical texts ('poetarum enarratio': Quintilian,
Institutio oratoria I.iv.2).[3] In terms of classical rhetoric, the above passage from
The Wanderer could be analysed according to the three phases of the production

---

[1] ASPR III, 136: 'Where has gone the steed? Where has gone the man? Where has gone the giver
of treasure? Where has gone the place of the banquets? Where are the pleasures of the hall?'
(trans. S. A. J. Bradley, Anglo-Saxon Poetry: an Anthology of Old English Poems in Prose Translation
(London and Melbourne, 1982), p. 324).

[2] The theme of ubi sunt, usually expressed by 'where are . . . ?' questions, has been thoroughly
investigated by J. E. Cross, ' "Ubi Sunt" Passages in Old English – Sources and Relationships',
Vetenskaps-Societeten i Lund Årsbok (1956), pp. 23–44, and idem, Latin Themes in Old English Poetry
(Bristol, 1962), pp. 2–5. On further topoi in The Wanderer, see below, pp. 25–6 and nn. 88–9; for
anaphora, see below, p. 23, n. 76.

[3] The quotations are taken from M. Fabi Quintiliani Institutionis oratoriae libri duodecim, ed. M.
Winterbottom, 2 vols. (Oxford, 1970). See also the concise definition of rhetoric by the late
antique encyclopedist Isidore of Seville, Isidori Hispalensis Episcopi Etymologiarum sive Originum
libri XX, ed. W. M. Lindsay, 2 vols. (Oxford, 1911), II.i.1. Some rhetorical principles can be
transferred to the writing of verse (poetics) without difficulty – the basic parts of both disciplines are identical and rhetoric had always been the one which was elaborated in detail. See H.
Lausberg, Handbuch der literarischen Rhetorik: eine Grundlegung der Literaturwissenschaft (Munich,
1960; repr. Stuttgart, 1990 with a preface by A. Arens), § 35. Rhetoric has been used for the
analysis of both prose and verse in modern scholarship.

of a text (*partes artis*) which pertain to both written and oral discourse: *inventio* (finding topics such as the *ubi sunt*), *dispositio* (arranging the parts of the text)[4] and *elocutio* (embellishing the text stylistically, for example with rhetorical questions and other figures and tropes).[5]

How and under what circumstances did the Anglo-Saxons acquire their knowledge of how to compose a text effectively? We should indeed be careful about attributing rhetorical features of Old English (and Anglo-Latin) texts to a direct influence of the *ars bene dicendi* because, generally speaking, there are no indications that scholars in Anglo-Saxon England (*c.* 700–1066) studied this discipline.[6] In order to understand the nature of Anglo-Saxon rhetorical learning it is first of all necessary to consider the different traditions of classical rhetoric together with their adaptation in Anglo-Saxon England while taking into account the specific literary culture of the time – the age of the *grammaticus*.[7]

---

[4] Thus, McPherson has suggested that an instance of the *ubi sunt* theme in *The Seafarer* 80b–83 (ASPR III, 145), belongs to the third part of a speech (*confirmatio*) within her theory that this elegy is a speech in reply to a first speech. See C. W. McPherson, 'The Influence of Latin Rhetoric on Old English Poetry' (unpubl. PhD dissertation, Washington Univ., 1980), pp. 175–98 and below, pp. 26–7.

[5] For the *partes artis*, see Lausberg, *Handbuch*, §§ 255–1091. The other two *partes* pertain to the oral medium only. These are *memoria* (learning the text by heart) and *actio* or *pronuntiatio* (performing the speech). To my knowledge, there is no indication that *memoria* and *actio* were of theoretical interest in Anglo-Saxon England. For techniques of *memoria* in the monastic culture, without a classical rhetorical background, see P. Riché, 'Le rôle de la mémoire dans l'enseignement médiéval', *Jeux de mémoire: aspects de la mnemotechnie médiévale*, ed. B. Roy and P. Zumthor (Montréal, 1985), pp. 133–48, esp. 133–41.

[6] The exceptional role of Alcuin will be discussed separately below, pp. 12–13. Knowledge of classical rhetoric in Anglo-Saxon England has been investigated above all by J. J. Campbell, 'Knowledge of Rhetorical Figures in Anglo-Saxon England', *JEGP* 66 (1967), 1–20; idem, 'Adaptation of Classical Rhetoric in Old English Literature', *Medieval Eloquence: Studies in the Theory and Practice of Medieval Rhetoric*, ed. J. J. Murphy (Berkeley, CA, 1978), pp. 173–97; L. M. Reinsma, 'Rhetoric in England: the Age of Aelfric, 970–1020', *Communication Monographs* 44 (1977), 390–403; idem, 'Ælfric: the Teacher as Rhetorician' (unpubl. PhD dissertation, Univ. of Michigan, 1978), esp. part I; R. Ray, 'Bede and Cicero', *ASE* 16 (1987), 1–15; H. Gneuss, 'The Study of Language in Anglo-Saxon England', *Bull. of the John Rylands Univ. Lib. of Manchester* 72 (1990), 1–32, at 28–32. See also the annotated bibliography by L. M. Reinsma, 'Rhetoric, Grammar, and Literature in England and Ireland before the Norman Conquest: a Select Bibliography', *Rhetoric Soc. Quarterly* 8.1 (1978), 29–48, and idem, 'Middle Ages', *Historical Rhetoric: an Annotated Bibliography of Selected Sources in English*, ed. W. B. Horner (Boston, MA, 1980), pp. 45–108. The present article presents the essential results of my *Traditionen der klassischen Rhetorik im angelsächsischen England*, Anglistische Forschungen 236 (Heidelberg, 1996).

[7] On the grammatical nature of Anglo-Saxon literary culture, see esp. Gneuss, 'The Study of Language', V. Law, *The Insular Latin Grammarians*, Stud. in Celtic Hist. 3 (Woodbridge, 1982) and the recent study by M. Irvine, *The Making of Textual Culture: 'Grammatica' and Literary Theory, 350–1100*, Cambridge Stud. in Med. Lit. 19 (Cambridge, 1994), esp. chs. 7–9.

TRADITIONS OF CLASSICAL RHETORIC

Before the emergence of the *artes* (*poetriae, dictaminis* and *praedicandi*) from *c.* 1100 onwards, the *ars bene dicendi* did not undergo a thorough transformation and adaptation to the needs of the day.[8] Rather, what we encounter in late antiquity are attempts to reduce this complex lore to manageable proportions. What is more, with the growing importance and status of the grammar teacher and the declining impact of rhetoric in a Christian culture focused on the interpretation or exegesis of the written word, rhetorical lore subtly entered the field of grammar. It is this last aspect which is of particular importance in the early Middle Ages. Therefore, two main traditions will be distinguished here: the rhetorical tradition of antiquity and the tradition of rhetoric within grammar.[9]

The rhetorical tradition of antiquity can be traced back to Greece but, because the Anglo-Saxons could not in general read Greek texts,[10] this survey starts from Roman antiquity. Rhetorical works in this tradition transmit, excerpt or discuss the *ars bene dicendi* as it is outlined by Cicero, the pseudo-Ciceronian *Rhetorica ad Herennium* and in Quintilian's *Institutio oratoria*.[11] Several types of textbooks

---

[8] On the later *artes*, see J. J. Murphy, *Rhetoric in the Middle Ages: a History of Rhetorical Theory from Saint Augustine to the Renaissance* (Berkeley, CA, and London, 1974), chs. 4–6, and literature cited in Knappe, *Traditionen*, pp. 4–6.

[9] On the following, and for details of the works referred to here, see Knappe, *Traditionen*, pp. 43–109 (part II). Earlier classifications of traditions of classical rhetoric include Reinsma, 'Rhetoric in England', pp. 393–403 (Augustinian, encyclopedic and grammatical traditions) and Gneuss, 'The Study of Language', pp. 28–31 (classical and grammatical traditions). The 'encyclopedic' and 'Christian' traditions are here subsumed within the rhetorical tradition of antiquity, and the full impact of the 'grammatical' tradition, which refers solely to the figures and tropes in the grammars in the studies mentioned above, is elaborated in the tradition of rhetoric within grammar.

[10] One notable exception is the school of Theodore and Hadrian in Canterbury in the late seventh century. See M. Lapidge, 'The Study of Greek at the School of Canterbury in the Seventh Century', *The Sacred Nectar of the Greeks: the Study of Greek in the West in the Early Middle Ages*, ed. M. W. Herren, King's College London Med. Stud. 2 (London, 1988), 168–94, and *idem* in *Biblical Commentaries from the Canterbury School of Theodore and Hadrian*, ed. B. Bischoff and M. Lapidge, CSASE 10 (Cambridge, 1994), esp. 240–2. See also M. C. Bodden, 'Evidence for Knowledge of Greek in Anglo-Saxon England', *ASE* 17 (1988), 217–46.

[11] On classical rhetoric in antiquity and late antiquity, see esp. the chronological survey in Murphy, *Rhetoric in the Middle Ages*, chs. 1–2; G. A. Kennedy, *The Art of Rhetoric in the Roman World: 300 B.C.–A.D. 300*, A Hist. of Rhetoric 2 (Princeton, NJ, 1972); T. M. Conley, *Rhetoric in the European Tradition* (Chicago, IL and London, 1994), chs. 1–4; B. Vickers, *In Defence of Rhetoric* (Oxford, 1988), ch. 1; M. L. Clarke, *Rhetoric at Rome: a Historical Survey* (London, 1953); D. L. Clark, *Rhetoric in Greco-Roman Education* (New York, 1957); C. S. Baldwin, *Medieval Rhetoric and Poetic (to 1400): Interpreted from Representative Works* (New York, 1928), chs. 1–5; J. O. Ward, '*Artificiosa eloquentia* in the Middle Ages', 2 vols. (unpubl. PhD dissertation, Toronto Univ., 1972), esp. I, 37–118; *idem, Ciceronian Rhetoric in Treatise, Scholion and Commentary*, Typologie des sources du moyen âge occidental 58 (Turnhout, 1995), pp. 76–104. Rhetoric is also very close to logic and dialectic; see the summary in Knappe, *Traditionen*, pp. 78–82, and below, p. 13, n. 31.

belong to this tradition. Apart from the ones already mentioned, these are late antique compendia and commentaries, chapters on rhetoric in the encyclopedias by Martianus Capella, Cassiodorus and Isidore of Seville and separate treatises both on basic rhetorical exercises (the *progymnasmata* or *praeexercitamina*) and on the rhetorical figures and tropes. Particularly the *praeexercitamina* and the treatises on the figures and tropes reflect an important cultural change in late antiquity. Juridical (forensic) rhetoric, which used to be the main concern of Ciceronian rhetoric, was declining at a time when the legal system had changed, and subsequently the other two *genera causarum*, deliberative and especially epideictic speeches in praise or censure of people, were gaining ground.[12] This led to rhetorical teaching which concentrated on the style of a speech and only to a lesser degree on its contents.[13] Finally, this tradition was controversially discussed by the Christians who, on the one hand, feared the power of the heathen art of persuasion and, on the other, were tempted to use their own rhetorical education against their religious opponents. It was St Augustine who, in bk IV of his *De doctrina christiana*, defended the potential use of the *ars bene dicendi* for the preacher (without discussing the rules). However, he also stated that learning from models can be of greater use than knowing rhetorical rules, 'Quoniam si acutum et fervens adsit ingenium, facilius adhaeret eloquentia legentibus et audientibus eloquentes quam eloquentiae praecepta sectantibus' (*De doctrina christiana* IV.iii.4).[14] The Christian teachers did not transform the art of rhetoric written for orators to suit the needs of the preacher.

The tradition of rhetoric within grammar is more complex. While the *ars rhetorica* was losing ground, other cultural conditions favoured the importance and enrichment of *ars grammatica*. As the indispensable foundation of all learning, the *recte loquendi scientia* retained its important status. Furthermore, Christian learning brought with it a different and more grammatically oriented approach.[15]

---

[12] For the *genera causarum* (*genus iudiciale, genus deliberativum* and *genus demonstrativum*), see Lausberg, *Handbuch*, §§ 61 and 139–254.

[13] On the developments in the so-called 'Second Sophistic' (*c.* 50–400) and the set speeches typical of the time, the *declamationes*, see Murphy, *Rhetoric in the Middle Ages*, pp. 35–42, Baldwin, *Medieval Rhetoric and Poetic*, pp. 8–50 and Kennedy, *The Art of Rhetoric*, pp. 301–472, esp. 428–61.

[14] *De doctrina christiana*, ed. W. M. Green, *Sancti Aureli Augustini opera VI*, CSEL 80 (Vienna, 1963), pp. 119–20: 'For those with acute and eager minds more readily learn eloquence by reading and hearing the eloquent than by following the rules of eloquence' (trans. D. W. Robertson, Jr, *Saint Augustine: On Christian Doctrine*, Library of Liberal Arts 80 (New York, 1958), 119). For the dilemma of the Church Fathers and the role of St Augustine, see J. J. Murphy, 'Saint Augustine and the Debate about a Christian Rhetoric', *Quarterly Jnl of Speech* 46 (1960), 400–10; *idem, Rhetoric in the Middle Ages*, pp. 46–64; H.-I. Marrou, *Saint Augustin et la fin de la culture antique*, 4th ed. (Paris, 1958); E. L. Fortin, 'Augustine and the Problem of Christian Rhetoric', *Augustinian Stud.* 5 (1974), 85–100. Cf. the discussion in Knappe, *Traditionen*, pp. 63–72.

[15] For surveys of grammar and grammarians in late antiquity, see in particular R. A. Kaster, *Guardians of Language: the Grammarian and Society in Late Antiquity*, Transformation of the Classical Heritage 11 (Berkeley, CA, 1988); *idem*, 'Islands in the Stream: the Grammarians of

Christian scholars were first and foremost concerned with the correct interpretation (exegesis) of the Holy Scriptures and other Christian writings. Therefore, they valued the second *officium* of *ars grammatica* very highly, namely *poetarum enarratio*, the interpretation of the poets (and also of prose).[16] For this grammatical task the exegetes did not hesitate to turn to rhetorical means. This tradition will be referred to as 'grammatical rhetoric'. In the wider sense of the term, grammatical rhetoric refers to rhetorical concepts which are used for interpretation but have not entered grammar textbooks. This is the case, for example, with the *genera dicendi* in commentaries on Vergil and in Cassiodorus's *Expositio psalmorum* where, among other things, a great number of figures and tropes in the rhetorical tradition are used for the interpretation of the psalms.[17] In the narrower sense of the term, grammatical rhetoric is apparent in the inclusion of rhetorical lore within grammar books as, for example, the treatment of the figures of sense in Charisius's grammar.[18] The main 'intrusion', to use James

Late Antiquity', *The History of Linguistics in the Classical Period*, ed. D. J. Taylor, Stud. in the Hist. of the Lang. Sciences, Amsterdam Stud. in the Theory and Hist. of Ling. Science III/46 (Amsterdam, 1987), 149–68; Irvine, *The Making of Textual Culture*, chs. 1–6; Marrou, *Augustin*, pp. 3–26 and 422–44.

16 Note also the flourishing of commentaries on Vergil. For the interpretation of prose by grammatical methods, see Quintilian, *Institutio oratoria* I.iv.2 and I.iv.4, and the definition of grammar by Cassiodorus (*Institutiones* II.i.1), quoted below, pp. 10–11. While rhetoric focuses on the production of texts, grammar is based on interpretation. These are the main tasks (*officia*) of the two arts although there is some overlap. Rhetoric, too, used to be concerned with interpretation (of prose), and the *ars recte loquendi* has certainly a productive aspect.

17 For the *genera dicendi* in commentaries on Vergil, see F. Quadlbauer, *Die antike Theorie der Genera Dicendi im lateinischen Mittelalter*, Österreichische Akademie der Wissenschaften, philosophischhistorische Klasse, Sitzungsberichte 241.2 (Vienna, 1962), 10–15. Cassiodorus's use of rhetorical figures and tropes in his commentary on the psalms and his sources are discussed in U. Schindel, 'Textkritisches zu lateinischen Figurenlehren (Anecdoton Parisinum, Cassiodor, Quintilian)', *Glotta* 52 (1974), 95–114; *Anonymus Ecksteinii: Scemata dianoeas quae ad rhetores pertinent*, ed. U. Schindel, Nachrichten der Akademie der Wissenschaften zu Göttingen I, philologisch-historische Klasse, 1987 no. 7 (Göttingen, 1987), introd., esp. pp. 5 and 45; J. M. Courtès, 'Figures et tropes dans le psautier de Cassiodore', *Revue des études latines* 42 (1964), 361–75. See Knappe, *Traditionen*, pp. 97–100. An index of the figures and tropes in Cassiodorus's *Expositio psalmorum* is provided *ibid*. Appendix B. This index is based on the marginal *notae* to the text reproduced in *Magni Aurelii Cassiodori Expositio psalmorum*, ed. M. Adriaen, 2 vols., CCSL 97–8 (Turnhout, 1958).

18 *Flavii Sosipatri Charisii Artis grammaticae libri V*, ed. K. Barwick, repr. with addenda and corrigenda by F. Kühnert (Leipzig, 1964), p. 371, line 29–p. 375, line 9. The figures of sense traditionally belong to rhetorical treatises only; see, for example, the typical statement by Donatus, *Ars maior* III.5, ed. L. Holtz, *Donat et la tradition de l'enseignement grammatical: étude sur l'Ars Donati et sa diffusion (IVe–IXe siècle) et édition critique* (Paris, 1981), pp. 603–74, at 663. Other intrusions of rhetorical lore into the grammars include *memoria* and *chria* in Diomedes's *Ars grammatica*; see *Grammatici latini*, ed. H. Keil, M. Hertz [for vols. 2 and 3: Priscian] and H. Hagen [for vol. 8: *Anecdota Helvetica*], 8 vols. (Leipzig, 1855–80) [=*GL*], I, 419, lines 22–5 and 310, lines 1–29, and fable ('de fabula') and narrative ('de historia') in Isidore's *Etymologiae* I.xl and xli. On these chapters in Isidore, see especially J. Fontaine, *Isidore de Séville et la culture classique dans l'Espagne wisigothique*, 2nd ed. (Paris, 1983), pp. 179–80, and Irvine, *The Making of Textual Culture*, pp. 261 and 234–41.

J. Murphy's term,[19] is that sections on the figures of diction and the tropes appear in a number of late antique grammars. Among these, bk III of Aelius Donatus's *Ars maior* (this book is sometimes also called *Barbarismus* because this is its first word) is the most important for the early Middle Ages. One has to be careful, however, about speaking of rhetorical lore in this case, because the figures and tropes in the grammars seem from very early on to have a distinct tradition from the rhetorical treatises; but it is not improbable that they originate in rhetorical teaching. Being defined as poetic licences (*virtutes orationis*), they are firmly connected to the vices of speech (*vitia orationis*) which make up the first part of the *Barbarismus*, and thus to the aspect of *recte loqui*.[20]

Grammatical studies can also be seen to transgress their proper sphere and enter the field of rhetoric in that they are concerned with the good production of text.[21] In this case we are dealing with the rhetorical aspect of grammar teaching. This development is usually not reflected in the definitions of the arts, which tend to be of a conservative nature. One remarkable exception, however, is Cassiodorus's definition of grammar (*Institutiones* II.i.1): 'grammatica vero est peritia pulchre

---

[19] J. J. Murphy, 'The Rhetorical Lore of the *Boceras* in Byrhtferth's *Manual*', *Philological Essays: Studies in Old and Middle English Language and Literature in Honor of H. D. Meritt*, ed. J. L. Rosier (The Hague, 1970), pp. 111–24, at 114.

[20] The term *Barbarismus* is henceforth used to refer to the sections in grammars which correspond to *Ars maior* III. For surveys of figures and tropes in the grammars, see U. Schindel, *Die lateinischen Figurenlehren des 5. bis 7. Jahrhunderts und Donats Vergilkommentar (mit zwei Editionen)*, Abhandlungen der Akademie der Wissenschaften in Göttingen, philologisch-historische Klasse, 3rd ser. 91 (Göttingen, 1975); *idem*, 'Die Quellen von Bedas Figurenlehre', *Classica et Mediaevalia* 29 (1968), 169–86; L. Holtz, 'Grammairiens et rhéteurs romains en concurrence pour l'enseignement des figures de rhétorique', *Colloque sur la rhétorique: Calliope I*, ed. R. Chevallier (Paris, 1979), pp. 207–20; *idem*, *Donat*, pp. 69–74 and 136–216; Murphy, *Rhetoric in the Middle Ages*, p. 32; *idem*, 'Rhetorical Lore', esp. pp. 111–19. On problems concerning the make-up and origin of the *Barbarismus*, see especially the discussions in K. Barwick, *Remmius Palaemon und die römische ars grammatica*, Philologus Supplement 15.2 (Leipzig, 1922), 89–108; M. Baratin and F. Desbordes, 'La "troisième partie" de l'*ars grammatica*', *The History of Linguistics in the Classical Period*, ed. Taylor, 41–66; D. M. Schenkeveld, 'Figures and Tropes: a Border-Case between Grammar and Rhetoric', *Rhetorik zwischen den Wissenschaften: Geschichte, System, Praxis als Probleme des 'Historischen Wörterbuchs der Rhetorik'*, ed. G. Ueding, Rhetorik-Forschungen 1 (Tübingen, 1991), 149–57. See also Knappe, *Traditionen*, pp. 86–97.

[21] This development (the close link between interpretation and production, i.e. the rhetorical principles of *ars grammatica* in late antiquity) has been noted by M. J. Irvine, 'Grasping the Word: "Ars Grammatica" and Literary Theory from Late Antiquity to the Carolingian Period' (unpubl. PhD dissertation, Harvard Univ., 1982), pp. 192, 309 and 356, n. 5 (for Anglo-Saxon England), *idem*, *The Making of Textual Culture*, pp. 7–8, 50–1, 54–5, 197, 206, 304, 319, 326, 426 and 440, and by Rita Copeland in her study of translation practice, 'As hermeneutics supplanted rhetoric as the master curricular practice, it also assumed the character of rhetoric': R. Copeland, *Rhetoric, Hermeneutics, and Translation in the Middle Ages: Academic Traditions and Vernacular Texts*, Cambridge Stud. in Med. Lit. 11 (Cambridge, 1991), 62; see also *ibid.* p. 55, and Knappe, *Traditionen*, pp. 100–7.

loquendi ex poetis illustribus auctoribusque collecta; officium eius est sine vitio dictionem prosalem metricamque componere; finis vero elimatae locutionis vel scripturae inculpabili placere peritia.'[22] This definition reflects the rhetorical nature of grammatical studies in that grammar is defined as the art of good or pleasing speech ('peritia pulchre loquendi') concerned with verse but also with prose interpretation ('auctoribusque') and production ('dictionem prosalem metricamque componere') with the aim of pleasing the listeners and readers ('placere'). These developments not only affected questions of style (*elocutio*), but also of invention and arrangement (*inventio* and *dispositio*). Other evidence from late antiquity, especially as found in the *Hermeneumata Celtis* from the early fifth century, points to the fact that Cassiodorus's definition of grammar does indeed mirror the practice of the time.[23] It was in fact as early as the first century AD that Quintilian (*Institutio oratoria* I.ix.6 and II.i, esp. II.i.2 and II.i.8–9) complained about grammar teachers infringing the field of the teachers of rhetoric especially with regard to set deliberative speeches (*suasoriae*) and basic rhetorical exercises (*praeexercitamina*) such as *prosopopoeia, narratio, laus* and others.[24] It was not pure chance that a grammar teacher, Priscian, translated the *Progymnasmata* by Hermogenes in his *Praeexercitamina*. Headings to this text in medieval manuscripts and its inclusion in collections of both rhetorical and grammatical works in the Middle Ages and today (for example, *Rhetores latini minores* and *Grammatici latini*) reveal that this text has never given up its intermediate position between rhetorical and grammatical studies.[25]

---

[22] *Cassiodori Senatoris Institutiones*, ed. R. A. B. Mynors (Oxford, 1937), p. 94: 'Grammar is skill in the art of cultivated speech – skill acquired from famous writers of poetry and of prose; its function is the creation of faultless prose and verse; its end is to please through skill in finished speech and blameless writing' (trans. L. W. Jones, *An Introduction to Divine and Human Readings by Cassiodorus Senator* (New York, 1946), p. 146).

[23] The *Hermeneumata Celtis* describe some aspects of language teaching practice in late antiquity, and rhetorical exercises are part of the grammarian's teaching; see A. C. Dionisotti, 'From Ausonius' Schooldays? A Schoolbook and its Relatives', *Jnl of Roman Stud.* 72 (1982), 83–125 (with an edition), esp. pp. 100–1, and P. L. Schmidt, '"De honestis et nove veterum dictis." Die Autorität der *veteres* von Nonius Marcellus bis zu Matheus Vindocinensis', *Klassik im Vergleich: Normativität und Historizität europäischer Klassiken*, ed. W. Voßkamp (Stuttgart, 1993), pp. 366–88, at 368–9. Cf. also Knappe, *Traditionen*, pp. 105–6.

[24] On basic exercises taught by the grammarian, such as paraphrases and *sententiae*, see Quintilian, *Institutio oratoria* I.ix.1–6.

[25] See *Rhetores latini minores: ex codicibus maximam partem primum adhibitis*, ed. K. Halm (Leipzig, 1863), pp. 551–60, and *GL* III, 430–40. On the headings in manuscripts which characterize the work as rhetorical but its author (translator) as a grammarian, see *Prisciani Caesariensis opuscula*, I: *De figuris numerorum, De metris Terentii, Praeexercitamina*, ed. M. Passalacqua, Sussidi eruditi 40 (Rome, 1987), introd., pp. xxxix and xliv. The manuscripts include this work in grammatical collections (especially from the eighth to the twelfth centuries) and rhetorical ones (especially from the fourteenth to the sixteenth centuries); see Knappe, *Traditionen*, pp. 124–5. A list of the manuscripts is given in Passalacqua's edition, introd., pp. xxix–xxx. See also her study of Priscian manuscripts, *I codici di Prisciano*, Sussidi eruditi 29 (Rome, 1978).

Gabriele Knappe

'ILLIS RHETORICAE INFUNDENS REFLUAMINA LINGUAE':
KNOWLEDGE OF THE TRADITIONS OF CLASSICAL RHETORIC IN
ANGLO-SAXON ENGLAND

The rhetorical tradition of antiquity

In his panegyric poem on York (*Versus de patribus, regibus et sanctis Euboricensis ecclesiae*), Alcuin claimed that rhetoric was taught as part of the classical *trivium* (grammar, rhetoric and dialectic) by his teacher Ælberht in eighth-century York:

> ille, ubi diversis sitientia corda fluentis
> doctrinae et vario studiorum rore rigabat,
> his dans grammaticae rationis gnaviter artes,
> illis rhetoricae infundens refluamina linguae.
> Istos veridica curavit cote polire . . .[26]

If indeed classical rhetoric was part of Ælberht's curriculum, this was probably unique in the whole Anglo-Saxon period. However, it would be dangerous to take Alcuin's statement at face value.[27] Although it cannot of course be positively excluded that Ælberht did teach some rhetoric to a small group of his students, it is more likely that the outstanding scholar Alcuin, who was the first and, for more than two hundred years, the only medieval writer of a textbook in the rhetorical tradition of antiquity (his *Dialogus de rhetorica et de virtutibus*, of *c.* 794), acquired his knowledge of rhetorical theory not in England but at the court of Charlemagne on the Continent.[28] There, Alcuin taught and wrote treatises on all

---

[26] *Alcuin: The Bishops, Kings, and Saints of York*, ed. P. Godman (Oxford, 1982), p. 112, lines 1432–6: 'There he watered parched hearts with diverse streams of learning and the varied dew of knowledge: skilfully training some in the arts and rules of grammar and pouring upon others a flood of rhetorical eloquence. Some he polished with the whetstone of true speech . . . .'

[27] It is quite possible that an *ideal* course of studies is being formulated here; see *Alcuin*, ed. Godman, p. 112, note to lines 1432–3. Likewise, the mention that Cicero was available in York ('rhetor . . . Tullius ingens', verse 1550) can be taken as a 'learned advertisement', *ibid.* introd., p. lxvi; but see also Schmidt, ' "*De honestis et nove veterum dictis*" ', p. 376. For Alcuin's booklist, see further M. Lapidge, 'Surviving Booklists from Anglo-Saxon England', *Learning and Literature in Anglo-Saxon England: Studies presented to Peter Clemoes on the Occasion of his Sixty-Fifth Birthday*, ed. M. Lapidge and H. Gneuss (Cambridge, 1985), pp. 33–89, at 45–9. For Ælberht's journeys to the Continent and their impact on the York library, see H. Gneuss, 'Anglo-Saxon Libraries from the Conversion to the Benedictine Reform', *SettSpol* 32 (1986), 643–88, at 655. See also the discussion in Knappe, *Traditionen*, pp. 166–71.

[28] See also Gneuss, 'The Study of Language', p. 29. Alcuin worked at the court of Charlemagne from 781 or 782 onwards, that is, he spent roughly ten years away from England before he wrote his work on rhetoric (and his poem on York). Notker Labeo's *Rhetorica nova*, Anselm of Besate's *Rhetorimachia* and Onulf of Speyer's *Colores rhetorici* are much later (first half of the eleventh century) and anticipate the development of the later medieval *artes*. For continental rhetorical studies after Alcuin, see Conley, *Rhetoric in the European Tradition*, ch. 4, and literature referred to in Knappe, *Traditionen*, pp. 177–84.

three subjects of the *trivium*. His *Dialogus*, written in the form of a dialogue between himself and Charlemagne, is an adaptation mainly of Cicero's *De inventione* and Julius Victor's *Ars rhetorica*.[29] While Alcuin's compilation is mostly traditional, slight adaptations have been noted. These are the important status of grammar, the discussion of the virtues which combines the Stoic and the Augustinian positions and the practical use of the treatise for Charlemagne as a secular ruler and judge.[30]

The evidence suggests that Alcuin was the only Anglo-Saxon who was well acquainted with the rhetorical tradition of antiquity. In fact, whereas dialectic was apparently known and to some extent studied in Anglo-Saxon England,[31] there is (despite Alcuin's testimony) no firm evidence as regards the rhetorical tradition of antiquity. An examination of the manuscript tradition, the evidence of surviving booklists and Anglo-Saxon statements of, or references to, this tradition reveal that hardly any of the texts were actually known.[32] Even Alcuin's *Dialogus* apparently did not reach Anglo-Saxon England.[33] Available were the encyclopedic works by Martianus Capella (in the later but probably also in the earlier period) and the Carolingian commentaries on Martianus Capella, Cassiodorus (bk II of the *Institutiones* was possibly known, especially in the earlier period) and Isidore's *Etymologiae* which were widely used.[34]

---

[29] See *The Rhetoric of Alcuin and Charlemagne*, ed. and trans. W. S. Howell, Princeton Stud. in Eng. 23 (Princeton, NJ, 1941), introd., pp. 22–33, and L. Wallach, *Alcuin and Charlemagne: Studies in Carolingian History and Literature*, Cornell Stud. in Classical Philol. 32 (Ithaca, NY, 1959), 35–47.

[30] On these three points, see Irvine, *The Making of Textual Culture*, pp. 325–7, S. Mähl, *Quadriga virtutum: die Kardinaltugenden in der Geistesgeschichte der Karolingerzeit*, Beihefte zum Archiv für Kulturgeschichte 9 (Vienna, 1969), esp. 124, and Wallach, *Alcuin and Charlemagne*, pp. 31–3, 48–59, 60–72 and 77–82, respectively, but also Irvine, *The Making of Textual Culture*, p. 325, and Ward, '*Artificiosa eloquentia*' I, 125–33. See the discussion in Knappe, *Traditionen*, pp. 161–6.

[31] For the three distinct periods of Anglo-Saxon learning, see Gneuss, 'The Study of Language', p. 5. Due to the decline of learning in the second period, only the first and the third periods are of importance here, i.e. (late) seventh and eighth, and late ninth (tenth) to the eleventh centuries. For a discussion of the knowledge of manuscripts including dialectical works and the study of this discipline by Aldhelm and in tenth-century Winchester (in the *Altercatio magistri et discipuli*), see Knappe, *Traditionen*, pp. 145–7, 251 and esp. at 185–8. For an edition and discussion of the *Altercatio*, see M. Lapidge, 'Three Latin Poems from Æthelwold's School at Winchester', *ASE* 1 (1972), 85–137, at 105–21 and 95–102.

[32] See the survey in Knappe, *Traditionen*, pp. 111–203, which is based on Gneuss, 'The Study of Language', *idem*, 'A Preliminary List of Manuscripts Written or Owned in England up to 1100', *ASE* 9 (1980), 1–60, Lapidge, 'Surviving Booklists', the relevant sections in *Sources of Anglo-Saxon Literary Culture: a Trial Version*, ed. F. M. Biggs, T. D. Hill and P. E. Szarmach, Med. & Renaissance Texts and Stud. 74 (Binghamton, NY, 1990) and *Texts and Transmission: a Survey of the Latin Classics*, ed. L. D. Reynolds (Oxford, 1983).

[33] On the reception of this work, see the discussion in Knappe, *Traditionen*, pp. 171–6. A list of the manuscripts and entries in medieval booklists is provided *ibid*. Appendix C.

[34] See Gneuss, 'The Study of Language', p. 9, n. 23, p. 29 and n. 106 and pp. 11–12 and nn. 36–7, and Knappe, *Traditionen*, pp. 127–35.

Additionally, there are some indications that Augustine's statements on the use of rhetoric for the preacher and probably also Hrabanus Maurus's views, which are based on Augustine and set out in bk III of his *De clericorum institutione* (*c.* 819), were known.[35] There are also tentative indications based on the analysis of Old English poetical texts that Priscian's *Praeexercitamina* were studied.[36] But neither Roger Ray's argument that Bede used rhetorical strategies nor Lupus of Ferrières's letter to Ealdsige of York (*c.* 849) in which he enquired after the full version of Quintilian's *Institutio oratoria* have the status of proof.[37]

From the rare statements on rhetoric which have come down to us, on the other hand, the Anglo-Saxons cannot be said to have rejected this art as such. There is certainly no need to postulate Christian distrust of this heathen art for Bede, Aldhelm or Ælfric.[38] In fact Bede, in his *Liber de schematibus et tropis*, stands in the Augustinian tradition by making use of secular learning for Christian purposes (here it is grammar), just like Cassiodorus before him. There are even indications that Aldhelm was familiar with some basics of classical rhetoric, perhaps through Isidore's *Etymologiae*.[39] However, when Felix of Crowland in his *Vita S. Guthlaci* (*c.* 730–40) praised the 'many . . . English scholars in our midst who make the waters of genius flow in pure and lucid streams among the flowers of rhetoric and amid the green meadows of literature',[40] he was probably referring to the tradition of rhetoric within grammar.

While Alcuin's *Dialogus* did not find much acceptance among his con-

[35] See Gneuss, 'The Study of Language', p. 28 and n. 103, p. 29, n. 106, and the evidence mentioned in Knappe, *Traditionen*, pp. 126–7 and 181–4. [36] See below, p. 26.

[37] For a discussion of Roger Ray's theory (in his 'Bede and Cicero' and earlier articles quoted *ibid.*), that Bede used Cicero's *De inventione* or Marius Victorinus's commentary on this work for argumentation strategies in his *Historia ecclesiastica* and his biblical commentaries, see Knappe, *Traditionen*, pp. 151–5. For Lupus's letter – as his subsequent letter addressed to Benedict III suggests, Lupus's request either had no success at all or he obtained a defective version – see Knappe, *Traditionen*, pp. 116–18, and literature cited there. For a discussion of rhetorical debts in Ælfric, as put forward by A. E. Nichols ('Ælfric and the Brief Style', *JEGP* 70 (1971), 1–12), see Reinsma, 'Ælfric', pp. 61–70, and Knappe, *Traditionen*, pp. 193–6.

[38] This opinion is expressed for Bede and Aldhelm by P. Riché, *Education and Culture in the Barbarian West: from the Sixth through the Eighth Century*, 3rd ed., trans. J. J. Contreni (Columbia, SC, 1976), p. 386 and p. 389 with n. 186, and for Ælfric and his time by Reinsma, 'Rhetoric in England', pp. 402–3. See the discussion in Knappe, *Traditionen*, pp. 18, 29–30, 144–56 and 393.

[39] See esp. *De virginitate (prosa)*, ed. R. Ehwald, *Aldhelmi opera*, MGH Auct. antiq. 15 (Berlin, 1919), 226–323, at 263–4, and Knappe, *Traditionen*, pp. 144–7. For Bede, see below, p. 17.

[40] *Felix's Life of Saint Guthlac*, ed. and trans. B. Colgrave (Cambridge, 1956), pp. 60–2: '. . . dum alii plurimi Anglorum librarii coram ingeniositatis fluenta inter flores rethoricae per virecta litteraturae pure, liquide lucideque rivantur . . .' These lines are placed in a commonplace passage on Christian eloquence, discussed in Knappe, *Traditionen*, pp. 156–7.

temporaries and successors on the Continent,[41] the pseudo-Alcuin 'Schemata' on the parts of philosophy, including the branch of *logica* with *rhetorica* and *dialectica*, were of interest in the ninth century.[42] These early Carolingian schematic representations which also include short definitions – they are somewhat exceptional in that they show a seven-part division of *physica* – are transmitted in many of the manuscripts of Alcuin's *Dialogus* and his *De dialectica*. Thus, an unpublished short prose text called 'Diffinitio philosophiae', which is based on the 'Schemata' and Alcuin's rhetorical and dialectical works, is found in a tenth-century manuscript known to the Anglo-Saxons (London, British Library, Royal 15. B. XIX, 91r–93r, possibly from Saint-Remi, Rheims).[43] Traditional classifications of *philosophia* (found above all in Isidore's *Etymologiae* II.xxiv and his *Differentiae* II.xxxix) were adapted in a number of early medieval texts.[44] Worthy of special note is an unpublished prose text called 'Pauca de philosophiae partibus' in Worcester, Cathedral Library, Q. 5, 72r–74v (Christ Church, Canterbury, s. x) which includes the computus among the liberal arts as part of *arithmetica* and, following Cassiodorus (*Institutiones* II.i.1) and Maximus Victorinus's *Ars grammatica*,[45] defines grammar (a part of *logica*) in a very inclusive way, thus fitting the basic disciplines of monastic education into the traditional model.[46]

What of the rhetorical theory of antiquity was transmitted to Anglo-Saxon England through the narrow channel of late antiquity could therefore have hardly been enough to satisfy an inquisitive mind or to arouse interest in this subject – for which there might not even have been serious need, considering the advanced role of grammar.

---

[41] See the references above, p. 13, n. 33, and esp. Murphy, *Rhetoric in the Middle Ages*, pp. 81–2.

[42] The 'Schemata' are ptd in PL 101, cols. 945–50, after Froben Forster (Regensburg, 1777). For the seven-part division of *physica*, which is based on Isidore's *Differentiae* and was part of the Irish educational tradition, see the study by B. Bischoff, 'Eine verschollene Einteilung der Wissenschaften', *Archives d'histoire doctrinale et littéraire du moyen âge* 25 (1958), 5–20 (repr. in his *Mittelalterliche Studien*, 3 vols. (Stuttgart, 1966–81) I, 273–88).

[43] The 'Schemata' and the 'Diffinitio philosophiae' are discussed in Knappe, *Traditionen*, pp. 172–6.

[44] The poetic texts known to the Anglo-Saxons (see Knappe, *Traditionen*, pp. 196–201) are: 'Verses on the Seven Liberal Arts' in London, British Library, Royal 13. A. XI (s. xi/xii), fol. 149 (unpublished); *Bibliotheca magnifica* in Cambridge, University Library, Gg. 5. 35 (St Augustine's Abbey, Canterbury, s. xi^med), 423v–425r (*Anecdota Bedae, Lanfranci, et aliorum: Inedited Tracts, Letters, Poems, &c. of Venerable Bede, Lanfranc, Tatwin and Others*, ed. J. A. Giles, Publ. of the Caxton Soc. 7 (London, 1851), 50–3); *Ad mensam philosophiae* in the same manuscript, at 440v (*Die Cambridger Lieder*, ed. K. Strecker (Berlin, 1926), p. 91; see also *ibid.* pp. 113–15).

[45] *GL* VI, 188, lines 1–3 and 6–12.

[46] See Knappe, *Traditionen*, pp. 201–3. The text is transmitted in a corrupt form; the bottom four or five lines of each page being illegible. For the inclusion of grammar in *logica*, see M. D'Alverny, 'La sagesse et ses sept filles: recherches sur les allégories de la philosophie et des arts libéraux du IXe au XIIe siècle', *Mélanges dediés à mémoire de Félix Grat* I (Paris, 1946), 245–78, at 249.

The tradition of grammatical rhetoric

A different picture emerges when we look at the tradition of rhetorical concepts used for the grammatical interpretation of texts, especially for exegesis. Not only did the Anglo-Saxons know most of the relevant works in this tradition: they also gave special attention to the figures and tropes in some of their own grammars, and glossed manuscripts reveal the ubiquitous presence of these studies.

In the wider sense, the tradition of grammatical rhetoric was above all present in Cassiodorus's *Expositio psalmorum*. Manuscripts of the whole work (150 psalms) or of parts of it were copied in Anglo-Saxon England.[47] Particularly in the earlier period, scholars paid close attention to the figures and tropes which are used and explained in this commentary on the psalms. Thus, a quite systematic excerpt of rhetorical figures and tropes taken from Cassiodorus's commentary on the first fifty psalms is included among the *glossae collectae* transmitted in the Leiden Glossary (St Gallen, *c.* 800). The glossary goes back to the school of Theodore and Hadrian in late-seventh-century Canterbury.[48] The Milan Biblical Glosses reveal that Theodore and Hadrian used both the grammatical and the Greek and Roman rhetorical figures and tropes, and probably also Cassiodorus's *Expositio psalmorum*, to explain the Bible.[49] Finally, unsystematic textual glosses transmitted knowledge of this tradition.[50]

With regard to works in the tradition of grammatical rhetoric in the narrower sense, many of the late antique grammars which include a *Barbarismus* (and also Carolingian commentaries from the ninth century) were known to the Anglo-Saxons.[51] Of special interest are four adaptations of the figures and tropes in textbooks which were written for advanced students in Anglo-Saxon England.

---

[47] See Gneuss, 'The Study of Language', p. 23, n. 79, and Knappe, *Traditionen*, pp. 217–20. See also *ibid.* pp. 208–13 and 221–9.

[48] The glosses are edited in *A Late Eighth-Century Latin-Anglo-Saxon Glossary Preserved in the Library of the Leiden University (MS. Voss. Q. Lat. Nº. 69)*, ed. J. H. Hessels (Cambridge, 1906), pp. 23–5 (xxviii.18–21, 24–88). For the background of the Leiden Glossary, see esp. M. Lapidge, 'The School of Theodore and Hadrian', *ASE* 15 (1986), 45–72, at 54–5 and 58. See Knappe, *Traditionen*, pp. 220–9, for an analysis of the fifty-eight glosses on the figures and tropes (from a total of sixty-nine) taken from Cassiodorus.

[49] See M. Lapidge in *Biblical Commentaries*, ed. Bischoff and Lapidge, esp. pp. 259–62. The corruption of the extant text makes the identification of sources very difficult. Knappe, *Traditionen*, pp. 204–17, discusses thirteen glosses, plus an explanation of *accessus ad auctores* based on the *Prolegomena in Aphthonii Progymnasmata*.

[50] There is no thorough investigation of rhetorical glosses in Anglo-Saxon manuscripts. For two glosses of rhetorical figures (*hypophora* and *anthypophora*), see J. J. Campbell, 'Knowledge of Rhetorical Figures', p. 18, and Knappe, *Traditionen*, pp. 248–9.

[51] See Knappe, *Traditionen*, esp. pp. 230–4, Gneuss, 'The Study of Language', *passim*, V. Law, *Insular Latin Grammarians* and *idem*, 'The Study of Latin Grammar in Eighth-Century Southumbria', *ASE* 12 (1983), 43–71.

Bede's *Liber de schematibus et tropis* (before *c.* 702) is the only one of these texts which deals with the figures and tropes exclusively. Nevertheless, it must be seen in the context of Bede's other grammatical writings (*De orthographia* and especially *De arte metrica*). With his grammatical sources (his main source is Donatus's *Ars maior*, bk III), the explicit reference to the grammarians[52] and his intention of making available for his students a means of interpreting the Bible in Jarrow, Bede is firmly established in the grammatical tradition. He defended the study of the figures and tropes for Christian purposes, showing that all these stylistic devices can already be found in Scripture. His examples are therefore taken from Christian literature, mostly from the Bible. For the terms, definitions and examples which correspond to Cassiodorus's *Expositio psalmorum*, he may have used an excerpt of rhetorical figures and tropes from this work. The Leiden Glossary, although it cannot count as a teaching manual, might be the extant first part of such a 'handbook'. Bede's *Liber de schematibus et tropis* was used both in England and on the Continent.[53]

In the later period, the first indication of the study of the figures and tropes is found towards the end of Abbo of Fleury's *Quaestiones grammaticales*. Abbo spent two years in Ramsey (985–7) and dedicated his book on grammar to his English students. It is, however, not clear whether the written text circulated in England.[54] Abbo's primary concern in the one paragraph which makes use of some parts of the *Barbarismus* (mentioned are *zeugma*, *soloecismus* and *hypallage*) is the explanation of a biblical passage by the figure *zeugma*. In omitting theoretical explanations, Abbo was surely writing for advanced students.[55]

In his Latin Grammar written in English (995) Ælfric included a short overview of the thirty parts of grammar (*triginta divisiones grammaticae artis*) according

---

[52] 'Quod grammatici Graece schema uocant, nos habitum uel formam uel figuram recte nominamus . . .' *De schematibus et tropis*, ed. C. B. Kendall, CCSL 123A (Turnhout, 1975), pp. 142–71, at p. 142, lines 6–7. All subsequent references to this work refer to pages and lines in this edition, hereafter cited as *DST*.

[53] A thorough investigation of Bede's sources (material from Cassiodorus's *Expositio psalmorum* and the now lost 'Christian Donatus' from the late fifth or early sixth century is used to complement Donatus's explanations) is Schindel, 'Die Quellen von Bedas Figurenlehre'. See the discussion in Knappe, *Traditionen*, pp. 234–43, and particularly pp. 238–9 for the possible use of a 'handbook' for the passages from Cassiodorus. The blending of two definitions, the fact that all terms and definitions taken from the first fifty psalms are also found in the Leiden Glossary and the agreement of only eight of the forty-two examples taken from the psalms with Cassiodorus point to the use of an excerpt where, as in the Leiden Glossary, only few examples from the psalms were included.

[54] See D. A. Bullough, 'The Educational Tradition in England from Alfred to Aelfric: Teaching *Utriusque Linguae*', *SettSpol* 19 (1972), 453–94, at 484.

[55] See *Abbon de Fleury: Questions grammaticales*, ed. and trans. A. Guerreau-Jalabert (Paris, 1982), p. 258 (§ 40), and the discussion in Knappe, *Traditionen*, pp. 250–5. Abbo was familiar with at least some basics of the rhetorical tradition of antiquity, but only grammar and dialectical subjects within grammatical considerations are dealt with (§§ 44–7).

to Isidore, among them the six chapters on the *Barbarismus* (*Etymologiae* I.xxxii–xxxvii). Isidore was not Ælfric's direct source for the *Barbarismus*. His Grammar follows the as yet unpublished 'Excerptiones de Prisciano' which were probably compiled on the Continent.[56] In his *Barbarismus*, Ælfric condensed even further his source's short synopsis of material taken from Donatus's *Ars maior* III (for *barbarismus, soloecismus,* [*cetera*] *vitia* and *metaplasmus*), Bede's *Liber de schematibus et tropis* (for *schemata* and *tropi*) and Isidore's *Etymologiae* I (used for additions). He paid special attention to the avoidance of the faults of diction, the *vitia*. Old English renderings for technical terms are restricted to *hiw* for *figura* and *species, wise* for *modus* (*tropus*) and *getacnung* for *tropus* (however, the last term translates *significatio*).[57] The few examples are also given in English. Ælfric's students could not learn much about the figures and tropes from his Grammar. It was written with beginners in mind, as he states in both prefaces, but besides discussing inflectional morphology in detail, it also mentions advanced grammatical studies such as metrics and the *Barbarismus* as later stages in grammatical education, 'forðan ðe stæfcræft is seo cæg, ðe ðæra boca andgit unlicð'.[58]

Finally, Abbo's student Byrhtferth of Ramsey presents some grammatical teaching, including Old English translations of the *Barbarismus* and all the seventeen figures of speech from Bede's *Liber de schematibus et tropis*, in his computistical *Enchiridion* (*c.* 1010–12).[59] Byrhtferth's sources are exclusively in the grammatical tradition.[60] His additional sources in his adaptation of Bede are

---

[56] See the detailed comparison (the *Barbarismus* is however not discussed) by J. M. Bender-Davis, 'Aelfric's Techniques of Translation and Adaptation as Seen in the Composition of his Old English "Latin Grammar" ' (unpubl. PhD dissertation, Pennsylvania State Univ., 1985) and V. Law, 'Anglo-Saxon England: Ælfric's "Excerptiones de arte grammatica anglice" ', *Histoire Epistémologie Langage* 9.1 (1987), 47–71. Ælfric's *Barbarismus* is edited in *Aelfrics Grammatik und Glossar: Text und Varianten*, ed. J. Zupitza, Sammlung englischer Denkmäler in kritischen Ausgaben 1 (Berlin, 1880; 2nd printing with a preface by H. Gneuss, Berlin, 1966), 294, line 4–295, line 14.

[57] See Knappe, *Traditionen*, pp. 256–70, for a comparison of Ælfric's *Barbarismus* with the 'Excerptiones de Prisciano' on the basis of Paris, Bibliothèque Nationale, nouv. acq. lat. 586, 127v–131r, and a discussion of Ælfric's aim. On Ælfric's grammatical terminology, see L. K. Shook, 'Ælfric's *Latin Grammar*: a Study in Old English Grammatical Terminology' (unpubl. PhD dissertation, Harvard Univ., 1939), E. R. Williams, 'Ælfric's Grammatical Terminology', *PMLA* 73 (1958), 453–62, Law, 'Ælfric's "Excerptiones" ', pp. 62–3, and particularly Gneuss, 'The Study of Language', pp. 13–18.

[58] From Ælfric's Old English Preface, ed. Zupitza, p. 2, lines 16–17; 'because grammar is the key which unlocks the meaning of books'.

[59] *Byrhtferth's Enchiridion*, ed. P. S. Baker and M. Lapidge, EETS ss 15 (Oxford, 1995), 88–90 (II.i.449–70; *Barbarismus*) and 162–8 (III.iii.21–119; *schemata*).

[60] On the use of Old English *hiw* for *schema* which renders 'form', not 'colour' (Latin *color* is used for figures and tropes in the later rhetorical tradition), see Gneuss, 'The Study of Language', p. 17, Knappe, *Traditionen*, pp. 272–4, but also Murphy, 'Rhetorical Lore', pp. 122–4. For the use of *color* for *schema*, see also G. Knappe, 'On Rhetoric and Grammar in the *Hisperica famina*', *Jnl of Med. Latin* 4 (1994), 130–62, at 142–3. On the *Barbarismus* in the *Enchiridion*, see R. Derolez,

Isidore's *Etymologiae* (or Julian of Toledo's *Ars grammatica*) for one example for
polyptoton (used wrongly for *homoeoptoton* by Byrhtferth), and above all the commentary on Bede's *Liber de schematibus et tropis* attributed to Remigius of Auxerre
which he probably found in the form of glosses in the manuscript of Bede's
text.[61] The only English example (for *polysyndeton*) can count as Byrhtferth's own
invention.[62] Byrhtferth did not extend Bede's work in any essential way. Rather,
he shortened and simplified much of what he found in Bede to such an extent
that roughly one third of the transmitted text of this passage remains difficult to
understand even if the reader knows by heart the psalms which are used as
examples. Byrhtferth gives Old English translations for the terms of seven
figures. These are mostly loan translations.[63] It must be kept in mind that it was
not Byrhtferth's intention to write a grammatical textbook. His sections on
grammar are bound up with his book on the computus in which he, according to
Reginald Berry, wanted to show that all phenomena of creation have a common
ground in the principle of the number.[64] In several places Byrhtferth strove to
show the connection between computus and grammar. The figures of speech
are not explicitly related to the computus, but as *hiw* 'form' they correspond well
with the (grammatical and computistical) *notae*. Thus, the signs of the alphabets,
the quantifying study of metrics, forms attained by the arrangement of words
(the figures of speech), the meaning of forms (*notae*) and the transferred
meaning of numbers (number allegory, discussed in part IV of the *Enchiridion*)
fitted into Byrhtferth's plan. The transferred meaning of words on the other

hand (the tropes) are left out. They may simply have transcended the competence of and potential use for the computist.[65]

The study of the figures and tropes in the grammatical tradition was thus integrated in advanced grammatical studies in both the early period and after the Benedictine Reform which created the conditions in which Abbo, Ælfric and Byrhtferth worked.[66] But even the most ambitious textbooks did not provide for the study of rhetoric.

OLD ENGLISH LITERATURE AND THE RHETORICAL ASPECT OF GRAMMAR TEACHING

A thorough and comprehensive investigation of rhetorical strategies in Old English and Anglo-Latin literature and its sources, if such a project is at all feasible, has not yet been carried out. Specific aspects, mainly concerning stylistic features in Old English texts, have however been the focus of a number of literary analyses. The following short overview is arranged according to the three *partes artis* which are relevant to the written medium.[67]

Elocutio

Particular points of interest concerning the impact of Latin figures and tropes include: the problem of judging whether stylistic arrangements were used intentionally and if they go back to the Latin tradition; how instructions for Latin could be employed in the Old English language and versification; the way in which both the Germanic and Latin poetic traditions complemented each other in vernacular (and also in Anglo-Latin) texts; and how the stylistic embellishment varies according to genre, author and purpose.

Firstly, it can be difficult to decide with certainty whether a particular figure (or, for that matter, any rhetorical technique) arose intentionally, with the background of Latin learning, or not. After all, as J. J. Campbell put it, '[we] must realize that factors of figurative language can usually be found operating in the language in its most natural state; that is, a completely untutored person competent in his own language has the resources for producing practically all the *figurae*

---

[65] For the grammatical aspects discussed in Byrhtferth's *Enchiridion* and its structure, see esp. Knappe, *Traditionen*, pp. 303–12 and 474.

[66] For figures and tropes in early glossaries and in textual glosses, see Knappe, *Traditionen*, pp. 243–9.

[67] For a detailed critical evaluation and bibliographical references, see Knappe, *Traditionen*, pp. 30–6 and 323–467 (pt IV). See also esp. the remarks in Gneuss, 'The Study of Language', pp. 31–2, Reinsma, 'Rhetoric, Grammar, and Literature', pp. 32–8, J. J. Campbell, 'Adaptation of Classical Rhetoric' and *idem*, 'Learned Rhetoric in Old English Poetry', *MP* 63 (1966), 189–201. The terms for the *partes artis* are here used to refer to their equivalents in a grammatically based culture which apparently lacked knowledge of the *ars bene dicendi*.

verborum and *figurae sententiarum*.[68] Attempts have been made to avoid the pitfall of attributing too many stylistic techniques to Latin learning. Thus, for example, Diane D. O'Connor, in her analysis of figures of repetition in forty-one Old English poems, introduced criteria for determining 'accidental' figures and distinguishing the Latin and Germanic traditions, for instance concerning *isocolon*: 'The figure is most complete when three or more cola are used together, and because the Germanic love of balanced pairs obscures any Latin influence on pairs of phrases, isocolon will only be discussed here when it involves at least three phrases.'[69] To give a second example, the high percentage of word pairs (synonyms) which render one Latin word in Old English prose translations, a feature which is especially typical of Wærferth's translation of Gregory's *Dialogi* and the *Old English Bede* (for example, *unclæne 7 besmiten* for Latin *pollutum*) is in accordance with the authors' aim to render the texts as clearly and precisely as possible. The word pairs therefore seem to point to educational and semantic considerations rather than to any specific classical rhetorical technique of amplification.[70] The frequency with which particular stylistic features are employed, the learned background of the text, the author's intention and a comparison with the sources might help to decide whether the figures and tropes were intended and based on Latin education.

Secondly, Old English writers did not apparently encounter too many difficulties when using Latin stylistic devices in their native tongue. There are of course limitations due to the nature of both the Old English language and versification. Such is the case with figures employing the repetition of final sounds or sound groups in a language with unaccented and reduced endings. It is thus doubtful whether the endings of '[earfoð]hwil*e*', '*þ*rowad*e*', '[breost]-cear*e*', 'hæbb*e*' and 'ceol*e*' in *The Seafarer* 3a–5a can count as an instance of

---

[68] 'Adaptation of Classical Rhetoric', p. 190. See also J. H. Bonner, 'Toward a Unified Critical Approach to Old English Poetic Composition', *MP* 73 (1976), 219–28, at 226–7.

[69] D. D. O'Connor, 'Rhetorical Patterns in Old English Poetry' (unpubl. PhD dissertation, Syracuse Univ., 1972), p. 40. *Isocolon* is defined in the rhetorical tradition only; it is the parallel arrangement of two or more cola (sentences, clauses or word groups); see, e.g., Quintilian, *Institutio oratoria* IX.iii.80. Likewise, O'Connor formulates restrictive rules for the identification of *paronomasia* (words similar in sound but not in meaning, word-play, which must be found within one line), *homoeoptoton* and *homoeoteleuton* (the repetition of the same case endings and the same syllable at the end of words, respectively; they must occur in more than four consecutive half-lines); see 'Rhetorical Patterns', pp. 46 and 94–8. Such criteria are, however, marked by a certain degree of arbitrariness. See Knappe, *Traditionen*, pp. 330–1, and also *ibid.* p. 373 and n. 3. On *paronomasia*, *homoeoptoton* and *homoeoteleuton*, see *DST* 147,90–148,102; 150,129–36; 149,115–28.

[70] See Knappe, *Traditionen*, pp. 377–9 (also on the debate on *cursus* forms) and literature cited there, particularly J. M. Hart, 'Rhetoric in the Translation of Bede', *An English Miscellany presented to Dr. Furnivall in Honour of his Seventy-Fifth Birthday* (Oxford, 1901), pp. 150–4, and S. M. Kuhn, 'Synonyms in the Old English Bede', *JEGP* 46 (1947), 168–76.

effective *homoeoteleuton*.[71] Similarly, *paromoeon*, which refers to the repetition of initial sounds but is not restricted to one line of poetry, is rare in Old English alliterative poetry, in which the constitutive repetition of sounds depends on the stressed syllable and is restricted by the line.[72] However, close adaptations (and also paraphrases) of Latin verse in Old English seem to prove that Anglo-Saxon poets recognized stylistic features in their sources and used or adapted them in the Old English alliterative line, as has been shown by Jackson J. Campbell and Claire W. McPherson. For example, *isocolon*, antithesis (for example, 'hot' and 'cold') and *homoeoteleuton* can be found in both languages in the following lines from the *Latin-English Proverbs*:

Ardor frigesscit,	nitor squalescit,
amor abolescit,	lux obtenebrescit.
Hat acolað,	hwit asolað,
leof alaðaþ,	leoht aðystrað.
Senescunt omnia,	que ęterna non sunt.
Æghwæt forealdað	þæs þe ece ne byð.[73]

The Old English poet was apparently eager to render the figures he discovered in the Latin (note also the rhyme of 'acolað – asolað') in his rhythmical alliterative lines, even at the cost of slightly mistranslating 'amor abolescit'.[74] It thus seems very likely that literary analysis in Anglo-Saxon grammar lessons (also by means of the figures and tropes in the grammars) was the basis for teaching the stylistic embellishment of texts in the schools, also for their use in the vernacular.[75]

---

[71] This example is considered to be *homoeoptoton* in O'Connor, 'Rhetorical Patterns', p. 160. See further Campbell, 'Learned Rhetoric in Old English Poetry', p. 197, n. 24.

[72] According to Bede, *paromoeon* is achieved by the repetition of word-initial consonants; see *DST* 148,108–149,114. On the characteristics of Old English poetry, including its formulaic character, themes and larger structures, see the summary in Knappe, *Traditionen*, pp. 331–9, and also D. G. Scragg, 'The Nature of Old English Verse', *The Cambridge Companion to Old English Literature*, ed. M. Godden and M. Lapidge (Cambridge, 1991), pp. 55–70.

[73] ASPR VI, 109: 'Hot grows cold, white becomes dirty, dear turns hateful, light becomes dark. Everything grows old which is not eternal.'

[74] For adaptations of Latin sources, see esp. Campbell, 'Learned Rhetoric in Old English Poetry', *idem*, 'Adaptation of Classical Rhetoric' (the quoted example is taken from there, p. 192) and McPherson, 'Influence of Latin Rhetoric', *passim*. See also Knappe, *Traditionen*, pp. 339–43. Some adaptations, for example *The Phoenix* (ASPR III, 94–113), show how freely Latin stylistic devices could be employed.

[75] Interesting examples for the grammatical rather than rhetorical basis of stylistic techniques are early 'glossary Latin' and the 'hermeneutic style' (which was current in tenth-century Anglo-Latin texts). See Knappe, *Traditionen*, pp. 193–4, and esp. M. Lapidge, 'The Hermeneutic Style in Tenth-Century Anglo-Latin Literature', *ASE* 4 (1975), 67–111. Concerning Old English as a literary language, there are indications in Ælfric's Grammar that some attention was also paid to the structure of the vernacular; see Gneuss, 'The Study of Language', p. 14.

Thirdly, Germanic and Latin stylistic devices were by no means mutually exclusive. Some of the features that are considered to be typical of the Germanic background of Old English literature find close correspondence in the Latin figures and tropes. For example, what Bartlett in her analysis of 'larger rhetorical patterns' calls the 'parallel pattern' (which covers the forms of Old English variation) might be influenced by antithesis, *anaphora* and the style of Latin homilies.[76] Similarly, the parenthetic exclamation, considered by Krapp to be typical of orally-delivered epics (for example, *Beowulf* 1422–1423a, at 1422b: *Flod blode weol / – folc to sægon – / hatan heolfre*), finds its counterpart in the Latin trope *parenthesis*.[77] In reverse, too, the Old English alliterative style had an impact on both Old English prose and Anglo-Latin texts.[78] The mixture of the two traditions resulted in the unique forms of Old English literature.

This takes us to the fourth point, namely stylistic variation according to genre, author and purpose. The lightest impact of Latin learning is to be expected in the most 'Germanic' genre, which is heroic poetry. Here, the influence of structural figures is usually acknowledged in scholarship, whereas figurative diction such as personification and 'synecdoche' (for example, Æschere is called *hand* in *Beowulf* 1343) is often attributed to the Germanic tradition.[79] But again, the kenning, for instance, coexists with the Latin tropes *metaphora*, *metonymia*, *antonomasia*, *synecdoche*, *catachresis* and *periphrasis*, and all of these constitute figurative

---

[76] See A. C. Bartlett, *The Larger Rhetorical Patterns in Anglo-Saxon Poetry* (New York, 1935), pp. 30 and 40–3, McPherson, 'Influence of Latin Rhetoric', p. 12, and Knappe, *Traditionen*, pp. 334–7 (on Bartlett's analysis). For *anaphora*, the repetition of words or word groups at the beginning of two or more consecutive verses or sense units, see *DST* 146,71–147,79.

[77] See G. P. Krapp, 'The Parenthetic Exclamation in Old English Poetry', *Mod. Lang. Notes* 20 (1905), 33–7; on *parenthesis*, see Lausberg, *Handbuch*, § 860, and *DST* 158,115–19. Bede defines *parenthesis* more specifically by stating that the interpolated utterance adds a reason to the statement. Swanton translates the passage from *Beowulf* thus: 'The flood welled with blood, with hot gore – the people gazed at it': *Beowulf*, ed. and trans. M. Swanton (Manchester, 1978), p. 103.

[78] See, for example, Ælfric's alliterative prose (summary of the discussion and references in Knappe, *Traditionen*, pp. 389–91). See also J. Bately, 'Old English Prose before and during the Reign of Alfred', *ASE* 17 (1988), 93–138, at 132. For the influence of Germanic stylistic devices such as alliteration, parallelism and variation on Anglo-Latin texts, see, for example, *Alcuin*, ed. Godman, introd., pp. ciii–cx, esp. at cv, and in particular A. H. Olsen, 'Old English Poetry and Latin Prose: the Reverse Context', *Classica et Mediaevalia* 34 (1983), 273–82. See also Knappe, *Traditionen*, pp. 326–9.

[79] See N. D. Isaacs, 'The Convention of Personification in *Beowulf*', *Old English Poetry: Fifteen Essays*, ed. R. P. Creed (Providence, RI, 1967), pp. 215–48 – the example is discussed on pp. 243–4. Through *synecdoche* the whole is designated by a part or vice versa (see *DST* 156,85–157,90). See also *Beowulf and the Fight at Finnsburg*, ed. Fr. Klaeber, 3rd ed. with first and second supplement (Boston, 1950), introd., p. lxviii. For a discussion of *elocutio* in heroic poetry and full bibliographical references, see Knappe, *Traditionen*, pp. 348–53. See also the particular case of the Old English elegies discussed in Knappe, *Traditionen*, pp. 366–73, and literature referred to there.

diction in a corpus of poetry in which even the most secular heroic specimens such as *Beowulf* show a definite influence of Christianity and the hagiographic poem *Andreas*, for example, makes extensive use of the native tradition.[80] On the other hand, it is certainly true that the Latin tropes lend themselves more readily to Christian metaphorical and allegorical poetry where they (and the figures) were handled with great skill within the requirements of Old English verse. In particular, figures of repetition, parallelization and of sound and tropes such as *metaphora* were used alongside formulas, alliteration and variation. Cases in point are the poems by Cynewulf, *Judith* and *The Dream of the Rood*. Note, for example, the elaborate use of stylistic devices in the Old English poem *Judith* which serves to allegorize the story.[81] Figures and tropes can also be found in Old English prose translations, where they enhance clarity, exactness and concreteness, and in the few independent pieces of prose such as Alfred's prefaces to his translations, for example the elaborate *metaphora* in his preface to the *Soliloquies*.[82] Stylistic embellishment even found its way into some versions of the *Anglo-Saxon Chronicle*, as was shown by Cecily Clark.[83] Among the Old English preachers Ælfric, as a teacher concentrating on clarity, brevity and figures of repetition, restricts himself most in the use of stylistic devices, while Wulfstan of York shows great skill especially with acoustic figures which were of particular use for orally delivered homilies and sermons (for example, rhyme, rhythm and the parallel structure in 'þær is wanung 7 granung 7 a singal sorh').[84]

[80] On Old English figurative diction, see Knappe, *Traditionen*, pp. 343–8, and literature cited there, esp. E. G. Stanley, 'Old English Poetic Diction and the Interpretation of *The Wanderer, The Seafarer* and *The Penitent's Prayer*', *Anglia* 73 (1955), 413–66. The kenning is usually defined as a two-part paraphrase of a concept whose metaphorical basis is specified by the first constituent which is taken from the same sphere of meaning as the referent (e.g. OE *ban-hus* 'bone-house', body'). *Metaphora* is a shortened comparison, transferring one expression into a different sphere. *Metonymia* is the substitution of a term by a similar one, often by the cause for the effect, the container for the contents or vice versa. *Antonomasia* is defined as the replacement of a proper name by a description. *Catachresis* is the inexact use of a noun to describe an object which does not have a designation of its own. *Periphrasis* is used to embellish a simple word or thought by naming it according to its characteristics. See *DST* 152,8–153,33, 155,53–63, 155,63–156,77, 153,34–154,48, and 157,99–158,106.
[81] See the discussion in McPherson, 'Influence of Latin Rhetoric', pp. 101–32. Studies of Christian poems are discussed in Knappe, *Traditionen*, pp. 354–66.
[82] See esp. Bately, 'Old English Prose', pp. 118–38, H. Sauer, 'König Alfreds Boethius und seine Rhetorik', *Anglistik: Mitteilungen des Verbandes Deutscher Anglisten* 7.2 (1996), 57–89 and literature referred to in Knappe, *Traditionen*, pp. 374–86.
[83] See C. Clark, 'The Narrative Mode of *The Anglo-Saxon Chronicle* before the Conquest', *England before the Conquest: Studies in Primary Sources presented to Dorothy Whitelock*, ed. P. Clemoes and K. Hughes (Cambridge, 1971), pp. 215–35, and Knappe, *Traditionen*, pp. 386–7.
[84] *The Homilies of Wulfstan*, ed. D. Bethurum (Oxford, 1957), p. 162 (IV.123): 'There is howling and groaning and perpetual sorrow.' This passage is discussed by D. Bethurum, 'Wulfstan', in *Continuations and Beginnings: Studies in Old English Literature*, ed. E. G. Stanley (London, 1966), pp. 210–46, at 234. On Ælfric, see particularly Reinsma, 'Aelfric', chs. IV and V, and the remarks in

While Old English writers were apparently at ease in combining Latin stylistic devices with the native tradition, it does not seem possible to prove by way of literary analysis that figures and tropes in the rhetorical tradition were used.[85] Due to the lack of evidence for rhetorical teaching in the tradition of antiquity, classical rhetorical influence on the level of *elocutio* should be attributed to grammatical studies only, that is, to formal instruction in the Latin figures and tropes (grammatical rhetoric in the narrower sense, and in the wider sense the study of Cassiodorus's *Expositio psalmorum*) and the deduction of devices through the close study of texts. Advising the students on how to employ these techniques belongs to the rhetorical aspect of grammar teaching.

Inventio and dispositio

An influence of the *ars bene dicendi* on the level of *inventio*, that is, the inventive procedure of finding out *what* to say (and in which order to put it),[86] will be evident in the use of *topoi* or *loci* in literary texts. *Topoi* are 'places' where arguments may be found. In the more general sense, *topoi* may be particular motives or themes which are transmitted through literary texts.[87] In the process of grammatical interpretation such literary 'commonplaces' may be abstracted and then applied during the creative process. Thus, we are here dealing with the rhetorical aspect of grammar teaching. The above-mentioned theme of *ubi sunt* is one example of this primarily grammatical procedure. Furthermore, the *sum*-series (found, for example, in *The Wanderer* 80b–84), particular conventions in descriptions of winter and the exordial tradition also belong here.[88] Of greater

---

P. Clemoes, 'Ælfric', *Continuations and Beginnings*, ed. Stanley, pp. 176–209. For a discussion of the stylistic devices used by Ælfric, Wulfstan and the Blickling homilists together with a note on the *Vercelli Homilies*, see Knappe, *Traditionen*, pp. 387–98, 449–59 and literature referred to there. See also below, pp. 27–8, n. 97.

[85] De Leeuw, for example, takes knowledge of the *Rhetorica ad Herennium* for granted; see W. L. De Leeuw, Jr, 'The Eschatological Homilies of Wulfstan: a Rhetorical Analysis' (unpubl. PhD dissertation, Auburn Univ., 1972), p. 3.

[86] *Dispositio*, which is concerned with the arrangement of the parts of a text, is closely interconnected with *inventio*; see Lausberg, *Handbuch*, §§ 260–452, esp. 444. For the systematic discussion of these two *partes artis* a separate treatment is chosen here.

[87] For the division into a general and a technical sense, see Knappe, *Traditionen*, pp. 398–9, based on E. R. Curtius, *Europäische Literatur und lateinisches Mittelalter*, 2nd ed. (Bern, 1954), pp. 79–80.

[88] See the discussion in Knappe, *Traditionen*, pp. 400–5. For the *ubi sunt*, see above, p. 5. The *sum*-series is discussed by J. E. Cross, 'On *The Wanderer* Lines 80–84, a Study of a Figure and a Theme', *Vetenskaps-Societeten i Lund Årsbok* (1958–9), 75–110; see also his *Latin Themes*. Both themes are primarily found in Latin homilies. An investigation of descriptions of winter is B. K. Martin, 'Aspects of Winter in Latin and Old English Poetry', *JEGP* 68 (1969), 375–90. On the Latin and Germanic background of exordial passages, see esp. M. Bridges, 'Exordial Tradition and Poetic Individuality in Five OE Hagiographical Poems', *ES* 60 (1979), 361–79. Themes from Germanic oral poetry are summarized in D. M. Jehle, 'Latin Rhetoric in the Signed Poems of Cynewulf' (unpubl. PhD dissertation, Loyola Univ. of Chicago, 1973), pp. 19–22.

interest to the influence of theoretical principles of classical rhetoric are *topoi*, in the technical sense of the word, as modes for arrangement and expression. They determine the structure of whole texts. Here again, however, we must in all cases consider the constitutive influence of model texts, such as the *topoi* of *consolatio* poetry in *The Wanderer*.[89] Likewise, prose and verse versions on the same topic, such as Aldhelm's *De virginitate*, are more probably based on the late antique genre *opus geminatum* than on the grammatical and rhetorical exercise of paraphrase (*conversio*), which demands full semantic correspondence of both versions.[90] While no evidence of actual rhetorical exercises that might have been taught in Anglo-Saxon schools is extant, Margaret Schlauch has shown the probability that in addition to the model of Latin poems, especially pseudo-Ovid's *De nuce*, the exercise of *prosopopoeia* (personification) had a considerable effect on the composition of the Old English poem *The Dream of the Rood*. Likewise, an impact of the exercise *encomium* (praise) on Old English literature, while difficult to prove, cannot be excluded.[91] Both these exercises are described in Priscian's *Praeexercitamina*.[92] Although there is no definite evidence that this textbook was known to the Anglo-Saxons, the potential value of these basic exercises with their intermediate position between rhetoric and grammar cannot be doubted.[93] Thus, while the use of forensic (juridical) techniques derived from the rhetorical tradition of antiquity cannot be proved,[94] the rhetorical prescriptions in Priscian's *Praeexercitamina* are not unlikely to have been part of the rhetorical aspect of Anglo-Saxon grammar teaching, thus complementing the teaching of techniques of text production based on literary models.

Textual traditions also played a major role in the arrangement of the parts of a text and in choosing the appropriate style for each part (*dispositio*). Thus, theories according to which whole poems, in particular *The Seafarer*, and speeches

---

[89] See J. E. Cross, 'On the Genre of *The Wanderer*', *Neophilologus* 45 (1961), 63–75, and the discussion in Knappe, *Traditionen*, pp. 406–7.

[90] See G. Wieland, '*Geminus stilus*: Studies in Anglo-Latin Hagiography', *Insular Latin Studies: Papers on Latin Texts and Manuscripts of the British Isles: 550–1066*, ed. M. W. Herren, Papers in Med. Stud. 1 (Toronto, 1981), 113–33, and *Alcuin*, ed. Godman, introd., pp. lxxviii–lxxxviii. See also Knappe, *Traditionen*, pp. 408–10, and above, p. 11, n. 24.

[91] See Knappe, *Traditionen*, pp. 411–20, and in particular the studies by M. Schlauch, 'The Dream of the Rood as Prosopopoeia', *Essays and Studies in Honor of Carleton Brown* (New York, 1940), pp. 23–34 (repr. *Essential Articles for the Study of Old English Poetry*, ed. J. Bessinger and S. Kahrl (Hamden, CT, 1968), pp. 428–41) and *idem*, 'An Old English *Encomium Urbis*', *JEGP* 40 (1941), 14–28. For a case of influence of technical *topoi* on *Beowulf*, put forward by G. I. Engelhardt, '*Beowulf*: a Study in Dilatation', *PMLA* 70 (1955), 825–52, see Knappe, *Traditionen*, pp. 420–2.

[92] Priscian, *Praeexercitamina*, ed. Passalacqua, pp. 45–6 ('De allocutione') and 42–4 ('De laude').

[93] See above, p. 11. Likewise, knowledge of this textbook in early medieval Ireland can only be established by way of literary analysis. See Knappe, 'On Rhetoric and Grammar', pp. 145–53.

[94] See the short summary in Knappe, *Traditionen*, pp. 422–3, and references given there.

functioning as verbal contests (flyting) in heroic poetry, for example the debate of Unferth and Beowulf (*Beowulf* 499–606), were composed according to the *ars bene dicendi* are neither easy to prove nor very probable.[95] A closer look at *The Seafarer* reveals that if it was indeed intended to be a speech, classical rhetorical theory was not heeded, and the general rhetorical principles in the speeches in *Beowulf* are much more likely to stand in the tradition of 'verbal duelling' in heroic narrative, which has been analysed by Ward Parks. The literary forms most closely akin to the classical oration are the homily and the sermon. It must, however, not be forgotten that exegetical homilies have a different background from classical rhetorical theory in being in the service of *enarratio*, that is grammatical exegesis, and are very much dependent on model homilies. In general, the following statement by Joshua H. Bonner should always be kept in mind: 'The elements of persuasion (*movere*) and teaching (*docere*) were, of course, retained in the sermon and homily, but to suggest that the sermon and homily were products of classical rhetoric would be a gross oversimplification. Both are distinctly medieval and Christian genres, and they seldom draw from formal classical rhetoric.'[96] These qualifications notwithstanding, it is not uncommon in scholarship to identify the parts of Old English homilies with the classical parts of a speech, that is, *exordium*, *narratio*, *confirmatio* and *peroratio*. These seem to correspond conveniently to the structure of Old English exegetical homilies in particular, where the pericope (*narratio*: the statement of the facts) and the exegetical part (*confirmatio*: the proof) are integral parts. If, on the other hand, the structure of some homilies of Ælfric, the *Blickling Homilies* and those of Wulfstan are scrutinized more closely, correspondences with – but also major deviations from – the *ars bene dicendi* come to light.[97] Thus, Ælfric's carefully

---

[95] For *The Seafarer*, see above, p. 6, n. 4, and Knappe, *Traditionen*, pp. 433–5. Twenty-two speeches in *Beowulf* are analysed according to the *ars bene dicendi* by G. Sander, 'Gliederung und Komposition des Beowulf' (doctoral dissertation, typescript, Mainz, 1955). The Unferth episode is looked at in P. Silber, 'Rhetoric as Prowess in the Unferð Episode', *Texas Stud. in Lit. and Lang.* 23 (1981), 471–83. But see also W. Parks, *Verbal Dueling in Heroic Narrative: the Homeric and Old English Traditions* (Princeton, NJ, 1990). For speeches in the *Battle of Maldon*, see E. R. Anderson, 'Flyting in *The Battle of Maldon*', *NM* 71 (1970), 197–202. See Knappe, *Traditionen*, pp. 424–33. See also *ibid.* p. 436, on the structure of Alfred's Preface to the *Pastoral Care* as put forward by B. F. Huppé, 'Alfred and Aelfric: A Study of Two Prefaces', *The Old English Homily and its Backgrounds*, ed. P. E. Szarmach and B. F. Huppé (New York, 1978), pp. 119–37, esp. 121–31.

[96] Bonner, 'Toward a Unified Critical Approach', p. 224. See also Knappe, *Traditionen*, pp. 437–40. For the view of the Church Fathers, see above, p. 8. Moreover, no rhetorical preaching manuals existed in late antiquity and the early Middle Ages.

[97] For such a comparison, see Knappe, *Traditionen*, pp. 440–59 and 464–6. This discussion is mainly based on the following analyses: L. G. Best, 'Classical *partitiones orationis* in the Homilies of Aelfric: an Overview' (unpubl. PhD dissertation, Univ. of Connecticut, 1977); M. A. Dalbey, 'Structure and Style in the *Blickling Homilies* for the Temporale' (unpubl. PhD dissertation, Univ. of Illinois, 1968); J. J. Campbell, 'Adaptation of Classical Rhetoric', pp. 178–89,

structured homilies often lack an introductory part (*exordium*) or mix it with the *narratio* or with explanations. Moreover, most of Ælfric's homilies are without a concluding part (*peroratio*) which, according to classical rhetorical theory, should be composed in the grand style, move the audience and convert them to moral living. As Luke M. Reinsma has shown, Ælfric appears primarily as a teacher, placing emphasis on instruction.[98] From a comparison of the structure of some of Ælfric's homilies with five exegetical *Blickling Homilies* which were written in the tenth century (but before the Benedictine Reform in England) by priests who are very unlikely to have had a formal rhetorical education, it becomes apparent that due to the less educated audiences pervasive methods of simplification are similar in both series, but are handled with more effect by Ælfric. Thus, we are dealing with a pedagogical preaching practice in the vernacular which is not heir to the classical oration but aims to teach (as in Ælfric) in the exegetical-grammatical tradition and to stir emotions (as in the *Blickling Homilies* and particularly Wulfstan of York) by following general rhetorical/educational principles.

In conclusion, Anglo-Saxon scholars, with the exception of Alcuin of York, do not seem to have been familiar with the rhetorical tradition of antiquity. However, they expressed themselves 'rhetorically', that is, in a good and effective manner. This situation seems to have been puzzling scholars for quite a long time but it can be explained by the tradition of rhetoric within grammar. It is thus essential to distinguish these two basic traditions for Anglo-Saxon England (and probably for the early Middle Ages in general) and to use the term 'classical rhetoric' with care. Working in a grammatical literary culture which aimed at the analysis and interpretation of literary texts, in particular with respect to the figurative language of the Bible and Christian literature in general, Anglo-Saxon writers and preachers could turn to literary models as inspirations for their own texts. Furthermore, both individual creativity, based on principles of education, and Germanic poetic techniques played their role. Thus, while rhetorical instruction in the classical sense cannot be claimed for Anglo-Saxon England, the *grammatici* were involved in teaching the figures and tropes in the tradition of grammatical rhetoric (as seen in Bede, Ælfric, Abbo and Byrhtferth), first of all for interpretative purposes and then also for text

---

esp. pp. 188–9 on Wulfstan's *Be christendome*; some remarks in R. Jurovics, '*Sermo Lupi* and the Moral Purpose of Rhetoric', *The Old English Homily*, ed. Szarmach and Huppé, pp. 203–20. On the *Vercelli Homilies*, see P. E. Szarmach, 'The Vercelli Homilies: Style and Structure', *The Old English Homily*, ed. Szarmach and Huppé, pp. 241–67. The structuring of Wulfstan's preaching has not yet received due attention in scholarship. Also, close comparisons with the sources in order to evaluate individual achievements of the Old English preachers have in many cases yet to be carried out.

[98] See Reinsma, 'Ælfric'.

production. Furthermore, strategies for text production derived from literary analysis were probably, in one or the other centres of learning, supported by Priscian's *Praeexercitamina*. All of these teaching methods constitute the rhetorical aspect of grammar teaching and account for the rhetorical quality of Anglo-Saxon literature.[99]

---

[99] I should like to thank Professor Helmut Gneuss, Professor Michael Lapidge and Dr Inge Milfull for their helpful comments on an earlier version of this article.

Cyninges fedesl:
the king's feeding in Æthelberht, ch. 12

LISI OLIVER

The twelfth-century *Textus Roffensis* contains a collection of early English laws, of which the first is attributed to Æthelberht of Kent, who reigned *c.* 580–616.[1] Although these laws remain to us only in a copy made some six centuries later, there are strong linguistic grounds, first proposed by Sievers and Liebermann, and recently elaborated on and expanded by myself, to assume that the text as we have it genuinely reflects a copy of an early original, albeit much changed by generations of scribal modernization.[2] Yet problems of interpretation often arise, among them the difficulty in the definition of hapax legomena: words which occur in the corpus of Old English only in this text. One such term is contained in Æthelberht, ch. 12,[3] which states: 'Cyninges fedesl XX scillinga forgelde.' This is presumably formulated along the lines of Æthelberht, ch. 8, which reads: 'Cyninges mundbyrd L scillinga.'

There is basic agreement among scholars as to the meaning, if not the precise interpretation, of *mundbyrd*: most would agree with Bosworth's definition of 'protection, patronage'. Along these lines, the clause can be interpreted as: '[For violating] the king's protection: 50 (of) shillings.' Using this as a template, one might translate Æthelberht, ch. 12, as: '[For violating] the king's *fedesl*: let [the perpetrator pay] 20 (of) shillings.'

There is, however, no consensus among previous interpreters of the laws as to the meaning of the term *fedesl*. The Latin version of 1640 of Johann de Laet, the first translator, printed by Hickes in 1703 (and reprinted by Harris in 1719),

---

[1] For recent discussion of the dating of Æthelberht's reign, see N. Brooks, 'The Creation and Early Structure of the Kingdom of Kent', *The Origins of Anglo-Saxon Kingdoms*, ed. S. Bassett (London, 1989), pp. 55–74, and I. Wood, 'The Mission of Augustine of Canterbury to the English', *Speculum* 69 (1994), 1–17.

[2] See E. Sievers, 'Altnordisches im *Beowulf?*', *BGDSL* 12 (1887), 168–200, at 174 n.; *Die Gesetze der Angelsachsen*, ed. F. Liebermann, 3 vols. (Halle, 1903–16); L. Oliver, 'The Language of the Early English Laws' (unpubl. PhD dissertation, Harvard Univ., 1995), in which I discuss in detail the arguments for archaism in the Kentish laws based on orthography, phonology, morphology and syntax.

[3] The manuscript is written continuously, with no breakdown into clauses. In Oliver, 'Language of Early English Laws', pp. 170–234 and 273–85 I argue for a new numeration based on the syntactic structure; pending publication of this analysis, I follow the standard breakdown for the sake of easy reference.

rendered it as *fidicina* 'female player on a lute', with the alternative *obsonatrix* 'woman who feeds' offered in brackets. In 1721, Wilkins wisely eliminated *fidicina*, leaving *obsonatrix* as the sole choice. A more conservative stance was taken by Thorpe, who in 1840 printed 'fed-esl', adding in his footnotes that 'there can be no doubt that this word is derived from *fēdan* "nutrire"; but whether the woman were the person fed or the feeder, *i.e.* a nurse, is not so clear'. This lead was followed by Schmid in 1858, who printed the word as it stands in the manuscript (with the addition of a macron over the first *e*), adding in a note, 'Ich wage das Wort fēdesl nicht zu übersetzen.'[4] Felix Liebermann, the great turn-of-the-century editor of the Anglo-Saxon laws, in 1903 translated the term as *Königskostgänger* 'king's boarder' (echoed by Eckhardt in 1958). In the 1921 supplement to *An Anglo-Saxon Dictionary*, Toller offered under definition II 'feeding: The word appears as a technical term in [the laws of Æthelberht]', with no indication as to what this 'feeding' implies. Attenborough in 1922 returned to the convention of leaving *fedesl* untranslated; but pointed out in a footnote that 'the word *fedesl* occurs elsewhere only as a translation of *altilis* ['fatted beast']'; Whitelock similarly left *fedesl*, with a note referring both to Liebermann's analysis and to the usual meaning of 'fatted animal'.[5]

In elucidating the meaning of *fedesl* it may be helpful to put the edict which contains the term in the larger context of the body of laws. Ch. 12 is the last of a series of laws dealing with payments owed to the king for various offences, summarized in Table 1.

As previously noted, Thorpe derived *fedesl* from *fēdan*, assuming that it meant a woman who was either 'the person fed or the feeder, *i.e.* a nurse.' Liebermann eliminates, I believe correctly, the possibility that *fedesl* is a woman, as it is difficult to imagine what 20-shilling-position fits between the 25 shillings for a 'grinding slave' and the 12 of the third rank of woman slave.[6] (This also excludes de Laet's *fidicina* 'female player on a lute', if, in fact, anyone but de Laet and Harris ever took that seriously).

[4] 'I do not dare translate the word *fedesl*.'
[5] G. Hickes and H. Wanley, *Linguarum Vett. Septentrionalium Thesaurus Grammatico-Criticus et Archæologicus*, 2 vols. (Oxford, 1703–5); D. Wilkins, *Leges Anglo-Saxonicae* (London, 1721); J. Harris, *The History of Kent* (London, 1719); *Ancient Laws and Institutes of England*, ed. B. Thorpe (London, 1840); *Die Gesetze der Angelsachsen*, ed. R. Schmid (Leipzig, 1858); *Gesetze der Angelsachsen*, ed. Liebermann; *Leges Anglosaxonum 601–925*, ed. K. Eckhardt (Weimar, 1958); T. N. Toller, *An Anglo-Saxon Dictionary: Supplement* (Oxford, 1921); F. L. Attenborough, *The Laws of the Earliest English Kings* (Cambridge, 1922); *English Historical Documents c. 500–1042*, ed. D. Whitelock (London, 1955; 2nd ed., 1979).
[6] *Ancient Laws and Institutes*, ed. Thorpe I, 7; *Gesetze der Angelsachsen*, ed. Liebermann III, 7. Puzzling is Liebermann's statement that 'laut des *forgieldan* bestand die Verletzung im Erschlagen, nicht im Schänden' ('on the basis of *forgieldan*, the injury consisted of killing, not of shaming'). But Æthelberht, ch. 4 uses *forgylde* as the verb of restitution for theft, and ch. 5 uses *gebete* as restitution for killing, so Liebermann's distinction between the two cannot be correct.

TABLE 1

Amount of restitution in Æthelberht chs. 2–12

ch. 2.	Injury to king's subjects at court:	50 shillings.
ch. 3.	Damage when king is at a subject's house:	2-fold restitution.
ch. 4.	Theft from king:	9-fold restitution.
ch. 5.	Killing person in the king's dwelling:	50 shillings wergeld.
ch. 6.	Killing a freeman:	50 shillings lordprice to king.
ch. 7.	Killing the king's man:	ordinary wergeld (100 shillings).
ch. 8.	Breach of king's peace:	50 shillings.
ch. 9.	Theft from a freeman:	3-fold restitution; king takes the rest.
ch. 10.	Lying with the king's maid:	50 shillings.
ch. 11.	'Grinding slave':	25 shillings.
	Third rank of female slave:	12 shillings.
ch. 12.	King's *fedesl*:	20 shillings.

Liebermann supports his interpretation of *Königskostgänger* with reference to two other sources. The first is from the laws of Hlothhere and Eadric (673×685?), ch. 15: 'Gif man cuman feormæþ III niht an his agenum hame (cepeman oþþe oðerne þe sio ofer mearce cuman) 7 man hine þonne his mete fede, 7 he þonne ænigum mæn yfel gedo, se man þane oðerne æt rihte gebrenge oþþe riht forewyrce' ('If someone puts up a guest for three nights in his own home (a merchant or another who has come over the border), and one feeds him his food there, and he then does ill to any man, that man shall bring the other to justice or do justice for him'). This clause has a somewhat different interpretation: a host has the responsibility to make sure that his guests obey the law. Liebermann's interpretation of *Königskostgänger* in Æthelberht, ch. 12, on the basis of Hlothhere and Eadric's phrase *hine his mete fede* 'feeds him his food', implies that a king is eligible for reparation if his guest or dependant is harmed, but, crucially, this implication is lacking in Hlothhere and Eadric's laws.

The other parallel Liebermann cites is from Ealdorman Æthelweard's *Chronicle*, written in the late tenth century. In the annal for 878 King Alfred is said to have had no reinforcements, 'excepto his qui regio pastu utebantur famulis', 'except servants who had royal maintenance'.[7] Following these examples, Liebermann maintains that the position of the *fedesl* to the king is parallel to that of the *hlafæta* 'bread-eater' listed as a dependant of the *ceorl* in ch. 25. In support of this argument is the evidence (which Liebermann neglects to mention) of their parallel position within the body of the text: the laws dealing

---

[7] *The Chronicle of Æthelweard*, ed. A. Campbell (Edinburgh, 1962), p. 42.

TABLE 2

Comparison of amounts of restitution to king and ceorl		
	King	*Ceorl*
mundbyrd	50 shillings	6 shillings
Female Slave		
1st rank	50 shillings	6 shillings
2nd rank	25 shillings	50 *sceatta*
3rd rank	12 shillings	30 *sceatta*
fedesl	20 shillings	
hlafæta		6 shillings

with the *fedesl* and the *hlafæta* are both last in their respective sections referring to the king and to the *ceorl*.

But although the position within the laws can be adduced to support Liebermann, the numbers do not match up in terms of the amounts of restitution, as shown in Table 2.

For both king and *ceorl* the *mundbyrd* is equal in worth to the top rank of female slave. However, there is a discrepancy in the last categories. Whereas the *ceorl*'s *hlafæta* is equal to his *mundbyrd* and top rank of slave, the king's *fedesl* is worth only forty per cent of these.

A more serious argument against Liebermann's analysis comes from the morphological formation of *fedesl*. Under the entry *fedels/fedesl* Toller cites the following Germanic glosses:

Old Saxon: *foedils* = *altile saginatum* 'fattened fatted beast'
Old High German: *fuotisal* = *pastio* 'pasture, feeding'

Toller also lists Icelandic *foeðsla* 'food', and thus in his definition II translates Æthelberht's *fedesl* as 'feeding'. Although Liebermann rejects the possibility of connection to Icelandic *foeðsla*, 'denn keine Spur besteht, dass es zwischen "Königsschutz" und Strafgeldfixum (50 bzw. 12 Sch.) eine dritte bestimmte Summe jenes Namens und sonst unbekannter Geltung gab',[8] I believe that it is precisely these cognates which give the clue to the interpretation in Æthelberht. All the parallels listed by Toller contain the Germanic suffix *-isla-*, which according to Ekwall 'is commonly used in Old Germanic languages to form

---

[8] 'for there is no trace that between "king's protection" and the base sum for punishment (50 and 12 shillings, respectively), there existed a third defined amount of this name and of otherwise unknown application'.

concrete nouns from verbs, especially weak *ia*-verbs'.[9] That we are dealing here with an *ia*-verb can be seen by Gothic *fōdjan* and Old Saxon *fōdian* 'to feed'; the **i* has fronted the **ō* to *ē* in OE *fēdan*. Formally, then, we can derive the nominal forms cognate with *fedesl* from Common Germanic **fōd-isla-*, which would regularly give OE **fēdisl* after *i*-umlaut:

Common Germanic **fōd-isla-* > Primitive Old English **fǣdisl(a)* > Archaic Kentish *fēdesl*.

The foregoing etymology crucially stops before Classical Old English, where the *-isl-* suffix regularly metathesizes.[10]

Most of the words containing this *-isl-* suffix, according to Ekwall, 'are instrumental in meaning'.[11] The affix is inherited from Common Germanic; according to Meid, the reflexes are 'überwiegend neutrale Verbalabstrakta'[12] although Brunner points out that in Old English these words are generally masculine rather than neuter (but crucially *not* feminine, which argues further against de Laet/Harris/Wilkins's and Thorpe's interpretations).[13] The instrumental force is clear from Meid's illustrations of this formation, such as Gothic *swartizl* 'ink' from **swartjan* 'to blacken', Old High German *irrisal* 'mistake' from *irren* 'to err', and ON *smyrsl* (cognate with the metathesized OE *smyrels*) 'fat, ointment' from *smyrja* 'to smear'. Looking at Ekwall's examples, it is obvious that this is the usual sense in Old English as well: *gyrdels* 'belt' = 'that which girds' from *gyrdan* 'to gird', *rēcels* 'incense' = 'that which smokes' from *rēcan* 'to smoke' and *brigdel(s)* 'bridle' from *bregdan* 'to drag to and fro'. From the verb *fēdan* 'feed' we would similarly expect a meaning such as 'that by which something/someone is fed', in fact, precisely the Icelandic *foeðsla* 'food', cited by Toller but rejected by Liebermann. Recall that in Old Saxon *foedils* glosses *altile saginatum* 'a fattened fatted beast', and in Old High German *fuotisal* glosses *pastio* 'pasture': both attestations support an instrumental reading.

This instrumental interpretation of the Germanic compound accords well

---

[9] E. Ekwall, 'The English Place-Names Etchells, Nechells', *Mélanges de philologie offerts à M. Johan Vising* (Göteborg, 1925), pp. 104–6.

[10] Metathesis is the switching of two contiguous sounds, as in OE *acsode* vs ModE *asked* vs dialectal *aksed*. This is generally a sporadic process: however Old English early developed a syllabic constraint against trisyllabic stems ending in [dental continuant]-[l]. That this metathesis holds for the *-isla-#* suffix and not for the *-sla-#* suffix (that is, for trisyllabic rather than bisyllabic stems) is demonstrated by the non-metathesized *cnosl* 'progeny, kin', *fæsl* 'offspring', *husl* 'eucharist', *rysl* 'fat', *susl* 'torment', *tæsl* 'teasle' and *gewrixl* 'interchange'. I have demonstrated in 'Language of the Early English Laws', pp. 135–51, that this metathesis must have been complete in both the northern and southern regions by the mid-eighth century: thus, *fedesl* would have already been an archaic form by the time of the compilation of the *Textus Roffensis*.

[11] Ekwall, 'English Place-Names in Etchells, Nechells', p. 105.

[12] 'overwhelmingly neuter verbal abstracts': W. Meid and H. Krahe, *Germanische Sprachwissenschaft*, 3 vols. (Berlin, 1967) III, 90.

[13] K. Brunner, *Altenglische Grammatik* (Tübingen, 1942), § 238, n. 2.

with the definition I offered by Toller for the metathesized *fedels* as 'fatling' or 'feeder'. As quoted above, Attenborough in his note to Æthelberht, ch. 12 states that 'the word *fedesl* occurs elsewhere only as a translation of *altilis* ["fatted beast"]'. The term 'elsewhere' is somewhat misleading: the form appears without metathesis in Old English exclusively in Æthelberht's laws; in all other occurrences the final -*sl* is metathesized to -*ls*. There are only five attestations of this metathesized version, according to computer search of the Anglo-Saxon corpus. All five of these appearances concur with Toller's definition I. The first two are both contained in late glossaries: one defines *fedels* as *altile* 'fatted [beast]', and another merely replaces the neuter *altile* with the masculine/feminine *altilis*. There are also two attestations of a partially-umlauted variant, *foedils*. In CorpGl 2 1.467 it glosses *altilia*, and in WerdGlC 566.15 *altile saginatum*.[14]

The only other attestation of the metathesized form is contained as the first element of a compound in the late-tenth-century list of stock at Yaxley, Huntingdonshire, preserved in a cartulary of Peterborough Abbey (S 1448).[15] The text, given here in the edition and translation by Robertson, reads as follows:

þis is þæt erfgewrit æt Geaceslea, þryttene wepmen weorcewyrþe 7 .v. wimmen 7 æhta geonge men 7 .xvi. oxan, faldreþere 7 .iii. hund scepa 7 .v. scep 7 .xxx. swina 7 hund-teonig fliccena 7 eal þa smean ðe þerto gebyriað 7 .xxx. forþer cornes 7 hundehtetig æcera gesawen 7 an egþwirf 7 .vi. bidenfate 7 .ii. cuflas 7 þry trogas 7 lead 7 trefet 7 .ix. winterstellas 7 .i. fedelsswin.

This is the inventory of the stock at Yaxley: 13 able-bodied men and 5 women and 8 young men and 16 oxen, a stalled ox and 305 sheep and 30 swine and 100 flitches of bacon and all the delicacies that belong to them, and 30 fothers of corn and 80 acres sown and 1 harrow (?) and 6 barrels and 2 tubs and 3 troughs and a cauldron and a trivet and 9 year-old stallions and 1 fat pig.[16]

There is clearly a differentiation between the 30 *swina* and the single *fedelsswin*: presumably the 30 are piglets not yet ready to be eaten, while the single *fedelsswin* could easily become tomorrow's pork chops. (A similar distinction is preserved in the Modern German doublet *Schwein* vs *Mastschwein*.) It is certainly difficult to

---

[14] *Microfiche Concordance to Old English*, ed. A. diP. Healey and R. Venezky (Toronto and Newark, DE, 1980); T. Wright, *Anglo-Saxon and Old English Vocabularies*, 2nd ed., ed. R. P. Wülcker, 2 vols. (London, 1884) I, cols. 120, 190. The editors of the *Dictionary of Old English*, Toronto, have pointed out in a personal communication that 'this glossary, found in the Antwerp–London Manuscript, is no longer considered to be Ælfric's . . . A discussion on the history of confusion of this glossary with Ælfric can be found in C. A. Ladd, 'The "Rubens" Manuscript and Archbishop Ælfric's Vocabulary', *RES* ns 11, no. 44 (1960), 353–63.'

[15] P. H. Sawyer, *Anglo-Saxon Charters: An Annotated List and Bibliography* (London, 1968), p. 406.

[16] *Anglo-Saxon Charters*, ed. A. J. Robertson, 2nd ed. (Cambridge, 1956), p. 75.

conceive that 'fat pig' is not the meaning of the final compound, as translated by Robertson.[17]

The semantic force of the *-isl-* suffix in Old English metathesized stems formed from the root *fēd-* matches that of all other Old English and Germanic verbal roots: that is, the suffix adds instrumental force with the meaning 'the means by which something/someone is X-ed'. But Liebermann's interpretation reverses the meaning from 'that by which the king is fed' to 'those whom the king feeds'; in short, he changes the semantics from 'feeder' to 'freeloader'. This would require an involved and otherwise unparalleled semantic shift of the term *fedesl* in Kentish: an inherited word, presumably with the meaning 'that which feeds' as predicted by the morphology everywhere else in the Germanic languages would have undergone a semantic shift in Kentish law to 'those who are fed' and be subsequently restored in Classical Old English to the meaning of 'that which feeds' or, more precisely, 'fatted beast' – in short, an unlikely scenario. Following the usage of other Germanic glosses and of the metathesized form in later Old English, one might translate the term as 'fatted beast' and tentatively render the law as follows: '[For stealing] a king's fatted beast, 20 shillings.' This is not a particularly satisfying interpretation, as we have no other references to a finite sum of restitution for theft: stealing from the king is recompensable by ninefold restitution (Æthelberht, ch. 4) and from a *ceorl* by threefold restitution (Æthelberht, ch. 9). This would also be the only specific property reference in Æthelberht's laws.

In place of the foregoing translation, I would like to offer an alternative analysis based on comparative glosses and early medieval legal/cultural parallels. The ninth-century Old High German glosses to Gregory's *Regula pastoralis* translate *pastionis* as *uueidines* or *futisales*.[18] The Latin *pastio* is a third-declension noun, closely related etymologically to the fourth-declension *pastus*, for which Du Cange, in the *Glossarium Mediæ et Infimæ Latinitatis*, gives as a secondary definition: 'PASTUS sumitur eadam notione, qua *Procuratio, convivium, cœnicatum, etc.* de quibus vocabulis, suis locis agimus, seu pro eo jure, quo vassalli et tenentes Principem ac Dominum statis ac definitis vicibus, vel diebus, vel etiam quoties per vassallorum prædia iter agebat, convivio tenebantur excipere: quod quidem jus in præstationes pecuniarias sæpenumero communitatum legitur' ('PASTUS is used for that same idea as *Procuratio, convivium, cœnicatum, etc.*, which terms we treat in their proper places, or according to that law by which vassals and tenants were obliged to welcome a prince or lord with provisions [*convivio*] at established and definite places or on (certain) days or, indeed, whenever (their) passage

---

[17] Thus also C. H. Whitman, 'Old English Mammal Names', *JEGP* 6 (1907), 649–56, who defines *fēdels* as 'fat beast; probably related to *fēdan*, to feed'. I am indebted to Ben Fortson for reminding me of the Modern German parallel.

[18] *Die althochdeutschen Glossen*, ed. E. Steinmeyer and E. Sievers, 5 vols. (Berlin, 1879–1922) II, 220.

proceeded through the estates of the vassals, which obligation indeed is said to have been commuted frequently in monetary payments').[19]

In other words, in the laws *pastus* has taken on the legal meaning of responsibility for feeding the king, either in kind or in monetary valuation. As an example, Du Cange cites chapter 8 of the *Concilium Romanum* (904):

Ut Pastus Imperatoris ab Episcopis et Comitibus *secundum antiquam consuetudinem* [emphasis mine] solvatur.

So that the Feeding of the Emperor be paid by the Bishops and the Counts *according to old custom.*

Ganshof discusses in detail support due from estates for the maintenance of the king in the Carolingian period.[20] More directly relevant to the practice in the early Anglo-Saxon territories is the charter of Wiglaf, king of Mercia, dated 836, given here in the citation by Du Cange with the translation by Whitelock:[21] 'liberabo a *Pastu* Regis et Principum' ('I will free them from *entertainment* of the king and ealdormen'). That this legal specification was extended from the fourth-declension *pastus* to the third-declension *pastio* can be seen in a ninth-century charter of Charles the Bald, which lists the equivalent terms: 'aut coenaticum, aut pastionem, aut laudaticum, etc.'. These are all synonyms for 'banquet'; all share the legal meaning 'restitution in lieu of feeding the king'. It is possible that the Old High German *fuotisal* and its Old English cognate *fedesl* have undergone a similar semantic specialization in early medieval legal texts, with the meaning 'feeding of the king or prince' either in kind or in monetary valuation.

There is support for the existence of this practice from the early vernacular laws in the British Isles. In the Anglo-Saxon territories, we find the custom described in the West Saxon law-code of Ine (*c.* 694) ch. 70.1: 'Æt X hidum to fostre X fata hunies, CCC hlafa, XII ambra Wilisc ealað, XXX hluttres, tu eald hriðeru oððe X weðeras, X gees, XX henna, X cesas, amber fulne buteran, V leaxas, XX pundwæga foðres ond hundteonig æla' ('From 10 hides for sustenance 10 vats of honey, 300 loaves, 12 vessels of Welsh ale, 30 of light (ale), 2 grown cattle or 10 wethers, 10 geese, 20 hens, 10 cheeses, a vessel full of butter, 5 lox, 20 poundweights of feed and 100 eels'). Here the term used is *fostre*, dative of the word which comes down to us in Modern English as 'foster'; the change in terminology may be a dialectal difference between West Saxon and Kentish. Charles-Edwards states that this foster 'may plausibly be thought of as a royal food render', although Liebermann supposes that it is 'nicht allein für

[19] I am indebted to Jesse Gellrich for help in the translation of this passage. This and following citations from C. Du Cange, *Glossarium Mediæ et Infimæ Latinitatis* (Paris, 1678) V, 206.

[20] F. L. Ganshof, *Frankish Institutions under Charlemagne*, trans. B. and M. Lyon (Providence, RI, 1968), pp. 34–45.   [21] Sawyer, *Anglo-Saxon Charters*, no. 190; *EHD* I, ed. Whitelock, no. 85.

den König fällig'.[22] Charles-Edwards presumably sees some sort of royal food render dating back to the earliest days of the Anglo-Saxon kingdoms, as he continues:

before *c.* 700 I doubt whether one had to pay the *feorm* of one night unless a royal household was there to be fed. The normal kind of food render, embracing the whole diet, could hardly be transported far, so that, if no one appeared to eat it, that was presumably the end of the obligation for that year . . . A regime of food renders, therefore, was common to the Celtic and Germanic parts of the British isles in the centuries after the departure of the Roman army and Roman mints.

Charles-Edwards's claim that this practice was common also in Celtic is well documented in Old Irish law, in which there is repeated reference to the terms *bés* 'the annual food-rent due by every base client . . ., the "fixed refection" . . . to be supplied by him in return for the fief . . . which he has received from his lord' and *bíathad*, which 'sometimes refers to the food-rent'.[23] The practice is also legislated in the Early Middle Welsh laws of Hwyel Dda (reigned 904–49 over first part and then all of Wales), where it is applied specifically to the king:

This is the measure of the King's *gwestfa* from a free *maenol* in winter-time: a horse-load of the best flour that grows on the land, and a meat steer; and a vat's quota of mead (nine fistbreadth in length diagonally, and the same in breadth); and seven thraves of single-bound oats as horse-fodder; and a three-year-old pig, and a salt flitch with fat three fingers' breadth thick; and a vessel of butter three fistbreadths deep without the heap, and three wide.[24]

This practice was common in the early medieval period in the British Isles; its persistence can be seen by references in Domesday Book to the practice known as the *firma unius noctis* ('farm of one night'), of which Stafford states: 'the farm of one night, more rarely referred to as the farm of one day, was a sum in cash, kind, or both, considered sufficient to support the royal court, in theory, for a single twenty-four hour period'.[25]

In conclusion, it seems possible that we are seeing in Æthelberht, ch. 12, a reference to the common early medieval practice of providing food render for the king. This would agree perfectly with the expected instrumental interpretation of 'feeding' dictated by the morphology. It is important to remember, however, that Æthelberht's laws never prescribe duties: they only establish restitution for offence. But as stated at the beginning of this

---

[22] '. . . not due to the king alone': *Gesetze der Angelsachsen*, ed. Liebermann III, 80; T. Charles-Edwards, 'Early Medieval Kingships in the British Isles', *The Origins of Anglo-Saxon Kingdoms*, ed. Bassett, pp. 28–39, esp. 30–1.   [23] *Críth Gablach,* ed. D. A. Binchy (Dublin, 1941), pp. 75–6.

[24] *The Law of Hywel Dda,* trans. D. Jenkins (Llandysul, 1986), p. 128.

[25] P. A. Stafford, 'The "Farm of One Night" and the Organization of King Edward's Estate in Domesday', *EconHR* 33 (1980), 491–502, at 491, n. 3.

discussion, the syntactic formulation of Æthelberht, ch. 12 parallels that of ch. 8: 'Cyninges mundbyrd: L scillinga.' ('[For violation of] the king's protection: 50 shillings.') The abstract noun *mundbyrd* (with its modifying genitive *cyninges*) stands alone in what is elsewhere the *gif*-clause, taking for granted the assumption of offence. Following this pattern, ch. 12 could be interpreted as follows: 'Cyninges fedesl XX scillinga forgelde'. ('[For violation of the responsibility for] the king's feeding, let him [who defaulted the responsibility] pay 20 shillings').[26]

---

[26] I would like to express my thanks to my colleagues who have been generous with their advice and patience in reading earlier versions of this article: chief (but not solely) among them Charles Donahue, Dan Donoghue, Joshua Katz, Jesse Gellrich, Calvert Watkins and Patrick Wormald, and also to Simon Keynes for his comments on an earlier draft of this paper submitted to this journal.

The Minster-in-Thanet foundation story

STEPHANIE HOLLIS

The story of how Domne Eafe[1] acquired the land for her monastery at Thanet when her brothers were murdered by a councillor of her cousin, Ecgberht of Kent (664–73), is variously related in a number of Latin and Old English works. The full version (involving Domne Eafe's tame hind and the death of the councillor) is found in three Latin Lives. These are: a *passio* of the murdered princes attributed to Byrhtferth, which is the earliest recorded account of the foundation of Thanet, dated *c.* 1000, and written for the monks at Ramsey, who believed the relics translated to their monastery in 978×992 to be those of Domne Eafe's brothers;[2] Goscelin's *Vita S. Mildrethae*, dated 1089×1099, and written for the monks at St Augustine's, Canterbury, who acquired the relics of Mildrith from Thanet in 1030; a *passio* of the murdered princes found in Oxford, Bodleian Library, Bodley 285, also from Ramsey, which was composed sometime between the mid-eleventh century and the early thirteenth.[3]

The same sequence of events is also related in an Old English fragment found in London, British Library, Cotton Caligula A. xiv (s. xi[med]), 121v–124v, which is

---

[1] 'Eormenburh, and oðre naman Domne Eafe' (Caligula). Contemporary charters have 'Æbba'. In references to Anglo-Saxon charters, S = P. H. Sawyer, *Anglo-Saxon Charters: an Annotated List and Bibliography* (London, 1968), followed by the number of the document; BCS = W. de G. Birch, *Cartularium Saxonicum*, 3 vols. (London, 1885–93). In references to *vitae* and *passiones*, BHL = *Bibliotheca Hagiographica Latina Antiquae et Mediae Aetatis*, ed. Socii Bollandiani, 2 vols. (Brussels, 1898–1901).

[2] Byrhtferth's *Passio SS Ethelberti atque Ethelredi regiae stirpis puerorum* (*BHL* 2643), in *Symeonis Monachi Opera Omnia*, ed. T. Arnold, 2 vols., RS (London, 1882–5) II, 3–13 (hereafter referred to as 'Arnold'). For attribution and dating, see M. Lapidge, 'Byrhtferth of Ramsey and the Early Sections of the *Historia Regum* attributed to Symeon of Durham', *ASE* 10 (1982), 97–122, at 98 and 119–20, repr. in his *Anglo-Latin Literature, 900–1066* (London, 1993), pp. 317–42.

[3] Bodley 285 (*Passio et translatio beatorum martyrum Ethelredi atque Ethelbricti* (*BHL* 2641–2)) and Goscelin's *Vita Deo dilectae virginis Mildrethae* (*BHL* 5960), ed. D. W. Rollason, *The Mildrith Legend: a Study in Early Medieval Hagiography in England* (Leicester, 1982), pp. 90–104 and 108–43. ('Rollason', followed by page number, refers hereafter to the editions of Bodley and *Vita S. Mildrethae* included in this study.) For dating and provenance, see Rollason, *Mildrith Legend*, pp. 18–21; for modifications, see R. Sharpe, 'Goscelin's St. Augustine and St. Mildreth: Hagiography and Liturgy in Context', *JTS* ns 41 (1990), 502–16; 'The Date of S. Mildreth's Translation from Minster-in-Thanet to Canterbury', *MS* 53 (1991), 349–54.

headed as a Life of Mildrith.[4] In these four accounts, and in most of the later, abbreviated versions, the story of Domne Eafe's foundation of her monastery is preceded by a genealogy, and it was followed by an account of Domne Eafe's daughter Mildrith, who succeeded her as abbess of Thanet (the account of Mildrith in Caligula A. xiv has been lost).[5] David Rollason, in his seminal study, terms this sequence 'the Mildrith legend'. As Rollason shows, the four versions named above ultimately derive from a common source. Paul Hayward, in a study of Byrhtferth's *passio* and Bodley 285, agrees with Rollason that Bodley 285 and Goscelin's *vita* probably share a dependency on a lost recension made at St Augustine's in the mid-eleventh century, and concludes that Byrhtferth's *passio* and Caligula are in independent lines of descent from the common archetype.[6]

An abbreviated version of the legend appears in the Old English account of the founding of the Kentish monasteries which is known as *þa halgan* or *The Resting Place of the Saints*.[7] Another incompletely preserved Old English text,

---

[4] *Leechdoms, Wortcunning, and Starcraft of Early England*, ed. O. Cockayne, 3 vols., RS (London, 1864–6) III, 422–8 (hereafter referred to as 'Cockayne'); also ed. M. J. Swanton, 'A Fragmentary Life of St. Mildred and Other Kentish Royal Saints', *AC* 91 (1975), 15–27, at 24–6. On provenance, see below, p. 45, n. 13. The rubric in Caligula A. xiv reads 'III. Id. Iulii. Natale Sanctae mildryðe uirginis.'

[5] Of the remaining versions discussed by Rollason (see *Mildrith Legend*, pp. 21–31), *þa halgan* omits the episode involving the tame hind and the death of Thunor, as do the Gotha version and Goscelin's *Vita S. Mildburgae*; Hugh Candidus mentions the death of Thunor, but omits the hind. Goscelin's *Vita S. Werburgae* and the *Genealogia regum Cantuariorum* – which are even more distantly related to the original – merely mention the murder of the princes in their genealogies of the Kentish royal house. It is possible that *þa halgan* (cited below, p. 42, n. 7) and Gotha, from St Gregory's Priory, Canterbury (cited below, p. 54, n. 43), represent independent traditions rather than later abbreviations (cf. Rollason, *Mildrith Legend*, pp. 23–5 and 28).

[6] See Rollason, *Mildrith Legend*, pp. 15–21 and 60–1; P. A. Hayward, 'The Idea of Innocent Martyrdom in Earlier Medieval England, ca. 700 to 1150' (unpubl. PhD dissertation, Cambridge Univ., 1994), pp. 101–20. Hayward (pp. 110–16) shows that there is no reason to believe that Byrhtferth's immediate source originated at Wakering, or that it differed from the source which lies behind Caligula and Bodley (cf. Rollason, *Mildrith Legend*, pp. 15–18). Rollason (who offers no stemma) states that the version represented by Caligula 'may have been known in Canterbury, since [Caligula] is very similar, given the difference in their language, to the Bodley 285 Text, which embodies a version written at St Augustine's Abbey, Canterbury, after Mildrith's translation' (p. 31). He suggests that Caligula, and the St Augustine's recension underlying Bodley (as well as Goscelin's *vita*), may have descended from a Thanet version which accompanied Mildrith's relics to St Augustine's (see also Rollason, *Mildrith Legend*, pp. 58–9). Bodley bears a closer resemblance to Caligula than do Goscelin's *vita* and Byrhtferth's *passio*, because it contains less interpolated material, but I argue below that there are significant differences which relate it more closely to the Latin versions. The existence of a lost St Augustine's recension is deduced by Rollason, *Mildrith Legend*, p. 19, from Bodley's statement that Mildrith's body rests before the high altar at St Augustine's, a state of affairs obtaining only in the period 1030 to *c.* 1059.

[7] *Die Heiligen Englands*, ed. F. Liebermann (Hanover, 1889), pp. 1–10, at 1–5. *þa halgan* is preserved in the *Liber vitae* of New Minster, Winchester (1031) and is dated to 725×974 by

London, Lambeth Palace 427 (s. xi²), fol. 211, is evidently a fragment of a text similar in kind to *þa halgan*.[8] Presumably, this fragment also related the story of the founder-abbess of Thanet and her daughter, since its acephalous opening refers to the translation of Mildrith's remains by her successor Eadburg. It is of interest here because it records the foundation story of another Kentish monastery, Minster-in-Sheppey, by Seaxburg (the East Anglian mother of Ecgberht of Kent). Like Caligula, Lambeth opens with a genealogy of the founder-abbess and the daughter who succeeded her, followed by an account of how the founder gained by her own efforts an independent legal title to the monastery's land.

Rollason concludes that the Mildrith legend originated at Thanet in the time of Mildrith's successor Eadburg (*c.* 732–51).[9] In his study, the Mildrith legend serves to illustrate the thesis that hagiography 'was not primarily a devotional genre out of touch with life beyond the monastery's or church's walls, [but] intimately concerned with wider attitudes and aspirations, a living genre with as much claim to have been in touch with the society in which it was written or read as medieval historical writing itself'. Rollason draws attention to what one might term 'reception opportunism' – the varied and conflicting forms of polemical endorsement that different groups of auditors and transmitters could draw from the legend over the course of the centuries. In the century of its origin, he argues, it served to enhance the prestige and sanctity of the Kentish royal house, but – as King Ecgberht's complicity in the murder of his cousins does not, in fact, redound to the glory of his house – the legend could, conversely, be used by the church 'to coerce . . . any of Egbert's successors who might be unco-operative with the story of his guilt'. In the later Anglo-Saxon period, the legend became 'relevant . . . to the problem of royal murders on the one hand and to the saintly ethos of a unified country on the other'. Finally, in post-Conquest Canterbury, when the canons at St Gregory's as well as the monks at St Augustine's claimed possession of Mildrith's relics, the legend was 'bound up with the petty jealousies of two squabbling religious houses'.[10] The 'wider attitudes and aspirations' that have

Rollason, *Mildrith Legend*, p. 28; see also above, p. 42, n. 5. I am indebted to Professor Lapidge for drawing my attention to S. Keynes's new dating of the *Liber vitae*, *The Liber vitae of the New Minster and Hyde Abbey, Winchester: British Library Stowe 944*, ed. S. Keynes, EEMF 26 (Copenhagen, 1996), 37–9.
[8] Ed. Cockayne III, 430–2; also ed. M. Förster, 'Die altenglischen Beigaben des Lambeth-Psalters', *ASNSL* 132 (1914), 328–35, at 332–3; Swanton, 'Fragmentary Life', p. 27. On dating, see below, p. 61, n. 76; on provenance, see below, p. 45, n. 13. Lambeth 427, fol. 211, is parallel to *þa halgan*, ed. Liebermann, *Heiligen*, pp. 5–7. (S. Hollis, 'The Old English "Ritual of Mildrith" (London, Lambeth Palace 427, fol. 210)', *JEGP* 97 (1998), 311–21, disagrees with Swanton, 'Fragmentary Life', p. 15, who suggests that Caligula and Lambeth 427, fols. 210–11, are the fragmentary remains of an amplified version of *þa halgan*.)
[9] See Rollason, *Mildrith Legend*, pp. 33–40.   [10] *Ibid.* pp. 69, 49 and 68.

significance for Rollason as a late-twentieth-century auditor and transmitter of the legend are the politics of kingship, and for him the salient feature of the legend is the murder of the princes – as it was to the Ramsey promoters of their cult, and to the Anglo-Norman writers whose primary interest was the deeds of kings.

In this article I shall argue that 'the Mildrith legend' was a monastic myth of origins that has bearing on the history of monastic women. In form, I am suggesting, it is the dynastic legend of a royal *Eigenkloster*, which relates how the founder-abbess gained the monastery's land and left it to her daughter. To me, its salient feature is a foundation story which affirms the monastery's traditional claim to the possession of its land. This, equally, is a reading of the legend that is of its time. But if we accept that the legend originated at Thanet in the time of Abbess Eadburg, we are bound to conclude that commemoration of the founder-abbess of Thanet and continued possession of the monastery's land were of greater concern to the originators of the legend than the problem of royal murders, or even the prestige and sanctity of the Kentish royal house to which the first abbesses belonged.

The cult of Mildrith, as we know it, is the creation of St Augustine's, whose abbot in 1030 took possession of Mildrith's remains, as well as the former monastery's land.[11] This translation, which appears to have greatly enhanced Mildrith's part in the original legend, undoubtedly gave St Augustine's a vested interest in the monastery's claim to its land. Canterbury was, arguably, the chief centre from which the legend was disseminated, but there is no evidence that the legend was a Canterbury creation, and it was evidently in existence at least thirty years before Mildrith's translation to St Augustine's, when Byrhtferth of Ramsey re-worked it as a hagiographical celebration of the murdered princes.[12] Caligula,

---

[11] See D. W. Rollason, 'Goscelin of Canterbury's Account of the Translation and Miracles of St. Mildrith (*BHL* 5961/4): an Edition with Notes', *MS* 48 (1986), 139–210, at 170–5.

[12] Cf. Swanton, 'Fragmentary Life', p. 15, who describes Caligula as representing 'the genuine Canterbury tradition in a relatively pristine state'. For St Augustine's versions of the legend, see Rollason, *Mildrith Legend*, pp. 19–21; for the St Gregory's Priory texts, see pp. 21–5. In particular, St Augustine's may have been responsible for the transmission of the legend to the west, which is marked by the appearance of feasts of Mildrith and other Mildrith legend saints in kalendars from that area; note, however, that at least one of these pre-dates Byrhtferth's *passio* (Salisbury, Cathedral Library, 150, 3r–8v, in *English Kalendars before A.D. 1100*, ed. F. Wormald, HBS 72 (London, 1934), no. 2; N. R. Ker, *Catalogue of Manuscripts containing Anglo-Saxon* (Oxford, 1957), no. 379, dates it 969×978). Some aspects of the earlier dissemination of the legend from Thanet which Rollason attributes to the political influence of Kent (*Mildrith Legend*, p. 49) are doubtful; its appearance in *Vita S. Mildburgae* and *Vita S. Werburgae*, for instance, may bear out the attribution of these Lives to Goscelin, and the existence of a Wakering version which he postulates as Byrhtferth's immediate source can no longer be accepted (see above, p. 42, n. 6). The legend may have been transmitted from Thanet to St Augustine's with Mildrith's relics, as Rollason suggests (*Mildrith Legend*, pp. 31 and 58–9); it is

in stating that Mildrith's body rests at Thanet, confirms the existence of the legend prior to 1030, and Rollason suggests that Caligula represents a Thanet version which accompanied Mildrith's relics to Canterbury.[13] The textual evidence he offers for concluding that the legend originated at Thanet in the time of Eadburg, however, is regarded as inconclusive.[14] His case is more securely based on the accumulation of circumstantial evidence.[15] Of this, the most significant fact is that Mildrith's remains were translated by her successor Eadburg to the new monastery church that she had built – which, in Eadburg's time, was effectively a form of canonization that abbesses were permitted to carry out[16] – and I hope to strengthen the case for attributing the origins of the legend to Thanet in the time of Eadburg by arguing that the circumstances in which Eadburg elevated Mildrith's remains explain the form that the legend takes, and also the prominence it gives to the origins of the monastery's territorial possessions.

The Latin versions of the legend were undoubtedly written by male religious. The Thanet community included men. But I also want to suggest that the Old English version in Caligula A. xiv is closer to the original Thanet

also possible that it was among the Thanet documents transferred to St Augustine's in the late eighth or early ninth century as a consequence of Viking raids, and/or of Archbishop Wulfred's assumption of the lordship of Thanet (see below, pp. 62–3, nn. 80–1). Possibly, in view of the legend's connection with Seaxburg (see below, p. 58, n. 64), Byrhtferth's source also came from Thanet, *via* Ely.

[13] Rollason, *Mildrith Legend*, p. 31. Like the Lambeth fragments (cited above, p. 43, n. 8), Caligula is preserved in an 'Exeter-type' script; linguistically, the Lambeth fragments have the regular forms of literary late WS, whereas some forms in Caligula suggest a Kentish provenance (Swanton, 'Fragmentary Life', p. 17). Ker, *Catalogue*, pp. 172–3 and 343, did not attempt to assign these fragments, and in view of the tendency of attributions to gravitate to the men's houses on which we are best informed, it should not be too readily assumed that Caligula and the Lambeth fragments were copied either at Exeter or at Canterbury (cf. Rollason, *Mildrith Legend*, p. 30).

[14] Hayward, 'Innocent Martyrdom', pp. 111–12, objects that Rollason's dating (*Mildrith Legend*, pp. 15–17) accepts at face value Byrhtferth's statement concerning the location of Mildrith's relics which may have arisen from careless abbreviation of his source. S. E. Kelly, 'The Pre-Conquest History and Archive of St Augustine's Abbey, Canterbury' (unpubl. PhD dissertation, Cambridge Univ., 1986), pp. 300–1, n. 16, casts doubt on Rollason's use of the form *Easterige* (*Mildrith Legend*, p. 16) as evidence of an early dating.

[15] See Rollason, *Mildrith Legend*, pp. 33–40, esp. 33–6.

[16] S 91 (BCS 177); *Charters of St Augustine's Abbey Canterbury and Minster-in-Thanet*, ed. S. E. Kelly, AS Charters 4 (London, 1995), no. 51. See also Seaxburg's translation of her sister Æthelthryth, *Bede's Ecclesiastical History of the English People*, ed. B. Colgrave and R. A. B. Mynors (Oxford, 1969), IV.19, pp. 292–4 (hereafter *HE*); and Pega's translation of her brother, *Felix's Life of Guthlac*, ed. B. Colgrave (Cambridge, 1956), pp. 160–2. E. W. Kemp, *Canonization and Authority in the Western Church* (London, 1948), pp. 36–55, traces the intervention of higher ecclesiastical authorities in the translation of relics in the centuries following the Council of Mainz in 813. See also below, p. 57, n. 56.

tradition[17] and that this tradition may have been created by monastic women. Comparison of Caligula with the two Ramsey *passiones* and Goscelin's *Vita S. Mildrethae* reveals that the underlying legend reflected aspects of early monasticism which were in conflict with the orthodox ideals of the Anglo-Saxon Benedictine reform and post-Conquest periods, and which were therefore modified and adapted by the authors of the three Latin Lives. This does not only confirm the view that Caligula is the closest surviving representative of a tradition which originated at an early Anglo-Saxon double monastery. It reveals a different kind of reception history from the one which Rollason deduces from focusing on the Latin Lives, wherein St Augustine's appropriation of the body of Mildrith and the Thanet lands epitomizes the transmission of the legend.

THE FOUNDATION STORY AND ITS GENEALOGY IN CALIGULA

Caligula opens with a genealogy which introduces Domne Eafe as the hero-protagonist of the ensuing story of how the Thanet monastery acquired its lands. The genealogy traces her descent from St Augustine's first royal convert, Æthelberht of Kent; there follows a report of her marriage to Merewalh of Mercia, their subsequent separation 'for the love of God', and a brief account of their saintly progeny. Unlike the genealogies of kings, this one includes queens (Bertha, Imme and Oslaf), and two sisters of kings – Æthelburg, who was a patron of Canterbury, and St Eanswith, who founded the monastery at Folkestone. Domne Eafe is thus established as a member of the Kentish royal house, who was, furthermore, linked by marriage to the Mercian royal line; she is also established as a member of a dynasty from which had sprung two generations of saintly women, who was herself the mother of three female saints (including Mildrith) and the holy child Merefin.[18] Women are entirely absent from Byrhtferth's genealogy, since his interest lies in the kingly descent of the murdered princes, but the female bias of the genealogy must have been a feature of the original, because it is also found in the Bodley *passio* and

---

[17] Hayward, 'Innocent Martyrdom', p. 106, observes: 'Like most OE homilies [Caligula] shows signs of being an abbreviated translation and is probably, therefore, derived from a now lost Latin life'; it appears to me, however, that Goscelin's *vita*, Byrhtferth's *passio* and, to a lesser extent, Bodley, represent rhetorical inflation. We can only presume, in the absence of conclusive evidence to the contrary, that the vernacular would not have been used for independent composition prior to Alfred's educational reform. Stylistically, there are no strong indications that Caligula is a *direct* translation from Latin; doubtless it is at some remove from the original (see below, p. 48, n. 24).

[18] Ed. Cockayne III, 422–4. Similarly, the genealogy in Lambeth traces the kinship between Seaxburg (mother of Ecgberht of Kent) and the sainted women of the East Anglian royal house with whom she is buried at Ely, i.e. her sisters Wihtburh and Æthelthryth, and her daughter Eormenhild (whose own daughter, Werburh, rests at Hanbury), with whom Seaxburg took the veil at Milton.

Goscelin's *vita*.[19] Caligula's account of Æthelburg is consistent with this bias. Bede's *Historia ecclesiastica*, surprisingly, makes no mention of any monastic women in Kent, despite the fact that his chief informant was Abbot Albinus of Canterbury. But he does give an account of Æthelburg being escorted back to Kent by Bishop Paulinus after the fall of her husband Edwin of Northumbria; he also tells us that Paulinus brought with him many precious things belonging to King Edwin which may still be seen in the church at Canterbury.[20] Only Caligula states that Æthelburg returned to Kent and Paulinus went with her, and that she brought *her* best treasures to the church at Canterbury, so that prayers might be said for her and for the soul of the king her father. Goscelin omits Æthelburg from the genealogy. Bodley (which Hayward regards as motivated by a desire for a 'more historically accurate text') echoes Bede.[21]

Bede gives no information on how founder-abbesses acquired their lands, although he does mention that Barking was founded for Abbess Æthelburg by her brother, Bishop Eorcenwald.[22] In most cases, the origins of the lands owned by early double monasteries are documented only in royal charters, which define them as the gifts of kings (and, occasionally, queens). The Thanet and Sheppey foundation stories thus stand in contrast to the available record, whose influence is discernible in modern scholars' tendency to describe abbess-ruled monasteries as having been founded by kings. Sheppey's land, according to Lambeth, was not a gift (liable to be taken back by the hand that gave it, and to involve debts of gratitude), but a purchase. Seaxburg bought it from her son when, prompted by an angelic warning of an imminent pagan invasion, she resigned the throne to him and retired to the monastery she had built at Sheppey; and the foundation story echoes the formulaic phrases employed in charters.[23] Lambeth's assertion that Seaxburg obtained for her monastery a papal privilege likewise affirms the monastery's autonomy.

Caligula's account of Domne Eafe's acquisition of the monastery land is a relatively straightforward narration of events, virtually unmarked by the hagiographical inflation and orthodox piety which characterizes the Latin

---

[19] Bodley, ed. Rollason, pp. 91–3; *Vita S. Mildrethae*, pp. 112–15. Cf. Byrhtferth's *passio*, ed. Arnold II, 3–5. Gotha contains no genealogy, but the female bias is also reflected to varying degrees in all other versions of the legend examined by Rollason, *Mildrith Legend*.

[20] *HE* II.20 (ed. Colgrave and Mynors, p. 204).

[21] Bodley, ed. Rollason, p. 92; cf. Caligula, ed. Cockayne III, 422. See Hayward, 'Innocent Martyrdom', pp. 116–17 and 107 (below, p. 48, n. 25). Other versions merely mention the return of Æthelburg and Paulinus and present her (apocryphally?) as the founder of Lyminge.

[22] See S. Hollis, *Anglo-Saxon Women and the Church: Sharing a Common Fate* (Woodbridge, 1992), pp. 111, n. 176 and 260.

[23] 'And heo ða æt him gebohte his dæl ðæs eardes to freodome in to ðam mynstre ða hwile ðe cristendom wære on engla lande gehealden', ed. Cockayne III, 432. See further below, p. 61, n. 76.

versions.[24] But Domne Eafe is more significantly reliant on the help of providence than Seaxburg, and the land which she acquires in her own right also
belongs to God (who will therefore assist in its defence). Caligula's version of
the story is that when Domne Eafe's orphaned brothers were entrusted to their
uncle King Ecgberht, his councillor Thunor, fearing that they would become
dearer to the king than he, urged the king to let him secretly do away with them
before they became a threat to the security of his line. The king, at first reluctant
to countenance the murder of his own kin, eventually gave his consent, and
Thunor hid the bodies in the king's hall. But by the power of God, the crime was
revealed, for early next morning the king saw a beam of light reaching through
the roof of the hall to heaven; terrified, he summoned Thunor and demanded
that he tell him what he had done with his cousins whom he had stolen from
him. Thunor replied that he had buried them beneath the throne; the king,
afraid that the beam of light presaged God's wrath, held a council which, with
the support of the archbishop,[25] advised that Domne Eafe should be recalled
from Mercia to choose as wergild whatever she and her closest friends thought
best. But just as the king's dealings with Thunor reveal the unreliability of his
words, this undertaking does not mean, in the event, what it seemed to. For the
locality is subject to negotiation, and so too is the amount: 'se cyning and hio
Domne Eafe ærest þæt land geceas' ('the king and Domne Eafe first chose the
place'), and when they arrived at Thanet, 'þa cwæð se cyning to hire hwylcne dæl
þæs landes hio onfon wolde hyre broðrum to wergilde' ('the king asked what
part of the land she would take as wergild for her brothers'). She said she wanted
no more from him than her hind would run around. And the king said he would
gladly consent to that. But as the hind had been reared by Domne Eafe, the

---

[24] Ed. Cockayne III, 424–8. Caligula does describe the murdered princes as 'halgan æþelingas',
and says that Thunor 'gemartirode' them. It also says that they were 'swyðe gesceadwise and
rihtwise, swa hit Godes willa wæs', and claims that this provoked Thunor; but another motive is
provided by Thunor's fear that they would become dearer to the king than himself (ed.
Cockayne III, 424). This, purely secular, motive, and the king's subsequent demand that
Thunor tell him what he has done with the princes 'be his freondscipe' are found only in
Caligula (ed. Cockayne III, 426); the hagiographic description of the princes may therefore
represent additions to the original influenced by familiarity with the Ramsey cult. Caligula also
relates that the king became fearful at the divine miracle which revealed the princes' bodies, and
that he realized that he had angered God; but, in contrast to other versions, Caligula does not
develop this in the council scene. Apart from the report that Domne Eafe and her husband
separated by mutual consent and gave their children and worldly possessions to God (ed.
Cockayne III, 422–4), and the statement that Domne Eafe 'þæt wergild geceas þurh Godes
fultum' (ed. Cockayne III, 426), there is no attempt to portray Domne Eafe in pious terms.

[25] Byrhtferth (ed. Arnold II, 9 and 12) and Caligula (ed. Cockayne III, 426) name Deusdedit. Later
substitution of Theodore reflects Bodley's 'correction' of the legend against *HE* IV.1 (ed.
Colgrave and Mynors, p. 328); see Hayward, 'Innocent Martyrdom', pp. 116–17. Whether or
not Bede is unfailingly accurate, it appears that the originators of the legend believed that the
Thanet foundation dated to the time of Deusdedit.

author explains, it always ran ahead of her while she was out riding, and Domne Eafe contrived to ensure that the hind kept on running.[26] Thunor (still suspiciously eager to protect the king's interests), protests: 'Leof, hu lange wylt ðu hlystan þyssum dumban nytene þe hit eal wile þis land utan beyrnan? Wylt ðu hit eal ðære cwenon syllan?' ('Sir, how long will you pay heed to this dumb animal which will run about all this land? Will you give it all to the woman?') And straight away the ground opened and swallowed him. At this point Caligula breaks off; the three Latin Lives relate that the hind finished its circuit and a huge mound was heaped over the site of the cataclysm, which 'to this day' is still known as *Thunoreshlæw*.[27]

As told by Caligula, then, the foundation story affirms a twofold title to the monastery land. Explicitly, the royal grant is ratified by secular law and custom – adjudged to the founder as wergild by the king and his council, which also includes an archbishop. Implicitly, it expiates the king's concealed sin – a crime against God (to whom all hearts are open and from whom no secrets are hidden) which is made public by a sign from heaven, and avenged upon Thunor when he attempts to prevent the king from keeping his word; for although the king's responsibility is to a high degree displaced (and is therefore merely a sin of intention), Thunor in his last speech is the voice of the king's unexpressed thoughts, as he is the instrument of his private wishes when he murders the princes.

Only in Caligula is Domne Eafe's acquisition of the monastery's land presented as an achievement in which she plays an active role; it is thus the only version which is consistent with the genealogy's attention to the deeds of women. Caligula is unique in explaining that Domne Eafe exploited her knowledge of her tame hind's behaviour to gain most of Thanet instead of the small portion that the king implicitly hopes will suffice to fulfil his undertaking to his council. All three Latin versions agree with Caligula in having the king offer Domne Eafe whatever she chooses, to which she replies that she wants only as much land as her hind will encompass in a single lap (or, according to Byrhtferth, in one day); but by the omission of Caligula's explanation and by other concomitant alterations, Domne Eafe's removal of a substantial part of Thanet from the king's possession is presented in the Latin versions as a purely

---

[26] 'And hio ða hind swa dyde þæt hio him beforan hleapende wæs' (ed. Cockayne III, 426). Swanton, 'Fragmentary Life', p. 20, translates: 'And then the hind so acted that it leaped in front of them.' But Cockayne's translation – 'She then so managed that the hind kept running before them' – is supported by an earlier sentence, 'And hio ða swa dyde þæt hio wergeld geceas . . .' (ed. Cockayne III, 426), which Swanton translates: 'And she so arranged it that she chose that compensation. . .'.

[27] See Byrhtferth's *passio*, ed. Arnold II, 11–12, Bodley, ed. Rollason, p. 97; *Vita S. Mildrethae*, ed. Rollason, p. 118.

miraculous occurrence. The hind ceases to be the instrument of Domne Eafe's concealed intention (secretly in league with her as the king is in league with Thunor); she and the hind are merely the instruments of providence (as mindlessly irrational as Thunor takes them to be), and her deceptively modest request to the king manifests her exemplary humility and lack of avarice. Byrhtferth, for instance, relates that the holy woman, in meek reply, begged that the king would grant only as much land as a female deer which she had brought up, guided by divine instinct, could traverse in one day.[28] Consequently, it is only the Caligula author who asserts that Domne Eafe brought it about that, with the help of God, she obtained her choice of eighty hides of land in Thanet as wergild for her brothers.[29]

THE CONSTRUCTION OF THE STORY AND ITS AETIOLOGICAL FUNCTION

The foundation story, in the Caligula version, is a type of 'rash promise' story, widely attested in folklore, in which a knowing protagonist takes advantage of a magnanimously open offer and thereby gains what would not otherwise have been granted. Like the story of rash promise in the Middle English romance *Sir Orfeo*, the Caligula text both calls into question and affirms the king's fidelity to his word – it is necessary to trick him into keeping it. A story of rash promise related by Snorri Sturluson has in common with Caligula the fact that it is a toponymic story which furnishes an aetiological explanation of a landmark, and involves a woman acquiring from the king more land than he wanted to give, with the aid of animals with whom she has a concealed alliance. Gylfi, king of Sweden, rewarded Gefjun by granting her as much land as she could plough around in a day and a night. As she had four sons fathered by a giant, she turned them into oxen and together they laid claim to a large tract of land which they definitively removed from the king's possession. They dragged it into the harbour, and, Snorri relates, it is known to this day as Sealand.[30]

To a historically plausible claim concerning the origins of the monastery land (royal wergild),[31] have been added two integrally-related narrative

---

[28] Byrhtferth's *passio*, ed. Arnold II. Cf. Bodley, ed. Rollason, pp. 96–7; *Vita S. Mildrethae*, ed. Rollason, pp. 117–18.

[29] Ed. Cockayne III, 426. See also above, p. 49, n. 26. There is no parallel statement in *Vita S. Mildrethae* and Byrhtferth's *passio*. Bodley (ed. Rollason, p. 96) has: 'Elegit itaque (secundum Domini disposicionem) pro eorum precio terram quadraginta aratrorum, in loco qui appellatur Tenet.'

[30] *Snorri Sturluson: Edda, Prologue and Gylfaginning*, ed. A. Faulkes (Oxford, 1982), p. 7; see also *Ynglinga Saga*, in *Snorri Sturluson: Heimskringla* ed. B. Aðalbjarnarson, Íslenzk Fornrit 26, 2 vols. (Reykjavik, 1979) I, 14–15.

[31] To regard this claim as 'historically plausible' does not necessarily entail acceptance of its accuracy. Rollason, *Mildrith Legend*, p. 39, notes that there is no corroboration for the killing of

elements, both of a non-realistic, folkloric nature, which incorporate pre-Christian beliefs: a story of rash promise involving a deception with a tame hind, and the destruction of Thunor when he attempts to prevent its success. The role of the hind in delineating the territorial boundary is reminiscent of the practice of taking auguries from animal behaviour; according to Tacitus, the continental Germans attached particular significance to the behaviour of birds and horses.[32] *Thunoreshlæw* was evidently an ancient burial mound on or near the monastery's boundary. Burial mounds (usually described as 'heathen') figure in the bounds of a number of Anglo-Saxon charters;[33] they were associated with pre-Christian cults, and also with royal power,[34] and the name 'Thunor' (equated in glosses with Jupiter) clearly identifies this *hlæw* with

Domne Eafe's brothers but suggests that the raid of 676 on Kent by Domne Eafe's brother-in-law, Æthelred of Mercia, was an act of retaliation. One possible sign of conflict between Ecgberht of Kent and Domne Eafe's family is S 14 (BCS 40), dated *c.* 690, a grant from Oswine of Kent to Abbess Æbba of land at Sturry, which is described as land once possessed by Eormenred (her father) and formerly the property of Theodore (cf. S 13 (BCS 35)); *Charters of St Augustine's*, ed. Kelly, nos. 42–3. See also below, p. 59, n. 68.

32   *The Germania of Tacitus*, ed. R. P. Robinson (Middletown, CT, 1935), pp. 285–6. Cf. the report that Ramsey was founded where a bull chanced to scrape with its foot: *Chronicon Abbatiae Rameseiensis*, ed. W. D. Macray, RS (London, 1886), p. 9. For the stag as guide in Germanic and Frankish legends, see K. Helm, *Altgermanische Religionsgeschichte*, 2 vols. (Heidelberg, 1913) II, 82.

33   Relevant charters are listed by D. Bonney, 'Early Boundaries and Estates in Southern England', *Medieval Settlement: Continuity and Change*, ed. P. H. Sawyer (London, 1976), pp. 72–82, who argues that the holdings of early ecclesiastical parishes and churches were based on secular estates, and that the areas of land thus defined had been valid entities for at least a thousand years. See also D. Hooke, 'Burial Features in West Midlands Charters', *JEPNS* 13 (1980–1), 1–40: 'Location of the *hlæw* features on or near to boundaries of parishes takes on a new significance in the light of the known tendency for Anglo-Saxon burials to occupy boundary sites and may be presented as evidence for a connection between the two' (p. 24). Hooke considers that *hlæw* refers to Anglo-Saxon (as opposed to prehistoric) barrows; for the shift from isolated barrows to the barrow cemeteries more characteristic of Kent, see J. F. Shephard, 'The Social Identity of the Individual in Isolated Barrows and Barrow Cemeteries in Anglo-Saxon England', *Space, Hierarchy and Society*, ed. B. C. Burnham and J. Kingsbury, BAR Int. Ser. 59 (London, 1979), 47–79, esp. 48, 50 and 70–7. Neither the mound nor the name *Thunoreshlæw* have survived (see F. Hull, 'The Isle of Thanet, Kent, Late Fourteenth Century×1414', *Local Maps and Plans from Medieval England*, ed. R. A. Skelton and P. D. A. Harvey (Oxford, 1986), pp. 125–6; but note the grant by Eadmund (943) of land *to miclangrafe on tenet* (S 512 (BCS 780)).

34   See esp. the pagan priest who stands on a high mound to prevent missionaries from landing, in *The Life of Bishop Wilfrid by Eddius Stephanus*, ed. B. Colgrave (Cambridge, 1927), p. 28. D. Wilson, *Anglo-Saxon Paganism* (London, 1992), in a brief survey of burial mounds as cult centres, observes: 'Thunreslau [Essex] and Wodneslawe [Bedfordshire] are particularly interesting, in that each was the name of a later Saxon administration unit, a half-hundred . . . It is possible that here we have two examples of pagan cult sites continuing as meeting places in the Christian period' (p. 14). J. Simpson, 'The King's Whetstone', *Antiquity* 53 (1979), 96–101, at 99, considers relevant Scandinavian sources which associate the king sitting on a burial mound with contact with dead ancestors, claims to succession and law-giving.

paganism.[35] The foundation story, then, in relating Domne Eafe's capture for Christ of land in royal-pagan possession, simultaneously converts a pagan landmark to one with Christian significance. The perambulation of the tame hind, marking out the hallowed ground, gives vividly memorable definition to the monastery's boundary; if the irregular boundary shown on Elmham's fifteenth-century map of the former monastery gives a roughly accurate impression of the shape of the original bounds,[36] this feature of the story may also have provided an aetiological explanation of the boundaries.

REVISIONS TO THE THREE LATIN LIVES

In Byrhtferth's *passio*, the council does not meet to determine an offer of wergild to Domne Eafe; it merely provides an audience for the king's exhumation of the murdered princes. As this episode is found only in Byrhtferth's *passio*, it is presumably his invention. There follows an account of the princes' translation to Wakering and their posthumous miracles, which has evidently been derived from a different source.[37] Byrhtferth then returns to his principal source and relates the story of Domne Eafe and her daughter; in his version this is merely a sequel to his expanded hagiographical account of the martyrdom of the infant princes. The story of how Domne Eafe acquired the monastery land is germane to his purpose because, for him, it manifests God's retribution upon Thunor for

---

[35] See esp. M. Gelling, 'Further Thoughts on Pagan Place-Names', *Otium et Negotium: Studies in Onomatology and Library Science presented to Olof von Feilitzen*, ed. F. Sandgren (Stockholm, 1973), pp. 109–28, at 122. C. E. Fell, 'Edward King and Martyr and the Anglo-Saxon Hagiographic Tradition', *Ethelred the Unready*, ed. D. Hill, BAR Brit. Ser. 59 (Oxford, 1978), 1–13, at 10, plausibly suggests that *Thunoreshlæw* was a centre of the god's cult and the legend derived the councillor's name from the place-name. Byrhtferth (ed. Arnold II, 6), explains that as Thunor means 'thunder', he was rightly named, for he was unceasingly tormented by the deadly furies of wicked spirits whose hideous tumults ultimately sank him into the pit of hell.

[36] Reproduced by Rollason, *Mildrith Legend*, p. 10. On the complexities of Thanet's tenurial history and the fictive nature of the legend of the hind's course, see Kelly, 'St Augustine's Abbey', pp. 146 and 171–7.

[37] Byrhtferth's *passio*, ed. Arnold II, 9–10. Whereas Rollason, *Mildrith Legend*, pp. 15–18, assumed that Byrhtferth merely improved the style of his source (see above, p. 42, n. 6) and left its content unchanged, Hayward, 'Innocent Martyrdom', pp. 101–20, shows that Byrhtferth and the Ramsey monks, erroneously believing the relics translated to their monastery to be those of Domne Eafe's brothers, appropriated the legend, re-defining the murdered princes as infant innocents. As Hayward points out, there are a number of passages found only in Byrhtferth's *passio* which emphasize the nature of the princes' sanctity, and the eulogy of the brothers' virtues (ed. Arnold II, 4–5) reflects one of Byrhtferth's favourite themes, the mystic significance of numbers. Bodley's placing of the translation and miracles of the princes after its (truncated) account of Mildrith confirms the view that Byrhtferth interpolated these from another source (Goscelin's *vita* has no parallel account). Other features peculiar to Byrhtferth's *passio* which appear to represent his additions are the demonic characterization of Thunor (ed. Arnold II, 5–6) and the use of direct speech in Thunor's approach to the king and in the council scene (ed. Arnold II, 6–8).

his murder of the princes. The establishment of Domne Eafe's monastery is of interest to him because it allows him to assert that it was dedicated to Mary in memory of her physically pure brothers.[38] But the subsequent history of the founder and her daughter is of interest only because their holy lives add to the glory of their martyred male relations, and he therefore abridges his source at this point.[39]

Having written out the legal basis of Thanet's claim to its land by altering the purpose of the council, Byrhtferth obscures the land's status as wergild: the king subsequently, of his own accord, offers Domne Eafe whatever she wishes, because he wished 'to honour' her,[40] and there is no equivalent in Byrhtferth's *passio* of the term *wergild*, which is used repeatedly in Caligula. The fact that the Thanet foundation story asserts that the monastery was founded on land acquired as wergild marks it as a creation of the early Anglo-Saxon period; it is evidently problematic for Byrhtferth and the authors of the post-Conquest versions. Churchmen in the conversion period promoted wergild as a preferable alternative to the blood-feud. Bede, for instance, relates that Theodore averted continued warfare in the north by persuading the Mercians to accept wergild for a prince slain by the Northumbrians; he also relates that Eanflæd of Northumbria persuaded her husband Oswiu to found a monastery to pray for himself and her kinsman whom he had murdered – this story and the Thanet foundation story thus represent the transmutation of woman as peaceweaver between families to weavers of peace between their kinsmen and God.[41] But in

---

[38] Byrhtferth's *passio*, ed. Arnold II, 12; see also Bodley (ed. Rollason, pp. 97 and 102). Caligula contains no suggestion that Domne Eafe's monastery was founded in memory of her brothers (see above, p. 48, n. 24). In view of Ramsey's promotion of the cult of the princes (see above, p. 52, n. 37), the claim that Thanet was founded to commemorate them is suspect. It is also undermined by Byrhtferth's report that the princes were translated to Wakering (although Hayward, 'Innocent Martyrdom', pp. 113–14, considers that it is the latter claim which is spurious). Goscelin's *vita* states only that Domne Eafe's minster was dedicated to Mary (ed. Rollason, p. 119). But in his narration of the foundation story, he relates that Domne Eafe wanted to build a monastery 'pro sancta germanorum memoria et regis indulgentia' (ed. Rollason, p. 118). As related by Caligula, the foundation story implies that the establishment of the monastery mitigated the king's guilt, and Bodley's statement that Ecgberht helped Domne Eafe to build it (ed. Rollason, p. 98) is in line with this.

[39] Textual markers of Byrhtferth's handling of his source are: 'Igitur quoniam passiones sanctorum martyrum prout potuimus strictim praelibavimus, restat [ut] quomodo divina ultio super iniquissimum judicem, piissimae necis eorum auctorem, pervenerit, breviter tangamus' (ed. Arnold II, 11). 'Sane in monasterii regimine succedit . . . Mildrytha praedicta, sanctissima virgo, multa fulgens miraculorum gratia. Unde unum narramus miraculum . . .' (ed. Arnold II, 13). 'Praeterea dum spurcissimi persecutoris piorum marytrum subitum mortis interitum statuimus describere, postmodum infleximus oculos ad veneranda sororis neptisque eorum gesta . . . cujus gratia ad alia narranda eo succurrente est properandum' (ed. Arnold II, 13). See also Hayward, 'Innocent Martyrdom', pp. 111–12.   [40] Byrhtferth's *passio*, ed. Arnold II, 11.

[41] *HE* IV.21 and III.24 (ed. Colgrave and Mynors, pp. 400 and 292).

the Benedictine reform period, acceptance of wergild by monastics was felt to be inconsistent with their religious profession, and was prohibited by VIII Æthelred 25.[42] Disapproval is particularly noticeable in the version of the legend which was written at St Gregory's Priory; this omits the council altogether (as well as Thunor and the hind), and relates that the king offered Domne Eafe land, as if by that he might console her grief, and that she, reluctant to profit from the blood of her brothers in the manner of the worldly-ambitious Eve, established a monastery dedicated to Mary to pray for their souls.[43]

Both Goscelin and the Bodley author describe the land offered to Domne Eafe (ambiguously) as the price (*precium*) of her murdered brothers,[44] but they are more explicit than Byrhtferth in their attempts to gloss over the implication that Domne Eafe was not merely willing to receive compensation for her brothers, but maximized the amount by tricking the king. Goscelin transforms the council into a meeting presided over by the archbishop, in which the king's offer of land becomes purely a means of atoning for an offence against God. Goscelin has the king first offer Domne Eafe her choice of treasures,[45] which she refuses, because she does not want to accept as the price of her brothers the earthly wealth which she herself has forsaken, and because, being a disciple of the gospel, she prefers freely to pardon the king. But as he insists, and because she desires to found a monastery in memory of her brothers and for the *indulgentia* of the king, she asks the king how much land he will grant her at Thanet; although the king, here made eager by having been brought into a repentant state of mind, is willing to give her as much as she wishes, she asks for as much land as her female deer will encompass in a single burst.[46] Stripped of the explanation that Domne Eafe exploited her knowledge of the hind's habit of running ahead of her, her request – only *seemingly* modest in Caligula – appears a trifle eccentric. Bodley adds the explanation that the king realized by this request that Domne Eafe was acting on a divine

---

[42] VIII Æthelred 25 prohibits monastics from requiring or accepting wergild on the grounds that members of religious orders have forsaken their kin.

[43] *Vita sanctorum Aethelredi et Aethelberti martirum et sanctarum virginum Miltrudis et Edburgis* (*BHL* 2644ab + 2384a + 5964b), Gotha, Landesbibliothek, I. 81, 185v–188v, ed. M. L. Colker, 'A Hagiographic Polemic', *MS* 39 (1977), 97–108, at 99.

[44] *Precium*, in Bodley, ed. Rollason, p. 96, lines 29, 34 and 38, parallels the appearance of *wergild* in Caligula (ed. Cockayne III, 426, lines 16, 18 and 24). Cf. *Vita S. Mildrethae*, 'crudele esse iudicans ut quasi fraternum sanguinem alieno precio uenditaret' (ed. Rollason, p. 117); Gotha, 'fratrum scilicet suorum quasi sanguinis precio' (ed. Colker, 'Hagiographic Polemic', p. 99).

[45] Goscelin also uses this 'vocational test' motif in *Vita S. Edith*, ed. A. Wilmart, 'La Légende de Ste Édith en prose et vers par le moine Goscelin', *AB* 56 (1938), 5–101 and 265–307, at 43–7.

[46] *Vita S. Mildrethae*, ed. Rollason, pp. 117–18.

intimation, so that the gulled king's pleasure at Domne Eafe's reply in Caligula is transformed in Bodley into a manifestation of his willingness to fulfil the divine will.[47]

The effect of these revisions is that a straightforwardly narrated and coherent story of rash promise has become a hagiographic miracle story, in which Domne Eafe and her hind are merely the agents of an all-controlling providential will. The simultaneous elimination of Domne Eafe's ruse to maximize the opportunity opened up by the king's offer of wergild and her legal right to the possession of land, could be described as an incidental consequence of the Latin authors' disinclination to depict, in a hagiographic context, values which conflict with the orthodox ideals of their own time. To put that another way, the polemical purpose foreshadowed by Caligula's genealogy – commemoration of the founder-abbess and the means by which she acquired the monastery lands – is not one that the authors of the Latin Lives have an interest in perpetuating. In their terms, Domne Eafe is merely the female relative of the saint(s) they celebrate; what is needed for their polemical purposes is not a woman who tricks a king and gains a legal title to land, but an abbess who behaves with exemplary meekness and unworldliness.

MONASTIC CHRONICLE AND DYNASTIC LEGEND

Byrhtferth, as I have indicated, not only alters the nature of the foundation story, but re-configures the legend as a whole, elevating the murdered princes to prominence by his additions and abridging the account of Mildrith's life. Goscelin also re-shaped the legend in accordance with his hagiographic aim. In Goscelin's *Vita S. Mildrethae*, the story of Domne Eafe is merely a preamble to a Life of Mildrith, whose stated purpose is to explain how the Mercian-born Mildrith became an abbess in Kent.[48] Most of the *vita* is taken up with a highly rhetorical account of how Mildrith, having been sent by her mother to be educated at Chelles, was persecuted by the abbess there because she refused to marry a relative of hers, and how, miraculously avoiding her pursuers, she escaped in safety to Thanet, bringing with her the relics she obtained in France. The narration of this sequence amounts to some 4,500 words, which is a little less than half of the total length of the *vita*.[49] Bodley lacks a few of the details contained in Goscelin's account, but relates the same basic sequence in approximately 1,200 words.[50] Bodley's account of Mildrith is incomplete (it concludes with her consecration shortly after her return from Chelles, and thus lacks the two miracles associated with her, her death and

---

[47] Bodley, ed. Rollason, pp. 96–7. Bodley, however, resembles Caligula in presenting the council as a body which advises the king to negotiate with Domne Eafe a *precium* acceptable to her.

[48] *Vita S. Mildrethae*, ed. Rollason, p. 116.   [49] *Ibid.* pp. 119–34.

[50] Bodley, ed. Rollason, pp. 98–102.

burial and subsequent translation by Eadburg); but as it stands, its account of
Mildrith's life is only about twenty-five per cent longer than its narration of
the foundation story. Byrhtferth's summary conclusion to his account of the
foundation story (which devotes as much space to Domne Eafe as to her
daughter) states only that Domne Eafe had Mildrith educated abroad.
Byrhtferth may have subsumed the entire sequence in the statement that
Mildrith was graced with many miracles.[51] It is also possible that some of the
events of Mildrith's life related by Goscelin and Bodley did not appear in the
common archetype, but originated in the recension drawn on by Goscelin and
Bodley (which Rollason identifies as a lost Life of Mildrith made at St
Augustine's in the mid-eleventh century).[52]

What is evident, however, is that Goscelin's rhetorical exaggeration of the
events narrated by Bodley transform the legend into a Life of a female virgin-
martyr, unconventional only in the nature of its genealogy and the relative
length of its account of the saint's pious mother. Goscelin's *vita* confirms that
Domne Eafe's designation of her daughter as her successor was a feature of the
original legend; the practice was so common at early double monasteries that
Bede, though well aware that it was prohibited by the *Regula S. Benedicti*, has
Abbess Hereburg of Watton appeal to John of Beverley to save the life of her
daughter because she intends to appoint her as her successor.[53] Goscelin
renders the event in a manner acceptable to the orthodoxy of his own time:
Domne Eafe desires her daughter to relieve her of the rule of the monastery
because she is mortally ill (yet nevertheless manages to live on for a very long
time), and Archbishop Theodore grants permission.[54] This is not the only point
at which Goscelin appears to have regularized the powers exercised by early
abbesses which were recorded in his source by placing them under episcopal
supervision. Byrhtferth, for instance, states that Domne Eafe dedicated the
minster that she built; Goscelin says that the minster was dedicated by
Theodore.[55] There is no reason to assume that this originated in the recension

[51] Byrhtferth's *passio*, ed. Arnold II, 12–13.
[52] Note that Goscelin used a similar motif in his *Vita S. Wulfildae*, where he relates the assistance given by Wenflæd Abbess of Wherwell in King Edgar's pursuit of her niece Wulfhild (ed. M. Esposito, 'La vie de Sainte Vulhilde par Goscelin de Cantorbéry', *AB* 32 (1913), 10–26, at 14–16). The account of Mildrith also employs the hagiographic topos 'relic-theft-by-night-with-pursuit'; see P. J. Geary, *Furta Sacra, Thefts of Relics in the Central Middle Ages*, rev. ed. (Princeton, 1990), pp. 118–24. [53] *HE* V.3 (ed. Colgrave and Mynors, p. 460).
[54] *Vita S. Mildrethae*, ed. Rollason, pp. 135–6. Domne Eafe's appointment of Mildrith as her successor is implicit in Byrhtferth's *passio* (ed. Arnold II, 12–13) and explicit in *þa halgan* (ed. Liebermann, *Heiligen*, p. 5). It appears from S 17 (BCS 88), taken in conjunction with S 18 (BCS 96) and S 20 (BCS 99), that Mildrith's abbacy overlapped with her mother's lifetime for the period 696–9; see *Charters of St Augustine's*, ed. Kelly, nos. 45–6 and 10. But Kelly (pp. 158–9) regards this as a reason for concluding that S 17 is a fabrication.
[55] Byrhtferth's *passio*, ed. Arnold II, 12; *Vita S. Mildrethae*, ed. Rollason, pp. 118–19. Gotha also says Domne Eafe dedicated the minster (ed. Colker, 'Hagiographic Polemic', p. 99).

drawn on by Goscelin; Bodley merely states that King Ecgberht helped Domne Eafe to build the minster.[56]

Mildrith was, presumably, a more prominent protagonist than her mother in the original legend, since there is no evidence of Domne Eafe having been elevated to sainthood. But the generic model of the legend was not hagiography as Goscelin and Byrhtferth understood it, whose purpose is to celebrate the sanctity of an egregious individual. In essence, 'the Mildrith legend' is an account of the origins of the Thanet monastery and its founding abbesses;[57] its underlying generic model is monastic chronicle of the kind represented by Bede's *Historia abbatum* ('Lives of the Abbots of Monkwearmouth and Jarrow'), and – more pertinently here – by the *libellus* that he used in his *Historia ecclesiastica* for his account of the first two abbesses of Barking (which presumably owed its existence to the study of chronicles at the Barking school taught by Hildelith).[58] As Jones points out, Bede's History drew on an existing tradition of annals and chronicle records.[59] Further indication of the chronicle-like character of the written sources pertaining to Thanet is found in Goscelin's *translatio* of Mildrith, which traces the history of Thanet through three of its successive abbesses, Eadburg, Sigeburg and Selethryth; and in his reference to Selethryth's land disputes with Archbishop Wulfred, Goscelin remarks that her difficulties are abundantly clear in the annals of the ancient fathers and in the privileges and charters of her monastery.[60] This may suggest that the reign of Eadburg, to which the legend is attributed, initiated a chronicle tradition which continued under her immediate successors.

Where 'the Mildrith legend' differs from the Barking *libellus* is that it opens with a genealogy of the founder and relates how she gained the land for her monastery and was succeeded by one of her three saintly daughters. In effect, it presents a female monastic version of the royal dynastic legend which forms the prologue to *Beowulf*.[61] Royal genealogies enshrine inheritance of

---

[56] Bodley, ed. Rollason, p. 98. Goscelin also relates that Archbishop Cuthbert dedicated Eadburg's new church, thereby suggesting that he presided over the translation of Mildrith (*Vita S. Mildrethae*, ed. Rollason, pp. 142–3); no bishop is mentioned by Gotha, the only other Latin version which describes this translation (ed. Colker, 'Hagiographic Polemic', pp. 104–6). Æthelbald's charter ascribes the translation to Eadburg (S 91 (BCS 177)), and there is no presiding bishop at the translations carried out by Seaxburg and Pega (see above, p. 45, n. 16).

[57] Cf. *þa halgan* (above, p. 42, n. 5), which records the founding of the Kentish monasteries; its account of Mildrith is solely concerned with her role as abbess of Thanet (ed. Liebermann, *Heiligen*, p. 5).   [58] See Hollis, *Anglo-Saxon Women*, pp. 75–82.

[59] C. W. Jones, *Saints' Lives and Chronicles in Early England* (Ithaca, NY, 1947), pp. 27–30 and 43–50.

[60] Ed. Rollason, 'Translation and Miracles', p. 159.

[61] With D. N. Dumville, 'Kingship, Genealogies and Regnal Lists', *Early Medieval Kingship*, ed. P. H. Sawyer and I. N. Wood (Leeds, 1977), pp. 72–104, esp. 96–104, cf. H. Moisl, 'Anglo-Saxon Royal Genealogies and Germanic Oral Tradition', *JMH* 7 (1981), 215–48: 'Although the Anglo-Saxon royal genealogies are in their extant form products of ecclesiastical scholarship, the keeping of royal genealogies in early England . . . was a native, originally pre-Christian institution which the Church adopted' (p. 215).

rule and possession of the kingdom through the male line. As the preamble to the *Parker Chronicle* affirms, 'þæt uuærun þa ærestan cyningas þe West Seaxna lond on Wealum geeodon' ('these were the kings who first won the Wessex kingdom from the Welsh'), and their who-begats go back to Woden.[62] Here the convention is redeployed to establish a female dynasty whose achievements were not feats of arms but acts of piety (and ingenuity), wherein Augustine (whose mission landed at Thanet) figures as race-father in place of the god of war. *Inter alia* the double monasteries were miniature kingdoms ruled by royal women. In them it was possible to achieve the transference of land and property through the female line that women who ruled the kingdom at large were least able to achieve – as the Lady of Mercia's daughter found.[63] Seaxburg, too, who in the Minster-in-Sheppey foundation story resigns the kingdom to her son when a military leader is needed, is said to have been succeeded by her daughter at the monastery whose land she bought.[64] Like Hrothgar's building of the hall in *Beowulf*, the erection of the monastery church sets the seal of possession on the land that the monastic founder won.

But although Domne Eafe's ingenuity outwits the king, the vanquishment of Thunor is effected by a manifestation of divine brute force; an alliance of alterity (woman, animal and God) is ranged against Thunor as the representative of royal and pagan power,[65] whose role demonstrates the slaughter by which the royal dynasty is maintained. In this creation of a female monastic version of a dynastic legend, the hind which encircles the territory captured from the king plays a symbolic role. It is the female counterpart of the stag, which (as the Sutton Hoo whetstone-sceptre manifests) was an emblem of kings.

---

[62] *The Anglo-Saxon Chronicle MS A*, ed. J. M. Bately, The AS Chronicle: a Collaborative Edition, ed. D. Dumville and S. Keynes 3 (Cambridge, 1986), 1–2. 'The relationship between dynastic founder and war god to which [genealogies] point is, of course, appropriate [in that] it was by war that a *dux* could establish a kingdom and a royal line' (Moisl, 'Anglo-Saxon Royal Genealogies', p. 222).

[63] Ælfwynn was prevented from succeeding her mother as ruler of Mercia by her uncle, Edward of Wessex, who took her back to Wessex in captivity (*Mercian Register*, s.a. 919).

[64] Lambeth says that Seaxburg and her daughter Eormenhild both took the veil at Milton, of which Sheppey was a dependency. The report that Eormenhild succeeded her mother as abbess of Sheppey is found in a twelfth-century Ely life of Seaxburg (London, British Library, Caligula A. viii, fols. 111–12). The Ely life of Seaxburg is thought to have drawn either on Lambeth or on its archetype; see S. J. Ridyard, *The Royal Saints of Anglo-Saxon England: a Study of West Saxon and East Anglian Cults*, Cambridge Stud. in Med. Life and Thought 4th ser. 9 (Cambridge, 1988), 56–8 and 181, n. 26.

[65] In *Vita S. Mildrethae*, ed. Rollason, p. 118, Thunor's speech suggests that the relation of Domne Eafe and the hind resembles that of witch and familiar ('cantatricis femine et effrenate fere').

THE ORIGINS AND POLEMICAL PURPOSE OF THE LEGEND

That Eadburg of Thanet elevated her predecessor Mildrith, rather than the monastery's formerly-married founder, was fortuitous for St Augustine's. The decisive factor for Eadburg, however, might not have been Mildrith's virgin state, nor her (extremely modest) claim to visionary experience, nor even the ill-treatment that she may have suffered at the hands of the abbess of Chelles, but the fact that Eadburg's rule of Thanet coincided with Æthelbald of Mercia's overlordship of Kent. This need not have been the sole motive for the translation of Mildrith to the new church that Eadburg had built on Thanet,[66] but it does provide a pragmatic rationale for the legend's linking of Mildrith's life to the story of her mother's acquisition of the Thanet land and its genealogical preamble.

The foundation story, as I have suggested, embodies an extremely wary attitude to kings, and turns upon the dubious reliability of the king's word. Kings were undoubtedly a major threat to the property of women who had no powerful male kindred, as Abbess Eangyth's letter explaining her problems to Boniface demonstrates.[67] Women like Domne Eafe (having neither father, brothers, nor husband) were particularly vulnerable to the forcible appropriation of their land by kings – the fact that Domne Eafe alienates land from the king thus inverts a more usual state of affairs.

In actuality, however, the double monasteries of Kent appear to have derived significant practical benefits from the kings (and, occasionally, queens) to whom their abbesses were related. Substantial grants of land to the first abbess of Thanet, and to her daughter Mildrith, are recorded in charters of their royal kinsmen dating between 689 and 727.[68] Further, the 699 charter of Wihtred of Kent (who reigned 691–725, and was directly descended from Domne Eafe's cousin Ecgberht) pledged to the monasteries of Kent immunity from royal taxes and services and guaranteed his protection. For protection there is always a price, and Wihtred's price to the monasteries was that they should exhibit to him and to his successors such honour and obedience as they exhibited to the kings who preceded him under whom justice and liberty had been preserved for them.[69] For the continuance of the promised immunities, however, and for the

---

[66] However, nothing in the life of Mildrith suggests that she was the centre of a popular cult prior to her translation.

[67] *Die Briefe des heiligen Bonifatius und Lullus*, ed. M. Tangl, 2nd ed., MGH, ES 1 (Berlin, 1955), no. 14.

[68] See *Charters of St Augustine's*, ed. Kelly, nos. 40–4 and 46–8. Land-charters in favour of Æbba (Eafe) are S 10 (BCS 42), S 11 (BCS 41), S 13 (BCS 35), S 14 (BCS 40), S 15 (BCS 86) and S 18 (BCS 96); land-charters in favour of Mildrith are S 26 (BCS 846) and S 1180 (BCS 141). These charters post-date the reign of Ecgberht and, as they may be confirmations of early grants, they do not disprove the claim that the monastery was founded with wergild land.

[69] S 20 (BCS 99); *Charters of St Augustine's*, ed. Kelly, no. 10.

continued possession of their lands, the monasteries were dependent on the king keeping his word. But the considerations that originally prompted munificence – whether piety, family feeling, prestige enhancement, or even a desire to ensure the monasteries' loyal co-operation – were all good reasons for kings to respect the property of monasteries ruled by their own kin (even though the foundation story shows how precarious the bonds of kinship could be).

Æthelbald of Mercia, who assumed control of Kent after Wihtred's death, was predictably less generous. Two surviving charters grant Mildrith the tolls due on one ship. Eadburg was granted, *c.* 748, half the tolls on one ship, and that was on the strength of Æthelbald's relation to Mildrith; as his charter explains, the remission of tolls was granted for the sake of eternal reward and in consideration of his consanguinity with the holy abbess whose corpse Eadburg had translated from its former tomb, and honourably enshrined in the church she had built and dedicated to the apostles.[70] Æthelbald also renewed Wihtred's immunity;[71] but he does not appear to have kept his word. During the 740s an Abbess Bugga, whom I take to be Eadburg of Thanet, went to Rome. She too had problems, which she discussed with Archbishop Boniface, but they were not the fault of her kinsman Æthelberht II of Kent, since it was he who reminded Boniface of these discussions in a letter asking him for a favour.[72] Boniface wrote to Æthelbald in 747; he was glad to hear that Æthelbald gave generously to pious causes, but it scarcely compensated for the fact that no Christian king had ever treated the monastic orders as violently and extortionately as Æthelbald and his officials, and Boniface reminded him of the eternal damnation that had befallen his predecessor Ceolred for precisely the same crimes. (Ceolred, as it happens was, like Thunor, struck down suddenly by a bolt from heaven and, perhaps not coincidentally, a report of a vision which included an eye-witness account of Ceolred's eternal damnation circulated among monastic women.)[73] Specifically, Boniface charged Æthelbald with violating monastic privileges and alienation of property. At the same time, Boniface wrote to Archbishop Cuthbert at Canterbury condemning any layman who captured a monastery by force from either bishop, abbot or abbess and ruled it himself. As for the forced labour of monks on royal buildings and other

---

[70] See S 91 (BCS 177); cf. S 86 (BCS 149) and S 87 (BCS 150); *Charters of St Augustine's*, ed. Kelly, nos. 49–51. Discussed by S. E. Kelly, 'Trading Privileges from Eighth-Century England', *EME* 1 (1992), 3–28, esp. 5 and 7. Nothing is known of Eadburg's immediate successor Sigeburg, who was granted a remission of tolls by Offa of Mercia (S 143 (BCS 188)) and by Eadberht II, king of Kent (S 29 (BCS 189)); *Charters of St Augustine's*, ed. Kelly, nos. 52–3. She was presumably connected to the Kentish royal family.   [71] S 92 (BCS 178).   [72] *Briefe*, ed. Tangl, no. 105.

[73] *Ibid.* no. 73; the vision of a Much Wenlock monk which includes Ceolred's damnation (*Briefe*, ed. Tangl, no. 10) was obtained by Boniface for a monastic woman called Eadburg from Mildrith's sister, Mildburg of Much Wenlock, *via* Hildelith of Barking (Tangl dates it 716).

works, it was a thing unheard of anywhere except in England and an evil unknown in times gone by.[74] The 747 synod of *Clofesho* considered the problem of lay overlordship, but notwithstanding the fact that Boniface had urged Cuthbert to join with him in sounding the trumpet of excommunication against it, the synod professed itself unable to proceed with the matter owing to 'the power of tyrannical avarice'.[75]

In these circumstances, Eadburg would have been well advised to promote her monastery's connection with Mildrith, who was half Mercian by virtue of her mother's marriage. Eadburg's elevation of Mildrith evidently had a desirable effect on Æthelbald. And, centrally, the legend does assert the monastery's Mercian connection; the genealogy which introduces Domne Eafe presents her as the former wife of Merewalh, son of Penda of Mercia, and the story of how she gained the monastery's land by tricking a Kentish king, and subsequently left it to Mildrith, seems similarly calculated to make him favourably disposed to the monastery to which Eadburg had in turn succeeded.[76] The foundation story is also well designed to catch the consciences of kings and kings' officials, there being few whose throne did not rest, metaphorically, upon the bodies of inconveniently close kinsmen. Its most obviously persuasive feature is the destruction of Thunor, whose mound is constituted in Caligula as a permanent and highly visible monument to a royal official[77] who attempts to deprive a woman of land rightfully hers, without realizing that she has an all-seeing but invisible protector on her side.

CONCLUSION

It is inherently probable that foundation stories are the creation of the monasteries whose foundation they record. Caligula's version of the origins of the Thanet lands is demonstrably closer to the common archetype than are the two Ramsey *passiones* and Goscelin's *Vita S. Mildrethae*. Caligula relates a coherent 'rash promise' story, in which Domne Eafe – as the opening genealogy

---

[74] *Briefe*, ed. Tangl, no. 78.

[75] *Councils and Ecclesiastical Documents relating to Britain and Ireland*, ed. A. W. Haddan and W. Stubbs, 3 vols. (Oxford, 1869–71) III, 364.

[76] Lambeth, which relates the foundation of Sheppey by Seaxburg, an East Anglian widow of a Kentish king, similarly asserts a Mercian connection through the marriage of Eormenhild (Seaxburg's daughter and successor) to Wulfhere of Mercia. Lambeth appears of a later date than Caligula, perhaps *c.* 800. Rollason, *Mildrith Legend*, p. 31, deduces that Lambeth 'must be later than the Viking invasions of the ninth century'. This overlooks earlier Viking raids in Kent (see, e.g., S 160 (BCS 317)), and the possibility that other pagan invasions of Kent are referred to, e.g., that of the unconverted Cædwalla of Wessex in 686–7; but the formula 'as long as Christianity shall last' (see above, p. 47, n. 23) is not recorded in charters before the late eighth century.

[77] Both Bodley (ed. Rollason, p. 97) and *Vita S. Mildrethae* (ed. Rollason, p. 118) remark upon the memorial function of *Thunoreshlæw*.

foreshadows – is an active protagonist. The revisions in the three Latin Lives run counter to the essential nature of the story. By excising Domne Eafe's ruse with the tame hind, they present her purely as an instrument of the will of providence. By glossing over the story's claim that the monastery was founded on land obtained as wergild, they eliminate the legal basis of Thanet's traditional claim to its lands. Like Bishop Æthelwold, the authors of the Latin Lives affirm, in effect, that the rulers of monasteries are not the owners of their lands in any secular sense but stewards of property that belongs solely to God.[78] Their rewriting of this feature of the story confirms the view that the Thanet foundation story originated prior to the Benedictine reform period. The first promoter of Mildrith's cult was her successor Eadburg, and to have translated her remains without creating a legend of the saint would have been unusual. The foundation story carries a powerful warning to secular powers; this, and the linking of Mildrith's life to an account of how her mother gained the Thanet lands and a genealogy affirming the relationship of the first two abbesses to the Mercian royal house, are explicable in terms of Eadburg's translation of Mildrith during the overlordship of Æthelbald of Mercia.

Royal alienation of monastic lands was still regarded as a serious threat in the Benedictine reform period,[79] from which period the earliest surviving version of the legend dates. But, in view of the subsequent history of Thanet, the legend is unlikely to have arisen much later than the abbacy of Eadburg. There is no evidence that any of the Kentish double monasteries survived the Viking raids of the mid-ninth century, nor that Thanet had been re-founded before Byrhtferth's *passio* came into being.[80] Both of Eadburg's immediate successors – Sigeburg

---

[78] See the Old English 'Account of Edgar's Foundation of the Monasteries' (*Councils & Synods with Other Documents relating to the English Church: I 871–1066*, ed. D. Whitelock, M. Brett and C. N. L. Brooke, 2 vols. (Oxford, 1981) I, 142–53, at 152–3). The exhortations concerning monastic lands are specifically directed to abbesses.

[79] See *Regularis Concordia*, ed. T. Symons (London, 1953), p. 7; see also above, n. 78.

[80] The question of Thanet's survival beyond Cwenthryth (last recorded 826) is complicated by the presence of a church in Canterbury dedicated to Mildrith (presumed to owe its existence to the refuge acquired within the city walls in 804 (S 160 (BCS 317)), as well as by a contemporary report that, in 1013, the abbess of Thanet was captured in Canterbury by Danes. N. Brooks, *The Early History of the Church of Canterbury: Christ Church from 597 to 1066* (Leicester, 1984), p. 204, concludes that, notwithstanding possible indications of a short-lived restoration of the conventual life at Thanet in the early eleventh century, there is 'no certain evidence' that any of the Kentish double monasteries survived the Viking raids in the mid-ninth century. R. Fleming, 'Monastic Lands and England's Defence in the Viking Age', *EHR* 195 (1985), 247–65, shows that Kentish monastery lands were appropriated by Wessex kings in the mid- to late ninth century, but there are signs in the charters that, by the late tenth century, some of the land was returning to monastic possession. Goscelin's *translatio* (ed. Rollason, 'Translation and Miracles', pp. 159–62), and Gotha (ed. Colker, 'Hagiographic Polemic', p. 107), report the destruction of the monastery, but in neither account is it clear whether this took place shortly after the time of Cwenthryth or in the raids that began in the late tenth century. Goscelin says the monastery was

and Selethryth – might have been Kentish; but Selethryth had Mercian backing and was probably Offa of Mercia's nominee, and her successor, Cwenthryth, the last recorded abbess of Thanet, was the daughter of one of the Mercian over-lords of Kent. The Mercian connections of the first two abbesses of Thanet may have been of interest to Selethryth and Cwenthryth; the foundation story could have offered them and their community a certain amount of comfort and support. But as the threat to the monastery's possessions that Selethryth and Cwenthryth had to contend with was not kings but Archbishop Wulfred, who eventually succeeded in wresting control of the monastery from Cwenthryth,[81] the legend is unlikely to have been created in their time.

The genealogy which opens the legend implies an intention to celebrate the Thanet branch of a dynasty of monastic women descended from the Kentish royal house, and in conception the legend has more in common with chronicles such as Bede's *Historia abbatum* and the Barking *libellus* than with *vitae* dedicated to an individual. Goscelin's chronicle of the abbesses of Thanet from Eadburg to Selethryth in his *translatio* of Mildrith, and his reference to what he described as 'annals of the ancient fathers', suggest the inception of a tradition of chronicle-writing at Thanet in the time of Eadburg.[82] The Thanet community was no less capable of writing its originary history in the mid-eighth century than was Barking in the late seventh (or early eighth). Eadburg of Thanet cannot be conclusively proven to have been one of the abbesses who was in correspondence with Boniface.[83] But contact with Latin literacy can be assumed from Mildrith's sojourn abroad; Domne Eafe is specifically said to have sent her daughter overseas to be educated, and Bede (although seemingly unaware of the existence of a monastery in contact with Canterbury whose foundation can scarcely have been of less significance for the early church than that of Whitby or Ely) does affirm that the East Anglian kinswomen of Seaxburg went to monasteries like Chelles to gain an education.[84] In their celebration of monastic women as pioneer founders, land-

---

rebuilt as a parish church housing two or three parish priests; but St Augustine's had no incentive to recognize the existence of any refoundation at Thanet. (Cf. the testimony of a woman belonging to the Thanet community in Goscelin's *translatio*, ed. Rollason, 'Translation and Miracles', pp. 207–10; relative chronology is again elusive.)

[81] See J. Crick, 'Church, Land and Local Nobility in Early Ninth-Century Kent: the Case of Ealdorman Oswulf', *Hist. Research* 61 (1988), 251–69. Cf. Brooks, *Early History*, pp. 180–203.

[82] See above, p. 57, n. 60; for the transmission of Thanet documents to St Augustine's, see above, p. 44, n. 12.

[83] See P. Sims-Williams, 'An Unpublished Seventh- or Eighth-Century Anglo-Latin Letter in Boulogne-sur-Mer MS 74 (82)', *MÆ* 48 (1979), 1–22, at 22, n. 119.

[84] *HE* III.6 (ed. Colgrave and Mynors, pp. 236–8); Byrhtferth says that Mildrith was 'ecclesiasticis in transmarinis partibus disciplinis eruditam' (ed. Arnold II, 12), but cf. Bodley ('ad imbuendam litteratorie studiis discipline'), ed. Rollason, p. 98. See also above, p. 46, n. 17.

owners and builders, the text of Caligula A. xiv, and the related foundation story of Sheppey in Lambeth 427, present the history of monastic women that Bede (and later clerics) did not write,[85] and of all the surviving anonymous Old English writings, they have perhaps the best claim to be regarded as a record of traditions that were created by monastic women.

[85] See Hollis, *Anglo-Saxon Women*, esp. pp. 243–70.

Manus Bedae: Bede's contribution to Ceolfrith's bibles

RICHARD MARSDEN

Bede entered Wearmouth–Jarrow at the age of seven and thereafter, he tells us at the conclusion of his *Historia ecclesiastica*, spent all his life 'applying myself entirely to the study of the Scriptures'. He goes on, 'From the time I became a priest until the fifty-ninth year of my life I have made it my business, for my own benefit and that of my brothers, to make brief extracts from the works of the venerable fathers on the holy scriptures, or to add notes of my own to clarify their sense and interpretation.'[1] Bede's modest remarks preface an impressive list of his own works, which includes commentaries on Genesis, I Samuel, Kings, Proverbs, the Prophets, Mark, Luke, Acts and Revelation, and many other exegetical, didactic and historical volumes. Installed at Jarrow from about 679 until his death in 735, he contributed more than anyone to the intellectual distinction of early-eighth-century Northumbria. At the same time, the twin house of Wearmouth–Jarrow was winning lasting renown for the products of its scriptorium (or scriptoria). Not least among these were the three great Vulgate bible pandects which Abbot Ceolfrith caused to be made, an achievement celebrated by the chroniclers of the house, who included Bede himself.[2] One of these pandects, which we know today as the Codex Amiatinus, was dispatched to St Peter's in Rome in 716, then spent more than 900 years at Monte Amiata in the Appenines, and is now in Florence (Biblioteca Medicea Laurenziana, Amiatino 1). The other two were for use in the Wearmouth and Jarrow churches. One of these has been lost without trace, but the second survived in the cathedral priory of Worcester until the sixteenth century, when an entrepreneurial Nottinghamshire family made use of some of its torn-out leaves as document wrappers. Twelve of these, with some fragments of a

---

[1] V.24: '[C]unctumque ex eo tempus uitae in eiusdem monasterii habitatione peragens, omnem meditandis scripturis operam dedi . . . Ex quo tempore accepti presbyteratus usque ad annum aetatis meae lviiii haec in Scripturam sanctam meae meorumque necessitati ex opusculis uenerabilium patrum breuiter adnotare, siue etiam ad formam sensus et interpretationis eorum superadicere curaui' (*Bede's Ecclesiastical History of the English People*, ed. B. Colgrave and R. A. B. Mynors (Oxford, 1969), pp. 566–7).

[2] See Bede's *Historia abbatum*, ch. 15, in *Venerabilis Baedae Opera Historica*, ed. C. Plummer, 2 vols. (Oxford, 1896) I, 364–87, at 379–80, and the anonymous *Vita S. Ceolfridi*, ch. 20 (*ibid.* I, 388–404, at 395).

thirteenth, are now in the British Library under three different shelfmarks (Loan 81, Add. 37777 and Add. 45025).[3]

Wearmouth–Jarrow, Bede and bibles – the association is inescapable and it is inconceivable that the great scholar of scripture did not have a major role in the production of Ceolfrith's pandects; yet the task of defining that role with any precision has always proved difficult.[4] Recently, however, a major step forward has been made by Paul Meyvaert, who has thrown new light on Bede's involvement in the production of the celebrated opening quire of Amiatinus, with its array of illustrations and prefatory material.[5] One of his conclusions is that Bede was responsible for the presentation of the seated figure in the 'Ezra miniature' (on 5r) as a high-priest, as well as for the composition of the Latin couplet which is written above the painting. Meyvaert has suggested further that we may even see Bede's handwriting in two of the opening quire's three presentations of the division of scripture.[6] It is with this example in mind, therefore, that I here focus on the actual text of Ceolfrith's pandects, as it survives both in Amiatinus and in the 'sister' fragments, and reconsider the role of Bede both in its establishment and in its emendment.

BEDE AND THE CODEX AMIATINUS

If we assume that Ceolfrith did not instigate his great biblical project until he became abbot of Wearmouth–Jarrow in 689, that provides our *terminus post quem* for the bibles; and 716, the year in which the Codex Amiatinus was taken abroad, is the obvious *terminus ante quem*, for there is little doubt that Amiatinus was the third and last of the three pandects to be made. My assumption is that the project was not started as early as most commentators have thought but that the first two pandects (destined for the two home monastic churches) were made together, or in close succession, during the late 690s or even later, after an initial period of preparation.[7] They were followed, in no great haste, by Amiatinus, which was probably always planned as a presentation volume for St Peter's. When Ceolfrith became abbot, Bede was only about sixteen, but it is likely that he was a youth far advanced for his years, as the fact that he became a deacon at nineteen, rather than the more usual age of twenty-five, may indicate.[8] By the time Amiatinus left England in the early summer of 716, Bede was

---

[3] On the pandects, see R. Marsden, *The Text of the Old Testament in Anglo-Saxon England*, CSASE 15 (Cambridge, 1995), 85–106.

[4] See J. Chapman, 'The Families of Vulgate Manuscripts in the Pentateuch', *RB* 37 (1925), 5–46 and 365–403, at 366; P. Meyvaert, 'Bede the Scholar', *Famulus Christi: Essays in Commemoration of the Thirteenth Centenary of the Birth of the Venerable Bede*, ed. G. Bonner (London, 1976), pp. 40–69, at 50; and Marsden, *The Text*, pp. 202–6.

[5] 'Bede, Cassiodorus, and the Codex Amiatinus', *Speculum* 71 (1996), 827–83.

[6] *Ibid.* p. 841, n. 75.   [7] I present the arguments in *The Text*, pp. 98–106.

[8] P. Hunter Blair, *The World of Bede*, 2nd ed. (Cambridge, 1990), p. 5.

about forty-four. Thus there is little difficulty in envisaging his playing an important role in textual preparation from the start, perhaps in vetting and emending the exemplars which were to be used for copying (at least some of which are likely to have been the manuscripts which Bede regularly used in his studies), and perhaps even in checking the component quires of the pandects as they were produced. All of these were of course mammoth tasks in respect of three complete Vulgate bibles, which each comprised some thousand leaves of parchment.

The textual history of the medieval Vulgate is largely the story of the transmission of variant readings which had been introduced by accident or design and which were often, in the latter case, derived from pre-Vulgate sources. In assessing Bede's probable contribution to Ceolfrith's project, an obvious question to ask first is the extent to which he used in his own works what we may call 'Ceolfrithian' textual variants. This will almost invariably mean, of course, those which were used in the Codex Amiatinus, though for small parts of Sirach and III–IV Kings we have the corroboration of the leaves of the 'sister' pandect; textual differences between these and Amiatinus are few and minor.[9] May we assume that Bede, when citing scripture in his own works of exegesis and history, will have chosen the variants which were used in the pandects? By no means is this always the case. Often Bede does not use the Vulgate at all in his scriptural citations but, rather, one of the Old Latin versions which predated Jerome's revisions and the establishment of the Vulgate as we know it.[10] The reason for this is sometimes obvious, for Bede may be doing little more than copy a passage from a patristic source which itself included a scriptural citation in a pre-Vulgate version. The range of such sources available to him in the library of Wearmouth–Jarrow was extraordinarily wide.[11] The writers he turned to most often were Ambrose, Augustine, Gregory and Jerome, all of whom regularly cited from Old Latin scripture, sometimes consciously comparing the old readings (which they might refer to as 'Septuagint' readings) with those of the Vulgate.[12] Yet Bede's use of extracts from such writers does not mean that he automatically took over their scriptural variants, for there are occasions when he appears to have eschewed an Old Latin variant in his source in favour of a Vulgate one. This may or may not be the one which Amiatinus carries. Furthermore, even when Bede is not apparently quoting from a patristic work, and may be using a Vulgate source, he still does not necessarily choose Amiatinan variants.

[9] Marsden, *The Text*, pp. 190–201.
[10] For a discussion of Bede's use of the Bible, see *ibid.* pp. 202–19.
[11] See M. L. W. Laistner, 'The Library of the Venerable Bede', in his *The Intellectual Heritage of the Early Middle Ages: Selected Essays by M. L. W. Laistner*, ed. C. G. Starr (Ithaca, NY, 1957), pp. 117–49.
[12] Marsden, *The Text*, p. 11.

Although the pattern of usage varies greatly between Bede's various works, I estimate that, overall, there is a maximum of no more than sixty per cent agreement with Amiatinus.

A full study of the relationship between scriptural variants used by Bede in his works and those in Amiatinus has yet to be undertaken, but in the following ten examples, or groups of examples, I have attempted to give some idea of the complexity of that relationship.[13]

1. The wholesale use of a patristic source is illustrated by a citation of Song V.2 in Bede's *De temporum ratione*, written in 725. This comes in the middle of a long extract which he took verbatim from Ambrose's *Hexameron* and which thus has Ambrose's Old Latin version of the passage, with 'quoniam caput meum repletum est rore et crines mei guttis noctis', rather than the Vulgate version, 'quia caput meum plenum est rore et cincinni mei guttis noctium', which is what Amiatinus carries.[14]

2. However, in a similarly substantial borrowing from Gregory's *Moralia* for his commentary on Proverbs (apparently written between 720 and 730), Bede lifted some 400 words of commentary on Prov. XXX.29–33 and yet did not use Gregory's reading *pauebit* in verse 30 (which is also the correct Vulgate reading) but the Septuagint-derived *pauet*.[15] A few Vulgate manuscripts have this present-tense alternative, and one of them happens to be Amiatinus, but it seems that Bede may have taken the text of the citation from the commentary on Proverbs by Salonius, which uses *pauet* and to which much of his own commentary is heavily indebted.[16]

---

[13] In Vulgate citations below, my authority for the Old Testament text is *Biblia Sacra iuxta latinam vulgatam versionem ad codicum fidem, cura et studio monachorum Abbatiae pontificiae Sancti Hieronymi in Urbe O. S. B. edita*, ed. H. Quentin *et al.*, 18 vols. (Rome, 1926–95); Sirach is in *Biblia Sacra XII*. For the New Testament, I use *Nouum Testamentum Domini nostri Iesu Christi latine*, ed. J. Wordsworth and H. J. White, 3 vols. (Oxford, 1889–1954). Old Latin citations in Genesis and Sirach are from *Vetus Latina: Die Reste der altlateinischen Bibel nach Petrus Sabatier neu gesammelt und herausgegeben von der Erzabtei Beuron* (Freiburg, 1949–): II *Genesis*, ed. B. Fischer (1951–4) and XI.2 *Sirach (Ecclesiasticus)*, ed. W. Thiele (1987–). Greek scriptural citations are from *Septuaginta. Id est Vetus Testamentum graece iuxta LXX interpretes*, ed. A. Rahlfs, 2 vols. (Stuttgart, 1982). English translations of the Vulgate are given in the Douai-Reims version, sometimes emended. Other translations are my own, unless otherwise stated.

[14] *De temporum ratione*, ed. C. W. Jones, CCSL 123B (Turnhout, 1977), 363 (ch. xxviii); *Hexameron*, ed. C. Schenkl, CSEL 32.1 (Vienna, 1897), 134 (IV.7). The dates I give for Bede's works, usually without further comment, are those suggested by Plummer in *Baedae Opera*, pp. cxlv–clix, sometimes modified by the most recent editors of the works in question.

[15] Gregory, *Moralia siue expositio in Iob*, ed. M. Adriaen, CCSL 143B (Turnhout, 1985), 1497 (XXX.3); Bede, *In Proverbia Salomonis*, ed. D. Hurst, CCSL 119B (Turnhout, 1983), 146 (ch. iii). Theoretically, Bede's copy of Gregory could have had the variant verb, but it is in none of the manuscripts collated by Adriaen for his edition.

[16] *Expositio mystica in parabolas Salomonis et in Ecclesiasten* (PL 53, 967–95, at 988). On Bede and Salonius, see Laistner, 'The Library', pp. 136–8.

3. In his *Historia abbatum* (the work, written soon after 716, in which Bede actually records the making of Ceolfrith's pandects), a citation from Sir. XXXII.1 reads 'rectorem te *constituerunt*, noli extolli, *sed* esto in illis, quasi unus ex illis'.[17] This is not the version in Amiatinus, where the passage has what is taken to be its correct Vulgate form, 'rectorem te *posuerunt* noli extolli esto in illis quasi unus ex ipsis'. In respect of the verb used and the addition of *sed*, Bede's version in the *Historia abbatum* repeats the Old Latin version he had already used, between 709 and 716, in his commentary on Luke, which in turn came straight from Gregory's *Regula pastoralis*.[18] Following Gregory, however, he has *ducem* in the commentary, not the Vulgate variant *rectorem* used in his *Historia abbatum* and in Amiatinus. Perhaps this was a case of Bede citing a well-known passage from memory and mixing the vocabulary of two versions.

4. In his *In Cantica Canticorum*, composed between 720 and 730, Bede cites Joel II.28 in the Septuagint-derived Old Latin form, 'effundam de spiritu meo super omnem carnem', rather than the usual Vulgate version, 'effundam spiritum meum super omnem carnem'.[19] This probably results from his familiarity with the same words in Acts II.17. Twice in his *Retractatio* on Acts he cites Joel II.28 in this form.[20] It is a variant version which a handful of Vulgate manuscripts carry also, but not Amiatinus.

5. In his commentary *In Genesim*, the bulk of which was probably composed after 725, Bede cites Gen. XVI.7 in what is arguably its correct Vulgate form, including the words 'super fontem aquae in solitudine quae est in uia Sur', whereas Amiatinus has the apparently tautological version, 'in solitudine qui est in deserto Sur'. Bede will have known the version with 'in uia Sur' from Jerome's *Hebraice quaestiones*, which has the passage in its usual Old Latin form, 'in deserto quae est in uia Sur'.[21] Among Vulgate manuscripts, the Amiatinan version is shared only by the early-seventh-century Ashburnham Pentateuch (Paris, Bibliothèque Nationale, nouv. acq. lat. 2334), but others have a variety of versions involving both 'in uia' and 'in deserto'.[22] Presumably such Vulgate versions originated with the interpolation of 'in deserto' from Old Latin texts. There has been some argument about what form Jerome originally gave to the

---

[17] *Baedae Opera*, ed. Plummer I, 372; on the dating of the work, see p. cxlviii.
[18] *In Lucam*, ed. D. Hurst, CCSL 120 (Turnhout, 1960), 381 (VI.22); *Regula pastoralis* II.6 (*Grégoire le Grand: Règle pastorale*, ed. B. Judic, F. Rommel and C. Morel, 2 vols., Sources chrétiennes 381–2 (Paris, 1992) I, 212). [19] *In Proverbia Salomonis*, ed. Hurst, p. 193.
[20] *Retractatio in Actus apostolorum*, ed. M. L. W. Laistner, CCSL 121 (Turnhout, 1983), 116–17.
[21] *In Genesim*, ed. C. W. Jones, CCSL 118A (Turnhout, 1967), 200 (ch. iv); on the complex dating problems of this work, see Jones's discussion, pp. vi–x; *Hebraice quaestiones in libro Geneseos*, ed. P. de Lagarde, CCSL 72 (Turnhout, 1959), 20 (XVI.7). On the wide variety of other versions of this passage, see my *The Text*, p. 210 and n. 41, and *Vetus Latina* II, 181.
[22] See *Vetus Latina* II, 181–2, and *Biblia Sacra* I, 202.

verse in his revision of Genesis, but certainly 'in uia Sur' is supported by the Hebrew and Greek.[23] Bede will have been familiar with Palestinian geography, including the Sur desert, from another Hieronymian source, the *De situ et nominibus*, which he used for parts of his commentary on Genesis.[24]

6. Bede differs again from Amiatinus in a citation from Gen. III.2 in the same commentary on Genesis, where he uses the Vulgate reading *uescemur*, not the Amiatinan *edemus*, a variant not known to have been used in any other Vulgate manuscript.[25] This time, however, it is Amiatinus which has patristic support, for *edemus* is an Old Latin variant, used in two of Augustine's works on Genesis and in Lucifer's *De sancto Athanasio*.[26] In these sources, *edemus* is only one of several Old Latin variations in the passage they cite, but Amiatinus has none of the others. The two Augustinian works were not only known to Bede but were heavily used in his Genesis commentary, to the extent that his citation of Gen. III.1–3 is actually sandwiched between passages from *De Genesi ad litteram*, taken over verbatim. It is thus curious that in the wording of Gen. III.1–3 itself he eschews Augustine's Old Latin version in favour of the Vulgate, for which, presumably, an alternative source to Amiatinus was at hand.

7. In a passage in the first book of his commentary *In Proverbia Salomonis*, Bede cites Prov. V.19 with the opening words 'cerua carissima et gratissimus hinulus', which again is not the version in Amiatinus.[27] This has *gratissima* for *carissima*, a variation which clearly arose by mistake under the influence of the next but one word, and which is without any patristic or other support, as far as I know.[28] However, when Bede begins his interpretation of the verse, he writes, 'carissima *siue gratissima* ut quidam codices habent . . .' (my emphasis). The 'certain codices' containing the variant *gratissima* to which he refers may include Amiatinus and the two sister pandects.

8. By contrast, when Bede comes to Gen. VI.21 in the Genesis commentary, he does choose to use a unique Amiatinan reading, *manducari* for *mandi*, which again has no patristic support, as far as I know.[29] One historian of the Vulgate concluded that the reading was an innovation of Bede's, but this seems unlikely,

[23] See H. Quentin, *Mémoire sur l'établissement du texte de la Vulgate. Première partie, Octateuque*, Collectanea Biblica Latina 6 (Rome, 1922), 473–5; E. K. Rand, 'Dom Quentin's Memoir on the Text of the Vulgate', *Harvard Theol. Rev.* 17 (1924), 197–264, at 257; and Marsden, *The Text*, p. 210 and n. 41.

[24] Ed. P. de Lagarde, in his *Onomastica sacra* (Göttingen, 1887); see pp. 150, 156 and 180–1, and cf. Laistner, 'The Library', p. 130.   [25] *In Genesim*, ed. Jones, p. 60 (I).

[26] *De Genesis ad litteram*, ed. J. Zycha, CSEL 28.1 (Vienna, 1894), 332 and 362 (XI.1 and 30) and *De Genesi contra Manichaeos* II.xxvi (PL 34, 217); and *De sancto Athanasio*, ed. G. F. Diercks, CCSL 8 (Turnhout, 1978), 128 (II.xxxii).   [27] *In Proverbia Salomonis*, ed. Hurst, p. 51.

[28] My own fallibility as a copyist allowed the rather surprising 'grauissima' to appear for 'gratissima' in a previous discussion of this passage (*The Text*, pp. 115 and 212).

[29] *In Genesim*, ed. Jones, p. 111.

for there is no good reason why he should have changed a perfectly good Vulgate reading for the sake of it.[30] It is probable that *manducari* was already in the exemplar used both by Bede and by the copyists of the pandects.

9. There are a number of other cases of Bede's sharing with Amiatinus what are otherwise unrecorded variants, including one in his commentary *In Ezram*, where he cites I Esd. II.58 with 'trecenti XVII' (i.e. 'septemdecim').[31] This is in fact an error for 'trecenti nonaginta duo'. One or two other Vulgate manuscripts have erroneous readings here, but none shares 'trecenti septemdecim'. However, there is no reason why the erroneous number should have been noticed, for it is just one total out of many in a long list of the Israelite tribes and their constituent numbers who returned to Judea (but see below for a discussion of another mistake with numerals).

10. The most sustained use by Bede of distinctive, and frequently unique, Amiatinan readings is in his citations from Tobit, both in his commentary *In Tobiam*, written probably between 720 and 730, and in other works where he cites from the book (though this is rare). The unique readings, often involving whole sentences, include 'ingrediebantur' for 'ingressi fuissent' (III.8), 'palpitare coepit in siccum' for 'adtraxit eum in sicco et palpitare coepit' (VI.4), 'qui eos suscepit' for 'et suscepit eos Raguhel' (VII.1) and 'quae illi fecit' for 'quae circa illum ostenderat' (XI.20).[32] I have analysed these readings elsewhere.[33]

Tobit was certainly a special case among the books of scripture copied at Wearmouth–Jarrow. It is interesting that the same distinctive text was used by Alcuin for the Tobit quotations in his *De laude Dei*, a florilegium probably compiled by him in York during a return visit to England in 790–3.[34] None of his quotations from other biblical books shows any distinct affinities with Amiatinus, and this suggests that Tobit was unusual in being known in Northumbria at this time through a single recension, the one used at Wearmouth–Jarrow. That the same recension was in the sister pandects is proved by its survival in a tenth-century manuscript written in Cornwall, whose text of Tobit almost certainly originated in Worcester during a sister pandect's sojourn there.[35] With the possible exception of one reading, there is no evidence that the recension was in use on the Continent, and this has led to the conclusion that it was in fact a product of the Wearmouth–Jarrow scholars themselves, working perhaps to improve a defective exemplar text.[36] If this is so, Bede himself is likely to have had a hand in the work, which would have taken

---

[30] See Chapman, 'Families', p. 366, and cf. Marsden, *The Text*, p. 203.
[31] *In Ezram et Neemiam*, ed. D. Hurst, CCSL 119A (Turnhout, 1969), 254 (ch. i).
[32] *In Proverbia Salomonis*, ed. Hurst, pp. 6, 9, 11 and 17.   [33] *The Text*, pp. 171–9.
[34] *Ibid.* pp. 232–5.
[35] See my 'The Survival of Ceolfrith's *Tobit* in a Tenth-Century Insular Manuscript', *JTS* 45 (1994), 1–23 and *The Text*, pp. 179–81.   [36] *The Text*, p. 176.

place before Tobit was copied into any of the pandects. However, it seems to me unlikely that he ever checked the copy in Amiatinus, for probably he would not have missed a rare error, in XI.10, where 'occurrit Thobiam filio suo' is written for 'occurrit in obuiam filio suo'.

This is an appropriate place to note an apparent anomaly in the almost uniformly excellent work of the Wearmouth–Jarrow scribes and scholars. The Ceolfrithian text of Wisdom, as we have it in Amiatinus, is riddled with errors, some of them serious, such as 'inpossibile' for 'mirabile' (XVI.17) and 'ciuitate' for 'caecitate' (XIX.16). Almost certainly these were not made at Wearmouth–Jarrow but were in the exemplar used, and if this bad text was copied into Amiatinus we must conclude that it was copied into the other two pandects also. It is all the more surprising that so many errors were not spotted, and certainly it is impossible to think that Bede had anything to do with the copying of this book. Indeed, he uses Wisdom infrequently in his works, and when he cites passages which contain readings subject to variation he does not use the Amiatinan variant, even when it is not erroneous.[37]

In Tobit and Wisdom, we appear to see two extremes on the scale of Bede's involvement with Ceolfrith's bible project: intimate involvement with the text at one end and complete detachment at the other. The other examples I have given, however, are sufficient to show that in general there is no simple correlation between Bede's writings and Amiatinus in respect of the textual variants that he used. One of the greatest difficulties for us is that our perception of the Ceolfrithian text of scripture is almost entirely dependent on a witness which is silent after the early part of 716, whereas for the monks of Wearmouth–Jarrow the text lived on in the two sister pandects, which were in daily use and, I suspect, under regular scrutiny by Bede. Most of Bede's exegetical and historical works were written in the 720s and early 730s, when emendations to the text of Amiatinus were no longer possible but when they could of course still be made – and, as we shall see, were made – to the sister volumes.

BEDE AS TEXTUAL CRITIC

Bede's exegetical works provide ample evidence that he never stopped learning and reappraising and, where he thought it appropriate, modifying his textual conclusions. He was a lifelong and effective textual critic of the Bible, whether in its Greek or Latin versions, as M. L. W. Laistner established in his important article on two works written by Bede some twenty years apart but about the

[37] *Ibid.* pp. 158–63. The text of Psalms, which follows Jerome's 'Hebrew' version, is also problematical in Amiatinus, being apparently an emended version of a poor Irish text; see B. Fischer, *Lateinische Bibelhandschriften im frühen Mittelalter*, Vetus Latina: Aus der Geschichte der latenischen Bibel 11 (Freiburg, 1985), 32 and Marsden, *The Text*, p. 141.

same biblical book, Acts.[38] He wrote the first, the *Expositio*, probably between 709 and 716, and the second, the *Retractatio*, in the early 730s.[39] To a significant extent, the latter was a revision of the former. Taking both works together, Laistner showed that Bede did base his citations most often on the Ceolfrithian Vulgate text, at least as it is witnessed by Amiatinus, but that two other Vulgate manuscripts must have exerted their influence also. One of these transmitted a Spanish tradition, the other the same Irish tradition found in the gospelbook known as the Book of Armagh.[40] To add to the complexity, in addition to three Vulgate exemplars of Acts, Bede turned also to at least three different Old Latin versions. The most consistently used text is that exemplified in Oxford, Bodleian Library, Laudianus graec. 35, a Latin and Greek manuscript of Acts which dates from the sixth or seventh century and is very likely to be a manuscript actually used by Bede at Jarrow.[41] In these commentaries on Acts, Bede again and again draws attention to readings on which his various sources disagree, and in general he concedes authority to the Greek, or to Old Latin versions derived from them. Thus, in a quotation from Acts II.34, the earlier work has 'dicit dominus domino meo', but the later 'dixit dominus domino meo', and here Bede comments: 'Quidam codices habent *dicit dominus* sed Graeca exemplaria et in hoc libro et in psalterio habent *dixit dominus*.'[42] His citation of Acts VI.10 in the *Expositio* has the simple Vulgate version, 'et non poterant resistere sapientiae et spiritui quo loquebatur'. In the later work, however, Bede cites the same words and then writes, 'In Graeco habet plus . . .' and repeats the words but qualifies 'sapientiae' with 'quae erat in eo' and 'spiritui' with 'sancto', and then adds, 'propter quod redarguerentur ab eo cum omni fiducia'. The additions derive, indeed, from the Septuagint.[43]

Paul Meyvaert has argued that Bede, as a textual critic, may have been 'the most important forerunner of the Carolingian revival'.[44] His influence may have reached later continental scholars with a keen interest in improving the quality of texts, including Theodulf of Orléans, who we know read Bede's works.[45]

---

[38] 'The Latin Versions of Acts known to the Venerable Bede', in his *Intellectual Heritage*, pp. 150–64.

[39] *Expositio Actuum apostolorum*, ed. Laistner, CCSL 121 (Turnhout, 1983), 3–99 and *Retractatio in Actus apostolorum*, ed. Laistner, pp. 103–63. The dating of the *Expositio* is Plummer's (*Baedae Opera* I, cxlvii).

[40] Paul Meyvaert's observation that Bede's preface to Romans seems to derive from the *prologus Hilarii* in the Book of Armagh offers further confirmation that Bede had an Irish text to hand; see 'Bede's *capitula lectionum* for the Old and New Testaments', *RB* 150 (1995), 348–80, at 378.

[41] See Laistner, 'The Latin Versions', pp. 157–9, and P. Meyvaert, 'Bede and the Church Paintings at Wearmouth–Jarrow', *ASE* 8 (1979), 63–77, at 77.

[42] *Retractatio*, ed. Laistner, p. 116: 'Some codices have *dicit dominus* but the Greek exemplars, both in this book and in the psalter, have *dixit dominus*.' Bede's allusion is to Ps. CIX.1.

[43] *Retractatio*, ed. Laistner, p. 131.   [44] 'Bede the Scholar', p. 48.

[45] A. Freeman, 'Further Studies in the *Libri Carolini*', *Speculum* 40 (1965), 203–89, at 281.

J. D. A. Ogilvy has suggested a line of influence also from Bede to the celebrated textual critic, Lupus of Ferrières, via Alcuin and Alcuin's pupils, who in turn became teachers.[46] Lupus devoted himself to Cicero, but Theodulf, flourishing at the end of the eighth century, was responsible for what is now recognized as the first critical edition of the Vulgate, prepared from a wide variety of sources. The successive volumes produced at Orléans, of which six survive, constitute a work in progress, showing continuing emendation, mainly in the form of classified marginal annotations, some of them even made under the influence of a Hebrew scholar.[47] It is worth noting Bede's own frequent references in his exegetical works to what was in the Hebrew, though this information is derived mainly from Jerome.[48]

Bede had no illusions about the problems of transmitting scripture. He knew that many textual errors were not the result of deliberate variation but arose by accident in copying, and he highlighted numerals as a particular source of confusion for copyists.[49] Amiatinus itself (presumably unknown to Bede) illustrates this problem well in its text of the first book of Esdras. In II.64, the original attempt to express the figure 42,360 in Roman numerals, *XL II CCCLXL*, was wrong (though of course we do not know how far the exemplar may have been to blame), and it was still wrong after 'correction' to *XL II DCLX*, made at an unknown date. Bede, however, got it right in his commentary *In Ezram*.[50] The danger of the adverse influence of biblical citations familiar in the liturgy on copyists of Vulgate scripture was also known to Bede, and he commented specifically in his *Retractatio* on the incorrect use of *pentecosten* in Acts II.1.[51] Liturgical influence on Bede's own choice of variants is apparent in his commentary *In Canticum Abacuc*. The 'Song of Habakkuk', Hab. III.2–19, is one of seven Old Testament canticles prescribed for use in the Divine Office, and the version which Bede uses in the commentary is not that of the Vulgate but an Old Latin text characteristic of the Roman series of canticles.[52] Plummer noted the interesting fact that Bede

---

[46] *The Place of Wearmouth and Jarrow in Western Cultural History*, Jarrow Lecture 1968 (Jarrow, 1969), p. 7.

[47] See E. Dahlhaus-Berg, *Noua antiquitas et antiqua nouitas. Typologische Exegese und isidorianisches Geschichtsbild bei Theodulf von Orléans*, Kölner historische Abhandlungen 23 (Cologne and Vienna, 1975), 39–61; Fischer, *Lateinische Bibelhandschriften*, pp. 94–6 and 135–47; and Marsden, *The Text*, pp. 19–22.

[48] A. C. Dionisotti, 'On Bede, Grammars, and Greek', *RB* 92 (1982), 111–41, at 128–9.

[49] See Plummer, in his introduction to *Baedae Opera* I, lvi and n. 3.

[50] *In Ezram et Neemiam*, ed. Hurst, p. 256.

[51] *Retractatio*, ed. Laistner, p. 109 (II.1). See Meyvaert, 'Bede the Scholar', p. 49.

[52] *In Canticum Abacuc*, ed. J. E. Hudson, CCSL 119B (Turnhout, 1983) 381–409. On Bede's promotion of the Old Latin versions of the canticles, see H. Schneider, *Die altlateinischen biblischen Cantica*, Texte und Arbeiten 29–30 (Beuron, 1938), 47–8.

even uses the expression 'alia translatio' in this commentary to signify the Vulgate, though in most of his works this would signify an Old Latin version.[53] The Vulgate text of Habakkuk in Amiatinus seems not to have escaped the influence of the liturgical version either, but it is very probable that the readings in question were already in the exemplar used for copying at Wearmouth–Jarrow.[54]

Bede knew that the largest number of variants arose during the process of translation itself, as different translators solved problems in different ways. Hence the frequent references of the sort we have seen in the *Retractatio* to what 'the Greeks' or 'certain codices' have. Paul Meyvaert has drawn attention to the statement Bede made in his preface to the *Retractatio* on Acts, in the preparation of which he had found discrepancies between his Latin and Greek texts. I quote it at length in translation:

I have as yet not been able to determine whether some of the changes and omissions are due to the negligence of the translator, or to his use of different words, or whether we are dealing with a case of scribes altering the text and omitting words. I hesitate to suppose that the Greek exemplar itself was a faulty one. Let my reader therefore accept whatever comments I make on these matters as scholarly comments, and let him not on that account start to correct his own copy of Acts, unless perchance he discovers a very old manuscript of the Latin version which confirms these comments.[55]

Two points are of particular interest here. The first is Bede's reverence for the readings of the Greek texts, which he avers may sometimes be confirmed by the earliest (Old) Latin translations, and the second is his implicit acceptance that the emendation of scriptural manuscripts is a necessary task, so long as the alternative readings have authority. Applying this rule to some of the Amiatinan examples I gave above, we may perhaps assume that Bede would have had 'in deserto Sur' corrected in Gen. XVI.17, if he had become aware of the problem early enough; this may indeed have happened in the case of the sister pandects, which presumably had the same error and continued to be available. As for the variant *gratissima* in Prov. V.19, Bede obviously realized that it did not have ancient authority, for he notes simply that 'other codices' have it, but perhaps he considered it only of minor importance. In the case of the reading in Acts II.34, Amiatinus has *dicit* but Bede took *dixit* to be authoritative reading (that is, derived from the Greek). As the *Retractatio* was not written until some years after Amiatinus had left Northumbria, it would have been too late for Bede to have effected an emendation there, though it is tempting to assume that he would have done so if able to.

---

[53] *Baedae Opera* I, p. lv, n. 1.   [54] See my *The Text*, p. 215.
[55] *Retractatio*, ed. Laistner, p. 103; Meyvaert's translation, 'Bede the Scholar', p. 50.

EMENDATION IN AMIATINUS

Such assumptions, however, must be made with caution, for the fact is that emendations were indeed made to Amiatinus before June 716 and that at least one of them did involve a variant addition highlighted, like *dixit*, in the *Retractatio*. The emendation in question is the one made to Acts VI.10, which I discussed above. The extra eight words, deriving from the Septuagint, were not originally in Amiatinus, but they were added before the codex left England in 716. As originally written, the verse had ended conveniently with 'loquebatur' on a line by itself, so there was space to add 'propter quod redargue' immediately after it, but the rest of the addition, 'rentur ab eo cum omni fiducia', was put at the top of the column, signalled by a characteristic Wearmouth–Jarrow *signe de renvoi*, the diagonal line with a dot above and below. In their critical edition of the Vulgate New Testament, Wordsworth and White identified the addition as the work of the original scribe ('A¹'), with the implication that the words had been in his exemplar but were accidentally omitted at first. I think this is unlikely. Certainly the addition was written by one of the team of astonishingly consistent Wearmouth–Jarrow scribes, using a similar pen and ink, but its relative untidiness renders comparison with the main script difficult. Although we must certainly label the addition 'contemporary', there might still be many months, perhaps several years, between its execution and that of the main writing. It is most improbable that the extra words were already in the exemplar, for it would be a remarkable coincidence if the copyist (in the absence of any repetition of words which might provoke eye-slip) had managed accidentally to omit eight words which not only formed a complete clause but which also happened to be a Greek-derived addition which is rare in Latin manuscripts. The only Vulgate witness which Wordsworth and White recorded in their edition as having the addition as an original part of the text is the Book of Armagh (Dublin, Trinity College 52; their siglum D), whose influence on Bede in his *Retractatio* was of course noted by Laistner.[56] It seems to me likely, therefore, that a scribe was set to make the addition in Amiatinus by Bede, after the latter had encountered the amplified reading in the Irish-influenced exemplar which was among his three Vulgate versions of Acts. Along with many other variant readings, he would eventually draw attention to it in the *Retractatio*. What is thus confirmed (and it is scarcely surprising) is that, although this work was not written until about 725, the material which it incorporates had been accumulated over the intervening years since Bede's writing of the *Expositio*. If he had also become aware of the variant reading *dicit* in Acts II.34 before 716, we must assume that he did not consider it of enough importance to warrant an emendation in Amiatinus, despite its impeccable Greek pedigree.

---

[56] See above, p. 73.

Among other examples of Northumbrian emendation in Amiatinus, one of the most interesting occurs in the eighth chapter of Genesis, which includes the story of the raven which was sent out by Noah from the ark to seek dry land. The original text of Amiatinus in Gen. VIII.7 had the version 'qui egrediebatur et reuertebatur donec siccarentur aquae super terram', where the tense of the first two Latin verbs conveys the idea of the raven's continually going and returning to the ark – it 'went out and returned until the waters over the earth dried up'. This version accurately renders the Hebrew and is likely to have been in the Northumbrian exemplar imported from Italy; certainly it is in the other two surviving 'archetypal' Vulgate manuscript sources for the book, the seventh-century Tours Pentateuch (Paris, Bibliothèque Nationale, nouv. acq. lat. 2340) and the eighth-century Codex Ottonbonianus (Vatican City, Biblioteca Apostolica, Ottob. lat. 66).[57] I assume, too, that the same version had been copied already into the first two pandects in Northumbria. However, before Amiatinus left England an emendation was made. A *non* was inserted, in a small untidy hand, over the second verb of the passage, *reuertebatur* (on 15r), so that now we read that the raven went out but did *not* return to the ark. This negative version was not new. It originated in the Septuagint and was carried over into the Old Latin versions of Genesis, which characteristically have the form 'et exiens non est reuersus', with the verb in the perfect tense. Eventually the negative version reached many of the Vulgate manuscripts, too (modifying 'reuerte-batur'), and then the printed editions. In his *Hebraice quaestiones*, Jerome showed his awareness of the two possibilities, using a negative version for his lemma of Gen. VIII.7 but adding that 'in other cases' an alternative version was to be found.[58] Augustine offers in one of his works, on John, an interpretation of the negative version which assumes that the raven drowned in the flood, but in another, on the Heptateuch, he states that the question has been asked, whether the raven did in fact die or whether it found some other means to live, and he notes that many have conjectured that it rested on a floating corpse.[59] This theory is given extended treatment by Isidore, in his *Quaestiones in Vetus Testamentum*.[60]

---

[57] See *Vetus Latina* II, 119–20 and *Biblia Sacra* I, 169.

[58] *Hebraice quaestiones*, ed. de Lagarde, p. 10. He uses a different Old Latin version, not the one which reached the Vulgate; thus: 'Et de coruo aliter dicitur "emisit coruum et egressus est exiens et reuertens".' In the same place, Jerome notes a variation between what is in the Hebrew and the Latin earlier in the verse, but he does not seem to attribute the positive version of the raven's activities to the Hebrew.

[59] *In Iohannis euangelium tractatus*, ed. R. Willems, CCSL 36 (Turnhout, 1954), 63–4 (VI.19) and *Quaestiones in Heptateuchum*, ed. J. Fraipont, CCSL 33 (Turnhout, 1958), 5 (I.13).

[60] PL 83, 233. For a very useful account of patristic treatments of the raven, see M. McC. Gatch, 'Noah's Raven in *Genesis A* and the Illustrated Old English Heptateuch', *Gesta* 14.2 (1975), 3–15, at 4–6.

It is the negative version (with the imperfect verbs of the Vulgate, *egrediebatur* and *reuertebatur*) which Bede uses in his commentary *In Genesim*, and quite deliberately, for he analyses the passage very carefully and gives an explanation which compares the vagrancy of the raven, in not seeking again the window of the ark whence it flew, to the state of the Christian who refuses to leave the darkness of earthly delights, loving the wide paths of the world more than the confinement of a churchly existence.[61] Elsewhere, in *De Tabernaculo* and *Homeliae*, Bede sees in the recalcitrant raven a figure for those who, after baptism, become apostates.[62] It seems very likely to me, therefore, that Bede was responsible for the emendation in Amiatinus. His commentary on this passage was probably written after 721, yet it would not be surprising, in view of its prominence in the works of church writers, that the alternative reading came to his attention far earlier and that, as with the emendation in Acts, he caused the addition of *non* to be made in the period between the finishing of Amiatinus and its export.[63]

I have speculated elsewhere that Bede might himself have added *non* above Gen. VIII.7 in Amiatinus.[64] There can of course be no proof. We know from Bede's own comments that he did sometimes copy complete works himself, including, according to its prologue, his commentary on Luke,[65] but none of the claims that have been made over the years in respect of specific manuscripts alleged to be in Bede's hand can be substantiated. Durham Cathedral Library catalogues of the fourteenth and fifteenth centuries listed three such manuscripts, including a gospelbook, with the assertion that they were 'de manu Bedae'; and a fourth Durham manuscript has 'de manu Bedae' added in a fourteenth-century hand. However, there is no reason whatever to suppose that Bede did in fact copy any of these manuscripts. No doubt the attributions reflected old traditions, but these probably had more to do with the relic value of some Bede manuscripts than with good historical evidence.[66] As for the St Petersburg manuscript of the *Historia ecclesiastica* (known previously as the 'Leningrad Bede'), with its famous 'signature of Bede', there is now a consensus among scholars that the signature is a medieval forgery, associated with that same tradition of autograph manuscripts.[67]

---

[61] *In Genesim* II: '. . . cuius egressui atque itineri recte comparantur hi qui sacramentis quidem celestibus institui atque imbuti sunt, nec tamen nigredinem terrenae oblectationis exuentes, lata potius mundi itinera quam ecclesiasticae conuersationis claustra diligunt' (ed. Jones, p. 123).

[62] *Homeliae* II, ed. Hurst, CCSL 119A (Turnhout, 1969), 69 and I.12, ed. Hurst, CCSL 122 (Turnhout, 1955), 87, respectively.

[63] On the dating, see Jones's discussion, *In Genesim*, ed. Jones, pp. vi–x.   [64] *The Text*, p. 204.

[65] Meyvaert, 'Bede the Scholar', p. 49 and n. 39.

[66] See M. R. James, 'The Manuscripts of Bede', *Bede: his Life, Times and Writings*, ed. A. H. Thompson (Oxford, 1935), pp. 230–6.

[67] See P. Meyvaert, 'The Bede Signature in the Leningrad Colophon', *RB* 71 (1961), 274–86.

As I noted above, Paul Meyvaert has wondered whether the distinctive, rather sloping hand responsible for the summaries of scriptural division in two of the three diagrams in the first quire might be Bede's. He has pointed out further that, if the same hand made some of the corrections which appear throughout the Bible (as David Wright, who made the standard analysis of the calligraphy of Amiatinus, has indicated),[68] then these could be by Bede also. The handwriting in the diagrams is that of someone apparently writing quite fast and without the fastidious attention to the detail of letter forms which is so characteristic of the team of expert scribes of the main text, who wrote the Wearmouth–Jarrow uncial with such consistency between themselves. Notable in the less formal script is the absence of the controlled and stately roundedness and symmetry of the main script. There are longer descenders, with some longer than others, variation in the angle of slope of descenders and ascenders, which may even affect repeated letters within a single word, and huge variety in the detail of letter forms, such that it would be difficult to isolate any one example of u, o, p, l or d (to name only the most obvious cases) as the writer's characteristic form. It is indeed very likely that some of the corrections in Amiatinus are by the same person who wrote the diagram script. However, although the manuscript was very competently copied and errors were relatively few, they still amount cumulatively, through more than two thousand pages, to a considerable number, and there are also several hundred emendations, additions and annotations made during the centuries after the codex reached Italy. The variety of scripts and styles involved in all these alterations is huge, and the daunting task of dating and classifying all of them has yet to be tackled.

BEDE AND THE SISTER PANDECT

Finally, however, I turn from Amiatinus to the surviving leaves of the sister pandect and the alterations made to their text. These are comparatively few in number, but I believe that they reveal clearly a textual scholar at work. The eleven leaves plus fragments which are in London, British Library, Add. 37777 and 45025, have text from III–IV Kings, and the single leaf in Loan 81 has part of Sirach XXXV–XXXVII. Overall there are about a dozen corrections and six emendations in the leaves, all apparently made before the codex containing them left Northumbria, with some of the corrections probably by the original copyist himself.[69] Three of the emendations are relatively minor, but the other three are additions to the text, and these are of the greatest interest. Each of them, shown here in italics, is in the second chapter of IV Kings:

[68] 'Some Notes on English Uncial', *Traditio* 17 (1961), 441–56, at 443 and 452. I suggest examples in *The Text*, p. 185.

[69] *The Text*, pp. 195–9. My previous conviction (p. 195) that *suis* in III Kings XI.43, on Add. 37777, was added by a corrector has weakened after a recent reappraisal of the manuscript.

II.1   cum leuare uellet Dominus Heliam per turbinem *quasi* in caelum

II.11 et ascendit Helias per turbinem *quasi usque* in caelum

II.14 et pallio Heliae quod ceciderat ei percussit aquas *et non sunt diuisae*

The additions in II.1 and II.11 have both been written in a small, informal hand in the margin to the left of the main text. The first (pl. I) has been placed quite far out in the margin, where it is now bordered by a red decorative line associated with a new chapter number, added in the thirteenth or fourteenth century. It is accompanied by a *signe de renvoi*, consisting of a short oblique 'ticked' line with a dot above and below it, which parallels the same sign placed above the adjacent line of text, between *turbinem* and *in*. This way of signalling insertions was used commonly in Amiatinus also. The second addition (pl. II), 'quasi usque', stands in the margin immediately adjacent to the words it qualifies, which comprise a half-line of their own. The third, 'et non sunt diuisae' (pl. II), has been placed immediately after the phrase it complements, at the end of a conveniently short line.

Assessment of the number of people responsible for the additions is difficult. The first *quasi*, in II.1, is notable for a rather long **s**, which extends below the line and is written with a continuous movement of the pen, and a **q** with a fairly short descender. This contrasts with 'quasi usque' in II.11, where the **q** in both words has a very long descender and the **s** is written in two parts and confined within the normal two-line letter area. The first and second **u** in 'quasi usque' differ from each other, and neither quite resembles the **u** of *quasi* in II.1. Both additions have a very slight sloping tendency in relation to the main text script. The ink of the first has faded to a mid-brown; that of the second is almost as dark as the main script. In the case of 'et non sunt diuisae', an effort was made, it seems, to mimic the formal uncial of the main text, though the new script is considerably smaller and the **e** looks more minuscule than uncial. The bowl of the uncial **d** is exceptionally open and the **t** in both *et* and *sunt* has a very short horizontal stroke. The circle of the **o** is incomplete, with the gap at the start of the letter, to the left of a notional vertical line. Up to the **d** of *diuisae*, the addition has been written with the same generous use of space as in the main script, but the rest of *diuisae* has been squeezed and is untidy, no doubt owing to the difficulty of writing near the gutter of a bound book. The addition acquires a slight slope as it proceeds. The use of the digraph **æ** for *ae* parallels the occasional practice of the scribes of the main text when space is at a premium.

There are, then, obvious calligraphic differences between the three additions, and yet I believe that there are enough general similarities between the writing of 'quasi usque' in verse 11 and 'quae non sunt diuisae' in verse 14 to warrant the conclusion that these two additions, at least, may have been the responsibility of

REGUM ISRAHEL

uel ceterons bellum per
turbauerint ad quod

ibant bellas ethelis regis
de galgalis
dixitq; bellas ad belis regio
sede hic quoniam dns ad ioerne

I London, British Library, Add. 45025, 3r (detail, scale 13:10)

DIUISERUNT UTRUMQUE
ET ASCENDIT HELIAS PERTURBINEM
quasi usq· INCAELUM
HELISAEUS AUTEM UIDEBAT
ET CLAMABAT
PATER MI PATER MI CURRUS
ISRAHEL ET AURICA EIUS
ET NON UIDIT EUM AMPLIUS
ADPRAEHENDITQ; UESTIMENTA SUA
ET SCIDIT ILLA IN DUAS PARTES
ET LEUAUIT PALLIUM HELIAE
QUOD CECIDERAT EI
REUERSUSQ; STETIT SUPER RIPAM
IORDANIS
ET PALLIO HELIAE QUOD CECIDERAT
EI PERCUSSIT AQUAS ET NON SUNT DIUISA
ET DIXIT UBI EST DS HELIAE
ETIAM NUNC

II London, British Library, Add. 45025, 3v (detail, scale 9:10) one writer. It is perhaps less likely, but still possible, that he also wrote 'quasi' in verse 1.

But why were the additions made? Both 'quasi' and 'quasi usque' are of Septuagint origin (II.1 and 11: ὡς εἰς τὸν οὐρανὸν),[70] and the second, at least, seems to have been current in Old Latin texts, though the only witness I know is the fourth-century Lucifer of Cagliari.[71] The appearance of either in Vulgate manuscripts of any period is rare. The former, 'quasi' in II.1, is recorded in a Spanish bible of the tenth century, the Codex Gothicus (León, Real Colegiata de San Isidoro 2), and is a marginal addition in another of the twelfth century (Madrid, Academia de la Historia Aemiliana 2–3); and 'quasi usque' in II.11 is part of the original text of one eleventh-century Italian manuscript from Monte Cassino (Archivio della Badia, 572) and appears again as a marginal addition in the twelfth-century Spanish manuscript just noted. It is therefore all the more significant that Bede, who alludes frequently in his works to the taking up of Elijah to heaven, cites II.11 with the additional words at least twice.[72] In a chapter on the six ages of the world in his *De temporum ratione*, composed in 725, he writes 'helias curru igneo rapitur quasi usque in caelum'.[73] Here Elijah's translation is presented simply as an historical event and Bede makes no comment on the passage. However, when Bede cites the verse in his *In ascensione Domini*, one of the collection of homilies on the Gospels composed late in his life, between 730 and 735, the significance of the addition is made quite clear. Describing how the conversation between Elijah and Heliseus was suddenly interrupted by the fiery chariot, Bede is at pains to distinguish between Elijah's elevation and Christ's: 'cumque incedentes sermocinarentur ecce curru igneo repente raptus "Helias", ut scriptura ait, "ascendit *quasi* usque in caelum". Qua euectione significatur quod Helias non in ipsum caelum ut dominus noster sed in altum aeris huius sub-leuatus est ac deinde inuisibiliter ad paradisi gaudia relatus.'[74] Elijah has been taken up *as though* to heaven, yet not in fact to heaven proper, where Christ is, but simply to the heights of what we may call the upper atmosphere. However, an

---

[70] But ὡς is absent from Origen's recension.

[71] *De Athanasio* (I.xx): 'et ascendit Helias in commotionem quasi in caelum' (ed. Diercks, p. 36). This is the only Old Latin citation noted by P. Sabatier, *Bibliorum Sacrorum latinae uersiones antiquae seu uetus Italica*, 3 vols. (Rheims, 1743–9) I, 598–9.

[72] He does not seem to cite II.1 specifically anywhere.

[73] *De temporum ratione*, ed. Jones, p. 477 (ch. lxvi): 'Elijah was snatched away in a fiery chariot, as though into heaven'. On the dating, which is known from internal evidence, see Jones's introduction, p. 241.

[74] *Homeliae* II.15 (ed. Hurst, p. 287, my emphasis): 'And as they continued to converse together, behold: snatched away suddenly in a fiery chariot, as scripture says, "Elijah ascended *as though* into heaven". By this upwards flight it is made known that Elijah was not taken up to heaven itself, as our Lord was, but into the upper atmosphere, whence he was carried invisibly to the joys of paradise.' On the dating, see Hurst, p. vii.

even more explicit explanation of the importance of the limiting adverb *quasi* in respect of Elijah is given by Bede in that comparatively early work which I have discussed already, the *Expositio Actuum apostolorum*, apparently written in 709 or shortly after. Interpreting the words 'hic Iesus qui adsumptus est a uobis in caelum', which are spoken in Acts I.11 by the two angels who appear beside the disciples as they watch Christ ascend into heaven,[75] Bede explains: 'Ob duas illis causas angeli uidentur, ut uidelicet ascensionis tristitiam regressionis commemoratione consolarentur, et ut uere in caelum illum ire monstrarent et non *quasi* in caelum sicut Heliam.'[76]

Frequent reference to Elijah's elevation is made in the writings of Ambrose, and in two of his works which were known to Bede he stresses the distinction between Christ and the prophet.[77] In the *Expositio euangelii secundum Lucam* he writes, '[S]ed non Helias Christus; ille rapitur, iste regreditur; ille inunam [*sic*] rapitur, iste rapinam non arbitratus est esse se aequalem deo.'[78] And again in *De fide*, citing Matt. X.24 and stressing the significance of resurrection as a prelude to true elevation to heaven, he explains: 'Translatus erat Enoch, raptus Helias, sed "non est seruus supra dominum. Nullus" enim "ascendit in caelum nisi qui descendit e caelo" . . . Translatus ergo Enoch, raptus Helias, ambo famuli, ambo cum corpore, sed non post resurrectionem, non cum manubiis mortis et triumpho crucis uiderant illos angeli.'[79] It is a theme which, in a later age, Abbot Ælfric would carefully expound in a vernacular homily composed, like Bede's, on the theme of the Ascension.[80]

---

[75] Acts I.10–11: 'And while they were beholding him going up to heaven, behold two men stood by them in white garments, who also said: "Ye men of Galilee, why stand you looking up to heaven? This Jesus who is taken up from you into heaven shall so come as you have seen him going into heaven".'

[76] *Expositio*, ed. Laistner, p. 9 (my emphasis): 'The angels appeared to them for two reasons, namely to console them for the sadness of his ascension by reminding them of his return and to show that he had truly gone to heaven and not, like Elijah, *as though* to heaven.'

[77] On Bede's knowledge of Ambrose, see Laistner, 'The Library', pp. 145–6.

[78] *Expositio*, ed. C. Schenkl, CSEL 32.4 (Vienna, 1897), 274 (VI.96); cf. Phil. II.6: 'But Christ was not Elijah; the one was snatched away, the other will return; the one was snatched away, the other "thought it not robbery to be equal with God".'

[79] *De fide*, ed. O. Faller, CSEL 78 (Vienna, 1962), 160 (IV.1,8); cf. John III.13: 'Enoch was carried off, Elijah snatched away, but "the servant is not above his master"; for "none hath ascended into heaven but he who descended from heaven" . . . Therefore Enoch was carried off, Elijah snatched away, both as servants, both in the body – but not after resurrection, nor with the spoils of death and the triumph of the cross, had angels seen them.'

[80] *In ascensione Domini*: 'we rædað on ðære ealdan æ þæt twegen godes men. henoh. and helias wæron ahafene to heofonum butan deaðe. ac hi elcyað ongean þam deaðe. and mid ealle ne forfleoð; Hi sind genumene to lyftenre heofenan: na to rodorlicere. ac drohtniað on sumum diglum earde mid micelre strencðe lichaman and sawle. oð ðæt hi eft ongean cyrron on ende þisre worulde togeanes antecriste. and deaðes onfoð' (*Ælfric's Catholic Homilies: The First Series. Text*, ed. P. Clemoes, EETS ss 17 (Oxford, 1997), 352).

In view of Bede's acquaintance with Ambrosian exegesis on Elijah, and his use of the amplified version of IV Kings II.11 in his own exegetical works, I would suggest that his direct connection with the emendation in the sister pandect is highly likely. The similar alteration to II.1 will probably have been made by simple analogy at the same time, or later.

The third addition, that of 'et non sunt diuisae' to 'et pallio Heliae quod ceciderat ei percussit aquas' in IV Kings II.14, reflects a frequent emendation in the Septuagint.[81] Indeed, although it is not in the Masoretic Hebrew text, some commentators have considered it to be an original part of the passage, for it makes sense of the question which Heliseus asks, after he has struck the waters of the Jordan with Elijah's cloak the first time, to no apparent effect: 'ubi est Deus Heliae etiam nunc?'[82] It is as much an invocation as a question, and it is effective, for at the second attempt Heliseus succeeds in parting the waters of the Jordan. There is no recorded Vulgate use of the addition before its appearance in a number of early-ninth-century bibles, including those produced at Tours from about 800 onwards, but after this it spread widely and eventually became standard in all Vulgate manuscripts and editions.[83] The Ceolfrithian pandect fragment thus has the distinction of being our earliest known biblical witness to the amplification, even if it is there as an emendation rather than as an original reading. Gregory the Great shows his familiarity with the amplified Septuagint version in his *Dialogi*. He does not cite the passage in full but presents the actions of Heliseus (as given in the Septuagint version) as an exemplary parallel when he relates a miracle enacted by a monk called Libertinus. This devout man carried everywhere with him a shoe which had belonged to his late master and abbot, Honoratus (just as Heliseus kept possession of Elijah's cloak). Libertinus was able to bring a dead child back to life by laying the shoe on its chest, but only after he had also, showing due humility in respect of his own unaided powers, called on God in the name of Honoratus. Similarly, explains Gregory, only after Heliseus had invoked the name of his master, Elijah, did his attempts to divide the waters of the Jordan, by striking them with Elijah's cloak, succeed: 'Nam Heliseus quoque magistri pallium ferens atque ad Iordanem ueniens, percussit semel *et aquas minime diuisit*. Sed cum repente diceret: "Vbi est Deus Heliae etiam nunc?", percussit fluuium magistri pallio et iter inter aquas fecit.'[84] Bede does not appear to cite IV Kings II.14 in any of his works, and thus

---

[81] καὶ ἐπάταξεν τὸ ὕδωρ καὶ οὐ διέστη. The addition is lacking in the fourth-century Vaticanus and the fifth-century Alexandrinus manuscripts of the Greek Bible, however.

[82] See J. Robinson, *The Second Book of Kings* (Cambridge, 1976), pp. 26–7.

[83] Some manuscripts have 'quae non sunt diuisae'; see *Biblia Sacra* VI, 215–16.

[84] *Dialogi* I, ii, 7 (*Grégoire le Grand: Dialogues*, ed. A. de Vogüé, 3 vols., Sources chrétiennes 251, 260 and 265 (Paris, 1978–80) II, 30; my emphasis): 'Just as Heliseus, coming to the Jordan and taking his master's cloak, struck the first time, *but the waters did not divide*. But as soon as he had

the case for his interest in the expanded version is only circumstantial. Nevertheless, Laistner has noted Bede's 'profound admiration' for Gregory and his 'constant indebtedness' to him, and certainly Bede knew Gregory's *Dialogi*, along with several other works.[85] He could have been familiar with the addition from the Old Latin text of the *Codex grandior*, the pandect brought to Wearmouth–Jarrow from Rome by Benedict Biscop, and also perhaps directly from the Greek text of the Septuagint.[86] The case for his responsibility for the addition of 'et non sunt diuisae' to the pandect, as with the addition to the earlier verse in the same chapter, is I believe a fairly persuasive one.

The evidence of these three additions in the dozen surviving leaves of the sister pandect leads me to suspect that, if the whole had survived, we would find it liberally supplied with such emendations, and I do not doubt that Bede would have instigated them. As various textual cruces came to his attention during his writing of his exegetical works, over two decades, he decided that some at least were amplifications which it would be appropriate to add to the Jarrow pandect. We cannot know whether they were added only in this pandect (in which case this is the volume from which the leaves in the British Library survive) or into the Wearmouth volume also.

I conclude by taking speculation a stage further. It is quite possible that Bede had the emendations entered by an assistant – one of his pupils, perhaps. Yet it seems to me at least as likely that he wrote them himself and that it may therefore be Bede's hand that we see in the emendations to IV Kings on the sister pandect leaves. When I study the emendations, I am inevitably reminded of a script I have discussed already, that of two of the diagrammatic summaries of scriptoral division which appear in the opening quire of the Codex Amiatinus. The most obvious feature of this handwriting is of course inconsistency in the detailed formation of the letters, and inconsistency in itself cannot be a reliable criterion of comparison. Yet the additions on the leaves of Add. 45025 do seem to me to show the same range of variation as the script of the diagrams, the same degree of informality, the same sloping tendency (though it is far less pronounced), and also echoes of some of the details of letter form. To put the argument more guardedly: in my view, none of the words in the additions would look out of place in the diagrams. The same applies, incidentally, to the other corrections in the sister leaves, most of which involve single letters.

said, "Where is now the God of Elijah?", he struck the river with his master's cloak and made a path through the waters.' The only other church writer I have noted as using the expanded version of IV Kings II.14 is Hrabanus Maurus, in the ninth century, who cites the verse in his *Commentarius in Regibus* IV.2 (PL 109, 224).

[85] Laistner, 'The Library', p. 129; and see also p. 147.
[86] Marsden, *The Text*, pp. 130–2; and on Bede's direct use of Greek scripture, see Laistner, 'The Library', p. 140.

As I noted above, Paul Meyvaert has wondered whether the handwriting in the Amiatinan diagrams might be that of Bede, and it is tempting to use this to bolster my own argument that the emendations in the sister pandect are his also. But that would be to argue in a circle, with conjecture endlessly chasing speculation; the case cannot be proven. It is plausible enough, nevertheless, to imagine Bede (whether or not he wrote the text in the Amiatinan diagrams), steadily emending the Ceolfrithian biblical text during the second and third decades of the eighth century. His interest in textual criticism of the Bible is well established, as we have seen, and there is evidence enough that even in Amiatinus, which was available only until early 716, deliberate emendations were already being made, surely under Bede's influence, if not by his own pen. As I have pointed out already, our view of the 'Ceolfrithian' (perhaps we ought to say 'Bedan–Ceolfrithian') text of scripture is inevitably restricted, because it was all but cut off in 716. But the sister leaves offer us a glimpse of the Northumbrian after-life of that text, during the period when it was still in use daily by the Wearmouth–Jarrow brethren and under the scrutiny of Bede, who never stopped reading and learning and reappraising. If all three of the Northumbrian pandects had survived complete and could be compared, I suspect that they would together resemble in a modest way the bibles produced nearly one hundred years later under the direction of Bede's continental successor in textual study, Theodulf – constituting between them, that is, a critical edition of the Vulgate.[87]

[87] I acknowledge the generous input of George Hardin Brown and Paul Meyvaert during the preparation of this article, which began as a paper given at a conference on 'The Golden Age of Northumbria' at the University of Newcastle upon Tyne, July 1996.

The transmission and reception of Graeco-Roman mythology in Anglo-Saxon England, 670–800

MICHAEL W. HERREN

Rhetoricians, orators, and public speakers of all stripes, if asked the question, which Greek or Roman deity they should invoke in case of need, would surely answer 'Hermes' or 'Mercury'.[1] Members of this profession who also read early Latin–Old English glossaries might therefore be surprised to learn that the *deus oratorum* was none other than Priapus! This came as good news to me as one who occasionally looks for novel ways to arouse an audience. However, as I reflected further on the meaning of Épinal Glossary 10v32, my expectations wilted. *Oratorum* must be a simple error for *hortorum*, 'of gardens'. Priapus may be *fecundus*, but he is not *facundus*.

This article is unconnected to oratory; it has nothing at all to do with gardens, and Priapus is raised only as an example of a pagan god whose name was known to the Anglo-Saxons. It is not very usual to think of the Anglo-Saxons around the time of Bede as having an interest in Graeco-Roman mythology. However, the monastic education that developed in England during the course of the seventh century included the reading of the pagan poets. This held especially for Canterbury and Wessex. In the north, we have Bede, who, though instructed in the pagan poets, was not partial to them. To exemplify his attitude he wrote his *De arte metrica*, a textbook that relied wholly on the Christian poets for its examples.[2]

Pagan poets such as Vergil and Ovid would have evoked an unfamiliar world to barbarians educated in Christian schools in the early Middle Ages.[3] The

---

[1] This article is a revised and expanded version of a paper presented at the meeting of the Medieval Academy of America in Toronto, 17–19 April 1997.

[2] *Beda. Opera Didascalica. Pars I*, ed. C. W. Jones, CCSL 123A (Turnhout, 1975), 60–114; cf. in general R. B. Palmer, 'Bede as Textbook Writer: a Study of his *De arte metrica*', *Speculum* 34 (1959), 573–84. For the specific problem of Bede's use of Vergil and his attitude towards the pagan classics, see N. Wright, 'Bede and Vergil', *Romanobarbarica* 6 (1981–2), 361–79; repr. in his *History and Literature in Late Antiquity and the Early Medieval West* (Aldershot, 1995), no. XI.

[3] See generally M. W. Herren, 'Die Anfänge der Grammatikstudien auf den Britischen Inseln: von Patrick bis zur Schule von Canterbury', *ScriptOralia* 43 (Tübingen, 1992), 57–79; repr. in his *Latin Letters in Early Christian Ireland* (Aldershot, 1996), no. II.

Germanic peoples in England in the seventh and eighth centuries doubtless retained a knowledge of their own pagan lore; to this would have been added a Christian foundation consisting of the study of the scriptures, the history of doctrine, in some cases canon law. However, the world of Jupiter and Juno and their kin would have been largely alien. Access to the Latin pagan poets would have been limited to a tiny number of churchmen with highly developed literacy skills. These faced a series of daunting tasks: acquisition of many archaic Latin forms and grammatical conventions; mastery of quantitative metre; and familiarization with the content of an alien religion and mythology. As everyone learns on first looking into anyone's Homer, a tremendous amount needs to be contextualized.

The process of contextualizing the Latin poets began well before the Anglo-Saxon period. The late fourth century produced the elementary commentary: Donatus, Servius and Philargyrius all produced *ad lineam* commentaries on Vergil's works.[4] These included much useful information on the gods, their attributes and their genealogies in addition to grammatical detail. The late fifth or early sixth century brought with it the revival of the mythological handbook: collections of stories about the gods and heroes. The prototype is the *Mitologiae* of Fulgentius (*c.* 500),[5] which was followed in the Carolingian period by the first of the collections attributed to the 'Vatican Mythographers'.[6] A third type of *Hilfsmittel* was the encyclopedia, especially Isidore of Seville's, written in the early seventh century,[7] of which much was repeated by Hrabanus Maurus in the ninth.[8] There one finds simple lists of deities' names with etymologies (*Etym.* VIII) or of monsters and portents familiar from classical texts (*Etym.* XI).[9]

It is perhaps tempting to believe that it was pagan literature alone that spurred the creation of reference works at the beginning of the Middle Ages. While it is

---

[4] See, in general, G. Funaioli, *Esegesi virgiliana* (Milan, 1930).

[5] *Fabii Planciadis Fulgentii V.C. Opera*, ed. R. Helm (Leipzig, 1898); translation in L. G. Whitbread, *Fulgentius the Mythographer* (Columbus, OH, 1971).

[6] See the new edition in the Belles Lettres series of 'the First Vatican Mythographer' by N. Zorzetti: *Le premier mythographe du Vatican* (Paris, 1995), esp. p. xi. The editor situates this recension between Remigius of Auxerre and the *Ecloga Theoduli*.

[7] The standard edition is still that of W. M. Lindsay, *Isidori Hispalensis Episcopi Etymologiarum sive Originum Libri XX*, 2 vols. (Oxford, 1911). A new multi-volume edition, with modern language translations, is being produced in the Belles Lettres series, Paris, under the general editorship of J. Fontaine.

[8] *De universo libri XXII*, PL 111, 9–614; see esp. XV.6, 'De diis gentium' (*ibid.* cols. 426–36). A new edition of this work is being prepared by W. Schippers, Memorial University, Newfoundland.

[9] See especially J. Fontaine, 'Le "sacré" antique vu par un homme du VIIe siècle: le livre VIII des *Étymologies* d'Isidore de Séville', *Bulletin de l'Association Guillaume Budé*, Lettres d'humanité 48 (1989), 396–405; further, K. N. MacFarlane, 'Isidore of Seville on the Pagan Gods (*Origines* VIII.11), *Trans. of the Amer. Philosophical Soc.* 70.3 (1980), 3–40.

true that pagan literature was indeed the primary factor, we should recall that Christian poetry also added impetus. The Christian poets of the fourth and fifth centuries especially – Proba, Prudentius, Paulinus, Dracontius among others – are rich in pagan allusions. Indeed, we observe that pagan–Christian poetic syncretism had its roots in the fourth century.[10] This is expressed at the most superficial level by the phenomenon of Christian poets employing words with pagan associations to express Christian teaching: heaven is called *Olympus*, hell is *Cocytus* or *Tartarus*, and God himself is sometimes given the epithet *Tonans*, ('thunderer'), frequently applied by pagan poets to Jupiter. At a more sophisticated level, we find the interweaving and reinterpretation of pagan tales as counterparts to biblical exempla. A fine example of this occurs in the anonymous poem 'De Sodoma', which juxtaposes the conflagration of Sodom with the destruction wrought by Phaethon in his fall, drawn from Ovid's *Metamorphoses*.[11] Early Anglo-Saxon readers would therefore have been obliged to cope with some of the same requirements to supply context for the Christian poets as they would have for the writings of Vergil, and, as the early Latin–Old English glossaries prove, the information was largely available from Christian writers.

Thanks to the survival of a letter by Aldhelm to Leuthere, bishop of Wessex,[12] we know that Latin poetry formed an important part of the curriculum at the school of Canterbury conducted by Theodore and Hadrian, and thanks to another letter (or fragment of a letter) by Aldhelm to Hadrian,[13] we may conjecture that it was under this master that Aldhelm learned about the groupings of 'letters, words, feet, poetic figures, verses, accents, and rhythms' – to cite his own words.[14] From Aldhelm's voluminous writings and those thought to derive from his circle we can form a good idea of the poets read at Aldhelm's own school at Malmesbury. The most heavily cited Christian poets were Juvencus and Caelius Sedulius.[15] Aldhelm had an excellent knowledge of the three major poems by Vergil;[16] he may have used Ovid's *Metamorphoses* for his

[10] The use of Vergil by Christian writers from late antiquity onwards is particularly striking. See the detailed study by P. Courcelle, *Lecteurs païens et lecteurs chrétiens de l'Énéide* (Paris, 1984).

[11] *Incerti de Sodoma*, ed. R. Peiper in *Cypriani Galli Poetae Heptateuchos*, CSEL 23 (Vienna, 1881), 217–18, lines 99–113; Ovid, *Met.* II.19–400.

[12] *Ep.* I, ed. R. Ehwald in *Aldhelmi Opera*, MGH, Auct. antiq. 15 (Berlin, 1919), 475–8; M. Lapidge and M. W. Herren, *Aldhelm: the Prose Works* (Cambridge, 1979), pp. 152–3.

[13] *Ep.* II, ed. Ehwald, p. 478; Lapidge and Herren, *Prose Works*, pp. 153–4.

[14] *Ep.* I, ed. Ehwald, p. 477: '. . . quomodo videlicet ipsius metricae artis clandistina instrumenta litteris, logis, pedibus, poeticis figuris, versibus, tonis, temporibus conglomerentur'; Lapidge and Herren, *Prose Works*, p. 152.

[15] See the *Index Locorum* in Ehwald's edition, pp. 544–6. For a detailed study of the knowledge of Juvencus and Sedulius in Anglo-Saxon England, see M. Lapidge, 'The Study of Latin Texts in Late Anglo-Saxon England', in his *Anglo-Latin Literature, 600–899* (London, 1996), pp. 470–83.

[16] Ehwald, *ibid.*

Aenigmata.[17] He apparently knew Lucan's *Pharsalia*, and remarkably, quotes lines from the opening of the same poet's lost *Orpheus*.[18] Doubtless some of the citations in Aldhelm's metrical treatises are derived second hand from grammarians, especially Priscian.[19] Priscian's *Institutiones grammaticae* are crammed with citations of Latin poems, and many of these bear upon Graeco-Roman mythology.[20]

What books were available in England in the seventh and eighth centuries to provide the needed *accessus ad auctores*? First and foremost, there was Isidore's *Etymologiae*, with the sections on the pagan gods and monsters already noted. There is a good deal of evidence to suggest that this text was already circulating in Ireland well before the end of the seventh century.[21] Indeed, the transmission of the *Etymologiae* to Anglo-Saxon England may have occurred via Ireland in light of the evidence for its early use there,[22] strengthened by the discovery of a late-seventh- or early-eighth-century fragment of the text in Irish script with Old Irish glosses in a manuscript closely linked to Glastonbury.[23] Glastonbury is in Aldhelm's diocese of western Wessex, and Aldhelm was probably the first English writer to consult the *Etymologiae* for his own compositions, especially his *Enigmata* or 'Riddles'.[24] The *Etymologiae* were also a source of the earliest

---

[17] See esp. no. XCV, 'Scylla', cited and discussed below, pp. 95–6. If Aldhelm knew Ovid directly, such knowledge would have been unique in his period. There are no full manuscripts of the *Metamorphoses* prior to the eleventh century, with only fragments and scattered quotations surviving from the Carolingian period. See R. J. Tarrant's entry in *Texts and Transmission: a Survey of the Latin Classics*, ed. L. D. Reynolds (Oxford, 1983), pp. 276–84. M. Manitius, *Geschichte der lateinischen Literatur des Mittelalters*, 3 vols. (Munich, 1911–31) I, 137, points out that examples of verses drawn from Ovid are wholly lacking in the metrical portions of the *Epistola ad Acircium* (i.e. the *De metris* and the *De pedum regulis*).

[18] F. Porsia, *Liber monstrorum: Introduzione, edizione, versione e commento* (Bari, 1976), p. 64; M. Lapidge, '*Beowulf*, Aldhelm, the *Liber monstrorum* and Wessex', in his *Anglo-Latin Literature, 600–899*, pp. 271–312, at 289.

[19] For Aldhelm's early use of Priscian, see V. Law, *The Insular Latin Grammarians* (Woodbridge, 1982), p. 21.

[20] Priscian manuscripts of the Carolingian period, especially those associated with the schools of north-eastern France, are rich in mythological glosses. These will be listed and discussed in a forthcoming study on the transmission and reception of Graeco-Roman mythology in western Europe in the period 600–900.

[21] B. Bischoff, 'Die europäische Verbreitung der Werke Isidors von Sevilla', in his *Mittelalterliche Studien: Ausgewählte Aufsätze zur Schriftkunde und Literaturgeschichte*, 3 vols. (Stuttgart, 1966–81) I, 171–94, esp. 180–6.

[22] M. W. Herren, 'On the Earliest Irish Acquaintance with Isidore of Seville', *Visigothic Spain: New Approaches*, ed. E. James (Oxford, 1980), pp. 243–50; repr. Herren, *Latin Letters*, no. III, pp. 243–50.

[23] J. P. Carley and A. Dooley, 'An Early Irish Fragment of Isidore of Seville's *Etymologiae*', *The Archaeology and History of Glastonbury Abbey. Essays in Honour of the Ninetieth Birthday of C. A. Raleigh Radford*, ed. L. Abrams and J. P. Carley (Woodbridge, 1991), pp. 135–61. The manuscript was certainly at Glastonbury in the later Middle Ages (*ibid.* pp. 136–7).

[24] N. Howe, 'Aldhelm's *Enigmata* and Isidorian Etymology', *ASE* 14 (1985), 37–59.

surviving Latin–Old English glossary, the Épinal–Erfurt Glossary, thought by most scholars to have been composed in Wessex in the last quarter of the seventh century.[25] They were heavily used in the composition of the *Liber monstrorum*,[26] to which we shall turn presently. Boniface used the first book of the *Etymologiae* in his *Ars metrica*.[27] Finally, and perhaps most interestingly, an epitome of the *Etymologiae* with Old English glosses dating to *c.* 700 was recently identified in a manuscript written in northern France *c.* 800.[28]

Next is Servius's commentary on the works of Vergil. The evidence for the transmission of this important text before the Carolingian Renaissance is rather sparse. Apart from Isidore's use of this work,[29] most of the evidence appears to be Insular. Servius was in all likelihood a source of the Irish recension of the Philargyrius commentary on Vergil, compiled in the seventh or eighth century.[30] The evidence for England is more concrete. Servius was used as a separate source for the compilation of the epitome of Isidore's *Etymologiae* just discussed,[31] and thus would have been available in England by *c.* 700. Servius is named by Alcuin as one of the authors available in the library at York around the middle of the eighth century[32] – though we cannot be sure that Alcuin is referring to the commentary on Vergil and not the metrical works ascribed to Servius entitled *De finalibus* and *De centum metris*. There is, however, a more concrete indication of the circulation of this commentary in England: the very earliest extant fragment of Servius was written in Anglo-Saxon minuscule dated to the first half of the eighth century.[33] It was found in Germany near Fulda, thus suggesting a connection to the mission of Boniface, allegedly a member of Aldhelm's circle and himself an author of a grammar as well as of the *Ars metrica* mentioned above.

[25] M. Lapidge, 'An Isidorian Epitome from Anglo-Saxon England', *Anglo-Latin Literature, 600–899*, pp. 183–223, at 190–1.   [26] See Porsia, *Liber monstrorum*, p. 67 and *app. font.*, *passim*.
[27] *Bonifatii (Vynfreth) Ars Grammatica, accedit Ars grammatica*, ed. G. J. Gebauer and B. Löfstedt, CCSL 133B (Turnhout, 1980), 109–13.
[28] Paris, Bibliothèque Nationale, lat. 1750; E. A. Lowe, *Codices Latini Antiquiores*, 11 vols. and Supp. (Oxford, 1934–71; 2nd ed. of vol. II, 1972) [hereafter *CLA*], Supp. no. 1674. For a full discussion, see Lapidge, 'An Isidorian Epitome'.
[29] See the entry by P. K. Marshall in *Texts and Transmission*, ed. Reynolds, p. 385.
[30] M. W. Herren, 'Classical and Secular Learning among the Irish before the Carolingian Renaissance', *Florilegium* 3 (1981), 118–57, at 136; repr. *Latin Letters*, no. I, p. 35.
[31] Lapidge, 'An Isidorian Epitome', p. 195.
[32] 'Quid Probus atque Focas, Donatus Priscianusve,/Servius, Euticius, Pompeius, Comminianus', *Versus de patribus regibus et sanctis Euboricensis ecclesiae*, ed. E. Dümmler, MGH PLAC I, 204, lines 1555–6; see also the discussion in the edition by P. Godman, *Alcuin: the Bishops, Kings and Saints of York* (Oxford, 1982), p. 127, n. to line 1557.
[33] Formerly Spangenberg, Pfarrbibliothek, s.n. (*CLA* Supp. no. 1806). This manuscript should now be identified as Marburg, Hessisches Staatsarchiv 319 Pfarrei Spangenberg Hr Nr. 1 (s. viii[1]); cf. B. Bischoff, V. Brown and J. John, 'Addenda to *Codices latini antiquiores* (II)', *MS* 54 (1992), 286–307, at 307; Lapidge, 'An Isidorian Epitome', p. 195 and n. 43.

Two other texts available in England at an early date are of value for transmitting mythological information. These are bk I of Orosius's *Historia aduersus
paganos* and bk XVI, ch. 8 of Augustine's *De ciuitate Dei*. Orosius is another work
with an early Irish *fortuna*,[34] and an Irish stage in the formation of the Latin–Old
English glossaries has been posited.[35] There are 'well-defined batches of
lemmata from Orosius's *Historia adversus paganos* in Épinal-Erfurt',[36] and a section
'De Orosio' in the Leiden Glossary.[37] The *Historia*, of course, is not a reference
work. Its value for transmitting mythological information is restricted to the first
book which incorporates euhemerized figures of Greek mythology into a history
of the world. Aldhelm used bk I (*Adv. pag.* I.xiii.2), citing both author and work in
a reference to the minotaur: 'Orosius in prosa historica: "Informe", inquit, "pro-
digium Graeciae luminibus saginabant", id est Creticum Minotaurum.' Curiously,
Aldhelm used this passage in his *De pedum regulis* to illustrate denominative
verbs![38] The author of the *Liber monstrorum* found his description of battle ele-
phants in the same source.[39] We know of one other early author with Insular
connections who excerpted the mythological section of Orosius, namely the
author of the so-called *Cosmographia* of 'Aethicus Ister', who wrote *c.* 700.[40] This
writer used Orosius chiefly for his description of the Amazons, which he wove
into his section dealing with the travels of Aethicus in Scythia.[41]

The second work is Augustine's *De ciuitate Dei*, where there is a list of literary
monsters in XVI.8. This work was heavily excerpted by the author of the *Liber
monstrorum*.[42] Aldhelm, too, cites the *De ciuitate Dei*,[43] though he did not exploit it
for mythological content. Another indication of early Anglo-Saxon interest in
Augustine's work is found in a tiny collection of excerpts in Leiden Voss. Q. 69,
36r–v, which follows immediately upon the Latin–Old English glossary known
as the Leiden Glossary. It begins 'Agustinus in .xii. libris de ciuitate dei . . .'.

With this groundwork completed. it will now be possible to examine what
was known about Graeco-Roman mythology and how it was utilized in seventh-
and eighth-century England; from this we may proceed to form an overall
impression of what may have been the prevailing attitudes towards this pursuit.
Let us turn again to Aldhelm, abbot of Malmesbury and afterwards bishop of

---

[34] Herren, 'Classical and Secular Learning', p. 133; repr. *Latin Letters*, no. I, p. 27.

[35] J. D. Pheifer, *Old English Glosses in the Épinal–Erfurt Glossary* (Oxford, 1974), p. xlvii; *idem*, 'Early Anglo-Saxon Glossaries and the School of Canterbury', *ASE* 16 (1987), 17–44, at 28–9 and 44.

[36] *Ibid.*   [37] *Ibid.*   [38] Ed. Ehwald, p. 167.   [39] Lapidge, '*Beowulf*', p. 288.

[40] For a summary of what is known about this writer, see the introduction to the edition by O. Prinz, *Die Kosmographie des Aethicus* (Munich, 1993), pp. 1–84. (I am preparing a new edition for the Oxford Medieval Texts series.)

[41] Ed. Prinz, pp. 178–81; see also the *Index Locorum*, pp. 327–8.

[42] Porsia, *Liber monstrorum*, pp. 66–7.

[43] Sometimes explicitly by author and work, as at *De virginitate*, c. IX (ed. Ehwald, p. 237): '. . . si-quidem beatus Augustinus in libro civitatis Dei. . .'

Sherborne, head of an important school, and the centre of a scholarly circle that included the poet Æthilwald and possibly the learned Boniface.[44] Aldhelm's influence on Anglo-Latin literature in the tenth and eleventh centuries is now well documented.[45] The impact of his latinity on that of his contemporaries and students has also been noticed.[46] However, his importance for the transmission of Graeco-Roman mythology has not been sufficiently recognized, although his contribution in this area was truly significant. It embraces glossarial activity, the use of mythological motifs in his own poetry, and a possible role in the creation of a handbook of mythology.

Aldhelm himself pretended to deprecate this pursuit, playfully labelling it a frivolous exercise characteristic of Irish scholarship, but hardly worthy of the attention of sober English study. In his letter to a certain Wihtfrith about to sail to Ireland to pursue his studies, Aldhelm chided his recipient for choosing a region that spurned the study of the Bible in favour of the worldly philosophers. Then he went on to say:

Quidnam, rogitans quaeso, orthodoxae fidei sacramento commodi affert circa temeratum spurcae Proserpinae incestum – quod abhorret fari – enucleate legendo scrutando sudescere aut Hermionam, petulantem Menelai et Helenae sobolem, quae, ut prisca produnt opuscula, despondebatur pridem iure dotis Oresti demumque sententia immutata Neoptolemo nupsit, lectionis praeconio venerari aut Lupercorum bacchantum antistites ritu litantium Priapo parasitorum heroico stilo historiae caraxare . . .[47]

We have come full circle to Priapus, our *deus oratorum*! Aldhelm must have invoked precisely this god in order to formulate such a fine example of *praeteritio*. He set out to criticize the study of mythology as a danger to the faith, but it would appear that he was more interested in proving that he knew as much about matters mythological as any Irish teacher, and therefore Wihtfrith would do better to stay at home than expose himself to dangers abroad. In his own *Enigmata*, metrical riddles based on the riddles of Symposius, Aldhelm makes

---

[44] For a brief biography of Aldhelm and list of his writings, see Lapidge and Herren, *Prose Works*, pp. 5–19.

[45] See especially M. Lapidge, 'The Hermeneutic Style in Tenth- Century Anglo-Latin Literature', in his *Anglo-Latin Literature, 900–1066* (London, 1993), pp. 105–49.

[46] Manitius, *Geschichte* I, 138.

[47] *Ep.* 3, ed. Ehwald, p. 479. 'What, pray, I beseech you eagerly, is the benefit to the sanctity of the orthodox faith to expend energy by reading and studying the foul pollution of base Proserpina, which I shrink from mentioning in plain speech; or to revere, through celebration in study, Hermione, the wanton offspring of Menelaus and Helen, who, as the ancient texts report, was engaged for a while by right of dowry to Orestes, then, having changed her mind, married Neoptolemus; or to record – in the heroic style of epic – the high priests of the *Luperci*, who revel in the fashion of those cultists that sacrifice to Priapus . . .' (Lapidge and Herren, *Aldhelm: the Prose Works*, p. 154).

Michael W. Herren

frequent use of Graeco-Roman mythological motifs. Let us examine some of the more striking examples.

V. IRIS
Taumantis proles priscorum famine fingor[48]

The probable source of this line is *Anth. Lat.* 543.1, labelled 'Tristicha de arcu caeli'; it begins: 'Thaumantis proles varianti veste refulgens.'[49] In this riddle, Aldhelm omits the most obvious biblical allusion to the rainbow (Gen. IX.12), connecting the natural phenomenon instead to Iris, the classical personification of the rainbow, beginning with her genealogy.

VIII. PLIADES
Nos Athlante satas stolidi dixere priores[50]

A fuller reference to the Pleiades occurs in Aldhelm's *De metris*: 'Quid referam Atlantidas patronimico dictas vocabulo, quas Graecorum traditio a pluralitate pliades, Latina a verno tempore vergilias?'[51] ('What shall I say of the daughters of Atlas who take their name from their father, whom the Greek tradition names *Pleiades* from their plurality, while the Latin calls them *vergilias* from the vernal season?') This remark seems to be a blend of phrasing and information taken from Servius, Servius Auctus and Isidore. (The derivation of *vergiliae* from *ver* is found in Isidore, *Etym.* III.xxi.13.)

XXVIII. MINOTAURUS
Sum mihi dissimilis vultu membrisque biformis
Cornibus armatus, horrendum cetera fingunt
Membra virum; fama clarus per Gnossia rura
Spurius incerto Creta genitore creatus
Ex hominis pecudisque simul cognomine dicor.[52]

The last line dealing with the origin of the name is probably due to Isidore, *Etym.* XI.iii.38. A full account of the minotaur story is given by Servius at *Aen.* VI.14. As we have seen, Aldhelm introduced what might be viewed as a gratuitous reference to the minotaur in his discussion of the verb *sagino*.

---

[48] Ed. Ehwald, p. 100. 'In the writings of the ancients I am conceived as the child of Thaumas' (Lapidge and Rosier, *Aldhelm: the Poetic Works*, p. 71).
[49] See Lapidge and Rosier, *Aldhelm: the Poetic Works*, p. 248, n. 4, where it is suggested that Aldhelm knew the 'African Anthology'.
[50] Ed. Ehwald, pp. 101–2. 'The stupid ancients said that we were the offspring of Atlas' (Lapidge and Rosier, *Aldhelm: the Poetic Works*, p. 72). [51] Ed. Ehwald, p. 72.
[52] Ed. Ehwald, p. 109: 'I am two-shaped, being different with respect to my face and my limbs: I am armed with horns, but my other limbs constitute a terrifying man. I am known by report through the fields of Cnossos, having been born a bastard of an unknown father in Crete. My name is taken from that of man and beast together' (Lapidge and Rosier, *Aldhelm: the Poetic Works*, p. 75).

XLV. FUSUM

In saltu nascor ramosa fronde virescens,
Sed fortuna meum mutaverunt ordine fatum,
Dum verbo per collum teretem vertigine molam:
Ex quo conficitur regalis stragula pepli.
Tam longa nullus zona praecingitur heros.
Per me fata virum dicunt decernere Parcas;
Frigora dura viros sternant, ni forte resistam.[53]

The spools of the fates were a commonplace, and there is nothing here to suggest a particular source. One notes that Aldhelm here mingles the natural and the mythological functions of the spindle, as he did in the instance of the rainbow (Iris).

LVII. AQUILA

'Armiger infausti Iovis et raptor Ganimedis'
Quamquam pellaces cantarent carmine vates,
Non fueram praepes, quo fertur Dardana proles,
Sed magis in summis cicnos agitabo fugaces . . .[54]

The words 'armiger . . . Ganimedis' suggest *Aen.* V.254–5 as the source. The passage is interesting because it so perfectly illustrates the ambivalence of early medieval Christian writers to pagan tales. Jupiter is *infaustus*, which assuredly he is not in Vergil, and the *vates* are *pellaces* ('seductive'). Yet Aldhelm cannot resist the allusion to the eagle that carried off Ganymede, even though he insists that the eagle *he* is describing is a different bird altogether!

XCV. SCILLA

Ecce, molosorum nomen mihi fata dederunt
(Argolicae gentis sic promit lingua loquelis),
Ex quo me dirae fallebant carmina Circae,
Quae fontis liquidi maculabat flumina verbis:
Femora cum cruribus, suras cum poplite bino
Abstulit immiscens crudelis verba virago.
Pignora nunc pavidi referunt ululantia nautae,
Tonsis dum tradunt classes et caerula findunt

[53] Ed. Ehwald, p. 117. 'I was born in the forest, green on a leafy bough, but fortune changed my condition in due course, since I move my rounded shape twirling through the smooth-spun thread; from this is made the royal covering of a robe. No hero (anywhere) is girded by a belt as long as mine [*scil.* the distaff]. They say that the Parcae decree the fates of men through me' (Lapidge and Rosier, *Aldhelm: the Poetic Works*, p. 79).

[54] Ed. Ehwald, p. 123. 'Although deceitful poets might sing in their verses (that I am) the weapon-bearer of unlucky Jove and the abductor of Ganymede, I was not that bird by whom the youth [i.e. Ganymede] was carried off; rather I chase fleeing swans high in the air. . .' (Lapidge and Rosier, *Aldhelm: the Poetic Works*, p. 82).

Vastos verrentes fluctus grassante procella,
Palmula qua remis succurrit panda per undas,
Auscultare procul, quae latrant inguina circum.
Sic me pellexit dudum Titania proles,
Ut merito vivam salsis in fluctibus exul.[55]

The account of the poisoning and mutilation of Scylla is told in succinct form by Servius at *Aen.* III.420, but Aldhelm gives more detail. Indeed, his account agrees more closely with the tale of Scylla given in Ovid *Metamorphoses* XIII.70–XIV.74.[56] Here we have another example of Aldhelm's delight in displaying his knowledge of mythology for its own sake, as he did in the riddle on the minotaur.

XCVII. NOX

Florida me genuit nigrantem corpore tellus
Et nil fecundum stereli de viscere promo,
Quamvis Eumenidum narrantes carmine vates
Tartaream partu testentur gignere prolem.[57]

The information that Night is the mother of the Eumenides can be found in Servius's commentary to *Aen.* VI.250 and in Vergil's own text at *Aen.* XII.846, though Vergil calls them the *Dirae* in that passage. The fourth verse of the *Enigma* is undoubtedly taken from the same Vergilian passage. A play on the connection of night to the *Dirae* occurs in line 9 (not cited above): 'Diri latrones me semper amare solebant' ('Cruel robbers always were wont to love me'). Normal events are connected to mythological ones through etymology.

One other aspect of Aldhelm's penchant for mythological study is his use of mythological language in non-mythological contexts. We have already seen one example in his *ars metrica*. Another occurs in the sole surviving example of his rhythmical poetry:[58]

---

[55] Ed. Ehwald, p. 142. 'Look, the Fates gave me the name of dogs – thus does the language of the Greeks render it in words – ever since the incantations of dread Circe, who stained the waters of the flowing fountain with her words, deceived me. Weaving words, the cruel witch deprived me of thighs together with shins, and calves together with knees. Terrified mariners relate that, as they impel ships with oars and cleave the sea, sweeping along the mighty waves while the tempest rages, where the broad blade of the oar runs through the water, they hear from afar the howling offspring that barks about my loins. Thus the daughter of Titan [*scil.* Circe] once tricked me, so that I should live as an exile – deservedly – in the salt waves' (Lapidge and Rosier, *Aldhelm: the Poetic Works*, p. 91).

[56] Cf. Lapidge and Rosier, *Aldhelm: the Poetic Works*, p. 254, n. 85; cf. above, pp. 89–90 and n. 17.

[57] Ed. Ehwald, p. 143. 'Flowering earth bore me, black, from her body; and I produce nothing fecund from my sterile womb, even though the poets, telling in their verse of the Eumenides, claim that I gave birth to the race of Tartarus' (Lapidge and Rosier, *Aldhelm: the Poetic Works*, p. 92).

[58] For the attribution, see Lapidge in Lapidge and Herren, *Aldhelm: the Prose Works*, pp. 16–17.

Carm. rhyth. I.76–8
Septem late lampadibus
Pliadis pulchra copula
Ab Athlantis prosapia . . .[59]

The dense little poem deals with a storm and the destruction of a church's roof. The detail of the mythological origin of the Pleiades might be somewhat surprising in this context. However, the same poem contains an allusion to the 'compact which holds the winds in check',[60] doubtless a reference to the tale of Aeolus and the winds in bk I of the *Aeneid*. Other examples can be found in this poem and also, if to a lesser degree, in the imitative rhythmical octosyllables written by Aldhelm's protégé Æthilwald.[61] They point to an avid interest, even delight, in the language, tropes and exempla of Graeco-Roman mythology that are provided by the earlier Latin poets.

Another important class of evidence for this interest is glossography. Anglo-Saxon England created the earliest known dictionaries comprising Latin and a vernacular language. These include both the so-called *glossae collectae*, organized according to the authors excerpted, and alphabetical glossaries. The former is represented by the Leiden Glossary, which survives in a manuscript written at St Gallen around the turn of the eighth century.[62] Except for a short section at the beginning, organized alphabetically, the glossary consists of batches of lemmata and glosses drawn from the Bible and popular patristic writers: Orosius, Eusebius's *Historia ecclesiastica* in Rufinus's translation, Cassiodorus's *Expositio psalmorum*, and the like. The extant Leiden Glossary is a representative of a larger family of similarly organized glossaries.[63] Many of its entries have precise or close parallels in the alphabetically organized glossaries, Épinal–Erfurt and Corpus. It has been argued plausibly that the archetype of the Leiden family was also a principal source of Épinal–Erfurt and Corpus.[64]

The Épinal–Erfurt Glossary,[65] basically a single alphabetical glossary that survives in two early copies, was compiled probably in southern England in the late

---

[59] Ed. Ehwald, p. 526. 'And likewise, the beautiful constellation of the Pleiades, offspring of Atlantis, with its seven gleaming lights lies hidden' (Lapidge and Rosier, *Aldhelm: the Poetic Works*, p. 178).

[60] *Carm. rhyth.* I.23, ed. Ehwald, p. 525: 'Cum fracto venti federe' (Lapidge and Rosier, *Aldhelm: the Poetic Works*, p. 177); cf. Vergil, *Aen.* I.50–141.   [61] Ed. Ehwald, pp. 528–37.

[62] See below, pp. 100–1.

[63] For a list of manuscripts of the 'Leiden family' of glossaries, see M. Lapidge, 'The School of Theodore and Hadrian', *Anglo-Latin Literature, 600–899*, pp. 163–8.   [64] *Ibid.* pp. 153–4.

[65] There is as yet no complete critical edition of this work. The Old English glosses only are ed. Pheifer, *Old English Glosses*. For the complete glossary one must still consult G. Goetz, *Corpus Glossariorum Latinorum*, 7 vols. (Leipzig, 1881–1923) V, 337–401. There is a diplomatic edition by O. Schlutter of the Épinal copy only (cited below, p. 98, n. 67), and a facsimile edition by B. Bischoff *et al.*, *The Épinal, Erfurt, Werden and Corpus Glossaries*, EEMF 22 (Copenhagen, 1988).

seventh century.[66] The mythological entries that can be extracted from it are rather sparse and consist largely of terse identifications of gods and heroes, some in the vernacular. I cite from Schlutter's diplomatic edition of the Épinal manuscript,[67] with my explanations in square brackets:

2v 35 (col. 3)	amphitrite mare
3r 34 (col. 3)	bel pater saturni
5r 36 (col. 2)	feton solis et climinae filius
6r 27 (col. 1)	hercolus [= hercoles] fortis
7v 16 (col. 2)	minerba palla deartium [= minerua pallas dea artium]
8r 9 (col. 2)	mars martis tiig.
9v 12 (col. 2)	pliadas sifun sterri
10v 32 (col. 2)	priapus deus oratorum [= (h)ortorum]
11r 23 (col. 1)	pan incibus [= incubus?]
11r 19 (col. 2)	penates domicilia sacra
11r 20 (col. 2)	pieridae quasi laptucae [= lapithae?]
13v 35 (col. 1)	theologia deigeneologia [= dei genealogia]
13v 21 (col. 3)	thyeasteas comesationes [lemma without gloss?]
14v 38 (col. 2)	tripodia mensa appollinis
14v 4 (col. 3)	tritonia genus est ferri [!] in mare

The glosses come from a variety of sources: Isidore, Orosius and Rufinus, among others.[68] Perhaps the most interesting aspect of these scanty and occasionally corrupt notes is the introduction of vernacular glosses. While the gloss 'sifun sterri' on *Pliadas* merely identifies the constellation, the gloss 'Tiig' on *Mars* is quite interesting. 'Tig' or 'Tiw' is the name of a Germanic war god, and thus provides early evidence of an attempt to correlate the Germanic and Graeco-Roman pantheons.[69]

Next is the Corpus Glossary, comprising two alphabetical glossaries preserved in Cambridge, Corpus Christi College 144 (s. viii/ix).[70] The second of the two glossaries repeats a large portion of Épinal–Erfurt while adding an equal amount of new material.[71] In examining the mythological glosses we can

---

[66] Épinal, Bibliothèque municipale, 72 (2) and Erfurt, Amplon., Fol. 42. The Épinal copy has recently been redated to *c.* 700: see T. J. Brown, 'The Irish Element in the Insular System of Scripts to circa A.D. 850', *Die Iren und Europa im Frühmittelalter*, ed. H. Löwe, 2 vols. (Stuttgart, 1982) I, 109, n. 12. See Pheifer, 'Early Anglo-Saxon Glossaries', p. 44.
[67] Schlutter, *Das Epinaler und Erfurter Glossar. I. Teil.* See above, p. 97, n. 65.
[68] Pheifer, *Old English Glosses*, pp. xli–lvii.
[69] See E. A. Philippson, *Germanisches Heidentum bei den Angelsachsen*, Kölner Anglistische Arbeiten 4 (Leipzig, 1929), 113–23. (I wish to thank Roberta Frank (Toronto) for this reference.)
[70] *CLA* II, no. 122; N. Ker, *Catalogue of Manuscripts Containing Anglo-Saxon* (Oxford, 1957), p. 49 (no. 36).
[71] I follow the edition of W. M. Lindsay, *The Corpus Glossary* (Cambridge, 1921). There is an older edition by J. H. Hessels, *An Eighth-Century Latin–Anglo-Saxon Glossary Preserved in the Library of*

see that the Corpus compiler reproduces without alteration several glosses found also in Épinal–Erfurt, as in the case of Corpus A509 and 529 'Amfrite/Amphitrite mare', H54 'Herculus [*sic*] fortis' and F130 'Foeton solis et Climenae filius'. At other times the Corpus compiler adds information to that given by the Épinal–Erfurt glossator, as at M49–50 'Mars Martis', where he mistakenly adds a note connecting the name to *mas, maris*, 'male' or 'husband'. However, the glossator also inserts many new entries, for example Acheron, Charybdis, Ciclops, Cinthia, Erebum, Eumenides, Euterpe, Helicon (MS Helson), Ilia and Iliacus, Iouem, Iris, Melpomene (MS Melfoben), Mulcifer, Naides, nimpha, Oedipia (MS Oethippia), Orcus, Pieris, Tempe, Tenarum, Tethys (MS Thedis), Titania, Titica (for Tethica?), Tisifone, and Titan (MS Titon). The number of Old English equivalents for Graeco-Roman divinities is also expanded. Lindsay's remarks are in round brackets, mine in square:

> E351 E[u]rynis: Walcyrge
> E354 Eumenides: haehtisse [!]
> I479 Iouem: þuner
> O231 Orcus: heldiobul
> S359 Smus (for Erinyis?): wellyrgae (for Walcyrgae?)
> T79 Tempe: sceadugeardas
> T158 Titica: uuefl [??]
> T159 Tisifone: Uualcyrge

As is evident, three of the entries (E351, S359 and T159) are glossed by *waelcyrige* (i.e. Valkyries), literally 'chooser of the slain'. In their original manifestation, the Valkyries selected those who were to die in battle; they meted out fates.[72] The entry at I479 *Iouem: þuner* makes the obvious correlation between Jupiter and thunder or Thor, god of thunder.[73] This finds a Latin reflex in the frequent references to God as *Tonans*, 'Thunderer' in the poetry of Aldhelm. *Tempe* (T79) is aptly glossed by *sceadugeardas*, 'places of shade', as is *Orcus*, god of the underworld, by *heldiobul*, 'devil of hell'. The mysterious *haehtisse*, yet another gloss to *Eumenides*, identified by Lindsay as Old English, is illuminated by an entry in the Leiden Glossary: 'Eumenides filiae noctis. i. hegitissae', the last being a corruption of *Hecates*, 'of Hecate'. What looks like an Old English gloss is, apparently, a corrupt Graeco-Latin form, presupposing an unattested **Hecatissa*. One entry remains a puzzle to me, namely T158 'Titica: uuefl'. If *Titica* stands for *Tethica* < *Tethys*, a sea nymph, then OE *uuefl*, 'woof' or 'warp' is totally inappropriate; one can assume only that the gloss has been misplaced.

Corpus Christi College, Cambridge (MS N°. 144) (Cambridge, 1890). For the position of this glossary in the complex of Old English glossaries, see Pheifer, *Old English Glosses*, pp. xxviii–xxxi.
[72] Philippson, *Germanisches Heidentum*, pp. 67–8.   [73] *Ibid.* pp. 136–41.

We now come to the Leiden Glossary, contained in Leiden, Universiteits-bibliotheek, Voss. Q(uarto) 69, part II, fols. 20–36.[74] The manuscript was written presumably at St Gallen and is dated s. viii/ix.[75] Unlike Épinal–Erfurt and Corpus, the Leiden Glossary is not arranged alphabetically (except for two short sections at the beginning), but consists rather of *glossae collectae*, arranged by author or text.[76] On fol. 34 is an item entitled 'De diuersis nominibus', in fact a list of mythological lemmata and glosses culled from different sources. There is only a little overlap with the two glossaries already discussed. The entries are:

Themisto insula, Calipso insula. Pan deus arcadiae uel pastorum. Arcades gens dicitur quae colebat pan. Polideuces polux, ulixes hominum fortissimi . . . Nereus deus maris . . . Carus (sc. Charon) nomen hominis qui transportare dicitur in infernum . . . Centaurus nauis unus de nauibus aeniae (Verg. *Aen.* V.122) . . . Bachus liber pater dionisius non (= nomen) unius hominis est. /f. 34v/ Floralia bacchanalia saturnalia liberalia ulcanalia: festiuitates uel sacra paganorum est . . . Manes anime mortuorum . . . Epul castor per pullux per castor . . . parcae quae minime parcent . . . Eumenides filiae noctis .i. hegitissae [*scil.* Hecates].

It is perhaps of some interest that the explanations found here have a distinctly euhemeristic cast.[77] Calipso is an island rather than a goddess. Carus (Charon) is the name of a *man* who transports (*scil.* souls) to hell. Centaur is the name of one of Aeneas's ships, while Castor and Pollux are reduced to names to be used in oaths. Nevertheless, the entries bear witness to a continuing interest in explaining mythological and Graeco-Roman religious references in Latin literature.

In addition to the mythological glosses in the section 'De diuersis nominibus' entries of mythological interest occur scattered throughout works excerpted by name or by author. It would appear that at least two sets of excerpts of Eusebius's *Historia ecclesiastica* in the translation of Rufinus were made, one set appearing under the title (Hessels, iv and v), the other, under the name of Eusebius (Hessels, xxxv). This could indicate that the excerptors had access to two or more glossed copies of Eusebius's work or, alternatively, that extensive scholia in the exemplar were excerpted in different ways at different times. This is shown by the example of *Oedipia*, which occurs in three different spellings, with three entirely different explanations:

Hessels, iv. Oedipia: obscene; Dapes: carnium infantium
Hessels, v. Oedippa: de odippo
Hessels, xxxv. Oethipia: coitum matris et sororis; sicut manichei in occultis; idest in occulta loca idolorum

---

[74] Ed. J. H. Hessels, *A Late Eighth-Century Latin–Anglo-Saxon Glossary Preserved in the Library of the Leiden University* (Cambridge, 1906).   [75] *CLA* X, no. 1585.

[76] Pheifer, *Old English Glosses*, p. xliii; Lapidge, 'The School of Theodore and Hadrian', pp. 150–68.

[77] For an overview of euhemeristic interpretations in the Middle Ages, see J. D. Cooke, 'Euhemerism: a Medieval Interpretation of Classical Paganism', *Speculum* 2 (1927), 396–410.

The first part of the third entry recurs as the entry for Corpus O130. The first entry is wholly confusing until one notices that the immediately preceding entry is 'Thesteas: indiscretas concubitas'. It would seem that the glosses to *Thesteas* and *Oedipia* were switched. *Thesteas*, in the form *Thiesteas*, appears again in section xxxv, where it is glossed – or at least joined to – *commessationes*, thus identical to Épinal 13v21 (allowing for a slight variation in spelling). While there are over-laps between Épinal–Erfurt, Corpus and Leiden, no one of these glossaries contains all the glosses found in the other two, at least to go by the sample pro-vided by the mythological entries. This in turn suggests that there must have been a substantial set of *glossae collectae* that was the basis of the selections in Leiden as well as those of the two alphabetical glossaries.

Not all of the mythological entries in Leiden are impressive for their learning. Apart from the reversal of glosses pertaining to Oedipus and Thyestes, there are other oddities. In Hessels xxxv ('De Eusebio') *Miherculi* is glossed by *mifortis*. *Fortis* is a gloss to Hercules (*Herculus* in Corpus H54). The glossator seems to have understood the word as a vocative ('my Hercules', 'my strong one') rather than as an oath with the archaic element *me-*. In section xxxvii ('De Clemente' = ps.-Clementine *Recognitiones*) Penelope appears as the wife of Achilles ('Paenilopis: uxor achilis')! In section xxviii ('In libro Antonii' = Cassiodorus [!], *Expositio psalmorum*) Typhon (*MS* Tifon) is confused with Typhoeus, and Iuno (*MS* Ionan) is presented as the daughter rather than the mother of Vulcan ('Ionan: filia uulcani'). In the same section Saturn is valiantly euhemerized as a king of the Greeks ('Saturnus: rex grecorum'). While some of these errors admit of explanations (for example, confusion of similar-looking names, eye-skip), it is hard to explain how Achilles acquired Penelope as a wife or how Vulcan managed to father his mother. Nonetheless, the glossaries are an impres-sive testament to the attempts made by the earliest Anglo-Saxon scholars to understand the Graeco-Roman mythological allusions in the texts they read.

We come now to the work that is without doubt the most important expression of Anglo-Saxon interest in classical mythology: the *Liber monstrorum*. The text was edited fairly recently with an Italian translation,[78] and is the subject of several recent studies.[79] Scholars are now in agreement that the work is a product of a Wessex school in the period of Aldhelm: the second entry in the first book deals with Hygelac, king of the Geats; there are close stylistic and lexical similar-ities to the writings of Aldhelm; entries in the Épinal–Erfurt Glossary are argu-ably drawn from this work. Its sources comprise Vergil, Ovid, Lucan, Servius,

---

[78] See the edition by Porsia, cited above, p. 90, n. 18.

[79] See esp. Lapidge, '*Beowulf*', as well as P. Lendinara, 'Il *Liber monstrorum* e i glossari anglosassoni', *L'immaginario nelle letterature germaniche di medioevo*, ed. A. Cipolla (Milan, 1995), pp. 203–15.

Augustine, Jerome and Isidore – precisely the complex of works known to Aldhelm.[80] Of decisive importance is the fact that the author of the *Liber* and Aldhelm both utilize the lost *Orpheus* of Lucan.[81] Interestingly, there is evidence of use of the *Epistola Alexandri ad Aristotelem*, the *Epistola Traiano* and the *De rebus in Oriente mirabilibus*.[82] Copies of the *Epistola Alexandri* and the *De rebus in Oriente mirabilibus* are found in London, British Library, Cotton Vitellius A. xv, the famous 'Nowell Codex' that contains the sole surviving copy of *Beowulf*.[83]

The *Liber* is divided into three books, each with its own preface written in the grand style. The first book is devoted to heroes and monsters that in the majority of cases have a human aspect. These range from the tragic figures of early Greek mythology such as Hercules and Orpheus to more popular figments such as the sciapods, cynocephali and their ilk. Also included are human marvels such as black people and pygmies. The second book is given over to unusual beasts, combining real but obviously exotic animals such as lions and tigers with fictional creatures such as the 'beast of Lerna' and the chimaera. The last book contains all scaly things, and like the previous books, mixes real vipers with snakes and dragons known from stories. Most of the entries are limited to descriptions of the named prodigies, but the work also contains encapsulated versions of tales, which the editor marks as interpolations. These include a second description of the Cyclops attached specifically to the tale of Ulysses, a description of the Scylla relating specifically to the *Aeneid*, and an entry marked as a tale: 'De fabula Proserpinae'. The *Liber*, therefore, was an invaluable guide to the heroes and prodigies of classical mythology. It could be consulted handily, as each book contains a detailed table of contents. Provided that one was not looking specifically for information about the pagan gods, the *Liber* offered more on Graeco-Roman mythology, and in more convenient form, than any other available source of the time.

The last quarter of the seventh century and, perhaps, the opening decades of the eighth might be looked upon as a sort of mini-renaissance of classical scholarship in Anglo-Saxon England. Classical poets were read in the schools of Canterbury and Wessex. They were studied not merely as models for metrical composition, but also for what they could impart about the world of pagan antiquity. Of special interest to teachers and students were the figures of Graeco-Roman mythology. Books were collected and scoured to gain information about the gods, heroes and prodigies found in pagan literature. Information gleaned from handbooks and glossed copies of 'mythophoric' works was gathered in the form of *glossae collectae*. These in turn became the basis of the more

---

[80] *Liber monstrorum*, ed. Porsia, p. 72.
[81] *Ibid.* p. 64; Lapidge, '*Beowulf*', p. 289.
[82] *Liber monstrorum*, ed. Porsia, pp. 70–1.   [83] *Ibid.* pp. 81–2.

convenient alphabetical glossaries, which could be consulted as reference works for reading the pagan poets or other writings requiring a knowledge of mythology. A new handbook was created to make information about heroes and monsters available in one place. Mythological figures and details became material for new poems. Perhaps of greatest interest is the fact that the Anglo-Saxons of the late seventh century were conscious of the relation between the gods and prodigies of Graeco-Roman mythology and the divinities and wondrous beings of their native religion and worked out a table of correspondences between the two mythological systems.

The mini-renaissance I speak of was localized and short-lived. It was basically limited to the area of Southumbria, specifically Kent and Wessex, and faded away probably in the second decade of the eighth century. Slight traces of its influence are still visible in the letters of Boniface, who, writing in a style strongly reminiscent of Aldhelm, could refer to death as 'exactrix invisi Plutonis',[84] or the letter of Ecgburg to Boniface referring to God as 'ille superi rector Olimpi'.[85] Bede, working in Northumbria, was unimpressed by all this. By the time of Alcuin, England was richer in classical texts than it was in the time of Aldhelm. Alcuin's famous 'metrical catalogue' of the library at York in the last quarter of the eighth century mentions Cicero and Aristotle, the latter doubtless a reference to a Latin translation of one of the philosopher's logical works, as well as Pompeius (Trogus) and Pliny and a host of grammarians in addition to the classical poets Vergil, Statius and Lucan. But Alcuin's 'classical interests' were directed to rhetoric and logic, and his numerous poems show only a passing interest in mythology, rarely going beyond the mention of a muse. However, movements rarely wholly die, and the seeds sown in this early period of Anglo-Saxon cultural history bore fruit in the Carolingian and later epochs.[86]

---

[84] *Ep.* IX, to Nihthard, ed. M. Tangl *et al.*, *Bonifatii Epistulae, Willibaldi Vita Bonifatii* (Darmstadt, 1968), p. 26.

[85] *Ep.* XIII, ed. Tangl *et al.*, p. 50.

[86] I am grateful to the Killam Foundation and the Humanities and Social Sciences Research Council of Canada for providing leave time and support money to enable me to carry out the research required for this paper.

A neglected early-ninth-century manuscript of the Lindisfarne *Vita S. Cuthberti*

DONALD A. BULLOUGH

For Janet Bately

Without the anonymous Lindisfarne *Vita S. Cuthberti*, written less than two decades after the saint's death in 687, our knowledge of aspects of the Iona–Lindisfarne tradition in the early Northumbrian church and of Cuthbert's life and death would be even more limited than it is.[1] Its medieval tradition is, however, very different from that of Bede's (prose) version of the Life, which, with its greater sense of literary form, composed in superior Latin, and with some additional or better evidence about its hero (although often omitting telling details), effectively drove the earlier work from its land of origin. The Lindisfarne *vita*'s later, post-1100, manuscript testimonies are exclusively in a closely-related group of continental legendaries (passionals); and the one extant pre-1066 English copy was among the books gifted to Saint-Vaast, Arras, *c.* 1070, by the former abbot of Bath, Sæwold.[2]

Despite its obvious interest and importance for students of early England and Scotland, the *Vita* was not seriously re-edited between the Bollandists' *editio princeps* of 1668 (from two manuscripts, at times very poorly transcribed) and Bertram Colgrave's admirable edition, with translation, of 1940.[3] Colgrave

---

[1] Edited and translated, together with Bede's prose *vita*, in B. Colgrave, *Two 'Lives' of Saint Cuthbert* (Cambridge, 1940), pp. 60–138, with notes at pp. 310–40. For its context and interpretation, see especially the contributions of J. Campbell ('Elements in the Background to the Life of St. Cuthbert and his Early Cult') and C. Stancliffe ('Cuthbert and the Polarity between Pastor and Solitary') to *St. Cuthbert, his Cult and his Community, to AD 1200*, ed. G. Bonner, D. Rollason and C. Stancliffe (Woodbridge, 1989), pp. 3–19 and 21–44.

[2] For the Saint-Vaast manuscript, see below, p. 107, n. 6. The evidence of glosses to copies of Bede's prose *Vita S. Cuthberti* in English books of the tenth and later centuries for an earlier, Northumbrian, manuscript of the Anonymous Life that has not survived is considered below, pp. 120–2.

[3] The unsatisfactory nature of the Bollandists' text (*Acta Sanctorum Martii* III (Antwerp, 1668), 117–24) may explain why Plummer included very few, but always apposite, references to it in his notes on Bede's account of Cuthbert in the *Historia ecclesiastica* (C. Plummer, *Venerabilis Baedae Opera Historica*, 2 vols. (Oxford, 1896) II, 265–71). Compare the characteristically oblique remarks of J. M. Wallace-Hadrill, 'Bede and Plummer' (1973), repr. in his *Bede's 'Ecclesiastical History of the English People': a Historical Commentary* [hereafter *Historical Commentary*] (Oxford, 1988), pp. xxxii–xxxiii: Plummer had (he observes) noted both the

recognized two sub-groups among the four Legendary manuscripts (HBPT), which are copies or part-copies of two different Trier-diocese compilations, made sixty or seventy years apart.[4] The basis of his edition, however, was an older group of three manuscripts, which go back (he supposed), 'although not directly', to the same 'Insular' exemplar, cautiously identified with the archetype.[5] It is headed chronologically by a manuscript of the ?tenth century from Saint-Bertin (Saint-Omer, Bibliothèque municipale, 267 (O_1)), this part probably written in that area by a possibly English-influenced hand. The second oldest and the one English-written copy (of s.xi *in.*?) is incorporated in a composite codex of *vitae sanctorum* (Arras, Bibliothèque municipale, 1029 (812): A),

Anonymous's and Bede's debt to Sulpicius Severus's *Vita S. Martini*, although 'whether directly or indirectly I am uncertain . . . *There is so much of Sulpicius in Venantius' Life of St. Martin that it may be from Venantius that the material was derived*' (my italics); and compare *Historical Commentary*, p. 170. At least with regard to the Anonymous, that uncertainty would surely have been dispelled by a simple comparison of the two texts. Venantius's *Life* is in verse with a distinctive proem and makes no use of Sulpicius's prefatory 'Ch. 1', the Anonymous's second preface is until its last sentence taken verbatim from Sulpicius; see further A. Thacker, 'Lindisfarne and the Origins of the Cult of St Cuthbert', *St. Cuthbert*, ed. Bonner *et al.*, pp. 103–22, esp. 110–12. Conversely and surprisingly, there is no clear evidence that Bede, who used both Paulinus of Périgueux and Venantius in the composition of his *Vita metrica*, was familiar at first-hand with Sulpicius's *Vita*: Thacker, 'Lindisfarne and the Origins of the Cult of St Cuthbert', p. 118. I have not seen C. E. Newlands, 'Bede and Images of Saint Cuthbert', *Traditio* 52 (1997), 73–109.

4   Colgrave, *Two Lives*, pp. 43–5, cf. pp. 16–20. The earlier Legendary is that in London, British Library, Harley 2800–2 (H), Brussels, Bibliothèque Royale, 207–8 (3132) (B) and – a late (fourteenth-century) and incomplete copy – Paris, Bibliothèque Nationale, lat. 5289 (P). The first of these is not merely from the Premonstratensian house at Arnstein (Lahn) but was evidently written there. Its similarities in both script and decoration with the 'Arnstein Bible' (London, BL, Harley 2798 and 2799) and the Arnstein copy of Hrabanus Maurus's *De Laudibus Sanctae Crucis* (BL, Harley 3045, in which the late-twelfth-century Arnstein library catalogue was added on fols. 48v–49r) argue that this earliest testimony to the Trier Legendary is a full generation older than Levison (W. Levison, 'Conspectus codicum hagiographicorum', *Passiones Vitaeque Sanctorum Aevi Merovingici*, ed. B. Krusch and W. Levison, MGH SS rer. Merov. 7 (Hanover, 1920), 529–706, at 537) and Colgrave supposed: see R. Schilling, 'Studien zur deutschen Goldschmiedekunst des 12. u. 13. Jhts.', *Form und Inhalt, Kunstgeschichtliche Studien Otto Schmitt zum 60. Geburtstag dargebracht*, ed. H. Wentzel (Stuttgart, 1950), pp. 73–88, esp. 76–80; D. H. Turner, *Romanesque Illuminated Manuscripts* (London, 1966), pp. 17–18, with colour pl. IV and pl. 9; H. Köllner, 'Ein Annalen-Fragment u. die Datierung der Arnsteiner Bibel in London', *Scriptorium* 26 (1972), 34–50 (without reference to Turner). The Brussels copy has been connected on very tenuous grounds with another Premonstratensian house, Knechtsteden (nr Neuss); but there is no doubt that its late-medieval home was the Carthusian house (S. Barbara) at Cologne. The February–April portion of the later legendary (for St Maximin, Trier) is Trier, Stadtbibliothek, 1151/453 vol. I (Colgrave's T). For a possible provenance of the Trier text of the *Vita Cuthberti*, see below, p. 110, n. 18.

5   *Two Lives*, p. 45. It will be argued below that the manuscripts O_1, A and O_2 (Saint-Omer 715: s. xii) are further removed from the archetype than Colgrave thought, although they descend from a common hyparchetype.

which has latterly been attributed to St Augustine's Canterbury: perhaps textually superior to O_1, it is unfortunately incomplete.[6] Colgrave's edition took no account of a much earlier manuscript, now at Munich, the contents of which include a text of the Anonymous *vita*; and although it was catalogued as such (but dated to the tenth century) more than a century ago, no scholar subsequently seems to have commented on the omission.[7]

THE MANUSCRIPT

Munich, Bayerische Staatsbibliothek, Clm. 15817 (hereafter M) is a Salzburg product of the 820s, latterly placed in its palaeographical context ('early Adalram', bishop 821–36) by the late Professor Bernhard Bischoff.[8] Fols. 1–53 provide a text of Augustine's *De pastoribus*, that is his *Sermo* xlvi, and 53r–99v, a text of *De ovibus*, that is Augustine's *Sermo* xlvii: they are among the Father's less common works, which the Salzburg scriptorium in Adalram's time seems systematically to have been copying.[9] The Augustine section ends at the end of a quire. The following fol. 100 is left blank; the *vita* is on 100v–119v, the leaves after fols. 111 and 113 being unnumbered. The rest of the codex (to 177v, with

---

[6] Saint-Omer 267: there is no satisfactory modern account of this manuscript, and I rely on Colgrave's summary description and two bad photographs; the scribe of the *Vita* consistently uses 'crossed d', 'wyn' etc. Arras 1029: H. Gneuss, 'A Preliminary List of Manuscripts Written or Owned in England up to 1100', *ASE* 9 (1981), 1–60, no. 781, where it is dated 'x ex, xi in. Bath?'; similarly M. Lapidge, 'Surviving Booklists from Anglo-Saxon England', *Learning and Literature in Anglo-Saxon England: Studies presented to Peter Clemoes on the Occasion of his Sixty-Fifth Birthday*, ed. M. Lapidge and H. Gneuss (Cambridge, 1985), pp. 33–89, at p. 61; but see now D. Dumville, *English Caroline Script and Monastic History* (Woodbridge, 1993), p. 147, where (n. 39) reference is made to M. Winterbottom's unpublished work on the manuscripts of the *Vita Dunstani* by 'B.'. It is no. 19 in the record of Sæwold's donation in Arras, Bibliothèque Municipale, 849 (539), ed Lapidge, 'Surviving Booklists', pp. 59–60.

[7] C. Halm *et al.*, *Catalogus Codicum manuscriptorum Bibliothecae Regiae Monacensis* IV.3 (Munich, 1878), 36. C. H. Beeson, *Isidor-Studien*, Quellen und Untersuchungen zur lateinischen Philologie des Mittelalters, IV.2 (Munich, 1913), 56, refers to it for its text of Isidore's *Synonyma* and correctly dates it 's.ix', but unfortunately misprints the subject of the *vita* as *S. Audbercti*!

[8] B. Bischoff, *Die Südostdeutschen Schreibschulen und Bibliotheken in der Karolingerzeit*, 2 vols. [hereafter Bischoff, *Schreibschulen*] (Wiesbaden, 1974–80) I, 141 (no. 118).

[9] The only other reported ninth-century copy of the two works in conjunction is a dismembered and defective Florus of Lyons book, Lyons, Bibliothèque de la Ville, 788, fols. 67–74 and 603, 1r–v, possibly from the same exemplar (late antique? or early Carolingian?); and Benedict of Aniane quoted *De pastoribus* extensively, in both his *Concordia* and the 816 Aachen Council *acta*, from a copy belonging to the same textual tradition. The same *sermo* in a different textual tradition is the opening item of a collection of Augustine's shorter writings in the Maurdramnus-script Corbie book, Paris, Bibliothèque Nationale, lat. 12210. For all this, see C. Lambot, 'Le sermon XLVI de Saint Augustin: *De Pastoribus*', *RB* 63 (1953), 165–210, esp. 166–9 (accepting the erroneous tenth-century dating of M). Augustine's major and minor works on baptism are in Salzburg, St Peter Stiftsbibliothek, a VIII 29 and in Munich, Bayerische Staatsbibliothek, Clm. 15814, for which see Bischoff, *Schreibschulen* II, 141–3 (nos. 119 and 121).

two unnumbered leaves) is a text of Isidore's *Synonyma*. The *Vita*'s heading, peculiar to this copy, is: 'IN NOMINE DOMINI. INCIPIT ACTUS VEL VITA SANCTI CUDBERCTI.'[10] The text that follows is an incomplete one, probably deliberately so rather than because of a defective exemplar. The initial *capitula* and Prefaces (bk I, chs. 1 and 2 in Colgrave's edition) are omitted. M's text opens, therefore, with 'I. De eo quod infans de illo profetavit' (O_1O_2 prophetavit; *alii om.*). After chs. 4–6, here numbered II, III, IV, with headings as in Colgrave's manuscript T, as reported by him (there are no headings in the manuscripts HBP), the text of M jumps to bk II, ch. 2 'V. De eo quod angelo *etc.*'. There is no numbering after 'VII. De delphino *etc.*'. The subsequent omissions are II.7, *capitula lib. III*, III.1; then III.6–IV.4 inclusive, IV.7, 8, 11, 12 and 16. The text finishes at *sanatus sit*, after which an explicit repeats the title.

Although the copyist's penmanship is of high quality (Bischoff thought that he was probably a well-trained disciple of the scribe of 1v–2),[11] his copying of the text is often careless, introducing many *errores proprii*: this is something he shares with the scribes of other early Salzburg and Saint-Amand manuscripts, including the oldest (pre-800) manuscript of Alcuin's letters.[12] As in the earliest copy of the letters made in the Salzburg cathedral scriptorium (Vienna, Österreichische Nationalbibliothek, lat. 808), however, he preserves the Northumbrian orthography *-erct-* or *-ercht-*, while the manuscripts O_1 and A adopt the West Saxon *-erht-*.[13] Furthermore, even in this incomplete Salzburg copy there are quite a number of places where the readings may have something to tell us about the *Vita*'s early transmission and suggest improvements to Colgrave's text.[14]

THE TEXT OF THE 'VITA'

Declaredly choosing the Saint-Bertin book O_1 as the basis of his 1940 text-edition 'because it is the oldest complete manuscript', Colgrave asserted that he

---

[10] The collection of material for the *Mittellateinisches Wörterbuch* at Munich includes no Carolingian-period example of *actus* used in this way: although Einhard's preface to his *Vita Karoli* famously has *vix imitabiles actus*, which even if it is (as Beumann supposed) an echo of Sulpicius's *Vita Martini* ch. 1 is not a quotation from it – the phrase in question reading *ne is lateret qui esset imitandus*.   [11] Bischoff, *Schreibschulen* II, 141.

[12] Vienna, Österreichische Nationalbibliothek, lat. 795, of which there is a complete facsimile under the title of *Alkuin-Briefe und andere Traktate*, with Introduction by F. Unterkircher, Codices Selecti 20 (Graz, 1969). Examples of careless copying are *Epistolae Karolini Aevi* II, ed. E. Dümmler, MGH Epist. 4 (Berlin, 1895), 60, 61, 63, 64, 167–9, 171 etc.: apparatus with siglum S.

[13] D. A. Bullough, 'What has Ingeld to do with Lindisfarne?', *ASE* 22 (1994), 93–125, at 96 and n. 12, and for the manuscript, below, p. 129. See also below (p. 130) for the autograph 'Cutbercht' of a late-eighth-century Salzburg-area scribe.

[14] For a collation of M, see the Appendix. I gratefully acknowledge the ready help of the Bayerische Staatsbibliothek in making the manuscript available for study and subsequently supplying photographs.

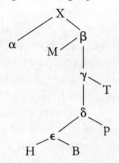

Fig. 1   The relationship of manuscripts of the *Vita S. Cuthberti.*

had normally adopted its (Carolingian) orthography. Arguably, at that time there is little else he could have done: but one consequence is that the Latinity of the anonymous Life is almost certainly made more like that of Bede's prose Life than would have been the case.[15] The nearest approximation to the Lindisfarne *Vita*'s original orthography must be that of the Dorbbéne (Schaffhausen) manuscript of Adomnan's *Vita Columbae*, penned at Iona *c.* 713, in conjunction with the 'Hibernian' spellings that have intermittently made their way into the 'Lindisfarne Gospels'.[16] Contemporary Iona/Lindisfarne usage is evidently reflected in, for example, M's *profetavit, profeta, Helias, harenosis locis, cepit* (for *coepit*), *celum* etc.; and in *remisionem* (one -*s*-), *ungere*, confusion between *des-* and *dis-*, etc., to all of which the gospelbook is testimony.[17]

On the evidence of readings other than *orthografica*, M clearly comes somewhere between the two major branches of the tradition, that is those represented

[15] Colgrave, in fact, not infrequently rejected the testimony of O₁ where he assumed – apparently – that it was due to scribal miscopying (or morphological error), as *exspecta-, planiciem, electioni, pussilla* (*Vita* II.3, *Two Lives* p. 80: the reading of both O₁ and A). The differences between the Latinity of the two *Vita*-authors are obscured in a contrary sense by Colgrave's preference for the evidence of twelfth-century manuscripts of Bede's *vita* over the earliest group, on which his edition should have been based: see below, p. 120, n. 58. For the orthography of the *Historia ecclesiastica*, compare 111–12 and 113, n. 28, below.

[16] For the former, see *Adomnán's Life of Columba*, ed. A. O. and M. O. Anderson, rev. M. O. Anderson (Oxford, 1991) and J.-M. Picard, 'The Schaffhausen Adomnán – a Unique Witness to Hiberno-Latin', *Peritia* 1 (1982), 216–49; for the latter (London, BL, Cotton Nero D. iv), see the facsimile edition *Evangeliorum quattuor codex Lindisfarnensis* ed. T. D. Kendrick, T. J. Brown *et al.* (Olten and Lausanne, 1960). See also Ludwig Bieler's remarks in *Adamnan's 'De Locis Sanctis'*, ed. D. Meehan, Scriptores Latini Hiberniae 3 (Dublin, 1958), 33–4 and the 'Index Orthographicus', pp. 124–6.

[17] Examples are *remis-* in Mark III.29, Luke I.77, Luke III.3; *ungere* (which has, however, ClLat. precedents) in Matt. VI.15, Mark VI.13, XIV. 8 etc.; *discendisset* in Matt. VIII.1 etc.; also *gravatum* for *grabattum* in Mark II.4 and 9, with which compare the *Historia ecclesiastica* spellings reported in n. 23.

respectively by the three 'early' manuscripts and the four 'late' ones (see fig. 1): but in the matter of 'inserted' phrases and common error it is closer to the latter than the former. M's exemplar β cannot, however, be identical with the common ancestor of the four Legendary manuscripts HBPT,[18] which already had the errors *Tesgeta, planicie, accepto, ad postremum, pro benedictione panis, deprecatus est, structuram, voce* (for *pace*), etc., which are not features of M.

Rather, both M and T's exemplar γ descend from a hyparchetype (β), evidently in Insular script, with the regular use of p (wyn) and $\eth$ and retaining many more of the Insular or 'Hibernian' spellings characteristic of the original Lindisfarne version than figure in Colgrave's printed text. Other such spellings were also to be found in the common ancestor α of O_1AO_2, but most have been eliminated in its copies.

Which, then, of M's readings should be admitted to the text of the Lindisfarne *Vita*?

In I.3 (p. 64), Colgrave inconsistently favoured HBP's *expectaret* and *in campi planicie* over the readings of O_1AT and now M (for the spelling *exspectans* also O_2; similarly Adomnán, *De locis sanctis* II.10): and even though he printed O_1's *exspectanda* in II.8 (p. 92). The use of a present participle where a personal form of the verb might be expected is a common phenomenon in early medieval Latin, however objectionable to later copyists.[19] Colgrave's translation suggests that he may have regarded *planicie* as adjectival ('level, even'), although this is not necessarily so. Jerome and other Fathers, however, like Cicero before them, regularly use the accusative after *congregare in*; and MO_1A's *planiciem* is clearly correct, with the meaning 'in an open space, in open country' (without any reference to the evenness or unevenness of the ground), as in Adomnan, *De locis sanctis* II.29 *factam esse campi planitiem*.[20]

---

[18] Wilhelm Levison showed ('Conspectus codicum hagiographicorum', *Passiones Vitaeque Sanctorum*, ed. B. Krusch and W. Levison, MGH SS rer. Merov., 7 (Hanover, 1920), 535–8) that among the sources of the two Trier Legendaries – but used by them independently – was a version of the (Carolingian-period) 'Salzburg Legendary', the earliest form or nucleus of which is Vienna, Österreichisches Nationalbibliothek, 420 (E. A. Lowe, *Codices Latini Antiquiores* [hereafter *CLA*], X (Oxford, 1963), no. 1479), written *c.* 800 at Saint-Amand (northeast France) but very quickly taken to Salzburg (so Bischoff, *Schreibschulen* II, 121–2 (no. 80)). Might the *Vita S. Cuthberti* have been among the additional texts included in that version (together with, for example, Alcuin's *Lives* of Vedastus and Richarius)? On the other hand, the Cuthbert *vita* in the slightly later 'Great Austrian Legendary' (which also used the 'Salzburg Legendary'), this part in Heiligenkreuz, Stiftsbibliothek, 11, of s.xii^{ex}, is said to be extracted from Bede's *Historia ecclesiastica*: D. Ó Riain-Raedel, 'Edith, Judith, Matilda: the Role of Royal Ladies in the Propagation of a Continental Cult', *Oswald, Northumbrian King to European Saint*, ed. C. Stancliffe and E. Cambridge (Stamford, 1995), pp. 210–29, at 226. (Professor Robert Bartlett kindly directed me to this book.)

[19] D. Norberg, *Manuel pratique de latin mediéval*, Connaissance des Langues (Paris, 1968), pp. 124, 127 and 145–6. Cf. the *Vita*'s *nesciebat etiam nec intellegens* (so O_1A) in II.7 (*Two Lives*, p. 92), which later copyists changed to *intelligebat* or *intellexit*.

[20] *Adomnán's 'De Locis Sanctis'*, ed. Meehan, p. 98.

In *Vita* II.2 (p. 78) the entire sentence *Panis enim . . . constituit* is very un-classical (where *evenit ut*, or in this case *ne*, would have been normal): but the editorial *ut* should surely be omitted; and *nisi tantum* (non-classical, but standard in late Latin for 'except only') substituted for (the classical but rare) *nisi tamen*. Colgrave's choice of HBPT's *pro benedictione panis* (translated 'as a blessed gift of bread') over MO₁AO₂'s *pro benedicto pane* is difficult to follow: the reference is to the 'blessed bread' also known as *eulogia*, the subject of a story in Adomnán's *Vita Columbae* II.13. (*Panis benedictione* in II.6 is the saint's blessing of bread brought to him by sick lay-folk, while the *benedictio* in the previous chapter is an unspecified blessed object.)[21]

In *Vita* II.8 (p. 92), *quia* β *quod* α: they are common alternatives in Late Latin and early medieval Latin and there are neither stemmatic nor other grounds for preferring one over the other. In the same chapter, M's *urbanis* supports O₁A's extraordinary *orbanis*, printed by Colgrave without comment and apparently regarded by him as an orthographical variant of *orfanis*. This may be the correct explanation; but objections can be raised. *b* for *v* is of course frequent, both in an initial position and intervocalically (Aldhelm, exceptionally, offers *bernaculus*, the *Vita Columbae* among others *berbices* and *corbus*); -*b*- for -*f*-, on the other hand, is extremely rare.[22] There are nonetheless isolated examples (and of the reverse, -*f*- for -*b*-, also) in both the 'Moore manuscript' and the St Petersburg (Wearmouth–Jarrow) manuscript of Bede's *Historia ecclesiastica*: in the latter *praebato* for *praefato* (with an early correction) at the beginning of *HE* I.15 and *praebuit* for *praefuit* twice, with *ruficundo* for *rubi*- in I.1; in the former *albabeti* – when listing, of all things, Bede's 'book on spelling' in V.24 – and *vagafundus* for *vagab*- (with an early correction) in II.12.[23] Since a later chapter of the Anonymous Life

---

[21] *Adomnán's Life of Columba*, ed. Anderson and Anderson, pp. 112, 104 and 102.

[22] It is not even acknowledged in the most recent extended discussions of *b/v* in Vulgar and 'Hibernian' Latin, such as B. Löfstedt, *Studien über die Sprache der langobardischen Gesetze* (Stockholm, 1961), pp. 149–59 and Picard, 'Schaffhausen Adomnán', pp. 238–9. For the (supposed) chronology of the 'collapsing' of intervocalic *b/v* compare A. Gratwick, 'Latinitas Britannica: was British Latin Archaic?', *Latin and the Vernacular Languages in Early Medieval Britain*, ed. N. Brooks, Stud. in the Early Hist. of Britain 1 (Leicester, 1982), 1–79, esp. 17–32 and 75, with the severe critique by D. McManus, '*Linguarum Diversitas*: Latin and the Vernaculars in Early Medieval Britain', *Peritia* 3 (1984), 151–88, at 165–74.

[23] See the complete facsimiles of the two manuscripts, *The Leningrad Bede*, ed. O. Arngart, EEMF 2 (Copenhagen, 1952), and *The Moore Bede*, ed. P. Hunter Blair, EEMF 9 (Copenhagen, 1959). The 'Moore manuscript', M, has many more 'Hibernicisms' or Vulgarisms than the St Petersburg manuscript, L, although confusion of *a* and *u* is much more common in the latter; and both have (for example) singling of -*ii* and gemination of consonants, if not often in the same place in the text! Both Plummer's and Colgrave and Mynors' editions of *HE* follow the 'm-text', which both those manuscripts transmit: but while Plummer sometimes (and very inconsistently) printed 'Hibernicisms' occurring in M, the Colgrave–Mynors text (apparently; the 'Textual Introduction' offers no guidance) often but by no means always admits 'Hibernicisms' found in L. Thus in *HE* I.14 and 15 (ed. Plummer I, 30–1; ed. Colgrave and Mynors, pp. 46–52)

shows familiarity with the ClLat. *orbare* (v.tr.) 'to deprive by death, to bereave' (adj. *orbus, -a, -um*), and a substantive *orbatus* is recorded from the twelfth/thirteenth centuries, it is not inconceivable that *orbanus* could be a Lindisfarne-Latin 'nonce word', formed by confusion between *orfanus* and *orbatus*: but this conjecture is perhaps unnecessary.

Also in II.8 (Colgrave, p. 92), M's and T's support for *spectanda* against *exspectanda* is justified by the context. O₁A's spelling might, however, be merely a (Lindisfarne?) orthographic variant: the late antique epithet *spectabilis* is spelt *expectabilis* in the Vienna, Nationalbibliothek, 420 (Saint-Amand, *c.* 800) text of the *Vita Lupi Trecensis*.[24] Conversely, M preserves the original Lindisfarne spelling *avenarum*: one which Bede, following Agroecius, was concerned to correct in his *De orthographia*, and about which Alcuin was even more specific ('Avena si ad germen sine h per v scribendum est, habena si ad retinaculum iumentorum per h et b scribitur').[25] The more familiar *freni* al. *-orum* in the later manuscripts presumably originated as a gloss.

The editorial *tacto* (p. 92, app. 66) is clearly correct, the 'restoration' of the fourth-declension *tactu* being presumably Carolingian (although if so it must have been made independently in more than one branch of the tradition). Similarly, Colgrave rightly printed O₁A's *medere* in *Vita* IV.17 (p. 136), although M has *mediri* and HBP the correct deponent form *mederi*.

In III.3 (p. 98), *maxilla* is surely correct: Judges XV.14–19 only has the singular, with both *in maxilla asini* and *de maxilla* in V.19. Relying on O₁'s *sibi*, Colgrave retained the nominative *suavitas* and translated '[he] declared that . . . he enjoyed . . . the sweetness of every kind of drink'. Such a construction seems very forced if not downright impossible: M(H)PT's *ibi esse suavitatem* gives a perfectly normal accusative-and-infinitive after *professus est*.

In III.4, the context favours MHB(P)'s *impetrasset*, despite MO₁A's *perpetraverunt* in II.6 and whatever the correct form of IV.9 (below) may be. Bede, in both *Vita (pr.)* and *HE*, consistently favours *impe-*; examples of *perpetrare* are peculiar to Pope Gregory's *responsiones* in *HE* I.27.[26] In *Vita* III.5, MPT's *enim*

Plummer has *acerba, improbos, Cantuarii*, Colgrave–Mynors *acerva* (the reading not only of L but also of M, C and N (Namur, Bibliothèque Communale, Fonds de la Ville 11)), *inprobos, Cantuari* (the reading of both L and M); in I.21 (ed. Plummer I, 40; ed. Colgrave and Mynors, p. 66) Plummer and Colgrave–Mynors alike print *curvatum*, although both L and M have *curbatum*; in V.19 (ed. Plummer I, 328; ed. Colgrave and Mynors, p. 526) Plummer prints *grabato* (*gravato* M), Colgrave–Mynors *grabatto* (so L). See further below, p. 113, n. 28.

24 *Passiones Vitaeque Sanctorum Aevi Merovingici*, ed. B. Krusch, MGH SS rer. Merov. 3 (Hanover, 1896), 300. For the manuscript, see Bischoff, *Schreibschulen* II, 121–2 (no. 79).

25 *Beda: De Orthographia*, ed. C. W. Jones, CCSL 123A (Turnhout, 1975), 12; but compare A. C. Dionisotti, 'On Bede, Grammars, and Greek', *RB* 92 (1982), 111–41, at 121; Alcuin, *De orthographia* versio II, Saint-Amand/Salzburg text (!) in Vienna 795, fol. 6.

26 Ed. Plummer I, 48–62; ed. Colgrave and Mynors, pp. 78–102.

alter is surely required after *habens* ('one of them having . . .'); compare *alter e duobus revertens* a few lines previously. Bede's re-writing of this chapter in his ch. 20 (ed. Colgrave, pp. 222–4) makes it uncertain what text-form he was using here.

In *Vita anon.* IV.5 (p. 118), *deposueruntque* imposes itself, *deportaveruntque* in the other main branch of the tradition having been influenced by the preceding *deportantes*, and making it unnecessary to regard the succeeding *in silva* as a solecism. *Mirabilia* is closer to the Vulgate; but for the subst. *mira* compare III.2 'in servis suis mira operantem' and *Vita Columbae* II.13 'Mira dicturus sum'.[27]

That M alone preserves the correct title of IV.6 (below, p. 136) is apparent from O_1's capitulum (ed. Colgrave, p. 108): 'De infante mulieris curato in mortale [*sic!*] et prophetia eius de tota familia.' Further support may be found in Bede's title for the corresponding chapter (ch. 33: ed. Colgrave, p. 258), which begins *Quomodo tempore mortalitatis morientem puerum*, although Bede himself generally prefers *pestilentia* to *mortalitas* (as indeed in this chapter).

The testimonies of M and A likewise establish the original title of *Vita* IV.9; and the former preserves also the doubtless authentic Lindisfarne spelling *anchorita*.[28] Copyists for whatever reason (corrections and/or abbreviations in the archetype, perhaps?) obviously had considerable difficulty with the text after Cuthbert's 'Surge et gaude.' The most economical solution seems to be to accept *indultum*, and translate 'brought about and acceded to'. (Bede, ch. 28, ed. Colgrave, p. 250 = *HE* IV.29, does not help here, although he introduces *impetrasse (se)* into his account of Cuthbert's praying, before 'Surge *etc.*').

M's text of *Vita* II.3 (ed. Colgrave, p. 80) shows that the fuller description of Æbba of Coldingham as *abbatissa famulantium Dei* was already in β. But should it be restored to the Lindisfarne text? Or is it an early addition, perhaps with public reading in mind? The contradiction with *a sanctimoniali vidua MATREQUE OMNIUM in Christo Æbba* – the more appropriate epithet for the head of a 'double monastery' – favours the latter.[29] The inclusion or exclusion of *humiliter* in the same chapter and of *et fidelis* after *probabilis* in IV.9 (ed.

---

[27] *Adomnán's Life of Columba*, ed. Anderson, p. 110.

[28] The claim implicit in Picard's comments in 'Schaffhausen Adomnán', p. 229, n. 9, that this was also Bede's normal orthography (and similarly *anchoretica* al. *-iticae* and *anchoritae*) is probably mistaken: in *HE* V.28 and 29, the 'Moore Bede' has these spellings, duly adopted by Plummer; but 'the Leningrad Bede', now generally accepted as a Wearmouth–Jarrow book written only a few years after Bede's death, has (as Colgrave and Mynors print at pp. 326 and 434) *anachoretica(e)* and *anachoritae*.

[29] Bede's account of the same episode (*Vita (pr.)* ch. 10: ed. Colgrave, *Two Lives*, p. 188) does not help with the textual problem directly, but his rephrasing is very instructive: favouring life-long virginity and perhaps indicating reservations about 'double monasteries', he characterizes Æbba as *sanctimonialis FEMINA et mater ancillarum Christi nomine*. In his account of the decline and destruction of Coldingham in *HE* IV. 26, however, she is *mater congregationis*.

Colgrave, p. 124) cannot be decided contextually or stemmatically, only on the basis of authorial style: and this, although hardly sufficient, suggests that *et fidelis* is an interpolation.[30]

The *in eodem quoque die* addition to Cuthbert's words in II.4 – a chapter which has acquired a degree of notoriety because of past attempts to identify the *Niuduera regio* in or adjacent to 'Pictland' with some part of south-west Scotland – requires fuller consideration. The day in question was Epiphany, described in all manuscripts of the *Vita* as that 'on which the Magi worshipped [Christ] with gifts and on which the Holy Ghost in the form of a dove descended upon him at his baptism in Jordan and on which he turned water into wine in Cana of Galilee to confirm the faith of his disciples' – a multiple symbolism that had a wide currency in the early church. Because the further reference to the miracle of the feeding of the 5000, *sancto A<u>gustino (at)testante*, figured only in the four Trier Legendary manuscripts, Colgrave reasonably supposed that it originated as a gloss, which in one branch of the tradition was subsequently inserted in the text; and he noted that an Epiphany sermon of Augustine's (actually pseudo-Augustine) speaks of all four reasons for celebration.[31] M is testimony to the presence of the passage already in β (late eighth–early ninth century, therefore?), and preserves the characteristic Insular spelling *Agus-*.[32] The erroneous word-order of M *might* be evidence that it was taken from a marginal gloss. The corresponding chapter in Bede's Life, however, describes the day simply as that *quam ipse per tot ac tanta suae miracula maiestatis inlustrare curavit*; while his homily for Epiphany is on the non-Roman pericope Matt. III.13–17, that is, Christ's baptism.[33] The Roman pericope is Matt. II.1–12; and the mass-sets in both Gelasian and Gregorian sacramentaries commemorate the manifestation of God in Christ to the Magi. In the Visigothic and Gallican liturgies, by contrast, the baptism of Christ, the

---

[30] Colgrave's translation of IV.9's *orationem inter eos frequentatam renovavit* as 'renewed their frequent prayers together' is hardly correct. *Oratio frequentata* is 'prayer performed (said) in common' or 'prayer said over and over again': the sense of the phrase is therefore that the two men 'resumed the practice of praying (*al.* repeating prayers) together'.

[31] *Vita*, ed. Colgrave, pp. 84 and 321. For the sermon, see below, p. 115, n. 36.

[32] As, for instance, in Cummian's *De controversia paschali*, ed. M. Walsh and D. Ó Cróinín, Stud. and Texts 86 (Toronto, 1988), 74, 80 etc.; in the authentic text of Bede's *Vita (pr.) Cuthberti* (below, p. 120 and n. 58); and consistently in Alcuin's letters (*Epistolae Karolini Aevi*, ed. Dümmler, nos. 19, 100, 111 etc., although the evidence is to be found more often in the apparatus than in the text).

[33] See further U. Lenker, *Die westsächsischen Evangelienversion und die Perikopenordnungen im angelsächsischen England*, Münchener Universitäts-Schriften, Texte und Untersuchungen zur Englischen Philologie 20 (Munich, 1997) (which became available too late for me to take account of it in the text), esp. 301–2. In some Carolingian lectionaries (e.g. that accompanying the 'Lorsch Gospels': Vatican City, Biblioteca Apostolica Vaticana, Vat. lat. 50, 116r–124v) this pericope was the one to be read on the Octave of Epiphany, and Bede's homily was correspondingly prescribed for that day in office-homiliaries.

changing of water into wine at the wedding at Cana and, in some places at least, the feeding of the five thousand were also commemorated: and there is evidence that (parts of) seventh-century Ireland observed the day similarly.[34] The Anonymous *Vita S. Cuthberti* points to Lindisfarne's familiarity with that observance at the beginning of the eighth century, whether or not it was reflected in the community's own liturgy[35] or known only through a sermon composed in a region where it had long been the normal practice.[36]

In III.5 (ed. Colgrave, p. 86) the wording of the quotation from Ps. XXXVI.25[37] presents a particular problem of transmission. Colgrave's text

---

[34] The Gallican/Visigothic evidence is best summarized, with key references, by H. Frank, art. 'Epiphanie (III. In der Liturgie)', *Lexikon für Theologie und Kirche*, 2nd ed., 3 (Freiburg, 1959), 941–4; but compare also Frank, 'Die Vorrangstellung der Taufe Jesu in der altmailändischen Epiphanieliturgie und die Frage nach dem Dichter des Epiphaniehymnus Inluminans Altissimus', *Archiv für Liturgiewissenschaft* 13 (1971), 115–32. The principal evidence from Ireland is an incompletely preserved mid-seventh-century sacramentary: *Das irische Palimpsestsakramentar im clm. 14429 der Staatsbibliothek München*, ed. A. Dold and L. Eizenhöfer, Texte und Arbeiten der Erzabtei Beuron 53/54 (Beuron, 1964), 51–7 (texts and editors' notes).

[35] As H. Mayr-Harting has rightly commented (*The Coming of Christianity to Anglo-Saxon England*, 3rd ed. (London, 1991), p. 164): 'where we are ignorant about the religious practices of the Irish monasteries in Northumbria, it is not to be assumed that they were in every way busy Romanizing themselves after the Synod of Whitby'. Cf. Bede's assertion in his *Vita (pr.)* ch. 16 (ed. Colgrave, p. 210), which has no precise counterpart in *Vita anon.* III.1 (ed. Colgrave, pp. 94–6), that *Erant autem quidam in monasterio fratres qui priscae suae consuetudini quam regulari mallent obtemperare custodie*: and, for the continuing use of the 'Gallican' psalter-version, below, p. 116, n. 39.

[36] The pseudo-Augustinian *sermo* no. 136 (*Clavis Patristica Pseudepigraphorum Medii Aevi* 1, ed. J. Machielsen (Turnhout, 1990), no. 921) is ptd PL 39, cols. 2013–15. Other sermons in circulation before 800 are seemingly dependent on it or on a common source; and either one of these or the pseudo-Augustine sermon itself is evidently among the sources of the proper *missa, inc.* 'Deus qui nobis ad relevandos', in the Visigothic ('Mozarabic') sacramentary: *Le Liber Mozarabicus Sacramentorum*, ed. M. Férotin, Monumenta Ecclesiae Liturgicae 6 (Paris, 1912), cols. 87–8. The manuscript transmission of *sermo* no. 136 depends on two overlapping collections, both probably put together by Caesarius of Arles, the so-called *collectio Germanica* in Munich, Bayerische Staatsbibliothek, Clm. 6298 etc., and the *collectio Gallicana*: for the latter, see R. Étaix, 'Nouvelle collection de sermons rassemblée par Saint Césaire', *RB* 87 (1977), 7–32, this sermon no. 36 (at 13); but unlike the preceding Epiphany sermon (which does not refer to the feeding of the five thousand) it seems not to be credited to Augustine in the manuscripts. The precise wording of the *Vita*'s characterization of Epiphany is indeed closer to the extant liturgical texts than to any published sermon: compare, e.g., *spiritus sanctus in specie* (as Luke III.21 but not the other Vulgate Gospels) *columbe . . descendit* with lines 29–30 of the *missa, Le Liber Mozarabicus*, ed. Férotin, col. 87; and *in eodem quoque die* with *in hac quoque die* (twice) in the Irish sacramentary *immolatio missae* for the feast, *Das irische Palimpsestsakramentar*, ed. Dold and Eizenhöfer, pp. 56 and 57. But while the Visigothic *inlatio* (*Le Liber Mozarabicus*, ed. Férotin, col. 89 lines 34–5), specifies the fishes in the form *pisce geminato*, in other respects the *Vita*'s additional clause is closer to the sermon's *de quinque panibus quinque millia hominum satiavit*: and here the *Agustino testante* makes a liturgical origin unlikely.

[37] The Anonymous's *ut impleatur prophetae dictum* is abnormal but not unparalleled: had he perhaps misremembered the source of the tag?

reads here *Iunior fui etenim senui*, which is the precise form of the *Gallicanum* version of the Psalter in most early manuscripts (including the Carolingian Court book Vienna, Nationalbibliothek, lat. 1861 and the Tours Bibles), although the 'Cathach of St. Columba', with other witnesses, and the modern Benedictine edition, have *et* in place of *etenim*.[38] M's *Iuvenior fui et senui* etc., is, however, categorically 'Roman', when all the other early evidence (including quotations elsewhere in the anonymous Life) points to the continuing use of the 'Gallican' version in early Irish-founded houses as well as in Ireland itself.[39] Where and at what point in the transmission of the *Vita* was M's 'Roman' form substituted? Before the text left England for the Frankish realms? In a lost intermediary between β and M, therefore?

PLACE-NAMES

Finally, there are the new testimonies to the Anonymous *vita*'s place-name forms, which are among the very earliest in 'English records'.[40] They are certainly not all of equal significance: M's *Hippe*, for Ripon, is evidently due to scribal carelessness, although preserving the initial *H-*.[41] In contrast, *Mailros* (if we follow the late Professor Kenneth Jackson) reflects careful recording and copying; and *Niuduera regio* in *Vita* II.4 is good additional testimony to this controversial district

---

[38] Colgrave correctly reports that *et* is the reading here of the three 'Trier' manuscripts.

[39] In *Vita Cuthberti* I.6, *foeni (-ae-) textorum* is the Ga(*llicanum*) reading of Ps. CXXVIII.6, where the Ro(*manum*) and all other pre-Vulgate Psalters, except Verona, Biblioteca Capitolare, I, have *aedificiorum*. (The indirect quotations in *Vita S. Cuthberti* I.6 and III.2 are inconclusive.) The lemmata of the eighth-century Psalter commentary from an unidentified ?'Columban' church in Northumbria, Vatican City, Biblioteca Apostolica Vaticana, Pal. lat. 68 (*CLA* I, 78) are overwhelmingly Gallican: see M. McNamara, *Glossa in Psalmos: the Hiberno-Latin Gloss on the Psalms of Codex Palatinus Latinus 68*, Studi e Testi 310 (1986). Paul Meyvaert has drawn attention to a possible link between the commentary's exegesis of Ps. CXLVIII and the iconography of the Ruthwell Cross: *The Ruthwell Cross*, ed. B. Cassidy (Princeton, NJ, 1992), at pp. 128–9. By contrast, when Bede produced his own prose version of the *vita*, he included at least fifteen quotations from the Psalter; and although some of them are only two or three words, and many are ones where the Ga. and Ro. versions are identical, several short phrases or individual words (e.g. in ch. 12 *Vita Cuthberti*, ed. Colgrave, p. 196: Ps. XXXIX.5 *spes eius* and *in sanias*) and two long quotations in particular – Ps. XXXIII.18 and 19 in ch. 5: Ps. CXIII.8 and 9 in ch. 18 (ed. Colgrave, pp. 170 and 218) – show clearly Bede's dependence on a *psalterium Romanum*. The account of Bede's Bible citations in Colgrave, *Two Lives*, p. 57, is unfortunately confused and misleading, and the italicization of his text is frequently erroneous.

[40] B. Cox, 'The Place-Names of the Earliest English Records', *JEPNS* 8 (1975–6), 12–66. For names in the *vita* (and for those in Bede's *vita prosaica* likewise), Cox relied exclusively on Colgrave's text, without reference to manuscript variants.

[41] Note that (*contra* Cox, *ibid.* p. 42) Ripon's early spellings with *Hryp-* or *Hrip-* include Bede's prose *Vita S. Cuthberti*, i.e. in the earliest and most trustworthy manuscripts. The *in Ripum* spelling is that of twelfth-century and later manuscripts: cf. the apparatus to Colgrave's edition, *Two Lives*, p. 175.

name.[42] M's *Cuncacaestir* in *Vita* I.6, for the place later called Chester-le-Street, is certainly to be preferred to *Kuncacester* (so O₁A) etc.: in the earliest manuscripts of Bede's *Historia ecclesiastica*, *-caestir* is the standard form or spelling of a place-name element signifying 'a (Roman) city or town or ['particularly in the North'] the remains of an ancient fortification . . .', as in this example.[43] In II.3, Colgrave adopted O₁A's *Colodesbyrig* for (as he assumed) Coldingham, against the testimony of the other manuscripts, now including M: he was surely wrong to do so, and *Colodesburg* must be regarded as the 'correct' text-form.[44] In the M text of *Vita* IV.10, Abbess Ælfflæd's account of a vision by Cuthbert describes it as taking place *in parrochia eius quae dicitur Osingaduum*. A gloss to a twelfth-century Durham copy of Bede's prose *Vita* which (I shall argue) is derived from a lost ?eighth-century manuscript of the Anonymous *vita* reads *nomen loci Osingædun*.[45] These two additional testimonies, especially in conjunction, must greatly strengthen the case against Colgrave's cautious identification – on the assumption of confusion of Insular *f* and *s* – with an Ovington.[46]

---

[42] K. Jackson, *Language and History in Early Britain* (Edinburgh, 1953), pp. 326–7, explained the spelling *Mailros* (cited from Bede, not from the Lindisfarne *vita*) as a 'Hibernicisation' of the Primitive Welsh toponym: 'the Irish monks substituted their own, cognate, *mail*, "bald", for Pr.W. *mel'; it has to be said, however, that there is no independent evidence that the seventh-century community was ever one of Irish-*origin* monks. There is still no satisfactory discussion of *Niuduera*, which must surely be located in Fife or Angus.

[43] A. H. Smith, *English Place-Name Elements*, 2 pts, EPNS 25–6 (London, 1956) I, 85–7; J. Campbell, 'Bede's Words for Places', in his *Essays in Anglo-Saxon History* (London, 1986), pp. 99–120, esp. 99–101 and 116–17. For the first element, from a Romano-British *Con-cang-*, see A. L. F. Rivet and C. Smith, *The Place-Names of Roman Britain* (London, 1979), p. 314. The entry in E. Ekwall's *Concise Oxford Dictionary of English Place-Names*, 4th ed. (Oxford, 1960), p. 101, has given the misleading impression that *Cunceceastre* etc. is not documented before the mid-tenth/early-eleventh-century *Historia de sancto Cuthberto* (in *Symeonis Monachi Opera Omnia*, ed. T. Arnold, 2 vols., RS (London, 1882–5) I, 208, 210).

[44] There is now sufficient evidence that the monastic *burh* familiar to Cuthbert and Coldingham were two different but adjacent sites: see L. Alcock, E. A. Alcock and S. M. Foster, 'Reconnaissance Excavations on Early Historic Fortifications and other Royal Sites in Scotland, 1974–80: 1, Excavations near St Abb's Head, Berwickshire, 1980', *Proc. of the Soc. of Antiquaries of Scotland* 116 (1980), 261–79; also, for the documented name-forms of the two places, W. H. F. Nicolaisen, *Scottish Place-names* (London, 1976), pp. 20–1 and 72–3. But the change to the *-byrig* (dat. sing.) form must surely have taken place in an Insular writing-centre.

[45] Colgrave, *Two Lives*, p. 262 app. 3; below, pp. 120–1.

[46] Cox, accepting Colgrave's conjecture as fact, interprets the name as 'Hill of Ofa's people': 'Place-Names of the Earliest English Records', p. 25. Is there any significance in the final *-m* in M as well as in the manuscripts TP? If so (as Prof. K. Cameron has observed in correspondence), the generic and name make no obvious sense. It is unfortunate that among the chapters omitted from M is *Vita* III.6. But O₁ and A's *Cocþædesæ* for Coquet Island is perfectly acceptable: Bede's *Vita (pr.) Cuthberti* ch. 24 (ed. Colgrave, p. 234, with the spelling *Coquedi*) refers to it as *insula quae Cocuedi fluminis hostio praeiacens ab eodem nomen accepit*. Cox, discussing the name in 'Place-Names of the Earliest English Records', pp. 19 and 43, had evidently forgotten that the river-name figures in the Ravenna Geographer, most probably as *Coccuveda*: see I. A. Richmond and O. G. S. Crawford (with linguistic notes by I. Williams), 'The British Section of the *Ravenna Cosmography*', *Archaeologia* 93 (1949), 1–50, at 14 and 29; Rivet and Smith, *Place-Names*, p. 311.

Of exceptional interest is the M-text's form of the place-name in *Vita* IV.5 (ed. Colgrave, p. 116). A certain Penna's account of the healing of a paralytic boy (recorded as *oratio recta*) says that it happened when the bishop was travelling from Hexham to Carlisle[47] and in mid-journey had set up his tents for two or three days *in regione ubi dicitur Aechsae*. This new testimony makes Colgrave's adoption of O_1O_2's aberrant spelling *Ahse*, against *Æhse* in A and *Echse* in TP, even less defensible, and points to an original *Æchs[a]e*. In consequence, an identification with the wall-station *Aesica*, that is, Great Chesters, first suggested by Cadwallader Bates a century ago but doubted by Colgrave, is greatly strengthened.[48] Kenneth Jackson declared *Aesica* to belong to a group of 'names whose etymologies and descendants, if any, are unknown', with an anomalous survival of intervocalic -s- (an early loss in British).[49] Granted the anomaly, the Old English form would be a borrowing in the late sixth/early seventh century, after syncope of -i- and subsequent metathesis.[50] Colgrave's further objection to the identification with *Aesica*, 'that Ahse is stated to be a region', has little cogency.

---

[47] *Ad civitatem quae Luel dicitur.* Bede's re-writing of this episode in *Vita (pr.) Cuthberti* ch. 32 (ed. Colgrave, pp. 256–8), and earlier in his *Vita metrica* ch. 26, omits the name of the informant (abandoning also the *oratio recta*-form of his report) and all the names of places. Revising the Anonymous's account (IV.8: ed. Colgrave, p. 122) of the bishop's presence at Carlisle in 685, however, Bede has previously changed *ad civitatem Luel pergens* to *venit ad Lugubaliam civitatem quae a populis Anglorum corrupte Luel vocatur.* ch. 27, ed. Colgrave, p. 242; *ad eandem Lugubaliam civitatem* also in ch. 28, Colgrave, p. 248, and in the corresponding passage in *HE* IV.29. The use of 'some written source' for the form *Lugubalia* is rightly assumed by Wallace-Hadrill in *Historical Commentary*, p. 172; but his further comment is not entirely happy since (following C. Thomas, *Early Christian Archaeology of Northern Britain* (Oxford, 1971), p. 18) it misrepresents what Bede has actually said in his *Vita (pr.)* and obscures the fact that *Luel* is the Pr. Cumbr. name-form (subsequent stages of the evolution of which are documented by Symeon of Durham) taken over by the English incomers. Was the 'written source' perhaps an inscription (cf. Rivet and Smith, *Place-Names*, p. 402) rather than the 'lost annals' or a similarly lost ecclesiastical source beloved of 'Arthurians' and others?

[48] C. Bates, 'The Names of Persons and Places Mentioned in the Early Lives of St Cuthbert', *AAe* ns 16 (1894), 81–92. G. W. S. Barrow, *The Kingdom of the Scots* (London, 1975), p. 67 n., says 'possibly represented by Haltwhistle'. This is perfectly possible topographically; but I know of nothing to support the suggestion, unless the alienation of its church by the king of the Scots, which took place a full five centuries later in ?1178 (*The Acts of William I, King of Scots 1165–1214*, ed. G. W. S. Barrow, Regesta Regum Scottorum 2 (Edinburgh, 1971), 251 (no. 197), cf. 270 (no. 227)), is somehow thought to do so. Note that the name-form *Hakatwisel* in the first of these, if correctly rendered, rules out Ekwall's explanation of the first element as OE *heafod* and points instead to *hacca*.

[49] Jackson, *Language and History*, pp. 523–5 and 324. Jackson's claim that *(A)Esica* etc. are to be regarded as 'fossilized spellings' (in both the *Notitia Dignitatum* and the Ravenna Cosmography!) is hardly acceptable: for a different view of *Clausentum* and a different approach to *Aesica*'s -s-, see Rivet and Smith, *Place-Names*, pp. 308–9 and 242.

[50] Is the -*ch*- of *Æchse* the Pr. Cumb. [X]? Compare Jackson, *Language and History*, pp. 565–73 and (simplified) 'The British Language during the Period of the English Settlements', *Studies in Early British History*, ed. N. K. Chadwick (Cambridge, 1954), pp. 74–5. There is inevitably no evidence for the 'normal' development after (Br.) *es*-.

The Lindisfarne *vita* is, in fact, part of the primary evidence for the existence in the early Northumbrian kingdoms of administrative *regiones* based on royal estate-centres (*vici regis* al. *regales*): and these *vici* were commonly at identifiable former Roman sites along the Wall or elsewhere.[51] To the east of *Aechse* was a better-documented *regio* linked with Hexham (but possibly originally centred on Corbridge), referred to as such in Stephen of Ripon's Life of Wilfrid of York and Hexham, which was composed only a few years later than the *Vita Cuthberti*. Another early *regio* within Cuthbert's diocese, but otherwise unlocated, is the one *quae dicitur Kintis* al. *Hintis* of *Vita anon.* IV.3.[52]

Hardly less interesting is the form of the river-name in the chapter (II.5) in which Ps. XXXV is quoted – the well-known one where an eagle provides the saint and his young companion with a fish for their mid-day meal. Bede's re-writing of this episode is not only more stylish, with more elaborate language put in the mouths of both men, but declares that they *agebant iter iuxta fluvium quendam*; by contrast, the Anonymous Life records, in all the manuscripts used by Colgrave, that the saint *proficiscebat iuxta fluvium Tesgeta*.[53] It has long been recognized that the *-s-* is a misreading of an Insular *f*, the river being the Teviot (the largest tributary of the Tweed): M's *Taefgeta* is the earliest 'correct' rendering of the early English name-form by several centuries.[54] Yet this may not be the one

---

[51] Such as the *vicus regis inlustris qui vocatur Ad Murum* al. *in villa regia . . . quae cognominatur Ad Murum* where Bishop Finan of Lindisfarne twice baptized kings and their followings from other English kingdoms: *HE* III.21 and 22; in the second passage it is described as being 'about twelve miles from the east coast', which accords reasonably well with an identification with Walbottle. The archaeological evidence for fifth-century 'high-status British' and sixth-century Anglo-Saxon reoccupation of sites on and near the Wall has been reviewed by K. R. Dark, 'A Sub-Roman Re-Defence of Hadrian's Wall?', *Britannia* 23 (1992), 111–20, esp. 111–13 and 119–20. Dark's speculations (esp. p. 118) on the possible implications for the region's post-Roman military and political history take no account of later evidence for local administrative *regiones* which may be of pre-English origin. For these, Barrow, *Kingdom of the Scots*, pp. 7–68, esp. pp. 19–22, 24–36 and 66–7, remains the most authoritative and best account.

[52] For Hexham and its *regio*, see *The Life of Bishop Wilfrid by Eddius Stephanus*, ed. B. Colgrave (Cambridge, 1927), pp. 44–6; Barrow, *Kingdom of the Scots*, p. 32; D. A. Bullough, 'The Place-Name Hexham and its Interpretation' (forthcoming). The location of the *regio quae dicitur Kintis* al. *Hintis* (Colgrave, *Two Lives*, p. 114) is unknown, except that it was in Cuthbert's diocese. Assuming that the spelling with *K-* is the more correct name-form, a connection with Brit. **cunetiu*, from which the river-names Kennet, Kent etc. are derived, is possible. *Hintis* is, however, the reading not only of the late manuscripts TP but also of a gloss to the corresponding chapter of Bede's *Vita (pr.) Cuthberti* (ch. 29) in post-1066 Durham manuscripts, the source of which I believe to be a lost eighth-century ?Wearmouth–Jarrow manuscript of the *Vita anon.* (below, pp. 120–2); for a Shropshire and Staffordshire place-name *Hints*, the latter an early Roman occupation site, compare Ekwall, *Concise Dictionary*, p. 241 with Jackson, *Language and History*, p. 519.   [53] Ed. Colgrave, *Two Lives*, pp. 196 (*Bedae Vita*) and 84 (*Vita anon.*).

[54] For the OE spelling *-æ-*, see Jackson, *Language and History*, pp. 324 and 326, and cf. 488 (the Devon Tavy). Note that the mid-tenth-/early-eleventh-century *Historia de S. Cuthberto* records a *Tefegedmuthe* in connection with Bishop Ecgred of Lindisfarne (830–45): *Symeonis Opera*, ed. Arnold I, 201.

that the anonymous Lindisfarne author had included in his text. For unexpectedly, even startlingly, there is indirect evidence that a lost older manuscript of the Anonymous Life recorded the river-name in its 'Primitive Welsh' form, or a good approximation to it at that stage in its evolution, that is, *Tabiad(e)*.

GLOSSES TO BEDE'S 'VITA S. CUTHBERTI' AS EVIDENCE FOR AN
EIGHTH-CENTURY MANUSCRIPT OF THE ANONYMOUS 'VITA'?

Glosses are a feature of copies of Bede's *Vita S. Cuthberti (prosaica)* in both pre-1066 and post-1066 manuscripts. The relationships between them need to be worked out fully by someone with regular access to all the manuscripts; but even a cursory study of the evidence available in print shows that groups of glosses recur in books several centuries apart (as in the case of other Latin-language works), in which the *Vita*-text with which they are associated may represent different traditions.[55] In the present context, two such books are directly relevant. The earlier is London, British Library, Cotton Vitellius A. xix (V in Colgrave's edition), written in a mid-tenth-century 'Anglo-Saxon Square minuscule' which establishes its origin at St Augustine's, Canterbury, although that was seemingly not its medieval home (which is unknown);[56] the later of the two is a twelfth-century Durham book, Cambridge, Trinity College O. 3. 55 (C_3 in Colgrave's edition).[57] In the tenth-century Canterbury book, Bede's prose *Vita* is on 1v–7r and 9r–84v, and is followed (to fol. 88) by his *Historia ecclesiastica* IV.31 and 32; the principal text in the concluding folios is Bede's *Vita metrica Cuthberti*.[58] The glosses to the *Vita prosaica* form three recognizable groups: first, Old English

[55] M. Lapidge, 'The Study of Latin Texts in Late Anglo-Saxon England: 1. The Evidence of Latin Glosses', *Latin and the Vernacular Languages*, ed. Brooks, pp. 99–140, repr. in his *Anglo-Latin Literature 600–899* (London, 1996), pp. 455–98 and 516, is concerned neither with hagiographic texts nor (directly) with post-1066 manuscripts: it nonetheless provides the best guide to glosses in general in early English books and to the proper methodology of their study.
[56] D. N. Dumville, 'English Square Minuscule Script: the Mid-Century Phases', *ASE* 23 (1994), 133–64, esp. 137 and 139; Gneuss, 'Preliminary List', no. 401. The added '*Alleluia* texts with neumes' on fols. 88 and 89 *might* provide a clue to its later home, but hitherto they have not done so.
[57] M. R. James, *The Western Manuscripts in the Library of Trinity College, Cambridge*, 3 vols. (Cambridge, 1902) III, 241–3 (no. 1227); Colgrave, *Two Lives*, pp. 21–2.
[58] It is beyond serious doubt that V, with the Æthelstan book, Cambridge, Corpus Christi College 183 (Colgrave's C_1) and the Christ Church, Canterbury book of s.x.ex, London, BL, Harley 1117 (H) – if it is not simply a copy of V *for this text* (for its text of the *Vita metrica* compare M. Lapidge, 'Artistic and Literary Patronage in Anglo-Saxon England', *SettSpol* 39 (1991), 137–98, at 174–5 (repr. in his *Anglo-Latin Literature 600–899*, pp. 37–91 and 499–500, at 74–5)) – should be the basis of any edition of the prose *Vita*. Colgrave unaccountably preferred a group of manuscripts of the twelfth century and later, with considerable implications for the text of the *Vita* and for our notions of Bede's Latinity, as was already pointed out in reviews of the edition by A. Souter in *JTS* 41 (1940), 321–4 and by M. L. W. Laistner in *AHR* 46 (1941), 379–81. Typical additional examples of the consequential changes to Colgrave's edition are (p. 220) *adpropians* (not *appropinquans*: compare *HE* IV.29, ed. Colgrave and Mynors, p. 440; already

ones – in fact, only two in number, compared with the thirteen to the verse *Vita* – printed by both Colgrave and Meritt; second, Latin lexical and occasional 'grammatical' or 'morphological' (syntactical) glosses, very unevenly distributed;[59] third, from ch. 12, glosses supplying the names of places and of persons omitted by Bede from his narration but discoverable from the text of the Lindisfarne *Vita*. In the third group are, for example, the glosses to Bede's *Vita* ch. 14: *nomen feminae Quenswith* and *nomen viculi Hruningaham*; and these have their precise counterparts in the Trinity College, Durham manuscript. Again, both manuscripts have as a gloss to ch. 15 (the healing of the wife of a reeve) *nomen uxoris Eadsuid*, whose name is not to be found in the 'received' text of the corresponding chapter (II.8) of *Vita anon.*[60] Similar glosses are to be found in subsequent chapters, although more frequently in the Durham book than in the Canterbury book; and a later Durham book, the fourteenth-century Oxford, Bodleian Library, Fairfax 6 (Colgrave's O$_3$), duplicates several of those in the Trinity College manuscript but has others which are unique to it.[61] A final category of glosses characteristic of the two Durham books, without any counterpart in V, is that of the names of witnesses to miracles whom Bede – and in one case the Lindisfarne author before him – had left anonymous: the priest Bæda (chs. 34, 35), the *minister* and priest Betwald and the brother Fridumund (ch. 35), the priests Cynimund (ch. 41) and Ceolbercht (ch. 46), from the communities at Lindisfarne or Jarrow and once (probably) from elsewhere.[62]

common in both the *Vetus Latina 'Itala'* and the Vulgate, although other patristic authors prefer the uncompounded *propiare*); (p. 240) *vespertina hora* (not *vespera*); (p. 274) *contra fidei fortitudinem* (not *c.f. virtutem*); the spellings *hymnos* and *harena* (always spelt *per aspirationem* by Bede), *sollemni-* (not *solenni-*), *Agustinus* etc.

59 For the terminology, see Lapidge, 'The Evidence of Latin Glosses', p. 106. A typical syntactical gloss is *id est similiter* to ch. 3's *Nec non etiam* (ed. Colgrave, p. 160): an early medieval reader could well require guidance on the force of the 'double negative'; cf. Norberg, *Manuel pratique*, pp. 116 and 171. Other characteristic examples are to *Vita*, chs. 4, 11, 21 and 28 (ed. Colgrave, pp. 164, 194, 226 and 248). Almost every gloss in this group (although apparently none from the other two groups) is repeated in H. Of particular interest for their linked 'text-history' is that to ch. 21: *scilicet debuit esse*; in both books it is over the word *iuxta*, but clearly belongs with *supponenda (erat)*.

60 Colgrave, *Two Lives*, pp. 200 (app. 9 and 13) and 204 (app. 7). The 'Lindisfarne' *Liber Vitae* always spells the name *Cuoen-* (four examples, plus one of *Cuoem-*). But both the Leningrad and the Moore manuscripts of *HE* spell Edwin's first wife *Quoenburga*.

61 The very first of the name-glosses not to be found in V, but common to C$_3$ and O$_3$, is *nomen presbyteri Tydi* to ch. 13 (ed. Colgrave, p. 192; corresponding to *Vita anon.* II.4, ed. Colgrave, p. 84 – with the spelling *Tidi* in M). Glosses to the later chs. of C$_3$ and O$_3$ include *nomen insule Cocue<dade>deseu* (ch. 24: ed. Colgrave, p. 234), *nomen comitis Sibca* (al. *Sibul*) (ch. 25: ed. Colgrave, p. 240; with which compare *Vita anon.* IV.7, ed. Colgrave, p. 120), *nomen loci Hintis. nomen comitis Hemni* (ch. 29: ed. Colgrave, p. 252) and *nomen loci Bædesfelth* (ch. 30: ed. Colgrave, p. 254). Apparently only in O$_3$ are *nomen viculi Medeluong* and *nomen presbiteri Tydi* (ch. 33: ed. Colgrave, p. 260), with which compare *Vita anon.* IV.6 (ed. Colgrave, p. 118).

62 Ed. Colgrave, pp. 262, 264, 266, 288 and 304 (apparatus).

It is the first of the place-name glosses in the two manuscripts V and C$_3$ that provides the distinctive early form of 'Teviot'. In the Canterbury manuscript at fol. 28, against Bede's *iuxta fluvium quendam* (*Vita pr.* ch. 12 = Colgrave p. 196) is *n[omen] fl[uvii] Tabiade*. At the same point in the text the twelfth-century Durham book has (at 10v) *n[omen] fl[uvii] Iccabicide* (sic!), a form or spelling readily explained as the misreading of a short-headed *t* and the open or Insular minuscule *a*.[63] On phonological grounds, Professor Jackson believed that English invaders of the North 'learned [the river-name] in the first half of the seventh century', his reconstruction of its Pr.W. form being *Tev'iad* (< Brit. *Tamiatis*) – with both lenited *m* (originally a strongly nasal, subsequently a weakly nasal, sound) and i-affection.[64] Of this, *Tabiad(e)*, with *b* for intervocalic *v*, is fully acceptable as the form or spelling of an early-eighth-century Lindisfarne scribe.

It is hardly credible that the series of witness-glosses in the two Durham books is pure invention; and in spite of the lateness of the testimony they surely have an identifiable (lost) written source: namely, entries made in the margins of a copy of Bede's prose *vita*, probably at Wearmouth–Jarrow, within a decade or two of its completion. The adding to a copy of Bede's *Vita prosaica* of the name-glosses extracted from a text of the Lindisfarne *vita*,[65] for which V is now the oldest manuscript testimony, could in theory have happened at any stage in the transmission of the Bedan text before V's mid-tenth-century date. But that it was done more or less contemporaneously with the witness-glosses now preserved only in the later manuscripts C$_3$ and O$_3$ is strongly suggested by the *Tabiad* gloss; and it is further supported by the inclusion among the glosses of at least one personal name, that is, *Eadswith*, which had already been lost from the Lindisfarne *vita*-text before the end of the eighth century (since it was evidently lacking in both β and in the common ancestor (α) of O$_1$AO$_2$).

THE CULT OF ST CUTHBERT ON THE EUROPEAN MAINLAND

Evidence for a lost eighth-century ?Wearmouth–Jarrow copy of the *Vita anon.* (if that is indeed the correct interpretation of the glosses) does little more than reinforce the now-established view of the early history of the saint's cult in England, although the precise form of its text at more than one point is certainly unexpected. In contrast, the dissemination and extent of his cult in Carolingian Europe remains ill documented and worse understood, in spite of the well-known dispatch to Lul of Mainz (in 764) of copies of Bede's verse and prose *Lives*, and the almost equally well-known *obiter* of Christopher Hohler that

---

[63] I am grateful to Dr S. Keynes and the Librarian of Trinity College for providing me with photocopies.   [64] Jackson, *Language and History*, pp. 488, 490 and 612–13; cf. pp. 413–15.

[65] The copy used by Bede in the composition of his own *Vitae Cuthberti*? Another copy, made possibly at Wearmouth–Jarrow? Compare the 'Romanizing' of the Psalter quotation in M (above, p. 116).

'Cuthbert is the one English saint who can be assumed to have been commemorated by any English missionary in the eighth century'.[66] Here the newly-identified manuscript text may do something to fill the more obvious gaps.

By a quirk of fate, none of the three or more prose *vita*-texts, whether Bede's or the Lindisfarne version, which figure in pre-900 library catalogues from places as far apart as Bobbio and Cologne, are now extant.[67] Cuthbert's *dies natalis* of 20 March is, however, entered in the several continental-written calendars that descend from a northern-English martyrological one,[68] in the *rotae sanctorum*

---

[66] *S. Bonifatii et Lulli Epistolae*, ed. M. Tangl. MGH, Epist. select 1 (Berlin, 1916), no. 116 (p. 251); C. Hohler, 'The Type of Sacramentary used by St. Boniface', *Sankt Bonifatius: Gedenkgabe zum Zwölfhundertsten Todestag* (Fulda, 1954), pp. 89–93, at 92; and below, p. 125. Lapidge has suggested a Fulda-Mainz connection pre-800 for the Bedan materials, including the unique copy of a 'first version' of the *Vita metr. Cuthberti*, in the mid-ninth-century German manuscript Besançon, Bibliothèque Municipale, 186: M. Lapidge, 'Bede's Metrical *Vita S. Cuthberti*', *St Cuthbert*, ed. Bonner *et al.*, pp. 77–93, at 84. The continental-European cult of the saint is otherwise barely touched on in that volume.

[67] At Bobbio a *vita [S.] Cuthberti* figures both in the main 'old' catalogue (which I believe to be in great part of the *early* ninth century at latest) and among the gifts of *Theodorus presbyter*, datable to the second third of the century; the two lists were edited from an early-eighteenth-century transcript as a single document by L. A. Muratori, whose text is most accessible in *Catalogi Bibliothecarum Antiqui*, ed. G. Becker (Bonn, 1885), pp. 64–73 (no. 32), the *vita* at 68 and 72; and from the same (?) transcript, with a much-improved text, by M. Tosi, 'Index MSS.rum Codicum Bobiensis', *Archivum Bobiense* 6/7 (1984–5), 135–44, the *vita* at 141–2 (no. 305) and 149 (no. 593). For the Cologne manuscript, see A. Decker, 'Die Hildebold'sche [*sic*; but falsely] Manuskriptensammlung des Kölner Domes', *Festschrift der 43. Versammlung deutscher Philologen u. Schulmänner, dargeboten von Höheren Lehranstalten Kölns* (Cologne, 1895), pp. 224–9 (also paginated 10–15), at 227 (no. 88). The mid-ninth-century Saint-Gallen catalogue has an entry *De miraculis Gudperti episcopi: Mittelalterliche Bibliothekskataloge Deutschlands und der Schweiz* 1, ed. P. Lehmann (Munich, 1918), p. 75; this was probably Bede's *Vita pr.* At Lorsch, a *vita sancti Cuthberti* figures among the works of Bede in the related catalogues of holdings *c.* 850 in Vatican City, Biblioteca Apostolica Vaticana, Pal. lat. 1877, fols. 1–34 and Pal. lat. 57, fols. 1–7, the former with a duplicate entry on the opening leaf ('sacristy' books?): see the conflate and chaotic edition in *Catalogi Bibliothecarum Antiqui*, ed. Becker, pp. 82–119 (as partly unscrambled by B. Bischoff, *Die Abtei Lorsch im Spiegel ihrer Handschriften*, 2nd ed. (Lorsch, 1989), pp. 19 and 26–8), at 100 (item no. 280), 82 (item no. 38) and 121 (item no. 24).

[68] I.e. in the ?Prüm manuscript (not Lorsch, and the calendar's Jarrow nucleus augmented at York *c.* 780, not Mainz) now Berlin, Deutsche Staatsbibliothek, Phillipps 1869, in the ?lower-Rhine manuscript now Milan, Biblioteca Ambrosiana, M. 12 sup., and in other books. The earliest reflection of the (abbreviated Hieronymian) martyrology is, I believe, the 'metrical calendar of York' (A. Wilmart, 'Un témoin anglo-saxon du Calendrier métrique de York', *RB* 46 (1934), 41–69, the text on 65–7; M. Lapidge, 'A Tenth-Century Metrical Calendar from Ramsey' (1984), repr. in his *Anglo-Latin Literature 900–1066* (London, 1993), pp. 343–86 and 489, at 345–6). I try to explain the whole complex in a forthcoming study provisionally titled 'The Eighth-Century "Schools of York" and the Calendar in Berlin Phillips 1869'. Cuthbert duly figures in the York text in the form *Cuthbertus denas tenuit ternasque kalendas* (ed. Wilmart, p. 66). In the later 'Metrical Calendar of Hampson' (P. McGurk, 'The Metrical Calendar of Hampson. A New Edition', *AB* 104 (1986), 79–125) the Cuthbert entry (*ibid.* p. 95) is *Tresdecimis sanctus Cuthberhtus scandit ad altum*, the text in London, BL, Cotton Julius A. vi having, however, the

associated with the seven-book version of the Carolingian Court-computus, and in other calendars of the ninth century, beginning with that from Fulda which Walahfrid Strabo copied into his 'vademecum', that is St Gallen, Stiftsbibliothek, 878. (Interestingly, the English royal martyr Oswald at 5 August is also in all of these *except* the Fulda calendar.)[69] Yet no ninth-century sacramentary has a proper mass for Cuthbert, even as an addition. The earliest in a continental book is that in the northern-French 'Ratoldus sacramentary', Paris, Bibliothèque Nationale, lat. 12052, characterized by Hohler as 'excessively rare and excessively odd', since (among other features) the saint is referred to in both prayers and *benedictio* as a martyr.[70] This may not be so 'odd' as it seems, and

'Northumbrian' orthography *Cuthberchtus*. The possibility of more links with the older 'martyrological calendar' tradition than McGurk recognized (*ibid.* p. 82) is suggested by the immediately preceding line *Gregorius fulget denis quadrisque kalendis* ('presumably the octave' of his *dies natalis, ibid.* p. 116): for in Milan, Biblioteca Ambrosiana, M. 12 sup. and some related calendars the *ordinatio sci. Gregorii pp.* is commemorated at 19 March.

69 *Rotae*: Vatican City, Biblioteca Apostolica Vaticana, Reg. lat. 309, fol. 2; Monza, Biblioteca Capitolare, f.9/176 (cclxvi), fol. 9. Fulda calendar: St Gallen, Stiftsbibliothek, 878, pp. 324–7; E. Munding, *Die Kalendarien von St. Gallen*, Text u. Arbeiten herausgegeben durch die Erzabtei Beuron, I/36 (Beuron, 1948), 19–20 and 35–91 (Cuthbert at 45); B. Bischoff, 'Eine Sammelhandschrift Walahfrid Strabos', *Mittelalterliche Studien*, 3 vols. (Stuttgart, 1966–81) II, 34–51, esp. 42–3. If Bischoff's 'absolute chronology' of Walahfrid's four successive script-styles is accepted, the calendar was necessarily copied *c.* 827–9: but for doubts, see A. L. Harting-Corrêa, *Walahfrid Strabo's "Libellus de exordiis..."*: *a Translation and Liturgical Commentary* (Leiden, 1996), pp. 11–12. Most of the early Oswald commemorations are brought together in an excellent recent study by A. Thacker, '*Membra Disjecta*: the Division of the Body and the Diffusion of the Cult', *Oswald*, ed. Stancliffe and Cambridge, pp. 97–127, at 115–17: the treatment of the relationships of the calendarial and martyrological texts needs, however, substantial amendment; compare provisionally the preceding note. The overlapping remarks of D. Ó Riain-Raedel, 'Edith, Judith and Matilda', pp. 210–11, are confused and confusing: Bede, *HE* III.13 does not attest the presence of an Oswald cult at Echternach but, as context and chronological reference show, at Utrecht and in Frisia; the Oswald entry in Wandelbert of Prüm's metrical martyrology is more likely to be dependent on the Phillipps 1869 calendar or its exemplar, since this also accounts for the otherwise inexplicable *Cassianus* at 15 July, and (rather than from Bede) quite possibly for Ciricus on the same day and perhaps Firminus at 25 September (cf. J. Dubois, 'Le martyrologe métrique de Wandelbert', *AB* 79 (1961), 257–93, at 271–2); while the tenth-century Fulda calendar 'now in St Gall' must surely be a reference to Basel, Universitätsbibliothek, N. II. 31.

70 C. E. Hohler, 'Some Service Books of the Later Saxon Church', *Tenth-Century Studies*, ed. D. Parsons (London and Chichester, 1975), pp. 60–83 and 217–27, at 66. The mass-set has been edited by N. Orchard, 'A Note on the Masses for St Cuthbert', *RB* 105 (1995), 79–98, at 97. The collect, in which Cuthbert is *martyr mirabilis atque potens anachorita*, is adapted from a prayer in the Bangor Antiphoner (*The Antiphonary of Bangor*, 2 vols., ed. F. E. Warren, HBS 4 and 10 (London, 1893–5) II, 32 (no. 124)), and seems not to be found elsewhere. The post-communion *Satiatis, Domine, numerum* is the same as that for St Aidan at 31 Aug. in the (later) English ?West-country sacramentary London, BL, Cotton Vitellius A. xviii, incompletely ptd in *The Leofric Missal*, ed. F. E. Warren (Oxford, 1883), pp. 303–7, here 306. For the distinctive preface, see below, p. 127.

would be even less so if the mass-set had been composed in a place in which (as in the Trier diocese later) the Lindisfarne *Vita S. Cuthberti* rather than Bede's was read. For in the concluding chapters of the former (but not, it seems, in Bede's *Vita*) the saint is referred to at least three times as '(holy) martyr', presumably in the Irish tradition of regarding as martyrs 'not only those who died for their faith, but also those whose ascetic discipline made their lives a kind of daily immolation for Christ'.[71] 'Ratoldus's' *praefatio* 'In hac die migrationis', in which the saint is not a martyr, is apparently incomplete: the full text is uniquely among the eleventh-century Durham additions to the pontifical, now Cambridge, Sidney Sussex College 100 (fol. 14).[72]

A quite different mass-set is to be found in a cluster of Fulda (Germany) sacramentaries written shortly before and shortly after 1000, using some distinctive prayers; it is this one that figures very soon afterwards in the English-origin 'Missal of Robert of Jumièges'. Three of its prayers had, however, already been copied into the 'Durham Collectar', and two of them, the *Super oblata* (*Secreta*) and *Ad complendum*, are also in the mass-set added at Durham to the Sidney Sussex pontifical.[73] It has recently been argued that the Fulda/Robert mass-set is of early/mid-eighth century origin (as indeed Christopher Hohler suggested forty years ago), whether put together in Northumbria or in the circle of Boniface, and that Alcuin was familiar with it and may even have made his own contribution to the final version. Such notions are very attractive and not lightly to be dismissed; equally, they are not easy to accept. (The issue here, of course, is not whether Cuthbert was commemorated – he clearly was – but whether he had a 'proper' mass-set (and office?) some two centuries before the

---

[71] *Vita* IV.15, 16 and 17 (ed. Colgrave pp. 132, 134, 136 and – possibly – 138); in IV.15, T substitutes other words for *martyris* (details in the collation *ad locc.* in the Appendix). For the Irish evidence, see L. Gougaud, 'Les conceptions du martyre chez les Irlandais', *RB* 24 (1907), 360–73; C. Stancliffe, 'Red, White and Blue Martyrdom', *Ireland in Early Mediaeval Europe*, ed. D. Whitelock, R. McKitterick and D. Dumville (Cambridge, 1982), pp. 21–46, the quotation in the text at 21.

[72] Compare Orchard, 'Masses for St. Cuthbert', p. 97, with *Two Anglo-Saxon Pontificals*, ed. H. M. J. Banting, HBS 104 (London, 1989), 169–70: the rest of the 'Sidney Sussex' mass-set is distinct from that of 'Ratoldus'. Hohler's suggestions ('Some Service Books', p. 67), tied in with a supposed West-country origin for the pontifical, of a Glastonbury origin for the Ratold mass-set has not won much favour: D. Dumville has latterly connected the pontifical with Oswald and Ramsey (*Liturgy and the Ecclesiastical History of Late Anglo-Saxon England* (Woodbridge, 1992), pp. 75–6 and *passim*). The origin of the mass can, however, be uncoupled from that of either book, although if it is 'West-country' it must be later than (probably) 944/5. Is there some link with the probably West-country origin of the 'Lanalet Pontifical' (and benedictional), Rouen, Bibliothèque Municipale, A.27 (368)), in which a benediction for St Benedict in the Benedictional of Æthelwold and the Canterbury Benedictional is adapted for Cuthbert (*Pontificale Lanalatense*, ed. G. H. Doble, HBS 74 (London, 1937), 92: retaining the phrase *quae in domo Dei ex vita patroni huius recitantur*)?

[73] Orchard, 'Masses for St Cuthbert', pp. 80–6, with a convenient tabulation at 95.

first documented texts.) Hohler noted that both the Secret (*Super oblata* in Fulda, with *pro ea nostrum gloriosa* for Robert's *per eam nostram gloriosa*) and Fulda's *Super populum* 'Deus qui sanctorum tuorum libenter . . . ab hostium insidiis protege semper et guberna' could not be traced in older sets; and this is still true. He also suggested that an eighth-century origin is strengthened by the use of the Secret in the Tegernsee mass for the *translatio* of its patron-saint Quirinus (16 June), which adapts other prayers from the 'Robert' Oswald mass-set: this may, however, be a two-edged argument, which could equally well be cited in support of a tenth-century date for the Cuthbert mass-set and the first diffusion of its prayers.[74] The Fulda etc. *Ad complendum* 'Deus qui nos sanctorum tuorum temporali . . .', on the other hand, is an adaptation of a collect for martyrs in the Luxeuil *Missale Gothicum*;[75] its presence as the prayer *super populum* (or as an alternative *postcommunio*) in Alcuin's mass for St Vedast is hardly proof that the

[74] Hohler, 'Some Service Books', p. 66; also in *The Relics of Saint Cuthbert*, ed. C. F. Battiscombe (Oxford, 1956), pp. 157–8; Orchard, 'Masses for St Cuthbert', pp. 86–7 and 94; *ibid.* pp. 83–4 for the *secreta* in the mid-eleventh-century Tegernsee-supplemented sacramentary, Cambridge, Fitzwilliam Museum, McClean 48 (84v). The *passio* of the otherwise unrecorded Roman saint Quirinus (at 25 March, *al.* 24: *Biblioteca Hagiographica Latina* [hereafter *BHL*], 2 vols. and Supplement (Brussels, 1898–1986) no. 7029) was composed at Tegernsee in or shortly before 921: see *Passiones Vitaeque Sanctorum Aevi Merovingici*, ed. B. Krusch, MGH SS rer. Merov. 3 (Hanover, 1896), 8; B. Schmeidler, *Studien zur Geschichtsschreibung des Klosters Tegernsee vom 11.–16. Jh.* (Munich, 1935), pp. 96–100. A *translatio* of the relics, previously brought from Rome, to a more distinguished place in Tegernsee's monastic church or in the complex of churches there on 16 June 804 is, however, recorded in a contemporary Freising charter and in an early-ninth-century addition to a calendar ultimately of Northumbrian origin: T. Bitterauf, *Die Traditionen des Hochstifts Freising*, 2 vols. (Munich, 1905–9) I, no. 197 (p. 188); R. Bauerreiss, 'Ein angelsächsische Kalendarfragment des bayrischen Haupstaatsarchiv in München' [*CLA* IX, 1236], *Studien und Mitteilungen O.S.B.* 51 (1933), 177–82, at 179. Only later was the 16 June commemoration understood as that of the arrival of the relics from Rome – the 'correction' of the document's testimony by H. Löwe and others being misconceived. It is not known when the church's original dedication, to the *Salvator mundi* (see *Passiones Vitaeque Sanctorum*, ed. Krusch, p. 15), was changed. The McClean 48 calendar, at 20 October, has *dedic. ecclesie S. Quirini*: but this is not reflected in the early-ninth-century collection of Tegernsee *tituli* in Karlsruhe, Landesbibliothek, Aug. perg. 205 and as an ?Ilmmünster addition to Munich, Staatsbibliothek, Clm. 19410. Finally, the beginnings of the cult of St Oswald in south and south-east Germany seems to be a phenomenon of the late tenth/eleventh centuries: Thacker, 'Membra disjecta', pp. 117–18 and 123–4; to whose evidence might be added the apparent lack of manuscript-texts of the *Vita Oswaldi* made up of extracts from Bede's *Historia ecclesiastica* (*BHL* no. 6361), exemplified by the Weingarten book Stuttgart, Landesbibliothek, HB. XIV. 6, 90r–99v, that are older than the twelfth century.

[75] Vatican City, Biblioteca Apostolica Vaticana, Reg. lat. 317: *Missale Gothicum*, ed. H. M. Bannister, 2 vols., HBS 52 and 54 (London, 1917–19) I, no. 457; *Missale Gothicum*, ed. L. C. Mohlberg, Rerum Ecclesiasticarum Documenta 5 (Rome, 1961), no. 457. It must be assumed that a considerable number of 'Gallican' mass-books similar to the Vatican 'Missale Gothicum' formerly existed; and it is impossible to say whether composers of new masses in the eighth century are less or more likely to have encountered the text in northern England (via Ireland?) or in Francia.

Cuthbert mass-set was his source. Other constituent parts of the Vedast mass-set (collect, *secreta* etc.) have good claims to being Alcuin's own compositions, and are also used for his mass for the Salzburg St Rupert in the 'Gregorian of Trento', for a mass or masses for St Boniface known from the Fulda sacramentaries and probably for a 'lost' mass for St Emmeram (Regensburg).[76] The claimed resemblance between the Fulda *praefatio* and that for the feast-day(s) of St Martin's in ninth-century Tours sacramentaries is only of the most general kind: it is significantly different from other prefaces attributable to Alcuin and includes none of his characteristic turns of phrase. He nowhere uses the term *aerias potestates* (although his disciple Hrabanus Maurus does); the opening words *In quo ita virtus* are almost unthinkable as Alcuin's; and clause- and sentence-endings of the form *talem fecit esse victorem, multiplici prostravit militia* and *nobis mirabile reliquit exemplum* are quite un-Alcuinian. Stylistic arguments for attributing the Cuthbert preface in the Sidney Sussex Pontifical to an Insular milieu, even to Alcuin, are considerably stronger![77] Yet the absence of a Cuthbert mass in a range of ninth-century 'Gregorian' sacramentaries, the supplementary

---

[76] *Le sacramentaire grégorien*, ed. J. Deshusses, I, 2nd ed., Spicilegium Friburgense 16 (Fribourg, 1979), 691; II, Spicilegium Friburgense 24 (Fribourg, 1979), 303; *Sacramentarium Fuldense saec. X*, ed. G. Richter and A. Schönfelder (Fulda, 1912), pp. 119–21, nos. 1025(=1031), 1026, 1027(=1033), 1028–9: in all three the *praefatio* is *inc.* 'Diemque natalicium'. The evidence for an Emmeram mass also composed by Alcuin is the two *Oratio[nes] in natali sancti Emmerammi marty<ris>* included in the collectar-pontifical of Bishop Baturich of Regensburg: *Das Kollektar-Pontifikale des Bischofs Baturich von Regensburg (817–848)*, ed. F. Unterkircher and K. Gamber, Spicilegium Friburgense 8 (Fribourg, 1962), 67 (nos. 114–15), corresponding to *Sacramentaire grégorien*, ed. Deshusses I, 691, nos. 59* and 62*. As Orchard notes ('Masses for St. Cuthbert', pp. 84–5) the 'St. Vaast' prayer (no. 63*) occurs also as a *super populum* in the mass for a confessor in the original, s. ix/x, section of the 'Leofric Missal', Oxford, Bodleian Library, Bodley 579 (*Leofric Missal*, ed. Warren, p. 173); but his further comment that the mass-set prayers 'are those of the late ninth-century sacramentary from St.-Maurice [cathedral], Tours, mediated through north-eastern France' may mislead. The mass *in natale unius confessoris* is a standard one in the Gregorian *supplementum 'Anianense'*, the fifth of a group of eight (*Sacramentaire Grégorien*, ed. Deshusses I, 412–17, Supplement mass-nos. XLVIII-LV), which is also present complete and with only minor variants in Paris, Bibliothèque Nationale, lat. n.a. 1589 (Tours cathedral), 80r–83v, and in Bodley 579, fols. 204–9 (with vigil masses intercalated) + 216 (*Leofric Missal*, ed. Warren, pp. 170–4 and 179); here, however, the masses in the main group have an added preface, sometimes also a *benedictio*, and – with one exception – a concluding prayer *ad populum*, all of which (except for a single preface) are lacking in the corresponding Tours mass-sets.

[77] The words *ita virtus . . . victorem cuius* are taken from an 'eighth-century Gelasian' preface found in (e.g.) *Liber Sacramentorum Gellonensis*, ed. A. Dumas and J. Deshusses, CCSL 159 (Turnhout, 1981), no. 1364 and *Liber Sacramentorum Engolismensis*, ed. P. Saint-Roch, CCSL 159C (Turnhout, 1987), no. 1241; for *aerias potestates*, see, e.g., Hrabanus Maurus, *Homiliae de festis praecipuis*, PL 110, cols. 9–134, at col. 60A (hom. no. 31). Alcuin uses *aereas turmas* in *Alcuin: the Bishops, Kings and Saints of York*, ed. P. Godman (Oxford, 1982), line 1328 and *hostis invisibilis* in *Epistolae Karolini Aevi*, ed. Dümmler, nos. 18 (p. 52), 19 (p. 56) etc. I hope to be able to demonstrate elsewhere the early Insular and other textual links of the Sidney Sussex Pontifical preface.

material of which includes masses now generally credited to Alcuin, becomes even more conspicuous in the Tours books that seem directly to reflect his work of compilation and organization:[78] all of which requires us to suppose that, having composed a distinctive preface, Alcuin or his disciples then took steps to ensure that the mass-set never circulated!

Nor can it convincingly be maintained that Alcuin was so disillusioned by Cuthbert's failure to protect Lindisfarne from the Northmen in the summer of 793 that he and his disciples turned their back on the cult. His dismay and distress at the time are indeed conveyed, from the comparative security and comfort of (probably) one of his possessions in northern France,[79] in a long verse-lament addressed in the first instance to the community; and in a series of letters to addressees in southern and northern England written before he rejoined the Frankish Court, then slowly returning north from Bavaria. When Alcuin eventually did so, he would – he assures Bishop Higbald – be intervening with the king to secure the release of some of the raiders' captives.[80] A few years later, when he was in residence at St Martin's, Tours, Alcuin sent copies of four of the letters, with others, to Salzburg. The *Vita Alcuini*, written in the 820s by someone who had obtained most of his information from one or more of his disciples, places him firmly in a tradition of learning that had descended, *vestigia per omnia sequentibus*, from Pope Gregory I and Augustine to Bede and Ecgberht via Cuthbert.[81]

---

[78] *Sacramentaire grégorien*, ed. Deshusses I, 46–7 and 64–6; *ibid.* II, 25–8.

[79] The evidence for which is assembled and discussed in my *Alcuin: Achievement and Reputation* (forthcoming), pt II ch. 3.

[80] *Poetae Latini Carolini Aevi* I, ed. E. Dümmler, MGH PLAC 1 (Berlin, 1881), 229–35 (*carm.* ix); *Epistolae Karolini Aevi*, ed. Dümmler, nos. 16–21, also (somewhat later) no. 22, with the promise that *cum domnus noster rex Karolus . . . domum revertetur, nos Deo iuvante ad eum venire disponimus* etc. in no. 20. For whatever reason, none of the letters is addressed to anyone on the Continent (for the later recopying and circulation of several of those addressed to English recipients, see below): and contrary to the impression sometimes given by modern works, there is no reference to the attack in any of the contemporary continental annals – nor in Irish Annals, which however record the *vastatio omnium insolarum Britanniȩ* in 794, and cf. the long annal for 825 which concludes with 'the martyrdom of Blamac . . . at the hands of the heathens' at Iona (*The Annals of Ulster*, ed. S. Mac Airt and G. Mac Niocaill (Dublin, 1983), pp. 250 and 282). Even the English record is less satisfactory than is commonly supposed. The 'correct' date of 8 June is found only in Simeon of Durham's *Historia Dunelmensis Ecclesiae* (in *Symeonis Opera*, ed. Arnold I, 50) although the 'Id. Ian.' date in *ASC* E (also D) (*Two of the Saxon Chronicles Parallel*, ed. C. Plummer, 2 vols. (Oxford, 1892–9) I, 57, cf. II, 62) is acceptable evidence that the version of the 'Northumbrian Annals' used by the Chronicler gave that date (omitted in the Byrhtferth version).

[81] *Vita Alcuini*, ch. 4, ed. W. Arndt (*Vitae Aliaeque Historiae Minores*, MGH SS, 15.1 (Hanover, 1887), 182–97, at 186). But also, more remarkably, via Theodore (of Canterbury), thus partially anticipating a later Aquitanian monk's view of the *traditio studii* in early England: L. Delisle, *Notices et extraits des manuscrits de la Bibliothèque Nationale et autres Bibliothèques* 35 (Paris, 1890), 241–357, at 311–2 (cited by J. Stevenson, *The 'Laterculus Malalianus' and the School of Archbishop Theodore*, CSASE 14 (Cambridge, 1995), 2, n. 3).

Others evidently felt much the same. More than a decade earlier than the *vita* is a litany included in the probably Aachen-written but then Werden manuscript, now Cologne, Erzbischöflische- und Dombibliothek, 106.[82] The last-named confessor in the litany's original text is *Luitgare*, Liudger of Werden and Münster (*ob.* 809); but, almost immediately, another five names were added including, as a marginal insertion, 'Chutberte Ecberte Beda'.[83]

None of the early English writings that would have given the Salzburg clergy and their bishop Arno a 'positive' view of Cuthbert, namely, Bede's metrical and prose *vitae* and his *Historia ecclesiastica* or Alcuin's 'York poem' which drew extensively on the first and last of these, can be shown to have been available to them *c*. 800.[84] The copies they had been sent of some of the letters written in the aftermath of the disasters of 793 necessarily offered a less encouraging picture; but when they were re-copied at Salzburg in 802/3, and again later, several of the clauses and passages that reflected badly on the Northumbrian saint were simply omitted or modified.[85] Moreover, while the 'Northumbrian Annals' incorporated in the *Historia Regum*[86] and Alcuin's letters and poem in their original text-forms agree on the material destruction at Lindisfarne and the fate of many members of its community, there is no suggestion that Cuthbert's burial-place had been despoiled. Later evidence indeed, without any recourse to the epithet 'miraculous', implies that it survived intact: the tradition – even if a false

---

[82] For its origin at the Aachen Court, the work – probably – of scribes temporarily there, see D. A. Bullough, *Carolingian Renewal: Sources and Heritage* (Manchester, 1991), pp. 239–40 and 252–3.

[83] The litany (Cologne, Dombibliothek, 106, fol. 74) is printed by M. Coens, *Recueil d'études bollandiennes* (Brussels, 1963), pp. 140–4, here 143. Note that neither E(c)gbert nor Bede figures in any pre-1100 litany of English origin, as may be gathered from *Anglo-Saxon Litanies of the Saints*, ed. M. Lapidge, HBS 106 (London, 1991): for Bede in the litany in Cambridge, Corpus Christi College 391, pp. 221–5 (Worcester, s. xi² but this part rewritten in s.xii¹), see *Litanies*, ed. Lapidge, pp. 115–19, at 117, and cf. *ibid.* p. 65.

[84] For the Bedan sources of the 'York poem's' account of Cuthbert, see *Bishops, Kings and Saints of York*, ed. Godman, lines 646–740 and notes, also the Introduction, *ibid.* pp. lii-liii. Surprisingly, there is no ninth-century copy of the *Historia* from either Salzburg or Saint-Amand, and no high-medieval copies that might depend on a lost Carolingian exemplar from either centre. In contrast, the earliest complete copy of the 'discipulus Umbrensium' version of Theodore's *Penitential* and book of canons (supplemented by a text of the *Interrogationes Augustini et Responsiones Gregorii*), Vienna, Nationalbibliothek, lat. 2195 (*CLA* X, 1508; Bischoff, *Schreibschulen* II, 84–5 (no. 3)) was written at Salzburg in Arno's earlier years.

[85] *Epistolae Karolini Aevi*, ed. Dümmler, nos. 17–20 are copied with omissions and/or slight modifications to the text in the Salzburg book Vienna, Nationalbibliothek, lat. 808, written in 802 or 803; and the same version of no. 19 is among the letters copied in Munich, Clm. 13581 (which, *contra* Bischoff, I believe to have been written in the Salzburg area, although not in its regular scriptorium). The small group of Alcuin's *carmina* copied in the Vienna manuscript concludes on fol. 233 with the last ten lines (only) of Alcuin's lament for the island-church: these do not contain any reference to the place (which in any case cannot be fitted into a hexameter) or to the saint; and there is no evidence to show whether Salzburg had been sent a copy of the entire poem. [86] *Symeonis Opera*, ed. Arnold II, 55.

one – that the (timber) church in which the saint had been buried in 687 was transported to Norham by Bishop Ecgred (830–45), and Cuthbert and Ceolwulf both re-buried there, is testimony of one kind; the still very visible coffin and associated relics are testimony of another.[87] None of this is encouraging to Hohler's assertion (to help explain the absence of pre-tenth-century Cuthbert masses) that 'his reputation received a mortal blow from his failure to protect his monastery of Lindisfarne from the Danes in 793'.[88]

A *Cutbercht*, who is skilled in several different Insular script-types, declares himself to be the scribe of a notable gospelbook (Vienna, Nationalbibliothek, lat. 1224), attributable on textual and other grounds to the Salzburg area *c.* 780/90. He was evidently a *peregrinus* from England, perhaps already in the last years of Bishop Virgil (*ob.* 784).[89] Had he brought with him a personal interest in his saintly namesake? Or was it only after Salzburg copyists had modified the texts of the letters they had been sent from Tours, in ways that obscured both the location of 'St Cuthbert's church' and why his intercessions were thought worth invoking, that a text of his *vita* was sought out? Did someone in the Salzburg *scola* wish to give the saint the historical context that he currently lacked? Or is this entirely too 'modern' a way of thinking? Was his abbreviated Life associated with Augustine's two works simply because he was a pastoral bishop?[90] To these and many other questions a single manuscript can give no

---

[87] For the latter, see *St Cuthbert*, ed. Bonner *et al.*, pt 3. For the former, see the *Historia de S. Cuthberto*, ch. 9 (in *Symeonis Opera*, ed. Arnold I, 201). The *Historia*'s account of the transfer to Norham is accepted without comment by E. Cambridge, 'Why did the Community of St. Cuthbert Settle at Chester-le-Street?', *St Cuthbert*, ed. Bonner *et al.*, pp. 367–95, at 371; but compare the more sceptical view of D. Rollason in the same volume, pp. 416–17 and esp. n. 17. That the church in which Cuthbert was originally buried was a wooden one is explicit (as Dr S. Keynes reminded me) in *HE* III.25 (ed. Plummer I, 181; ed. Colgrave and Mynors, p. 294). But as this same passage makes clear, its construction *non de lapide sed de robore secto* ('not of stone but of hewn oak') was the work of Aidan's successor Finan and not of Aidan, as the author of the *Historia* believed; and Bede adds that subsequently Bishop Eadberht covered the church's walls and roof with sheets of lead.

[88] Hohler, 'Type of Sacramentary', p. 92. Similarly, it cannot be assumed (as does A. Campbell, *Æthelwulf 'De Abbatibus'* (Oxford, 1967), p. xxx) that the devotions of Eadfrith teacher of Æthelwulf at the *tumbam Cudberchti corpore . . . almam* (lines 752–3, at p. 59) must have been before 793.

[89] *CLA* X, 1500; Bischoff, *Schreibschulen* II, 95–6 (no. 24). Bischoff believed that the same scribe was probably also responsible for corrections to the fragmentary *Prophets*, now Kremsmünster, Stiftsbibliothek, Fragm.I/1. (*CLA* X, 1462): *Schreibschulen* II, 85 (no. 4). There is, Bischoff emphasized (*ibid.* p. 58), no other Anglo-Saxon scribe at Salzburg in the Virgil/early Arno period. He does not figure in the Salzburg *Liber Vitae*; and his *floruit* seems to be too early for Alcuin's (epistolary) links with the church there to be invoked for his presence in the Salzburg area.

[90] And very different, therefore, from another English saint, the 'royal martyr' Oswald, whose cult was being actively promoted, although in a limited number of places, without an independent *Vita*: Thacker, '*Membra Disjecta*', esp. pp. 116–19 and cf. pp. 123–5.

answers. Over and beyond its interest for the text of the Lindisfarne *vita*, it is at present the only witness to a Cuthbert 'cult' in the (arch)diocese of Salzburg and its churches in the ninth century.[91]

APPENDIX

A COLLATION OF MUNICH, STAATSBIBLIOTHEK, CLM. 15817, 100V–119V

[Colgrave, *Two Lives*, does not have a line-numbering in his editions; it records variants with a 'footnote' numbering on each page, referred to here as 'app.']

Colgrave, p. 64

    (line 6) dedicimus (*alii* didicimus)

    (app. 11) praedestinatam (*with* O_2; *ed.* pre- *alii*)

    (app. 13) Cuthberchto

    (app. 15) Helias (*with* AO_2T; *ed.* Elias *with* O_1 [HB *omm.*])

    (app. 18) superans (*ed. with* O_1AO_2T; superavit HBP)

    (app. 21) exspectans (*with* O_1O_2; expectans AT; *ed.* expectaret *with* HBP)

    (app. 22) congregati sunt (*ed. with* O_1AT; *om.* sunt HBP)

    (app. 23) planitiem (planiciem O_1A; *ed.* planicie *with* HB(P?)T)

    (app. 35) neglegenti (*ed.* negligenti *with* O_1O_2A; negligente HB)

Colgrave, p. 66

    (app. 1) intellegens (*ed. with* O_1 1a man.; intellig- *alii*)

    (app. 5) coepit (with AO_2H; *ed.* cepit *with* O_1BPT)

    (app. 8, 9) retinens in mente (*ed.* in mente retinens *alii*)

    (app. 13) providentiam (providentia O_1; *ed.* -iam *alii*)

    (app. 16) Samuhel (*ed. with* O_1O_2; -uel AHBPT)

    (app. 21) adfirmavit (*ed. with* O_1A; affirmat O_2HBPT)

    (app. 25) *om.* et reliqua (*with* O_2P)

    (app. 26, 27: tit.) quod eum angelus sanavit (*with* T; *ed.* quod angelus sanavit eum *with* O_1O_2 [HBP *om.*])

    (app. 30) electioni (*with* O_1O_2; *ed.* electione)

    (app. 35) detenebatur (*with* T; *ed.* detin- *alii*)

    (app. 36) Nam quia (*ed. with* O_1AO_2; *om.* quia HBPT)

    (app. 42) adtingens (attingens HBPT; *ed.* tangens *with* O_1AO_2)

    (app. 43) deportatus (*ed. with* O_1AO_2T; deportatur et HBP)

    (app. 46) venire (*ed. with* O_1AO_2; venisse HBPT)

    (app. 48) propinquans (*with* AT; appropinquans O_2HBP; *ed.* adpropinquans)

    (app. 51) etiam (*ed. with* O_1AO_2; vero iam HB, iam TP)

[91] Thanks are due to Professor K. Cameron, Professor H. Hine and Mrs Veronica Smart for their critical comments on an earlier version of this paper, and above all to Dr Simon Keynes for his substantial editorial improvements. I take this opportunity of thanking also the Monumenta Germaniae Historica (Munich) and its successive presidents for their hospitality during 1991–5, which enabled me to explore the manuscript riches of the Munich Staatsbibliothek.

(4 lines from bottom) *om.* intrepida mente corporis infirmitatis r-
(app. 56–7) pro peccatis non obligasset (*ed. with* O₁AO₂T; n.o.p.p. HBPT)

Colgrave, p. 68

(app. 3) discendens (*ed.* desc-)
(app. 5) cocere (*ed.* coquere *with* O₁AO₂; coque HBPT)
(line 11) linere (*ed.* linire *alii*)
(app. 10) saluatus (*with* HBPT; *ed.* sanatus *with* O₁AO₂)
(app. 13) miseranti (*ed. with* O₁AO₂; -ante HBT)
(app. 21, tit.) caelum (*ed.* coelum *with* O₁O₂; A *om.*)
(line 15) adulescentia (*ed.* adolescentia ?*alii*)
(app. 24) Ledir (*ed.*; -yr B)
(app. 31) cognominatur (*with* P; *ed.* cognominabatur *with* O₁O₂ ?HBT; cognomibatur A)
(app. 32) discendentes et ascendentes (desc- et asc. HBT; *ed.* asc. et desc- *alii*)
(app. 37, 38) remque mirabilem illam (m.i. *marked superscript ?for correction*; *ed.* remque illam tam mirabilem *with* O₁AO₂; rem namque tam mirabilem HBT)
(app. 45) probavit (*with* HBPT; *ed.* probabat *with* O₁AO₂)
(app. 46) etenim (*ed. with* O₁AO₂T [HBP *om.*])

Colgrave, p. 70

(app. 3) Aedani (*with* H; *ed.* Aegdani)
(app. 6, tit.) in via pascebat (*with* AT; *ed.* pascebat in via)
(app. 8) *om.* ei (*with* HBPT)
(app. 10) Iuur (*with* HB; *ed.* Uuir *with* O₁AO₂?T)
(app. 14) Cuncacaestir (*ed.* Kuncacester *with* O₁A; Cuncacestir T, Concalestir H)
(app. 22, 23) nam quia (*ed. with* O₁AO₂; *om.* quia HBT)
(app. 27) distrato (*ed. with* O₁AT; distracto O₂HB)
(app. 35) faeni (*ed.* foeni *with* O₁AOT; feni BPT)
(app. 44) panno *corr.* ?-e (*ed.* panne *with* O₁A; panno HBPT)
(app. 45) lineo (*with* O₂ *corr.* HBPT; *ed.* linea *with* O₁A(O₂))
(app. 51) adiuuabit (*ed.* adiuuauit *with* O₁AO₂; -abat HBPT)
(app. 55) proficiscebat (*ed. with* O₁AO₂; proficiscebatur TP; profectus est HB)

Colgrave, p. 76

(app. 19) *om.* Dei
(app. 20) Cudberht
(app. 24) caput (*with* HBPT; *ed.* capud *with* O₁A)
(app. 25) cingentis (*ed. with* HBPT; -entes O₁AO₂)
(app. 27) Hippe [*sic*] (Hripe HBT; Hyrpae O₁; *ed.* Hrypae *with* A)
(app. 38) Mambrae
(app. 42) suscepto (*ed. with* O₁O₂A; accepto HBP)
(app. 46) fricans propter frigorem (*ed.* p.f.f.)
(app. 53) rennuentemque (*ed. with* O₁AO₂?T; renitentemque HB)
(app. 54, 55) et postremo (*ed. with* O₁O₂; ad (et B) postremum HBPT)

Colgrave, p. 78

(app. 1) consentientem (*with* HBPT; *ed.* consentiendo *with* O₁AO₂)
(app. 4, 5) hora tertiae (*ed.* hore tertiae *with* O₁; horae tertiae [-ciae] *alii*.)
(app. 6) oratione sumato (*ed.* o. consummata *with* ?O₂HBPT; o. consumata O₁A)
(app. 12) *om.* ut (*with* O₁AO₂T)

(app. 14) tantum (*with* HBP; *ed.* tamen O_1AO_2T)

(app. 15, 16) pro benedicto pane (*with* O_1AO_2; *ed.* pro benedictione panis, *with* HPBT)

(app. 22) cocebant (*ed.* coquebant *with* O_1AO_2T; coquebantur HBP)

(app. 26, 27) solum manducantem relinquerat (solum relinquerat manducantem O_1; *ed.* solum reliquerat manducantem *with* AO_2; s.m. reliquerat HTBP)

(app. 36) obstupefacto (*ed. with* O_1AO_2T; -actus HBP)

(app. 45) repletae (*with* O_2H; *ed.* replete *alii*.)

(app. 50) *om.* et (*with* T)

(app. 68) Pleggils (*with* T [HB *om.*]; Plecgilf O_1; *ed.* Plecgils *with* A)

(app. 69) Mailros (*ed. with* O_1AO_2; Meilros TP)

Colgrave, p. 80

(app. 1) accitus (*with* HBPT; *ed.* accersitus *with* O_1A)

(app. 4) Aebba; *add.* abbatissa famulantium Dei (*add.* abbatissa famularum Dei HTB; *add.* a. famulantium Deo P)

(app. 6) Colodesburg[92]

(app. 8) aliquot (*with* HB; *ed.* -quod ?*alii*)

(app. 11) coepit (*with* H; *ed.* cepit ?*alii* [*add.* namque HBP])

(app. 13, 14) Quo comperto (*ed.* Quo conperto *with* O_1A?T; Quod ut [*om.* P] compertum est HBP)

(app. 22) inobstinata (*ed. with* O_1AO_2)

(app. 25, 26) stetit (*with* HB; *ed.* iam enim *with* O_1AO_2T)

(app. 32) harenosis locis (*with* HB; *ed.* ar- *with* AT; O_1 *om.*)

(app. 35) adorabat (*ed.* orabat *with* O_1AO_2; oraret HBT)

(app. 46, 47) minsterio impleto (*ed. with* O_1AO_2; -um -um HBPT)

(7 lines from bottom) scopolosis (*ed.* scopu-)

(5 lines from bottom) morti (*ed.* mortem)

(app. 63) hominis Dei] *add.* humiliter (*with* TP; *add.* humiliter et HB)

Colgrave, p. 82

(app. 7) servitium (*with* HBPT; *ed.* servitionem *with* O_1AO_2)

(app. 10) Daniel

(app. 15) Animam [*sic*]

(app. 19, tit.) delphino (delphina A; *ed.* delfina *with* HBP (-o T)

(app. 15) sictorum [*sic*] (*ed.* Pictorum)

(app. 23) Niuduera regio (*ed. with* ?HBT; Niudþæralegio O_1A)

(app. 26) iterum (*ed.*; itineris O_1)

(app. 30–2) nam etenim post diem nataliciae (*ed.*; Nam etenim post nataliciae [*sic*] O_1AO_2; nam post diem natalicii HB; nam et post diem natalicium T; statim p.d.n. P)

(spp. 42) columbae (*with* H; *ed.* columbe *alii*)

(app. 44) Cana (*with* T; *ed.* Chana *alii*)

Colgrave, p. 84

(app. 2) suorum *add.* In eodem quoque sancto Agustino testante die [*sic*] de quinque panibus et duobus piscibus saturavit Dominus quinque milia hominum (In eodem die sancto Augustino testante (attest; PT) de --- hominum HBPT; *ed. om.*)

(app. 6) humano (*ed. with* O_1; humana AHBPT)

(app. 71) cultello (*with* HBPT; *ed.* cultella *with* O_1A)

---

[92] For the other manuscript-testimonies, see above, p. 117.

(app. 21) manente (*with* T; *ed.* manentes *alii*)

(app. 26) Tidi (*with* T; *ed.* Tydi *with* O_1AO_2; Tydius HB)

(app. 29) Heliae (*with* H; *ed.* Helie *with* $O_1A?O_2$)

(10 lines from bottom) profetavit

(app. 32) Tidi (*ed.* Tydi *with* O_1AO_2 [HB *om.*])

(app. 35) proficiscebat (*ed. with* O_1A; -batur HBPT)

(5 lines from bottom) Taefgeta (*ed.* Tesgeta *alii*)

(app. 36) *om.* et (*with* HBP)

(app. 44) respondit (*with* HBPT; *ed.* respondente *with* O_1A)

Colgrave, p. 86

(app. 2) aliquod (*with* HBPT; *ed.* aliquid)

(app. 3) sperantem (*ed. with* O_1A; sperare HBP)

(app. 9) speranti (*with* HBPT; *ed.* sperantibus *with* O_1A)

(app. 13) *om.* ergo (*with* T)

(lines 6–7: app. 17, 18) Iuvenior fui et senui (*ed.* Iunior fui etenim senui *with* O_1A)

(app. 19, 20) dignus namque est (*with* T; *ed.* dignus est namque *with* O_1A; dignus est enim HB)

(app. 26) precepit (*with* T; praecepit HB; *ed.* praeceperat *with* O_1A)

(app. 28) currens (*ed. with* ?HBPT; cucurrens O_1A)

(app. 38) aliisque (*ed.*; aliosque O_1)

(app. 42) gratias (*with* HB; *ed.* gratiasque *alii*)

(app. 44) voluntate Dei (*ed. with* O_1A?T; Domino HB)

(5 lines from bottom, tit.) profetia

(app. 64) profetali

Colgrave, p. 88

(app. 9) tardamini (*ed. with* O_1AT; tarde- HB)

(app. 11) proibiti (*ed. with* O_1; prohi- AHBPT)

(app. 20) strepidum (*ed.* strepitum *with* O_1AT)

(app. 23) instabiles (*ed.* instabiliter *with* O_1AT [HB *om.*])

(app. 30, 31) quod ignem (*ed. with* O_1; quae ignem HB; qui ex igne A; quidem [*om.* ignem] T

(app. 46) ante--------fallatos (*ed. with* O_1A)

(app. 55) perpetraverunt (*ed. with* O_1A; impetraverunt HBPT)

(app. 63) intellegere (*with* A; intellere O_1; *ed.* intelligere *with* ?HBPT)

Colgrave, p. 90

(tit.) demonio (*ed.* daem-)

(app. 50, 49) Hildmer (*ed.* Hildmaer *with* A; Hildimer TP)

(app. 51) lacrimabile (*with* O_1A; *ed.* -ilem *with* ?HBPT)

(app. 56) Cudberchtum (*ed.* Cuðberhtum *with* O_1A; Cuthbertum HBP, Cud- T)

Colgrave, p. 92

(app. 6) tunc (*with* HBP; *ed.* tamen *with* O_1AT)

(app. 8) intellegens (*ed. with* O_1A; igens T; intelligebat HB)

(app. 9) quia (*with* HBPT; *ed.* quod *with* O_1A)

(app. 11) accedere (*with* T; *ed.* accid- *alii*) quippe (*ed. with* O_1A; HBT *om.*)

(app. 29) urbanis [*sic*] (*ed.* orbanis *with* O_1A; orph- *alii*)

(app. 41–4) homini Dei spectanda erat (h. D. s. i. erat quia T; *ed.* homini Dei exspectanda [exp- A] erat *with* O_1A; sibi spectandam esse HB)

134

(app. 45) consulare (consolare T; *ed.* consolari *alii*)

(app. 53) avenarum (*ed.* habenarum *with* O₁A; freni HTB, frenorum P)

(app. 62) dixit (*ed.* diximus [O₁ *om.*])

(app. 66) tactu streni [*sic*] (*ed.* tacto freni *with* O₁A; tactu freni HBPT)

(app. 70) testata [*suprascript.*] *om.* est (*with* T)

Colgrave, p. 96

(app. 35–7) lapis in exteriore parte insulae (in exteriori parte insule [-ae B] lapis HBPT; *ed.* lapis in interiore parte insule [*sic*] *with* O₁A)

(app. 43–5) illi autem sine mora statim (ille sine mora statim O₁; Illi autem statim sine mora TP; illi autem statim H; *ed.* illi sine mora statim)

(app. 48) sibi (*ed. with* O₁; se HBPT)

(app. 50) relinquerunt (*with* O₁; *ed.* reliquerunt *with* ?HBPT [AO₂ ?*deff.*])

(app. 51) ergo (*ed. with* O₁; HBPT *om.*)

(app. 61) structura (*ed. with* O₁; -uram HBPT)

Colgrave, p. 98

(tit.) detulit (*ed.* dedit ei)

(app. 16) maxilla (*with* HBPT; *ed.* maxillis *with* O₁ [AO₂ *deff.*])

(app. 19, 20) orante eo statim et (*with* HBPT; *ed.* et orante eo statim *with* O₁ [AO₂ *deff.*])

(app. 26–8) a Deo donata omnis liquoris ibi esse suavitatem (*with* PT; a Deo ibi donata omnis liquoris esse suavitatem [sani- B] HB; *ed.* a D. d. o. l. sibi esse suavitas *with* O₁ [AO₂ *deff.*])

(app. 33) longitudinem (*with* O₁; *ed.* -tudine *with* ?HBPT

(app. 35–8) nam etenim illic (*ed. with* O₁, nam illic PT)

Colgrave, p. 100

(app. 2) constituere (*with* HBP; *ed.* construere *with* O₁T)

(app. 5) petrasset (impetrasset HB, in- P); *ed.* perpetrasset *with* O₁?T)

(app. 16) servi Christi (*with* T; *ed.* servi Dei *with alii*)

(app. 18) detollens (*with* P; *ed.* detulens *with* O₁; detulit HB [T *om.*])

(app. 30) paraverunt (*ed. with* O₁T; paruisset HB, -issent P)

(tit., app. 34) exterminatis (*with* T; *ed.* exterminandis *with* O₁)

(app. 37) servientem (*ed. with* O₁T; servivit HBP)

(app. 51) portum (*ed.* portum *with* O₁ [*corr. from* porte]; portu HBPT)

(app. 53) leni (*ed. with* O₁T; leui HBP [AO₂ *deff.*])

Colgrave, p. 102

(app. 1–4) igitur nec requies nec mora (*ed. with* O₁)

(app. 6) fodenti (*ed.* fodienti *with* O₁ *corr.* ?HBP; fodientem T)

(app. 10–12) penitens [*sic*] et merens (*ed.* sedens et merens *with* O₁T; merens resedit HBP)

(app. 22) curvi [*sic*] (*ed.* corvi *with* O₁O₂PT [HB *om.*])

(app. 25) pace (*ed. with* O₁AO₂; voce HBPT)

(app. 27) enim alter (*with* PT; alter HB; *ed.* enim *with* O₁AO₂)

(app. 40) linientes *corr. to* liniantes (*ed.* liniantes *with* O₁AO₂; linientes HBPT)

Colgrave, p. 116

(app. 54) dicentes (*with* T; *ed.* dicentis *alii*)

(app. 55) hagustaldes<e *eras. vel add.* 2ª *manu*?>quę (Hagustaldesæ A, -esae O₁, -ese O₂; Hagustaldense HBPT)

(app. 63) in regione ubi dicitur Aechsae (for *ed. and other testimonies, see above, p. 118*)

(app. 64) nam quia (*with* PT; nam HB; *ed.* namque *with* O₁AO₂)

Colgrave, p. 118

(app. 1) grabatto (grabbato P; *ed.* grabato ?*alii*)

(app. 2) deposueruntque (*with* HBPT; *ed.* deportaveruntque *with* O₁A)

(app. 8–10) bendicens eum (*ed.* benedicens eum et *with* O₁AO₂; benedicens Deum HBP; T *om.*)

(app. 21) mirabilia (*with* HBPT; *ed.* mira *with* O₁AO₂)

(line 16; tit.) curato] *add.* in mortalitate; profetia (*ed.* curato et prophetia *etc. with* O₁; for O₁'s *capitulum, see above, p. 113*)

(app. 28) Tidi (*with* O₁O₂T; *ed.* Tydi *with* ?A)

(app. 29–31) a me sepe (*with* PT; ante sepe HB; *ed.* a me *with* O₁AO₂)

(app. 41) praedicans (*with ed.* ; praedicavit HBPT)

(app. 55) haut (*with* HT; aut O₁A; *ed.* haud)

Colgrave, p. 124

(line 1, tit.; also lines 3–4, text) anchorita (*ed.* anachorita ?*alii*)

(line 2, tit.) secundum prophetiam eius (*with* A and *capitulum, ed. Colgrave, p. 108; ed.* prophetavit discessum suum *with* O₁O₂)

(app. 4) probabilis] *add.* et fidelis (*with* HBPT)

(app. 8) ante (*ed. with* O₁AO₂ [HTPB *om.*])

(app. 21) conloquium spiritalem querens (*ed.* conloquium spiritale querens *with* AH [quae-]BP[-uale]T; *om.* querens O₁O₂)

(app. 26) renovabit *corr. to* -avit (*ed.* renovavit *with* O₁AO₂)

(app. 69–71) secundum verbum tuum perpetratum et indultum recipies (*ed.* s.v.t. perpetratum et indubitatum recipies *with* AO₁; impetravi et indubitatum recipies O₂; s.v.t. donatum et indultum est T; s.v.t. impetratum et indultum recipies P)

(app. 74) longo (*with* HBPT; *ed.* longe *with* O₁AO₂)

(bottom line) *add.* Amen.

Colgrave, p. 126

(tit., app. 1, 5) vidit animam fratris (*with* T)

(app. 7) scientiae (*with* AO₂HB; *ed.* scientie *with* O₁)

(app. 9) quodam (*with* HBPT; *ed.* quadam *with* O₁AO₂)

(app. 13) Osingaduum (*ed.* Osingadun *with* O₁AO₂; Osingadum TP; HB *om.*)

(app. 16) miro (*with* HBPT; *ed.* mire *with* O₁AO₂)

(app. 23) caelum (*with* AO₂, coelum ?H; *ed.* celum *with* O₁)

(app. 24) *om.* angelorum (*with* HBPT)

(app. 26) collocatam (*with ed.*)

(app. 39) pastoralibus (*ed. with* O₁AO₂; pastoribus HB)

(app. 40) summa (*with* HB; *ed.* summo *with* O₁AO₂)

(app. 45–6) reversus abbatissae (*with* HBT[-e], r. abbati P; *ed.* r. ad abbatissam *with* O₁AO₂)

(app. 54) cantanti (*with* O₂ *corr* HBPT; *ed.* cantantibus *with* O₁AO₂)

(app. 58) *add.* et reliqua (*with* HBPT)

Colgrave, p. 130

(line 2, tit.) positus est (*ed.* sepultus est ?*alii*)

(app. 6) Cutberchtus *corr. to* Cudb-

(app. 7–9) ad Deum commendans ei animam (*with* PT; a. D. commendasset ei animam HB; ad celum commendans Domino A, ad caelum commendans Dominum O₁O₂; *ed.* ad coelum commendans Domino)

(app. 18) oblata (*ed. with* HBPT; oblato O₁AO₂)

(app. 20) vestimento (*ed. with* HBPT; vestimenta O_1AO_2)

(app. 23) volutus (*with* O2; involutus HBP; *ed.* curatus *with* O_1AT, *where* vel volutus *as gl.*)

(app. 24–6) gaudentem corpus incorruptibile requiescens (*ed. with* O_2T; gaudentium, incorruptibilem O_1A; *om.* requiescens HB)

Colgrave, p. 132

(app. 3–4) elevantes eum (*ed. with* ?PT; elevantes autem eum HB; elevatis eum O_1; elevantis eum A; elevatus enim O_2)

(app. 16) vicones (*with* T; *ed.* ficones *alii*)

(line 10, tit.) familiae; *om.* solus

(app. 26–31) pro amore martyris sui (*ed.* pro honore sancti martyris sui *with* O_1A; pro honore martyris sui ?P; pro honore dilecti Cudberti sui T; ad honorem martyris sui HB)

(app. 35–7) vociferantem et lacrimantem lacerantemque (*ed. with* O_1AO_2 [lacerat-] ?PT; et lacerantem HB)

(app. 42–3) edoctus erat a presbitero (*with* PT; *ed.* erat edoctus a presbitero *with* A?HB; erat edoctus a populo O_1O_2)

(10 lines from bottom) Tidi (*ed.* Tydi *alii*)

(app. 52) disperantibus (*ed. with* O_1A; desp- O_2HBPT)

(app. 58) Cudberchti

Colgrave, p. 134

(app. 1) effusum (*with* HBPT; *ed.* effusus *with* O_1AO_2)

(app. 9) crastinaque (*with* HBPT; *ed.* crastinoque *with* O_1A)

(app. 12) sanatum (*with* O_1O_2P; *ed.* sanatus *with* AHBT)

Colgrave, p. 136

(line 13, tit.) curatus est (*ed.* liberatus est *alii*)

(app. 41–3) nostri coenubii (nostri cenobii HBPT; coenobii nostri O_2; *ed.* cenobii nostri O_1A)

(app. 46–8) mediri coeperunt (*ed.* medere ceperunt O_1?T; medere coeperunt AO_2; ceperunt mederi HBP)

(app. 54) puer itaque (*ed. with* O_1AO_2)

(app. 56) *om.* ut (*with* HBPT)

(app. 64) deseminavit (*ed. with* O_1AO_2; disseminatum est HBPT [desem.])

(app. 73) martyris (*ed. with* AO_2; martyres O_1; confessoris HB [T *om.*])

(app. 78) vicones (*with* T)

Colgrave, p. 138

(app. 7–11) Domino laudem stans cantavit (*ed. with* O_1AO_2; D. l. s. cantare cepit T; stans D. l. cecinit HB)

(app. 15, 16) Domino quod pro meritis (*ed.* Domino quod meritis *with* AO_2; Domino quod merita O_1; quod pro meritis P; quod per merita T; quod meritis HB)

(line 8, tit.) pretermissis (*with* T *and capitulum [p. 108]*)

(app. 21–6) nam etenim de hoc sileo quomodo in multis locis (*ed. with* O_1AO_2T)

(app. 40) sciente (*with* APT; *ed.* scienti *with* O_1A *corr.* O_2)

(app. 41) necessaria (*ed. with* HBPT; necessario O_1AO_2)

(line 17) profetali

(app. 62) Uynfridi

The transmission of the 'Digby' corpus of bilingual glosses to Aldhelm's *Prosa de virginitate*

SCOTT GWARA

Aldhelm of Malmesbury's *Prosa de virginitate* (hereafter *Pdv*)[1] can be called one of the most enduring works of Anglo-Saxon scholarship.[2] Immensely influential in Aldhelm's lifetime, the text continued to be popular in England and on the Continent until Viking invasions put an end to native learning in the last half of the ninth century.[3] Yet by the 920s interest in Aldhelm's prose treatise had revived, inaugurating a new movement in 'hermeneutic' Latin that lasted, in some centres, beyond the turn of the twelfth century.[4] Fourteen English manuscripts of *Pdv* document the renewed interest in Aldhelm's work. Most of these manuscripts are heavily glossed, and, indeed, some preserve about 25,000 bilingual annotations ranging from single letters or symbols to entire paragraphs copied verbatim from Isidore's *Etymologiae*. The density of glossing is astounding, when contrasted with the length of *Pdv*, about 20,000 words.

---

[1] I use the following abbreviations: Ehwald = R. Ehwald, *Aldhelmi Opera*, MGH, Auct. Antiq. 15 (Berlin, 1913–19); Goossens = L. Goossens, *The Old English Glosses of MS. Brussels, Royal Library 1650 (Aldhelm's De Laudibus Virginitatis)* (Brussels, 1974); Gwara = S. Gwara, 'Literary Culture in Late Anglo-Saxon England and the Old English and Latin Glosses to Aldhelm's *Prosa de virginitate*', 2 vols. (unpubl. PhD dissertation, Univ. of Toronto, 1993); Isid. = *Isidori Hispalensis etymologiarum sive originum libri XX*, ed. W. M. Lindsay (Oxford, 1911); Ker = N. R. Ker, *Catalogue of Manuscripts Containing Anglo-Saxon* (Oxford, 1957); Lapidge and Herren = M. Lapidge and M. Herren, *Aldhelm: the Prose Works* (Cambridge, 1979); Lapidge and Rosier = M. Lapidge and J. Rosier, *Aldhelm: the Poetic Works* (Cambridge, 1985); Napier = A. Napier, *Old English Glosses, Chiefly Unpublished* (Oxford, 1900). All citations of glosses derive from my edition.

[2] *Pdv* was arguably composed in the 670s. The details of Aldhelm's biography derive mainly from William of Malmesbury's *De gestis pontificum anglorum* (ed. N. E. S. A. Hamilton, RS 52 (London, 1870)) in which bk V (pp. 330–443) comprises the *Vita Aldhelmi*. For a full overview of Aldhelm's career – his birth, education, travel, ecclesiastical honours and death – see Lapidge and Herren, pp. 5–10 as well as Lapidge and Rosier, pp. 5–9.

[3] See, for example, the *Index locorum* (II. Loci classici et ecclesiastici) to Ehwald, pp. 544–6; Lapidge's Appendix III ('Check-List of Sources of Aldhelm's Exemplary Virgins', Lapidge and Herren, pp. 176–8); T. J. Brown, 'An Historical Introduction to the Use of Classical Latin Authors in the British Isles from the Fifth to the Eleventh Century', *SettSpol* 22 (1975), 237–93, and, most recently, A. Orchard, *The Poetic Art of Aldhelm* (Cambridge, 1994) and *idem*, 'After Aldhelm: the Teaching and Transmission of the Anglo-Latin Hexameter', *Jnl of Med. Latin* 2 (1992), 96–133.

[4] Cf. S. Gwara, 'The Continuance of Aldhelm Studies in Post-Conquest England and Glosses to the *Prosa de virginitate* in Hereford, Cath. Lib. MS P.I.17', *Scriptorium* 48 (1994), 18–38. On the hermeneutic idiom, cf. M. Lapidge, 'The Hermeneutic Style in Tenth-Century Anglo-Latin Literature', *ASE* 4 (1975), 67–111.

Even after a century of research, discovering the transmission of such a large corpus of interrelated glosses remains problematical. Yet the transmission is central to Aldhelm studies: isolating the dissemination of glosses to *Pdv* means tracing the path of the Aldhelm revival as well as the origin of the hermeneutic Latin renaissance.[5] In my view, untangling the knotty relationships between so many layers of *Pdv* glosses should be tackled manuscript by manuscript. Hence, I aim here to discuss certain gloss strata in three *Pdv* copies preserving the most bilingual glosses: Oxford, Bodleian Library, Digby 146, Brussels, Bibliothèque Royale, 1650 and London, British Library, Royal 6 B. VII. Old English glosses in Brussels 1650 were first printed in 1830.[6] Vernacular glosses in Digby 146 and Royal 6. B. VII have been in print since 1900, when Arthur Napier published a substantial edition of Old English *Pdv* scholia. But even though thousands of Latin glosses circulated side-by-side with the Old English ones and were often written by the same scribe, editors have ignored their relevance for more than 150 years. When the Latin glosses in these manuscripts are considered as part of the transmission history, a new relationship emerges between these key *Pdv* witnesses. This new relationship not only documents the pre-eminence of Digby 146 as a source of Aldhelm scholarship but also discloses the conservative preservation of glosses to *Pdv*.[7]

---

[5] Cf. S. Gwara, 'Manuscripts of Aldhelm's *Prosa de virginitate* and the Rise of Hermeneutic Literacy in Tenth-Century England', *SM*, 3rd ser. 35 (1994), 101–59.

[6] F. Mone, *Quellen und Forschungen zur Geschichte der teutschen Literatur und Sprache* I (Aachen, 1830) pp. 329–442.

[7] Hereafter I refer to manuscripts by sigla according to the following list. My sigla differ from Ehwald's (p. 225) in some respects. A denotes the Yale fragment to which Ehwald had given two sigla: frgt. Oxon.=Bodl. Lib. MS th. d. 24, fols. 1–2; P=Cambr. Add. 3330. In my apparatus P denotes the Hereford *Pdv* copy, rather than Harley 3013, to which Ehwald assigned no siglum. The London fragment has been incorrectly cited in a number of sources as Add. 50483K, but re-catalogued as of 1997.

R2 London, BL, Royal 7. D. XXIV, 82r–168r: text s. x^1, gll. s. x^2; ?Glastonbury, ?Canterbury
R4 London, BL, Royal 5. E. XI: text s. x/xi, gll. s. xi^{in}–xi^{med}; Christ Church, Canterbury
S   Salisbury, Cathedral Library, 38: text, gll. s. x^{ex}; Christ Church, Canterbury
C1 Cambridge, Corpus Christi College 326: text s. x^2, gll. s. x^2–xi^{in}; Christ Church, Canterbury
C2 Oxford, Bodleian Library, Bodley 97: text, gll. s. xi^{in}; Christ Church, Canterbury
A   Cambridge, University Library, Add. 3330+
    New Haven, Yale University, Beinecke Library 401, 401A+
    London, BL, Add. 71687+
    London, BL, Add. 50483J+
    Oxford, Bodleian, Arch. A. fol. 131
    Oxford, Bodleian, th. d. 24, fols. 1–2+
    Coll. Martin Schøyen MS 187 (*olim* Aachen, Dr Peter Ludwig's Library; Malibu, J. Paul Getty Museum Ludwig XI 5)+
    Philadelphia, Free Library, John Frederick Lewis Coll. ET 121: text s. ix^{in}, gll. s. x^2; ?Glastonbury, ?Canterbury
P   Hereford, Cathedral Library, P. I. 17: text, gll. s. xii/xiii; ?Abingdon, Cirencester
The dates, origins and provenances of these manuscripts are discussed in Gwara I, pp. xxxvii–clvi.

THREE GLOSSED MANUSCRIPTS OF *PDV*

Oxford, Bodleian Library, Digby 146 (S.C. 1747) (O)

The Digby volume contains *Pdv* (fols. 1–95), Aldhelm's *Epistola ad Heahfridum* (95v–100v), and a version of *c.* 1200 of King Edward's martyrdom (101v–104r).[8] As an example of Style II Anglo-Caroline, the Digby volume must have originated in late-tenth-century Canterbury.[9] Although produced at Canterbury, Digby 146 migrated to Abingdon during its history. An early-sixteenth-century inscription appears on 1r: 'Liber monast<er>ii Abendonie quem Iohannes Clyffe fecit ligari A° . . .'[10] The date is now illegible. The volume was in the possession of Thomas Allen in 1622, but Sir Kenelm Digby donated it to the Bodleian a decade later.[11]

In Ker's view, the Old English Digby glosses can be divided into three groups according to scribe.[12] Group (i)[13] consists of about thirty glosses contemporaneous or virtually contemporaneous with the text and written at the same time as the first stratum of Latin glosses (s. x^ex).[14] These few glosses have peculiar affinities with the early layers in many *Pdv* manuscripts, notably London, British Library, Royal 7. D. XXIV.[15] Ker's second group of glosses, Group (ii), comprises additions 'in a very neat and minute hand probably of s. xi in. only on fols. 8–15'.[16] Ker concluded that these glosses were added after the main group of Latin glosses

---

[8] C. E. Fell, *Edward King and Martyr* (Leeds, 1971), pp. xix–xx and 1–16; cf. D. Rollason, 'The Cults of Murdered Royal Saints in Anglo-Saxon England', *ASE* 11 (1983), 1–22, at 2. The sheets are ruled dry-point, ruled nineteen lines to the page. The collation is complex, and Quire III preserves an unusual cancellation: I²(blank)+II⁸(3, 5 canc.)+III¹⁰(4, 5 canc.)+IV⁸–XIII⁸+XIV⁸(8 canc.) [end of *Pdv*]+XV⁸ (1, 3, 5, 7 canc.)+XVI² (a bifolium, blank).

[9] Curved elements in **b, c, d, e, o, p** and **q** are rotund. Unlike some coeval Canterbury scripts, however, Caroline **a** has no exaggerated top-stroke, and its back slants at 45°. Letter **e** has a negligible compartment; **g** boasts a comparable compartment with a grand, sweeping *cauda*, resembling that in some scripts of St Augustine's. Although the Caroline element of the Digby script dominates letter-forms, abbreviations and ligatures, the scribe still tends to incorporate **æ** in Latin, predominantly in final position. On the generic conventions of Style II Anglo-Caroline, cf. D. Dumville, *English Caroline Script and Monastic History* (Woodbridge, 1993).

[10] According to Napier, John Clyffe or Clyve can be identified in Dugdale's *Monasticon Anglicanum* and Oxford University Register for 1510 (Napier, p. xiii). Ehwald mistranscribed the name as 'Clysse' (Ehwald, p. 219).

[11] A. Watson, 'Thomas Allen of Oxford and his Manuscripts', *Medieval Scribes, Manuscripts and Libraries: Essays presented to N. R. Ker*, ed. M. Parkes and A. Watson (London, 1978), pp. 279–314.   [12] Ker, no. 320.

[13] I refer to Ker's 'Groups (i), (ii) and (iii)' as the products of 'scribes (i), (ii) and (iii)' or written in 'hands (i), (ii) and (iii)'. The terms are meant to be equivalent.

[14] This hand is not identified in Napier's edition of the Old English glosses.

[15] Cf. my discussion in 'Manuscripts'. Glosses from the first seven layers of Royal 7. D. XXIV ('Early Strata') form part of the first layer in Digby 146 (Ker's hand (i) and Napier's 'second Latin hand'). The Digby text was in fact copied from an apograph of Royal 7. D. XXIV.

[16] Ker, p. 382. In fact, this hand continues on later folios, e.g. 16r5 (*herebecn*).

but before the primary group of Old English glosses in his Group (iii). Few glosses in Group (ii), Ker mentions, have parallels in the Brussels manuscript. A comparison of respective examples cited by Ker and Napier shows that this hand corresponds to Napier's 'Second Hand'.[17] The third group of glosses disclosed by Ker's examination are the more than 5000 annotations 'on fols. 8–95 in a small and neat, but uncalligraphic hand, probably of s. xi med., which tends to slope either up or down the page'.[18] This hand corresponds to Napier's 'Ordinary Hand'. All the Old English glosses are written in Insular characters, except for some in the first layer and two in a twelfth-century script; these have an admixture of Insular and Caroline letter-forms, the latter being **a**, **g**, **r** and **s**.

In his edition of 1974, Louis Goossens did not explore the palaeography of Digby 146, and neither he nor Ker expanded on Napier's brief discussion of the Latin glosses. Napier divided these into two main hands. The first, called by him the 'ordinary Latin hand', contributed the majority of interlinear and marginal Latin glosses. The ink is light brown, and strokes are executed with a narrow-cut pen. Letters **m**, **n** and **r** taper at the ends and sometimes even look sharp at their terminations.

Napier's 'second Latin hand' added vernacular glosses only infrequently. Napier did not realize that this hand is identical to Ker's scribe (i), who contributed the first layer of Old English glosses. This scribe writes a large pure Anglo-Caroline script in black ink. The Caroline letter-forms lack formal features, but the tails of **a** and **t** occasionally curve upward at word-ends. Additionally, the scribe has made wide use of **&** for 'et'. Two *punctus* set off the abbreviations for *id est* and *scilicet*. According to Napier, the 'second Latin hand' ends at the bottom of 68r, and the 'ordinary Latin hand' continues glossing thereafter. My own examination reveals that the 'second Latin hand' appears throughout the later portion of the volume *intermittently* after 68r. No reason attributable to the manuscript explains why the marginal glossing should suddenly diminish here, and the change might reflect a defective exemplar or scribal caprice.[19] Occasional Latin glosses, some with Insular letter-forms (such as **r**), were also penned by Ker's scribe (iii). Furthermore, Ker's scribe (ii) seems to have contributed a small layer of Latin glosses with an attenuated duct having tall, sharp ascenders and descenders. This expert Anglo-Caroline script still betrays Insular forms in **a** and **r**. Like Ker's scribe (ii), these glosses are later than the first

---

[17] Napier, p. xiii.

[18] Ker, p. 382. Napier draws attention (p. xiii) to 'some few English glosses [which] have also been written . . . here and there by various different hands'. Thus *wrangwise* (30v16) and *ealswage* (70v8) are twelfth-century additions.

[19] For example, the glossing ends after the catalogue of male virgins and part-way into the list of female virgins. A monk might have deemed this part of the book less valuable or pertinent to his intended audience.

The transmission of the 'Digby' glosses to Aldhelm's Prosa de virginitate

stratum of Latin glosses, but come before the Old English glosses in Ker's hand (iii).

Brussels, Bibliothèque Royale, 1650 (olim 1580) (B)

Four scholars in this century have scrutinized and described the Brussels *Pdv*: G. Van Langenhove, N. R. Ker, R. Derolez and L. Goossens.[20] My own remarks derive partly from the work of these scholars.

The Brussels Aldhelm is foliated i+56+i, collated I⁸–VII⁸; it measures 28 × 44 cm, with a written space of 22.5 × 15 cm. Ruled in dry-point with twenty-two long lines per page, the manuscript was penned by a single scribe of s. xi[1] in a hand closely resembling the Style IV Anglo-Caroline from Canterbury in the second quarter of the eleventh century.[21] The letter forms **b, c, d, e, g, o, p, q** are rotund. Upper and lower members of **g** are proportional and sometimes connected by a small stem; **e** has a narrow upper compartment, unlike **a**, which is well-formed with a large upper member. Common ligatures are **rt, st** and **r+cc** form of **a**; & is used freely, even with *caudae* representing 'aet' or **e**- caudata plus **t**. Chapter-headings are written in uncial, and syntactic glossing, probably in the main scribal hand, appears consistently.

Four principal and contemporaneous glossing hands of s. xi[1] appear in Brussels 1650.[22] Ker's hand (1), a 'pointed, sloping' hand writing either in brown

---

[20] Respectively, *Aldhelm's De Laudibus Virginitatis with Latin and Old English Glosses: Manuscript 1650 of the Royal Library in Brussels* (Bruges, 1941); Ker, no. 8; 'De oudengelse Aldhelmglossen in HS. 1650 van de koninklijke Bibliotheek te Brussel', *Handelingen IX der Zuidnederlandse Maatschappij voor Taal- en Letterkunde en Geschiednis* 1955, 37–50; Goossens, pp. 5–8, 28–32, 37–52.

[21] The volume once belonged to a single codex of 242 folios comprising three items, but now broken up into four fragments. In addition to the Brussels portion there is: (a) Antwerp, Plantin-Moretus Museum MS 47 (Salle iii.68) + (b) London, British Library, Add. 32246 [Ker 2]; (c) Antwerp, Plantin-Moretus Museum MS 190 (Salle iii.55) [Ker 3]. The flyleaves of these manuscripts contain additions of s. xi[1], which Ker used to localize the composite codex to Abingdon. Ker relied most heavily on forty-nine elegiac couplets by an unknown Herbert (of Fleury?) to Wulfgar, identified as abbot of Abingdon 989–1016 (ptd. E. Dümmler, 'Lateinische Gedichte des neunten bis elften Jahrhunderts', *Neues Archiv* 10 (1884), 351–3). Ker insisted that '[s]cholia to the *Excerptiones*, two supply-leaves ... the verses [to Wulfgar] and [two] glossaries ... are in a pointed, slightly forward-sloping hand which occurs also in [Brussels] 1650' (Ker, p. 3). In other words, the earliest stratum of glosses in Brussels 1650 was written in the same hand as the verses to Wulfgar. Speculating that the elegiac verses were addressed to Wulfgar of Abingdon and further theorizing that the eleventh-century provenance of this manuscript was Abingdon, Ker could reach only one conclusion concerning the Brussels glosses: unless the scribe travelled from elsewhere, all of them must have been added at Abingdon. Unfortunately, Ker's reasoning not only contradicts the palaeographical record (cf. Dumville, *English Caroline*, pp. 102, 136 and 154) but also makes no sense in the textual history of *Pdv* manuscripts which I present here.

[22] Goossens discusses the palaeography in his volume (pp. 45–52), and I have not recorded all of his observations here. Hands A, B, C, CD and R appear in chronological order, except for A and B. Scribes A and B never gloss the same words, so their relative chronology cannot be gauged by this formal method. Ker describes these hands in his *Catalogue* entry.

(earlier) or black (later) ink, corresponds to Goossens's Hand A. This scribe may have preceded or followed another represented by Ker's hand (2), which Goossens calls Hand B. Ker describes this contribution as 'a small upright hand which occurs only about fols. 34–45'. There are few glosses in this hand. Goossens cautiously suggests that scribe (2) may have collaborated with scribe (1), but acknowledges that there is no evidence for the assumption except the divisions of their respective contributions in the Brussels volume.[23] (The work of scribe A comes first.) Ker's hand (3) corresponds to Goossens's Hand C. In Ker's words, it is 'a spreading, slightly sloping hand, using rich brown ink, later than hand (1), but generally like it . . .' This glossator has taken lemmas from the text and glossed them in the outer margins,[24] as if he were preparing *glossae collectae* for a glossary.

There are at least two different strata of glosses in Ker's hand (3), as distinguished by distinct shades of ink. Goossens first noted the variance. He described the first layer as dark brown to black, contributing the interlinear Old English glosses; the second layer, in a somewhat smaller format and in light brown ink, comprises the marginal glosses and most of the interlinear Latin ones.[25]

Ker's hand (4), called CD in Goossens's edition, is at times difficult to distinguish from hand (3). In Ker's terms, it is a 'clumsy, square hand, using generally brown ink of poor quality'. Ker notes, too, that some glosses by this scribe are written in red ink, and Goossens describes these as the 'last layer of the glossing'.[26] CD wrote almost no Latin glosses. Goossens paid careful attention to this hand, in which he was able to perceive the work of at least two and maybe more scribes. His appellation CD is therefore intended to be a catch-all for various glossing contributions as distinct from those made by A and B – Ker's hands (1) and (2).

London, British Library, Royal 6. B. VII (R5)

This Royal manuscript[27] preserves approximately 500 Old English glosses as well as thousands of Latin ones, almost all of which were written in the same semi-rotund Exeter hand as the text. The duct of the main hand in Royal 6. B. VII is relatively wide, with almost all circular elements in the letters **b, c, d, g, o, p, q** perfectly round. On occasion the scribe clips the left-hand curve of these letters, giving a 'left-leaning' aspect. Characteristic of this main hand is a 'left-leaning' Caroline **a** with open upper member and correspondingly compressed

---

[23] Goossens, p. 51. Goossens assumes that the scribes copied an exemplar.
[24] Cf. R. Derolez, 'Zu den Brüsseler Aldhelmglossen', *Anglia* 74 (1957), 153–80.
[25] Goossens, p. 48.   [26] Ker, p. 7; Goossens, p. 50.
[27] Cf. G. Warner and J. Gilson, *Catalogue of Western Manuscripts in the Old Royal and King's Collections* (London, 1921), p. 136.

lower member, rotund **e** with tiny upper compartment and angular cross-stroke, negligible serifs on **m** and **n**. Abbreviations and *nomina sacra* are infrequent, although regular in form.[28] The script is purely calligraphic, a minuscule of the late eleventh century with distinct pen-lifts and highly mannered features (in particular **st** and **rt** ligatures, **&**, and **e**-caudata). Although the elegant script, overall accuracy of text and care of execution imply that Royal 6. B. VII was a *de luxe* copy of *Pdv*, misplaced and erroneous glosses belie its superior production.

The identical script recurs in a gloss hand of Cambridge, Trinity College 315 (fols. 26–7, 36v12–39v1, from St Mary's Leicester) and in the main hand of Cambridge, Trinity College 1475 (a holograph).[29] Generically resembling the style of more or less coeval Exeter manuscripts (such as London, BL, Cotton Cleopatra B. xiii or Cambridge, Corpus Christi College 191), the main Royal hand is nevertheless asymptomatic of the Leofrician script developed at the Exeter scriptorium. According to Elaine Drage, who catalogued all eleventh-century Exeter books in her monumental Oxford thesis, 'the nucleus of [Royal 6. B. VII] was probably written at Exeter towards the end of the eleventh century, since . . . it is both more decorated than is usual for the bulk of "Exeter" manuscripts and the illuminated initials show affinities with those in books imported from Normandy to Exeter, probably by Bishop Osbern (1072–1103)'.[30] The main hand of Royal 6. B. VII therefore represents the second generation of the Exeter house style.

Royal 6. B. VII has been ruled in dry-point with twenty-five long lines per page and collated by Drage *before* rebinding in 1983: (fols. i+1–53+i+54–55+i), I[8]–VI[8], VII[6] (fols. 49–53+i), VIII[3] (fols. 54, 55+i). The collation presently reads: iii+I[2]+II[6]+III[1](a singleton)+IV[8]–VIII[8]+IX[1](a singleton)+ X[4](now all singletons)+XI[1](a singleton)+XII[2] (a bifolium)+iii. Now re-bound with individual quires sewn to paper guards, the book measures 30 × 20 cm, with a written area of 22 × 15 cm. Because the lines are so widely spaced and the glosses so carefully positioned, the manuscript appears

---

[28] These features are, of course, characteristic of the script developed by the Canterbury scribe Eadwig Basan and practised at Christ Church from the second quarter of the eleventh century onwards. Eadwig's script appears in the Hanover Gospel Book (Hanover, Kestner-Museum, W. M. XXIa, 36) and in London, BL, Cotton Vespasian A. i, pt ii. By *c.* 1040 this Canterbury model was imitated in major scriptoria across southern England and formed the basis for the Exeter script of Leofric's scriptorium. Even so, there are appreciable differences between the Exeter script and Eadwig's experimentations: Canterbury books often have a Canonical Capital display script, compressed lower member on **a**, and the tendency, apparent early at Tours, to link the upper fillips of letters across the bounding line.

[29] T. A. M. Bishop, 'Notes on Cambridge Manuscripts, Part III: MSS. Connected with Exeter', *Trans. of the Cambridge Bibliographical Soc.* 2 (1954–8), 192–9, at 198–9.

[30] E. Drage, 'Bishop Leofric and the Exeter Cathedral Chapter 1050–1072: a Reassessment of the Manuscript Evidence' (unpubl. D.Phil. dissertation, Oxford Univ., 1978), p. 372.

to have been ruled for glossing.[31] The volume was not catalogued in the Exeter inventory of 1327, and its later history is virtually unknown.[32]

THE SO-CALLED 'DIGBY' (OR 'ABINGDON') FAMILY OF VERNACULAR *PDV* GLOSSES[33]

In the course of editing some 7,000 Old English glosses to *Pdv* for his compendium, Arthur Napier observed that hundreds of identical glosses appear in more than one manuscript. To account for the relationship between these glosses, Napier prefaced his edition with a theory of the gloss transmission. In a brief digression he reasoned that the vernacular glosses in seven manuscripts belong to two families, the 'Digby group' and the 'Salisbury group'.[34] To the 'Digby group' Napier assigned Brussels 1650, Digby 146, Royal 6. B. VII and Hereford, Cathedral Library P. I.17. Old English glosses in these books, he concluded, 'are closely related and ultimately come from one original'.[35] In fact, Napier viewed the Old English glosses in Digby 146 as an apograph copy of those in a lost exemplar which he designated 'Y'.[36] In his opinion, the Old English glosses in Brussels 1650 also derive from this exemplar.[37] Napier alleged that glosses in the third manuscript of his 'Digby' family, Royal 6. B. VII, stem from a hyparchetype of 'Y', or, in his terms, 'X'.[38] This hyparchetype was 'presumably free from the Kenticisms characteristic of [Digby 146] and [Brussels 1650]'.[39] Finally, Napier concluded that glosses in Hereford P. I.17 descended from those in Digby 146.[40]

Working from the advantage of shared error in his opening remarks on the Digby glosses, Napier established that both Brussels and Digby have identical errors in a number of glosses. Eleven examples are cited, but I omit two as mistaken.[41] Forms in parentheses represent corrections which Napier supplied:

---

[31] The spacing may be coincidental, however, insofar as many Exeter manuscripts have widely separated lines, a characteristic of Eadwig Basan's innovative script; cf. Cambridge, Corpus Christi College 191 (Exeter, s. x$^{3/4}$).   [32] Drage, 'Bishop Leofric', p. 372.

[33] For the Brussels manuscript, Louis Goossens has discerned a number of hands which he terms 'A', 'B', 'C', 'CD' and 'R'. I adopt Goossens's inventory, which is represented in my edition by superscript lower-case letters. Thus, B^c denotes scribe C in the Brussels manuscript. The reference numbers in each gloss citation refer to the number of the lemma in my edition: 13934, the final lemma glossed in any annotated copy of *Pdv*, indicates the sequential number of that lemma in the list of lemmata. Reference numbers followed by a lower-case letter are simply additions to the corpus, either discovered after the edition was complete or simply corrected.

[34] The term 'group' went undefined in Napier's book. It seems to mean any manuscripts having a majority of their Old English glosses in common with one another. The evidence of shared error figures only in Napier's 'Salisbury group'.   [35] Napier, p. xxiii.   [36] *Ibid.* p. xxiv.

[37] *Ibid.* pp. xxiv–xxv.   [38] *Ibid.* p. xxiv.   [39] *Ibid.* p. xxv.   [40] *Ibid.*

[41] Glosses 4369 and 8975. Napier found most of these errors by collating Old English glosses in Royal 6. B. VII.

4637 SPIRITVS] *orþas* B^{cd} O (*orþes*, gen. sg.)

5839 INEXPERTO] *oncuþum* B^{cd} O (*uncuþum*)

7806 CVNICVLI] *crepeles* B^{cd}: *crypeles* O (*crypelas*, nom. pl.)

7959 NITEBANTVR] *hi higde* B^{c} O (*higdon*, pl.)

8696 DOLIVM] *cype* B^{c} O (*cyfe*)

10675 FACVLAS] *sandbærde brynas* B^{cd}: *sandbærnde brynas* O (*sambærnde*)

11787 THERMARVM] *baþana* B^{c}: *baþena* O (*baþa*)

11827 RIPARVM] *stæþ/<e>na* $B^{a,cd}$: *stæþena* O (*staþa*)[42]

13351 ASSENTATRIX] *gehwæriende* B^{c} O (*geþwæriende*)

On balance, only a handful of these glosses represent common errors which can be weighed as evidence of dissemination.[43] Yet Napier concluded from these few correspondences that the Old English glosses in Brussels and Digby are 'very closely related'.[44]

The Old English glosses in Brussels and Digby were found to be linked, but Napier claimed that the Digby glosses could not have been the source of the Brussels corpus. In the first instance, he noted that Brussels often has 'better' readings than those in Digby, a circumstance which suggested to Napier that the Digby glosses could not have engendered the Brussels corpus.[45] Napier gives thirty-one examples of this point, two of which are inaccurate. The remaining twenty-nine are cited below:

974 CARMINE] *tælsumum leoþe* B^{a}: *on gelsumum le'o'ðe* O

1405 IN COMPARATIONE] *on wiþmetenysse* B^{cd}: *unwiðmetenesse* O

1653 AMBRONIBVS] *gifrum* B^{a}: *grifrum* O

1781 AEMVLORVM] *wiþerwinnena* B^{cd}: *wiþerwinna* O

2068 TRIBVNATVM] *ealdordom* B^{cd}: *ealdordomum* O

2134 EPITAPHION] *byriensang, 7 bergelsleoð* B^{c}: *ł sang* B^{cd}: *byriensang, leoþsang* O

2627 DEBITO] *neadwisum ł neadþearflicum* B^{cd}: *neadwisum, <n>eadþearflicum* O[46]

2705 CLAVSTRA] *fæstenu* B^{cd}: *fæstenum* O

3395 LAPSVM] *forwyrd ł sllide* B^{cd}: *forwyrd, sliden* O

4692 DOCVMENTVM] *healic lar* B^{cd}: *healic lac* O

4978 VELAMENTO] *under wæfelse* B^{cd}: *under wæfesse* O

---

[42] Altered from *stæþa* B^{a}.

[43] Some of Napier's putative errors, in particular the grammatical ones, do not illuminate the transmission. In 4637 the lemma SPIRITVS must be genitive singular (cf. Ehwald 258.4), although both Old English glosses are nominative or accusative plural. Similarly, the lemma CVNICVLI (7806) must be nominative (Ehwald 279.25), but it has been glossed as if it were genitive. These semantic errors might have originated with the earliest *Pdv* glossator, and they are not incontestably spurious. Gloss 7959 is likewise an ambiguous indicator of dissemination, for unparallel *higde* might have arisen in a manuscript reading NITEBATVR. *Higde* only appears as an error because of Digby's plural verb. More valuable are 11787 and 11827, although *baþana* for *baþa* and 11827 *stæþena* for *staþa* could arguably represent morphological changes from strong to weak nouns. Such errors are not necessarily deviations, if morphological. [44] Napier, p. xxiv. [45] *Ibid.* [46] *eadþearflicum* **O**.

5359 RECIPROCIS] *edlæcendum* B^{cd}: *edlædendum* O

6546 PLANTA TENVS] *oþ þa fotwelmes* B^{cd}: *oþ þa formylmas* O

7014 FVRIBVNDVS] *se gehatheort* B^{cd}: *gehathord* O

7423 BOMBICINIS] *sylcenum, sidenum* B^a: *godwebbenum* B^{cd}: *godewebbum, sidenum* O

7524 CAPTIOSIS] *7 hedendlicum, of hæftlicon* B^a: *of hæftlicon, hydenlicum* O

7548 PALMAM] *sigelean ł edlean* B^{cd}: *sigelean, edlead* O

7642 SVRAS] *spærliran* B^c: *sprerliran* O

8285 AGGLOMERANTVR] *wæran gegædrede* B^{cd}: *wæron gegærode* O

8731 NVDITAS] *scamfæst necednys* B^{cd}: *sceamfestnys* O

8973 INTEMPESTE] *smeltre* B^{cd}: *swyltre* O

9239 MASSAS] *clyna* B^c: *clyne* B^{cd}: *cnynas, clot* O

9488 LAVDABILI] *of lofflicere* B^{cd}: *of leoflicere* O

10749 FONTIBVS] *wilspringum* B^{cd}: *wylsrin* O

10756 HORRISONO] *egeslicum* B^c: *egeslico* O

10870 RADERETVR] *of ascoren* B^c: *on ascoren* O

12300 DECLINAVIT] *he forbeah* B^{cd}: *he forbead* O

12871 LENOCINIA] *forspen* B^{cd}: *sporspen* O

13262 TALOTENVS] *þa ancleo<w>* B^c: *oþ þa ancneow* O⁴⁷

Unfortunately, Napier compromised his position at the start by failing to infer the textual transmission from shared error. Most of the 'errors' he identified involve the omission or misreading of one or two letters (e.g. 974, 1653, 2627, 2705, 4692, 4978, 5359, 7548, 7642, 8285, 8973, 9239, 10870, 12300 and 13262), and such examples hardly constitute the kind of solid evidence which editors rely on to group textual witnesses. For example, gloss 2705 has no editorial value. Any scribe writing *fæstenum* could have omitted the nasal suspension when he saw that the lemma called for a neuter plural noun. A copyist could likewise have added the abbreviation to *fæstenum* out of carelessness. Sound changes, too, could account for 4978 (ls>ss) and 7524 (ndl>nl), just as morphological slips might explain 1781 and 2068. Ultimately, Napier ought to have questioned his rigid adherence to 'correct' spellings of Old English as evidence of dissemination. Almost all of the examples he provided to illustrate his position are equivocal.

In the same vein, Napier supplied ambiguous citations to illustrate a second, equally indefensible, position. Napier contended that 'the still more numerous cases in which [Digby 146] has a better reading than [Brussels 1650] shows that the latter is not the original of [Digby 146]'.⁴⁸ He lists twenty examples and states that they are 'almost unnecessary' to prove his point:⁴⁹

---

⁴⁷ *w* altered from *f* B^c.   ⁴⁸ Napier, p. xxiv.

⁴⁹ Because he relied on Bouterwek's edition of the Brussels glosses (C. Bouterwek, 'Angelsächsische Glossen (1): die ags. Glossen in dem Brüsseler Codex von Aldhelms Schrift De Virginitate', *Zeitschrift für deutsches Alterthum* 9 (1853), 401–530), Napier's examples corresponding to 3014 and 4065 are no longer valid. Gloss 1169 has been shifted from the section dealing with better readings in B against those in O; it is erroneously included there.

253 PRORETA] *plichtere ł ancremen* B^{cd}: *plihtere, ancremen* O
368 ROSCIDO] *dæaweinlicre* B^{cd}: *deawigre* O
468 AMOENA] *þa mergen* B^{cd}: *þa mæran* O
689 DISCVRSIBVS] *mid f'l'ugulum færeldum* B^{cd}: *mid flugelum færeldum* O
703 VICE] *fram < ?> gewrisce* B^{cd}: *gewrixle* O
1169 BOMBICINVM] *siden ł seolcel* B^{cd}: *seolcen, sinden* O
2015 POSTERITATIS] *towurdre æftergencnyssum* B^{cd}: *towurdre æftergencnesse* O
2324 ARDORIS] *feortwitnysse* B^{cd}: *fyrewitnesse* O
2476 INFECVNDA] *uneacniendli[endri]ce* B^{cd}: *uneacniendlicere* O
2499 VLTRO CITROQVE] *hider 7 þrideres* B^{cd}: *hider 7 þyderes* O
2969 MORIBVNDAE] *swlentendes* B^{cd}: *swyltendes* O
3044 SVGGESTIONIS] *tinctincge* B^{cd}: *tyhtinge* O
3244 LIBERORVM] *erferda* B^{cd}: *yrfwerda* O
3289 VERBOSITAS] *malelung* B^c: *maþelung* O
3833 MORARVM] *lentincga, lentincga* B^{cd}: *lettincga* O
3847 FVNDITVS] *grundulga* B^c: *grundlunga* O
7505 THALAMI] *bedbures* B^{cd}: *brydbures* O
7627 STRICTVRAE] *bidingce* B^{cd}: *bindingce* O

Some of Napier's glosses simply exhibit orthographical variance: 253 (*plichtere/plihtere*), 689 (*f'l'ugulum/flugelum*), 3244 (*erferda/yrfwerda*). Furthermore, both glosses to 7505 are legitimate nominal compounds, and neither can claim precedence. In cataloguing the preceding variants, then, Napier did not consider that a spelling – or word – in either manuscript could be due to scribal corruption or correction. For some glosses Brussels preserves a better reading. That fact might mean that the Digby copyist was sometimes careless, accidentally adding a nasal suspension (2705) or miscopying an *r* (4692). More often, the Digby manuscript gives a better reading, arguably implying that the Digby scribe was correcting mistakes he came upon in the exemplar. In this respect, would it be hard for a native speaker of Old English to perceive the proper words in such corruptions as *gewrisce* (*gewrixl* 703), *seolcel* (*seolcen* 1169), *feortwitnysse* (*fyrewitnysse* 2324), and *uneacniendliendrice* (*uneacniendlice* 2476)?[50] Ker and Goossens showed how the process of correction and corruption worked when they examined certain errors arising in Digby 146.

Given that they were based on so brief an analysis, Napier's generalizations were unjustifiable. The simple fact that the Digby glosses were written primarily in a single hand and the Brussels glosses in five hands or more should have prompted Napier to review his argument. He relied, however, on Bouterwek's edition of 1853 of the Brussels glosses, which does not discuss the palaeography of the manuscript. Hence, Napier confidently reckoned that the Old English glosses in both Brussels and Digby descend from the same source,

[50] Similarly in 2499, 2969, 3847 and 7627.

which he later called 'Y'. The fanciful transmission that Napier alleged for the compilation of this 'Y' archetype (p. xxv) reflects his biased evidence.

Ultimately, Napier's investigation boasts a more pernicious shortcoming than its fruitless comparisons: his classification rests solely on the *Old English* glosses preserved in the *Pdv* manuscripts familiar to him. Thousands of Latin glosses were neglected, presumably because Napier could not find any common link between the Old English and Latin contributions in the manuscripts he studied. The Latin glosses, it turns out, are essential to understanding the gloss transmission and cannot be overlooked.

Louis Goossens legitimized Napier's methodology in 1974, although he made significant modifications to Napier's fictitious stemma. In particular, he dismantled Napier's transmission of the 'Digby' family and even rejected the term 'Digby group'. Goossens preferred 'Abingdon group', and his reasons stem from the transmission which he proposed. For example, Goossens refined Ker's proposal that the Old English glosses in Digby 146 were copied directly from Brussels 1650.[51] Napier's hypothetical 'X' and 'Y' archetypes were illusory, Goossens implied, and the phrase 'Digby group' a misnomer.[52] Nowadays, one gloss family is incongruously named after a manuscript, the other after a conjectural provenance.

Goossens had considerably more to say than Napier about Royal 6. B. VII. He argued that glosses in Royal 6. B. VII descended directly from Brussels 1650, rather than from Napier's lost manuscript 'X'.[53] He has reaffirmed this claim in a recent article.[54] Yet Goossens's ingenious hypothesis fails to account for all the Old English Royal glosses, as well as for thousands of Latin ones. For this reason alone, his theory invites criticism.[55]

Unfortunately, Napier's and Goossens's classifications inadequately describe the relationship of Old English and Latin glosses in *Pdv* manuscripts. Neither scholar credits the value of Latin glosses, which bear significantly on the dissemination. Goossens alone discusses the various scribal hands, which record the growth of the gloss corpus, but he does so for one manuscript only. In the following pages, then, I offer a reassessment of the dissemination of this

---

[51] See below, p. 151.

[52] 'Napier's "Digby group" may suggest that [Digby 146] is the central member of the group, which is not the case. "Abingdon group" is a better term because both [Brussels 1650] and [Digby 146] are Abingdon MSS., whereas [Royal 6. B. VII] and [Hereford P. I.17] are closely connected with them' (p. 22).   [53] *Ibid.* pp. 23–5.

[54] 'Latin and Old English Aldhelm Glosses: a Direct Link in the "Abingdon Group" ', *Anglo-Saxon Glossography*, ed. R. Derolez (Brussels, 1992), pp. 141–9.

[55] *Ibid.* p. 27. Goossens had earlier qualified his own prodigious efforts: 'In nearly all cases it will be impossible to establish direct relationships among the Old English glosses: it is good to remember in this respect that for each [manuscript] which has come down to us several others must have been lost in the course of time' (p. 21).

important corpus of glosses. In my discussion, I refer periodically to the 'Digby' or 'Abingdon' groups. By retaining the nomenclature, I try to show where Napier's and Goossens's categories remain viable. For all intents and purposes, however, the distinctions are both impressionistic and casual.

THE RELATIONSHIP OF OLD ENGLISH GLOSSES IN BRUSSELS HAND CD TO GLOSSES IN THE 'ORDINARY HAND' OF DIGBY 146

Any serious study of the 'Digby' glosses to *Pdv* must begin with the Brussels (B) and Digby (O) manuscripts. The codices contain, by far, the largest number of Old English Aldhelm glosses, and they are surpassed only by Royal 7. D. XXIV in the number of Latin ones. The relationship of Old English glosses in B and O is complex, but Ker and Goossens left a roadmap to the transmission of certain gloss strata. Their analyses suggest persuasively that the bulk of Old English glosses in Digby 146 was copied directly from Brussels 1650.

Writing in 1955 René Derolez pointed out that the Old English Digby glosses represent a copy of those in Brussels 1650,[56] and Ker advanced Derolez's position, apparently independently, two years later:

... there does not seem to be any serious objection to the theory which Napier rejected, that the Digby glosses were copied from [Brussels 1650], if we may assume that the copyist tried to correct mistakes in his exemplar and to alter some of the dialectal forms. Some of the forms can best be explained as errors in copying from [Brussels 1650], e.g. in gl. 26 'torhtte' [=245], the spelling *tt* may be due to the alteration in [Brussels 1650] of 'torhta[.]' (originally 'torhtas'?) to 'torhtæ', the second t and flat-topped æ following it resembling *tte*. The reading 'horrescunt' in [Brussels 1650][57] has given rise to the gloss 'andþrac[h]iaþ' in both manuscripts (gl. 3185) [=7476], although Digby has correctly 'herescunt'.[58]

Goossens accepted Ker's reasoning. He suggested that the systematic method of copying confirms that Brussels 1650 was the direct source for most of the Old English glosses in Digby 146. In fact, almost every Old English gloss in Brussels is accounted for in Digby. Even Goossens's 'exceptions' support his hypothesis, for he mistakenly assumed that 'there is no counterpart in O for B 1–78, 80–86, 88–96 and 98'.[59] These glosses have been *erased* in O. Few glosses were therefore omitted from the corpus, in Goossens's words, 'only the duplications, some of the marginal gll. by hand 3 in B, and the last OE gl. in B, which is no gl. to the text'.[60] This kind of manuscript collation, arguably intended to bring both manuscripts into conformity, is reflected in other glossed *Pdv* copies.

Following Ker's approach, Goossens identified five other erroneous glosses in Digby 146 which can be traced to a misreading of Brussels entries:

---

[56] Cf. 'De oudengelse Aldhelmglossen'.   [57] Only B has this variant.   [58] Ker, pp. 382–3.
[59] Goossens, p. 26.   [60] *Ibid.*

1851 BELLICOSAS] *wiglic/'h'ear<d>lice* B^{c,cd}: *wihearde* O

The gloss was altered from *wiglice*; 'h' and 'ardlice' were added by CD, and 'd' was altered from 'l'. This badly executed correction gives rise to *wihearde* in O, whereas two glosses in B were intended: *wiglice* and *heardlice*.

2134 EPITAPHION] *byriensang, 7 bergelsleoð* B^c: *1 sang* B^{cd}: *byriensang, leoþsang* O

In the Brussels manuscript the gloss *licleoð* is emended to *licsang*, with 'sang' written above 'ð' in *licleoð*. This has produced the erroneous *leoþsang* in O.

2053 TEXTRINVM] *web/lic gewurc* B^{a,cd}: *weblic, geweorclic* O

In B *gewurc* is written above *weblic* and engenders the nonce-word *geweorclic* in O.

2535 BIS TINCTO] *twyhiw<um>* B^c: *twyhiwædum* O

The gloss in B has been corrected from *twyhiwe* by erasure and substitution of 'u' with nasal suspension. In Goossens's view, confusion accounts for the gloss *twyhiwædum* in O.

3625 PROCVMBERE] *h'n'ipte* B^{cd}: *hnimpte* O

Goossens explains that the Brussels gloss is situated just below the lemma COR-RVERET, 'in which the first *r* is 2-shaped and consequently has a horizontal bottom stroke looking like a long mark of abbreviation over *h'n'ipte*'.[61]

This additional evidence strongly supports the argument that Digby was collated against Brussels. Obviously, there may have been an intermediary exemplar, but none is demonstrable through an examination of the glosses. I therefore concur with Ker and Goossens: the meticulous method of transcription suggests that the Old English glosses were copied *directly* from Brussels into Digby.

The Brussels CD glosses form a vast corpus attesting to the intensive study of *Pdv*. As a corpus, however, the glosses have few parallels, apart from scratched glosses preserved in three manuscripts with connections to Canterbury. Until these scratched glosses are fully edited and profitably compared to those in the Brussels corpus, neither the origin nor the dissemination of the 5,500 Old English glosses in Brussels 1650 will be known. Simply speaking, no substantial comparable *Pdv* glosses exist prior to the date of the CD scribe. Hence, the CD corpus, ostensibly copied from an exemplar, has no extant source.

THE RELATIONSHIP OF GLOSSES IN BRUSSELS HAND C (FIRST
STRATUM) AND ROYAL 6. B. VII (MAIN STRATUM)

The Old English and Latin glosses written by the five identifiable Brussels scribes and by the 'Ordinary Hand' of Digby 146 represent a significant portion of glosses in these manuscripts. Thus far, however, only the 'Ordinary Hand' glosses in Digby and the CD glosses in Brussels can be accounted for in

---

[61] *Ibid.*

terms of their textual history. Glosses in the Digby 'Ordinary Hand' derive from Brussels, but what is the source of the Brussels hands other than those by CD? For the present, I shall set aside glosses in HANDS A and B, and examine the glosses in HAND C. These, we may recall, are in two separate layers. The first layer comprises interlinear Old English and Latin glosses. The second layer comprises marginal glosses in Latin (mainly on 8r and 9v–11r)[62] and the series of *glossae collectae* which turn up in the margins from 19r–53v. These different layers imply that the glosses in HAND C may have had two discrete sources, and the evidence of collation suggests the same. Before setting out this evidence, however, my position can helpfully be formulated in advance.

First, apart from the *glossae collectae*, the marginal scholia in the second layer of Brussels scribe C appear to derive from a source from which the Digby marginalia also descend. A collation of the common glosses implies this relationship without making it certain. Secondly, the interlinear glosses in the first stratum of HAND C must have come from Digby 146, for HAND C of Brussels 1650 incorporates errors which can be traced unequivocally to the Digby manuscript. Some of these same errors, as well as comparable ones, appear in Royal 6. B. VII. The nature of the errors common to Brussels HAND C (first layer) and Royal 6. B. VII (main glossing hand) proves that an antecedent manuscript was the source for both of them.

In his book Goossens surmised that 'with comparatively few exceptions, the gll. of [Royal 6. B. VII] were copied from those in [Brussels 1650] at a stage when the glossing there had not yet been completed'.[63] He repeats this very hypothesis with the same wording in his article of 1992. From the outset, however, the hypothesis is unfeasible, since *all* the Brussels glosses had been added by s. xi[med], and the Royal manuscript postdates these accretions.[64] To salvage Goossens's argument, one would have to postulate an intermediary exemplar which was copied from Brussels at the stage Goossens alleges and which came into possession of the Exeter community in time for the Royal copy to be made. Because establishing an intermediary superficially appears to resolve several problems, let us assume that such an intermediary existed and proceed to Goossens's evidence.

---

[62] Goossens (p. 48) claimed that these do not pertain to the text. In fact, the lemmas to these legitimate glosses appear throughout. [63] Goossens, p. 23.

[64] Goossens nowhere cites Drage's work, and the dates of the gloss-hands in the manuscripts (cf. Goossens, p. 17) rest on outdated descriptions. Moreover, his argument calls for justification on grounds of provenance. If glosses from Brussels 1650 were copied into Royal 6. B. VII, either Brussels 1650 must have been at Exeter or the Royal scribe must have travelled to the foundation housing the Brussels volume, either Canterbury or Abingdon. Neither hypothesis can be verified from known evidence.

Goossens made a series of arguments in favour of his thesis that the glosses in R5 descend directly from those in B.[65] Primarily, he asserted that 489 Old English glosses in R5 – a substantial majority – agree with those in B. 356 of these glosses occur in HAND C, about 109 in HAND A and 24 in HAND B.[66] By contrast, only twenty-nine CD glosses appear in R5,[67] and none in HAND R (in red ink).[68] How, Goossens asked, could a corpus of glosses represented by three hands in one manuscript appear as one hand in another volume, if the glosses in the later manuscript were not copied from the earlier? Goossens had concluded in his edition, 'if the glossator of R5 did not copy from B, he must have drawn his material from the same sources (or sources very similar to) those of the first, second and third hands in B, which is not very likely'.[69]

Goossens subsequently broadened his base of evidence and further refined his analysis. He maintained that there are even greater correspondences between the Latin glosses in R5 than between the Old English glosses: 'Our strongest argument comes from the Latin glosses in MS. R5. They agree for about 95% with glosses in MS. B and with few exceptions are identical with them.'[70] Having made this statement, Goossens recognizes a problem: as many as forty-four Old English glosses in Royal 6. B. VII are not present in Brussels.[71] Goossens endeavours to dismiss these glosses, but nine of them can only be explained as having arisen from another source.[72] Goossens would have been rewarded by examining the Latin glosses at this stage of his argument. Dozens of them, too, are not in B:[73]

1141 DEFORMATVR] i. non deformatur R5: i. non deturpatur O
1252 PVTANTVR] i. estimamus uel putamur R5: i. estimamus O
1353 CVM CONSTET] i. certum est R5: i. testum est O
1615 DINOSCITVR] s. illa superbia, arrogantia R5: s. illa superbia O
1951 RECESSIBVS] i. occultationibus, i. uisceribus R5: i. uisceribus O
2160 APOSTOLICAE] i. episcopalis R5
2409 PLENE] i. omnino, aduerbialiter R5: i. omnino O
2944 FACTIOSAM] i. fraudulentiam R5: i. falsam O

---

[65] Goossens, pp. 23–4; *idem*, 'Aldhelm Glosses', p. 142.
[66] Goossens, 'Aldhelm Glosses', p. 142.   [67] *Ibid.* p. 143.   [68] *Ibid.* p. 144.   [69] *Ibid.* p. 23.
[70] Cf. Goossens, p. 24: 'The agreement between [Royal 6. B. VII] and [Brussels 1650] is much greater here than for the Old English glosses, especially as regards the number of gll. that were taken over. On folio 5R e.g., the glossator of Royal 6. B. VII took over only one OE gl. against 70 Latin gll., on folio 6R no less than 87 Latin gll., but not a single OE gl.'; cf. Goossens, 'Aldhelm Glosses', p. 142.   [71] Goossens, 'Aldhelm Glosses', p. 147.   [72] *Ibid.* p. 148.
[73] Not to mention: 3927, 3984, 4005, 4333, 4700, 4715, 4763, 4792, 4952, 5224, 5351, 5409, 5554, 5590, 5616, 5734, 5957, 5991, 5993, 6032, 6073, 6099, 6507, 6594, 6668, 6863, 6926, 6990, 7403, 7411, 7525, 7577, 7683, 7738, 7908, 8070, 8402, 8458, 8495, 8578, 8663, 8824, 9067, 9277, 9368, 9807, 9841, 9939, 9987, 10251, 10289, 10480, 10681, 10811, 10852, 10921, 11044, 11816, 12084, 13564, 13575 and 13808.

3052 DEDITI] i. locupletati R5: i. subiecti O
3397 CAEREMONIAS] i. obseruationes R5
3478 SVPREMAM] i. ultimam R5
3592 SVB CONO] i. summa parte R5: sublimis summus grandis excelsus preclarus O
3597 PRAEPETI] i. ueloci R5: i. celeri O
3724 CENSVRAM] i. estimationem uel mensuram R5: i. iudicium O
3878 CONGESSIMVS] i. collegimus R5: i. congregauimus O
3892 PROCERITAS] i. celsitudo uel altitudo R5: i. magnitudo uel status, longitudo O
3914 CREDATVR] s. qui, mercatur R5

No doubt Goossens would have conjectured that these glosses stem from his source and that they would have been added in the transitional stage we have allowed for.

Superficially, Goossens's argument seems fine. Certainly, the intimate relationship between glosses in R5 and B^c is beyond doubt. In fact, if Goossens had printed all the Latin entries in the Brussels codex and compared them to those in Royal 6. B. VII, he would have noted examples of shared error in R5 and B^c which buttress his case:

1886 INFLEXIBILE] innodabile R5 B^c: inenodabile O
3463 VERBORVM] seruorum R5 B^c:[74] sermonum O
3774 FLAMMIVOMA] a flamma et umbo R5 B^c: a flamma et uerbo O
4161 SOFISTAE] sophistica facta R5 B^c: sofistica ficta O
4389 PROCACIBVS] inprudentibus R5 B^c: inpudentibus O
4541 PROPALAT] presens pro pretereo R5: presens pro preterio B^c: presens pro preterito O
4646 LATEBRARVM] sacratorum R5 B^c: secretorum O
4910 SEMITAM] uitam R5 B^c: uiam O
5012 EVENTVM] quod deuenit R5 B^c: quod euenit O
5032 GLORIA] honora R5 B^c: honore O
6431 OBLIQVO] turto uel curuo R5: curto uel curuo B^{c75}

Obviously, there is a material connection between the glosses in HAND C of Brussels and the glosses in Royal 6. B. VII. Alas, it never struck Goossens that an equally close connection exists between glosses in Royal and Digby, manuscripts which are about 100 years apart in date. After discerning that the *Old English* glosses in Digby had been copied from B, Goossens neglected to collate the *Latin* Digby glosses with those in R5 and B. In fact, hundreds of Latin glosses are unique to these three manuscripts. Furthermore, Goossens overlooked errors common to R5 B^c and O, such as 183 PANDO] curruu R5 B^c O.[76] He also

---

[74] Corrected to *sermonum* B.   [75] For *torto uel curuo.*   [76] Altered to *curuo* B^c.

neglected errors common to O and R5 alone, such as 5392 PERITORVM] pre-dentium R5 O (for *prudentium*, omitted in B). Several errors common to Royal 6. B. VII and Digby 146 stand corrected in B as well:

4381 QVAESTVVM] lucrarum R5 O: lucrorum B^c
5479 MARTIRIZARETVR] cruaretur R5 O: cruciaretur B^c
6806 VICTORIA] tropheti R5 O:[77] trophea B^c[78]

These variants prove that the glosses in Royal 6. B. VII must be related to those in Digby 146 as well as to those in Brussels 1650. Could the Latin glosses in Digby, like the Old English ones, have also come from Brussels? The dating of the gloss hands makes this impossible. In fact, a closer look at more substantive errors demonstrates beyond any doubt that an intermediary copy of certain Digby glosses must be the source of glosses in the first stratum of Brussels HAND C and the main stratum of Royal 6. B. VII. I call this Digby apograph *O.

In the following erroneous glosses, distinguishing features in the layout and script of the Digby manuscript account for glosses in Brussels and Royal. Three kinds of error characterize the Digby apograph which gave rise to the glosses in these manuscripts. In several places a copyist of Digby truncated a gloss, leading to an ungrammatical transcript. He also took marginal material spreading into the line as part of an interlinear annotation; the resulting glosses are often non-sensical. Finally, he mistakenly copied sections of long interlinear glosses, so that the last portions of them, often a word or two, appear over adjacent lemmas. By reference to these varieties of error arising in an apograph of O, we can interpret seemingly inexplicable glosses in R5 and B:

2130 LAMENTABILE] lamentabile flebile luctuosum funes R5: flebile luctuosum B^c: Lamentabile flebile luctuosum funestum plorabile lacrimabile O

2132 QVOD] funes B^c
In the Digby copy of *Pdv* the gloss to LAMENTABILE reads (19v1):

lamentabile flebile luctuosum funes
tum plorabile lacrimabile

The first line ends at *funes*, and a scribe has only copied to this point, thereby omitting *-tum*. The erroneous gloss appears in B (9r3), except that *funes* is taken as a gloss for the later lemma QVOD. The same error occurs in R5 (11r20). Note that *funes*, which makes no sense, might have been mistaken for *funus*.

2175 RADICIBVS] radices dicuntur R5 B^c: Radices dicuntur que in imo atque in occulto site sunt O

---

[77] *tropheti* altered to *trophea* O.
[78] And possibly 6439 SVSPICIONVM] iudiciarum R5: iudiciorum B^c: indiciarum O.

The marginal gloss in O (19v11) reads as follows:

Radices dicuntur
que in imo atque
in occulto
site sunt

The scribe of the Digby apograph only bothered to copy out the first line of the gloss before realizing he had no space to complete it. His brief transcript is taken over in Brussels (9r10) and Royal (11v3).

2180 SPISSA] i. spissum densum, i. in unum collectum R5 O: densa, in unum collecta B^c
O reads *densum* (19v13), with the interlinear gloss *in unum collectum* directly above the following lemma VIRGVLTORVM. This format has confused a copyist, who took the second part as a gloss to VIRGVLTORVM. In R5 (11v4) and B (9r10) this same arrangement is duplicated.

2260 VVLNVS] i. aporia, cura, i. angor R5 B^c O
The word *angor* appears above the following lemmas IN MENTE in the Digby manuscript (20r13). It is treated as a separate gloss to that term both in R5 (11v19) and B (9v4).

3389 VOCIS] i. uox dicitur R5: uox dicitur quicquid sonat O
3390 MVGITVM] i. quicquid sonat R5 B^c
In manuscript O (27r14) the gloss to VOCIS reads as edited above, but the final words *quicquid sonat* are written above the following lemma MVGITVM. These words have been taken as a gloss to this lemma and are written separately with *i.* in R5 (16r9–10). The first, nonsensical, half of the gloss is omitted in B (14r1).

3442 TENERITVDINE] i. tenerum molle fragile, i. flexum flexibile R5: i. tenerum fragile molle flexum flexibile B^c: i. tenerum fragile molle flexum flexibile O
In O (27v6) the long interlinear gloss runs across the line, and the words *flexum flexibile* occur just above the following lemma VIRGINITATI. In B (14r9–10) a similar arrangement crops up, but the words have been shifted to suggest that they gloss VIRGINITATI. In R5 (16r18–19) they were separated from the first part of the gloss and taken as an interpretation of VIRGINITATI as well.

3569 MINVTATIM] i. gradatim, i. ordinatim R5: i. gradatim, ordinatim B^c: i. gradatim uel ordinatim O
In O (28r16) there is no Latin gloss to the preceding lemma ABSCISO. *Gradatim* was taken as a gloss to this word and became misplaced in the Digby apograph. The misplacement shows up in R5 (16v18) and B (14v10), and the single gloss *ordinatim* was written above MINVTATIM in both manuscripts.

6878 FERRO FORTIOR] i. semina frugum R5 B^c: Ferrum dictum ... O
The long marginal gloss in O (48r11), which comes from Isidore, *Etym.* XVI.xxi.1, reads as follows:

Ferrum dictum quod farra i. semina frugum
terre condeat idem et calips
a calibes flumine
ubi ferrum optima acie temperatur
unde et abusiue dicitur calips
ipsa materies

The words *semina frugum* appear directly above the lemma FERRO FORTIOR, since the gloss runs into the text. The gloss was then truncated in an apograph, and the error appears in R5 (28v5) and B (27r16).

8042 POLLVENDO] comminando R5 B^c: contaminando O
The gloss in O (55v14) is correct. Yet the ascenders in POLLVENDO divide the word at *contamin//ando*. A corruption arose in this way, and the error appears as *comminando* with various marks of abbreviation in R5 (32v1) and B (31v22).

These entries are conclusive evidence that the glosses common to B^c (first layer) and R5 stem from a manuscript copied from O. No reasonable alternative explanation accounts for the errors discussed above as well as for other errors common only to Digby and Royal, to Digby and Brussels, and to Digby, Brussels and Royal together. Yet a common exemplar not only explains the unusual, irreproducible errors appearing identically in Royal 6. B. VII and Brussels 1650. More conveniently, it accounts for errors unique to glosses in each of these codices.

In my view, this hypothetical copy of O (=*O) must have had even more corruptions similar to the ones just described but not introduced into R5 or B, either because the error was corrected or because the gloss was never copied. Glosses 3389–90, cited above, illustrate my reasoning. At this point in *Pdv* Digby 146 contained a relatively long interlinear gloss which became divided in my alleged transcript. The division is fortuitously recorded in R5, but the Brussels codex has only half of the gloss: 'quicquid sonat'. A scribe, possibly scribe C, eliminated the useless gloss 'uox dicitur' here. This scribe, or the scribes of any intervening archetypes, may have made similar emendations to correct faulty readings arising from Digby. Other (admittedly problematic) examples in the Brussels corpus are:

8075 CYCLADIBVS] i. uirginilibus uestibus R5: uirginalibus B^c: uirginalibus uestibus O
Apart from the minor error *uirginilibus*, the glosses in R5 (32v6) and O (56r3) are identical. The gloss in B, however, makes no sense (32r6). Looking at O, we can see one way this gloss may have arisen: the final term *uestibus* extends into the margin and may have been taken as a gloss to the following lemma. If the Digby apograph preserved this format, the Brussels scribe might mistakenly have omitted the final term. The scribe of R5 may have noticed the misplacement and put matters right.

8722 GVRGITIS] i. fluminis, proprie latus altus in flumine R5: fluminis, est proprie latus
B^c: i. fluminis, Gurges est proprie lacus altus in flumine O

In Digby 146 the final words *in flumine* are written over the following lemma (60r5). They may have been mistakenly attached to it in the apograph and re-located correctly only in R5 (32v6). Note that the Insular **c** has given rise to the common error *latus* in R5 and B^c (34v5).

Comparable scribal confusions which appear in R5 are more obviously attributable to a Digby apograph. We have seen, for example, that long interlinear glosses were often truncated and the various parts reassigned to preceding or following lemmas. Many more examples of this phenomenon are documented in the Royal copy of *Pdv*, and they attest to a more corrupt transcript of Digby 146 than the Brussels text does. In other cases an unnoticed abbreviation engenders a serious mistake.

952 VERTICEM] cacum R5: cacumen B^c O
The nasal suspension above the 'm' in O (12v3) is placed high, and the word runs directly into the glossword for the following lemma. A scribe seems to have been missed the abbreviation, giving rise to the meaningless *cacum* in R5 (6r16). The Brussels scribe recognized the mistake in his exemplar (4v14).

1562 ROSCIDIS] i. humidis, i. rore madidis R5 B^c O
In Digby (16r7) as in Brussels (6v22) this entire gloss is placed interlinearly, and it runs over the following lemma OCVLORVM. In R5 (8r18) the second half *rore madidis* appears as a separate gloss to OCVLORVM with the abbreviation *i.*

2011 PATERNAE] s. terram repromissionis R5 B^c O
In Digby (18v9) and Brussels (8v4) this long gloss extends over the following lemma GENERATIONIS. In R5 it is separated (8r18), the first half *terram* glossing PATERNAE, the second half *repromissionis* glossing GENERATIONIS.

2529 TINCTVRAE] tinctus luridus infectus coloratus R5 B^c O
This long interlinear gloss covers several words in Digby (21v19) and Brussels (10v5). The final term *coloratus* appears over the verb SPLENDVISSE. While all the glosses are correctly placed in Brussels, in the Royal manuscript (12v19–20) *i. coloratus* occurs separately above SPLENDVISSE.

4050 PATENTE] i. aperiente, i. manifestante R5 B^c O
In Digby (31r1) and Brussels (16r22), these interlinear glosses extend beyond the lemma, and *manifestante* is written over the following lemma VOCE. *Manifestante* appears as a separate gloss to VOCE in R5 (18v1).

5060 BIGARVM] bige ubi duo i. curru iunguntur R5: curruum B^c: i. bige ubi duo equi curru iunguntur O
In Digby 146 the interlinear gloss to BIGARVM runs over a large part of the line (36v12). The words *curru iunguntur* appear above SVBIVGALES. While HAND C in B writes simply *curruum* as a gloss (20r19), a reflex of the layout in O appears in R5 (22r9): *curru iunguntur* is a separate gloss to SVBIVGALES, and *equi*, which in O straddles the lemmas BIGARVM SVBIVGALES, is missing. The gloss makes no sense, perhaps explaining why it was omitted in B.

8442 STOLIDA] i. rori stulta R5: stulte B^c: stulta O

The interlinear gloss to STOLIDA in O (58r16) is straightforward, but a marginal gloss to the preceding lemma GINGINIS gives rise to an error in the hypothetical apograph:

> Gingiue a gignendis
> dentibus nominatae
> facte sunt
> etiam ad dec
> orem dentium hor rori
> potius quam orna
> mento existerent

The word *horrori* in this gloss has been divided in two by the capital 'S' of SIC, just preceding STOLIDA. The glossator therefore took *rori* as part of the gloss and wrote *rori stulta* in his apograph. This appears in R5 (33v15). The Brussels scribe probably recognized that *rori* made no sense in the context ('foolish to dew'!) and omitted it from his text (33v3).

Although these errors occur only in R5, their obvious affinities with the varieties of error common to R5 and B^c imply that they were in the Digby apograph that gave rise to the Brussels HAND C glosses. Omissions of such mistakes in either manuscript are attributable to the vigilance of scribes, who corrected or omitted these problematic entries.

Because layers of glossing in Digby 146 can be dated palaeographically, the Digby apograph was indisputably penned after the glosses by Ker's scribe (i) (=Napier's 'second Latin hand') and Napier's 'Ordinary hand' but before the Old English glosses by Ker's scribe (ii) (=Napier's 'Second hand'), that is *c.* 980×1020. The evidence derives from collation. Glosses in Ker's hand (ii) appear neither in Brussels HAND C nor in the main hand of Royal 6. B. VII, whereas glosses in hand (i) and in Napier's 'Ordinary hand' crop up consistently. Incidentally, because Digby 146 preserved about thirty Old English glosses in its earliest stratum and because these glosses were copied into the Digby apograph, some redundant glossing arose in Digby when the vernacular glosses were transferred from Brussels 1650.

THE CORRESPONDENCE OF GLOSSES IN BRUSSELS HANDS A, B AND C TO GLOSSES IN ROYAL 6. B. VII

Goossens wrongly derived glosses in R5 from those in B, and his reasoning needs to be considered in more detail. He contended that glosses in three hands which elsewhere correspond closely to glosses in one hand must have given rise to them. His evidence is, as outlined above, 109 glosses in HAND A, 24 glosses in HAND B and 356 glosses in HAND C which are common to glosses in R5. In the following instances I provide some of his uncited examples, Old English glosses found in Royal 6. B. VII which agree with those in Brussels HAND A:[79]

255 NAVCLERV] *rowendes* R5: *nowend* B[a80]
1192 DACTILOS] *clistro* R5: *clystra, fingerappla* B[a]
1335 CAVLICVLVS] *stela* R5 B[a]
1719 GENVINIS] *toðreomum* R5: *to<þ>reomum* B[a81]
2510 FVCO] *dæge* R5: *deage* B[a]
2684 PASTINARE] *tyddrian* R5: *tidrian* B[a]
2830 TORTIS] *aþrawenum* R5: *geþrawenum* B[a]
2847 CAESARIE] *fexe* R5 B[a]
2857 INDRVTICANS] *ticgende* R5 B[a]
2909 CONDICIO] *ræden* R5 B[a]
3273 GRANIGERA] *of gornbærre* R5: *cornbærum* B[a]
4033 ANFRACTVS] *woge, hylcas* R5: *hylcas* B[a]
4135 GLAREAS] *ceoslas* R5: *stancislas* B[a]
4310 FLAMINIA] *sacerhadas* R5 B[a]

An adjustment to Goossens's argument renders it plausible. If B, O and *O were housed together, who could say that a scribe did not copy a hundred glosses from Brussels 1650 into the Digby apograph, whence they could have been transmitted into an archetype of the Royal book? Yet one fact, misinterpreted by Goossens, vitiates this conclusion. In 1974 Goossens argued that the Royal glosses were copied from Brussels after scribe C made alterations to the Brussels corpus, specifically after modifying glosses in HANDS A and B. His position reverses the cart and horse. Scribe C, in fact, systematically *collated* his source with A and B's glosses in the Brussels *Pdv* copy. Hence, glosses, partial glosses and merographs in HANDS A and B already corresponded to glosses in scribe C's exemplar. There are instances, for example, where the C scribe added words to make Brussels agree with his own source:

2764 BIPERTITAM] i. in duas partes diuisam R5: diuisam B[a]: in duas partes B[c]: i. in duas partes diuisam O
Diuisam existed already in HAND A. Scribe C simply added *in duas partes* to make the texts uniform.

3652 MONARCHIAE] i. unius principatus R5: principatus B[a]: unius B[c]: i. unius principatus O
Scribe A had already written the gloss *principatus* in the Brussels codex. (The word stands in other manuscripts as well.) Scribe C added the term *unius* to make the Brussels gloss agree with the gloss in his exemplar.

6062 SACELLA] i. templum idolorum R5: i. templa B[a] O: idolorum B[c]
Again, scribe C collates the Brussels manuscript with his source.

[79] Goossens finds categorical alterations in these glosses, but there is no reason to consider these here.   [80] Altered to *nowendes* by scribe CD.   [81] *topreomum* B[a].

6178 NEGOTIVM] i. opus uel labor uel causa R5: i. labor Bᵃ O: i. opus uel causa Bᶜ
Collation is evident here, as in numerous other examples.

The abundant examples of this kind of collation are enhanced by even more evidence of collation. Scribe C also altered A and B's readings and expanded their merographs, presumably to make them match those of his source:

1963 EXPEDITIONVM] *fyrda* Bᵃ alt. to *fyrdunga* Bᶜ (R5 reads *fyrdunga*)
3353 DIVTVRNA] *longa* Bᵃ alt. to *longæua* Bᶜ (R5 and O read *longeua*)
3798 MACHINAS] *seara* Bᵃ alt. to *searacræftas* Bᶜ (O reads *searacræftas*)
3944 SPVRCAE] *scand* Bᵃ alt. to *scandlicre* Bᶜ (O reads *sceadlicere*)
5454 INSOLESCAT] *awo* Bᵃ alt. to *awolfige* Bᶜ
9965 MVSCIPVLIS] *feal* Bᵇ alt. to *feallan* Bᶜ
11086 PROCERVM] *ealdorman* Bᵇ alt. to *ealdormanna* Bᶜ

In the same way, CD later altered some of scribe C's glosses: 1851 BELLI-COSAS] 7 *wiglice* R5: *wiglice* Bᶜ alt. to *wiglice, heardlice* Bᶜᵈ.[82] Goossens now maintains – without palaeographical evidence – that some of these CD alterations were made by the Royal scribe![83]

Evidently, if glosses in Brussels 1650 did not quite correspond to glosses in his exemplar, the C scribe emended them. What would he have done if the glosses did correspond? It seems likely that if glosses were already present in Brussels HANDS A and B, the glossator would not have bothered to write a duplicate. Let us rehearse the circumstances of copying. Scribe C comes across an apograph of Digby which he intends to collate with Brussels 1650. The Brussels manuscript already has a few hundred glosses written in HANDS A and B, but this sparse glossing could be usefully augmented by such collation. Scribe C begins copying glosses into Brussels, but where he finds a gloss in HAND A or B which matches one in his exemplar, he does not copy out the gloss a second time; he passes on. Where slight differences exist, he brings both manuscripts into conformity by correcting A or B's glosses. For this reason, glosses in three hands in Brussels (A, B and C) could correspond to a single layer in Royal 6. B. VII and need not give rise to it.[84]

Of course, this interpretation of events requires that a core of glosses

---

[82] Goossens, pp. 24–5.
[83] Goossens, 'Aldhelm Glosses', p. 149: 'Obviously, if my assumptions are correct, CD must here be identical with the 'glossator of [R5]'.
[84] The hypothesis also explains what Goossens claimed was a 'striking difference in the way [the Royal glossator] treats the glosses by C as compared with those by A and B' (Goossens, 'Aldhelm Glosses', p. 146). Glosses in Brussels HANDS A and B appeared 'changed [in Royal 6. B. VII] more often than not' (*ibid.* p. 147) than glosses in HAND C. The corpus of glosses in HANDS A and B circulated in many other manuscripts, and probably in many divergent spellings. Such glosses might have gone unaltered by the scribe who copied from the Digby apograph.

represented by HANDS A and B and by elements of Hand C was present in a layer of glosses in the Digby apograph. In fact, this core of glosses circulated in almost every extant *Pdv* manuscript, and it resembled the glosses comprising the earliest gloss strata of Royal 7. D. XXIV. I call this common core of Old English and Latin glosses the 'Common Recension'.[85] For present purposes, isolating the 'Common Recension' does not warrant the lengthy discussion it would require. We need only acknowledge here the working hypothesis that Brussels HANDS A and B encompassed a layer of glosses also in scribe C's exemplar.

DIFFERENCES BETWEEN GLOSSES COMMON TO BRUSSELS HAND C (FIRST STRATUM) AND ROYAL 6. B. VII (MAIN STRATUM) COMPARED TO THE LATIN GLOSS CORPUS IN DIGBY 146

Glosses in the Digby apograph plausibly resembled those common to the main glossing hand in R5 and to HANDS A, B and C in Brussels: thousands of Latin glosses alongside a few hundred Old English contributions. By the time the R5 and B^c glosses were copied, however, this hypothetical Digby transcript (*O) differed substantially from Digby. Theoretically, any number of intervening copies could have existed between the Digby apograph and its descendants, just as several copies of the Digby apograph could have existed. Hence, the glosses in R5 which are not found in the Digby or Brussels volumes may have been added either to the Digby apograph or to a copy of it. To avoid confusion I have not designated any intermediary manuscript copy between the Digby apograph and Royal 6. B. VII.

The transparent relationship between Royal 6. B. VII and Brussels 1650 belies occasionally stark differences between the glosses shared by R5 and B^c and by O. In respect to these differences, three important observations must be recorded and discussed. In the first instance, many glosses common to R5 and B^c are neither in O nor in any other extant manuscript:

1930 VENENOSA] i. temperantia R5 B^c
1946 MVNICIPES] i. principes R5 B^c
1954 LATIBVLIS] i. cubilibus R5 B^c
1988 AMBRONIS] i. deuorantibus R5 B^c
2218 SE EXALTAT] i. eleuabitur R5 B^c
2934 HOC] *pis* R5 B^c
3240 IVGALITAS] s. est R5 B^c
3375 FISCALE TRIBVTVM] fiscus, i. prumptuarium cesaris inde fiscale R5 B^c
3380 DITATVS] muneratus R5 B^c
3383 PRAEDITVS] i. ornatus R5 B^c
3404 MELOTE] i. mantile R5 B^c
3464 FACVNDIA] i. eloquentia R5 B^c

---

[85] Gwara I, pp. clvii–cxciii.

3487 THIMIAMA] i. odoramentum incensi R5 B^c
3531 MVNERIBVS] i. donis R5 B^c
3694 IMPORTVNA] i. improba R5 B^c
3697 DELERAMENTA] i. stoliditates R5 B^c
3712 EXTITISSE] i. mansisse R5 B^c

These glosses are probably unique to the Digby apograph which gave rise to the Royal and Brussels HAND C corpus.

Second, many glosses common to R5 and B^c diverge radically from the surviving glosses in O, while others are only slightly different. The following random samples exemplify the degree of these differences:

906 IRRIGABAT] infundebat R5 B^c: perfundebat O
1409 PROPENSIVS] diligentius R5 B^c: plenius O
1482a FRETVS] fructus R5 B^c: functus O
1484 INDVSTRIA] sollertia R5 B^c: curiositate O
1532 RATIBVS] nauibus R5 B^c: medicinis O
1845 FRETI] fructi R5 B^c: functi O
1919 INPORTVNVS] improbus uel inmitis R5 B^c: ferus uel inmitis O
1936 EXPLODATVR] excludatur uel eiciatur R5 B^c: deleatur O
2211 CONFIDVNT] consperant R5 B^c: sperant O
2321 COMPVNGVNTVR] conpuncti R5 B^c: constringuntur O
3032 PROMVLGARE] statuere R5 B^c: demonstrare O
3072 INDVSTRIA] sollertia R5 B^c: assiduitate O
3241 AD PROPAGANDAM] ad extendendam uel protelandam R5 B^c: ad manifes-
    tandam O
3358 HACTENVS] hucusque R5 B^c: usque huc O
3374 VECTIGAL] pupplica exactio R5 B^c: fiscalia O
3391 REBOASSE] uociferasse R5 B^c: tonasse O
3392 DESCRIBITVR] memorabitur R5 B^c: memoratur O
3403 FRETVS] fructus R5 B^c: functus O
3405 INORMEM] magnum R5 B^c: maximam O
3465 FRETVS] fructus R5 B^c: functus O
3481 GRATISSIMVM] amantissimum R5 B^c: optatissimum O
3506 LIQVIDO] manifeste R5 B^c: clare uel perspicue O
3543 EBDOMADIBVS] septenis uel septies R5 B^c: curriculis O
3732 FERCVLORVM] epularum R5 B^c: diliciarum O
3749 INORME] tam magnum R5 B^c: inmane O

The substitutions range from slight rewordings to utterly distinct terms, and deliberate emendation probably accounts for many of them. *Infundebat*, for example, appears to have been made morphologically parallel to IRRIGABAT of 906, just as *consperant* of 2211 to CONFIDVNT. Some alterations, too, represent corrections: one Digby glossator misconstrues RATIBVS (*medicinis*), and the mistake has been corrected to *nauibus*. Still other readings are refinements of sense. The substitution of *sollertia* for *curiositate* in 1484 INDVSTRIA privileges a superior interpretation: '. . . cum sudoris industria efficatur antecessor'.[86] The persistent quality of 'sollertia' displaces the milder 'curiositas'. *Diliciarum* for FERCVLORVM in 3732 ('ut . . . opulentas regalium ferculorum dilicias . . . in tenerrima pubertate contempserint') mischaracterizes the phrase.[87] Because *dilicias* follows *ferculorum* in the text, it is an inadequate rendering. The more apposite gloss *epularum* therefore appears as a correction in Brussels 1650 and Royal 6. B. VII. Finally, four occurrences of FRETVS (1482a, 1845, 3403 and 3465) in which the gloss *functus* in O corresponds to the gloss *fructus* in R5 and B imply that a glossator emended to suit his own linguistic idiosyncrasies. Such alterations as these manifest a careful and intelligent editor who interpreted as he wrote. Glosses to 3241, 3391 and 3405 may also show his intervention.

My third, and most important, observation raises questions of transmission. In a number of cases, glosses which are common to R5 and B[c] but which are not found in O correspond to glosses in earlier *Pdv* manuscripts, giving the impression that they are not isolated annotations:[88]

4368 MANVBIAS] predas R4 S R3 C2 C1
4759 TORQVENTES] uertentes R4 S R3 C2
6312 NVGACITER] inutiliter R4 S R3 C2 C1

These glosses which do not stem from O can be explained either as accretions, or as prior contributions, to the Digby apograph. Of course, determining an exact explanation of the copying of these glosses would be fruitless. The simple fact that Brussels and Royal glosses are found in other *Pdv* manuscripts but not in Digby implies widespread contamination. Again and again, scribes sought to compare *Pdv* copies and to transfer glosses among them.

THE RELATIONSHIP BETWEEN GLOSSES IN BRUSSELS HAND C (SECOND STRATUM) AND THE MARGINAL GLOSSES IN DIGBY 146

The first stratum of HAND C in Brussels 1650 bears an obvious paternity. Yet a problem remains in the derivation of the second gloss stratum of C, which consists mainly of marginal Latin glosses and Latin *glossae collectae* with Old English interpretations. There is no precedent for the *glossae collectae*, and they were probably assembled as the scribe read the text. In almost every instance, the Old English *interpretamentum* derives from a gloss in HANDS A or B:

7827 DE CLATRIS] clatru *pearruc* B[c]: *pearr<u>cum* B[a] [89]
7836 LASCIVVS] lasciuus *grædig* B[c]: *grædig* B[a]

---

[86] Ehwald 238.14: '. . .[he] is made the leader by the effort of his labour'.
[87] Ehwald 252.9–10: '. . .[that] they spurned the rich delights of regal feasts in their innocent youth'.   [88] For sigla, see above, p. 140, n. 7.   [89] Altered from *pearricum* B[a].

7837 SCORTATOR] scortator *wemmend* B^c: *wemmend* B^a
7838 VAGABVNDIS] uagabundus *woriend* B^c: *woriendum* B^a
8102 MVNICIPIO] Municipium *fæsten* B^c: *fæstene* B^a
8110 SVB DISTRICTO] Districtus *þear</l>'e'wis* B^c: *þearlwisum* B^{a 90}
8116 A TRAMITE] tramite *stige* B^c: *fram stige* B^a
8152 GRASSARETVR] Grassor *ic onhige* B^c: *onhigede* B^a
8644 ANACHORESEOS] Anachoreseos *ænyttes* B^c: *aenetes* B^b
8676 STROFAM] Stropha fraus *facn* B^c: *fanc* B^b
8876 ARCHIMANDRITA] Archimandrita *hehfæder* B^c: *hehfæder* B^b

Such glosses as these demonstrate that the C scribe was working from the Old English glosses already present in the manuscript. The glossary entries in the margins are therefore explicable simply as points of interest.

Unlike the *glossae collectae* in HAND C, however, the dense marginal glossing on fols. 8–11 poses an interpretative obstacle. These glosses correspond almost word for word to marginal glosses in Digby 146. Now, the errors we have uncovered in Royal 6. B. VII and the first layer of HAND C in Brussels show that Digby must have had dense marginal glossing *before* the presumed Digby apograph was penned. Otherwise, errors traceable to the intrusion of marginal glosses into the line could not have been made. Could the marginal glosses in Digby have been the source of those in the second stratum of HAND C in Brussels? The evidence is unclear, mainly because of the lack of shared error. Yet among the marginal glosses in B are two which could not have come from O:

2556 TOPAZIO] ex uirenti genere est. Topazius omnium gemmarum in se habet pulchritudines omnium uincit honores [Topazius . . . honores *om.* O] Topazion lapis pretiosus in quo sicut alii adfirmant omnium colores fulgent B^c O

2833 CALAMISTRO] Calamistro i. ac<u> [aco MS] ferreo in similitudine calami[i] facto in quo crines obtorquentur ut crispi sint quem in cinere cale'sce're solent qui capillos crispant ut calamistrati sint B^c: Calamistratus a calamistro, i. acu ferreo in calami[s] similitudine facto in quo crines obtorquentur ut crispi sint O

These marginal glosses are lifted from Isidore's *Etymologiae*, which gave rise to most of the marginal glosses in O.[91] In both of the cited instances, however, B^c has an additional phrase from Isidore which is not found anywhere in Digby 146. These additions might derive from the hypothetical Digby apograph, in which a scribe has added some other sections of Isidoriana where he noted unsatisfactory glosses. However, the first section in B 2556, which is missing in O, is so similar to the second section, which is common to B and O, that this hypothesis seems unlikely. The copyist of O would more reasonably have left

---

[90] l altered.
[91] Cf. M. C. Bodden, 'Evidence for Knowledge of Greek in Anglo-Saxon England', *ASE* 17 (1990), 217–46.

out extraneous material rather than resort to Isidore for further information on a term already heavily glossed. In my view, then, these marginal glosses probably stem from the same source which gave rise to the marginal glosses in O. The errors *calamii* in B^c and *calamis* in O likewise raise expectations that both sets of marginalia are related. Tentatively, then, I suggest that the second layer of Brussels glosses in HAND C derives from a text closely related to the long marginal glosses in O.

THE DIGBY APOGRAPH (*O), CANTERBURY AND EXETER

The existence of an apograph of Digby 146 dating from *c.* 980 × 1020 and the textual transmission which I propose raise two collateral issues: where was the apograph copied, and how did it, or a version of it, get to Exeter? In answer to the first question, only one centre makes sense as the origin of the Digby apograph: Canterbury. Despite their Abingdon provenance and the meticulous research of N. R. Ker, both Digby 146 and Brussels 1650 are Canterbury volumes. Exeter, then, must have applied to a Canterbury foundation for a copy of *Pdv*.

To answer the second question and ascertain why and when a *Pdv* copy should have come into the possession of the Exeter *familia*, we have to speculate on Exeter's historical background as well as on the relevance of *Pdv* to its community. Patrick Conner's recent study of Exeter proposes two phases of intellectual activity at the late Anglo-Saxon minster. The period between 968, when Sidemann was sent to Exeter with monks from Glastonbury 'to establish the new Benedictine monasticism in an important, active minster'[92] and 1003, when Exeter was ravaged by Swegn, witnessed a staggering intellectual reprise. This renewal is documented by an increasing number of manuscripts from about the time when Sidemann would have been promoting change at Exeter, roughly 968 × 977. Attributable Exeter manuscripts from this decade include traditional school authors: Amalarius, Bede, Boethius, Cassian, Hrabanus Maurus, Isidore, Persius and Prudentius.[93] In my view, *Pdv* would fit into the intellectual concerns of an abbot who was trained at Glastonbury and who would have been interested in fashionable textbook authors. As I have stated elsewhere, 'Glastonbury rated as a centre of Aldhelm scholarship not only for its resources and patronage but also for its celebrated alumni.'[94] The mania for Aldhelm which was sweeping England during Sidemann's Exeter and Crediton years can be traced directly to a coterie of Glastonbury reformers, Sidemann among them. At this historical moment, it would be fitting for Sidemann to acquire a copy of *Pdv*

---

[92] P. Conner, *Anglo-Saxon Exeter: a Tenth-Century Cultural History* (Woodbridge, 1993), p. 30.
[93] *Ibid.* pp. 3–8, items 12, 15, 17, 28, 31–3, 46 and 48–9.
[94] Gwara, 'Manuscripts', p. 157.

Scott Gwara

from Canterbury, perhaps a generation of the Digby apograph, and to inaugurate the study of Aldhelm in his growing community. Monks in tenth-century Exeter would no doubt prize the literary sophistication which Aldhelm's *œuvre* represented.

The second phase of intellectual growth at Exeter took place under Bishop Leofric (d. 1072), who moved the episcopal see from Crediton to Exeter in 1050. Admittedly, Leofric either obtained or produced many books, but it seems unlikely that the exemplar of Royal 6. B. VII came from Canterbury during his episcopate. Canterbury had suffered from devastation and fire first in 1011 and again in 1067,[95] and its foundations could no longer be held rich in books. Furthermore, except at Abingdon (it seems), *Pdv* had lost the pre-eminence it had long held as a model of Latin style. An interest in Aldhelm's Latin prose could therefore be seen as antiquarian rather than current. In fact, the Exeter *Pdv* was written in the generation after Leofric's death, as if it were answering to a non-scholastic interest. The volume was probably intended to commemorate Aldhelm's sanctification in 1078 under Bishop Osmund of Salisbury.[96] Around the time of Aldhelm's translation, the Exeter community probably saw fit to prepare a superior copy of *Pdv* from an exemplar of presumed antiquity. Thus, Royal 6. B. VII may represent the second-generation copy of the Digby apograph. Although speculative, then, it seems most likely that Exeter acquired *Pdv* from Canterbury during Sidemann's time or just afterwards and in the wake of the Aldhelm revival. Certainly the copying of *Pdv* in this era would corroborate Conner's profile of late-tenth-century Exeter as a mainstream foundation nurturing intellectual trends.[97]

[95] N. Brooks, *The Early History of the Church of Canterbury* (Leicester, 1984), pp. 55–6.
[96] By William of Malmesbury's testimony; cf. Hamilton, *Gesta pontificum*, pp. 423–5.
[97] The preceding work derives from my Ph.D. dissertation (cited above), which incorporates an edition of all Old English and Latin glosses to the *Prosa de virginitate*, fully lemmatized, from the fourteen glossed manuscripts of English provenance. I owe a considerable debt to Professors A. G. Rigg and Michael Herren, who corrected innumerable mistakes and challenged me to refine points I might otherwise have left vague. I have benefited, too, from Professor David Dumville's expert advice on palaeography and dating. I am also grateful to the Dictionary of Old English, University of Toronto, for access to their microfilm manuscript archive. The Centre for Medieval Studies, University of Toronto, and the Associates of the University awarded me research grants to consult most of the *Pdv* manuscripts *in situ*.

Exeter Book Riddle 74 and the play of the text

JOHN D. NILES

Riddle 74 is one of a handful of Old English riddles of the Exeter Book that have stubbornly resisted a solution.[1] As Bruce Mitchell and Fred C. Robinson remark, 'scholars have suggested answers . . . but none satisfies all the conditions set forth in the poem'.[2] Peter Clemoes finds the attributes that are ascribed to this particular riddle-subject to be 'so paradoxical that it seems impossible to name their possessor at all'.[3] Riddles normally do have answers, however, and this one is no exception. My first aim in this article is to offer an answer to Riddle 74 that will put debate to rest as to its intended solution.

Ascertaining the answer to the riddle is not my only purpose, however. Like almost any short specimen of Old English verse, Riddle 74 can be used as a lever by which large objects may be moved. A second aim of this essay is to assess the criteria for validity in interpretation, both in regard to the literary riddle (as opposed to social riddling) and as a general problem in human understanding. The question of how to determine linguistic meaning in general, I shall claim, can be clarified using Riddle 74 as a test case. A third aim of the paper is to examine the ludic qualities of the Exeter Book riddles and, by extension, of poetry of other kinds. I will suggest that there is reason to regard poetry in general, not just in the Anglo-Saxon context, as a species of play, a special type of extended riddling. Finally, approaching Riddle 74 as a microcosm, I will suggest that the corpus of Old English riddles provides a useful vantage point for examining the worldview of the Anglo-Saxons. Through their bold use of metaphor, the riddles play with conceptual categories and habits of thought that were taken for granted in the culture of their time. Although my subject is only five lines of verse, it therefore involves questions of some magnitude.

---

[1] The riddle is no. 74 in *The Exeter Book*, ed. G. P. Krapp and E. V. K. Dobbie (New York, 1936), ASPR 3 (henceforth cited as K–D), and I shall follow common practice in referring to it by that number. It is no. 72 in *The Old English Riddles of the Exeter Book*, ed. C. Williamson (Chapel Hill, NC, 1977), henceforth W in short citations. For assistance in the preparation of this essay I am indebted to the University of California, Berkeley, for a Humanities Research Fellowship and sabbatical leave during 1997–8; to the President and Fellows of Clare Hall, Cambridge; and to Andy Orchard, Donald Scragg and John Lindow for advice on particular points.

[2] B. Mitchell and F. C. Robinson, *A Guide to Old English*, 5th ed. (Oxford, 1992), p. 240.

[3] P. Clemoes, *Interactions of Thought and Language in Old English Poetry*, CSASE 12 (Cambridge, 1995), 185.

John D. Niles

TEXT, TRANSLATIONS AND IMAGINED SOLUTIONS

The manuscript context of Riddle 74 is well known and need not detain us long, though it has a bearing on my arguments. In modern editions the riddle consists of five printed lines of verse. In its unique manuscript source it appears as three lines of writing at the foot of 126v of the Exeter Book.[4] It is one of ninety-five riddles, according to the usual count,[5] that are written out in two main sets. The first set, nos. 1–59 (101r–115r), is preceded by a large and miscellaneous group of poems, the last of which are *Deor* (fol. 100) and *Wulf and Eadwacer* (100v–101r). The second set, nos. 61–95, occupies 124v–130v and concludes the Exeter Book. Between the two sets, a dozen other poems are written out in the same hand: *The Wife's Lament* (fol. 115), seven devotional poems (115v–122v), another version of Riddle 30 (122v), Riddle 60 (122v–123r), *The Husband's Message* (fol. 123) and *The Ruin* (123v–124v). No titles are given for any of these texts and there are no sectional divisions in the manuscript, so that the poems succeed one another without special distinctions other than capitalization of their first word on a new line and the marking of their last word with full-stop punctuation. There has naturally been some debate as to which of these poems belong to the riddle genre and which do not.[6] While the versified version of the Lord's Prayer (122r) is clearly not a riddle, some readers have thought that *The Husband's Message*, for example, is. Speaking of the group of items that extends from Riddles 30b and 60 through the three capitalized sections of *The Husband's Message* to the *Ruin*, Anne Klinck suggests that 'the compiler seems to have thought that all six were riddle-like.'[7] Certainly there is reason to conclude that the compiler of the manuscript (or its archetype) was a 'creative antholo-

---

[4] A facsimile has been published as *The Exeter Book of Old English Poetry*, with introductory chapters by R. W. Chambers *et al.* (London, 1933). For information with a possible bearing on the manuscript's early history, see P. W. Conner, *Anglo-Saxon Exeter: a Tenth-Century Cultural History* (Woodbridge, 1993), esp. pp. 48–94 (on paleographical context) and pp. 95–147 (on codicology) and, for a more sceptical view, R. Gameson, 'The Origin of the Exeter Book of Old English Poetry', *ASE* 25 (1996), 135–85. Besides K–D, W and the facsimile, other editions that I have consulted are *Codex Exoniensis*, ed. B. Thorpe (London, 1842); *The Riddles of the Exeter Book*, ed. F. Tupper, Jr (Boston, MA, 1910); *Old English Riddles*, ed. A. J. Wyatt (Boston, MA, 1912); *Die altenglischen Rätsel*, ed. M. Trautmann (Heidelberg, 1915); *The Exeter Book*, pt 2, ed. W. S. Mackie, EETS os 194 (Oxford, 1934); *Old English Riddles*, ed. F. H. Whitman (Ottawa, 1982); *Die altenglischen Rätsel des Exeterbuchs*, ed. H. Pinsker and W. Ziegler (Heidelberg, 1985); and *The Exeter Anthology of Old English Poetry: an Edition of Exeter Dean and Chapter MS 3501*, ed. B. J. Muir, 2 vols. (Exeter, 1994).

[5] There are ninety-one riddles according to the Williamson count. The reason that this count varies from the K–D count is disagreement as to whether K–D riddles 1–3, 75–6 and 79–80 constitute separate poems or are parts of single poems. Williamson favours the latter conclusion and numbers these as riddles 1, 73 and 76, respectively, with the rest of his numeration adjusted accordingly.   [6] See the more extended discussion of genre on pp. 198–9 below.

[7] A. L. Klinck, *The Old English Elegies: a Critical Edition and Genre Study* (Montreal, 1992), p. 197.

gist',[8] gathering materials from various sources and making an effort to put like things together, but what these principles of likeness were is not altogether clear, nor were they necessarily followed consistently.

Riddle 74 is a good test case for larger arguments because it is short and complete, there are no disputes about its genre, and it presents almost no textual difficulties.[9] In line 5 the manuscript reading *forð* 'forth', a nonsensical reading, is emended by almost universal agreement to *ferð* 'spirit, soul', yielding a verse that is grammatical, that makes sense in this context, and that is paralleled twice elsewhere in the riddles.[10] The text thus emended reads as follows, as punctuated by its most recent editor:

> Ic wæs fæmne geong,   feaxhar cwene,
> ond ænlic rinc   on ane tid;
> fleah mid fuglum   ond on flode swom,
> deaf under yþe   dead mid fiscum,
> ond on foldan stop –   hæfde ferð cwicu.[11]

In essence, the art of riddling is the art of deceptive speech. Here, as in over half of the riddles of the Exeter Book, the thing or object whose name is to be guessed speaks in its own voice.[12] The speaker-subject tries to disguise its identity[13] not through the usual human strategems of silence or lies, but rather through the artful use of metaphor and other forms of deliberate ambiguity.

---

[8] *The Exeter Book*, ed. Muir II, 624.

[9] Since the manuscript text is unpunctuated apart from capitalization of *Ic* (line 1) and the inclusion of a full stop after *cwicu* (last line), there are various possible ways of punctuating the text in modern editions. These options have caused no more than minor debate, however, and I will pass over the question of punctuation now before returning to it after offering my proposed solution.

[10] Cf. Riddle 10 (W8), verse 6a: *Hæfde feorh cwico*, 'I had a living spirit'; Riddle 13 (W11), verse 3a: *hæfdon feorg cwico*, 'they had living spirits'. To judge from these parallels, *ferð* functions as a variant of *feorh* or *feorg*, 'life, soul'. Williamson, following *An Anglo-Saxon Dictionary*, ed. J. Bosworth and T. N. Toller (Oxford, 1898), with *Supplement*, ed. T. N. Toller (1921) and *Revised and Enlarged Addenda* by A. Campbell (1972) (henceforth cited as B–T), lists *ferð* separately from *feorh* in his glossary and glosses it 'mind, spirit, life', but the two words seem to be used interchangeably.

[11] *The Exeter Anthology*, ed. Muir I, 369; text identical with W, p. 109. What follows is a hyperliteral word-for-word translation: 'I was (a) woman/girl young, (a) hair-gray woman/queen, and (a) peerless warrior/man in/at one time/season/hour; (I) flew among birds and in/on (the) sea swam, dived under (the) wave dead among fish/fishes, and stepped/walked on land – (I) had/held (a) spirit/soul (or souls) living.'

[12] *Riddles of the Exeter Book*, ed. Tupper, p. lxxxix, lists fifty riddles in this category.

[13] I shall try to avoid referring to the speaker by any third-person-singular pronoun, as by its grammatical gender the wording 'he', 'she' or 'it' can prejudice a solution. Where the resulting awkwardness becomes intolerable I shall use 'it', with the justification that the neuter pronoun is the least likely to mislead, seeing that most of the Exeter Book riddles have an inanimate solution.

The speaker must be identified in defiance of four paradoxes. It was female but also male; it was a young maiden but also a mature woman; it moved about not just in one medium but on land, in and on the sea, and in the air; and at one time or another it was both quick and dead.

Before I review proposed answers to this riddle, a glance at its published translations may be in order, for translations can easily predispose a reader in the direction of one or another solution. As has often been remarked, any act of translation (even the hyperliteral translation I have given above, n. 11) is at the same time an act of interpretation. Every translator of a work puts a different spin on the text, and these different spins, even if slight, can be instructive.[14] Moreover, verse is difficult to translate compared with prose, and Old English alliterative verse is notoriously difficult to render transparently. With no intent either to blame or praise this work as poetry in its own right, I will reproduce three translations of Riddle 74 that are likely to be well known. One is by Michael Alexander, the second by Kevin Crossley-Holland, and the third by Craig Williamson.[15]

Alexander translates the riddle as follows:

> I was in one hour an ashen crone
> a fair-faced man, a fresh girl,
> floated on foam, flew with birds,
> under the wave dived, dead among fish,
> and walked upon land a living soul.

Here, noticeably, the first three main substantives come in a different order from what we see in the Exeter Book. Alexander has the speaker change from *crone* to *man* to *girl*, whereas in the original text the speaker changes from maiden to mature woman to man. The negative connotation of Alexander's 'crone' is absent from the OE noun *cwene*, or at least is very muted there.[16] Alexander's

---

[14] For discussion of this aspect of translation theory with examples drawn from *Beowulf*, see my 'Rewriting *Beowulf*: the Task of Translation', *College Eng.* 55 (1993), 858–78.

[15] The following examples are taken, respectively, from *The Earliest English Poems*, trans. M. J. Alexander (Harmondsworth, 1966), p. 101, repr. with no change in his *Old English Riddles from the Exeter Book* (London, 1980), p. 73; *The Exeter Riddle Book*, trans. K. Crossley-Holland (London, 1978), p. 91, repr. with no change in his *The Exeter Book Riddles* (Harmondsworth, 1979), p. 90; and *A Feast of Creatures: Anglo-Saxon Riddle-Songs*, trans. C. Williamson (Philadelphia, PA, 1982), p. 134. Other translations of Riddle 74 that I have consulted are by Thorpe, *Codex Exoniensis*, p. 487; *Anglo-Saxon Riddles of the Exeter Book*, trans. P. F. Baum (Durham, NC, 1963), pp. 51–2; *The Riddles of the Exeter Book*, trans. H. H. Abbott (Cambridge, 1968), p. 41; *Old English Riddles*, ed. Whitman, p. 213; and *Die altenglischen Rätsel*, ed. Pinsker and Ziegler, p. 117.

[16] *Dictionary of Old English*, ed. A. C. Amos *et al.* (Toronto, 1987– , henceforth *DOE*), fascicle C, s.v. *cwene*. The word normally means 'woman' or 'wife'; specialized senses are 'queen, empress', 'princess' or 'concubine' (in reference to a priest's consort, or perhaps common-law wife). The word is used of the Virgin Mary as well as of historical queens of good repute.

'crone' has an ashen complexion rather than ash-grey hair,[17] while his man is 'fair-faced', a rather free rendering of OE *ænlic*, which literally means 'peerless' or by extension 'excellent, beautiful, elegant'.[18] The four verbs of motion, too, come in a different sequence. Alexander's speaker first *floated*, then *flew*, then *dived*, then *walked*, whereas the speaker of the original riddle first flew, then swam, then dived, and then stepped on land. From the practical standpoint of riddle-solving, these small departures from the Exeter Book text could be misleading, for through them a code is scrambled that might be suggestive of a solution. In Alexander's poem, also, the speaker 'walked upon land a living soul', whereas it is not clear that the original speaker had a living soul at the same time as it stepped on land. It might have had life at some prior stage of its existence; the OE past tense *hæfde* encompasses pluperfect usages.

Crossley-Holland's version reads as follows:

> I was once a young woman,
> a glorious warrior, a grey-haired queen.
> I soared with birds, stepped on the earth,
> swam in the sea – dived under waves,
> dead amongst fishes. I had a living spirit.

Although this translation is more literal than the preceding one, again the order of the first three main substantives is altered. Crossley-Holland's speaker changes from *young woman* to *warrior* to *queen* (far from a crone!) instead of from a young woman to a mature one to a warrior. The adjective 'glorious' is another loose rendering of *ænlic*, a word that need not imply fame. The speaker's movement progresses from *air* to *earth* to *sea*, not from air to sea to land. Again, these departures from the Exeter Book text could interfere with a solution.

Craig Williamson faithfully reproduces the speaker's movement from air to sea to land. Like Alexander, however, he avoids rendering *hæfde ferð cwicu* with a syntactically equivalent phrase and so his speaker is unambiguously alive at the same time as it moved about. In a more dramatic departure from the original wording, he reduces the number of substantives in the first series from three to two:

> I was a gray girl, ash-haired, elegant,
> And a singular warrior at the same time.
> I flew with the birds and swam in the sea,
> Dove under waves, dead among fish,
> And stood on the shore – locking in a living spirit.

---

[17] OE *feax* denotes 'hair', as in ch. 33 of the Laws of Æthelberht, where *feaxfang* 'pulling someone's hair' is a legal offence subject to compensation of fifty *sceattas*, or the same amount that was exacted for rape of a slave of the second class (ch. 16): *The Laws of the Earliest English Kings*, ed. and trans. F. L. Attenborough (Cambridge, 1922), pp. 8 and 6 respectively.

[18] B–T; *DOE*, fascicle Æ, s.v. *ænlic*.

Instead of a three-stage transformation from maiden to matron to man, Williamson offers the metamorphosis of a girl into a warrior. From the standpoint of riddle-solving, this is an unfortunate loss. The noun *fæmne*, despite its etymological descent from Latin *femina*, normally denotes 'maiden' rather than 'woman',[19] and when qualified by the adjective *geong* it must have that meaning. The noun *cwene*, however, denotes a mature woman. Despite the enduring appeal of the 'warrior-maiden' motif in both fiction and life,[20] something potentially important having to do with age and maturity is absent from this translation.

Two other points relating to the translation of Riddle 74 deserve notice. (1) The second line of the OE poem ends with the phrase *on ane tid*. Taken literally this phrase would seem to mean 'at the same time', as it does for example in an anonymous twelfth-century homily printed by Belfour,[21] and that is how Williamson translates it. Alexander translates the phrase 'in one hour', a variation on the same sense. Crossley-Holland prefers to translate it as 'once', as in 'once upon a time'. As I shall argue, this latter choice happens to be an attractive one. Although I will not yet try to resolve the meaning of *on ane tid*, I wish to make note of the translators' different ways of handling it; for that difference, I believe, results from the calculated ambiguity of the Exeter Book text, which leads us down a false track at every turn. (2) The noun *ferð* in line 5 (the product of reasonable emendation), though almost always taken as grammatically singular since the verb that governs it is singular, could also be grammatically plural. As a neuter a-stem monosyllabic noun with a long syllable, it takes no plural inflection. The *-u* inflection of the accompanying adjective *cwicu* does not help us here, for though one might expect it to indicate plurality, the same inflectional vowel (in the variant spelling *-o*) appears elsewhere with *cwic* in the riddles in a phrase that can only be taken in the singular.[22] 'I had a living spirit' is thus the usual translation of the last verse, though 'I had living spirits' or 'I held living spirits' or even 'he, she or it held living spirits' remain possible alternatives.

---

[19] B–T, s.v. *fæmne*.

[20] For a discussion of this theme in British popular literature, see D. M. Dugaw, *Warrior Women and Popular Balladry, 1650–1850* (Cambridge, 1989). Although the theme has been exploited by writers from the time of *Hervarar Saga* to that of Maxine Hong Kingston's *The Woman Warrior* (New York, 1976), its relevance to this riddle cannot be assumed.

[21] 'Uton nu bihealden þa wunderlice swiftnesse þare sawlæ. Heo hafæð swa mycele swiftnesse, þ heo on ane tid, ȝif heo wyle, bisceawiæð heofenum 7 ofer sæ flyhð, lond 7 burȝa ȝeondfaræð' ('Let us now consider the marvellous swiftness of the soul. It has such great speed that at a single time, if it wishes, it contemplates the heavens and flies over the sea and journeys through lands and cities'): *Twelfth-Century Homilies in MS. Bodley 343*, ed. A. O. Belfour, EETS os 137 (London, 1909), 88. This particular example is relevant to the solution to Riddle 74 that is proposed by Erhart-Siebolt (see below pp. 176–7).

[22] For the plural, see verse 3a of Riddle 13 (W11); for the singular, verse 6a of Riddle 10 (W8), as cited above, p. 171, n. 10.

If Riddle 74 remains unsolved, this is not because of a failure of will on the part of would-be solvers. Over the century and a half since the Exeter Book was first published, at least nine different solutions have been proposed.[23] It will be useful to review these briefly.

The first solution, 'cuttlefish', was offered by Franz Dietrich in 1859.[24] Dietrich retracted his suggestion six years later for lack of evidence,[25] but John Walz then took up the cause.[26] Aldhelm's *Enigma* 16, 'Luligo', whose title is translated by Pitman as 'flying-fish' but that literally denotes 'cuttlefish' (Latin *lolligo*), bears some resemblance to Riddle 74.[27] According to Pliny the cuttlefish could fly out of water.[28] But since no authority claims that the cuttlefish is hermaphroditic; since Aldhelm's riddle says nothing about either a sex change or life-in-death; and since the change from *fæmne* to *cwene* remains unexplained, a connection here is unlikely.

Moritz Trautmann's 'water in its various forms' (1894, 1905, 1915) is ingeniously argued.[29] The *fæmne geong* is a fresh spring (OE *burne*, a feminine noun); the *feaxhar cwene* is an ice floe;[30] and the *rinc* is snow (OE *snaw*, a masculine noun). Snow flies through the air; ice floats in the sea, and ice also melts into the sea when it 'dies', or dissipates; and water flows on land in the forms of streams or, as waves, rolls over the shore. The objection has been made that water is not alive, that it has no *ferð cwicu*. In his note of 1915 Trautmann evades this difficulty by suggesting that that phase, taken in the plural, refers to fish and other aquatic creatures, who are 'held' by the water of seas, pools and rivers. If no better

[23] For a list of solutions to Exeter Book riddles proposed through the 1970s, see D. K. Fry, 'Exeter Book Riddle Solutions', *OEN* 15.1 (1981), 22–33, at 25 for Riddle 74.

[24] F. Dietrich, 'Die Räthsel des Exeterbuchs: Würdigung, Lösung und Herstellung', *Zeitschrift für deutsches Altertum* 11 (1859), 482.

[25] 'Die Räthsel des Exeterbuchs: Verfasser; weitere Lösungen', *ibid.* 12 (1865), 248.

[26] J. A. Walz, 'Notes on the Anglo-Saxon Riddles', *Stud. and Notes* 5 (1896), 266–7.

[27] *The Riddles of Aldhelm*, ed. and trans. J. H. Pitman (New Haven, CT, 1925), pp. 10–11. Aldhelm's riddle describes a creature with scales that swims with fish and flies with birds, but that cannot breathe air. There was evidently some confusion in the Anglo-Latin tradition: the cuttlefish, a cephalopod mollusc related to the octopus, does not have scales.

[28] Pliny, *Historia naturalis*, vol. III (bks 8–11), ed. and trans. H. Rackham (London, 1940), ix. 45 (pp. 218–19).

[29] Trautmann offered this solution without any supporting argument in 'Die Auflösungen der altenglischen Rätsel', *Beiblatt zur Anglia* 5 (1894), 46–51. He argued his case fully in 'Alte und neue Antworten auf altenglischen Rätsel', *Bonner Beiträge zur Anglistik* 19 (1905), 201–3, and confirmed and nuanced it in his edition of 1915, *Die altenglischen Rätsel*, p. 128.

[30] The *feaxhar cwene* could also be frost, I might add. Frost might seem long-haired and is clearly greyish; cf. 'hoar-frost', though the earliest use of this word is *c.* 1290, according to the *Oxford English Dictionary*, 2nd ed., vol. VII (Oxford, 1989), henceforth *OED*. This connection is supported by Riddle 93 (W89), lines 13–14, where the adjective *har* and the noun *feax* appear in conjunction with frost: *hwilum hara scoc / forst of feaxe*, 'sometimes grey frost shook from his hair' (according to one possible translation of this grammatically difficult clause).

solution were available I would be tempted to opt for Trautmann's, with some uncertainty as to why the iceberg is a feminine personification as well as with some doubt as to whether ice, when it melts away into its matrix and alter ego of water, can legitimately be called 'dead'.[31]

Frederick Tupper argued vigorously for the solution 'siren' (1903, 1906, 1910).[32] His proposal has attracted intermittent support despite the very peripheral place of the siren in Anglo-Saxon lore; but can we seriously imagine the speaker to be a transsexual birdlike siren that has dived among fish and has died by being turned to stone? Here is one instance where Tupper's classical learning has led him into the realm of fancy.

Ferdinand Holthausen's proposal 'swan' (1925), on the other hand, seems more literal than one might wish.[33] The cygnet, in his view, is the *fæmne geong*. The adult female, with a few grey feathers still attached, is the *cwene*, while (with some special pleading) the female is also the *rinc*, since OE *swan* 'swan' is a grammatically masculine noun. A swan does indeed fly, swim, dive, and step on land. But if a swan is meant, it would have to be a dead swan unless we accept Holthausen's suggested emendation of *dead* 'dead' to *dreag* 'moved'. Given the neat antithesis of the quick and the dead in lines 4–5, no other editor or translator has adopted this course. Recently Peter Kitson has proposed an ingenious variation on the 'swan' solution that sidesteps the problem of the speaker's 'death' by postulating that allusion is being made to the former belief that rather than migrating, certain waterbirds lie hidden for long periods of the year like fishes beneath the surface of the sea. He therefore takes the bird in question to be the *ylfetu* 'whooper swan', a winter migrant to the British Isles from circumpolar regions.[34] Since OE *ylfetu* is a feminine noun, the female personification of the speaker in line 1 is explained. Kitson does not attempt to explain why the same creature is described as a masculine *rinc* in line 2, but leaving this point aside, his solution is the most persuasive among the non-metaphorical ones that have been offered to date.

Erhardt-Siebold's solution of 'soul' (1946, 1952) is based on a parallel between Riddle 74 and a fragment from the writings of the pre-Socratic

[31] P. Baum, *Anglo-Saxon Riddles*, suggests that if 'water' is the solution, then a more specific answer would be 'rain': he sees here a 'gentle shower, a heavy downpour, in the sea its natural form (its life) is lost; a little imagination can see it as hail walking on the ground' (p. 51). But this proposal makes little sense of *feaxhar cwene* and *ferð cwicu*.

[32] F. Tupper, 'Originals and Analogues of the Exeter Book Riddles', *Mod. Lang. Notes* 18 (1903), 100; 'Solutions of the Exeter Book Riddles', *ibid.* 21 (1906), 103–4; *The Riddles of the Exeter Book* (1910), pp. 214–15.

[33] F. Holthausen, 'Anglosaxonica Minora', *Beiblatt zur Anglia* 36 (1925), 220.

[34] P. Kitson, 'Swans and Geese in Old English Riddles', ASSAH 7 (1994), 79–84. Cf. Donoghue, '*An Anser*' (see below, p. 207)

philosopher Empedocles.[35] The sinful soul, according to Empedocles, is doomed to a cyclic metempsychosis that starts from earthly forms (a young man, a maiden and a plant), moves thence to air (in the form of a bird), thence to water (in the form of a fish), and finally back to land (equated, here, with a fish out of the sea). This proposed solution lacks either contextual or textual likelihood. There is no other evidence for knowledge of the Empedocles fragment in Anglo-Saxon England, while neither the *feaxhar cwene* of the OE riddle nor the phrase *dead mid fiscum* is explained. One thing we do know about the soul, whether in its Empedoclean or its Christian form, is that it does not die.

F. H. Whitman offers the answer 'writing', or 'quill pen used for writing' (1968, 1982).[36] The solution works well for Riddle 51 (W49, 'Pen and Fingers'), so why not here as well? Feathers (or the birds who once wore them) do fly through the air and swim in the sea, while in Riddle 51 a quill pen does dip into an inkwell (the 'sea of ink', as it were) and leaves 'tracks' on a manuscript page (the land on which the riddle-creature steps). Important details of Riddle 74 remain unexplained, however. Whitman can perhaps be permitted to collapse the *fæmne geong* and the *feaxhar cwene* of line 1 into a single thing, the quill pen, but what of the *ænlic rinc* of lines 1–2 and the fishes of line 4?[37]

Another solution proposed recently is Kiernan's 'sea-eagle' (1974).[38] Like Holthausen's swan, the sea-eagle is at home in the air, in or on the sea, and on the shore. Kiernan must face the same objection as Holthausen, however: what to do with *dead mid fiscum*? Rejecting the route of textual emendation, Kiernan appeals to medieval exegesis. The medieval Latin *Physiologus* recounts a legend to the effect that the eagle – not, however, specifically the sea-eagle – 'when he grows old, seeks a well, and by diving into it renews himself' (p. 520). As for the sex-change of lines 1–2, the riddle describes parthenogenesis, which Kiernan relates to both the Virgin Mary and vultures, in a tradition going back to Ambrose. He then has the task of relating vultures to the eagle, and specifically to the sea-eagle, which however is not grey but white. The exegetical route, when superimposed on a literalist base, becomes so complex as to seem unwieldy and leaves us with a dead (but now resurrected) parthenogenic bird freshly emerged from the baptismal font.

---

[35] E. von Erhardt-Siebold, 'The Anglo-Saxon Riddle 74 and Empedokles' Fragment 117', *MÆ* 15 (1946), 48–54, and 'Note on Anglo-Saxon Riddle 74', *ibid.* 21 (1952), 36–7.

[36] F. H. Whitman, 'OE Riddle 74', *ELN* 6 (1968), 1–5; *Old English Riddles*, ed. Whitman (1982), pp. 144–8. The goose-feather solution is pursued by H. Göbel, 'Studien zu den altenglischen Schriftwesenrätseln', *Epistemata: Würzburger wissenschaftliche schriften, Reihe Literaturwissenschaft* 7 (Würzburg, 1980), in an article I have not seen.

[37] Whitman makes bold but rather desperate attempts to relate the *rinc* to the nib of the pen and the *fiscas* to the cuttlefish, whose black fluid was sometimes used for ink in the ancient world though not, apparently, in Anglo-Saxon England.

[38] K. Kiernan, 'The Mysteries of the Sea-Eagle in Exeter Riddle 74', *PQ* 54 (1974), 518–22.

In the notes to his critical edition of 1977, finally, Williamson has proposed the solution 'ship's figurehead in the form of a girl'.[39] This solution, like Whitman's pen, depends on our taking the *fæmne geong* and the *feaxhar cwene* of line 1 as a single thing, here an ash-haired girl, with reference to both the hair of a carved figurehead and the grey colour of wood that has been subject to weathering. The figurehead is dead, but it is made of what was once living wood. The figurehead can be called a *rinc*, in Williamson's view, because it charges the waves like a beautiful warrior. There is a historical/contextual problem with this solution, however. Despite Williamson's suggestion to the contrary, neither archaeology nor art history provides evidence that shipwrights of this period fashioned figureheads in the shape of young women. Although zoomorphic or draconic figureheads are known from the Anglo-Saxon and Viking periods, nowhere do we find carvings in the shape of a girl.[40] The solution is subject to doubt whether or not Williamson's reading of the metaphors is accepted.

It therefore seems that over the century and a half since Riddle 74 was first published, scholars have hunted through both physical nature and material culture without finding a viable solution.[41] They have scoured the myths and texts of the ancient classical world for clues and have come up with empty hands. They have thumbed through Pliny's natural history and the medieval *Physiologus*, they have applied the art of medieval exegesis, and they have stretched their personal powers of imagination to the utmost without evident success. No convincing parallel has been cited either from the medieval Latin tradition or from elsewhere in the Exeter Book. Critics remain as baffled as ever by the paradoxes of female in male, of young in old, of life in death, of a creature that seems to know no physical limits to its powers of motion.

THE LITERARY RIDDLE AND THE FOLK RIDDLE

How do we proceed, then, in this impasse? If we were dealing with social or 'folk' riddling, there would be no problem. Spoken riddles 'presuppose at least two parties, the poser and the solver, and constitute a dialogue between the

---

[39] *The Old English Riddles of the Exeter Book*, pp. 349–52.

[40] See R. Bruce-Mitford, 'Ships' Figure-Heads of the Migration Period', in his *Aspects of Anglo-Saxon Archaeology* (London, 1974), pp. 175–87.

[41] Other solutions to Riddle 74 have been proposed, but only the ones I have discussed call for serious consideration. E. Müller opted for 'sun', during the boom years of solar mythology: *Die Rätsel des Exeterbuchs* (Cöthen, 1861), p. 19. L. Bragg, *The Lyric Speakers of Old English Poetry* (Rutherford, NJ, 1991), posits a human speaker and takes that speaker's words literally, despite the difficulty one might have imagining what person could have satisfied the claims made in these five lines. In its blithe self-referentiality, Bragg's reading of the riddle is a concise expression of the school of thought that a poem means what it feels like: 'This solution may not be the one intended by its author, but it is the one that brings this riddle to life for me, and that causes me to think most deeply about my own experiences' (p. 52).

two'.[42] In the human contexts that are studied by anthropologists and folklorists who have set up camp in the field, the 'correct' answer to a riddle is whatever the poser says is right. According to the rules of the game, the poser alone has the authority to declare a solution. What is black and white and red all over? The newspaper, you say? No: it is a blushing zebra. A blushing zebra, you say? No, it is a sunburned zebra, or a skunk with diaper rash, or a chocolate sundae with ketchup on it, or a squashed nun, or a penguin that cut himself shaving.[43] There is no escaping either the poser's authority or his wit. The riddler is the *magister ludi*, whose decision is final.

In the Anglo-Saxon context, however, we have no riddle performers, only riddle texts. The artful and uncompromising textuality of the Exeter Book riddles is in part what makes them so interesting from a literary perspective, for some of them pose as brisk a challenge to the intelligence and imagination of their readers as is offered by any other poetry of this time. Let us therefore consider what light can be cast on the art of the Exeter Book riddles by consideration of a literary riddle of more recent date.

A poem written by the American poet Emily Dickinson (1830–86) will serve well for our purposes. It is headed '1463' in the author's unique holograph collection, a neatly handwritten set of fascicles that was discovered after her death and that has come to be regarded as one of the greatest achievements of American poetry. Like the poems of the Exeter Book, this poem stands alone in its manuscript context without title or explanatory notes. It reads as follows in Thomas Johnson's edition, which is a semi-diplomatic one:[44]

> A Route of Evanescence
> With a revolving Wheel –
> A Resonance of Emerald –
> A Rush of Cochineal –
> And every Blossom on the Bush
> Adjusts it's tumbled Head –
> The mail from Tunis, probably,
> An easy Morning's Ride –

Some creature or thing is being described in oblique, metaphorical terms. How can we tell what it is?

As many answers might be proposed for this riddle as have been proposed for

---

[42] N. F. Barley, 'Structural Aspects of the Anglo-Saxon Riddle', *Semiotica* 10 (1974), 143–75, at 143–4.

[43] Most of these solutions are drawn from D. Ben-Amos, 'Solutions to Riddles', *Jnl of Amer. Folklore* 89 (1976), 249–54. This issue of that journal (no. 352), ed. E. Köngäs Maranda, is devoted to the riddle.

[44] *The Complete Poems of Emily Dickinson*, ed. T. H. Johnson, 3 vols. (Cambridge, MA, 1963) III, 1010. Capitalization, punctuation and the apostrophe in line 6 follow Dickinson's usage.

Exeter Book Riddle 74 if it existed only in Dickinson's manuscript fascicles, but only one answer would be right. Dickinson herself named the solution no fewer than five times in personal letters when she sent this poem to friends.[45] The object to be guessed is a hummingbird, the bird that James Audubon described as a 'glittering garment of the rainbow'.[46] The revolving wheel of line 2 is the blur of the hummingbird's wings, which (scientists tell us) beat at the rate of 80 beats per second in ordinary forward flight and, reportedly, up to 200 beats per second during courtship. The emerald and cochineal are features of the iridescent coloration of the particular North American hummingbird that Dickinson had in mind: probably the male ruby-throated hummingbird (*Archilochus colubris*), which has a range from Central America to Canada and which frequents summer gardens in that part of Massachusetts where the Dickinson family made their home. The phrase 'Route of Evanescence' neatly evokes the hummingbird's unique 'now-you-see-it, now-you-don't' manner of flying: the hummingbird can hover virtually motionless, then accelerate almost instantaneously to a speed of 50–60 km/hour in forward flight. The blossoms on the bush are shaking slightly, somewhat dishevelled after their quasi-sexual encounter with the bird. Tunis represents any exotic location, and yet the hummingbird, like any otherworldly messenger, seems to flit effortlessly between the land of iridescent imaginings and any person's back garden.

While poem '1463' is obviously a literary riddle, and while Dickinson wrote other poems in the same genre, neither this one example nor her riddle poems as a group demand analysis separate from her verse taken as a whole. Rhetorically, 'A Route of Evanescence' functions very nearly like any of her other 1,775 lyric poems. It offers comparable challenges and pleasures. In one after another of her poems can be traced the same oblique approach to a subject, the same bold use of metaphor, and the same fondness for personification as is evident here, whether her subject is the death-watch, a train in motion over the hills, a mood of intense despair, or delight in one of the creatures of nature.

Furthermore, the process of reading 'A Route of Evanescence' – the process of unriddling this text – is the same that is at work when we read any of Dickinson's poems. With any of them she plays similar games with the reader. We feel the same initial bafflement at the aggressive alterity of the text. We are challenged to draw on all the resources of our imagination to resolve the problem posed by this alterity so as to enter into the thought-world of the speaker. Then, if all goes well, comes the sudden pleasure of guessing the right answer – or, in other words, understanding the literal subject of the poem.

[45] *Ibid.* pp. 1011–12.
[46] Quoted by P. A. Johnsgard, *The Hummingbirds of North America* (Washington, DC, 1983), p. 11. I rely on Johnsgard for the technical information given elsewhere in this paragraph. Johnsgard's pl. 16C is a colour illustration of the ruby-throated hummingbird.

Finally and most importantly, we can then savour our insight and work out its implications, attentive to the nuances of every phrase and sometimes astounded by Dickinson's genius for metaphor.

Just as Old English Riddle 74 is to the whole Exeter Book anthology, then, so Dickinson's poem '1463' is to her body of poetry as a whole. Whether we are speaking of formalist poetics or of reader-response theory, the art of a riddle is a quintessence of the art of the more lyrical type of poetry. This is a point to which I will return.

One troublesome question needs posing here, however. Suppose we had no confirmation from Dickinson's private correspondence that 'hummingbird' is the subject of poem '1463'. By what standards could we still conclude that this is the right answer and that all other possible answers are wrong? To return to the Anglo-Saxon context: how can one judge if any one solution to Riddle 74 is so superior to others that it can be declared 'the' solution? What makes for validity in interpretation, anyway?

I mean this to be a practical question, not an abstract one. There are pragmatic principles of criticism that we employ all the time and that still beg for clarification. Let us then take a moment to consider their basis.

WHAT MAKES FOR VALIDITY IN INTERPRETATION?

Thirty years ago, E. D. Hirsch's classic study *Validity in Interpretation* staked out one position in a debate that subsequently has taken many forms.[47] In brief, according to Hirsch, a work means what its author claims it means, or what readers can reasonably deduce to have been the author's intent based on signs that are evident in the text. The ascription of intentionality to the figure of the author-as-God is no clear-cut matter, however, as has often been pointed out. The author may be dead and may have left no statement as to his or her intentions. Even if still alive, the author may be lying, or drunk, or otherwise untrustworthy as a witness. Or it could be that by happenstance, the author has hit upon some combination of words whose import, though meaningful to some readers, was never consciously intended. In the Old English period, very few authors can be visualized in conjunction with the texts that have come down to us. Almost all the poetry is of anonymous origin, and the concept of authorship during this period of formulaic composition, massive debts to prior sources and frequent scribal rewriting has rightly become one of the most contested points of literary criticism.[48] The argument from intention should not be dismissed – someone, somewhere must have meant something by the texts that we read today! – but it is fraught with difficulties.

---

[47] E. D. Hirsch, Jr, *Validity in Interpretation* (New Haven, CT, 1967).

[48] C. B. Pasternack, *The Textuality of Old English Poetry*, CSASE 13 (Cambridge, 1996), 12–21, reviews the problematics of authorship and audience in the Anglo-Saxon context without exhausting this potentially explosive subject.

Running counter to all arguments based on intentionality is a vein of thought, prominent in critical studies postmarked in Paris in recent years, to the effect that no one can possibly make meaningful statements in a medium as slippery as language, and that if someone does try to make meaningful statements, then no one else can possibly construe them. Writing partly to shun the nihilistic abyss that has been opened up by deconstruction, partly to provoke old-school positivists, Stanley Fish has marked out a hermeneutical position that allows for the identification of meaning in a text, yet from a standpoint opposite to that of Hirsch.[49] Meaning is not to be ascertained by trying to enter into an author's consciousness, nor is it inscribed immutably in the text, as some New Critics used to imagine. Rather, it occurs within the individual reader as that person responds to the stimulus of the text. For obvious practical reasons, few critics are willing to embrace the pure relativism that this view entails in its 'hard' form. Fish suggests two possible ways of mitigating the drawbacks of pure relativism: authority and convention. The meaning that a competent or authoritative person ascribes to a text is preferable to a meaning that is declared by anyone else; or, alternatively, acceptable meanings are distinguished from unacceptable ones by judgement of an interpretative community of competent members. In other words (to caricature this argument somewhat cruelly), meaning is what Stanley Fish says it is, or it is what a group of Stanley Fish's friends says it is. 'Soft' relativism of this kind, too, can have only slight appeal to medievalists, few of whom are likely to grant any one scholar or circle of scholars the authority to declare solutions to literary problems. When we try to solve Riddle 74, we have no access to the interpretative community of the Anglo-Saxons themselves, and modern-day specialists in Old English (the best available substitute for that community) have arrived at no consensus of opinion. We still need to know how to proceed.

Paul Armstrong's thoughtful study *Conflicting Readings: Variety and Validity in Interpretation* reviews such debates from a philosophical perspective and makes a case for a middle ground that allows for limited pluralism within a phenomenological framework.[50] Mistrusting the double absolutisms of authorial intention and radical relativism,[51] Armstrong offers three tests for validity in interpretation: *inclusiveness*, *intersubjectivity* and *efficacy*. In brief, what he means by these terms is that first of all, an interpretation, to be valid, should be complete and should involve 'consistency-building' among various elements. Second, it should prove acceptable to the members of an interpretative community. Third, it should lead to new insights and continued comprehension of the subject.

[49] S. Fish, *Is There A Text in This Class? The Authority of Interpretive Communities* (Cambridge, MA, 1980).
[50] P. B. Armstrong, *Conflicting Readings: Variety and Validity in Interpretation* (Chapel Hill, NC, 1990).
[51] Paradoxically, 'hard' relativism can be called an absolutist position, for it categorically denies a locus for validity in interpretation outside the mind of the individual interpreter.

Although there is nothing unreasonable about Armstrong's approach, we might note that it more accurately helps us locate what has been regarded as a valid interpretation in the past than it tells us how to discover merit in a proposed new reading. Armstrong's criterion of 'efficacy', for example, looks forward toward the possible consequences of a hermeneutical discovery; but before we can be aware of such consequences, we sometimes need to have achieved historical distance from the problem in question. As for Armstrong's appeal to 'intersubjectivity', this is essentially a nuanced version of Fish's argument for the authority of the interpretative community, and it is subject to similar objections. In any historical era or among any group of interpreters, consensus may harden into dogma regarding the truth-value of particular claims: Marxist claims among Marxists, for example, or exegetical claims among medieval theologians, or Freudian claims among mid-twentieth-century psychoanalysts who are not in the Jungian camp. Interpretations that are accepted by consensus of one group, and that are even thought to yield brilliant insights, may be unacceptable to another equally vocal, well-credentialled group. Moreover, consensus positions die hard, for they are rarely shaken by solutions that proceed from initial assumptions that fall outside the parameters accepted by the group. Michel Foucault responded as follows to the charge that by failing to affiliate himself with any consensus group, he forfeited the right to represent anyone or any values:

[One critic has pointed out] that in these analyses I do not appeal to any 'we' – to any of those 'we's' whose consensus, whose values, whose traditions constitute the framework for a thought and define the conditions in which it can be validated. But the problem is, precisely, to decide if it is actually suitable to place oneself within a 'we' in order to assert the principles one recognizes and the values one accepts; or if it is not, rather, necessary to make the future formation of a 'we' possible . . .[52]

If we accept Foucault's defence, then what is sometimes needed is an interpretative judgement or question that is both new and so powerful that it can create a new consensus; but this process of acceptance may take time, and it does not necessarily happen at all.

Whether the arguments that I have summarized in the preceding paragraphs are found appealing or appalling, some of us may remain impatient about the need for reasonable ways to test solutions for a poem like Riddle 74. The one book written by an Anglo-Saxonist that directly addresses the question of validity in interpretation, Stanley B. Greenfield's *The Interpretation of Old English Poems*, now seems somewhat dated, however well reasoned it is.[53] Greenfield offers no

---

[52] *The Foucault Reader*, ed. P. Rabinow (Harmondsworth, 1986), p. 385.
[53] S. B. Greenfield, *The Interpretation of Old English Poems* (London, 1972), esp. ch. 1: 'Towards a Critical Framework' (pp. 1–29).

system for testing validity. Instead, working against the grain of the 'historical' (that is, exegetical) mode of criticism that was especially popular during the 1950s and 1960s, he argues in favour of interpretations that engage closely with the language of the text, working out from there to the historical context. Greenfield seems to hope that in specific instances, his readers will accept as valid his nuanced *ad hoc* resolutions of one critical problem or another.

Finding available no master key to the door labelled 'interpretation', I therefore have drawn up a working list of criteria that ought to be satisfied if a riddle solution is to be found valid.[54] The principles are four in number. Each can be expressed in both a positive and a negative form.

First, a valid solution must be *philologically exact*, to the extent that any of us is capable of judging and practising good philology, which itself is a contestable enterprise that has to be positioned within a hermeneutical system. To speak in negative terms, the solution contains no howlers, or at least not any howlers that are crucial to the point being made. Nothing in the interpretation does violence to the specific language of the text, according to all reasonable standards of lexicography and textual criticism. No word or phrase is forced to mean anything other than what it can reasonably be expected to mean, given the linguistic conventions of the era in question – conventions that do, of course, encompass implicit rules for acceptable metaphors, kennings, puns, irony and other sorts of double meanings.

Second, a valid solution is *comprehensive*. As with Armstrong's criterion of inclusiveness, no potentially important aspect or detail of the text is left out; nothing is left unexplained. The solution is not just declared; it is developed step by step on the basis of a reasonable and sufficient body of evidence. As we have seen, for example, the cuttlefish and quill-pen solutions to Riddle 74 founder on the unexplained male/female paradox, and so neither of these readings is attractive. Moreover, the solution does not contradict itself. It functions smoothly within whatever system of belief or analysis is activated by this solution. To take an example from riddle-solving: the Empedoclean soul, through metempsychosis, can change its shape and age and sex, but it cannot be both living and dead. Erhardt-Sieboldt's solution to Riddle 74 must therefore be rejected.

Third, the solution makes for a good *historical/contextual fit*. It is not anachronistic. It does not stand in intolerable opposition to whatever else is

---

[54] Barley, 'Structural Aspects of the Anglo-Saxon Riddle', raises the issue of validity, but only in the course of a short paragraph (p. 152). More helpfully, he then works through the process by which specific riddles can be disambiguated. Heeding Ben-Amos, 'Solutions to Riddles', we should not forget that in a social context, riddling is a deliberate and sometimes even tyrannical manipulation of truth. A riddle has multiple solutions, any of which can be considered valid by its solver, even though only one is accepted by the person posing the riddle at a given moment.

known about the historical period during which the work in question was composed, the author who composed it (if that disputed category 'authorship' is invoked), the genre (or the nexus of genres) that is at stake, the intellectual tradition to which the work appears to pertain, and the sources and analogues of the work (if sources and analogues to it are known, or can be located). The solution is therefore in alignment with the possible expectations of an original audience. This is not to say that any of these factors will determine the meaning of the work in question. Any author who writes a work that is worth being read is capable of pushing generic expectations to their limit, so that interpretation must be prepared to go beyond genre at times. Certain interpretations of certain works, still, can be ruled out as historically impossible, while others may appear so implausible as to impede belief. To return to Emily Dickinson's hummingbird riddle, for example, if one were to propose the solution 'a rainbow-coloured helicopter just arrived from North Africa', every detail of the poem would be accounted for consistently, but the answer is still a cultural absurdity.

Finally, the proposed solution not only satisfies all the first three criteria I have named. It also has an aesthetic appeal to it, deriving from its relative simplicity, that can be summed up under the name *elegance*. The solution has an 'inner click', to use an expression favoured by Leo Spitzer.[55] It is not clumsy. It is no more involved or ingenious than it needs to be. There are no transsexual dead birds lurking about. A correct riddle solution engenders a minor rapture that is akin to what a mathematician experiences when, after years of labour, he or she discovers an elegant solution to a complex problem. Trautmann's 'water in its various forms' is a solution to Riddle 74 that has some elegance about it, for example, whether or not one accepts it, for through one leap of the imagination it transforms what had seemed an exotic creature into something utterly familiar.

If these four intertwining principles of validity do indeed constitute a practical basis for determining correctness in riddling – always in the absence of a flesh-and-blood riddler who will set us straight, of course – then what must also be granted, I believe, is that what we are developing is a system of practical criticism that can come to grips with the problem of validity in interpretation in general. What holds true for the special genre that we call the literary riddle should also hold true for poetry in general, or indeed for any kind of interpretative activity that is done by remote control rather than in face-to-face personal encounters. If what we want is a pragmatic basis for arriving at relative probabilities among many competing possibilities of meaning, then this four-point programme provides a reasonable point of departure.

---

[55] L. Spitzer, *Linguistics and Literary History* (Princeton, NJ, 1948), pp. 7 and 19.

UNRIDDLING RIDDLE 74

Some while ago, I promised that I would offer a solution – *the* uniquely acceptable solution, as I like to think – to Exeter Book Riddle 74. I will now do so. We can then see whether this new solution satisfies reasonable criteria for validity any better than other proposed solutions do.

The best heuristic strategy in this instance is to start at the end of the riddle and work step by step backwards. *Hæfde ferð cwicu*, the speaker concludes: 'I had a living spirit', if we give these words their face value. This last verse may give us a crucial hint. The speaker of this poem seems to have changed from a 'quick' state to a 'dead' one. Let us then take as our initial act-of-faith assumption that the speaker is an artefact that has been made from some formerly living thing. It is then an object akin to the war-horn and drinking-horn of Riddle 14 (W12), which used to be the horn of an ox, or the leather of Riddles 12, 38 and 72 (W10, W36 and W70), which used to be the hide of a living ox; or the inkhorns of Riddles 88 and 93 (W84 and W89), which used to be antlers on the head of a stag; or the battering ram or other wooden object of Riddle 53 (W51), which used to be a tree; or, for that matter, it must be like the cross in the poem known as *The Dream of the Rood*, which tells its own life story from the time that it grew up as a tree in the forest. Other examples could easily be cited. The Exeter Book includes a goodly number of 'transformation' riddles that attempt to mystify the reader by juxtaposing two stages of life in a manner that highlights the continuity of material substance through profound changes of form and function.[56]

What kind of an artefact speaks here, then? The middle of the poem tells us. It is something mobile. It is something that – speaking metaphorically, we may assume – 'flies', 'swims', 'dives', and yet also 'steps on land'. A tentative answer to the riddle can now be proposed: it is a *ship*. But let us be sure to visualize this ship correctly, for it is not a modern ship, of course, but rather a ship of the kind that would have been familiar to English-speaking people during roughly the eighth to tenth centuries AD, the apparent period when the poems of the Exeter Book were being written and compiled. Let us pursue this hypothesis.

Ships, especially those with sails, metaphorically fly like birds. This is what Beowulf's ship does, for example, when it is speeding on its way from the hero's homeland to the coast of Denmark:

> Gewat þa ofer wægholm   winde gefysed
> flota famiheals   fugle gelicost . . .[57]

[56] P. Sorrell, 'Oaks, Ships, Riddles and the Old English *Rune Poem*', *ASE* 19 (1990), 103–16, at 109, n. 26, lists as other examples of 'transformation' riddles nos. 26, 28, 73 and 83, with reference also to 9, 12, 27 and 77.

[57] *Beowulf*, ed. F. Klaeber, 3rd ed. (Boston, MA, 1950), p. 9 (lines 217–18): 'Then the foamy-necked floater [the ship] departed over the ocean, impelled by the wind, most like a bird . . .'

Ships obviously swim on the sea, metaphorically speaking. When travelling in high seas, they also metaphorically dive beneath the waves, as any sailor knows who has seen waves cascading over the prow. And what do ships do at the end of their journeys – Viking-style ships, that is? They are not normally anchored offshore. They are beached, and thus metaphorically they step onto the land, as Beowulf's same ship does on its return voyage from Denmark to the land of the Geats:

> Ceol up geþrang
> lyftgeswenced,   on lande stod.[58]

So the speaker-subject of Riddle 74 could be a ship or boat. We may now be halfway to a solution, but only halfway, for lines 1–2 must still be interpreted. Their use of metaphor is not impenetrable, however. What is a ship or boat made of? Wood. While the *ænlic rinc* of line 2 could be the ship itself – ocean-faring ships of the Viking Age were indeed singularly beautiful objects – the feminine item or items evoked in line 1 must be something different. Let me suggest that what is designated is the wood of the ship when it was a living tree.[59]

If we pursue this possibility, then the *fæmne geong* of line 1 is the tree in the form of a sapling, while the *feaxhar cwene* must be the mature tree from which timber is cut. Although the compound adjective *feaxhar* is unique to this poem and is therefore a small riddle in itself, its two components are commonplace and the simplex *har*, 'grey' or 'old and grey', occurs many times with reference to trees. One famous example is the *Anglo-Saxon Chronicle* entry for the year 1066. Here a *har* apple tree is said to mark the site near Hastings where King Harold Godwinson fought to the death against Duke William of Normandy:

> þis wearð þa Harolde cynge gecydd, 7 he gaderade þa micelne here, 7 com him togenes æt þære haran apuldran.[60]

A scanning of the charters of the Anglo-Saxon period will turn up no fewer than thirty-six references to *har* trees that served as boundary markers in a local landscape. Nine of these instances refer to thorn trees (OE *þorn*, denoting one or another type of hawthorn), seven of them to willows (OE *wiðig*), no fewer than nineteen to apple trees (OE *apeltreo*, with many variant spellings), and there

---

[58] *Ibid.* p. 71 (lines 1912b–1913): 'The ship sped ashore, it came to rest on land.'
[59] This suggestion is in accord with the system of Old English poetic diction, for ship-kennings in Old English can take a word for 'wood' as their base; examples are *brimwudu, flodwudu, sæwudu, sundwudu* 'sea-wood' and *wægbord, wægþel* 'wave plank' (B–T). Similarly, the simplex nouns *beam* 'beam' and *bord* 'board' can metaphorically designate 'ship'; see B–T, *beam* sense IV, *bord* sense III; *DOE*, *bord* sense 2.
[60] *The Anglo-Saxon Chronicle MS D*, ed. G. P. Cubbin, The AS Chronicle: a Collaborative Edition 6 (Cambridge, 1996), p. 80: 'This news was then brought to King Harold, and he then mustered a great army and came against him [Duke William] at the old grey apple-tree.'

is one solitary hazel (OE *hæsel*).⁶¹ *Har* is an adjective that is especially appropriate to old, well-established trees because of their tendency to host a robust collection of lichens, which often take the form of crusty patches or bushy growths on trunks and limbs.⁶² The *feaxhar cwene* must be an old tree covered with lichens.

If this line of reasoning is correct, is there a way of deciding what particular kind of hoar-headed tree the riddler had in mind? I think there is. Old oak trees are often conspicuous for their abundant growths of lichens. They also host mistletoe, an epiphyte that is specific to oak and that might contribute to its hoary aspect. The knight-errant Sir Gawain, in *Sir Gawain and the Green Knight*, for example, passes through woods consisting of *hore okez ful hoge a hundreth togeder*,⁶³ and we may assume that full-grown oak trees of the Anglo-Saxon period were no less hoary in appearance than their later medieval or modern counterparts. More importantly, oak wood is specific to the shipwright's trade. Although various woods are known to have been used in early boat construction,⁶⁴ oak was the favoured timber for sturdy sea-going vessels in northwest Europe during the Anglo-Saxon period, just as it has been in more recent times. Material evidence from all over the North Sea culture zone confirms this observation. The Nydam boat from Schleswig, which can be dated to the period 350–400 AD, is built entirely of oak, with planks eighty-two feet long by twenty inches broad. According to one authority, 'it must have been in ships of the Nydam type that the Anglo-Saxons reached Britain'.⁶⁵ The Sutton Hoo ship, of the early seventh century, is likely to have been of oak, according to the best authorities.⁶⁶ The ship from Kvalsund, western Norway, roughly contemporary with the

---

⁶¹ *A Microfiche Concordance to Old English*, ed. A. diP. Healey and R. L. Venezky (Toronto and Newark, DE, 1980), s.v. *haran*. The specific charters, using the *Microfiche* system of numeration (which gives cross-references to published sources), are S nos. 142, 179, 378, 411, 412, 455, 470, 491, 508, 558, 560, 563, 609, 690, 695, 766, 800, 847, 881, 896, 911, 916, 962, 967, 969 (*apuldran*), 969 again (*wiðig*), 993, 999, 1001, 1006, 1010, 1272, 1314, 1380, 1542 and 1819.

⁶² See B–T (both main volume and supplement by Toller), s.v. *har*; note also the *OED*, s.v. *hoar*, sense 3: 'The meaning may have been "grey" simply, or with lichen, and so "grey with age", "old, ancient".'

⁶³ *Sir Gawain and the Green Knight*, ed. J. R. R. Tolkien and E. V. Gordon, 2nd ed., rev. by N. Davis (Oxford, 1967), p. 21 (line 743): 'huge, hoary oaks, a hundred together'.

⁶⁴ I have found reference in the archaeological literature to ash, aspen, poplar, larch, elm, lime and pine being used in northern regions; this list is unlikely to be exhaustive.

⁶⁵ A. E. Christensen, 'Scandinavian Ships from Earliest Times to the Vikings', *A History of Seafaring, Based on Underwater Archaeology*, ed. G. F. Bass (London, 1972), pp. 159–80, at 164.

⁶⁶ 'Although it has proved impossible to make any formal identification of the wood used, the wood grain, preserved in the iron oxides from the rivets, has a denseness similar to that of oak and it is probable that oak planking was used': A. C. Evans and R. Bruce-Mitford, 'The Ship', ch. 5 (pp. 345–435) of *The Sutton Hoo Ship Burial* I, ed. Bruce-Mitford, 3 vols. (London, 1975), at 354.

Sutton Hoo ship, is made of oak planking with ribs of pine.[67] The Oseburg ship (*c.* 800 AD) and the Gokstad ship (850–900 AD), from the Oslo fjord area, are both built of oak throughout, while the Tune ship, a less well preserved ship from Oslo fjord (also 850–900 AD), is all of oak except for the cross-beams and rudder, which are of pine.[68] Sometimes half-shaped oak timbers were stored submerged in water so that they would stay supple until such time as a ship was to be built; examples are two pieces of oak meant for the prows of a large ship that were found in Sunnanå, Ryfylke, and are now to be seen in Stavanger Museum.[69]

A complete and precise solution to Riddle 74 can now be offered. The elusive speaking object is an *ac*, or oak-tree, which has been cut down and made into a *bat*, or boat.

One wonders why this solution has caused so much difficulty, for it is very much in keeping with riddling strategies used elsewhere in the Exeter Book. Riddle 73 (W71), for example, directly preceding the *ac/bat* riddle, has the answer *æsc/gar*, or (in modern English) 'ash wood/spear'. Although the text of Riddle 73 is marred by a large burn-hole that adds to its enigmatic character – evidently the mark of someone's red hot poker set down to cool for a while – the speaker tells of how it grew up on a patch of open ground, where the earth and the clouds of heaven nourished it (it too was then *cwic*, 'alive', line 4), until such time as unidentified enemies killed it, hauled it away, and shaped it to their own design (*on bonan willan*, 'to the killer's [or killers'] will', verse 7a). Riddle 30 (W28), which also uses first-person address, describes a tree or log (perhaps OE *beam*) that is variously considered as a living thing and as firewood, a cup and a cross. Riddle 92 (W88), yet again using first-person address, is thought to yield the solution 'beech tree (OE *boc*), from which a book is made'. These riddling strategies are not unique.[70]

How does this solution resolve the sex-change paradox of lines 1–2? The answer is simple, though it may seem a nasty trick. It depends on our declaring the answer to the riddle in the language of the riddler, not in modern English. OE *ac* is a feminine noun. OE *bat* is masculine. There is grammatical play here, as was possible since grammatical gender was emphatically tied to male and female categories in nature. As Ælfric writes in his *Grammar*:

---

[67] Christensen, 'Scandinavian Ships'.

[68] A. W. Brøgger and H. Shetelig, *The Viking Ships: their Ancestry and Evolution*, trans. K. John (Oslo, 1953), pp. 112, 147 and 154.   [69] *Ibid.* p. 108.

[70] As Williamson notes (*Old English Riddles*, p. 345), 'The motif of the flourishing tree, uprooted and carried off to another fate, is common to *Rids.* 71 [=K–D 73] and 51 [=K–D 53, 'battering-ram'] and also to *The Dream of the Rood* (lines 28ff.), and perhaps to the lost beginning of *The Husband's Message*.' Williamson also observes that the author of the *Rune Poem* plays on this double meaning of 'ash tree' and 'spear' in those lines (81–3) that accompany the *æsc* rune.

Æfter gecynde syndon twa cyn on namum, *masculinum* and *femininum*, þæt is, werlic and wiflic. Werlic cyn byð *hic vir* 'þes wer', wiflic *hæc femina* 'þis wif'. þas twa cyn synd gecyndelice on mannum and on nytenum.[71]

Trautmann was of the opinion that play upon grammatical gender was basic to the art of personification in the riddles. 'The Old English riddles, when they personify X, respect the gender very carefully', he claims: 'a thing whose name is masculine, they always represent as a man, feminine, as a woman'.[72] Although Trautmann exaggerates – the solution to some riddles is an idea, not a specific word, and hence a 'right' answer can be expressed by synonyms of one or another gender[73] – his claim holds true at least some of the time, and that is sufficient to show plausibility here. Tupper, in his discussion of grammatical gender as a clue to riddling, cites at least fifteen possible instances where grammatical gender is 'invoked to the reader's aid'.[74] One example is Riddle 73(W71), whose solution 'spear' is concealed in the masculine inflection of *frodne* in line 3, for both *gar* 'spear' and *æsc* 'ash wood', the material source of the spear, are masculine in gender. Another example is Riddle 21 (W19), whose precise solution *sylh* 'plough' (a feminine noun) is coded in the feminine inflections of *me...gongendre* (9a) and *me...hindeweardre* (14b–15a).

The play in Riddle 74 between the feminine oak tree and the masculine boat is consistent with gender biases that were firmly entrenched in Anglo-Saxon society and that have not lost all their power in subsequent eras. Trees are rooted to one spot, just as women are traditionally associated with hearth and home. Ships – those of the Viking age, in particular – are daring rovers, as men have been known to be. It is not surprising that systems of poetic diction that were in use among the skalds are based on these same metaphors. Just as trees can have feminine qualities, women can be called by the names of trees, as Snorri Sturluson notes in ch. 31 of his *Skaldskaparmál*.[75] Ships, in a poetic context, are

---

[71] *Aelfrics Grammatik und Glossar*, ed. J. Zupitza (1880; repr. with new foreword, Berlin, 1966), p. 18, lines 5–9, with my own capitalization and punctuation: 'As to gender: there are two genders in nouns, masculine and feminine; that is, male and female. The male gender is *hic vir* "this man", the female is *haec femina* "this woman". These two genders occur naturally among both human beings and beasts.' Ælfric then defines the neuter gender as *naðor cynn, ne werlices ne wiflices*, 'neither gender, neither male nor female'.

[72] M. Trautmann, 'Alte und neue Antworten auf altenglischen Rätsel', *Bönner Beiträge zur Anglistik* 19 (1905), 167–215, at 181.   [73] *Old English Riddles*, ed. Whitman, pp. 135–6.

[74] *Riddles of the Exeter Book*, ed. Tupper, p. lxxxix. See the end of his long footnote on pages lxxxix–xc for examples.

[75] 'Woman is called in metaphorical speech by all feminine tree-names'. See also ch. 46: 'woman is the Willow, or Dealer, of that gold which she gives; and the willow is a tree. Therefore, as is already shown, woman is periphrased with all manner of feminine tree-names.' *The Prose Edda of Snorri Sturluson*, trans. A. G. Brodeur (New York, 1923), pp. 143 and 177, respectively. For examples of woman-kennings based on oak trees, see *Lexicon Poeticum Antiquae Linguae Septentrionalis*, ed. F. Jonsson, 2nd ed. (Copenhagen, 1966), s.v. *eik*, and for

also sometimes periphrased as trees[76] and often bear a masculine, heroic aura. To judge from a book on Viking ships that was published in the 1950s, this heroic resonance still plays a strong part in the aesthetics of seafaring:

A ship is built to swim the sea, to run through the water and shed it again; it should be strong to withstand the wind and the waves, and there should be room on board for people and goods. We all know how a ship labours in a storm, wrestling with the sea, rising and heeling over till all its timbers creak and groan. Then we see that a ship is alive, that it has a personal will of its own to take on a fight with the elements and see it through . . .[77]

The strongly masculine ethos that permeates to the language of this description scarcely needs pointing out. As evoked by this expert in shipbuilding and sailing, the ship is no inert object. Rather it is a living thing that *swims, runs, sheds water,* is *large and strong, labours, wrestles* and *groans aloud.* It has the unyielding moral character of a warrior who is keen to take on a fight and see it through to the end. So we may be right: the young maiden of line 1 is a slender oak sapling; the *feaxhar cwene* is a hoary old oak tree, able to provide timbers of the size and tensile strength required for the planks, ribs and other parts of a ship; and the *rinc* or warrior is the strong, beautiful ship itself, battling the waves as it courses forward.

There remains one thorn in Riddle 74 still to be removed, however: the phrase *on ane tid* (line 2). The usual sense of this phrase, as previously noted, is 'at one time'. How can the speaker have been a sapling, a mature oak tree and a ship at the same time?

It was not, of course. There are two quite different ways by which a riddler could declare this question to have no force. First, the riddle need not be punctuated as modern editors and translators have done. The problem of *on ane tid* disappears if we group the poem's phrases as follows, in modern translation: '*I have been a young maiden, a hoar-headed woman, and a peerless warrior. At a single time I flew among birds and swam in the sea; I dived under the wave, dead among fish, and stepped*

<hr />

close discussion of one example, see A. G. Brodeur, *The Art of Beowulf* (Berkeley, CA, 1959), p. 249. Male tree-kennings are also commonplace, of course; that fact does not negate the evidence cited here.

[76] R. Meissner, *Die Kenningar der Skalden* (Bonn, 1921), notes in his section 85, on ship-kennings, that Old Norse court poets used words for tree or wood to designate the keel or mast of a ship, hence the ship itself: 'Es ist der lebende Baum, der sein Dasein als Schiff weiterführt, wobei vor allem an Kiel oder Mast gedacht wird' (p. 208). This usage is consistent with what we find in Latin exegetical tradition, where the image of the ship as a figure of *Ecclesia* rests upon the association of the *lignum* 'wood' of the Cross with the wood of which the ship is made, so that *lignum* alone can serve as a synecdoche for 'ship': see P. and U. Dronke, *Growth of Literature: the Sea and the God of the Sea,* H. M. Chadwick Memorial Lectures 8 (Cambridge, 1997), p. 12.

[77] Brøgger and Shetelig, *The Viking Ships,* pp. 104–5.

onto the shore. I had a living spirit.[78] It is the ship's motion that is single and undivided, not the speaker's identity as maiden, matron and man. Perhaps everyone since Thorpe has been punctuating Riddle 74 the wrong way; a clever syntactic strategem has worked.

Even if one rejects this choice and retains the riddle's conventional modern punctuation (which has nothing but convention to recommend it), all the demands of sense are satisfied if one looks hard at the wording of the phrase in question. *Tid* is a vague term in the Anglo-Saxon temporal vocabulary. A *tid*, or a space of time, can be as short as one hour. It can be as long as the twelve doleful years – *twelf wintra tid* – during which Grendel ravaged the deserted hall Heorot (*Beowulf* verse 147a). For Ælfric, *tid* often denotes a particular festival time like Eastertide. Ælfric also uses the word with reference to the whole period of thirty-three years during which Christ dwelled on earth in human form.[79] In his *Grammar and Glossary* Ælfric glosses *post multum tempus* as *æfter mycelre tide*, 'after a long *tid*', so a single *tid* can clearly be of long duration.[80] The whole history of the world, Ælfric declares in his first homily for Pentecost, can be divided into three *tida*, three ages:

þreo tida sind on þissere worulde: an is seo þe wæs butan æ; oðer is seo ðe wæs under æ; seo þridde is nu æfter Cristes tocyme.[81]

It is nothing magical, then, for a sapling to become a tree and a tree to be turned into a ship in a single *tid*. The reader may have been tricked into thinking that these different modes of being were simultaneous, when what the poet said is no more than that they existed *on ane tid*.

[78] My translations of *ic wæs* as 'I have been' (in the perfect tense) and *hæfde* as 'I had' (in a pluperfect sense) deserve comment. In the Old English text, all six verbs are in the simple past tense. As Bruce Mitchell points out in 'Linguistic Facts and the Interpretation of Old English Poetry', *ASE* 4 (1975), 17–24, and in *Old English Syntax*, 2 vols. (Oxford, 1985), §§ 633–44, the Old English past tense is sometimes to be translated in Modern English by a perfect or pluperfect construction. Normally either semantic context or the presence of a limiting adverb, however, clarifies the temporal meaning of a verb if something other than the simple past is meant. Although critics and translators of poetry have sometimes opted for pluperfect translations in a clause where nothing marks the verb as something other than the simple past, Mitchell argues that the burden of proof is on those who claim that the pluperfect is meant (*Old English Syntax*, § 644). In a riddle, however, are overt markers for perfect or pluperfect constructions necessarily to be expected, when the whole art of the riddle is to deceive? No linguistic 'facts' determine the answer to this question. We have a choice of interpretative options, and our choice determines a semantic context wherein the action of the verb is to be understood. For examples of changes in the sense of past-tense verbs in *The Wife's Lament* and *The Dream of the Rood*, see K. Wentersdorf, 'The Situation of the Narrator in the Old English *Wife's Lament*', *Speculum* 56 (1981), 492–516, repr. in *Old English Shorter Poems: Basic Readings*, ed. K. O'Brien O'Keeffe (New York, 1994), pp. 357–92, at 358–61.

[79] *Homilies of Ælfric: a Supplementary Collection*, ed. J. C. Pope, 2 vols., EETS os 259–60 (Oxford, 1967–8) II, homily 14 (for the sixth Sunday after Pentecost), lines 1–2, p. 515.

[80] *Aelfrics Grammatik*, ed. Zupitza, p. 270, lines 6–7.

[81] *Ælfric's Catholic Homilies. The First Series. Text*, ed. P. Clemoes, EETS ss 17 (Oxford, 1997), p. 355: 'There are three ages in this world: the first was when there was no law, the second was under law [that is, Mosaic law], the third is now after the advent of Christ.'

The 'oak/boat' solution to Riddle 74, I therefore maintain, satisfies all the criteria that I have identified as constituting a practical basis for interpretation. The answer is *philologically exact*. No word has been twisted from its literal meaning or used in a special sense, apart from appropriate metaphorical extension. The answer is *complete and self-consistent*. Every word of the riddle, every image, has been accounted for in a manner that is free of contradiction. I hope that the answer is *elegant*, but of that the reader has to judge. What of its *contextual fit*? Is the proposed solution anachronistic, generically scandalous, or otherwise monstrous on contextual grounds? Absolutely not. None of the conventions of the riddle genre is violated by this solution, and some are aptly fulfilled. The solver's first task was to reject overly literal interpretations and thereby to crack into the riddler's system of metaphor and personification. The next task was to think historically: what relevant class of object was made from a living thing during the Anglo-Saxon period? The answer fairly leapt forth when we looked at the riddle's exact wording, with its sundry verbs of motion and its 'hoar-headed woman'. A bizarre bundle of contradictions soon resolved into a familiar object. Although I suspect that ocean-going ships were as special and unusual to most Anglo-Saxon villagers as bullet trains are to most English farmers today, they were well known. As for the oak, it was literally one of the building-blocks of the Anglo-Saxons' world. It was as natural to their surroundings as hummingbirds were to Emily Dickinson's garden. And the idea of a tree being cut down and transformed into an object of some kind is clearly one that poets of this time delighted in.

As a way of clinching this argument, let me add two final pieces of evidence that will confirm the 'oak/ship' solution through the comparative method that was championed long ago by Tupper[82] and that remains a keystone of the riddle-solver's art.

The first exhibit pertains to runology – another kind of riddling, as we have seen. The transformation of oak tree into ship that is the subject of Riddle 74 is not unique to that poem. It also serves as the organizing principle of stanza 25 of the *Rune Poem*. The author's strategy in that poem is first to give the symbol for each rune in the futhorc, then to provide a short verse passage that begins with that rune-name and that tells us something more about the item that is named. Here is the passage on the *ac* rune:[83]

---

[82] Tupper begins his learned discussion of the Exeter Book riddles with a section on 'The Comparative Study of Riddles' (pp. xi–xxvi), berating prior scholars for neglecting this aspect of their subject.

[83] *The Old English Rune Poem: a Critical Edition*, ed. M. Halsall (Toronto, 1981), p. 92: 'The oak is food for flesh [i.e. yields acorns to feed swine] for the children of men; often it travels over the gannet's bath [the ocean]; the open sea tests whether the oak keeps good faith.' In her commentary on this stanza (p. 153), Halsall notes that 'the oak becomes a kind of amphibian', for it both stands *on eorþan* (on earth) and moves *ofer ganotes bæþ* (upon the sea). She also notes that seafaring is traditionally described in 'somewhat heroic terminology'.

ᚪ (ac) byþ on eorþan   elda bearnum
    flæsces fodor;   fereþ gelome
    ofer ganotes bæþ;   – garsecg fandaþ
    hwæþer ac hæbbe   æþele treowe.

We see the oak tree in two moments of its existence: first in the woods, where it provides food for pigs,[84] and then turned into the timber of a ship that traverses the high seas, just as in Riddle 74. By synecdoche, the *ac* 'oak wood' is the ship itself.

The second exhibit relates directly to this same stanza. As Paul Sorrell has pointed out,[85] stanza 25 of the *Rune Poem* is not only riddle-like in its structure. It is the next thing to a true riddle, for it represents an Anglo-Saxon analogue to an international riddle-type that is discussed as number 828 in Archer Taylor's standard collection *English Riddles from Oral Tradition*.[86] This riddle-type has been recorded from Lithuania to Jamaica. Sorrell traces it as far back in time as a seventh-century Latin collection from Bobbio, northern Italy. Since Aldhelm is believed to have known this collection,[87] it is possible to suppose a direct line of influence from the Bobbio text to the *Rune Poem* and the Exeter Book, although nothing in my argument depends on the ascription of either of these Old English texts to a specific source. What is important is that the folk riddle that underlies stanza 25 of the *Rune Poem* and that is worked into complex literary form in Exeter Book Riddle 74 has long been common currency in the West. Folk riddles of Taylor type 828 are usually put into the voice of an imagined speaker, who declares one or another variation on the theme 'When I was alive, I fattened the living. Dead, I carried the living.'[88] A Latvian version omits the feeding motif and dispenses with the first-person singular mode of address but still draws attention to the towering tree that is the material source of the ship: 'Living, it bears a green crown. Dead, it bears the living.'[89] Riddle-type 828 has many variant forms, but its regular answer is 'ship' or 'boat', a vessel that is made of dead wood and transports living people. The popularity of this international riddle type indicates a measure of 'folk' consent to the paradoxical wisdom that Anne Michaels ascribes to the character named Athos in her novel *Fugitive Pieces*: 'The great mystery of wood is not that it burns, but that it floats'.[90]

---

[84] This subject is frequently represented in medieval manuscript illustrations of the labours of the months; for Anglo-Saxon examples, see J. C. Webster, *The Labors of the Month in Antique and Medieval Art* (Evanston, IL, 1938), pp. 53–5, with pl. 33b, item 3 (showing September from London, BL, Cotton Julius A. vi) and pl. 34b, item 3 (showing September from London, BL, Cotton Tiberius B. v).   [85] Sorrell, 'Oaks, Ships, Riddles'.

[86] A. Taylor, *English Riddles from Oral Tradition* (Berkeley, CA, 1951), pp. 309–11: 'The Dead Bears the Living: A Ship'.

[87] Sorrell, 'Oaks, Ships, Riddles', p. 104 and n. 8.

[88] A Lithuanian example, from Taylor, *English Riddles*, p. 309.   [89] *Ibid.* p. 310.

[90] A. Michaels, *Fugitive Pieces* (London, 1998), p. 28.

This connection between Exeter Book Riddle 74 and Taylor riddle-type 828 is instructive from the hermeneutical perspective that was adopted earlier in this paper, for it neatly illustrates the point that the process of reading riddles – which is essentially the same process as problem-solving in general, if that prior argument is accepted – is an intellectual adventure that oscillates between a perceived problem, a set of critical assumptions, an imagined solution to that problem, and a set of tests, with each element in this web of relationships remaining subject to modification in a process of feedback. Under the name 'the hermeneutical circle', this process of oscillating between assumptions and tentative conclusions is sometimes condemned as if it were a cycle to be escaped, when what it amounts to is the essential means by which human beings gain experiential knowledge in the world. As Paul Ricoeur has emphasized, the process of textual interpretation is never mechanical; rather it is a complex provisional enterprise that is grounded and humanized in moments of personal commitment:[91]

Understanding is entirely mediated by the whole of explanatory procedures that precede it and accompany it . . . We are not allowed to exclude the final act of personal commitment from the whole of objective and explanatory procedures that mediate it . . . The 'hermeneutical circle' . . . remains an insuperable structure of knowledge when it is applied to human things, but this qualification prevents it from being a vicious circle.

To keep to Riddle 74 as an example of this hermeneutical process: once one accepts 'ship' as a possible solution to the riddle, then one is in a position to perceive it as a special example of a large class of similar riddles; and once this taxonomical triumph is achieved, then new insight follows that affects the contours of the problem itself. Line 5 of the Old English text can now be read in a different light, with the noun *ferð* taken in the plural and the verb *hæfde* read in a pluperfect sense. The phrase *hæfde ferð cwicu* can now be read as 'I contained living spirits.'[92] This meaning is undoubtedly the 'right' one from a comparative perspective, for in Taylor riddle type 828 the 'dead' carries the 'quick', that is, the ship carries people. If no editor or translator of Riddle 74 (except for Trautmann, in his own way) has opted for such a translation of *hæfde ferð cwicu*, that fact is not surprising, for no one yet either has entertained 'ship' as a solution or has noted the parallel with riddle type 828. In other words, here is an instance where Ricoeur's philosophy of interpretation is confirmed and where

[91] P. Ricoeur, 'The Model of the Text: Meaningful Action Considered as a Text', in his *From Text to Action: Essays in Hermeneutics, II*, trans. K. Blamey and J. B. Thompson (London, 1991), pp. 144–69, at 169.

[92] For this observation I am indebted to my former student Mary Bucholtz, who arrived at this insight before I had become aware of international riddle-type 828.

the comparative method in riddle analysis can offer a hint, and possibly even a correction, to textual philology.[93]

I have no wish to push this plural reading of line 5 to the exclusion of the equally valid singular reading 'I had a living spirit'. As we have seen, the latter reading encodes an important clue to the speaker's identity as an artefact made from what was once a living thing. What I do mean to suggest is that artful ambiguity is present in the grammar of line 5, just as artful ambiguity concerning gender is found in lines 1–2. A plurality of possible answers concerning the number of *ferð* in question is consistent with the riddler's mission of tripping readers up while teasing them with wisps and fragments of a solution, thus forcing only half-hearted acts of interpretative commitment on the part of a reader who remains perplexed.

RIDDLING OUT IMPLICATIONS

Before concluding this essay I wish to develop two points of interest that have been raised only glancingly thus far. First, through their teasing rhetorical strategies, how do Riddle 74 and the other riddles of the Exeter Book illustrate the ludic vein in poetry in general? And second, through their commonplace subjects and their arresting use of metaphorical imagery, how do the riddles serve as a microcosm of the Anglo-Saxon thoughtworld?

In the early medieval context, the distinction between literary riddles and 'folk' riddling is actually more problematic than I have made it appear. On one hand, the Exeter Book riddles come down to us only as written texts. The voices of their posers, assuming there once were posers, cannot now be heard. On the other hand, Old English poetry in general was meant to be voiced aloud. It was a social medium to its core. Poets maintained the trope of bodily presence and physical voice long after Old English verse had developed from its oral roots and had become a supple medium for writers. Very often, Anglo-Saxon poets use the rhetoric of an oral/aural mode of address when there can be no question of speakers being present.[94] Poetry, like riddling, thus presents itself rhetorically as a public and interactive form of communication even when we encounter it on the manuscript page. From a sociological perspective, Old English poetry uses the language of metaphor

---

[93] Since the comparative method as used here depends on the work of folklorists, my results give reason to question the claim that the relevance of late medieval, renaissance, or early modern English folklore to Old English riddles is 'doubtful at best' (Williamson, *Old English Riddles*, p. 22).

[94] W. Parks comments on this oxymoron of 'speaking books' in his fine article 'The Traditional Narrator and the "I Heard" Formulas in Old English Poetry', *ASE* 16 (1987), 45–66; cf. J. M. Foley, 'Texts That Speak to Readers Who Hear: Old English Poetry and the Languages of Oral Tradition', *Speaking Two Languages: Traditional Disciplines and Contemporary Theory in Medieval Studies*, ed. A. J. Frantzen (Albany, NY, 1991), pp. 141–56.

and paradox so as to astonish in order to elicit the participative energies of the group.[95]

Although the wish to astonish is a crucial part of the literary riddle, that desire is by no means restricted to riddling, for in their style and form, the Exeter Book riddles are a quintessential example of the Anglo-Saxon *ars poetica*.[96] From a formalist perspective there is little that distinguishes them from any other type of short poem known to the Anglo-Saxons.[97] Riddles draw on the full resources of the poetic word hoard; their syntax is interlaced in the customary poetic manner, which differs so noticeably from that of prose; and they are densely impacted to the point of being difficult to understand, even when one knows their answers. They are artful in their use of alliteration and other aural effects, as Andy Orchard has shown with reference to Riddle 74.[98] They use the conventional figures of rhetoric (or at least the figures of rhetoric can be traced in them, whether or not consciously deployed).[99] More than half the riddles use direct first-person address, as poetry in the lyric mode traditionally does.[100] Above all, the riddles are flamboyant in their display of figurative language. Their soul is metaphor. They thrive on personification and paradox. Some of them have an extraordinary exuberance, as do the storm riddles (nos. 1–3 = W1), which Charles W. Kennedy praises extravagantly as examples of the poet's

---

[95] R. Abrahams, 'The Literary Study of the Riddle', *Texas Stud. in Lit. and Lang.* 14 (1972), 177–97, argues strongly that social riddling is a group enterprise, a test of wits that is open to all members of a community, as opposed to its being a test of knowledge that is directed to an elite, as some have claimed.

[96] Arguments along this line have been opened up by J. F. Adams, 'The Anglo-Saxon Riddle as Lyric Mode', *Criticism* 7 (1965), 335–48, and M. Marino, 'The Literariness of the Exeter Book Riddles', *NM* 79 (1978), 258–65.

[97] Williamson (pp. 25–6), following earlier editors and commentators, distinguishes two main kinds of Old English riddle: one that begins with the conventional opening *Ic eom* or *Ic wæs* and one that begins typically with *Ic seah* or *Ic gefrægn* or *Wiht is*. Needless to say, these markers are not sufficient to identify a riddle as such. Some riddles lack them, while the same phrases occur in poems that are not riddles. All scholars agree that riddles either state or imply a question, but that does not take us far toward a definition.

[98] A. Orchard, 'Artful Alliteration in Anglo-Saxon Song and Story', *Anglia* 113 (1995), 429–63, at 437.

[99] M. Nelson, 'The Rhetoric of the Exeter Book Riddles', *Speculum* 49 (1974), 421–40.

[100] E. G. Stanley, 'Old English Poetic Diction and the Interpretation of *The Wanderer, The Seafarer,* and *The Penitent's Prayer'*, *Anglia* 73 (1955), 413–66, repr. in *Essential Articles for the Study of Old English Poetry*, ed. J. B. Bessinger, Jr and S. J. Kahrl (Hamden, CT, 1968), pp. 458–514, at 487–90, identifies the use of first person singular verbs as characteristic of the elegies and frequent in the riddles. Note further Bragg, *The Lyric Speakers of Old English Poetry*. W. R. Johnson, *The Idea of Lyric: Lyric Modes in Ancient and Modern Poetry* (Berkeley, CA, 1982), devotes a good deal of his first chapter, on defining lyric poetry, to a discussion of first-person address and the 'I/thou' relationship that use of the first-person pronoun establishes.

art.[101] F. H. Whitman writes with similar enthusiasm about Riddle 5 (W3), which has the answer 'shield'. In his view, this riddle 'seems to have become more than itself, in its emotional life more a poem, with the riddling properties delegated to a position of secondary importance'.[102] The fact that Whitman can speak of this riddle as having an 'emotional life' tells us much about the unusual degree of poetic animation to be found in this genre. The Exeter Book riddles are not just versified social riddles; they push the language of Old English poetry to its very limits.

Given this similarity between the art of the riddles and the art of Old English poetry in general, questions have naturally arisen concerning the genre of the poems that are inscribed in the later parts of the Exeter Book. Some scholars have wondered which riddles are really riddles, since some of them seem to give their answers away. Other poems in this section of the manuscript are riddle-like and yet lack the specific turns of phrase (such as *saga hwæt ic hatte* 'say what I am called') that mark out a riddle as such. Riddle 60 (W58), for example, which begins *Ic wæs be sonde sæwealle neah* ('I stood on the sand close by the sea-wall'), has sometimes been classed as a lyric monologue (or part of a lyric monologue) as opposed to a riddle. The poetic monologue that immediately follows it, *The Husband's Message*, has sometimes been classed as a riddle or a cluster of riddles.[103] Various readers have regarded *Wulf and Eadwacer* as a riddle. Anne Klinck likens it to the riddles on the basis of 'its brevity, its cryptic style, and its use of animals'.[104] Arnold E. Davidson has suggested that, though not technically a riddle, *Wulf and Eadwacer* is meant to be deciphered on the basis of hints and allusions: 'the very fact that the poem can be read in so many different ways suggests that it might be ambiguous and perhaps deliberately so'.[105] Interpretations of *Deor*, too, 'tend to view the poem as a puzzle to be solved'.[106] The riddling qualities of *The Ruin* are familiar to its readers: the 'answer' to that poem has been thought to be the ruins of Bath, but that specific place-name is nowhere mentioned and may be deliberately suppressed. *The Wife's Lament*, too,

---

[101] 'Nowhere else in Old English verse do we find a treatment of natural phenomena comparable in length, realism, or descriptive skill': C. W. Kennedy, *The Earliest English Poetry* (Oxford, 1943), p. 142.   [102] Whitman, *Old English Riddles*, p. 47.

[103] For discussion of these two poems' genre and their vexed relationship, see Klinck, *The Old English Elegies*, pp. 20, 56–60 and 197–9.   [104] *Ibid.* p. 49.

[105] A. Davidson, 'Interpreting *Wulf and Eadwacer*', *Annuale Mediaevale* 16 (1975), 24–32. Similarly, H. Aertsen accepts the possibility that the author of this poem 'allowed . . . multiple readings on purpose' so as to lend it the appeal of an enigma: '*Wulf and Eadwacer*: a Woman's *cri de coeur* – For Whom, For What?', *Companion to Old English Poetry*, ed. H. Aertsen and R. H. Bremmer, Jr (Amsterdam, 1994), pp. 119–44, at 120. On pp. 125–9 Aertsen discusses in some detail the 'riddle' interpretations of *Wulf and Eadwacer*.

[106] A. Olsen, 'Old English Women, Old English Men', *Old English Shorter Poems*, ed. O'Brien O'Keeffe, pp. 65–83, at 69.

has recently been solved as a riddle and has been given the solution 'sword'.[107] Wisely stopping short of such a radical reinterpretation, Karl P. Wentersdorf still advocates reading that poem as if it were a riddle: 'Today's reader seems compelled . . . to select one of a number of possible versions of the story line if there is to be a coherent evaluation of the poem as a work of art', he writes.[108] In other words, first you read *The Wife's Lament* and opt for one of its possible plots, then you experiment with the implications of your choice and evaluate how coherent they are. This is the method of riddle-solving – and, as we have seen, of interpretation in general[109] – with the difference that with the riddles, one posits a single item-as-answer rather than a life story. Many of the speakers of the riddles, however, tell their own life-story in brief, so that this distinction can break down.

Not just poems in the immediate manuscript context of the riddles flaunt an enigmatic quality. Poems from earlier parts of the Exeter Book partake of it as well. Benjamin Thorpe, the book's first modern editor, lamented that a number of these poems rely on, yet withhold, special knowledge that would render their meaning accessible. He found *Widsith* 'eminently calculated to excite, without gratifying, curiosity', while *The Wanderer* he found 'isolated, apart from every historic or legendary notice' that might explain it.[110] *The Seafarer*, too, is notoriously enigmatic for its use of a system of paranomasia whereby words such as *dryhten* 'lord' and *dreamas* 'joys' are first used in a secular context and then in a spiritual one, where their sense is transformed. Guessing the literal subject of *The Seafarer* is much like guessing the answer to a riddle. The inclusion of a series of such texts in the Exeter Book suggests, though it cannot prove, that the compiler of that anthology had a fondness for poetry that offered a challenge to the reader and that in some way had to be 'solved'. Certainly it is an interesting fact that the riddles of the Exeter Book are untitled, and hence offer a genuine experience of mystification, whereas their Latin analogues are titled and thus hand their

---

[107] F. Walker-Pelkey, '*Frige hwæt ic hatte*: "The Wife's Lament" as Riddle', *Papers on Lang. and Lit.* 28 (1992), 242–66.   [108] Wentersdorf, 'The Situation of the Narrator', pp. 357–8.

[109] Armstrong, in *Conflicting Readings* (esp. pp. 17–18), argues that any act of interpretation depends on an initial 'act of faith' that permits exploration of a subject. He accepts that different interpreters may opt for different initial stances, so that all that is available to them in the end is consistency within a system, not absolute truth. By arguing that one's initial choice of assumptions is an ethical act that may have political consequences, he aligns himself with Hirsch (and, with lesser emphasis, Ricoeur) as opposed to Fish. One could regard Armstrong's book as an effort to rationalize and humanize what could otherwise be a distastefully narcissistic relativism.

[110] B. Thorpe, *Codex Exoniensis*, p. viii. More recently R. North, discussing the genre of *The Wanderer*, has concluded that 'riddle' seems 'a good term for this poem of a notably veiled allusive style': see his 'Boethius and the Mercenary in *The Wanderer*', *Pagans and Christians: the Interplay between Christian Latin and Traditional Germanic Cultures in Early Medieval Europe*, ed. T. Hofstra *et al.* (Groningen, 1995), pp. 71–98, at 92.

solutions away. If the compiler of the Exeter Book did have a taste for the enigmatic, then that person probably shared a set of aesthetic assumptions that were held widely in Anglo-Saxon times. *The Dream of the Rood* (from the Vercelli Book) and the *Rune Poem* (from a manuscript destroyed in 1731) are only two examples, among many that could be cited, of poems from other manuscript sources that pose a deliberate challenge to the reader, withholding basic information that has to be guessed.[111] Only certain Old English poems are true riddles, but any number challenge readers to use their wits and make use of their prior knowledge in extraordinary ways.

The experience of reading and solving the Exeter Book riddles is thus very much like that of reading practically any Old English poem. Not just from a rhetorical perspective but also from a phenomenological one, riddles are a distillation of the poetic art. This is not to deny their special generic characteristics. Riddles require a single answer that can be declared either 'right' or 'wrong', for example, while other poems ask for more complex or nuanced responses. Still, guessing the answer to a riddle is not the end of things; it is rather more like their start. 'After the riddles have been solved', as has been noted more than once, 'they become most interesting'.[112] Once you find what seems to be the answer, you go back through the text, testing your answer against every detail and examining both that text and your own ordinary conceptual categories according to the insights that are provoked by your answer. This is essentially what we do when reading any demanding text. The result of this process of mental exploration is a revised knowledge of the world and of one's place in it. J. R. Hall has described this process well, speaking of the enigmatic art of the Old English

---

[111] Both of these poems have been linked with the riddles. M. Irvine examines *The Dream of the Rood* as a riddle-like text in 'Anglo-Saxon Literary Theory Exemplified in Old English Poems: Interpreting the Cross in *The Dream of the Road* and *Elene*', *Old English Shorter Poems*, ed. O'Brien O'Keeffe, pp. 31–63, at 35–8. M. Halsall, in her edition of *The Old English Rune Poem*, pp. 25–6 and 85, concludes that the lost original of that poem did not include the names of the runes. If this reasonable surmise is correct, then a member of the original audience could not have read the poem correctly without a prior knowledge of runes. The poem would thus have been an exercise in cryptography, on top of its other challenges.

[112] E. T. Hansen, *The Solomon Complex: Reading Wisdom in Old English Poetry* (Toronto, 1988), p. 127, paraphrasing M. Marino, 'The Literariness of the *Exeter Book* Riddles', p. 259. Throughout ch. 5 of her book (pp. 126–52), Hansen discusses the art of the Exeter Book riddles not with an eye to their solutions, but rather as poems with conventional features and as an ostensible speech situation. She likens them to the charms, in particular, as well as to the wisdom debate or monologue, and she discusses these genres within the general context of 'wisdom literature', a class of writings that she sees as challenging the normal categories through which people construct reality. Similarly, W. Tigges, 'Snakes and Ladders: Ambiguity and Coherence in the Exeter Book Riddles and Maxims', *Companion to Old English Poetry*, ed. Aertsen and Bremmer, pp. 95–118, compares riddles and maxims as two entries to a single body of knowledge and set of perceptions. It may be asked to what extent the qualities that Hansen and others associate with 'wisdom literature' are confined to that class of writings or are characteristic of poetry in general.

Rune Poem: 'Like a riddle-master, the rune-poet uses wordplay, antithesis, and ambiguity to challenge the reader to enlarge his perspective and deepen his sensitivity to the world in which he lives and moves and has his being.'[113]

The power that Hall ascribes to the rune-poet or that other writers have ascribed to the riddle-master, I suggest, is no different from what is deployed by the poets of the Exeter Book in general.[114] When we first approach a poem like *Wulf and Eadwacer* or *The Seafarer* or *The Dream of the Rood*, we are likely to be baffled by the way it plunges us into the midst of an unknown scene. Then at some point in our reading, if all goes well, we realize what scene is invoked, what plot is unfolding, what imagined subject is being addressed. Armed with this knowledge (or, more cautiously, furnished with this hypothesis), we then go back to the beginning of the poem and read through it again, now understanding it with pleasure if our proposed 'answer' works out, perhaps still enjoying a stringent hermeneutical challenge if it does not.

What I am suggesting is that there is much to be gained from considering Old English poetry in general as a form of play. Again and again, at every level of this poetry from the kenning to the story line, one can see the workings of the 'double task of revealing and concealing'[115] that is the special mode of the riddles. To speak of poetry as play is not a new departure, of course. Johan Huizinga described poetry in terms of game theory nearly fifty years ago in his classic study *Homo Ludens*, which called attention to the origins of culture itself in play.[116] More recently Wolfgang Iser has mounted a similar argument from a contemporary phenomenological perspective. In his view, 'authors play games with readers, and the text is the playground'.[117] The formalized structures of poetry – the special diction, syntax and rhetoric that are characteristic of all poetic languages – serve to open up the play space. Conventional formulas, such as *ic wæs*, *ic seah*, *ic gehyrde* or *we gefrugnon* in the Old English context, announce the start of the game. The disfigurement of language that is such an overt and pleasurable part of much archaic and medieval poetry, alienating verse from the language of everyday life, alerts readers that a ritualized ludic activity has begun. The process of reading a literary text of any kind is thus an activity akin to what

---

[113] J. R. Hall, 'Perspective and Wordplay in the Old English *Rune Poem*', *Neophilologus* 61 (1977), 453–60, at 458.

[114] *The Rune Poem* is riddle-like but is not part of the Exeter Book. On the other hand, some of the poems included in the Exeter Book are not particularly enigmatic. My generalization therefore applies not to this one poetic codex, but rather to a type of poetry that is commonly practised there and that is sometimes practised elsewhere.

[115] Nelson, 'The Rhetoric of the Exeter Book Riddles', p. 424.

[116] J. Huizinga, *Homo Ludens: a Study of the Play-Element in Culture*, trans. R. F. C. Hull (1949; repr. London, 1970, with introduction by G. Steiner), ch. 7 ('Play and Poetry'), pp. 141–58. On pp. 156–8 Huizinga discusses riddles and poetry as two closely related forms of expression.

[117] W. Iser, *Prospecting: From Reader Response to Literary Anthropology* (Baltimore, MD, 1989), p. 250.

children or any of us do in rule-governed games, where the object is not simply to win or lose but rather to extend ourselves, through imaginative role-playing, into new configurations of reality.

CONCLUSION: POETRY AS EVIDENCE FOR WORLDVIEW

My argument thus far can be summarized as follows. Although social riddling is sometimes dismissed as a mere pastime, the Anglo-Saxon literary riddle can be regarded as a kind of 'pure' poetry that depends for its effect less on its readers getting the right answer than on their engagement with the poetics of riddle production. Paradoxically, through phrases like *saga hwæt ic hatte* 'say what my name is' – as if a flesh-and-blood person were in a position to hear this command and respond to it – the literary riddles of the Exeter Book make strong gestures toward face-to-face communication. In this regard the riddles are no different from Old English poetry in general, which regularly 'speaks' to its 'audience' as if it were being voiced aloud in a social situation. In its brevity, its use of the first-person voice, and its reliance on metaphor, personification and paradox, Riddle 74 is a distillation of the Anglo-Saxon poetic art – an art that thrives on the fiction that it is a gift of words, an act of verbal exchange.

Since written literature has never wholly shed this underlying fiction of orality,[118] the process of reading the Exeter Book riddles thus typifies the process of reading poetry in general. No matter if we are reading Riddle 74 or *The Dream of the Rood*, Dickinson's poem '1463' or any of a number of other modern lyrics. Whatever poem we turn to, to the extent that the author addresses an imagined audience and conceals as he or she reveals, we are invited to take part in a play of the text that stretches our intellectual faculties beyond their usual limits. It is only to be expected that the criteria by which we can reasonably judge correctness in riddling are no different from the criteria by which interpretations of any kind can be tested. Riddles are not unique. In their compactness, they provide an entry to the most basic hermeneutical issues.

The last point that I wish to make, even if briefly, is that study of the riddles has much to contribute to our understanding of the worldview of the Anglo-Saxons. Since 'worldview' is not a term in common parlance among medievalists, the sense in which I am using it should be explained.

Anthropologists and folklorists have long been accustomed to analysing what is special about a people's 'outlook on life,' '*Weltanschauung*', or 'vision of the world'. As is now recognized, study of a people's 'outlook on life' also includes

[118] We still routinely speak of an author's 'audience', for example, as if readers were listening to speech rather than deciphering visual glyphs. Some modern authors (like Henry Fielding in *Tom Jones*) address the reader familiarly, as if in personal conversation, thus adapting a 'listener-response' rhetoric that has long been conventional in sermons, as in the prologues and epilogues of plays.

how they themselves are implicated in the world that they perceive and that they partially construct through their imaginings. The present concept of 'world-view' thus encompasses a people's strategies of selfhood as well as their concept of all that constitutes external reality. It is widely assumed that worldview is patterned, not random, and that all the elements of a culture that are open to scholarly analysis, including 'kinship data, grammar, child-rearing details, agricultural techniques, or any one of a thousand bits and pieces of culture' (to quote Alan Dundes),[119] are potentially subsumed in this patterning, though the place of every detail in this scheme may not be equally clear. Worldview is largely invisible to those who share it, for people do not normally have an anthropologist's vantage point on their own culture and cannot easily stand outside their own mind in order to observe it. For scholars of cultures that are remote from us either spatially (for example, the Fiji Islands) or temporally (for example, Anglo-Saxon England), the value of studying worldview is twofold. First, it may promote insight into those bedrock structures of thought and feeling that form the basis of private identity and that justify the institutions of social power in any given time and place. Second, it may enhance understanding of any one element of culture – this hoe, this festival, or this text – by showing how that detail is expressive of a much larger system.

Partly because of their utterly mundane literal content, partly because of their flamboyant use of figures of speech, the Exeter Book riddles provide an illuminating entry to the worldview of the Anglo-Saxons. More than any other documents from their time, they play with the bric-à-brac of daily life. They give life to things that are so often seen that they are no longer seen. As has long been recognized, the riddles 'stand forth as the most important contemporary contributions to our knowledge of the everyday life of their time'.[120] They evoke image after image that has no place in the loftier world of heroic poetry or scriptural narrative: the four teats of the milch-cow, for example, or the pedlar's pack of wares. Wim Tigges claims that in their 1,630 lines of verse – five per cent of the extant Old English poetic corpus – riddles constitute '*the* environment of images *par excellence*' of the earliest English

---

[119] A. Dundes, 'Thinking Ahead: a Folkloristic Reflection of the Future Orientation in American Worldview', *Anthropological Quarterly* 42 (1969), 53–71, repr. in his, *Interpreting Folklore* (Bloomington, IN, 1980), pp. 69–85 and 264–5, at p. 70. Other influential studies of worldview include R. Redfield, 'Primitive World View and Civilization', in his *The Primitive World and its Transformations* (Ithaca, NY, 1953), pp. 84–110, and C. Geertz, 'Ethos, World-View and the Analysis of Sacred Symbols', *Antioch Rev.* 17 (1957), 421–37, repr. in A. Dundes, *Every Man His Way: Readings in Cultural Anthropology* (Englewood Cliffs, NJ, 1968), pp. 301–15. A. Gurevich, *Historical Anthropology of the Middle Ages*, ed. J. Howlett (Chicago, IL. 1992), ch. 1 (pp. 3–20), reviews the importance of 'worldview' in recent historiography under the guise of many different names, including *mentalité*, 'collective consciousness' and 'picture of the world'.

[120] *Riddles of the Exeter Book*, ed. Tupper, p. lxxxvi.

poetry.[121] It is thus to the riddles that one naturally turns if one wishes to discover how the Anglo-Saxons thought and felt about the basic elements of their lifeworld.

The riddles remind us that no object is merely an object. When singled out by a poet's or artist's attention, an ordinary thing becomes luminous with spirit. Very often it takes on a human face and form. This is what happens in the riddles, where 'dead' objects speak about their lot in terms that living people will understand. By endowing with soulful sentience a single reed growing by the shore, for example, a poet not only imparts information about the natural world but also communicates human feelings of loneliness. Sometimes the emotions that are lodged in the riddles can only be recognized if one has competence in the power relations that shaped the Anglo-Saxon social world. The riddles stress lordship, obedience, fear. They dwell on the service of man to master.[122] Whitman sees in them a 'preoccupation with valor and suffering' that matches their concern with 'the spirit of comitatus'.[123] As Tigges has remarked, the riddles thus have a social function, for they 'confirm the social relationships of their day by metaphorically applying these to randomly presented phenomena or objects'.[124]

Edward B. Irving, Jr, agrees that useful information can be extracted from study of the riddles.[125] By 'useful information' he is not only speaking of ornithology, leather-working, the technology of script and countless other aspects of the Anglo-Saxons' material world. He also means information with a bearing on the history of human sensibility, particularly among people of ordinary status. If we take the anthropomorphic figures of the riddles as surrogates for real people, then the riddles have much to say about downtrodden members of society. There is the battered shield who is beaten down without heroic recourse in Riddle 5 (W3), for example; or there is the female fox or badger of Riddle 15 (W13), who runs and hides and fights desperately to defend its young; or there is the sword of Riddle 20 (W18), who is a peerless warrior and yet also, in Irving's view, 'a vain and swaggering murderer, shielded by the protection of an indulgent patron' (p. 205). These poems give shelter to elements that find no place in the Anglo-Saxon heroic world. Irving sees in the riddles a robust cynicism that complements the effulgent surfaces of war and weaponry that are held up for admiration in such poems as *Beowulf* and *Waldere*.

---

[121] Tigges, 'Snakes and Ladders', p. 95, with reference to a phrase, 'environment of images', that A. Lee uses to good effect in his book *The Guest-Hall of Eden: Four Essays on the Design of Old English Poetry* (New Haven, CT, 1972), p. 231.

[122] See *Riddles of the Exeter Book*, ed. Tupper, p. lxxxviii; Tigges, 'Snakes and Ladders', p. 99; Hansen, *The Solomon Complex*, pp. 137–8. [123] Whitman, *Old English Riddles*, p. 51.

[124] Tigges, 'Snakes and Ladders', p. 109.

[125] E. B. Irving, Jr, 'Heroic Experience in the Old English Riddles', *Old English Shorter Poems*, ed. O'Brien O'Keeffe, pp. 199–212, at 199.

The riddles not only present objects in anthropomorphic guise; they also arrange them in anthropocentric systems of order. Virtually everything that they name has a function. What the riddles prize above all is the way things turn to the welfare of humankind. Rarely is the 'raw' stuff of nature introduced (a deer's antlers, an ox's hide) without its being brought into relation to the 'cooked' elements of culture (a pair of inkwells, a set of leather goods). The riddles thus domesticate the wild and the natural and turn it to human use.

As anthropologists have stressed, it is in part through posing and solving riddles that people test the conceptual boundaries of their world, rendering abstract relations concrete and endowing common things with sentience. Through such games, people construct the world of thought and feeling that they inhabit.[126] By composing and interpreting poetry in general, people do much the same thing. The Anglo-Saxons were no different from ourselves in that regard. Their riddles – and their poetic texts in general – not only mirror a world; they constitute a mental world as well.

Riddle 74 can serve as an example of this cosmoplastic tendency. Basic features of the Anglo-Saxon worldview are on display here in a mere five lines of verse. A speaker celebrates its free movement in the open air, on the sea, and on the earth. What if the speaker is a ship? Cannot a ship, like a person, delight in the power of motion? A ship is not only mobile, however; it is also *ænlic*. It is a singularly beautiful (and expensive) product of craftsmanship. As such, it shouts out its owner's wealth and social status. The ship is not solely admired as artefact and symbol, however. It is also seen in relation to the stuff out of which it was made: the living oak tree out of which it was hewn by the woodsman's effort and the carpenter's skill. That oak tree too is presented in anthropomorphic terms. She is a woman who has grown from slender, virginal youth to grey-headed old age. The epithet *feaxhar* with which the speaker's life as a mature tree is evoked reveals the poet's eye for an aged oak as an observable thing in nature, variegated in appearance. Nature, material culture and human spirit here cohabit a single body. Moreover, delight in the physical world is consistent with an appreciation of mutability. Through its paradoxes, the riddle neatly expresses the impending presence of death in life, the lingering traces of life in death, the constant inconstancy of earthly things. Equally typically, Riddle 74 is self-conscious about its own use of language. It plays with grammatical duplicity as well as with metaphor. Riddle 74 thus explores the ways in which, in sites opened up by its inevitable ambigu-

[126] See M. D. Lieber, 'Riddles, Cultural Categories, and World View', *Jnl of Amer. Folklore* 89 (1976), 255–65. Barley, 'Structural Aspects of the Anglo-Saxon Riddle', writes about riddles from an anthropological perspective with attention to their world-building capabilities, as does I. Hamnett, 'Ambiguity, Classification and Change: the Function of Riddles', *Man* ns 2 (1967), 379–92.

ities, speech enables the language-user to flirt with the actions and things that words denote.

In sum, even the five lines of Riddle 74 point unerringly to how the Anglo-Saxons conceived of a human being as a creature who delights in *physical movement* and dreads confinement, who uses the divine gift of language to *speak* the world into both 'real' and contrary-to-fact configurations, who identifies aesthetic beauty with the *craftsmanship* that shapes the things of nature into new forms, who sees the whole of nature as a field for human *use*, who seeks to *control* both the external world and other human beings through exercise of the art/wealth/power nexus, and who freely acknowledges, for good and for ill, both the *mutability* of existence and the liberating *potential* in things whereby the future is latent in the present, like the idea of a spear or a plank embedded in a tree, while the past continues to reside in the present, as happens on every occasion when the poet or seer breaks into speech or the author lifts his pen. These conceptions (and others like them) were not unique to the Anglo-Saxons, of course. To some degree, though not to the extent that we may naively think, they are perhaps 'simply human'. Still the strong effort of scholarship should always be to historicize such conceptions as 'reality', 'the world', or 'human nature' so as to expose them as aspects of worldview – that is, as period-specific creations of language that become accepted so widely that they achieve the status simply of truth.

Whether or not there is merit in the argument that poetry itself is a form of riddling play, whether or not anyone will sign up for my four-step programme for validity in interpretation, and whether or not the claim is persuasive that even one very short poem can encode essential elements of the Anglo-Saxon worldview, I hope that readers have profited from the exercise of close reading that has been undertaken here. Among the pleasures of reading the poetry of any period is that provided by close scrutiny of a single text. Sometimes, as with poets of the stature of Dickinson, the pleasures of reading increase in proportion to the challenge a text provides. Since the Exeter Book riddles are not only artful but, taken collectively, have been called 'certainly the most difficult text in the field of Anglo-Saxon',[127] their pleasures for some readers must be substantial.

Even if, for reasons that I cannot anticipate, my proposed 'oak-boat' solution to Riddle 74 is rejected, I hope that the process of playing with that text may still have been rewarding, with its byways among grammar and semantics, birds and boats, metaphors and metamorphoses. Some readers who delight in open-endedness may even be content to leave Riddle 74 unsolved, for opting for one interpretation naturally means opting out of others. As Iser remarks, any decision about the meaning of a text 'will eclipse countless aspects brought to view

---

[127] *Riddles of the Exeter Book*, ed. Tupper, p. vii.

by the constantly shifting, constantly interacting and hence kaleidoscopically iterating positions of the game, so that the game itself runs counter to its being brought to an end'.[128] In other words, the process of playing the Exeter Book game may be more fun than winning it. If the solution that I have offered gains enough converts to pass Armstrong's 'intersubjectivity' test, however, then a degree of closure will have been brought to a mental contest that has baffled some very learned and thoughtful people over the past 150 years. We will have unriddled the quick and the dead; and that, I think, is enough for one article.

[128] Iser, *Prospecting*, p. 252.

Addendum. I regret that D. Donoghue's study 'An *Anser* for Exeter Book Riddle 74', *Words and Works: Studies in Medieval Language and Literature in Honour of Fred C. Robinson*, ed. P. S. Baker and N. Howe (Toronto, 1998), pp. 45–58, appeared in print too late for discussion here.

Body and law in late Anglo-Saxon England

KATHERINE O'BRIEN O'KEEFFE

This article explores some textual dimensions of what I argue is a crucial moment in the history of the Anglo-Saxon subject. For purposes of temporal triangulation, I would locate this moment between roughly 970 and 1035, though these dates function merely as crude, if potent, signposts: the years 970×973 mark the adoption of the *Regularis concordia*, the ecclesiastical agreement on the practice of a reformed (and markedly continental) monasticism, and 1035 marks the death of Cnut, the Danish king of England, whose laws encode a change in the understanding of the individual before the law. These dates bracket a rich and chaotic time in England: the apex of the project of reform, a flourishing monastic culture, efflorescence of both Latin and vernacular literatures, remarkable manuscript production, but also the renewal of the Viking wars that seemed at times to be signs of the apocalypse and that ultimately would put a Dane on the throne of England. These dates point to two powerful and continuing sets of interests in late Anglo-Saxon England, ecclesiastical and secular, monastic and royal, whose relationships were never simple. This exploration of the subject in Anglo-Saxon England as it is illuminated by the law draws on texts associated with each of these interests and argues their interconnection. Its point of departure will be the body – the way it is configured, regarded, regulated and read in late Anglo-Saxon England. It focuses in particular on the use to which the body is put in juridical discourse: both the increasing role of the body in schemes of inquiry and of punishment and the ways in which the body comes to be used to know and control the subject.

As a way of bringing several problems into focus, I wish to read two texts together and against each other. The first of these is an entry from the mid-eleventh-century C-text of the *Anglo-Saxon Chronicle*, recording the murder of Alfred ætheling in 1036. The second, though chronologically earlier, text is the *Translatio et miracula S. Swithuni*, written at Winchester around 975 by Lantfred, a Frankish monk, probably from Fleury.[1] These two texts, history and hagiography, have markedly different expectations and interests. The one records violent mutilation; the other records miracles of healing. The one concerns itself with deadly political struggles during the last life-breaths of the Cerdicing dynasty;

---

[1] See M. Lapidge, *Anglo-Latin Literature, 900–1066* (London, 1993), pp. 36–7.

the other seeks to glorify a new and powerful *patronus* for the previously eclipsed Old Minster in the royal city of Winchester. But, as I shall argue, they converge powerfully in their take on the body and the subject of law.

In exploring the implications of the body as sign of something other than itself, my interest lies in the textual dimensions of the Anglo-Saxon *subject*, that being who fills the position of 'I' in a sentence, thus one who is subject *of* and *to* discourse, and, at the same time, one who is also subject of and to power. Investigation of the 'subject' exploits the dual possibility of the word to signify that grammatical subject about whom things are predicated and the social subject who is the object of power. It situates an analysis of the individual within discursive structures – in the present instance, secular and canon law – examining ways in which the subject is called forth within complex webs of interlocution. And, in its focus on the body, it seeks to avoid two positivities: face value acceptance of an Anglo-Saxon definition of the primacy of the soul and, similarly, of present-day reflexes of the mind/body split. In such discussions, the familiar word 'self' is unhelpful as much from its imprecision in analyses of discourse and of power as from the weight of historical interpretation freighted on 'self'. Scholarship on the nature of the 'self', particularly as it appears in Old English poetry, has been too ready to read in the Old English word *sylf* a reflex of the modern English word. As illustration one might use the famous exchange of essays by J. C. Pope and Stanley Greenfield on the force of *sylf* in *The Seafarer*, where the end point of the exchange was the transformation of the reflexive pronoun into a substantive, giving the Seafarer a 'self'.[2] Pope's first translation clearly recognizes the word's reflexive function. But his second analysis requires *sylf* to mark a separate consciousness ('alone'). In Greenfield's second argument, 'for myself' skates back and forth over the slippery border of grammar and semantics. That is, while Greenfield acknowledges that *sylf* is grammatically a reflexive pronoun, he begs the question by claiming that his translation uses the word's 'semantic and not its grammatical property', that is, that in the name of semantics he can read *self/sylf* as 'by and for the speaker's *self*' (emphasis added), producing a substantive self.[3] Focus on the body, then, is strategically a defamiliarizing manoeuvre and analytically an opportunity to examine some culturally specific ways in which body and individual are constructed in late Anglo-Saxon England. The first part of the

---

[2] J. C. Pope, 'Dramatic Voices in *The Wanderer* and *The Seafarer*', *Franciplegius: Medieval and Linguistic Studies in Honor of Francis Peabody Magoun, Jr.*, ed. J. B. Bessinger and R. P. Creed (New York, 1965), pp. 164–93; S. B. Greenfield, '*Min, Sylf*, and "Dramatic Voices in *The Wanderer* and *The Seafarer*" ', *JEGP* 68 (1969), 212–20; J. C. Pope, 'Second Thoughts on the Interpretation of *The Seafarer*', *ASE* 3 (1974), 75–86; and S. B. Greenfield, '*Sylf*, Season, Structure and Genre in *The Seafarer*', *ASE* 9 (1981), 199–211.

[3] S. A. J. Bradley's widely used (and normally reliable) translation of *The Seafarer*, at line 1, 'I can tell the true riddle of my own self', equips the Seafarer with a confessional personality and illustrates how far current interpretation in the field assumes an identity between modern and medieval self-consciousness (*Anglo-Saxon Poetry* (London, 1982), pp. 332–5, at 332).

argument examines the implications of a particular nexus of discourse and power in the annal for 1036 in the C-text of the *Anglo-Saxon Chronicle*.

The appearance of the body in the C-text is regulated, by and large, by conventional usage, though the annal of the events of 1036 marks a significant departure from such conventions. In general bodies appear modestly and unremarkably in the *Chronicle*, for almost always they are quite dead. The form of their mention is standard if not frequent: upon mention of the death of a person of rank, the place of burial is noted with 'and his (her) body lies at X'.[4] This is not to suggest that the body goes unremarked in the written discourse of Anglo-Saxon England. One might take as an early example Bede's *Historia ecclesiastica*, whose account of Gregory's letter to St Augustine includes a lengthy discussion of the particulars of the female body for women's ritual periods of cleanness and defilement and the effect of what are delicately called 'illusions' on male ritual purity.[5] Similarly, the church's numerous canonical strictures on fasting, prohibitions of consanguienous marriage, or specification of the times during which marital intercourse was licit all appear in discourse on the body designed for its regulation.[6] The so-called 'Old English Handbook for a Confessor' (Cambridge, Corpus Christi College 265 and elsewhere), grounding the other world in this one, expects the penitent to confess sins of the body in somatic detail:

Ic andette eal þæt ic æfre mid eagum geseah to gitsunge oððe to tælnesse, oððe mid earum to unitte gehirde, oððe mid minum muðe to unnytte gecwæð. Ic andette þe ealles mines lichamon synna, for fel and for flæsc, and for ban and for sinuwan, and for æddran and for grislan, and for tungan and for weleras, and for goman and for teð, and for feax and for mearh, and for æghwæt hnesces oððe heardes, wætes oððe driges.[7]

---

[4] See, for example, 755 C 'and his lic lið on Wintanceastre. . . .'; see also 783, 856, 861, 868, 875, MR 918, MR 924, 978, 981, 1016 and 1050. The body makes a different appearance in the *Chronicle* beginning with the account of Æthelred's reign. See especially ASC 993 and 1006 for brief mention of Æthelred's blinding of Ælfric's son, Ælfgar, and of Wulfgeat's sons, Wulfheah and Ufegeat. At 1014 the C-text notes that Cnut has aristocratic hostages taken by his father mutilated by cutting off hands, ears and noses. See also the murder of Bishop Ælfheah, 1012, where C alone adds 'hine þær ða bysmorlice acwylmdon' to the details of his death by beating.

[5] *Bede's Ecclesiastical History of the English People*, ed. B. Colgrave and R. A. B. Mynors (Oxford, 1969), I.27, *interr*. 8 and 9. On the authenticity of the *Libellus responsionum*, see R. Means, 'A Background to Augustine's Mission to Anglo-Saxon England', *ASE* 23 (1994), 5–17.

[6] See, for example, *Die Canones Theodori Cantuariensis und ihre Überlieferungsformen*, ed. P. W. Finsterwalder (Weimar, 1929): *Canones Theodori*, items 56 (abstaining), 42 (masturbation), 68 (prohibiting naked intercourse); *Canones S. Gregorii*, items 78–81 and 107; '*Canons of Edgar*', item 25.

[7] R. Fowler, 'A Late Old English Handbook for the Use of a Confessor', *Anglia* 83 (1965), 1–34, at 17–18: 'I confess all that I ever saw with my eyes in avarice or calumny, or heard with my ears in vanity, or spoke with my mouth in idleness. I confess to you all the sins of my body, for skin and flesh, and for bone and sinew, and for vein and gristle, and for tongue and cheeks, and for gums and teeth, and for hair and marrow, and for anything soft or hard, wet or dry.' Dorothy Whitelock suggests that 'Wulfstan may have written parts of the text, and have had a hand in the compilation' (*Councils and Synods with other Documents relating to the English Church*, ed. D. Whitelock, M. Brett and C. N. L. Brooke, 2 vols. (Oxford, 1964–81), I, 313, n. 5).

In the context of regulation, the law codes are of especial interest, not simply for their cataloguing of crimes and punishments, but for the matrices they offer in which bodies and body parts are counters within an economy of pain, payment and value.

The following argument focuses on the use which the *Chronicle* writer makes of the body, the juridical discourse upon which he draws, and the opportunity it affords us to speculate on the ways in which the subject is formed through such discourse. It analyses the conjunctions between the annal for 1036, elements of the law codes, and two treatments of the miracles of St Swithun.

1036. Her com Ælfred, se unsceððiga æþeling, Æþelrædes sunu cinges, hider inn and wolde to his meder, þe on Wincestre sæt, ac hit him ne geþafode Godwine eorl, ne ec oþre men þe mycel mihton wealdan, forðan hit hleoðrode þa swiðe toward Haraldes, þeh hit unriht wære.

> Ac Godwine hine þa gelette   and hine on hæft sette,
> 7 his geferan he todraf,   and sume mislice ofsloh;
> sume hi man wið feo sealde,   sume hreowlice acwealde,
> sume hi man bende,   sume hi man blende,
> sume hamelode,   sume hættode.
> Ne wearð dreorlicre dæd   gedon on þison earde,
> syþþan Dene comon   and her frið namon.
> Nu is to gelyfenne   to ðan leofan gode,
> þæt hi blission   bliðe mide Criste
> þe wæron butan scylde   swa earmlice acwealde.
> Se æþeling lyfode þa gyt;   ælc yfel man him gehet,
> oðþæt man gerædde   þæt man hine lædde
> to Eligbyrig   swa gebundenne.
> Sona swa he lende,   on scype man hine blende,
> 7 hine swa blindne,   brohte to ðam munecon,
> 7 he þar wunode   ða hwile þe he lyfode.
> Syððan hine man byrigde,   swa him wel gebyrede,
> ful wurðlice,   swa he wyrðe wæs,
> æt þam westende,   þam styple ful gehende,
> on þam suðportice;   seo saul is mid Criste.[8]

The outrage which the C-text voices at the mutilation of the *æþeling* Alfred and of his men is not the voice of genteel horror at the culturally shocking. Mutilation of whatever origin must have been commonplace in daily life, from the twisted limbs and gaping, festering sores presented for healing at holy places, to the casual acts of violence which were the hallmarks of victorious

[8] *The Anglo-Saxon Minor Poems*, ed. E. V. K. Dobbie, ASPR 6 (New York, 1942), 24–5.

marauders, to the excruciating forensic exactments in compensation for rapes, thefts, adulteries and other crimes outlined variously in the law codes. We know that such acts took place, and the bodies of their survivors would have been their witness – but about these the C-text tells us nothing. Whence comes this memorializing of the events for 1036 – events about which D is circumspect and E is silent?

The players in this drama are Emma, wife to Æthelred and later to the Dane Cnut, and their sons (variously) Edmund Ironside, Harold Harefoot, Harthacnut, Edward, later king, and the unfortunate Alfred.[9] When Cnut became sole king of England, Edward and Alfred, the two sons of Æthelred and Emma, were in their early teens and in exile in Normandy. Their mother, the Norman Emma, had stipulated in her treaty of marriage to Cnut that only a son of her body would succeed Cnut to the throne of England,[10] a provision to disinherit Cnut's sons, but which effectively disinherited her own sons by Æthelred, Edward and Alfred, when she bore Cnut a son, Harthacnut.[11] Cnut's sudden death in 1035, apparently without provision for succession, threw England once again into turmoil. Into this stew the hapless Alfred *æþeling* makes his appearance in 1036. The C- and D-texts claim that he travelled to England on a filial visit to his mother. The truth is difficult to discern. Later, Norman sources indicate that Edward made an initial sortie into England which appears to have been repulsed.[12] John of Worcester describes both æthelings travelling to England from Normandy with a number of Norman soldiers.[13] William of Poitiers makes the throne the objective of each brother.[14] The *Encomium Emmae* has Alfred alone depart from Flanders by way of Boulogne and with only a few men, lured by a letter from Emma supposedly forged by Harold.[15] For all the rhetoric of the *Encomium*, in its narrative of the capture and torture of Alfred's men it is markedly less specific than the C-text: in the *Encomium* none but a tenth of Alfred's men was spared. Guiltless they are condemned without hearing, and

[9] See F. Barlow, *Edward the Confessor* (London, 1970), p. 30.
[10] *Encomium Emmae Reginae*, ed. A. Campbell, Camden 3rd ser. 72 (London, 1949), 11–14 (II.16).
[11] On the politics of inheritance, see S. Keynes, 'The Æthelings in Normandy', *Anglo-Norman Stud.* 13 (1990), 173–205.
[12] See William of Jumièges, *Gesta Normannorum Ducum,* ed. E. M. C. Van Houts, 2 vols. (Oxford, 1992–5) II.106–8 (VII.6), and William of Poitiers, *Gesta Guillelmi,* ed. R. H. C. Davis and M. Chibnall (Oxford, 1998), pp. 2–6.
[13] *The Chronicle of John of Worcester II,* ed. R. R. Darlington and P. McGurk, trans. J. Bray and P. McGurk (Oxford, 1995), pp. 522–5. On the use of sources for the reigns of Æthelred and the Danish kings, see R. R. Darlington and P. McGurk, 'The "Chronicon ex Chronicis" of "Florence" of Worcester and its Use of Sources for English History before 1066', *Anglo-Norman Stud.* 5 (1983), 185–96, esp. 193–4. [14] Barlow, *Edward the Confessor,* pp. 45–6.
[15] *Encomium,* ed. Campbell, III.4 (p. 42).

variously slain, enslaved, or kept in chains.[16] The detail is kept for the torture of Alfred.[17]

This background, complicated as it is, is essential to any understanding of the appearance of the body in the C-text for 1036. Politically, the body makes its uncomfortable appearance in the C-text in the record of years of turmoil caused by a challenge to the throne and then by the chaos resulting from an uncertain succession. Alfred's body (ineligible for succession by its blinding) is thus made to stand in the C-text for one line of succession. And his treatment (and the treatment of his men) is evoked to argue against Earl Godwine and Harold Harefoot, and the outrage of the text is directed against them. The politics of the C-text's anti-Godwinist sentiments aside, the narrative stance of the entry for 1036 asks us to attend to its reading of the bodily signs inflicted on Alfred and his men.

It is not merely the cruel treatment of these men which inspires the passion of the entry. It is the significance of that treatment which evokes its anger and protest. At four points in the entry the text asserts the innocence of the captives. Alfred is *se unsceððiga æþeling* caught in the grip of a usurper (though popular support seemed to be turning to Harold, the text notes that *hit unriht wære*). The men who were murdered rest in bliss with Christ, because they are *buton scylde*. And the soul of Alfred, whose body rests in a place of honour at Ely, is likewise with Christ. These repeated protestations of innocence are much in excess of a chronicle of events and interpret these events by challenging a very powerful matrix for interpreting the body. In the frame in which the C-text presents them, these events are given a greater significance than the unchristian barbarities and signs of dishonour narrated in the *Encomium Emmae*, for the C-text reads these mutilations in the context of the forensic exactments of the law codes of the two fathers, Æthelred and Cnut. To view those eyeless, noseless faces, those

---

[16] 'Unde huiuscemodi tortores canibus deteriores digne omnia dicunt secula, qui non miliciae uiolentia sed fraudium suarum insidiis tot militum honesta dampnauerunt corpora. Quosdam ut dictum est perimebant, quosdam uero suae seruituti mancipabant; alios ceca cupidine capti uendebant, nonnullos autem artatos uinculis maiori inrisioni reseruabant. Sed diuina miseratio non defuit innocentibus in tanto discrimine consistentibus, quia multos ipsi uidimus quos ex illa derisione eripuit caelitus sine amminiculo hominis ruptis manicarum compedumque obicibus' (Campbell translates: 'Hence all ages will justly call such torturers worse than dogs, since they brought to condemnation the worthy persons of so many soldiers not by soldierly force but by their treacherous snares. Some, as has been said, they slew, some they placed in slavery to themselves; others they sold, for they were in the grip of blind greed, but they kept a few loaded with bonds to be subjected to greater mockery. But the divine pity did not fail the innocent men who stood in such peril, for I myself have seen many whom it snatched from that derision, acting from heaven without the help of man, so that the impediments of manacles and fetters were shattered' (*Encomium*, ed. Campbell, III.6, pp. 44–5)). John of Worcester reports that 600 men were killed at Guildford s.a. 1036 (*The Chronicle of John of Worcester*, ed. Darlington and McGurk, p. 522).   [17] *Encomium,* ed. Campbell, III.6 (pp. 44–7).

scalpless heads, arms without hands, legs without feet is to read upon their bodies the legal exactment of punishment for crimes.

An overview of the earliest English law codes shows them to offer an intricate and shifting system of exchange among rank, offence, bodily injury and money. Their interest is in satisfaction, and compensation lies within the family or social group. That said, there are suggestive instances of condign punishment. The laws of Wihtred, king of Kent (695), specify flogging as an alternative punishment to a six-shilling fine for servants or slaves.[18] (Social standing is a crucial determinant here.) Such punishments escalate. The penalty exacted from a slave for rape is castration.[19] The laws of Ine specify that a much-accused freeman may have his hand or foot struck off if finally taken in the act.[20] In the earlier codes, condign punishment and monetary compensation occasionally exchange places. For example, the laws of Alfred specify that the thief of church goods must pay simple compensation and a fine as well as have his hand struck off, though that hand may be 'redeemed' by its equivalent in wergeld.[21] The penalty for slander is the loss of the tongue, though this too may be redeemed.[22] At the same time, various acts of physical violence, construed as acts of dishonour, are accorded monetary compensation (for example, putting someone in bonds, cutting the hair, the beard, or inappropriate tonsuring).[23] Injuries which are visible are more heavily compensated than those which are not seen.[24] Æthelstan (in a law that looks to the Continent for precedent) punishes counterfeiting by the loss of the hand which made the money, though the accused may request the ordeal of hot iron.[25] Even allowing for its specification of condign punishment for particular crimes and its substitution of certain corporal punishments for the unfree, what is notable in the present context is that the preoccupation of early Anglo-Saxon law is overwhelmingly with legal composition for crime, detailing the wergelds (man-prices) for individuals of various ranks and the financial penalties and degrees of compurgation required for numerous classes of offences.

---

[18] E.g. Wihtred 10, 13 and 15; but see 26, specifying that a thief caught with the goods may either be killed, sold into slavery or redeemed. The laws are cited from *Die Gesetze der Angelsachsen*, ed. F. Liebermann, 3 vols. (Halle, 1903–16), I. Compare the *Capitulare Haristallense* (779), ch. 23: 'De latronibus ita precipimus observandum, ut pro prima vice non moriatur, sed oculum perdat, de secunda vero culpa nasus ipsius latronis abscidatur; de tertia vero culpa, si non emendaverit, moriatur' ('Concerning thieves, we direct that it be attended to in this way, that for the first time he is not to be put to death, but lose an eye, for the second offence let the nose of the thief be cut off, for the third offence, if he does not mend his ways, let him be killed') (*Capitularia regum Francorum,* ed. A. Boretius, MGH Leges sec. ii, I (Hanover, 1883), 51).

[19] Alfred 25.1 (Liebermann, *Gesetze* I, 64).

[20] Ine 18 and 37 (Liebermann, *Gesetze* I, 96 and 104).

[21] Alfred 6 and 6.1 (Liebermann, *Gesetze* I, 52).   [22] Alfred 32 (Liebermann, *Gesetze* I, 66).

[23] Alfred 35–35.6 (Liebermann, *Gesetze* I, 68).

[24] See Alfred 45.1, 49–49.1, 66.1 (Liebermann, *Gesetze* I, 78, 80 and 84). Compensation is double for *visible* wounds.   [25] II Athelstan 14.1 (Liebermann, *Gesetze* I, 158).

By contrast, I should argue, Æthelred's law code of 1008 (V Æthelred), the first datable code bearing Archbishop Wulfstan's mark, offers a first glimpse into the changing understanding of the Anglo-Saxon subject of law. This code orders that men ought not be punished by death for slight offences.

[3] 7 ures hlafordes gerædnes 7 his witena is, þæt man Cristene men for ealles to lytlum to deaðe ne fordeme.
[3.1] Ac elles geræde man friðlice steora folce to þearfe 7 ne forspille for lytlum Godes handgeweorc 7 his agenne ceap, þe he deore gebohte.[26]

In contrast to the fairly common death penalty for theft,[27] V Æthelred specifies that punishments are to be devised which spare the lives of thieves specifically in the interest of their salvation. The *friðlice steora* of 3.1 corresponds, as Dorothy Whitelock has noted, to excerpts from Latin canons (probably continental) in a section of an important manuscript, London, British Library, Cotton Nero A. i, annotated by Archbishop Wulfstan himself, where punishments allowing the transgressor opportunity to save his soul are described by the phrase *per penas saluandi [sunt]*.[28] The text below is given from Nero A. i, fol. 157:

Sunt namque his temporibus iudices seculares qui pro modico commisso homines statim morti adiudicant, parui pendentes monita apostoli, dicentis: castigate et non mortificate. Castigandi sunt enim rei diuersisque modis, arguendi et non statim necandi, sed per penas saluandi, ne anime pro quibus ipse dominus pasus [*sic*] est, in eterna pena dispereant. Alii uinculis et flagris; alii autem fame uel frigore const[r]ingendi sunt; alii quoque pellem, capillos et barbam simul perdentes turpiter obprobria sustineant; alii adhuc acrius const\r/ingantur, id est, membrum perdant, oculum uidelicet uel nasum, manum uel pedem seu aliud ali\q/uid membrum.[29]

---

[26] Liebermann, *Gesetze* I, 238: 'And the decree of our lord and his councillors is that Christian men should not be condemned to death for all too small offences. But *friðlice* punishments are to be otherwise devised at the need of the people, and God's handiwork and his own purchase which he bought so dearly should not be destroyed for small offences.' For *friðlice* to describe punishments that keep the criminal within the 'frið' (= 'life-sparing'), see *English Historical Documents c. 500–1042*, ed. D. Whitelock, Eng. Hist. Documents I, 2nd ed. (London, 1979), p. 443, n. 1.

[27] VI Athelstan 1.1 specifies the death penalty for any thief over twelve years of age who steals anything over twelve pence (Liebermannn, *Gesetze* I, 173).

[28] *English Historical Documents*, ed. Whitelock, p. 443, n. 1. Whitelock's reference to 'penas salvandi' here is slightly misleading, since Wulfstan, while specifying a range of penalties, is referring to the efficacy of punishment itself. See below, pp. 217 and 226, n. 55.

[29] 'There are in these times secular judges who for a small crime condemn men immediately to death, thinking of no account the admonition of the apostle, saying "Punish and do not put to death." Indeed, the culprits ought to be punished by various means, they ought to be charged and not immediately killed, but to be saved through punishments, lest their souls, for which the Lord himself suffered, be undone in eternal punishment. Some by chains and whips, others, however, ought to be bound by hunger and cold; let others, losing at the same time skin, hair and beard, suffer disgrace shamefully; others should be restrained still more sharply; that is, let

Such punishments, unspecified in Æthelred's rather vague code, take the form of mutilations which enacted on the bodies of those convicted at once the penalty and the ineradicable memorials of their crimes. Their mutilated bodies became texts of their behaviour and its lawful consequences. Specifying such an enactment of crime and punishment upon the body, Cnut's law codes of 1020–3, also authored by Wulfstan, provide that an adulterous woman, for example, is to lose her nose and ears.[30] But the 'mercy' of a mitigated sentence as alternative to death, called for by Wulfstan in Cnut's voice, is made most explicit in the case of the recidivist thief:

[30.4] And æt þam oðrum cyrre ne si þær nan oðer bot, gif he ful wurðe, butan þæt man ceorfe him ða handa oððe þa fet oððe ægþer, be þam ðe seo dæd sig.
[30.5] 7 gif þonne gyt mare wurc geworht hæbbe, þonne do man ut his eagan, 7 ceorfan of his nosu 7 his earan 7 þa uferan lippan oððon hine hættian, swa hwylc þyssa swa man þonne geræde, ða þe ðærto rædan sceolon: swa man mæg styran 7 eac þære sawle beorgan.[31]

Within the range of law texts here cited, action on the body is reassigned meaning over time as compensation for wrongdoing shifts from an external, and in some ways communal, responsibility satisfiable by compurgation and fine (as is paramount in the late-ninth-century laws of Alfred), to an internal guilt in the eleventh-century codes (in a mutilation which forever after forces the body to confess to its guilt as part of the process of salvation). At this point it would

---

them lose a body part, namely an eye or ear, a hand or foot, or some other member.' For a facsimile, see *A Wulfstan Manuscript containing Institutes, Laws, and Homilies. British Museum Cotton Nero A. i*, ed. H. R. Loyn, EEMF 17 (Copenhagen, 1971). The text is printed with small differences in *Die Hirtenbriefe Ælfrics*, ed. B. Fehr, Bibliothek der angelsächsischen Prosa 9 (Hamburg, 1914; repr. Darmstadt, 1966), 245 from Cambridge, Corpus Christi College 190. Nero A. i, CCCC 190 and 265 are part of a complex of manuscripts identified by Dorothy Bethurum as containing Wulfstan's 'Commonplace Book': see her 'Archbishop Wulfstan's Commonplace Book', *PMLA* 57 (1942), 916–29.   [30] II Cnut 53 (Liebermann, *Gesetze* I, 348).

[31] II Cnut 30–30.1 (Liebermann, *Gesetze* I, 332 and 334), 30.4: 'And on the second occasion there is to be no other remedy, if he is guilty, but that his hands, or feet, or both, depending on the deed, are to be cut off'; 30.5: 'And if, however, he has committed further crimes, his eyes should be put out and his nose and ears and upper lip cut off, or he should be scalped, whichever of these they may decide who must make the judgement; thus one can punish and also save the soul.' Cf. *Leis Willelmi* 40, 'Prohibemus, ne pro parvo forisfacto adiudicetur aliquis homo morti; sed ad plebis castigacionem al[i]a pena secundum qualitatem et quantitatem delicti plectatur. Non enim debet pro re parva deleri factura, quam ad ymaginem suam Deus condidit et sanguinis sui precio redemit' ('We forbid that for a small offence a man may be condemned to death, but for the correction of the people let another punishment, according to the quality and gravity of the crime, be exacted. Nor, indeed, should anyone be destroyed for a small offence, whom God made in his image and redeemed at the cost of his blood') (Liebermann, *Gesetze* I, 516). For juridical mutilation in the reign of Henry I, see C. W. Hollister, 'Royal Acts of Mutilation: the Case Against Henry I', *Albion* 10 (1978), 330–40.

be useful to turn from the legal background of the story of the torture and death of Alfred ætheling and his companions to what hagiography can reveal about the juridical context for reading the body in late Anglo-Saxon England, specifically, Lantfred's *Translatio et miracula S. Swithuni* (*c.* 975) and Wulfstan Cantor's versification of it some twenty years later.

Lantfred's text celebrated the miracles associated with the translation of St Swithun's remains to within the Old Minster at Winchester (971).[32] If the body appeared rarely and discretely in the *Chronicle*, the opposite is the case with the *Translatio et miracula S. Swithuni*. There the text is virtually littered with the bodies of the blind, the deaf, the crippled and the diseased of all sorts. The shrine itself at the Old Minster must have become a kind of bedlam: Lantfred describes how the crowds of supplicants groaning in pain from suppurating wounds, penitential tortures, pitiable illnesses and forensic mutilations filled the area within and around the shrine while waiting for a cure. Swithun himself was rather a mystery. All that is known of him are the dates of his episcopate at Winchester: 852 until his death in 863.

According to Lantfred's account, three years before Swithun's translation on 15 July 971, the saint appeared to a blacksmith to inform him that he was no longer content with his burial place outside the west wall of the Old Minster and wished to be translated within the church. He instructed the blacksmith to find one Eadsige, formerly a canon of the Minster expelled in Æthelwold's monastic reform, and have that Eadsige tell Æthelwold to order the translation. This was all a bit much for the blacksmith, who delayed. And it was a bit much for Eadsige as well, who delayed further. In the meantime, two remarkable miracles occurred. In the first, a hunchbacked cleric from Alderbury was told in a dream to fast and pray outside the west wall of the Old Minster (Swithun's place of burial), and he would be cured. When his remarkable cure was effected, some of the brothers assumed that it was done by the power of St Martin of Tours, whose tower overlooked the site from the west. But the now-cured cleric testified that the miracle was Swithun's. The other miracle, immediately before the translation, effected the cure of a man paralysed from a stitch; its significance will be considered below.

Although the four miracles involving Swithun and the law are the focus of this argument, their primary interest lies in the ways they produce the body as a

---

[32] The present published state of Lantfred's text is unsatisfactory. The partial text in *Acta SS., Iul.* is incomplete and is supplemented (though not perfectly) by E. P. Sauvage, 'Sancti Swithuni Wintoniensis episcopi translatio et miracula auctore Lantfredo monacho Wintoniensi', *AB* 4 (1885), 365–410. A complete edition by Michael Lapidge is forthcoming in *Winchester Studies* 4.2. Citations of the text as well as translations in this article are from Lapidge's edition and are keyed to *Acta SS* and *AB* for ease of reference. On Lantfred's training at Fleury, see J. P. Carley, 'Two Pre-Conquest Manuscripts from Glastonbury Abbey', *ASE* 16 (1987), 197–212, at 210.

site at which secular law and divine power meet. Considered as a whole, as the opening miracles attest, Lantfred's collection is about healing: the two significant miracles that most clearly promoted the translation of the holy body were the cure of the hunchback cleric and the cure of the citizen of Winchester suffering from paralysis. These miracles are designed as testimonies to Swithun's power to heal, and there are two important themes that weave through the collection. The first of these is that the power of cure at the Old Minster operates through Swithun, whose body rests there. The healing of bodies continues after the translation, and Swithun's mortal remains are of crucial efficacy.[33] The second theme is the ways in which the healed bodies are to be interpreted. The lengthy discussion of the significance of the healing of the paralytic from Winchester, stricken after seeing the three hags, takes an ancient theme and points it for a contemporary purpose.

Quod idcirco actum fore credimus, quatinus sciret uniuersus indubitanter populus quod per meritum sancti pontificis Suuithuni languidus ab omnipotente Domino fuisset curatus. Infirmus uero ipse ideo meruit sanitatem recipere quia non dubitauit in fide, sed permansit in prece . . . Tria namque miracula in hoc egro cernimus esse peracta: mulierum uisionem, ac sancti patris piam commonitionem, necne languoris medicationem. Percutitur dolore corporis ut suscipiat uigorem mentis, quia 'Deus castigat ac corrigit omnem filium quem diligit.' Commonetur ut medicinam requirat, quatinus se infirmum prius peccatis confiteatur et intelligat; et sic demum sanitatem animae percipiat, quoniam omnipotens angelorum creator et hominum non desiderat mortem delinquentium sed expectat nefandarum in melius conuersionem mentium, ne cogatur districtum exercere iudicium quod impiis supplicium confert sempiternum. Qui si ita studuerit animam a uitiis purgare, quemadmodum ipse curatus est somate absque dubio merebitur hereditare felicitatem caelestis patriae.[34]

---

[33] One should not overlook the economic and political advantages to the shrine in having a resident powerful healer, and Lantfred's text repeatedly notes the critical proximity of Swithun's body: e.g., 'ad sancti praesulis corpusculum deferrent' (*Acta SS* text, ch. 6), 'cupiens accedere ad sanctum Christi famuli corpusculum' (*Acta SS*, ch. 15), 'in qua quiescebat sanctus corpore Christi praesul' (*Acta SS*, ch. 23), 'ad templum illud in quo corpus sancti presulis venerabatur' (*Acta SS*, ch. 24). Examples could be multiplied. The intersection of monastic and royal interests in Swithun and the Old Minster are illustrated by the making of a sumptuous reliquary for the saint's remains. Wulfstan Cantor describes the splendid reliquary in which part of the saint's body was kept, fabricated by order of King Edgar from materials including silver, gems and 300 pounds of gold (*Frithegodi monachi breuiloquium uitae beati Wilfredi et Wulfstani Cantoris narratio metrica de sancto Swithuno*, ed. A. Campbell (Zurich, 1950), pp. 141 and 143). See also R. N. Quirk, 'Winchester Cathedral in the Tenth Century', *ArchJ* 114 (1959), 28–68, at 41–2; and M. Biddle, '*Felix Urbs Winthonia*: Winchester in the Age of Monastic Reform', *Tenth-Century Studies, Essays in Commemoration of the Millennium of the Council of Winchester and Regularis Concordia*, ed. D. Parsons (London, 1975), pp. 123–40 and 233–7, at 136.

[34] Lapidge, ch. 3; Sauvage, pp. 393–4: 'I think that it happened in this way so that the entire populace would know without any doubt that the sick man had been cured by the omnipotent Lord through the merit of the holy bishop Swithun. Accordingly, the sick man himself had deserved

The man, healed in body and in soul, is cured because of his faith. This particular healing is quite explicit in its emphasis on the body: the bodies of the naked hags are loathsome to see; Swithun, himself, appears as a being of marvellous height and shining like the sun; and the paralytic regains the use of his body, though losing his shoe in the bargain. The health of his soul is directly tied to the health of his body: 'percutitur dolore corporis ut suscipiat uigorem mentis'.[35] Reciprocally, confession of his sins allowed him to be cured. The paralytic cured in soul and body echoes Luke V.17–26: 'Quid est facilius dicere: "Dimittuntur tibi peccata", an dicere: "Surge et ambula?" Ut autem sciatis quia filius hominis habet potestatem in terra dimittendi peccata (ait paralytico), "Tibi dico surge, tolle lectum tuum, et vade in domum tuam."' The power to forgive sins is signified by the healing of the man's body, and spiritual health inside is read from the change on the outside. The healing of the soul with the body, illness as metaphor for sin, and the Divine Physician are all commonplaces in the discourse of saintly miracles. In this sense, Swithun's miracles of healing are no different from those of any other saint. Nor, for the most part, is Lantfred's emphasis on the efficacy of Swithun's relics and on the salutary effect of his translation unusual. The typicality of these miracles of healing shows us what is most important in the cult, that the body of the saint, analogous to the body of Christ, connects heaven and earth. But the relics, as Patrick Geary has observed in another context, *were* the saint.[36] The saint would reclaim his body at the end of time, but for now, the laity could see and sometimes even touch these powerful links with the other world.

What appear to be different in status are the miracles treating individuals who are not sick but who have run foul of the law. In these stories we see not only the guilty but the innocent, and the reading of the body, so straightforwardly invited in the cures of the sick, becomes, in the stories of

to obtain his health because he did not waver in his faith but persevered in his prayers . . . For we may distinguish three miracles performed through this sick man: the vision of the women, the kindly admonition of the holy father, and the curing of the disease. He is struck down with bodily anguish so that he might acquire strength of mind, since "God chastizeth and he scourgeth every son whom He receiveth." He is warned that he would require medicine, so that he might first admit and realize that he was diseased through sin; and thus at length he could obtain the health of his soul, since the omnipotent creator of angels and men does not desire the death of sinners but anticipates the conversion of wicked hearts for the better, so that He will not be compelled to exercise that severe judgement which confers eternal punishment on the wicked. If someone shall thus desire to purify his soul from sin, just as that sick man was cured in his body he will without doubt deserve to inherit the blessedness of the heavenly kingdom.'

[35] In the *Etymologiae* Isidore notes of *anima* that when it knows, it is referred to as 'mind' ('dum scit, mens est'): *Isidori Hispalensis episcopi etymologiarum siue originum libri xx*, ed. W. M. Lindsay (Oxford, 1911), XI.xiii.25.

[36] P. J. Geary, *Furta Sacra: Thefts of Relics in the Central Middle Ages* (Princeton, NJ, 1978), p. 39.

law, a rather more problematic matter. In the four stories discussed below, dealing with bodily punishment, innocence and guilt, the suppliants of St Swithun are a parricide, a slave (crime unspecified), a thief and an innocent man. Read together, these stories witness various lines of power as they were articulated in England in the later tenth century in canon law and secular law. We might begin with the parricide. This suppliant arrives at the shrine of the saint loaded down with particularly harsh irons, bound by nine iron bands which ate into the swollen flesh of his trunk and arm. He had been condemned by his bishop to wander from place to place, dragging the instruments of his penitence, and now, in the holy resting place of Swithun's body, he begs relief from his agony. St Swithun obliges. Despite the detail of the suppliant's anguish, neither the penalty nor the story is original.[37] For the most serious of sins (especially homicide within the family) the bishop reserved to himself the assigning of penance. And for such sins, pilgrimage, often without end, barefoot and sometimes in chains, was prescribed. It does not take long to realize that such a practice would fill the roads with the most serious of criminals. And although Charlemagne prohibited the practice in 783, his sanction against it was to no avail.[38] Even though the parricide's story is, in a sense, typical in hagiography, its currency testifies as well to penitential options in late Anglo-Saxon England, corroborated by three letters collected by Archbishop Wulfstan, designed to accompany such sinners, letters of introduction recounting their crimes and begging prayers for them. One of these letters was addressed to the pope.[39] CCCC 265, a manuscript otherwise associated with Wulfstan, details as well the chaining of a parricide with devices made from the iron of his own weapon, fastened triply around the waist and arm, and pre-

[37] Compare, for example, the *post mortem* miracle of St John, abbot, who frees a sinner loaded with penitential chains after he begs relief at the monastery of Moutier-Saint-Jean: *Acta sanctorum ordinis s. Benedicti*, ed. J. Mabillon, 9 vols. (Paris, 1668–1701) I, 641. This miracle is inserted in a ninth-century manuscript of Gregory of Tours's *Liber in gloria confessorum*, where the sinner is named as a fratricide 'pro enormitate criminis ferreis circulis alligatus' ('fettered with iron rings for the magnitude of his crime'). See *Gregorii episcopi Turonensis miracula et opera minora*, ed. B. Krusch, MGH, Scriptores rer. Merov. I.2 (Hanover, 1885), 353. Compare the *Miracula ss. Floriani et Florentis* (*Acta SS*, Sept. VI, 431–2).

[38] See C. Vogel, 'La discipline pénitentielle en Gaule des origines au ixe siècle', *Revue des sciences religieuses* 30 (1956), 1–26 and 157–86, at 10. See also his 'Les rites de la pénitence publique aux xe et xie siècles', pp. 137–44; 'Le pèlerinage pénitentiale', pp. 116–17 and 130–2; and 'Pénitence et excommunication dans l'eglise ancienne et durant le haut moyen âge', pp. 16–22, esp. p. 17, all in his *En rémission des péchés: Recherches sur les systèmes pénitentiels dans l'église latine*, ed. A. Faivre (Aldershot, 1994).

[39] See R. A. Aronstam, 'Penitential Pilgrimages to Rome in the Early Middle Ages', *Archivum Historiae Pontificiae* 13 (1975), 65–83, at 72. Aronstam edits Wulfstan's three letters from Copenhagen, Kongelige Bibliothek Gl. Kgl. Sam. 1595. The letters are also printed by M. Bateson, 'A Worcester Cathedral Book of Ecclesiastical Collections, made c. 1000 A.D.', *EHR* 10 (1895), 712–31 at 728 (from CCCC 265).

scribes that the chains should come off only after true penitence at holy places.[40]

The story of the parricide reminds us as well that the distinction between sin and crime (*peccatum* and *crimen*) in Anglo-Saxon society was drawn somewhat differently from our own, and their differing kinds of satisfaction would only much later be neatly divided between religious and secular spheres.[41] The satisfaction achieved by the parricide at Swithun's tomb is the result of a durative, public, highly visible and deeply shaming set of practices where action on the body of the sinner permitted him the opportunity to cleanse his soul. Such a penitent set off on his pilgrimage with hair and beard shaved off, shoeless, barely clad, or clad in the *cilicium*, a kind of hair-shirt. It was expected that his body would be wasted with fasting and the rigours of the journeys.[42] Action on the parricide at Swithun's tomb, then, is understood in two ways: as manifest healing (earlier in the *Translatio et miracula* Swithun is described as another Angel Raphael[43]) and as release (where the saint holds the power of the keys). The falling off of the irons is a visible sign of God's forgiveness. In short, in his spectacular progress, at every stage, such a penitent was, and was meant to be, read.

A very different kind of crime, punishment and outcome structure the story of the Frankish thief. In this curious subversion of civil justice a thief, literally caught in the act, lies in a dungeon awaiting imminent execution.[44] The thief remembers hearing about St Swithun, and praying to him (though not even knowing his name) he finds that his chains have fallen off and the bars on the prison door have miraculously come undone. (The falling off of chains and the release from prison are tropes one can trace in the hagiography of the early

---

[40] 'Sepe etiam et nos vidimus ipsi parricidas jejuniis macerari vinclisque ferreis quantotiens coartari, ita ut proprio quis circumcinctus ense medius cum quo iracundus perculit, trinisque vinclis adhibitis, uno vinciretur brachio <et> numquam solvi aliquem nisi vera penitentia subveniente sacris solveretur in locis' ('We have also often seen that parricides are wasted by fasting and just as often constrained with iron chains – just as one man encircled around his middle with his own sword, with which he had struck while enraged, with triple chains used, was fastened on one arm – and that none is ever released unless he is freed through true penitence undertaken in holy places') (Bateson, 'A Worcester Cathedral Book', p. 725). Cf. *Capitularia Ansegisus* II.41, which specifies handing over incorrigible parricides (and some others) to the secular authorities (MGH, Leges sec. II, 1). These capitula occur in Oxford, Bodleian Library, Hatton 42, bk I, 47r and 194v, annotated by Wulfstan. See N. R. Ker, 'The Handwriting of Archbishop Wulfstan', *England Before the Conquest: Studies in Primary Sources presented to Dorothy Whitelock*, ed. P. Clemoes and K. Hughes (Cambridge, 1971), pp. 315–31. See also *Capitulare Missorum Generale*, item 32 (802) for the homicide within the family: 'statim se ad penitentiam sibi compositam sumit, et ita ut episcopus eius sibi disponat absque ulla ambiguitate' ('he undertakes immediately the penance assigned to him, and just as his bishop arranges, without any equivocation') (MGH Leges, sec. II, 1). Cf. item 37, where the *missi* are to take into custody for the good of his soul a criminal who spurns penitence.

[41] See Fehr, *Die Hirtenbriefe Ælfrics*, pp. 244–5.   [42] Vogel, 'Le pèlerinage pénitentiale', pp. 130–1.

[43] Lapidge, ch. 3; Sauvage, p. 395.   [44] Lapidge, ch. 34; Sauvage, pp. 399–401.

Middle Ages, and particularly, though not exclusively, in Gregory of Tours's *De virtutibus S. Martini*.) English saints credited with *post mortem* releases of the imprisoned include Edward Martyr, Æthelwold, Dunstan, Erkenwold, Mildreth and Cuthbert.[45] Bishop Ecgwine has his self-imposed penitential chains unlocked by a miraculously appearing key.[46] But the Frankish thief's relief at his deliverance through the miracle is local, particular and of especial interest in this context. The text records his joy – '. . . gauisus est eximium/ se euasisse periculum/ atque mortis interitum/ utriusque perpetuum . . .' – that he had escaped a double death in the immediate death of the body and the eternal death of the soul.[47] Such an expectation of 'twin' deaths is the trigger for Wulfstan's modification of royal law.

The last two, complementary, stories to be considered have St Swithun help a slave and a wrongly accused innocent man.[48] In the first, a slave accused (apparently correctly) of a substantial crime is forced by a reeve named Eadric to undergo the ordeal instead of accepting composition by Flodoald, the slave's owner.[49] In the single ordeal by hot iron, the accused is required to carry a red-hot pound of iron nine feet and have his hand bandaged for three days. The condition of the hand after that time would indicate the accused's innocence or guilt.[50] After the ordeal by hot iron is enacted, Flodoald, nearly despairing of the

---

[45] *Edward King and Martyr*, ed. C. Fell (Leeds, 1971), p. 15; Wulfstan's Life of Æthelwold, in *Wulfstan of Winchester: the Life of St Æthelwold*, ed. M. Lapidge and M. Winterbottom (Oxford, 1991), p. 68 (ch. 46); Osbern's Life of Dunstan, PL 137, 455–74 at 468C–9C, and his Life of Ælfheah, PL 147, 584; *The Saint of London: the Life and Miracles of St Erkenwald. Text and Translation*, ed. E. G. Whatley (Binghamton, NY, 1989), pp. 116–19 and 217 [Miracle 3]; D. W. Rollason, 'Goscelin of Canterbury's Account of the Translation and Miracles of St Mildrith (*BHL* 5961-4): An Edition with Notes', *MS* 48 (1986), 139–210, at 188; [H. Hinde], *Symeonis Dunelmensis Opera et Collectanea* I, Surtees Soc. 51 (London, 1868), 168–70, at 169.

[46] M. Lapidge, 'The Digby-Gotha Recension of the Life of St Ecgwine', *Vale of Evesham Hist. Soc. Research Papers* 7 (1979), 39–55, at 44 (ch. 6).

[47] Lapidge, ch. 34, Sauvage, p. 401. Lapidge trans.: 'He rejoiced that he had escaped/ so great a danger/ as well as the perpetual oblivion/ of either sort of death.'

[48] See P. Wormald, 'A Handlist of Anglo-Saxon Lawsuits', *ASE* 17 (1988), 247–81 (items 154 and 155).

[49] Lapidge, ch. 25; *Acta SS*, Iul. I, ch. 33–5. Wulfstan Cantor provides the additional detail that the ordeal takes place at the royal vill at Calne (*Narratio*, II, 306–7). D. Whitelock examines the legal background to the versified version of this story in Wulfstan's *Narratio* ('Wulfstan *Cantor* and Anglo-Saxon Law', *Nordica et Anglica. Studies in Honour of Stefán Einarsson*, ed. A. H. Orrick (The Hague, 1968), pp. 83–92; repr. in her *History, Law and Literature* (London, 1981)).

[50] See R. Bartlett, *Trial by Fire and Water: the Medieval Judicial Ordeal* (Oxford, 1986), pp. 32–3: 'It [ordeal] was *lex paribilis*, or *apparens*, or *aperta* – "the manifest proof". It was a device for dealing with situations in which certain knowledge was impossible but uncertainty was intolerable.' See also P. R. Hyams, 'Trial by Ordeal: the Key to Proof in Early Common Law', *On the Laws and Customs of England: Essays in Honor of Samuel E. Thorne*, ed. M. S. Arnold *et al.* (Chapel Hill, NC, 1981), pp. 90–126, at 111: 'The *spectaculum* presented a visible sign "so that the rest seeing this might be freed from their incredulity through God's mercy." ' See Liebermann, *Gesetze* I, 406–7,

outcome, prays for help to St Swithun.[51] When the slave's hand is unbandaged after three days, the reeve and his men see a clean hand, although Flodoald sees on the hand the putrefying signs of the slave's guilt. A miracle, to be sure, but of what? At issue in this story is the ability to read the signs of guilt. After the punctilious reeve chose to pursue a form of mutilation possibly leading to a sentence of death over an exchange of money (and the life of the slave!), God, through the mediation of St Swithun, prevented him from 'reading' the bodily sign correctly. As a result, Flodoald gives the slave to St Swithun, and the reeve loses the silver he had been promised.

If there is something satisfying about the thwarting of the punctilious reeve, the story of the freed thief who had been caught in the act is rather shocking. But the two stories, read together with the story of the parricide, combine to show two powerful notions in the late-tenth-century theory of guilt and punishment which cross ecclesiastical and secular boundaries: that forensic action on the body is 'readable' (but for the miracle the slave would have been executed for his crime), and that a swift sentence of death endangers the soul of the criminal (release of the thief and the slave removes them from certain damnation). In the conduct of the ordeal, the forensic exactment is evidentiary, not penal: the body is set up to confess its guilt, and punishment, if necessary, will follow. At the time of this story, the ordeal was generally reserved for untrustworthy men (that is, men who had bad reputations or who had previously failed at an oath or ordeal (II Cnut 22)), foreigners (II Cnut 35 = *feorran cuman*), and those accused of specific offences). Carolingian practice generally permitted the oath to reputable free men, but specified ordeal for the untrustworthy, for foreigners and for the unfree.[52]

(Ordo II.4): '... et ut caeteri hoc uidentes ab incredulitate sua, te miserante, liberentur' ('that the rest, seeing this, might be freed from their disbelief'). The text in Cambridge, Corpus Christi College 44, fol. 362, indicates a range of offences and hoped for efficacy: 'Hac itaque fiducia, exauditor piissime, hoc ferrum ... quaesumus, ut per nostram benedictionem santifices, ut, quicumque sacrilegii, furti, homicidii, adulterii quarumque aliarum noxa deprehensus ... hoc ferrum ... igne calidatum ... tangere presumpserit ..., indignationis tue incendio in conspectu adstantium ardeat ... ut omnis populus credat te ... in hoc iudicio afuisse' ('and so with this assurance, most blessed lord who hears our prayers, we beg that you may sanctify this iron through our blessing so that anyone, taken in the crimes of sacrilege, theft, homicide, adultery, or any others, who will have presumed to touch this iron heated by fire, may burn in the flame of your displeasure in the sight of those present, so that all the people may believe that you have been present in this trial') (Liebermann, *Gesetze* I, 416).

[51] If the slave's crime was theft, *pace* Whitelock, Flodoald ran the risk of being accused as an accessory (especially since he appeared to know the slave would fail at the ordeal). On the lord as accessory to theft by his slave, see II Æthelstan 3.1 (loss of slave and payment of wergild for the first offence; at the second offence he lost all that he owned); VI Æthelstan 2.1 (death for harbouring a thief). As discussed below, as a foreigner, Flodoald's legal status was problematic.

[52] See the Council of Tribur, ch. 22a, in *Capitularia regum Francorum*, ed. A. Boretius and V. Krause, MGH, Leges sec. ii, 2 (Hanover, 1897), 225; Regino of Prüm, PL 132, 342, and Bartlett, *Trial*, pp. 31–2.

Such a distinction is not surprising, since an unsupported man would have no compurgators to swear to his innocence. Without a web of communal support, in the complementary truth processes of oath-swearing and ordeal, the body of the unsupported man had to give its own evidence. (There is no confession here, in the Foucaultian sense, for no verbal discourse was produced. But truth is at issue, and truth is not uttered by the accused but read on the surface of the body.) By contrast to evidentiary process, the penal exactment of death is simply an ending. It produces no knowledge about the criminal and, curiously, would appear not even to make satisfaction. (Indeed, the Frankish thief's fear of a double death strongly suggests that he perceived that submitting to execution was insufficient satisfaction for his earthly crimes and put his soul at risk. Thus his sincere entreaty of God and St Swithun could reasonably produce a reprieve.) We might compare the Wulfstan text on the salvific effect of punishments discussed above.

Quite the opposite case is the narrative of an unnamed innocent man accused of robbery and condemned to its horrible punishment.

Prenotato denique tempore, glorioso rege Eadgaro precipiente, ad deterrendos quosque malos horribili poena talis lex est constituta in Anglorum prouincia: ut si quispiam cleptes in tota uel predo inueniretur patria, caecatis luminibus, truncatis manibus, auulsis auribus, incisis naribus, et subtractis pedibus excruciaretur diutius; et sic demum decoriata pelle capitis cum crinibus, per omnia pene membra mortuus relinqueretur in agris, deuorandus a feris et auibus atque nocturnicanibus.[53]

The remarkable similarities of these penalties to those mentioned in Cnut's code of 1020–3 (= II Cnut) led Dorothy Whitelock to suggest that they reflect a lost code of Edgar, one used by Wulfstan in drafting Cnut's laws.[54] Simon Keynes, modifying Whitelock's view, suggests that the story indicates that comprehensive mutilation was instituted in the reign of Edgar (early 970s) and that it must have remained in force throughout Æthelred's reign, only surfacing in the codes

---

[53] 'At the aforesaid time and at the command of the glorious King Edgar, a law of great severity was promulgated throughout England to serve as a deterrent against all sorts of crime by means of a dreadful punishment: that, if any thief or robber were found anywhere in the country, he would be tortured at length by having his eyes put out, his hands cut off, his ears torn off, his nostrils carved open and his feet removed; and finally, with the skin and hair of his head shaved off, he would be abandoned in the open fields dead in respect of nearly all his limbs, to be devoured by wild beasts and birds and hounds of the night.' Lapidge, ch. 26; Sauvage, pp. 409–10.

[54] Whitelock, 'Wulfstan *Cantor* and Anglo-Saxon Law', p. 86. The so-called Laws of Edward and Guthrum 10 specify 'Gif limlæeo lama, þe forworht wære, weorþe forlæten, 7 he æfter þam ðreo niht alibbe, siððan man mot hylpan be bisceopes leafe, se ðe wylle beorgan sare 7 saule' ('If a [judicially] maimed and crippled man, who was convicted, has been abandoned, and after three days he is still alive, after that time, with the bishop's permission, one may help him who wishes to save his injured body and his soul'). Whitelock argues persuasively that this law shows Wulfstan's hand and is to be dated 1002–8, i.e. before V Æthelred. (*Councils and Synods*, ed. Whitelock *et al.* I, 302–3).

of Cnut.[55] My interest here is not so much in the aetiology of the laws as it is in the reading of the body they generate while producing a particular subject. Lantfred's unfortunate innocent undergoes savage mutilation: he is afflicted in all the body parts just mentioned (losing his hands, nose, eyes and ears), though his scalp and feet are left to him: 'qui mox comprehensus a nefandis criminatoribus et condempnatus a legislatoribus, caesus per supradicta penitus membra: relicti sunt insonti pedes cum uita, et cutis illi capitis miseranda minime est subtracta'.[56] He is then returned to his unhappy family in whose care he suffers for almost four months. (It is worse for him in Ælfric's account: there he suffers for seven months.[57]) Lantfred's narrative, whose main interest is, after all, in the power of Swithun, appears to lose track of the man's miseries. For although at the shrine of Swithun the man miraculously regains both hearing and sight, no further mention is made of his hands or nose. Convinced that his ruined eyes are beyond healing, he asks only for his hearing or for death. He prays:

Alme Deus munificens
cosmi sator omnipotens:
insontem caesum miserum
me respice, rex omnium;
caesis auditum auribus
redde meis diuinitus
uel mortem citam tribue,
Christe saluator optime,
necne uitam post obitum
mihi deprecor caelestem.[58]

After the miracle, the reader is asked to marvel at the healing of the blinded man's ruined eyes, as the text notes, 'Non legimus in sanctarum codicibus scripturarum

---

[55] S. Keynes, 'A Tale of Two Kings: Alfred the Great and Æthelred the Unready', *TRHS*, 5th ser. 36 (1986), 195–217, at 212. Although Keynes is inclined to think that the 'merciful' aspect of comprehensive mutilation was in effect at the time of Edgar, that is certainly not the motivation attributed to the legislation by Lantfred and Wulfstan Cantor. Rather, it is Archbishop Wulfstan who transforms the purpose of such punishment from deterrent ('ad deterrendos quosque malos horribili poena') to salvation ('per penas *salvandi* [sunt]'), refiguring identical punishments as notional mercy. See also S. Keynes, 'Crime and Punishment in the Reign of King Æthelred', *People and Places in Northern Europe 500–1600: Essays in Honour of Peter Hayes Sawyer*, ed. I. Wood and N. Lund (Woodbridge, 1991), pp. 67–81, at 72–3.

[56] 'Who was immediately seized by wicked executioners and condemned by the judges to be mutilated in all the aforementioned parts of his body: only the feet of the guiltless man were left him with his life, and the wretched skin of his head was not stripped off him': Lapidge, ch. 26; Sauvage, p. 409.

[57] *Ælfric's Lives of Saints*, ed. W. W. Skeat, 2 vols., EETS os 76, 82, 94 and 114 (London 1881–1900) I, 440–71, at line 270. In Ælfric's account, the man loses only eyes and ears (lines 267–9).

[58] 'King of all things, look upon me,/ a wretched man guiltlessly mutilated:/ restore my hearing to my wounded ears/ through divine intervention/ or else grant me a speedy death.'

quempiam cecatum hactenus recepisse lumen oculorum preter hominem istum.'[59]
Cecatum – it is the nature of the blinding that produces wonder at its healing.
Unlike death, mutilation is evidentiary: its result produces knowledge about the
criminal. In this sense, a judicious application of the law of comprehensive
mutilation has the same end-product as the ordeal, even though each is effected at
a different point in the process of accusation. The body of Lantfred's mutilated
and miraculously healed man speaks doubly: it attests gloriously to the power of
God in its healed parts (as Ælfric will later remind us in his Old English account of
St Swithun[60]), but its still-mutilated hands and nose speak to the power of the
king. The latter point is made clear in a subsequent treatment.

While Lantfred merely describes Edgar's penalties for theft, two decades later
in his versification of Lantfred's narratives, Wulfstan Cantor praises Edgar's
judicial zeal:

> Stat praedicta pii lex et sententia regis,
> in commune bonum quam sanxerat ille benignus,
> unus quisque suis securo ut pectore lucris
> plena pace frui posset sine murmure damni.
> exploratores siluarum densa peragrant,
> predonesque locis inuestigantur opacis,
> et membris caesi prebent spectacula plebi,
> perculerat terrorque animos formidine cunctos . . .
> (II.453–60)[61]

Wulfstan Cantor's emphasis on the efficacy of punishment resides in the *spectacle*
of the mutilated bodies ('et membris caesi prebent *spectacula* plebi' (emphasis

---

[59] 'I have not read anywhere in the books of holy writ about anyone – except this man – having
regained his eyesight who had been blinded to such an extent.' There is an interesting slippage
in the various versions of this statement. In Sauvage's Rouen manuscript (whose text is admittedly lacunose), the sentence reads 'Hoc namque miraculum in hoc est valde mirandum,
quoniam non legimus quempiam cæcatum recepisse lumen oculorum præter hominem istum'
(p. 410), omitting 'hactenus' and suggesting that the wonder of the miracle lies in the cure of
one who had been blinded (rather than one who had gone blind through illness). Wulfstan
Cantor moves 'hactenus' with similar result:

> [O]bstupuit natura, suas quia perdit habenas,
> hactenus in mundo quoniam sibi talia numquam
> contingerant, aliquem post lumina prendere uisum
> caecata, et reducem post nubila cernere lucem,
> hunc praeter solum, patris medicamine fotum (II.507–11).

[60] See Skeat, *Ælfric's Lives of Saints* I, 458, at lines 276–89.
[61] 'Thus stands the aforesaid law and judgement of the pious king, which he in his benignity had
decreed for the common good, that anyone might be able to enjoy his own possessions with an
easy heart in full peace without grumbling of loss. Searchers travel the thickets of the woods,
and robbers are discovered in shady places, and, mutilated in their limbs, they furnish a spectacle to the people; and terror struck all hearts with fear . . .' (II.453–60).

added)), which proclaims both the guilt of the bodies and the just power of the king. Unlike Foucault's liturgy of punishment elaborated in *Discipline and Punish*, where the spectacle resides in the community's watching the criminal body being destroyed and thus witnessing both the docility of the body and the prince's power, the spectacle, as Wulfstan defines it, resides in the show of the altered body itself.[62] Such spectacle is designed to produce *post factum* knowledge about the body of the criminal as well as remind the onlooker of the king's punishment and his power. As Wulfstan implies, sight of those mutilations reveals all that need be known about the bodies that suffered it. They are marked, punished, guilty. It is precisely this spectacle, implicit in Lantfred's account of the wrongly mutilated man, and, I should argue, in the *Chronicle* entry for 1036, that must interest us.

In the annal for 1036, with which this article began, the repeated assertion of guiltlessness protests the reflex of mapping guilt upon the body, codified by the replacement of communally satisfiable fines by a mutilation which signalled an internalizing of guilt. The unwilling bodies of the men in Alfred's party become a spectacle, textualized by their mutilation (whose effects must have appeared forensic), and are in turn, of necessity, retextualized by the chronicler. The mutilated body of the ætheling is a powerful metaphor to illustrate the injustice and guilt of the opportunist Godwine and of the illegitimate Harold. But that metaphor could cut both ways, for the discourse of the mutilated body could equally point to the guilt of the sufferer. This the chronicler contests by pious prayers for the dead men and by pointed and detailed mention of the honourable resting place of Alfred's body.[63]

The thief caught in the act and the innocent man mutilated for theft each in different ways illustrate the action of criminal penalties exacted for transgression of the law. Although Lantfred's story is of a Frankish thief, the penalty he faced was consistent with those in contemporary English laws. And the innocent man's fate, not codified in the written law that survives until II Cnut 30.1, may well have been promulgated two generations earlier. In drawing these connections, however, I do not assume that the occasionally draconian stipulations of the various law codes were universally applied and map for us to any degree a faithful picture of social practice. Two famous records of legal proceedings suggest the reverse. The Fonthill Letter (s. x^{in}) recounts the dubious activities of Helmstan, godson of Ealdorman Ordlaf and apparently a man of substance in his own right. Though a convicted thief, he still managed to swear an oath to secure his property. Subsequently, when theft of cattle was proved against him, he lost all his property, only to have at least some of it returned to

---

[62] M. Foucault, *Discipline and Punish: the Birth of the Prison*, trans. A. Sheridan (New York, 1978), p. 34; originally published as *Surveiller et punir: naissance de la prison* (Paris, 1975).

[63] The *Encomium Emmae*, ed. Campbell, p. 46, and the *Liber Eliensis*, ed. E. O. Blake, Camden 3rd ser. 92 (London, 1962), 160, both report miracles at the ætheling's tomb.

him at a later time.[64] Similarly, Æthelstan the priest, taken in chains as a thief, is redeemed when his elderly kinsman, the priest Herulf, uses church treasure to sway Bishop Oscytel.[65] This took place during Edgar's reign. Æthelstan's later, perjured oath, made on the body of St Æthelthryth, appears not to have incurred its canonical penalty. These instances, and that of the robber-priest Leofstan, are salutary reminders that one cannot infer from the law codes or from canon law any confident estimate of the percentage of prosecutions that resulted in conviction. Certainly, rank and connections helped Helmstan avoid the noose and probably helped the two priests as well. And a judicious offering of gifts (seen, apparently, in Flodoald's case) seems not to have been unknown. The readings of the cases that I offer here suggest not that the laws and canons reflect society, but rather that they are a repository (however imperfect) of notions about the individual before the law. These notions make up a substantial part of the web of interlocutions in which the Anglo-Saxon subject is implicated and through which he comes into being.

In particular terms, we have seen that the body of Alfred functions metonymically for his line, but the bodies of his tortured men demand a broader reading. Indeed, the chronicler's apologetic points to a pressing reading of the body in socio-legal terms. We might note a literalization of this 'reading' in the canonical cases of CCCC 265. There the fantasy (if it was only fantasy) of a particular power/knowledge is materialized in the punishment of a thief in holy orders. After flogging inscribes his body, the word *fur* is branded (*prenotatum*) on his face. Another account, that of a priest taken in adultery, specifies that after various corporal punishments, he had the legend 'hoc est profanus adulter' tattooed on his forehead.[66] That the body is inevitably 'read' is

---

[64] For an edition and commentary, see S. Keynes, 'The Fonthill Letter', *Words, Texts and Manuscripts: Studies presented to Helmut Gneuss on the Occasion of his Sixty-Fifth Birthday*, ed. M. Korhammer (Cambridge, 1992), pp. 53–97. Keynes's observation, '. . . one does not doubt for a moment that behind every oath-swearing lurked every kind of intrigue and abuse' (p. 75) is apposite. On the date of the Fonthill Letter, see M. Gretsch, 'The Language of the "Fonthill Letter" ', *ASE* 23 (1994), 57–102.

[65] See *Liber Eliensis*, ed. Blake, ch. 32–3. A. Kennedy gives an important account of legal procedure in 'Law and Litigation in the *Libellus Æthelwoldi episcopi*', *ASE* 24 (1995), 131–83, at 152–3.

[66] Bateson, 'A Worcester Cathedral Book', p. 726. These are extraordinary punishments, better understood as notional retributions rather than expressions of fact. The 'Apostolic Canons' in the Dionysio-Hadriana, item 25 (see *Ecclesiae Occidentalis Monumenta Iuris Antiquissima: Canonum et Conciliorum Græcorum Interpretationes Latinae*, ed. C. H. Turner, 2 vols. in 7 pts (Oxford, 1899–1939) I, 18) specifies degradation. Compare the so-called Laws of Edward and Guthrum 3 (showing Wulfstan's hand), which specify wergild or fine for a man in orders who fights or commits theft, perjury or adultery. Similarly, VIII Æthelred 27 (and I Cnut 5.3) specify degradation if appropriate penance is not done. The Penitential of Theodore (*Die Canones Theodori Cantuariensis*, ed. Finsterwalder), item 127, specifies degradation for the priest who commits homicide or fornication; item 140 specifies degradation for a priest or deacon taken in fornication, perjury, or theft, but not excommunication (=Apostolic Canon 25).

demonstrated by both sets of miracle texts. But those texts' interactions with the corpus of Anglo-Saxon law, especially in its move from external settlement to internal guilt, inflected by the continental canons to which I have referred, suggest that the time span between 970 and roughly 1035 saw a significant development in the construal of the Anglo-Saxon subject of law, where the notion of punishments that assisted salvation sought to extend the reach of law inward into the soul.

Mutilation designed for the living body serves multiple purposes. Whatever its function as deterrence, juridical mutilation produces a body about which things may be known. The spectacle of such a body continually announces both crime and punishment, and I should argue that it is precisely the force of this spectacle that the *Chronicle* entry for 1036 tries to counter. Even more interesting, however, is the development that Wulfstan's reinterpretation of mutilation indicates. The formulation *per penas salvandi [sunt]*, by construing juridical mutilation as a mercy, by making it a happy alternative to eternal death, makes the criminal a partner in his punishment. By working on the body, it extends the power of the law (previously satisfied by external compensation) inward into the criminal's soul.[67] Such a refiguring of legal purview, produced by a synergism of monastic and royal concerns for regulation, produces an unexpected knowledge of the sinner/criminal as its by-product. Such knowledge is not thought of as self-knowledge, but rather knowledge for those who see the sinner/criminal. And, significantly, the truth-function of this knowledge is not accomplished by verbal confession, marked by Foucault from its canonical adoption by the Fourth Lateran Council (1215) as a kind of point of departure for the western deployment of law. To ground his argument about the modern subject, Foucault produced a picture of medieval confession and penitence at once monolithic and startlingly precocious.[68] For the period before the twelfth century it was

---

[67] Earlier codes mention the king's moral obligation, but not in terms of individual souls: e.g. Ine Preface: 'ic ... wæs smeagende be ðære hælo urra sawla 7 be ðam staþole ures rices, þætte ryht æw 7 ryhte cynedomas ðurh ure folc gefæstnode ...' ('I was thinking about the salvation of our souls and about the security of our kingdom, that right law and right statutes be secured throughout our people') (Liebermann, *Gesetze* I, 88). Similarly Alfred Preface, 49.7 (*ibid.* I, 44 and 46).

[68] Foucault, *Discipline and Punish*, p. 33: 'The Middle Ages had organized around the theme of the flesh and the practice of penance a discourse that was markedly unitary'; p. 58: 'Since the Middle Ages at least, Western societies have established the confession as one of the main rituals we rely on for the production of truth: the codification of the sacrament of penance by the Lateran Council in 1215, with the resulting development of confessional techniques, the declining importance of accusatory procedures in criminal justice, and abandonment of tests of guilt (sworn statements, duels, judgments of God) and the development of methods of interrogation and inquest. ... All this helped to give the confession a central role in the order of civil and religious powers.' On the shifting nature and significance of the act of confessing, see Vogel, 'Le pèlerinage pénitentiale', pp. 116–17. Vogel makes it clear that an *aveu* could be made to a priest or to a *senior* (i.e. father or mother superior) and was a private matter. *L'aveu* as such is not sacramental confession.

neither. The by-product of such sweeping generalization was the production of a Middle Ages linked to modernity as its crucial origin, but also as its other and opposite. This version must be unthought. Other it may be, but opposite it is not. The silent, spectacular confession of ordeal and punishment is another road to truth that characterized the conduct of law and the production of certain forms of legal knowledge before the thirteenth century. It is a road to truth produced from without, like *fur* inscribed on the forehead, which did not lead to verbal confession as we know it, but rather is a road foreclosed. Yet the troubled bodies travelling that road must concern us.

I should like to conclude with a kind of postscript on the *Nachleben* of the hapless Alfred *æþeling*, the account of whose murder began this inquiry. In the *Annales de Wintonia*, Godwine is a villain who plots to destroy both Alfred and Edward (later the Confessor) so that his own son Harold (briefly king after Edward's death) could succeed.[69] In this account, he is responsible for the decimation of Alfred's men, the comprehensive mutilation of the rest, and the excruciating murder of the ætheling by unwinding his entrails around a tree. But the greatest focus of this story now is on the body of Alfred's mother, Emma. After succeeding to the throne, Edward the Confessor (whose affection for his mother in real life was demonstrated in 1043 by his stripping her of all her lands and possessions and sending her into exile) is tricked into accusing Emma of sexual misconduct with the bishop of Winchester and treason. To vindicate herself and the bishop, she demands trial by ordeal and is judged liable to the ordeal by ploughshare – nine of them, four for herself, five on behalf of the bishop. She is brought back to Winchester and spends the entire night before her ordeal in prayer to St Swithun. At the one moment she falls asleep, Swithun appears to her. 'Flamma non nocebit te', he tells her. Before submitting to the ordeal, walking barefoot over the nine red-hot ploughshares, she speaks before the king: ' "Domine", inquit, "et fili. Ego illa Emma quae te genui, pro te de tuis impetita de crimine in te et Eluredum filios meos, et de consensu turpitudinis et proditionis cum hujus sedis episcopo, invoco hodie Deum testem *in corpus meum*, ut peream, si quid horum quae mihi imposita sunt *vel mente* commiserim" '[70] (emphasis added). She is brought to the ordeal by a cohort of weeping bishops, all crying out, 'Sancte Swithune, Sancte Swithune, tu illam adjuva', with such a roar that the crowd could not hear the church bells tolling.[71] The ordeal is

---

[69] See *Annales Monastici*, ed. H. R. Luard, 5 vols., RS (London, 1864–9) II, 17–25 [*Annales Monasterii de Wintonia*]. Luard dates the *Annales Monastici* to about 1200.

[70] 'My lord . . . and son. I, the Emma who bore you, before you charged by your people with a crime against you and Alfred, my sons, and charged with conspiracy of infamy and treason with the bishop of this seat, I call upon God today to be witness on my body, that I may perish, if I have committed any of the charges brought against me even in my mind' (*Annales Monasterii de Wintonia*, p. 23). [71] 'St Swithun, help her' (*Annales de Wintonia*, p. 23).

enacted, and although she walked over each of the nine glowing ploughshares, placing her full weight on each, she neither noticed the iron nor felt the fire. 'Ducite me . . . ad filium meum: ut videat pedes meos, et sciat quia nihil mali passa sum'.[72] In the happy denouement, Emma, restored to her all possessions, gave nine manors to St Swithun, one for each of the ploughshares. The much-relieved bishop did the same.[73]

---

[72] 'Lead me . . . to my son: that he may see my feet and know that I have suffered no harm.' (*Annales de Wintonia*, p. 24).

[73] Research on this article was supported by an NEH Senior Summer Fellowship (1997), by a John Simon Guggenheim Fellowship and by the Institute for Scholarship in the Liberal Arts, College of Arts and Letters, University of Notre Dame. I should like to thank Ewa Płonowska Ziarek and Paul E. Szarmach, who read early drafts of the essay and made many helpful suggestions; Patrick Wormald, who permitted me to read in advance the portion on Lantfred in his forthcoming book on Anglo-Saxon law; and Michael Lapidge, who made work on Lantfred immeasurably easier by allowing me to use and cite his forthcoming edition. Needless to say, any errors are mine alone.

Two composite texts from Archbishop Wulfstan's 'commonplace book': the *De ecclesiastica consuetudine* and the *Institutio beati Amalarii de ecclesiasticis officiis*

CHRISTOPHER A. JONES

The great monument of tenth-century Anglo-Saxon monastic liturgy, the *Regularis concordia*, has been particularly fortunate in its twentieth-century devotees. The most prominent was Dom Thomas Symons, who published numerous learned articles on the text and, in 1953, an edition and translation that are still immensely valuable.[1] More recently, Lucia Kornexl has re-edited the *Concordia* with its continuous Old English gloss from London, British Library, Cotton Tiberius A. iii, and provided an exhaustive collation against the second Latin copy in London, British Library, Cotton Faustina B. iii.[2] Building on this detailed editorial work, Kornexl's introductory chapters also suggest new and helpful ways of regarding the transmission of this text and the authority of its two extant manuscripts.[3]

From these and other advances in the study of the *Concordia* itself, the way

---

[1] *Regularis Concordia Anglicae Nationis Monachorum Sanctimonialiumque: The Monastic Agreement of the Monks and Nuns of the the English Nation*, ed. and trans. T. Symons (London, 1953). Just before his death Symons also collaborated on a new edition of the text, published as *Regularis Concordia Anglicae Nationis*, ed. T. Symons and S. Spath, with M. Wegener and K. Hallinger, *Consuetudinum Saeculi X/XI/XII Monumenta: Introductiones*, ed. K. Hallinger, Corpus Consuetudinum Monasticarum 7.1 (Siegburg, 1984), 155–67 (prolegomena), and *Consuetudinum Saeculi X/XI/XII Monumenta Non-Cluniacensia*, Corpus Consuetudinum Monasticarum 7.3, ed. K. Hallinger (Siegburg, 1984), 61–147 (edition). This edition is valuable more for its accompanying explanatory notes than for its text, which is based on the poorer of the two extant manuscripts (London, British Library, Cotton Faustina B. iii).

[2] Both manuscripts were copied at Christ Church, Canterbury, and are now usually dated to s. xi^med, though earlier scholarship tended to date the Faustina copy earlier. On the manuscripts, see *Die Regularis Concordia*, ed. Kornexl (cited below, n. 3), pp. xcvi–cxxix.

[3] *Die Regularis Concordia und ihre altenglische Interlinearversion*, ed. L. Kornexl, Texte und Untersuchungen zur englischen Philologie 17 (Munich, 1993); summarized in English as 'The *Regularis Concordia* and its Old English Gloss', *ASE* 24 (1995), 95–130. In the following pages I quote the Latin text from Kornexl's edition, cited as *Reg.con.*, by her section and line numbers (the section divisions correspond to those of Symons's edition of 1953).

now lies open to consider in greater detail the influence of Bishop Æthelwold's 'national customary' on the monastic and secular churches of the late Anglo-Saxon period. The handful of Latin and Old English derivatives, or 'reflexes', of the *Concordia* have attracted notice rarely, and then usually only to corroborate or supplement details in the parent-text. In the introduction to his edition of 1953, Symons included a brief list of extant documents that reflect the influence of the *Concordia*, and this list has been expanded and improved in a helpful survey lately assembled by Joyce Hill.[4] Despite the almost forty years that separate these surveys, Hill's discussion alerts us that the two most important daughter-texts of the *Concordia* still await thorough studies of their own. The first, Ælfric's so-called *Letter to the Monks of Eynsham*, was edited in 1892 and has recently found its way into the series Corpus Consuetudinum Monasticarum – though less, one senses, as a document worthy of study in its own right than as a text ancillary to the *Concordia*.[5]

A second substantial witness to the reception of the *Concordia* is the set of excerpts preserved in two manuscripts and bearing the title *De ecclesiastica consuetudine* (hereafter *DEC*). The *DEC* consists of passages from the *Concordia* adapted for secular churches and supplemented from the *Liber officialis* (or *De ecclesiasticis officiis*), an allegorizing treatise on the liturgy by Amalarius of Metz (d. 852 or 853).[6] Symons and Kornexl often refer to the *DEC* in the commentary to their respective editions, and its value for clarifying some points in the *Concordia* is indeed great. But the *DEC* and another set of excerpts adjacent to it, titled *Institutio beati Amalarii de ecclesiasticis officiis* (hereafter *IBA*), have also figured prominently – and controversially – in discussions of Ælfric's pastoral writings

---

[4] *Regularis concordia*, ed. Symons, pp. lvi–lviii; an abridgement of this list appears in Corpus Consuetudinum Monasticarum 7.1, 164. See also J. Hill, 'The "Regularis Concordia" and its Latin and Old English Reflexes', *RB* 101 (1991), 299–315, and *Die Regularis Concordia*, ed. Kornexl, pp. cxlix–clv.

[5] *Excerpta ex Institutionibus Monasticis Æthelwoldi Episcopi Wintoniensis Compilata in Usum Fratrum Egneshamnensium per Ælfricum Abbatem*, ed. M. Bateson in *Compotus Rolls of the Obedientiaries of St Swithun's Priory, Winchester*, ed. G. W. Kitchin, Hampshire Record Soc. (London, 1892), pp. 171–98 (Appendix VII). Here I cite (as *LME* and section no.) the more recent edition, *Aelfrici Abbatis Epistula ad Monachos Egneshamnenses Directa*, ed. H. Nocent, with C. Elvert and K. Hallinger, in *Consuetudinum Saeculi X/XI/XII Monumenta Non-Cluniacensia*, ed. Hallinger, 155–85. On the dismissive view of the Eynsham letter by editors of this series, see introductory remarks in Corpus Consuetudinum Monasticarum 7.1, 158 and 160. A new edition, with translation and commentary by the present author, is forthcoming in the series Cambridge Studies in Anglo-Saxon England.

[6] *Liber officialis*, ed. J. M. Hanssens as vol. II of *Amalarii Episcopi Opera Liturgica Omnia*, 3 vols., Studi e Testi 138–40 (Rome, 1948–50). All quotations hereafter are from Hanssens's text, cited by book, chapter and section numbers of his edition. On Amalarius's career, see Hanssens's prolegomena (*Amalarii Episcopi Opera* I, 58–82) and A. Cabaniss, *Amalarius of Metz* (Amsterdam, 1954).

and Eynsham letter. The history of that problem will require some consideration below. The debate bears mentioning here, however, simply to underscore
that, despite their proximity to studies of the *Regularis concordia* and Ælfric's
canon (not to mention the Anglo-Saxon reception of Amalarius), the excerpts
in question have never been adequately edited.[7] The present article therefore
addresses three largely inseparable issues: establishment of the texts of the
DEC and *IBA* (edited in the Appendix), analysis of their sources and, finally, a
review of their relations to the *Concordia* and to Ælfric's Eynsham and pastoral
letters.

MANUSCRIPTS AND ESTABLISHMENT OF THE TEXTS

The *DEC* and *IBA* are preserved in two manuscripts exemplifying Archbishop
Wulfstan's 'commonplace book': Cambridge, Corpus Christi College 190 and
Rouen, Bibliothèque Municipale, 1382 (U. 109).[8] Cambridge, Corpus Christi
College 190 (siglum O) is a composite volume made up of two manuscripts: one
of s. xi[1] (pp. iii–xii and 1–294) in Latin, the other of s. xi[med] and xi[2] (pp. 295–420),
mostly in Old English. The origins of the Latin and original Old English quires
are unknown, although the two volumes were bound together as early as 1327
and probably as early as 1070, when the composite book appears to have been
included among Bishop Leofric's gifts to Exeter Cathedral.[9] The *DEC* and *IBA*
occur in the Latin portion of the manuscript on pp. 213–25 and 229–37 within a

---

[7] A very incomplete transcription, from a single manuscript, was included as an appendix to
Bernhard Fehr's edition of Ælfric's pastoral letters. See 'Anhang III: Teile aus Aelfrics
Priesterauszug', in his *Die Hirtenbriefe Ælfrics in altenglischer und lateinischer Fassung*, Bibliothek der
angelsächsischen Prosa 9 (Hamburg, 1914; repr. with a 'Supplement to the Introduction' by P.
Clemoes, Darmstadt, 1966), 234–49. The *DEC* and *IBA* are edited, with omissions, on pp.
234–40 (§§ 1–13) and 241–3 (§§ 17–32). Fehr prints complete only those portions of the *De
ecclesiastica consuetudine* transcribed for him by Karl Jost (see p. 234, n. 3); these are §§ 3 and 5–7
of my edition, below. The item which I include as § 12 of the *DEC* has been edited by J. E.
Cross, 'A Newly-Identified Manuscript of Wulfstan's "Commonplace Book", Rouen,
Bibliothèque Municipale, MS 1382 (U.109), fols. 173r–198v', *Jnl of Med. Latin* 2 (1992), 63–83,
at 77–8.

[8] For the theory of Archbishop Wulfstan's 'commonplace book', see M. Bateson, 'A Worcester
Cathedral Book of Ecclesiastical Collections, made c. 1000 A.D.', *EHR* 10 (1895), 712–31; D.
Bethurum, 'Archbishop Wulfstan's Commonplace Book', *PMLA* 57 (1942), 916–29; D.
Whitelock, 'Archbishop Wulfstan, Homilist and Statesman', *TRHS*, 4th ser., 24 (1942), 25–45,
at 30–5; H. Sauer, 'Zur Überlieferung und Anlage von Erzbischof Wulfstans "Handbuch"',
DAEM 36 (1980), 341–84; and the introduction by J. E. Cross and J. M. Tunberg to *The
Copenhagen Wulfstan Collection: Copenhagen Kongelige Bibliotek Gl. Kgl. Sam. 1595*, EEMF 25
(Copenhagen, 1993).

[9] The standard accounts of CCCC 190 include: Bateson, 'A Worcester Cathedral Book'; M. R.
James, *A Descriptive Catalogue of the Manuscripts in the Library of Corpus Christi College, Cambridge*, 2
vols. (Cambridge, 1909–12) I, 452–63; *Hirtenbriefe*, ed. Fehr, pp. xvii–xix, with Clemoes's
'Supplement', pp. cxxx–cxxxi; Bethurum, 'Archbishop Wulfstan's Commonplace Book'; N. R.
Ker, *A Catalogue of Manuscripts Containing Anglo-Saxon* (Oxford, 1957), pp. 70–3 (no. 45).

block of texts chiefly liturgical in character, including: Ælfric's first Old English pastoral letter to Wulfstan (pp. 188–201) and his excerpts on the seven ecclesiastical grades (pp. 201–5);[10] excerpts on the canonical hours from Hrabanus's *De clericorum institutione* II.i–vii (pp. 205–12);[11] an *ordo lectionum* for the Night Office, known as *Ordo romanus XIII A* (pp. 212–13);[12] then the *DEC*, followed by excerpts concerning the Ember Days and the excommunication and reconciliation of penitents (pp. 225–9);[13] then the *IBA*, followed by numerous penitential canons (pp. 238–45) and *ordines* for Ash Wednesday and Maundy Thursday (pp. 245–64).[14] Most of these texts can be found in at least one other manuscript within the family derived from Wulfstan's 'commonplace book'.[15]

The division of these many excerpts into discrete 'texts' is a hazardous business, and the isolation of the *DEC* and *IBA* as distinct items demands some justification. Surveying this material, some readers have assumed that the manuscript title *De ecclesiastica consuetudine* in CCCC 190 applies to the great sprawl of liturgical and penitential excerpts between pp. 213–64.[16] While it is possible to view this entire portion of the manuscript as a loose collection of material for use in secular churches, certain internal divisions do suggest themselves: the *ordines* for the public dismissal and reconciliation of penitents on Ash Wednesday and Maundy Thursday (pp. 245–64) straddle the liturgical–penitential divide, but the remaining texts seem to fall decidedly into one category or the other. Fehr printed excerpts from the entire series under the title 'Teile aus Aelfrics Priesterauszug', although he inclined towards the view that the heading 'Consuetudo ecclesiastica' (as he called it) was meant to include only the extracts from the *Concordia* (pp. 213–25) and from Amalarius (pp. 229–37), and perhaps a part of the following penitential matter.[17] That the penitential text which follows the *IBA* begins imperfectly and without a rubric at the top of p. 238 sug-

---

[10] Fehr collates the pastoral letter as 'Brief III' (*Hirtenbriefe*, pp. 146–221) and the excerpts on the ecclesiastical grades as *De septem gradibus aecclesiasticis* (*Hirtenbriefe*, Anhang V, pp. 256–7).

[11] Ed. PL 107, cols. 325–8.

[12] Not collated in *Les Ordines romani du haut moyen âge*, ed. M. Andrieu, 5 vols., Spicilegium Sacrum Lovaniense, Études et Documents 11, 23–4, 28 and 29 (Louvain, 1931–61) II, 481–8. Andrieu did collate the closely related copy of this *ordo* preserved in our second manuscript, Rouen 1382; see item 1 in Cross's inventory and discussion of this manuscript, cited above, p. 235, n. 7.   [13] Partially edited by Fehr in Anhang III, *Hirtenbriefe*, pp. 240–1 (§§ 14–16).

[14] Ed. (with some omissions) by Fehr, *ibid.*, pp. 243–9 (§§ 33–48).

[15] The most convenient and accurate overview is by Sauer, 'Zur Überlieferung', p. 383 (manuscript O, 'Textblock IX').

[16] E.g. Sauer, 'Zur Überlieferung', p. 383; Hill, 'The "Regularis Concordia"', pp. 305–6.

[17] *Hirtenbriefe*, ed. Fehr, p. cxxv (§ 265). On this point he appears to have changed his mind since an earlier article, 'Das Benediktiner-Offizium und die Beziehungen zwischen Ælfric und Wulfstan', *Englische Studien* 46 (1912–13), 337–46. There he speaks (p. 342) of the Amalarian extracts as a separate text: 'Es folgen nun nach der *Consuetudo* [= *DEC*] längere stücke aus Amalarius [= *IBA*], ferner *ordines* für bestimmte offizien usw ...'

gests that this was a separate item, the beginning of which was already lost in the exemplar of CCCC 190.[18]

There would be further reason to view the *DEC* (at least pp. 213–25) and the *IBA* as distinct texts amid the surrounding confusion, if only because their choice of sources and methods of adaptation are internally consistent. Fortunately, J. E. Cross's discovery of the *DEC* and *IBA* in a second manuscript now permits a more confident sorting of the pieces in CCCC 190.[19] Rouen, Bibliothèque Municipale, 1382 (U. 109) (siglum R) is a miscellany of homiletic, hagiographical, liturgical and canonistic materials copied by numerous hands of the eleventh century. Only the last section of the manuscript (173r–198v) appears to be the product of an English scriptorium of the first half of the eleventh century.[20] Cross's detailed inventory of the contents of this portion of the manuscript has conclusively established its associations with Wulfstan's 'commonplace book'. Only the first five items in Cross's inventory need concern us; these are: (1) a copy of *Ordo romanus XIII A* (173r); (2) the *IBA* (173r–176v); (3) a Latin Ember Day sermon (176v–178r); (4) the *DEC* (178v–182v); and (5) another short item on the Ember Days (182v–183r, *Qualiter quattuor tempora agantur*).[21] Differences in sequence apart, this is more or less the same group of texts found in CCCC 190, pp. 213–27 and 229–37, the chief discrepancy being the transposition of the two items concerning the Ember Days. Taking Cross's items 4–5 as a unit, I include the piece *Qualiter quattuor tempora agantur* as part of the *DEC* below, though its affiliation remains the least certain of all the texts here examined: in CCCC 190 it is found as the last chapter of the *IBA* (or the first text thereafter). On the other hand, the *Qualiter quattuor tempora agantur* does consist of excerpts from the *Regularis concordia* supplemented by teaching from Amalarius's *Liber officialis*; it not only commands these sources in much the same way as other segments in the *DEC*, but neatly rounds out the discussion of the liturgical seasons in that text.[22] The Rouen

---

[18] The *IBA* ends at line 24 on p. 237, and the last ruled line of the page has been left blank. Elsewhere the scribe has been perfectly willing to begin a new text on the last line of a page (cf. p. 213). The table of contents in CCCC 190, apparently copied from the exemplar, is too incomplete to offer sure guidance: it notes the last item of my *IBA* ('XCI. De quattuor tempora [sic] qualiter agantur'), but its next item ('XCII. De incestuosis et homicidis') does not begin until p. 241. Perhaps no more than a single leaf was missing from the exemplar following the *IBA*.   [19] See Cross, 'A Newly-Identified Manuscript', pp. 65–7 (items 2 and 4).

[20] Cross, 'A Newly-Identified Manuscript', pp. 63–4; see also Sauer, 'Zur Überlieferung', p. 345; R. A. Aronstam, 'The Latin Canonical Tradition in Late Anglo-Saxon England: the *Excerptiones Egberti*' (unpubl. PhD dissertation, Columbia Univ., 1974), p. 23 and n. 42.

[21] Cross edits both of the Ember Day items (his items 3 and 5) in 'A Newly-Identified Manuscript', pp. 73–8.

[22] Fehr recognized the affinities between the item *Qualiter quattuor tempora agantur* and the earlier selections from the *Concordia*, and this led him to view all the intervening Amalarian material in CCCC 190 as part of the *De ecclesiastica consuetudine*; see his *Hirtenbriefe*, p. cxxv (§ 265).

manuscript thus preserves a more coherent ending of the *DEC*, and I think it likely that the Ember Day sermon that occurs in the corresponding position in CCCC 190 is a substitution.[23]

THE INTERRELATION OF VERSIONS *O* AND *R*

Both manuscripts exhibit numerous corruptions and scribal errors in their texts of the *DEC* and *IBA*. Clearly neither manuscript is a copy of the other, nor can it be assumed that both copies necessarily descend from a single common exemplar, given what is now understood about Wulfstan's practice of revising and recopying his florilegia-texts at the source.[24] Not all the differences, moreover, are passive copying errors. Substantial interpolations in manuscript O justify our speaking of variant versions of the *DEC*. Generally, features that distinguish the two versions are of the type often seen among multiple copies of texts preserved in manuscripts of Wulfstan's 'commonplace book'. Two major additions, amounting to entire sections, appear in O but not in R. The first, in *DEC* 1,[25] is a hortatory passage developed, in part, from the Mass lections of the first Sunday in Advent; the second, in *DEC* 4, equals roughly two-thirds of the total Amalarian material on Septuagesima contained in O. In the latter instance, the portion not found in R appears as discrete pendant in O (headed 'ALIA' and beginning on a new line with a *littera notabilior*). While it is possible that a scribe

[23] Cross notes in his edition of these Ember Day texts (see above, p. 237, n. 21) that both also occur in manuscripts other than CCCC 190 and Rouen 1382. The *Qualiter quattuor tempora agantur*, which I would associate with the *DEC*, also occurs in Oxford, Bodleian Library, Barlow 37. The Latin sermon, beginning 'Quattuor esse tempora totius anni manifestum est', is found in CCCC 190, Rouen 1382, Barlow 37, and also Copenhagen, Kongelige Bibliotek, Gl. Kgl. Sam. 1595 as well as in London, BL, Cotton Nero A.i, but the versions vary considerably. Cross also lists three other manuscripts that are not associated with the 'commonplace book' family.

[24] This hypothesis explains the remarkable differences in arrangement and content of entire 'text-blocks' in the 'commonplace book' manuscripts (Sauer, 'Zur Überlieferung', p. 379). On the basis of textual evidence alone, Sauer (*ibid.* p. 377) posits at least four original versions in Wulfstan's possession, now represented by: (1) Copenhagen 1595 and (2) Cotton Nero A. i, as well as (3) one now-lost archetype from which descends CCCC 190, and (4) another from which descend the closely-related CCCC 265 and Barlow 37. Several manuscripts in the family, moreover, preserve corrections and revisions supposedly in Wulfstan's own hand, on the identification of which see N. R. Ker, 'The Handwriting of Archbishop Wulfstan', *England Before the Conquest: Studies in Primary Sources presented to Dorothy Whitelock*, ed. P. Clemoes and K. Hughes (Cambridge, 1971), pp. 315–51, repr. in his *Books Collectors and Libraries: Studies in the Medieval Heritage*, ed. A. G. Watson (London, 1985), pp. 9–26. Now also of crucial importance is J. M. Tunberg's analysis of the codicology of one first-generation copy of Wulfstan's collection (Copenhagen 1595); her observations suggest how certain practices in Wulfstan's scriptoria could account for the apparent multiplicity of 'commonplace book' archetypes; see Cross and Tunberg, *The Copenhagen Wulfstan Collection*, pp. 27–8.

[25] References to the *DEC* and *IBA* employ the section numbers I have assigned in the editions, below.

has omitted such segments when copying R, or that they simply were not present in his exemplar, an overview of all differences between O and R suggests that R witnesses an earlier form of the excerpts and O a subsequent, significantly expanded version. The R version, for example, adheres closely to the *Concordia* in its description of the special *Kyrie*-chant that was to conclude Tenebrae on each of the last three nights of Holy Week (*DEC* 7). The same material is much augmented in O, where the simple *Miserere*-petitions of the cantors at the western end of the church are expanded and given in detail.[26] Likewise, at Easter Vespers, O but not R (or the *Concordia*) inserts the verse 'In resurrectione tua' following an unspecified sequence hymn (*DEC* 10). Other differences are minor by comparison: once, for example, the compiler of the excerpts has apparently forgotten to secularize 'abbot' to 'priest', and R preserves the unaltered, O the adapted reading (*DEC* 2).

TEXTUAL VARIANTS AND THE COMPILER'S SOURCES

Another distinguishing feature of the O version is its preservation of the correct order of readings, chants and prayers for the Vigil of Pentecost, where most other derivatives of the *Concordia* show extraordinary corruption. This detail raises the issue of the relation of the *DEC*-compiler's sources to the extant manuscripts of the *Concordia* and *Liber officialis*. The Pentecost Vigil *ordo* is garbled and incomplete in R and seriously corrupt in both surviving manuscripts of the *Concordia* itself.[27] If R preserves the excerpts in a form similar to the one underlying the expanded version in O, the redactor of the latter sorted out the mess admirably.[28] The corresponding portion of the text in R is incomplete (probably by an error of haplography), but what is present there hints that the exemplar of R preserved the erroneous order of readings seen in the text of the *Concordia* in Faustina B. iii. Both versions of the *DEC* exhibit other notable variants closer to the Faustina copy than to Tiberius A. iii. In preserving the correct order of readings, chants and prayers for the Easter Vigil, for example,

---

[26] Thus *DEC* 7: (1) 'Qui passurus aduenisti propter nos, miserere nobis'; (2) 'Qui <prophetice promisisti>, Ero mors tua, O mors: Domine miserere nobis'; (3) 'Vita in ligno moritur, infernus ex morsu expoliatur: Domine miserere nobis'. Ælfric's Eynsham letter (§ 33) follows the shorter form found in the *Concordia* and R. See also *Regularis concordia*, ed. Symons, p. 36, n. 6. The additional verses in O appear in a form of this devotion included on p. 562 of the 'Red Book of Darley' (Cambridge, Corpus Christi College 422; Winchester, s. xi^med); cf. R. J. Hesbert, *Corpus Antiphonalium Officii*, 6 vols., Rerum Ecclesiasticarum Documenta, Series Maior 7–12 (Rome, 1963–79), II ('Cursus monasticus'), no. 74c.

[27] *Reg.con.* 58.1404–14; see also Kornexl's extensive commentary and bibliographical references (*ibid.* pp. 353–6).

[28] The only flaw in the O version is the omission of the canticle 'Cantemus Domino' after the first lesson, 'Temptauit Deus'; cf. *Reg.con.* 58.1407 and apparatus. If the version in O was developed from a form of the text similar to R, the presence of this canticle (correctly) in R but not O is difficult to explain.

both O and R agree with Faustina against Tiberius.[29] The *DEC* and Faustina also agree that the verse said or sung between Nocturns and Lauds of Easter Sunday shall be 'Surrexit Dominus de sepulchro', against Tiberius's 'In resurrectione tua, Christe'.[30] These and a few other minor variants suggest that our excerpts descend from an exemplar of the *Concordia* closer to Faustina B. iii than to Tiberius A. iii.[31] A collation of the manuscripts of the *DEC* individually against those of the *Concordia* clarifies the picture a little more, inasmuch as R tends to be closer to the source than O is – hardly a surprising conclusion if R represents the excerpts in an earlier form, and O in a subsequently expanded and revised form. As already mentioned, R shares with the source (and in particular with Faustina B. iii) remarkable errors in its *ordo* for the Vigil of Pentecost. The R version also follows the *Concordia* in limiting the summer observance of Wednesday and Friday processions before the principal Mass to the period from the Octave of Pentecost until 1 October, while in O the period extends 'ad Kalendas Nouembris' (*DEC* 5).[32]

Other conjunctive readings in R and one or both manuscripts of the *Concordia* suggest the beginnings of a pattern,[33] but with only two manuscripts of the excerpts to compare and so many unanswerable questions about the *Concordia* itself, little more can be said about the form of the source known to the original compiler of the *DEC*. Kornexl's analysis leaves little hope that the details of the *Concordia*'s transmission are recoverable: neither of the two complete manuscripts of the work necessarily represents the authoritative version of Æthelwold's text – if such a version ever existed.[34] Even so, collation of the two versions of the *DEC* with the critical apparatus of Kornexl's edition raises no serious challenges to the hypothesis that: (1) someone first compiled the excerpts using a copy of the *Concordia* similar to the one in Faustina B. iii; (2) he

---

[29] *DEC* 9; cf. *Reg.con.* 48.1171–7, plus apparatus and commentary.

[30] *DEC* 10; cf. *Reg.con.* 52.1260.

[31] E.g. (*Fa* = Faustina B. iii, *Ti* = Tiberius A. iii): *DEC* 7 sufficiat: sufficiat *Fa*, sufficit *Ti*; and *DEC* 11 colamus: colamus *Fa*, colimus *Ti*. Also *DEC* 9 and *Fa* omit the phrase *et pacem non dare nisi qui communicent* found in the Tiberius manuscript (*Reg.con.* 49.1196–7), though the grammatical awkwardness of the phrase, the redundancy of its teaching and its conspicuous lack of an Old English gloss all suggest to Kornexl a late and clumsy addition (*Die Regularis Concordia*, ed. Kornexl, pp. 320–2).

[32] Cf. Ælfric, *LME* 29: 'et ab octauis Pentecostes usque ad Exaltationem sanctae Crucis [*scil.* 14 September]'. The disagreement among the witnesses reflects some inevitable misunderstanding about the date of the transition from the summer to winter horarium. Most of the changes in the Office took place from 1 October, although the summer hymnal remained in use until 1 November; the summer schedule of meals and work, however, lasted only until 14 September. See *Regularis concordia*, ed. Symons, p. xxxv.

[33] E.g., *DEC* 2 conplectione *R*, complectione *Fa*, completione *O Ti*; also *DEC* 7 Dehinc *R Fa Ti*, Deinde *O*; and *DEC* 10 eatur *R Fa Ti*, eant *O*. But cf. *DEC* 6 oblatum *R*, oblationem *O Ti Fa*.

[34] *Die Regularis Concordia*, ed. Kornexl, pp. cxliv and cvii–cviii.

or a later redactor then revised and supplemented these; (3) the versions of the *DEC* extant in R and O represent consecutive stages in this process.

Finally, the *DEC* specifies certain liturgical forms mentioned only vaguely, or not at all, in the *Concordia*. These details are naturally of great interest to historians of the liturgy, and Symons called attention to most of them in his extensive publications on the *Concordia*. I have already mentioned some supplementary matter found only in O, such as the expanded instructions for the *Kyrie*-chant after Tenebrae, but numerous other details occur in both manuscripts and therefore appear to predate the reworking of the excerpts into the form now seen in CCCC 190 (although whether or not they go all the way back to the first compiler's exemplar of the *Concordia* cannot be known). On Ash Wednesday, for example, after the imposition of the ashes, *DEC* 5 specifies the *preces* to follow Ps. LXVI as 'Peccauimus, Domine: Adiuua nos'; the processional chants 'Iuxta uestibulum' and 'Inmutemur habitu' are then given instead of the vague 'antiphonas, quae in antiphonario continentur' of the *Concordia* (34.785–6).[35] Another addition later in the same passage (*DEC* 5) directs that on Ash Wednesday, contrary to the usual Lenten practice, the single meal of the day shall precede Vespers (no other text derived from the *Concordia* contains this provision). Less noticeable departures also occur among the instructions for the offices of Easter Day: in the processions to and from the baptismal font (immediately following the final collect for Vespers), *DEC* 10 specifies that the antiphons 'Sedit angelus' and 'Christus resurgens' shall accompany the psalms 'Laudate pueri' (Ps. CXII) and 'In exitu Israel' (Ps. CXIII), respectively.[36]

The textual evidence of the Amalarian material in both the *DEC* and *IBA* strongly suggests that the compiler(s) knew the *Liber officialis* in the revised, greatly abridged form which appears to have been the only version of the text available in pre-Conquest England. Because the anonymous compiler's reliance on this source for his excerpts has at times invited comparisons to Ælfric's methods in the *Letter to the Monks of Eynsham*, the use of the *Liber officialis* and of a few other previously unacknowledged sources may be more profitably examined in the context of the 'authorship' debate.

AUTHORSHIP AND RELATION TO ÆLFRIC'S EYNSHAM LETTER

The usual notions of 'authorship' are not well suited to anonymous composites such as the *DEC* and *IBA*. The possibility remains, however, of identifying their typical methods and use of sources that bear comparison with those of

---

[35] As Symons noted, these are the processional chants found in the 'Portiforium of St Wulfstan' (Cambridge, Corpus Christi College 391; Worcester, s. xi[med]).

[36] *Reg.con.* (53.1287–90) does not specify the antiphons, nor does Ælfric at *LME* 48.

known authors. Similarities between these excerpts and Ælfric's *Letter to the Monks of Eynsham* have been acknowledged since Mary Bateson included, in her edition of the latter, cross-references to passages in the *DEC*, cited only as 'CCCC 190'. Bateson's text, and her subsequent article on the manuscript family now known as Wulfstan's 'commonplace book', may have called the attention of Bernhard Fehr to the *DEC* and adjacent texts in CCCC 190.[37] Today it is universally accepted that CCCC 190 and other manuscripts of the 'commonplace book' family, although they contain certain items by Ælfric, exhibit far stronger ties to the interests and works of Archbishop Wulfstan. Fehr attempted at first, however, to view the contents of CCCC 190 as a reference book compiled by Ælfric for use in the writing of his pastoral letters.[38] Not surprisingly, among the Latin texts in CCCC 190 that Fehr originally cited to argue the Ælfrician associations of the manuscript was the *De ecclesiastica consuetudine*, which, in its selection and use of sources, does bear a superficial resemblance to Ælfric's *Letter to the Monks of Eynsham*. Both Ælfric and the anonymous compiler drew from the *Regularis concordia* and the *Liber officialis* details about the liturgies and symbolic meanings of the church year, and did so most heavily for the important and exceptional rites of the *triduum sacrum* and Easter Day. The *DEC* and *IBA*, adjacent to each other in both manuscripts (of which Fehr knew only one), do approximate some of the content of the Eynsham letter, albeit in a simplified form adapted for use in secular churches. Though it would have supported his case, Fehr did not note the additional similarity lent by the presence of *Ordo romanus XIII A* adjacent to the *DEC* and *IBA*, again in both manuscripts. This *ordo lectionum*, or one close to it, provided the framework of Ælfric's *ordo* of readings for the Night Office in the last part of the Eynsham letter.[39]

Fehr never claimed that the 'Consuetudo ecclesiastica' in CCCC 190 (including the texts I distinguish as the *DEC* and *IBA*) was dependent on the Eynsham letter or vice versa, for he recognized that each must have drawn upon the *Concordia* and *Liber officialis* independently of the other.[40] He did argue, however,

---

[37] Bateson, 'A Worcester Book'. Fehr was also influenced by E. Feiler's study of the so-called 'Old English Benedictine Office', published as *Das Benediktiner-Offizium, ein altenglisches Brevier aus dem 11. Jahrhundert: Ein Beitrag zur Wulfstanfrage*, Anglistische Forschungen 4 (Heidelberg, 1901). This edition and study prompted Fehr's article cited above, p. 236 n. 17.

[38] Fehr, 'Das Benediktiner-Offizium', p. 338. Fehr even suggested an Eynsham origin for the Latin core of CCCC 190.

[39] I.e., *LME* 70–80. See J. R. Hall, 'Some Liturgical Notes on Ælfric's Letter to the Monks at Eynsham', *Downside Rev.* 93 (1975), 297–303; also M. McC. Gatch, 'The Office in Late Anglo-Saxon Monasticism', *Learning and Literature in Anglo-Saxon England: Studies presented to Peter Clemoes on the Occasion of his Sixty-Fifth Birthday*, ed. M. Lapidge and H. Gneuss (Cambridge, 1985), pp. 341–62, at 352–62. The copy of *OR XIII A* in Rouen 1382 was collated as manuscript *S* by Andrieu (see above, p. 236, n. 12).   [40] *Hirtenbriefe*, ed. Fehr, p. cxxv, n. 1.

that both the 'Consuetudo ecclesiastica' (or 'Priesterauszug') and the Eynsham customary ('Klosterauszug') were compiled by Ælfric as preliminary texts from which to draw for his Old English pastoral letters to Archbishop Wulfstan, which at times (Fehr asserted) translate these 'Auszüge' directly.[41] Perceiving a lack of editorial finesse in the 'Consuetudo ecclesiastica' in particular, Fehr even went so far as to claim that Ælfric must have compiled this work before the Eynsham letter because 'der Priesterauszug ist . . . gewöhnliche Handwerkerarbeit. Der Klosterauszug ist die feinere Arbeit und ist wahrscheinlich aus dem Priesterauszug hervorgegangen'.[42]

Fehr had the misfortune to have been preparing his edition of the pastoral letters before the theory and implications of the 'commonplace book' idea had been fully worked out. Once the case had been made that CCCC 190 exemplifies Wulfstan's collection rather than Ælfric's, Fehr's attribution of the 'Priesterauszug' to Ælfric was left to stand or fall on the internal evidence of its sources and methods and on its alleged ties to the Eynsham letter and *pastoralia*.[43] Dorothy Bethurum dealt the Ælfrician attribution another blow when she hinted, following a remark by Whitelock, that the method by which the compiler of the *DEC* drew from his sources without attempting to synthesize them is more characteristic of Wulfstan's practice than Ælfric's.[44] Finally, Peter Clemoes moved to demolish what was left of Fehr's original case: not only was Fehr wrong about the relevance of CCCC 190 to Ælfric's works, Clemoes asserted, but he also seriously misjudged the similarities among the 'Priesterauszug', the Eynsham letter and the pastoral letters:

This seems to be a case in which [Fehr] allowed his interpretation of the evidence to be influenced by his preconceived theory of the nature of CCCC 190's authority. A detailed comparison of the ways in which Ælfric's letter to the monks of Eynsham, his second English pastoral letter for Wulfstan and the *De Ecclesiastica Consuetudine* reproduce the *Regularis Concordia* shows that all the significant correspondences are between the two

---

[41] He variously implies that the 'Priesterauszug' and 'Klosterauszug' are 'Vorbereitungsarbeiten' (*ibid.* p. xlvii), 'Vorarbeiten' (*ibid.* p. cxxv), or 'Vorstufen' (*ibid.* p. cxxvi).

[42] *ibid.* p. cxxvi.

[43] See Whitelock, 'Archbishop Wulfstan', p. 33, n. 1. Yet Whitelock did not see her revision of Fehr's theory about the manuscript as necessarily refuting Ælfric's authorship of the 'Priesterauszug'. It is difficult to determine, however, whether Whitelock's definition of the *De ecclesiastica consuetudine* included only the excerpts from the *Concordia* (with their Amalarian interpolations), or also the subsequent passages from Amalarius (my *IBA*) or any other part of Fehr's 'Priesterauszug'.

[44] *The Homilies of Wulfstan*, ed. D. Bethurum (Oxford, 1957), p. 345, with ref. to Whitelock, 'Archbishop Wulfstan', p. 34. Bethurum finally leaves the question open: 'the evidence is not sufficient for certain attribution to either [*scil.* Wulfstan or Ælfric]'. Fehr had also acknowledged the different methods of the 'Priesterauszug' and the Eynsham letter (*Hirtenbriefe*, pp. cxxv–cxxvi). Bethurum's statements imply a grouping of all the liturgical and penitential texts on pp. 213–64 of CCCC 190 under the single title *De ecclesiastica consuetudine*.

letters, and that there is no necessary connection between them on the one hand and CCCC 190's piece on the other . . . There seems to me no reason to connect this piece with Ælfric at all.[45]

Clemoes thus solidified the argument that manuscript context alone supports no link between the *DEC*, or any isolated text preserved in Wulfstan's 'commonplace book', and the writings of Ælfric. The observations in Clemoes's article and again, more briefly, in his 'Supplement to the Introduction' included in the 1966 reprint of Fehr's edition discouraged further analysis of similarities between the *DEC* (and, by implication, the *IBA*) and Ælfric's letters. While Clemoes's point about the manuscript context remains unassailable, his supporting remarks (quoted above) about the dissimilarities between the Eynsham and the pastoral letters on the one hand, and the *DEC* on the other, now admit some qualification.

To support the claim that 'all the significant correspondences are between the two letters [*scil*. Eynsham and Brief III]', Clemoes introduces two examples which, on review, beg the question they were meant to answer. To demonstrate that the *Letter to the Monks of Eynsham* and *DEC* drew upon the *Regularis concordia* independently of each other, he must discount one clear instance of agreement between the *DEC* and Eynsham letter against their apparent common source.[46] In their descriptions of the correct way to introduce the three Passion narratives read in Holy Week (that is, on Palm Sunday, Wednesday and Good Friday), Ælfric's letter and the *DEC* agree in their wording against both manuscripts of the *Concordia*. A synoptic comparison illustrates the difficulty (italics indicate correspondences between the *DEC* and Eynsham letter):[47]

Reg.con. 36.865–70:	*DEC* 6:	*LME* 32:
Ea die ad passionem dicitur 'Dominus uobiscum,' sed 'Gloria tibi, Domine' non respondetur.	*Eadem die ad passionem Domini diaconus dicat 'Dominus uobiscum' et respondent 'Et cum spiritu tuo.' Sed cum dicit 'Passio Domini nostri' nullus respondeat 'Gloria tibi Domine.'*	*Eadem die ad passionem domini diaconus dicat 'Dominus uobiscum' et respondent omnes 'Et cum spiritu tuo.' Sed cum dicit 'Passio domini' et reliqua, nullus respondeat 'Gloria tibi domine.'*

---

[45] P. Clemoes, 'The Old English Benedictine Office, Corpus Christi College, Cambridge, MS 190, and the Relations between Ælfric and Wulfstan: A Reconsideration', *Anglia* 78 (1960), 265–83, at 276–7; see also his 'Supplement to the Introduction' in the 1966 repr. of *Hirtenbriefe*, ed. Fehr, pp. cxlvi–cxlvii.

[46] See Clemoes, 'The Old English Benedictine Office', p. 276, n. 3, and 'Supplement to the Introduction', *Hirtenbriefe*, ed. Fehr, p. cxlvi, n. 94.

[47] I have substituted single quotation marks for the editors' original italics (indicating liturgical incipits).

Similiter et in reliquis	Similiter et in reliquis	Similiter ad illam passionem
passionibus excepta	passionibus excepta	quae legitur in quarta feria.
parasceuę passione, ubi	Parasceuae passione, ubi	Ad illam uero quae legitur
neutrum dicatur, nec	neutrum dicatur nec	in sexta feria non dicatur
'Dominus uobiscum' nec	'Dominus uobiscum' nec	'Dominus uobiscum' nec
'Gloria tibi, Domine.'	'Gloria tibi Domine.'	'Gloria tibi domine.'

The *DEC* and Ælfric coincide at the instruction about the Palm Sunday gospel, but then the Eynsham letter goes its own way while the *DEC* and *Concordia* agree in their formulas for Wednesday and Friday. Clemoes would explain the initial correspondence between the letter and the *DEC* as a result of common indebtedness to 'a version of the *Regularis Concordia* slightly different from any now extant'.[48] This solution is plausible, but the picture is complicated by the discovery that Ælfric and the *DEC* here draw on a common *external* source. Just before this passage in the Eynsham letter, Ælfric has used material from Amalarius's *Liber officialis* to explain the significance of Palm Sunday and its ceremonies (*LME* 32). The directions about the Passion readings immediately follow and, because of their similarity to corresponding matter in the *Concordia*, might appear to mark Ælfric's return to that source. But comparable details about the Passion readings also occur in the *Liber officialis*, and it is Amalarius's wording, rather than the *Concordia*'s, that informs Ælfric's instruction for Palm Sunday and, less certainly, for the other two days as well. The relevant sentences, moreover, are found only in copies of the two-book redaction of the *Liber officialis* (called by its modern editor the *Retractatio prima*) that was available in Anglo-Saxon England:[49]

Eadem die ad passionem Domini diaconus dicat: 'Dominus vobiscum', et respondent omnes: 'Et cum spiritu tuo'; sed cum dicit 'Passio Domini' et reliqua, nullus respondeat 'Gloria tibi Domine'.

. . . Et ad illam passionem [*scil.* on Wednesday] diaconus dicat: 'Dominus vobiscum', et respondent omnes: 'Et cum spiritu tuo', sed cum dicit 'Passio Domini' et reliqua, nullus respondeat 'Gloria tibi Domine'.

---

[48] 'Supplement to the Introduction', *Hirtenbriefe*, ed. Fehr, p. cxlvi, n. 94.

[49] See D. N. Dumville, *Liturgy and the Ecclesiastical History of Late Anglo-Saxon England: Four Studies*, Stud. in Anglo-Saxon Hist. 5 (Woodbridge, 1992), 116 and 135, and *idem*, 'Breton and English Manuscripts of Amalarius's Liber officialis', *Mélanges François Kerlouégan*, ed. D. Conso, N. Fick and B. Poulle (Paris, 1994), pp. 205–14. The transmission of the *Liber officialis* is notoriously complex. The *Retractatio prima* may be the work of a late-ninth-century French or Breton redactor working from the text of Amalarius's third, revised edition (i.e., the one incorporating changes inspired by a visit to Rome in 831). Into the abridgement (or *Retractatio prima*) the redactor also occasionally spliced material of his own, which Hanssens prints in a special appendix (see below, p. 246, n. 50). On the textual history of the *Liber officialis*, see the prolegomena to Hanssens's edition in *Amalarii Episcopi Opera* I, 120–200, esp. pp. 129 and 198 on the *Retractatio prima*.

... Ad illam passionem [*scil.* on Friday] diaconus non dicat: 'Dominus vobiscum', sed: 'Passio Domini' et reliqua, nullo respondente: 'Gloria tibi Domine'.[50]

Ælfric did not immediately turn back to the *Concordia* for these details, but simply continued the borrowing from Amalarius already begun in the preceding remarks on Palm Sunday.[51] The compiler of the *DEC* appears to have drawn his first instruction from the *Retractatio prima* of the *Liber officialis*, as Ælfric did, but the latter two from the *Concordia*.

What the *DEC* and Eynsham letter ultimately share in this passage, then, is an interpolation from the *Retractatio prima* of the *Liber officialis*. It is highly unlikely that Ælfric and the compiler of the *DEC*, working independently of each other, both made the same subtle alteration of the *Concordia* by using the *Liber officialis* in much the same way. Conceiveably, some prior, unknown redactor used the *Retractatio prima* to supplement the *Concordia*, and this augmented text underlies the Eynsham letter and the *DEC* separately. Against this prospect, however, Ælfric expressly takes the credit for introducing Amalarian teaching into the *Concordia* in the preface to his *Letter to the Monks of Eynsham*,[52] and he makes comparable use of the *Liber officialis* in other contexts throughout his career.[53]

Clemoes's second example of agreement between the Eynsham letter and *DEC* resolves itself in a similar way: 'the *Letter to the Monks of Eynsham* and Brief III [*scil.* the second Old English pastoral letter to Wulfstan], but not the *Regularis Concordia* or the *Priesterauszug*, specify that the number of candles extinguished during the night Office on the last three days of Holy Week shall be twenty-four.'[54] In fact, the mention of twenty-four candles does occur in the 'Priesterauszug', though among the Amalarian excerpts (my *IBA* 11) that follow those from the *Concordia* (my *DEC*). This Amalarian *locus*, or a variation of it,

---

[50] All printed by Hanssens (*Amalarii Episcopi Opera* II, 561–2) as *Lectiones a textu discrepantes longiores* II.3, 4 and 6 pertaining to *Liber officialis* I.x.1–2, I.xi.14 and I.xiii.12.

[51] He may also have been influenced by the arrangement of the comparable matter in the *Concordia*, where the three provisions are grouped together at the end of instructions for Palm Sunday. In the *Retractatio prima* of the *Liber officialis*, each provision occurs separately in the chapters devoted to each of the three occasions.

[52] *LME* 1: 'Tamen ne expertis tam salubris doctrine remaneatis, aliqua quae regula nostra non tangit, huic cartule insero uobisquae [*sic*] legenda committo addens aetiam aliqua de libro Amalarii presbiteri.' The final participial phrase suggests that Ælfric himself has introduced the supplementary material from the *Liber officialis*.

[53] For the use of Amalarius as a supplementary source in the *Catholic Homilies*, for example, see the citations by M. Förster, 'Über die Quellen von Ælfrics exegetischen Homiliae Catholicae', *Anglia* 16 (1894), 1–61, at 48–9; and, more doubtfully, by B. Fehr, 'Über einige Quellen zu Aelfrics Homiliae Catholicae', *Archiv* 130 (1913), 378–80. Ælfric's most extensive use of Amalarius in the vernacular occurs in the homily for Septuagesima Sunday; see *Ælfric's Catholic Homilies. The Second Series. Text*, ed. M. Godden, EETS ss 5 (London, 1979), Homily V, pp. 41–51, at 49–51, lines 234–87.

[54] 'Supplement to the Introduction', *Hirtenbriefe*, ed. Fehr, p. cxlvii, n. 96.

certainly accounts for the mention of twenty-four candles in both the Eynsham letter and, probably, in the second Old English pastoral to Wulfstan.[55] Once more Ælfric and the compiler of the 'Priesterauszug' make comparable uses of material from the *Liber officialis* to supplement the teaching of the *Concordia*.

However fair Clemoes's appraisal of the manuscript context, then, the presence of Amalarian interpolations at these points forms a link that is difficult to explain unless Ælfric exercised some influence, direct or indirect (through the text of his Eynsham letter), on the compilation of the *DEC*. Fehr had already observed that neither the Eynsham letter nor the 'Priesterauszug' depends solely on the other, but that both must draw directly on the *Concordia* and *Liber officialis*. Some differences in choice and arrangement of material are therefore allowable – analagous to the duplicate and triplicate provisions among the pastoral letters, perhaps. The absence from one text of material found in the other does not by itself indicate a different compiler. But Fehr also admitted that there appear to be differences in method between the 'Priesterauszug' (including my *DEC* and *IBA*) and the Eynsham letter. He claimed that the former consists of verbatim passages from the *Concordia*, to which the compiler simply appended Amalarian excerpts without attempting a more thorough integration. Moreover, among these sets of excerpts there are, Fehr asserted, no characteristically Ælfrician interpolations from other sources.[56] The 'Priesterauszug', in other words, is thought to show none of the deep engagement with its sources that the Eynsham letter does – a quality Clemoes invoked as 'the characteristic stamp of Ælfric's mind'.[57] Fehr dismissed this incongruity by viewing the 'Priesterauszug' as a prior, rough outline of a text and the *Letter to the Monks of Eynsham* as a later, more sophisticated reworking of the same sources.[58] Bethurum, Clemoes and others were naturally wary of that solution, and they argued that this very discrepancy of method amounted to evidence *against* Ælfric's authorship.[59]

Neither Fehr nor his opponents could build a convincing case because both

---

[55] *LME* 33; cf. Brief III.24 (ed. Fehr, p. 154). Some of Ælfric's interpretation of Tenebrae, however, cannot be traced to standard versions of the *Retractatio prima*, indicating his reliance on a variant text of that recension (see below, p. 255).

[56] *Hirtenbriefe*, ed. Fehr, pp. cxxv–cxxvi: 'Dieser Priesterauszug unterscheidet sich nun allerdings in einem Punkte deutlich vom Klosterauszug. Er ist immer wörtliche Kopie Aethelwolds und bringt lange Auszüge aus Amalarius als Anhang. Aelfricsche Zutaten selbständiger Art fehlen. Der Klosterauszug aber unternimmt gerne kleine stilistische Aenderungen im Latein Aethelwolds und arbeitet Amalarius und einige allerdings wenige eigene Zutaten organisch in den Aethelwoldschen Grundstock hinein.'

[57] 'Supplement to the Introduction', *Hirtenbriefe*, ed. Fehr, p. cxlvii: 'the *Priesterauszug* bears none of the characteristic stamp of Ælfric's mind: its method of quoting whole passages of the *Regularis Concordia* verbatim lacks any of the active comprehension which Ælfric brings to bear on this source in his *Letter to the Monks of Eynsham* and in Brief III, and which is so characteristic of his work as a whole.'   [58] See above, p. 243, n. 41.

[59] See above, n. 57, and p. 243, n. 44.

sides misrepresented the compiler's method in the *DEC* and *IBA* and relied on overly-general assertions about Ælfric's habits of adapting Latin sources. To take up the second issue first, comment on the method of Ælfric's Latin *abbreviationes* has tended only to see and praise in them features already familiar from his Old English: brevity, clarity and synthesis.[60] This tendency has allowed to pass unexamined some features of Ælfric's Latin-to-Latin writings distinct from his Latin-to-Old English ones, and has promoted a view of all his Latin works as *abbreviationes* of a uniform type. The effects of such generalization are strongly felt in the argument that the *DEC* and, presumably, the *IBA* do not bear the 'stamp of Ælfric's mind' while the Eynsham letter does. In fact, both Fehr and his later challengers overstated the extent and integrity of synthesis achieved in the *Letter to the Monks of Eynsham*: contrary to the impression given by Bethurum and Clemoes, significant portions of that text do consist of verbatim extracts from the sources,[61] and, although Ælfric's incorporation of supplemental matter into his customary is sometimes seamless, more often he keeps the Amalarian teaching separate and simply appends it to the relevant material from the *Concordia* – the very method of the *DEC*-compiler on two occasions.[62] Surely it is also relevant that the Eynsham letter is a public, comparatively polished work; Ælfric may even have compiled it with a broader audience in mind than his Eynsham monks alone.[63] By contrast, the excerpts in Wulfstan's 'commonplace book' are, as Fehr surmised, the sort of rough, working texts typically

[60] On Ælfric's Latinity, viewed against the background of the 'hermeneutic' style then in vogue, see M. Lapidge, 'The Hermeneutic Style in Tenth-Century Anglo-Latin Literature', *ASE* 4 (1975), 67–111, at 101; repr. with addenda in his *Anglo-Latin Literature, 900–1066* (London, 1993), pp. 105–49 and 474–9, at 139. For an inventory of Latin works attributed to Ælfric and a detailed discussion of his abbreviation of the *Vita S. Æthelwoldi*, see *Wulfstan of Winchester: the Life of St Æthelwold*, ed. and trans. M. Lapidge and M. Winterbottom (Oxford, 1991), pp. cxlvi–clv. A fuller account is forthcoming in C. A. Jones, '*Meatim sed et Rustica*: Ælfric of Eynsham as a Medieval Latin Author'.

[61] Extensive verbatim borrowings from the *Concordia* occur in *LME* 17–22, 29–30, 32–4, 36, 40, 45–6, 49, 52, 65–6 and 68–9. For verbatim quotation of the *Liber officialis*, see especially *LME* 27–8 and 30. In fact, Ælfric's Latin writings as a whole show a strong reliance on the wording of their immediate sources. For example, the extracts on the ecclesiastical grades preserved in Boulogne-sur-Mer, Bibliothèque Publique, 63, and in numerous manuscripts of the Wulfstan's 'commonplace book' (see above, p. 236, n. 10), are almost universally attributed to Ælfric, though they consist in large part of verbatim quotation of Isidore and the Aachen Council of 816.

[62] See *DEC* 6 and 12. For Ælfric's silent interpolation of Amalarian or other material, see *LME* 22 (on the feast of the Holy Innocents, from *Lib.off.* I.xli.2) and 25 (on Candlemas, from *Lib.off.* IV.xxxiii.18). Usually, however, Ælfric keeps the Amalarian teaching separate, introducing paraphrases or direct quotation from the *Liber officialis* with the words 'Amalarius' and 'Amalarius dicit . . .'; see, e.g., *LME* 24, 30–2, 35 and 43.

[63] The grounds for this speculation are discussed in ch. 3 (on the manuscript context) and in the commentary to *LME* 12, 25 and 68 in my forthcoming edition of the Eynsham letter.

found in a reference collection. It is hard to proceed, then, from the observation that the *DEC* and *IBA* are less polished works than the Eynsham letter to the conclusion that Ælfric could not have assembled the former.

But the terms of the contrast collapse altogether when we leave assumptions about Ælfric's methods in the Eynsham letter to examine the methods actually present in the *DEC* and *IBA*, only to find that these too have suffered misrepresentation. First, the *DEC* and *IBA* are hardly slavish in their adherence to the sources. Although there is much direct quotation, minor alterations and adaptations abound, and abridgement is frequently and intelligently carried out. A few select passages may illustrate the variety of the compiler's practice (italics indicate portions of the *Concordia* used verbatim in the *DEC*):

1. *Reg.con.* 31.687–98:

In cuius noctis [*scil.* Christmas] *uigilia* in quarto responsorio, ut honorificentius agatur, duo simul cantent. *Euuangelium post 'Te deum laudamus' ab* abbate *more solito legatur.* Dicta oratione, sub silentio egrediantur ministri, ut calcient se, lauent et induant sub festinatione, *omnibus*que *signis motis agatur missa. Post hęc, laudes matutinales.* His finitis, incipiant laudes de omnibus sanctis more solito <si nondum *diei aurora eluxerit*>. Si autem eluxerit, post missam celebrentur matutinalem, quę *in* lucis *crepusculo* celebranda est. *Dehinc, tempore oportuno, signo pulsato, canant primam.*[64]

DEC 2:

In cuius noctis uigiliis euangelium post 'Te Deum laudamus' a sacerdote more solito legatur et <oratio> dicatur. Sicque motis omnibus signis agatur missa. Post haec matutinales laudes, quas sequatur missa <matutinalis> cum in crepusculo aurora diei eluxerit. Dehinc tempore oportuno, signo pulsato, canant primam.[65]

The *DEC* does not simply parrot the source. The necessary change of 'abbot' to 'priest' occurs here and elsewhere and could have been carried out

---

[64] 'At Nocturns on Christmas night the fourth respond shall, for extra solemnity, be sung by two cantors. After the "Te Deum laudamus" the gospel shall be read by the abbot, as is usual; and when the prayer has been said the ministers shall go out silently, change their shoes, wash and vest quickly; then all the bells shall peal and the Mass shall be celebrated. Matins shall follow, after which, if day has not yet dawned, Lauds of All Saints shall be begun in the usual way; if, however, it is already daybreak, that Office shall be said after the Morrow Mass which must itself be said in the early dawn. Then, at the proper time, when the bell rings the brethren shall sing Prime' (*Regularis concordia*, trans. Symons, pp. 28–9).

[65] 'At Vigils on that night, after the "Te Deum laudamus" the gospel shall be read by the priest, as is usual, and the collect shall be said. And so, when all the bells have been set ringing, Mass shall be said. After these things [come] Lauds, followed by the matutinal Mass when, at first light, the day has begun to dawn. Then, at the proper time, at the sound of the bell they shall sing Prime' (all translations from the *DEC* and *IBA* are my own).

mechanically,[66] but the adaptation of the *Concordia* for secular churches required more substantial intervention. The compiler omits the custom of having two cantors sing the fourth responsory, and he drops the reference to the Office of All Saints. The absence of these may be a concession to lower standards or limited resources among the secular clergy (Ælfric retains both customs in the Eynsham letter).[67] The *DEC*-compiler was also willing to abbreviate severely, when necessary:

2. *Reg.con.* 48.1158–64 and 1169–71:

DEC 9:

Sabbato sancto, hora nona, ueniente abbate in aecclesiam cum fratribus, nouus, ut supra dictum est, afferatur ignis. Posito uero cereo ante altare, ex illo accendatur igne. Quem *diaconus more solito benedic*ens, hanc orationem quasi uoce legentis proferens dicat: 'Exultet iam angelica turba celorum' . . . *Benedictione peracta*, ascendat *subdiaconus* ambonem. *Legat lectionem* primam: '*In principio* creauit'.[68]

Sabbato Sancto diaconus more solito cereum benedicat. Benedictione peracta legat subdiaconus lectionem 'In principio'.[69]

There are of course parts of the *DEC* that do quote long sections of the *Concordia* (for example, *DEC* 3), but to characterize the method of the entire text as that 'of quoting whole passages of the *Regularis Concordia* verbatim' is too facile. The same lessons can be demonstrated by the compiler's use of the *Liber officialis* in the *IBA*, where similarly purposeful interventions occur:

3. *Liber officialis* I.iv.4 and 5:

IBA 7:

(4) . . . *Hoc enim sufficit hic commemorare, quod quadraginta a* supradicto dominico *duo dies* supersint usque ad baptismum, et fiunt quadraginta duo; *tot enim mansiones habuerunt filii Israhel,* qui baptizati sunt in

Hoc sufficit hic commemorari, quod in Quadragesima .xl. duo sunt dies a die dominico quem .xl. nominamus. Tot enim mansiones habuerunt filii Israel quando exierunt de terra Aegipti ad terram

---

[66] See *Hirtenbriefe*, ed. Fehr, pp. cxxiv–cxxv. The compiler failed to change *abbas* in *DEC* 3 and numerous references to *fratres* are left unaltered.

[67] *LME* 18. Brief III mentions no special customs for Christmas.

[68] 'On Holy Saturday at the hour of None, when the abbot enters the church with the brethren, the new fire shall be brought in, as was said before, and the candle which has been placed before the altar shall be lit from that fire. Then, as is the custom, a deacon shall bless the candle saying, in the manner of one reading, the prayer "Exultet iam angelica turba coelorum." . . . After the blessing the subdeacon shall go up into the pulpit and shall read the first lesson: "In principio creavit"' (*Regularis concordia*, trans. Symons, p. 47).

[69] 'On Holy Saturday the deacon shall bless the candle in the usual way. After the blessing the subdeacon shall read the lesson "In principio"'.

mari Rubro, *quando exierunt de terra Aegypti*
de dura servitute, et pervenerunt ad terram
promissionis ... (5) *Merito, qui ad caelestem*
patriam tendunt, eodem numero mansionum
satagunt, quo filii Israhel ad terram promissionis
venerunt ...[70]

promissionis. Et merito qui ad caelestem
patriam tendunt eodem numero
<mansionum> satagunt quo filii Israel ad
terram promissionis uenerunt.[71]

The relevant passage is included in the *Retractatio prima*, but the omissions seen in the *IBA* are not attributable to variant readings common to that redaction. Some very intelligent improvements appear here, such as the relative clause 'quem ... nominamus' in place of 'supradicto dominico', which would be puzzling excised from its original context. More importantly, the compiler simplifies the overburdened allegorical reading by omitting the references to baptism on Holy Saturday, leaving only the numerological significance of the forty-two days. Ælfric does not use this section of the *Liber officialis* in the letter to his monks, but the quiet, sensible methods of adaptation in the above passage (not an isolated example) invite comparisons to his handling of Amalarian material in the Eynsham letter.

Even more valuable as evidence of the author's intellectual habits are other interpolations that occur throughout the *DEC* and *IBA* but have passed largely unnoticed. Fehr was certainly aware that the *DEC* includes additions from the *Liber officialis* woven among its excerpts from the *Concordia*, and he mentioned two specifically in the section on Septuagesima.[72] But not even Fehr fully appreciated the extent and potential significance of these and other interpolations. I have identified several of these extra sources in the *apparatus fontium* of the

---

[70] 'Suffice it to recall here that from the aforementioned Sunday [*scil.* I Lent] there are still forty days [plus] two until the rite of baptism, making a total of forty-two; for that was the number of habitations had by the sons of Israel, who were baptized in the Red Sea, when they went forth from their harsh slavery in the land of Egypt and came to the promised land ... Those who are heading towards their heavenly home are rightly satisfied with the same number of habitations as the sons of Israel had on their journey to the promised land.' The reference is to the itinerary of the Israelites given in Num. XXXIII.1–49.

[71] 'Suffice it to recall here that in Lent there are forty-two days from the Sunday we call Quadragesima. For that was the number of habitations had by the sons of Israel when they went out of Egypt into the promised land. And those who are heading towards their heavenly home are rightly satisfied with the same number of habitations as the sons of Israel had on their journey to the promised land'.

[72] *Hirtenbriefe*, ed. Fehr, p. cxxv, n. 1; the latter of these occurs in manuscript O only; see my source apparatus to *DEC* 4. Subsequent analyses of the *DEC* have rested on general assertions that easily obscure this point: e.g., Whitelock ('Archbishop Wulfstan', p. 33, n. 1) speaks of 'a text made up of passages from Æthelwold's *Regularis concordia* and Amalarius', where it is not clear whether she means the *DEC* with its Amalarian interpolations or the *DEC* plus the *IBA*; similarly Bethurum (*Homilies of Wulfstan*, p. 345) refers to 'passages inserted from Amalarius', but since she apparently considers the *DEC* to include all the texts on CCCC 190 pp. 213–64, her reference is also unclear.

edition, below; because their significance and extent are hard to gauge from that format, however, a summary of them here may prove useful.

In the whole of *DEC* 1, nothing is drawn from the *Concordia*. The statement about the omission of the *Gloria* in Advent may come from Amalarius, although the liturgical prescription by itself would have been commonplace enough. It does occur at *IBA* 1, however, and Ælfric includes an analogous comment in *LME* 16. There follows (in manuscript O only) a long hortatory passage (source unknown) which consists in part of quotations from the epistle reading for the Mass of the first Sunday in Advent (Rom. XIII.11–14).[73] The next interpolation is less obtrusive and adds to the Epiphany customs of the *Concordia* a detail about omission of the invitatory, perhaps from *Liber officialis* IV.xxxiii.1.[74] I have already mentioned the interpolations from the *Liber officialis* concerning Septuagesima (*DEC* 4); these were identified by Fehr and overlap only partially the extensive Amalarian matter Ælfric introduced in the corresponding section of the Eynsham letter (§ 26). A significant interpolation from *Liber officialis* I.x.1 (with distinctive *Retractatio prima* variants) follows the customs from the *Concordia* for Palm Sunday, already discussed.[75] In *DEC* 8 the custom of not kneeling at the prayer for the Jews in the *orationes solemnes* does not come from the *Concordia* and may reflect the influence of *Liber officialis* I.xiii.17 (though this instruction is also a commonplace in liturgical *ordines*).[76] Furthermore, *DEC* 9 smoothly blends phrases from the *Liber officialis* with those of the *Concordia* (on the absence of torches at the gospel procession in the Easter Vigil Mass) in a way similar to Ælfric's version of the same passage.[77] Finally, interpolations also occur in *DEC* 12 (on the Ember Days),[78] where the compiler adds to the whole of *Regularis concordia* 61 an impressive supplement drawn from several points in Amalarius's text.[79]

To summarize: the compiler of the *DEC* displays an impressive familiarity with the *Liber officialis*, the probable source of significant details added at four points (*DEC* 4, 6, 9 and 12). Similar and even more illuminating interpolations occur in the *IBA*. *IBA* 5 (*De Yppapanti*) begins with a brief quotation from *Liber*

---

[73] *DEC* 1, starting at my third sentence ('In tempore quoque . . .').
[74] *DEC* 2: 'In qua etiam nocte <inuitatorium> amittimus.'   [75] *DEC* 6; see above, p. 245.
[76] The Amalarian passage is probably the source of the same detail at *LME* 43.
[77] The wording of *DEC* 9 is closer to the *Concordia* than to Ælfric, but *DEC* 9 and *LME* 46 both contain the detail (probably from *Liber officialis* I.xxxi.8) that incense only precedes the gospel in imitation of the holy women who brought spices to Christ's tomb. The exact interrelations are complex; see commentary to *LME* 46 in Jones, *Ælfric's Letter.*
[78] As noted above (pp. 237–8), the exact relation of this item to the *DEC* is questionable; it follows my *DEC* 11 only in the Rouen manuscript.
[79] I.e., *Liber officialis* II.i.1, II.ii.6 and 12 and II.iii.12. This selection in part reflects the prior abridgement represented by the *Retractatio prima*, but the compiler still shows fair skill in choosing and recombining the sentences.

officialis IV.xxxiii.18 (including a significant reading peculiar to the *Retractatio prima*), followed by an unidentified exhortation that combines a reference to the bearing of candles to church on Candlemas with a quotation of the beginning of Ps. XLVII.10, the Mass introit (or gradual) for the feast of the Purification. The remainder of the section explains the events commemorated on this feast (that is, the presentation of Jesus in the Temple and the ritual purification of the Virgin). The compiler quotes the beginning of the gospel of the day (Luke II.22–3), followed a judicious selection of comments from Bede's exposition of this pericope.[80]

Two other major interpolations occur near the end of the excerpts. In *IBA* 14 the compiler again introduces his subject with a quotation from Amalarius (*Liber officialis* I.xxxiv.1 and 2) describing the significance of the introit, collect, epistle, gradual and *Alleluia*-verse ('Pascha nostrum immolatus est Christus' etc.) of the Mass for Easter Day. He then drops the thread of Amalarius's commentary and, seizing on the word 'Pascha' from the *Alleluia*-verse, proceeds to explain the meaning of that word and the rich typology of the Lord's 'passing over' (*transitus*). This interpolation consists of a patchwork of three separate *loci* drawn from chs. 61 and 63 of Bede's *De temporum ratione*.[81] Finally, there is another significant use of Bede in the compiler's discussion of Pentecost (*IBA* 16), which begins and ends with selected material from *Liber officialis* I.xxxv.3 and I.xxxix.1. In between, however, the compiler has mingled at least two comments from Bede's *Expositio* of Acts, describing the significance of the tongues of flame and drawing the commonplace parallel with God's fiery appearance on Mount Sinai.[82]

These interpolations lay unrecognized during the earlier debate, but now they prompt the speculation: if the same person compiled both these sets of excerpts, it seems he enjoyed a thorough familiarity with the *Regularis concordia* and Amalarius's *Liber officialis* and at least some knowledge of Bede's commentaries on Luke and Acts, as well as his *De temporum ratione*. The *DEC* passages on Palm Sunday and Tenebrae, discussed above, allow that the Eynsham letter itself may have served as an additional source. On the basis of all this evidence, it is tempting to wonder if Fehr's attribution may have been right, albeit for the wrong reasons. The compiler obviously commanded several sources well known to Ælfric, whose Eynsham and pastoral letters and, to a lesser extent,

---

[80] Bede, *In Lucae euangelium expositio* I.ii.22, lines 1662–6 and 1691–6, in *Bedae Venerabilis Opera, Pars II: Opera Exegetica 3*, ed. D. Hurst, CCSL 120 (Turnhout, 1960), 61–2.

[81] Bede, *De temporum ratione liber*, c. 61, lines 14–16, and c. 63, lines 7–9, 11–13 and 32–4, in *Bedae Venerabilis Opera, Pars VI: Opera Didascalica 2*, ed. C. W. Jones, CCSL 123B (Turnhout, 1977), 450 and 454–5.

[82] Bede, *Expositio actuum apostolorum* II.1, lines 34–6, and II.3, lines 46–8, in *Bedae Venerabilis Opera, Pars II: Opera Exegetica 4*, ed. M. L. W. Laistner, CCSL 121 (Turnhout, 1983), 16.

Old English homilies attest his knowledge of the *Concordia* and *Liber officialis*. Ælfric drew heavily from Bede's *De temporum ratione* (though not the sections quoted at *IBA* 14) for his Old English *De temporibus anni*. His knowledge of Bede's exegetical writings is well established, and he may even have used Bede's commentary on Luke II.22 (the source of the interpolations at *IBA* 5) for his Old English homily for the feast of the Purification.[83] In his Old English homily for Pentecost, Ælfric appears to have used Bede's homily for that occasion, though not his commentary on Acts.[84]

The sort of unequivocal analogues that would confirm links between the *DEC/IBA* and Ælfric's known writings are not forthcoming: Fehr and Clemoes would certainly have noticed them long ago. Bethurum's suggestion that Wulfstan was responsible for the excerpts rests on a barely tenable distinction between the habits of Ælfric and Wulfstan as Latin authors. The sources of the *DEC* and *IBA*, at any rate, now look rather less like the archbishop's usual fare. Wulfstan knew at least portions of the *Liber officialis*,[85] but I am unaware of evidence (other than the disputed *DEC* itself) that he took a direct interest in the *Concordia*. Ælfric did translate portions of it for his second Old English pastoral letter for Wulfstan, though whether this was at the archbishop's specific request is uncertain. None of Wulfstan's known writings suggests a command of Bede's aforementioned exegetical or scientific works.

The evidence here gleaned hardly encourages positive claims for Ælfric's 'authorship', but a connection of some kind no longer seems so remote. If Ælfric is not responsible for the expanded version of the *DEC* in O, he or someone under his direction may still have compiled the base text, similar to the form preserved in the Rouen manuscript, and sent this to Wulfstan or whoever carried out the subsequent revisions. We are otherwise left to explain the coincidence that someone working independently of Ælfric or his works (1) used Amalarian commentary and other sources to supplement the customs of the *Regularis concordia*, then in turn (2) drew from Bede's exegetical and scientific

---

[83] See Förster, 'Über die Quellen', p. 24 (§ 81); but cf. C. L. Smetana, 'Ælfric and the Early Medieval Homiliary', *Traditio* 15 (1959), 163–204, at 187.

[84] Förster, 'Über die Quellen', p. 20 (§ 75). The homily includes one sentence that is close to the Bedan interpolation at *IBA* 16, but Ælfric is probably only translating the quite similar words in his chief source, Gregory the Great's *Homiliae in euuangelium XL*, no. XXX: 'in linguis igneis apparuit Spiritus, quia omnes quos repleverit ardentes pariter et loquentes facit' (PL 76, col. 1223C); cf. *Catholic Homilies I*, no. 22 (*In die sancto Pentecosten*): 'Se halga gast wæs gesewen on fyrenum tungum bufon þam apostolon for þan ðe he dyde þæt hi wæron byrnende on godes willan. 7 bodiende ymbe godes rice' (*Ælfric's Catholic Homilies. The First Series. Text*, ed. P. Clemoes, EETS 17 (Oxford, 1997), 359).

[85] See, e.g., Bethurum's commentary to items VIII.a–c [sermons on baptism] in her *Homilies of Wulfstan*, pp. 302–4 and 311–20, supplemented by J. E. Cross, 'Wulfstan's *Incipit de baptismo* (Bethurum VIIIa): a Revision of Sources', *NM* 90 (1989), 237–42.

writings to supplement Amalarius. The strongest argument against adding these excerpts to Ælfric's Latin canon lies not in any of the objections voiced by Bethurum or Clemoes, but in an apparent discrepancy between the content of Ælfric's exemplar of the *Liber officialis* and that used by the compiler of the *DEC* and *IBA*. The Eynsham letter makes clear that Ælfric's copy of the *Retractatio prima* contained an unusual version of that text, similar to one now uniquely preserved in Salisbury, Cathedral Library, 154 (Salisbury, s. xi^ex).[86] In the Salisbury manuscript, variant matter actually replaces the original Amalarian text from which *IBA* 10–11 (at least) derive. Whether the same omission pertained in Ælfric's exemplar cannot be known, and even if it did, the authentic *Retractatio prima* text could have been supplied from an additional copy, though this leads to the awkward conclusion that Ælfric deliberately used the variant text in one circumstance and not in another. This extraordinary complication urges that the origin and transmission of the composite texts remain open questions. Their surprisingly complex relationships with the *Concordia*, the *Liber officialis*, the Eynsham letter and other sources nevertheless demand far greater recognition than they have received. These 'excerpts' demonstrate, above all, an intelligent and resourceful application of reformed monastic liturgy and scholarship for the wider benefit of the eleventh-century Anglo-Saxon church.[87]

---

[86] See C. A. Jones, 'Ælfric, Amalarius, and Salisbury, Cathedral Library, MS. 154' (forthcoming).

[87] I owe thanks to the late J. E. Cross, who patiently responded to my early queries about these texts, and to Antonette DiPaolo Healey, Roberta Frank, David Townsend and Michael Lapidge, all of whom read drafts of the study and edition and saved me from numerous errors. All faults that remain are entirely my own.

APPENDIX

EDITORIAL PROCEDURES

The following editions are based on photostats and microfilms generously made available by Corpus Christi College, Cambridge, the Dictionary of Old English and the Library of the Pontifical Institute of Mediaeval Studies, Toronto, and, for section twelve of the *DEC*, the Bodleian Library, Oxford. For permission to publish the excerpts as they appear in CCCC 190, I am grateful to the Master and Fellows of Corpus Christi College, Cambridge.

The base manuscript is CCCC 190 (= O), pp. 213–25 and 229–37, with variants from Rouen 1382 (= R), 173r–176v and 178v–183r, reported in the apparatus. For § 12 of the *DEC* only, variants are also reported from Oxford, Bodleian Library, Barlow 37, 40r–v. To facilitate close comparison with the extant manuscripts of the *Regularis concordia* and Ælfric's Eynsham letter, as well as with the *Liber officialis*, it has seemed advisable to include orthographic variants, excepting (for reasons of space) the fluctuation of *e, ę, æ, œ* and *ae*. 'Tailed'-e (*ę*) has been transcribed *ae* or *e*, as phonologically correct.

With only two manuscripts – which in fact appear to represent two different versions – it has seemed best to print the 'expanded' version (O) with limited editorial intrusions. Emendations taken over into the text of O are indicated by angled brackets, and all variant readings, including the original reading of O where that of R has been preferred, are signalled by superscript lower-case letters keyed to the critical apparatus (this series of letters beginning anew from *a* within each numbered section). In addition to the manuscript sigla, the following abbreviations also occur in the apparatus: *ed.* = my conjecture, *Reg.con.* = *Regularis concordia, Lib.off.* = *Liber officialis* and *R1* = *Retractatio prima*. Section numbers and modern punctuation are my own. Abbreviations are expanded silently and attempt to follow the orthography and morphology of the scribe of O. Because the text of the *DEC* so often wavers between connected prose and lists of incipits, the expansion of abbreviations for 'antiphon', 'tract', 'psalm' and 'collect' is often difficult, and further complicated by both scribes' tolerance of declensional variants of some of the commonest technical terms (e.g., alternate nominatives 'psalm*um*' and 'psalm*us*', 'tractu*m*' and 'tract*us*', 'capitulum' beside 'capitulo' and 'capitula'). Where my expansion is doubtful, the manuscript form is given in the apparatus. The spelling and inflection of foreign words such as *Pascha, Parasceue* and *Pentecoste* are inconsistent, and in most cases I have not emended them in O.

Superscript numerals running in a single series through each of the two texts refer to the necessarily brief *apparatus fontium* that follows the editions. There the same abbreviations are used as noted above (*Reg.con., Lib.off., R1*), plus *LME = Letter to the Monks of*

256

Eynsham, and a few others that should be obvious (e.g., *De.temp.rat.* = Bede, *De temporum ratione*). It is not possible in so small a space to indicate the precise relation of text to source, but the following conventions have been observed: where the source citation immediately follows the lemmata and colon, the reader may understand that the borrowing is verbatim or nearly so. The word 'from' preceding the source citation indicates that the passages of the *DEC* or *IBA* represent only a part of the section cited or a mixture of verbatim quotation with paraphrase, additions or omissions. A preceding 'cf.' signals an analogue or a possible but unverifiable source. Single quotation marks set off liturgical incipits and other quoted matter. I have not identified biblical quotations or liturgical incipits when these have already been identified in the printed editions to which the source apparatus refers.

To provide a liturgical commentary in so limited a space has not been possible, though features of the *DEC* that depart significantly from the *Concordia* have already been discussed in the preceding pages. For any provision borrowed directly from that source, the reader may consult the introductions and commentary of Symons and Kornexl, as well as the *apparatus explicatiuus* in the Corpus Consuetudinum Monasticarum.

DE ECCLESIASTICA CONSUETUDINE

[1] ITEM^a DE ECCLESIASTICA^b CONSUETUDINE. Ab^c Aduentu Domini 'Gloria in excelsis'^d non^e canitur antequam celebretur missa in nocte Natale Domini. Sciendum quoque est quia in festiuitatibus apostolorum 'Credo in unum' post euange-lium^f ut in dominicis diebus canendum est.[1] In tempore quoque Aduentus Domini nos oportet unanimiter laudare nomen Domini et gaudere in Domino: 'Sobrie ergo et iuste et pie' uiuere,[2] scientes 'quia hora est iam nos de somno surgere'[3] dum expectamus beatam spem et aduentum Domini: 'non in commessationibus et ebrietatibus, non in contentione et emulatione'[4] diem natiuitatis Domini, sed in sobrietate et castitate et omni sanctitate nos oportet expectare, ut digni efficiamur percipere sacrosanctum corpus et sanguinem Domini nostri Iesu Christi in die natale sui. Et hoc christianorum nullus debet neglegere, quia Dominus in euangelio dicit: 'Nisi manducaueritis carnem filii hominis et biberitis eius sanguinem, non habebitis uitam in uobis.'^g[5]

[2] DE NATALE DOMINI.^a Vespere Natale Domini canantur antiphonae congruae de ipsa temporis completione^b ad psalmos. In cuius noctis uigiliis^c euangelium^d post 'Te Deum laudamus' a sacerdote^e more solito legatur et <oratio>^f dicatur. Sicque motis^g omnibus signis agatur missa. Post haec matutinales laudes,^h quas sequatur missa <matutinalis>ⁱ cum in crepusculo aurora diei eluxerit.^j Dehinc tempore oportuno, signo pulsato, canant primam.[6] Ad uesperam ipsius diei dicantur antiphonae 'Tecum principium'. Reliquis uero tribus diebus dicantur antiphonae de ipsis sanctis cum psalmis ipsi <sollempnitati>^k competentibus. His peractis rursum repetatur^l 'Tecum principium' usque Octabas Domini.[7] Hinc usque Epyphaniam^m Domini psalmi ad uesperumⁿ ad feriam pertinentes cum antifonis^o dicantur. In uigilia Epyphaniae^p Domini ieiunium minime exequitur. Ad psalmos ipsius uesperae antifonae^q dicantur de

eadem[r] sollempnitate.[88] In qua etiam nocte <inuitatorium>[t] amittimus.[9] Ceteris diebus, post Octabas Domini uidelicet et Epiphaniorum primum <diem>,[u] nec <signa>[v] pulsantur simul nec 'Gloria in excelsis[w] Deo'[x] canitur (nisi alia festiuitas interuenerit) usque octauum diem, qui sollempniter cum .xii. lectionibus celebratur.[10]

[3]   DE PURIFICATIONE.[a] In[b] Purificatione sanctae Mariae sint cerei ordinati in ecclesia ad quam fratres ire[c] debent ut inde petant luminaria. Euntes autem silenter incedant psalmodie dediti et omnes albis[d] induti si fieri potest uel aeris permiserit temperies. Et intrantes ecclesiam agant[e] orationem cum antifona[f] et collecta ad uenerationem ipsius sancti cui ecclesia ipsa ad quam itur[g] dedicata est. Deinde abbas stola et cappa indutus benedicat[h] candelas et conspergat aqua benedicta et thurificet,[i] et sic accepto cereo ab aedituo psallentibus cunctis accipiant[j] singuli singulas acceptasque accendant.[k] Inde reuertentes canant antifonas[l] quae adsunt usquequo ueniant ante portam ubi, decantata antifona[m] 'Responsum[n] accepit Symeon',[o] dicatur oratio 'Erudi quaesumus Domine', post quam ingrediantur ecclesiam canentes responsorium[p] 'Cum inducerent'. Hoc decantato dicant orationem dominicam,[q] dehinc sequatur <tertia>.[r] Qua finita, si processionem induti non egerunt, induant se <et missam>[s] celebrantes teneant luminaria in manibus donec post oblationem ea sacerdoti[t] offerant.[11]

[4]   DE SEPTUAGESIMA.[a] In Septuagesima[b] mutatur cantus laetitiae in tribulationem[c] et 'Gloria in excelsis Deo'[d] intermittitur.[12] Cruces atque reliquiae occultantur usque Pascha.[13] Sabbato Sancto item mutatur cantus tribulationis in <letitiam>,[e] quantoque antea erat rarior tanto tunc erit[f] preciosior.[g] ALIA: In Septuagesima itaque oportet nos luctum penitentiae peragere ut captiuus populus <inuitus>[h] peregit annos septuaginta in peregrinatione, et luctus penitentiae conuertatur nobis simul in gaudium in resurrectione Domini.[14] Populus Dei pro peccatis in Babylonia detentus est captiuus sub numero septuagenario, quo numero completo reuersus est in Hierusalem. Et quod illi inuiti sustinuerunt per annos septuaginta nos uoluntarie pro peccatis nostris sustineamus,[15] saltem quasi per dies .lxx.,[16] quibus mereamur esse participes in <caelestis>[i] Hierusalem sempiternis gaudiis.[j]

[5]   DE CAPITE IEIUNII.[a] Quarta[b] feria Capitis Ieiunii, nona decantata, sacerdos stola ornatus benedicat cyneres, quibus benedictis imponat[c] cyneres capitibus singulorum. Canentque antifonam[d] 'Exaudi nos Domine'. Psalmus[e] 'Saluum me fac Deus'[f] et 'Gloria Patri'. 'Kyrrieleison'. 'Pater noster'. Psalmus[g] 'Deus misereatur nostri'. Preces[h] 'Peccauimus Domine: Adiuua nos'.[i] Collecta.[j] Tunc uadant ad[k] ecclesiam quo ire habent canentes antiphonas[l] 'Iuxta uestibulum' et '<Inmutemur>[m] habitu'.[n] Venientes autem ad[o] ecclesiam <quo>[p] eunt, canant antifonam ad uenerationem ipsius sancti cui ipsa ecclesia[q] dedicata est. 'Kyrrieleison'. 'Pater noster'. Psalmus[r] 'Ad te leuaui'. Preces et[s] collecta. Statimque incipientes letaniam reuertantur ad matrem ecclesiam ac hinc more solito[t] agatur missa.[17] Peracta missae celebratione non quadragesimali[u] usu[v] uesperas ante refectionem celebrent, sed primo refectionem fratrum agant, dehinc tempore oportuno uesperas celebrent.[18] Iste ordo processionis semper teneatur quotiens processio[w] agitur, sed aliis temporibus semper antiphona 'Exurge[x] Domine' dicatur <prima>[y] cum psalmo et 'Gloria'. 'Kyrrieleison'. 'Pater noster'. Psalmus[z] 'Deus misereatur'.[aa] Preces[bb] et collecta. Tunc uadant quo ire habent.[19] His peractis induant se

258

ministri altaris postquam ingressi fuerint ecclesiam cum processione, prolongata letania quantum ad hoc sufficiat, et sic peragant ministeria sua.[20] A Capite Ieiunii .iiii.[cc] et .vi. feria processionem custodiant usque in Cenam Domini, et ab Octabis Pentecosten usque ad Kalendas[dd] Nouembris.[ee]

[6]   DE DIE PALMARUM.[a] In die palmarum fratres sub silentio ordinatim eant ad ecclesiam ubi palmae sunt, et intrantes ecclesiam agant orationem cum antifona[b] et collecta. Finita oratione, a[c] diacono legitur[d] euangelium[e] 'Turba multa' usque 'Ecce mundus totus post eum abiit'. Quod sequatur benedictio palmarum. Post benedictionem aspergantur aqua benedicta[f] et thus cremetur. Dehinc, pueris inchoantibus antifonam[g] 'Pueri Hebreorum', distribuantur ipsae palmae et sic[h] egrediantur. Venientes autem ante ecclesiam subsistant donec pueri decantent[i] 'Gloria laus' cum uersibus. Quibus finitis, incipiente cantore responsorium[j] 'Ingrediente',[k] aperiantur portae. Ingressi teneant palmas in manibus usque dum offertorium cantetur, et eas post oblationem[l] ordinatim offerant sacerdoti.[21] ITEM:[m] Dies[n] palmarum dicitur, id est uictoriarum.[o] Eadem die[p] Dominus de Bethsaida descendit Hierusalem. Quare uenit Hierusalem Beda in Marco ex testimoniis scripturarum promit dicens: 'Appropinquante[q] autem Christi[r] passione, appropinquare[s] Dominus uoluit loco passionis.'[22] Eadem die ad passionem Domini diaconus dicat 'Dominus uobiscum' et respondent[t] 'Et cum spiritu tuo.' Sed cum dicit 'Passio Domini nostri'[u] nullus respondeat 'Gloria tibi Domine.'[23] Similiter et in reliquis passionibus excepta Parasceuae passione, ubi neutrum dicatur nec 'Dominus uobiscum' nec 'Gloria tibi Domine.'

[7]   DE CENA DOMINI.[a] Quinta[b] feria, quae et Cena Domini dicitur, nocturnale officium agatur secundum quod in antifonario[c] habetur,[24] et 'Gloria Patri' in psalmis et responsoriis[d] non dicatur.[25] Euangelii[e] antifona[f] finita nihilque iam cereorum luminis remanente agant tacitas genuflexo more preces.[26] Vel, si priori ita placuerit, sint duo[g] in dextera parte[h] canentes 'Kyrrieleison' et duo[i] in sinistra 'Christe eleison',[j] duoque in occidentali 'Qui passurus aduenisti propter nos, miserere nostri.'[k] Tunc chorus 'Christus Dominus factus est obediens usque ad mortem.'[l] 'Kyrrieleison'. 'Christe eleison'. 'Qui <prophetice promisisti>,[m] Ero mors tua, O mors: Domine miserere nostri.' Chorus 'Christus Dominus'. 'Kyrrieleison'. 'Christe eleison'. 'Vita in ligno moritur, infernus ex morsu expoliatur:[n] Domine miserere nostri.' Chorus 'Christus Dominus'.[o] Qui ordo trium noctium uniformiter teneatur.[27] Prima in Cena Domini sonore dicta et canonico[p] more, scilicet 'Deus in nomine',[q] 'Beati'[r] usque 'Legem pone', tunc, dicto uersu, genu flexo peragant cetera silenter. Sed priore preueniente[s] ad confessionis locum, facto signo agant confessionem. In ceteris horis similiter residua capitula: ad .iii.[t] 'Legem pone' usque 'Defecit'; ad .vi. 'Defecit'[u] usque 'Mirabilia'; ad .viiii.[v] 'Mirabilia'[w] usque 'Ad Dominum cum tribularer'.[x] Vespere similiter sonora uoce unusquisque psalmus cum antifona[y] et uersus et euangelium,[z] et cetera[aa] silenter. Completorium aeque sonore et <canonico>[bb] more, et preces agant tacite.[28] Ea enim die post tertiam[cc] fratres discalciati lauent pauimenta[dd] ecclesiae, sacerdotibus interim cum ministris altaris benedicta aqua sacra altaria lauantibus. Et non fit celebratio missae in aliquo altari donec lauetur.[29] Sexta peracta celebretur missa pauperibus, dehinc[ee] collectis in locum congruum lauent fratres et extergant pedes pauperum atque osculentur, denturque eis cybaria.[ff][30] Dehinc hora

congrua agatur nona.[31] Post haec celebratio missae ad quam 'Gloria Patri' minime[gg] dicatur et 'Dominus uobiscum', nisi ab episcopo tantummodo ubi crisma conficitur. A quo etiam in eucharistiae acceptione pacis osculum presbyteris,[hh] ter 'Agnus Dei' decantato, solummodo detur. In qua missa sicut[ii] et in[jj] sequentium dierum communicatio praebetur cunctis fidelibus, reseruata nihilominus[kk] ea die eucharistia[ll] quae sufficiat ad[mm] communicandum altera die. <Peracta>[nn] missae celebratione omnes ad mixtum <pergant>.[oo][32] Post mixtum sacerdos suum peragat[pp] mandatum, quo peracto uesperas celebrent. Deinde[qq] refectionem agant, post quam tempore congruo fratrum agatur mandatum[33] et cetera.

[8] DE PARASCEVE.[a] In[b] die Parasceuae agatur nocturna laus sicut supra dictum est[34] et ceterae horae <tacite>[c] canonico more. Eadem die primo subdiaconus legat lectionem Oseae 'In tribulatione sua'. Sequitur tractus[d] 'Domine audiui'. Postea datur oratio a[e] sacerdote cum genuflexione[f] 'Deus a quo et Iudas'. Deinde lectio 'Dixit Dominus ad Moysen'. Sequitur tractus 'Eripe me'; postea passio.[35] Post haec celebrentur orationes sollempnes – omnes orationes cum genuflexione,[g] excepta pro Iudaeis.[36] Quibus expletis statim praeparetur sancta crux ante altare, sustentata hinc et inde a duobus diaconibus. Tunc canent 'Populus meus' et cetera.[37] His peractis egrediantur diaconus et subdiaconus[h] de secretario cum corpore Domini quod pridie remansit et calice cum uino non consecrato et ponant super <altare>.[i] Tunc sacerdos ueniet ante altare et dicat uoce sonora[j] 'Oremus: Praeceptis salutaribus moniti'[k] et 'Pater noster', inde[l] 'Libera nos' usque 'Per omnia saecula saeculorum.' Et sumat sacerdos de sacrificio[m] et ponat in calice <nihil>[n] dicens, et communicent omnes cum silentio. Hoc expleto uespertinum officium agat unusquisque priuatim in loco suo. Quo peracto refectorium petant.[38] Completorium uero unusquisque in loco suo stans semotim ac silenter decantet.[o][39]

[9] DE SABBATO SANCTO.[a] Sabbato Sancto diaconus more solito cereum benedicat. Benedictione peracta legat subdiaconus lectionem 'In principio'. Sequitur oratio 'Deus qui <mirabilia>'.[b] Secunda[c] lectio 'Factum est in uigilia'. Tractum[d] 'Cantemus'.[e] Oratio[f] 'Deus cuius[g] antiqua'. Tertia lectio[h] 'Apprehendent'.[i] Tractum 'Vinea'.[j] Oratio[k] 'Deus qui nos'.[l] Quarta[m] lectio 'Haec est hereditas'. Oratio[n] 'Deus qui ecclesiam tuam'. Tractum[o] 'Sicut ceruus'. Collecta 'Concede quesumus'. Finita oratione inchoentur letaniae <septene>.[p] Postea descendant ad fontes canentes letanias quinas. Sequitur consecratio fontis. His expletis redeant[q] ad altare cum letania terna, et antequam cantetur[r] 'Gloria in excelsis Deo' dicat cantor alta uoce 'Accendite' .iii.,[s] et tunc inluminentur omnia luminaria. Et <sacerdote incipiente>[t] 'Gloria in excelsis Deo' pulsentur omnia signa ecclesiae. Sequitur collecta 'Deus qui hanc sacratissimam'. Epistula 'Si consurrexistis'. 'Alleluia: Confitemini'.[u] Tractum[v] 'Laudate Dominum'. Ante euangelium[w] non portantur luminaria in ipsa nocte sed incensum tantum[40] ad imitationem[x] mulierum, quia hoc tantummodo obtulerunt mulieres, ut dicit euangelium[y] 'Cum transisset sabbatum' et reliqua.[41] Finito euangelio[z] dicat sacerdos 'Dominus uobiscum. Oremus'. In ipso die non cantatur[aa] offertorium nec 'Agnus Dei' nec communio, sed interim dum communicantur 'Alleluia, alleluia'.[bb] Psalmus 'Laudate'.[cc] Dehinc antifona[dd] 'Vespere autem'.[ee] Psalmus[ff] 'Magnificat'. <Sic>[gg] sacerdos missam ac uespertinalem sinaxim una compleat[hh] oratione.[ii] Completorium sonoriter celebretur[jj] more canonicorum.[42]

[10] DE DIE SANCTO PASCHAE.[a] In[b] die sancto Paschae inprimis ad nocturnam dicat sacerdos 'Domine labia mea', 'Deus in adiutorium meum'[c] cum 'Gloria', statimque cantor incipiat <inuitatorium>.[d] Tunc tres[e] antiphonae cum tribus psalmis. Quibus finitis uersus conueniens dicatur, deinde .iii.[f] lectiones cum responsoriis.[43] Deinde sacerdos incipiat ymnum 'Te Deum laudamus', post cuius finem dicat sacerdos 'Surrexit Dominus de sepulchro'[g] uerbotenus, et initiet matutinas dicens 'Deus in adiutorium'. Et a cantore ilico inchoentur antifonae cum psalmis[h] 'Dominus regnauit'. Psalmis[i] iure peractis cum antifonis, capitulo[j] a presbytero[k] uersuque 'Surrexit', ut mos est, a puero dicto, initietur antiphona in euangelio.[l] Qua peracta dicatur collecta.[44] Ad primam quattuor[m] psalmi: 'Deus in nomine'[n] et 'Confitemini'[o] (prima tantum feria). 'Beati' usque 'Legem pone'.[p] Capitula. Versus 'Haec dies'[q] directe a puero et reliqua. Ad .iii.[r] 'Legem pone'[s] usque 'Deficit' cum 'Alleluia'. Gradale[t] 'Haec dies' sine uersu. 'Dominus uobiscum'. Collecta. Similiter ad .vi. et[u] ad .viiii.[v] Ad uesperas[w] psalmi[x] 'Dixit Dominus', 'Confitebor', 'Beatus uir' cum antifonis[y] sine capitula. Gradale 'Haec dies' sine uersu. 'Alleluia' cum uersu. Sequentia.[z] Versus 'In resurrectione <tua>'[aa].[bb] Postea inchoetur antiphona in euangelio.[cc] 'Dominus uobiscum'. Collecta. Dehinc eant[dd] ad fontes, psalmum[ee] 'Laudate pueri'[ff] cum antiphona[gg] 'Sedit angelus' <canentes>,[hh] quam sequatur collecta. Inde[ii] reuertentes chorum <adeant>[jj] psalmum 'In exitu' decantantes cum antiphona 'Christus[kk] resurgens', quam propria sequatur collecta. Completorium more peragatur canonicorum. Finitis enim[ll] psalmis subsequitur <capitulum>[mm] et uersus. Exhinc 'Nunc dimittis' cum antiphona concinatur,[nn] consequentibus eius horae[oo] precibus cum collecta et benedictione.[45] Vespera uero Octabarum Paschae ordo iam regularis pleniter inchoetur.[46]

[11] INCIPIUNT LECTIONES DE PENTECOSTEN.[a] Incipiunt orationes cum lectionibus atque canticis quae dicuntur in uigiliis Pentecosten[b] ante descensum[c] fontis. Prima lectio 'Temptauit Deus Abraham'.[d] Sequitur oratio 'Deus qui in Abrahae'.[e] Secunda[f] lectio 'Scripsit Moyses'. Canticum 'Adtende caelum'.[g] Sequitur oratio 'Deus qui nobis'.[h] Tertia[i] lectio 'Apprehendent'.[j] Canticum 'Vinea facta est'. Sequitur oratio 'Deus qui nos ad celebrandum'. Lectio quarta 'Audi Israel'. Canticum[k] 'Sicut ceruus'. Sequitur oratio 'Omnipotens sempiterne'.[l] Finita oratione inchoantur letaniae septenae ad introitum ante altare. Postea descendat sacerdos cum <scola>[m] canente letanias quinas ad fontes benedicendos. Sequitur oratio et praefatio.[n] His expletis redeunt ad altare cum letania terna, quo finito dicat sacerdos 'Gloria in excelsis'. Sequitur[o] collecta 'Praesta quaesumus'. Postea legitur epistola 'Cum Appollo[p] esset' et cantatur[q] 'Alleluia: Confitemini' et tractus[r] 'Laudate',[s] deinde missa secundum ordinem. Post refectionem uero tempore congruo uesperae ceteraque celebrantur more solito.[47] Illa dominica nocte tribus[t] psalmis totidemque lectionibus cum responsoriis agatur[u] nocturna laus, ut[v] <in antiphonario>[w] titulatur. Ceteris horis[x] diei et ebdomadae sequentis regularis ordo tenetur, sed et uesperae sabbati et ipsius diei sancti normaliter psallant.[48] Illa ebdomada Pentecosten sollempniter celebratur sicut[y] et Paschalis, excepto quod ieiuniorum diebus 'Gloria in excelsis' non canitur et 'Alleluia' pro gradalibus[z] canitur et uesperae de Omnibus Sanctis dicuntur.[aa] Rursus in Octabis[bb] Pentecosten dominica non repetitur 'Spiritus Domini' eo quod septem tantum colamus dona Spiritus Sancti, sed agitur illa ebdomada de sancta Trinitate.[49]

[12] QUALITER QUATTUOR TEMPORA AGANTUR.[a] Quattuor[b] Temporibus quae ecclesiastice custodiuntur[c] ad missae celebrationem[d] <dicitur>[e] a diacono 'Flectamus genua'[f] quadragesimali[g] more, sed et abstinentia ciborum[h] cum magna custodiatur diligentia, excepto dum in Pentecosten ebdomada euenerit. Tum[i] enim aliquantulum remissius pro tantae sollempnitatis reuerentia agi oportet, ut diximus.[j]50 Ab antiquis Romanis grece et latine legebantur .xii. lectiones quattuor Temporibus propter duas causas: unam quia aderant Greci quibus incognita erat latina[k] lingua, aderantque Latini quibus incognita[l] erat greca.51 At quia quattuor tempora annorum nos incendunt[m] ad amorem Dei quattuor ieiunia facimus, per singula quaeque[n] tempora <suum>[o] ieiunium. In unoquoque ieiunio .iii. dies sunt[p] quia unumquodque tempus .iii.[q] menses habet. Pro unoquoque mense[r] singuli dies ieiunio consecrantur, id est .iiii. et .vi. et .vii. feria: quarta quia in ea Iudaei fecerunt consilium[s] ut occiderent Christum; .vi.[t] occiderunt[u] eum; .vii.[v] Romanorum more ieiunio[w] concluditur propter tristitiam[x] .xii. apostolorum quam habuerunt pro nece[y] Domini.52 Per singulas quoque orationes solemus genuflexionem[z] facere in .xii. lectionibus, excepto Octauis[aa] Pentecosten:[bb] in <sola>[cc] illa oratione de camino ignis non flectimus genua[dd] ut separata sit nostra oratio quae est ad unum uerum Deum ab errore gentilium, sicut Nabuchodonosor[ee] errauit[ff] quando compellabat populum ut adorarent statuam quam fecit.[gg]53

Apparatus criticus

[1]   [a] Item *O*: Hec *R*. [b] Ecclesiastica *O*: Ecclestica *R*. [c] Ab *O*: b *R*. [d] excelsis *O*: excelsis Deo *R*. [e] non *O*: t̄i *? abbrev., prob. a corruption of* non *R*. [f] euangelium *O*: euuangelium *R*. [g] In tempore quoque …uitam in uobis *O: om. R*.

[2]   [a] De Natale Domini *O: om. R*. [b] completione *O*: conplectione *R*. [c] uigiliis *O*: uigilia *R*. [d] euangelium *O*: euuangelium *R*. [e] a sacerdote *O*: ab abbate *R*. [f] oratio *R*: oratione *O*. [g] motis *O*: modis *R*. [h] matutinales laudes *O: transposed R*. [i] matutinalis *ed.*: matutinales *OR*. [j] eluxerit *O*: eduxerit *R*. [k] sollempnitati *R*: sollempnitate *O*. [l] repetatur *O*: repitatur *R*. [m] Epyphaniam *O*: Epiphania *R*. [n] ad uesperum *O*: a uesperam *R*. [o] antifonis *O*: antiphona *R*. [p] Epyphaniae *O*: Epiphania *R*. [q] antifonae *O*: antiphone *R*. [r] eadem *O*: eade *R*. [s] sollempnitate *O*: sollemnitate *R*. [t] inuitatorium *R*: uitatorium *O*. [u] diem *R*: die *O*. [v] signa *R*: signum *O*. [w] excelsis *O*: excelsis *corr. from* exelsis *R*. [x] Deo *O: om. R*.

[3]   [a] De Purificatione *O: om. R*. [b] In *O*: n *R*. [c] ire *O*: irae *R*. [d] albis *corr. from* albi *O*: albis *R*. [e] agant *O*: agunt *R*. [f] antifona *O*: antiphona *R*. [g] itur *O*: iturum *R*. [h] benedicat *O*: benedic *R*. [i] thurificet *O*: turificet *R*. [j] accipiant *corr. from* accipient *O*. [k] accendant *O*: accedant *R*. [l] antifonas *O*: antiphonas *R*. [m] antifona *O*: antiphona *R*. [n] Responsum *O*: Responnsum *R*. [o] accepit Symeon *O: om. R*. [p] responsorium *O: om. R*. [q] dominicam *O*: dominica *R*. [r] tertia *R*: tercia *O*. [s] et missam *R Reg.con.*: et ad missam *O*. [t] sacerdoti *with* ti *smeared and rewritten above O*.

[4]   [a] De Septuagesima *O*: De Septuagessima *R*. [b] Septuagesima *O*: Septuagessima *R*. [c] tribulationem *O*: tribulatione *R*. [d] Deo *O: om. R*. [e] letitiam *R*: laetitia *O*. [f] erit *O: om. R*. [g] preciosior *O*: pretiosior *R*. [h] inuitus *Lib.off.*: intutus *O*. [i] caelestis *ed.*: caelesti *O*. [j] Alia … gaudiis *O: om. R*.

[5]   [a] De Capite Ieiunii *O: om. R*. [b] Quarta *O*: uarta *R*. [c] imponat *O*: inponat *R*. [d] antifonam *O: om. R*. [e] Psalmus *O: om. R*. [f] Deus *O: om. R*. [g] Psalmus *O: om. R*. [h] Preces *O: om. R*. [i] nos *O*: nos Deus *R*. [j] Collecta *O: om. R*. [k] ad *O: om. R*. [l] antiphonas *ed.*: A. *O: om. R*. [m] Inmutemur *R*: Imutemur *O*. [n] habitu *O: om. R*. [o] ad *O: om. R*. [p] quo *R*: qua *O*. [q] ipsa ecclesia *O: transposed R*. [r] Psalmus *O: om. R*. [s] et *O: om. R*. [t] solito *O*: solita *R*. [u] quadragesimali *O*: quadragessimali *R*. [v] usu *O*: morte *R*. [w] pro-

cessio *O*: processo *R.* [x] Exurge *O*: Exsurge *R.* [y] prima *R*: primam *O.* [z] Psalmus *O*: *om. R.* [aa] misereatur *O*: misereatur nostri *R.* [bb] Preces *O*: et Preces *R.* [cc] .iiii. *O*: quarta *R.* [dd] Kalendas *O*: Calendas *R.* [ee] Nouembris *O*: Octobris *R.*

[6] [a] De Die Palmarum *O*: *om. R.* [b] antifona *O*: antiphona *R.* [c] a *O*: ad *R.* [d] legitur *O*: legatur *R.* [e] euangelium *O*: euuangelium *R.* [f] aqua benedicta *O*: *transposed R.* [g] antifonam *O*: *om. R.* [h] sic *O*: sic *corr. from* sis *by another hand R.* [i] decantent *O*: cantant *? corr. to* cantent *R.* [j] responsorium *O*: *om. R.* [k] Ingrediente *neumed O*: Ingrediente Domino *R.* [l] oblationem *O*: oblatum *R.* [m] Item *O*: *om. R.* [n] Dies *O*: Deus *R.* [o] uictoriarum *O*: uictimarum *R.* [p] die *O*: diem *R.* [q] Appropinquante *O*: Adpropinquante *R.* [r] Christi *O*: Xpisti *R.* [s] appropinquare *O*: adpropinquare *R.* [t] et respondent *O*: *om. R.* [u] nostri *O*: *om. R.*

[7] [a] De Cena Domini *O*: *om. R.* [b] Quinta *O*: uinta *R.* [c] antifonario *O*: antiphonario *R.* [d] responsoriis *O*: in responsoriis *R.* [e] Euangelii *O*: Euuangelii *R.* [f] antifona *O*: antiphona *R.* [g] duo *O*: .ii. *R.* [h] parte *O*: *om. R.* [i] duo *O*: .ii. *R.* [j] Christe eleison *O*: Christeleison *R.* [k] Qui . . . nobis *O*: Domine miserere *R.* [l] Tunc chorus . . . ad mortem *O*: Tunc omnis clerus simul, Christus Dominus factus est obediens usque, ita ter *R.* [m] prophetice promisisti *ed.*: propheticae promsisti *O.* [n] Vita . . . expoliatur *neumed O.* [o] Kyrrieleison Christe eleison Qui prophetice promisisti Ero mors tua O mors Domine miserere nobis Chorus Christus Dominus Kyrrieleison Christe eleison Vita in ligno moritur infernus ex morsu expoliatur Domine miserere nobis Chorus Christus Dominus *O*: *om. R.* [p] canonico *O*: canonica *R.* [q] nomine *O*: nomine tuo *R.* [r] Beati *O*: Beati inmaculati *R.* [s] preueniente *abbrev. as both* pre- *and* per- *O.* [t] Legem pone tunc . . . ad .iii. *O*: *om. R.* [u] Defecit *O*: a Defecit *R.* [v] .viiii. *O*: nonam *R.* [w] Mirabilia *O*: ad Mirabilia *R.* [x] usque Ad Dominum cum tribularer *O*: usque in finem *R.* [y] antifona *O*: antiphona *R.* [z] euangelium *O*: euuangelium *R.* [aa] et cetera *O*: et cetera *corr. from* ettera *R.* [bb] canonico *R*: canonica *O.* [cc] tertiam *O*: .iii. *R.* [dd] pauimenta *O*: pauimento *R.* [ee] dehinc *O*: deinde *R.* [ff] cybaria *O*: cibaria *R.* [gg] Patri minime *O*: patr munime *R.* [hh] presbyteris *O*: presbiteris *R.* [ii] sicut *O*: *?* sac *(obscured by stain) R.* [jj] in *O*: *om. R.* [kk] nihilominus *O*: nihil omnium *R.* [ll] eucharistia *O*: eucharistie *R.* [mm] ad *O*: *om. R.* [nn] Peracta *R*: Peractae *O.* [oo] pergant *ed. Reg.con.*: peragant *O*: pergant mandatum *R.* [pp] sacerdos suum peragat *O*: sacerdotes suum peragant *R.* [qq] Deinde *O*: Dehinc *R.*

[8] [a] De Parasceue *O*: *om. R.* [b] In *O*: n *R.* [c] tacite *R*: tacito *O.* [d] tractus *O*: *om. R.* [e] a *O*: ab *R.* [f] genuflexione *O*: genuflectione *R.* [g] genuflexione *O*: genuflectione *R.* [h] subdiaconus *O*: subdianus *R.* [i] altare *R*: altari *O.* [j] uoce sonora *O*: *om. R.* [k] moniti *O*: *om. R.* [l] inde *O*: in ebd *? corrupt abbrev. R.* [m] sacrificio *O*: sancto sacrificio *R.* [n] nihil *R*: *om. O.* [o] decantet *O*: decante *R.*

[9] [a] De Sabbato Sancto *O*: *om. R.* [b] mirabilia *ed.*: mirabili *OR.* [c] Secunda *O*: .ii. *R.* [d] Tractum *O*: Tractus *R.* [e] Cantemus *O*: Cantemus Domino *R.* [f] Oratio *O*: Collecta *R.* [g] cuius *O*: cui *R.* [h] Tertia lectio *O*: .iii. *R.* [i] Apprehendent *O*: Adprehendent *R.* [j] Tractum Vinea *O*: Trachtus Vinea facta est *R.* [k] Oratio *O*: Collecta *R.* [l] nos *O*: nos ad celebrandum *R.* [m] Quarta *O*: *om. R.* [n] Oratio *O*: Collecta *R.* [o] Tractum *O*: Trachtus *R.* [p] septene *R*: sep *O.* [q] redeant *O*: redeunt *R.* [r] cantetur *O*: cantatur *R.* [s] Accendite .iii. *O*: ter Accendite *R.* [t] sacerdote incipiente *R*: sacerdos incipiens *O.* [u] Confitemini *O*: Confitemini Domino *R.* [v] Tractum *O*: Trachtus *R.* [w] euangelium *O*: euuangelium *R.* [x] imitationem *O*: imitatione *R.* [y] euangelium *O*: euuangelium *R.* [z] euangelio *O*: euuangelio *R.* [aa] cantatur *O*: cantantur *R.* [bb] alleluia$_2$ *O*: *om. R.* [cc] Laudate *O*: Laudate Dominum omnes gentes *R.* [dd] Dehinc antifona *O*: Canitur dehinc ad uesperas *R.* [ee] autem *O*: autem sabbati *R.* [ff] Psalmus *O*: *om. R.* [gg] Sic *ed.*: Sic sic *O*: Sicut *R.* [hh] compleat *O*: conpleat *R.* [ii] oratione *O*: oratio *R.* [jj] sonoriter celebretur *O*: sonoritur celebriter celebretur *with* celebreter *corr. from* celebretur *R.*

[10] [a] De Die Sancto Paschae *O*: *om. R.* [b] In O: n *R.* [c] meum *O*: *om. R.* [d] inuitatorium *R*: uitatorium *O.* [e] tres *O*: tertia *R.* [f] .iii. *O*: tertia *R.* [g] Surrexit Dominus de sepulchro *O*: Surrexit Dominus de se *with* Dominus *added above line R.* [h] psalmis *O*: psalmo *R.* [i] Psalmis *O*: Psalmus *R.* [j] capitulo *O*:

capitulo etiam *R.* [k] presbytero *O*: presbitero *R.* [l] euangelio *O*: euuangelio *R.* [m] quattuor *O*: .iiii. *R.* [n] nomine *O*: nomine tuo *R.* [o] Confitemini *O*: Confitemini Domino *R.* [p] usque Legem pone *O*: Retribue *R.* [q] Haec dies *O*: Haec est dies *R.* [r] .iii. *O*: tertiam *R.* [s] Legem pone *O*: Psalmus a Legem pone *R.* [t] Gradale *O*: *om. R.* [u] et *O*: *om. R.* [v] .viiii. *O*: nonam *R.* [w] uesperas *O*: uesperam *R.* [x] psalmi *O*: a p̄s *R.* [y] antifonis *O*: antiphonis *R.* [z] cum uersu Sequentia *O*: cum uersu sequente *R.* [aa] tua *ed.*: t̄ *abbrev. as if* ter *O*. [bb] Versus . . . tua *O*: *om. R.* [cc] euangelio *O*: euuangelio *R.* [dd] eant *O*: eatur *R.* [ee] psalmum *O*: *om. R.* [ff] pueri *O*: pueri Dominum *R.* [gg] cum antiphona *O*: *om. R.* [hh] canentes R: cane***s *partially illegible O.* [ii] Inde *O*: Inde uero *R.* [jj] adeant *R*: audeant *O*. [kk] Christus *O*: Cristus *R.* [ll] enim *O*: cum *R.* [mm] capitulum *ed.*: cap̄ *O*: capitło *R.* [nn] concinatur *O*: concinitur *R.* [oo] horae *O*: ore *R.*

[11] [a] Incipiunt . . . Pentecosten *O*: De Pentecosten *R.* [b] Pentecosten *O*: Pentecostes *R.* [c] descensum *O*: discensum *R.* [d] Deus Abraham *O*: Deus cum cantico Cantemus *R.* [e] Abrahae *O*: Habrahe *R.* [f] Secunda *O*: *om. R.* [g] Adtende caelum *O*: Vinea facta est *R.* [h] nobis *O*: nobis prophetarum *R.* [i] Tertia *O*: .iii. *R.* [j] Apprehendent *O*: Adprehendent *R.* [k] Vinea . . . Canticum *O*: *om. R.* [l] sempiterne *O*: sempiterne Deus *R.* [m] scola *R*: stola *O*. [n] praefatio *O*: praephatio *R.* [o] Sequitur *O*: Siquitur *R.* [p] Appollo *O*: Apollo *R.* [q] cantatur *O*: cantantur *R.* [r] tractus *O*: trachtus *R.* [s] Laudate Dominum *R.* [t] tribus *O*: .iii.bus *R.* [u] agatur *O*: agitur *R.* [v] ut *O*: et *R.* [w] in antiphonario *R*: in antifonario *corr. from* intifonario *O*. [x] horis *O*: choris *R.* [y] sicut *O*: scē *R.* [z] gradalibus *O*: gadalibus *sic corr. from* galibus *R.* [aa] dicuntur *O*: *om. R.* [bb] Octabis *O*: Octobis *R.*

[12] [a] Qualiter Quattuor Tempora Agantur *O*: *om. R*: Item De .IIII. Temporibus *D.* [b] Quattuor *OR*: Quatuor *D.* [c] custodiuntur *OR*: custodiunt *D.* [d] celebrationem *OR*: celebracionem *D.* [e] dicitur *RD*: *om. O.* [f] genua *OR*: ge *D.* [g] quadragesimali *OD*: quadragessimali *R.* [h] ciborum *OD*: cyborum *R.* [i] Tum *OR*: Tunc *D.* [j] oportet ut diximus *O*: oportunum diximus *RD*: oportunum duximus *Reg.con.* [k] latina *OD*: *om. R.* [l] incognita *OD*: incognati *R.* [m] incendunt *O*: inpendunt *R*: impendunt *D*: impediunt *Lib.off.* [n] quaeque *OR*: quoque *D.* [o] suum *RD*: sua *O.* [p] ieiunio .iii. dies sunt *OD*: *om. R (rest of line blank).* [q] .iii. *OD*: tertia *R.* [r] mense *OD*: *om. R.* [s] fecerunt consilium *OR*: *transposed D.* [t] .vi. *O*: sexta *RD.* [u] occiderunt *OD*: occiderent *R.* [v] .vii. *OD*: septima *R.* [w] ieiunio *OR*: ieiunium *D.* [x] tristitiam *OR*: tristiciam *D.* [y] pro nece *O*: de morte *RD Lib.off.* [z] genuflexionem *O*: genuflectionem *RD.* [aa] Octauis *O*: Octb̄ *R*: Octauas *D.* [bb] Pentecosten *OR*: Pentecostes *D.* [cc] sola *RD*: sole *O.* [dd] genua *O*: genua unquam *RD.* [ee] Nabuchodonosor *OR*: Nabugodonosor *D.* [ff] errauit *OD*: erraut *R.* [gg] fecit *OD*: f. *R.*

Apparatus fontium

[1] Ab Aduentu . . . canendum est: *cf. IBA* 1 *and LME* 16.

[2] Sobrie . . . uiuere: *from* Titus II.12.

[3] quia hora . . . surgere: Rom. XIII.11.

[4] non in . . . emulatione: *from* Rom. XIII.13.

[5] Nisi . . . uobis: John VI.54.

[6] Vespere . . . primam: *from Reg.con.* 31.685–98.

[7] Ad uesperam . . . Octabas Domini: *Reg.con.* 31.708–13.

[8] Hinc . . . sollempnitate: *Reg.con.* 32.727–31.

[9] In qua . . . amittimus: *? from Lib.off.* IV.xxxiii.1; *cf. IBA* 4 *and LME* 24.

[10] Ceteris . . . celebratur: *from Reg.con.* 32.731–8.

[11] In Purificatione . . . offerant: *Reg.con.* 33 *(entire).*

[12] mutatur . . . intermittitur: *from Lib.off.* IV.xxxiii.18 *(? and* I.i.17*); cf. IBA* 6 *and LME* 26.

[13] Cruces . . . Pascha: *Lib.off.(R1), lect. discr. long.* II.i.9–10; *cf. LME* 30.

[14] in peregrinatione . . . Domini: *? from Lib.off.* I.i.11.

[15] Populus . . . sustineamus: *from Lib.off.* I.i.2 *and* 6; *cf. IBA* 6.

[16] saltem . . . dies .lxx.: *cf. IBA* 6.

[17] Quarta feria . . . agatur missa: *from Reg.con.* 34.770–90.

[18] Peracta . . . celebrent: *? neither Reg.con. nor LME.*

[19] Iste ordo . . . habent: *from Reg.con.* 34.791–4 *and* 783–5; *cf. LME* 29.

[20] His peractis . . . sua: *Reg.con.* 34.794–6 *and* 798.

[21] In die . . . sacerdoti: *from Reg.con.* 36.845–65.

[22] Dies palmarum . . . passionis: *? from Lib.off.(R1)* I.x.1; *cf. LME* 32.

[23] Eadem die . . . tibi Domine: *Lib.off.(R1), lect. discr. long.* II.3; *cf. Reg.con.* 36.865–70 *and LME* 32.

[24] Quinta . . . habetur: *Reg.con.* 37.871–3.

[25] Gloria . . . dicatur: *? from Lib.off.* IV.xxi.6: *cf. IBA* 10 *and LME* 33.

[26] Euangelii . . . preces: *Reg.con.* 37.878–9 *and* 890.

[27] sint duo . . . teneatur: *from Reg.con.* 37.879–92.

[28] Prima . . . tacite: *from Reg.con.* 39.916–34.

[29] lauent pauimenta . . . lauetur: *Reg.con.* 40.941–5.

[30] Sexta . . . cybaria: *from Reg.con.* 40.946–53.

[31] Dehinc . . . nona: *Reg.con.* 41.956.

[32] Post haec . . . pergant: *from Reg.con.* 41.967–80.

[33] Post mixtum . . . mandatum: *from Reg.con.* 42.980–4.

[34] In die . . . dictum est: *Reg.con.* 43.1013–14.

[35] Eadem die . . . passio: *Reg.con.* 43.1021–8.

[36] Post haec . . . Iudeis: *Reg.con.* 43.1035; *also perh. Lib.off.* I.xiii.17; *cf. IBA* 12 *and LME* 43.

[37] Quibus expletis . . . et cetera: *Reg.con.* 44.1040–4.

[38] His peractis . . . petant: *from Reg.con.* 47.1132–44.

[39] Completorium . . . decantet: *Reg.con.* 47.1149–52.

[40] diaconus more solito . . . tantum: *from Reg.con.* 48.1158–49.1193.

[41] ad imitationem . . . et reliqua: *from Lib.off.* I.xxxi.8; *cf. LME* 46.

[42] Finito euangelio . . . canonicorum: *Reg.con.* 49.1193–1201 *and* 1204–5.

[43] inprimis ad nocturnam . . . responsoriis: *from Reg.con.* 50.1213–21.

[44] incipiat ymnum . . . collecta: *from Reg.con.* 52.1257, 1259–63 *and* 1266–71.

[45] Ad primam . . . benedictione: *from Reg.con.* 53.1273–95.

[46] Vespera . . . inchoetur: *Reg.con.* 54.1299–1300.

[47] Incipiunt orationes . . . more solito: *Reg.con.* 58 *(entire).*

[48] Illa dominica . . . psallant: *Reg.con.* 59.1428–34.

[49] Illa ebdomada . . . Trinitate: *Reg.con.* 59.1434–42.

[50] Qualiter . . . diximus: *Reg.con.* 61 *(entire).*

[51] Ab antiquis . . . erat greca: *from Lib.off.* II.i.1.

[52] At quia . . . nece Domini: *from Lib.off.* II.ii.6 *and* 12.

[53] Per singulas . . . fecit: *from Lib.off.* II.iii.12–13.

INSTITUTIO BEATI AMALARII DE ECCLESIASTICIS OFFICIIS

[1] ITEM ALIQUA[a] INSTITUTIO BEATI AMALARII[b] DE ECCLESIASTICIS OFFICIIS. Primitus de Aduentu Domini: Ideo 'Gloria in excelsis Deo'[c] intermittitur in diebus Aduentus Domini et nocte[d] Natiuitatis Domini reditur ut eo magis ad memoriam nobis reducatur tunc <primo celebratum>[e] esse ab angelis.[1] Et ideo in festiuitatibus apostolorum 'Credo in unum' semper canitur quia dominicum simbolum[f] illi <primo>[g] concordi animo simul celebrabant.[2]

[2]   DE MISSA IN NOCTE. Missam quam celebramus in nocte Natiuitatis Domini <Thelesphorus>[a] apostolicus constituit propter recordationem angelorum qui nocte[b] concinerunt[c] 'Gloria in excelsis'.[3]

[3]   DE MISSA INNOCENTUM. De missa Innocentum praetitulatur in antifonario[a] sic: '"Gloria in excelsis[b] Deo" non cantatur[c] nec "Alleluia" sed quasi in tristitia ducitur dies illa.' Compositio[d] officii[e] praesentis coniungi nos uult animis deuotarum feminarum quae in morte Innocentum doluerunt et planxerunt. Sicut separat[f] nos ab actu malorum Iudaeorum in Cena Domini siue in Parasceue siue in Sabbato amittendo oscula[g] siue cetera consueta, ita coniungit in praesenti festiuitate[h] dolori deuotarum[i] feminarum. Causa earum tristitie amittimus 'Gloria in excelsis Deo' et[j] 'Alleluia'.[4]

[4]   DE THEOPHANIA . In Theophania amittimus <inuitatorium>[a] reducentes ad memoriam <fraudulentam>[b] inuitationem Herodis, qui propterea magos inuitauit congregauitque scribas et principes Iudaeorum ut disceret ubi Christus nasceretur, quem cogitauit occidere.[5]

[5]   DE YPPAPANTI.[a] Oportet nos cereos accensos[b] in[c] manibus portare in Yppapanti,[d] quod in praesentatione sui unumquemque sanctum significat habere opera sua in quibus clarus et lucidus appareat cetibus sanctorum angelorum.[6] Teneamus igitur lumen in manibus et clamemus laudantes Dominum ac dicentes: 'Suscepimus Deus misericordiam tuam',[7] id est lumen aeternum Christum Dominum.[e] Octaua die circumcisus est puer Iesus secundum legem Moysi. 'Et postquam impleti sunt dies purgationis eius, secundum legem tulerunt illum in Hierusalem ut sisterent illum Domino, sicut scriptum est in lege Domini quia omne masculinum adaperiens uuluam sanctum Domino uocabitur.'[8] Decretum quidem legis erat paruulum ad templum Domini deferri darique hostiam pro eo. Non enim filius Dei, <non>[f] mater Domini sancta uidelicet et immaculata[g] semper uirgo Maria uictimis hostiarum quibus purgarentur <indigebant>,[h] sed ut nos[i] a legis uinculo solueremur, sicut Dominus Christus, ita et beata semper uirgo Maria legi est sponte subiecta.[9]

[6]   DE SEPTUAGESIMA.[a] In[b] Septuagesima mutamus cantum[c] laetitiae in tribulationem ut eo[d] trahatur ad nostram memoriam cui affectui[e] debitores sumus ex nostris mentibus, et ut educatu[f] humilitatis perueniamus ad passionem Domini.[10] Populus Dei in Babilonia detentus est captiuus sub numero septuagenario,[g] quo numero completo reuersus est in Hierusalem. Quod illi inuiti sustinuerunt per annos .lxx. nos uoluntarie pro peccatis nostris sustineamus[11] saltem[h] quasi[i] per dies .lxx.[j][12]

[7]   DE QUADRAGESIMA.[a] Hoc sufficit hic commemorari, quod in Quadragesima .xl. duo[b] sunt dies[c] a die dominico quem .xl.[d] nominamus. Tot enim mansiones habuerunt[e] filii Israel[f] quando exierunt de terra Aegipti[g] ad terram[h] promissionis.[i] Et merito qui ad caelestem patriam tendunt eodem numero <mansionum>[j] satagunt quo filii Israel ad terram promissionis uenerunt.[13]

[8]   DE PASSIONE DOMINI.[a] Dies Passionis Domini computantur duabus <ebdomadibus ante Pascha, quoniam in duobus <temporibus>[b]>[c] huius mundi scribitur et informatur eadem passio. In illis diebus[d] amittimus per .xiiii. dies in solis

responsoriis 'Gloria Patri' quoniam per humilitatem ueniendum est ad passionem Christi.[e14]

[9] DE DIE PALMARUM.[a] Turba[b] 'quae uenerat ad diem festum, cum audisset quia uenit Iesus Hierosolimam, acceperunt ramos palmarum et processerunt obuiam ei.' In memoriam illius <rei>[c] nos per ecclesias nostras solemus portare palmas[d] et clamare 'Osanna'. Decima enim die mensis primi agnus Dei[e] qui in Pascha immolatur domum introduci iussus est. Ita et Dominus noster decima die eiusdem mensis, hoc est ante dies .v.[f] Paschae, in ciuitatem in qua pateretur ingressus est.[15]

[10] <DE CENA DOMINI.>[a] Amalarius dicit: Quinta feria Christus ueteri <legi>[b] finem dabat.[16] Dixit enim 'Non bibam de hoc genimine[c] uitis', et reliqua.[17] Romanus ordo praecepit ut a quinta feria usque in Sabbato Sancto nudata sint altaria, quod aliud non significat nisi fugam apostolorum. Vestimenta altaris Christi sancti sunt de quibus dictum est: 'Et relicto eo omnes fugerunt.'[18] Notandum[d] quoque est quod omnis doctrina pastoris taceatur in ecclesia in his diebus. Non <dicitur>[e] 'Deus in adiutorium',[f] non datur benedictio legentibus, admonitio[g] lectionis non ministratur. Ideo haec non fiunt quia pastor noster Christus recessit et arietes gregis, qui iam praedestinati erant ut pastores fierent ecclesiae,[h] dispersi sunt. Inuitatorium[i] non cantent cantores[j] ut doceant malum conuentum uitare suos, qualis[k] fuit apud Iudaeos de nece Christi. Quanto propinquius instant passioni, tanto se plus humiliant in officio suo.[19] Christus enim humiliauit semet ipsum 'factus obediens usque ad mortem.' Igitur in istis diebus siue noctibus penitus amittunt[l] 'Gloria Patri',[m] et omnis salutatio deest[n] in istis tribus[o] diebus ad[p] uitandam[q] salutationem pestiferam qualem diabolus per Iudam exercuit. Necnon[r] tintinnabula[s] signa deponuntur, et lignorum sonus necessarie[t] pulsatur ut conueniat populus[u] ad ecclesiam.[20]

[11] DE EXTINCTIONE LUMINUM.[a] Accenduntur in .v. feria et .vi. et .vii.[b] per singulas noctes .xxiiii. lumina ante introitum fratrum extingunturque per singulas antifonas[c] et responsoria,[d] et fiunt simul .lxxii. inluminationes et extinctiones. Extinctiones enim luminum significant defectum laetitiae .lxxii.[e] discipulorum quam habuerunt quamdiu Christus iacuit in sepulchro.[21]

[12] DE PARASCEVE.[a] Parascheue[b] praeparatio interpretatur quia eo uidelicet die Iudaei quae in sabbato necessaria erant praeparabant.[22] Et discendum est ex decretalibus Innocentii papae quare missa non cantetur in[c] .vi. et .vii. feria. 'Nam utique', inquid,[d] 'constat apostolos biduo isto in tristitia et in merore fuisse et propter metum Iudaeorum se occultasse. Quod utique non dubium est, in tantum eos ieiunasse biduum memoratur, ut traditio ecclesiae[e] habeat isto biduo sacramenta penitus non celebrari.'[23] Dominus enim dixit pridie: 'Non bibam de hoc genimine', et reliqua.[f] Ratus ordo est ut expectemus usque dum Dominus noster consecret sacramenta corporis et sanguinis sui in cruce et noua ea faciet per sanctam resurrectionem suam.[24] Per omnes orationes sollempnes quae dicuntur in Parasceue[g] post passionem genuflectionem facimus, excepto[h] quando oramus pro perfidis Iudaeis. Illi illudendo genuflectebant et idcirco uitamus genuflectionem in oratione pro Iudaeis.[25]

[13] DE SANCTO SABBATO.[a] Nobis[b] praeceptum est a papa Zosimo benedicere cereum. Cera humanitatem Christi significat. Iste cereus qui praefigurat humanitatem

Christi inluminatus benedicitur quia humanitas Christi, postquam assumpta est a diuinitate, semper fuit inluminata.[26] Qui cereus ideo nouo[c] igne accenditur ut[d] designet Christi doctrinam nouam quae est in nouo testamento.[27] Post epistulam cantatur prius 'Alleluia', quod est ebreum.[e] Ebrea mater linguarum,[f] latina inferior est;[g] ideo 'Alleluia' praeponitur hic.[28] In commemoratione[h] quoque[i] primae uitae quam habuit primus Adam 'Alleluia' canitur, et quia non fuit sempiterna tractus sequitur, ut in lingua humiliori humilitas posterioris[j] uitae[k] recordetur.[29] In tempore sacrificii silent cantores reducendo ad memoriam silentium et sacrificium mulierum[30] quae ausae non fuerant respondere angelo cum ad eas locutus est dicens: 'Nolite expauescere', et reliqua:[l] 'et[m] exeuntes fugerunt de monumento; inuaserat enim[n] eas[o] timor et tremor.'[31] 'Sanctus, Sanctus, Sanctus' cantant,[p] quod est angelorum cantus, quia non tacuerunt angeli[q] de eius resurrectione sedentes ad caput et ad pedes, ut Iohannes narrat.[r] Iterum 'Agnus Dei' <reticent>[s] cantores quia Maria dicebat: 'Domine si <tu sustulisti>[t] eum', et reliqua. Quem[u] credebat <furto>[v] sublatum non credebat tollere peccata mundi.[32]

[14] DE DIE SANCTO PASCHAE.[a] Die[b] sancto Paschae[c] <in introitu>[d] per <ora>[e] prophetarum praesentat se Christus ex resurrectione Patri suo in ecclesia sua dicens: 'Resurrexi'. Oratio prima demonstrat aditum esse apertum sanctae ecclesiae regni caelestis per <capitis>[f] sui resurrectionem. Epistula admonet[g] nos ut separati sumus a uitiis in quibus certauimus per dies quadragesimales.[h] <Responsorius>[i] monstrat quantum laetari oporteat <eos>[j] qui purgentur a uitiis. In[k] 'Alleluia' monstratur in quo sit tota causa laetitiae, id est quia 'Pascha nostrum immolatus est Christus.'[33] Pascha transitus dicitur: transitum enim de morte ad uitam, de corruptione ad incorruptionem, de pena ad gloriam Dominus resurgendo facere dignatus est.[34] In Exodo enim scriptum est ubi agnus immolari .xiiii. die primi mensis ad uesperam <mandatur>:[l] 'Et comedetis festinantes: est enim phase, id est transitus, Domini.' Transiuit enim Dominus nocte illa per terram Egypti percutiens primogenita[m] Aegiptiorum[n] et signatas agni sanguine domus filiorum Israel liberans.[35] Ipse enim uerus <est>[o] agnus qui abstulit peccata mundi, nocte uidelicet transitus dominici, id est resurrectionis eius a morte,[p] qua[q] impium[r] triumphando fideles saluare dignatus est.[36]

[15] DE LETANIA MAIORE. Romani unum diem, id est .vii. Kalendas Mai, colunt, quem uocant Letania Maior,[a] <non in ieiunio>.[b] Letania deprecatio est. <Potest>[c] enim serena mens et aliena a uoluntate mala precari[d] Deum quamuis manducet sobrie carnem meridie et laetetur de resurrectione Domini.[37] Alii tamen ieiunant processionemque agunt sicut et Romani.[e]

[16] DE PENTECOSTEN. Tempus Pentecosten[a] inchoatur prima[b] die resurrectionis et currit usque ad diem[c] quinquagesimum[d] post Pascha.[38] Illi dies <.l.>[e] futuram uitam informant in qua est requies et laetitia sempiterna. Et eandem laetitiam numerus quinquagenarius[f] significat, qui apud Ebreos[g] <iubileus>[h] appellatur eo quod fit[i] iubilatione plenus.[39] Pentecosten sicut et Pascha apud Ebreos[j] celebris dies erat. In die sancto Pentecosten misit Dominus Spiritum Paraclitum discipulis sicut promisit, 'apparueruntque[k] illis dispertitae linguae tamquam ignis.'[40] Nam sicut hic discipulis sic et Moysi in ignis uisione Deus apparuit, dicente <Exodo>:[l] 'Totus enim mons Sinai[m] fumigabat eo quod descendisset Dominus super eum in igne.'[41] Spiritus Sanctus in igne et linguis

apparuit quia omnes quos impleuerit ardentes pariter et loquentes facit.[42] Et quia Spiritus Sancti septiformis est gratia, iure sollempnitas aduentus eius per septem[n] dies laude ymnorum debita simul et missarum celebratione colitur.[43]

Apparatus criticus

[1] [a] Item aliqua *O*: Incipit *R*. [b] Amalarii *O*: Amalari *R*. [c] Deo *O*: *om. R*. [d] nocte *O*: in nocte *R*. [e] primo celebratum *R Lib.off*.: celebratum primus *O*. [f] dominicum simbolum *O*: illud symbolum *R*. [g] primo *R*: primus *O*.

[2] [a] Thelesphorus *R*: Thalesphorus *O*. [b] nocte *O*: nocte illa *R Lib.off*. [c] concinerunt *OR*: cecinerunt *Lib.off*.

[3] [a] antifonario *O*: antiphonaria *R*. [b] excelsis *O*: excelsis *corr. from* ecelsis *R*. [c] cantatur *O*: cantantur *R*. [d] Compositio *OR*: compositor *Lib.off*. [e] officii *O*: officis *R*. [f] separat *R*: seperat *O*. [g] oscula *O*: osecula *R*. [h] festiuitate *O*: festiuitati *corr. from* festiuitate *R*. [i] deuotarum *O*: deuota *R*. [j] et *O*: *om. R*.

[4] [a] inuitatorium *R*: uitatorium *O*. [b] fraudulentam *R*: fraudulentiam *O*.

[5] [a] Yppapanti *O*: Yppopanti *R*. [b] accensos *O*: ascensos *R*. [c] in *O*: *om. R*. [d] Yppapanti *O*: Yppopanti *R*. [e] Christum Dominum *O*: *transposed R*. [f] non *R*: nam *O*. [g] immaculata *O*: inmaculata *R*. [h] indigebant *ed.*: indiebant *OR*. [i] nos *O*: ad nos *with* ad *expunged R*.

[6] [a] De Septuagesima *O*: *om. R*. [b] In *O*: n *R*. [c] cantum *O Lib.off*.: tantum *R*. [d] eo *O*: ex eo *R Lib.off*. [e] affectui *O*: adfectui *R*. [f] educatu *O*: edocatu *R*. [g] septuagenario *O*: septugenario *perh. corr. from* septugenerio *R*. [h] saltem *O*: saltim *R*. [i] quasi *O*: *om. R*. [j] .lxx. *O*: id est planctum *added above* .lxx. *perh. as a gloss to the object of the sentence (*Quod*) R*.

[7] [a] De Quadragesima *O*: *om. R*. [b] duo *O*: uero *R*. [c] sunt dies *O*: *transposed R*. [d] .xl. *O*: Quadragesimam *R*. [e] habuerunt *O*: habuerint *R*. [f] Israel *O*: Israhel *R*. [g] Aegipti *O*: Egypti *R*. [h] terram *O*: terra *R*. [i] promissionis *O*: promissionis *corr. from* promissiones *R*. [j] mansionum *ed. Lib.off*.: mansionem *OR*.

[8] [a] De Passione Domini *O*: *om. R*. [b] temporibus *ed.*: teporibus *R*. [c] ebdomadibus ... temporibus *R*: ebdomada diebus duabus ebdomadibus *O*. [d] diebus *O*: *om. R*. [e] Christi *O*: Xpisti *R*.

[9] [a] De Die Palmarum *O*: *om. R*. [b] Turba *O*: urba *R*. [c] rei *ed. Lib.off*.: regi *OR*. [d] palmas *O*: palmaru *with* u *erased R*. [e] Dei *O*: *om. R*. [f] dies .v. *O*: *transposed R*.

[10] [a] De Cena Domini *R*: *om. O*. [b] legi *R*: legem *O*. [c] genimine *O*: gemine *R*. [d] Notandum *O*: Non tandum *R*. [e] dicitur *ed. Lib.off*.: dic̄ *O*: dicit *R*. [f] adiutorium *O*: adiutorium meum *R*. [g] admonitio *O*: ammonitio *R*. [h] ecclesiae *O*: et ecclesiae *R*. [i] Inuitatorium *O*: Et uictatorium *R*. [j] cantores *O*: cantatores *R*. [k] qualis *O*: quale *R*. [l] amittunt *O*: amittat *R*. [m] Patri *O*: Patri et reliqua *R*. [n] salutatio deest *O*: salut****est *erasure R*. [o] tribus *O*: tribus *R*. [p] ad *O*: ad *with* d *erased R*. [q] uitandam *O*: uitandum *R*. [r] Necnon *R*: Nec *with* non *inserted above O*. [s] tintinnabula *O*: compana *R*. [t] necessarie *O*: necessaria *R*. [u] populus *O*: populos *R*.

[11] [a] Luminum *O*: Liminum *R*. [b] .v. .... .vi. .... .vii. *O*: quinta ... sexta ... septima *R*. [c] antifonas *O*: antiphonas *R*. [d] responsoria *O*: responsorios *R*. [e] .lxxii. *O*: septuaginta duorum *R*.

[12] [a] Parasceue *O*: Parascephe *R*. [b] Parascheue *O*: Parasceue *R*. [c] in *O*: iii *R*. [d] inquid *OR*: inquit *Lib.off*. [e] ecclesiae *O*: ecclesesiae *false abbrev. R*. [f] genimine et reliqua *O*: genimine uitis usque dum illud bibam uobiscum nouum et reliqua *R*. [g] Parasceue *O*: Parascephe *R*. [h] excepto *O Lib.off*.: excepta *R*.

[13] [a] Sancto Sabbato *O*: *transposed R.* [b] Nobis *O*: obis *R.* [c] nouo *O*: uouo *R.* [d] ut *O*: *om. R.* [e] ebreum *O*: ebrea *R.* [f] linguarum *O*: est linguarum *R.* [g] est *O*: *om. R.* [h] In commemoratione *O*: In memoratione *corr. from* Imemoratione *R.* [i] quoque *O*: *om. R.* [j] posterioris *O*: posterioris *corr. from* posteriores *R.* [k] uitae *O*: uitet *added at line end R.* [l] expauescere et reliqua *O*: expauescere Iesum queritis surrexit et reliqua *R.* [m] et *O*: sed *R.* [n] enim *O*: enim *added above R.* [o] eas *O*: eos *R.* [p] cantant *O*: cantores cantant *R.* [q] non tacuerunt angeli *O*: angeli non tacuerunt *R.* [r] narrat *O*: narrant *R.* [s] reticent *R Lib.off.*: recitent *O.* [t] tu sustulisti *R Lib.off.*: tulisti *O.* [u] Quem *O*: Qui *R.* [v] furto *R*: furtu *O.*

[14] [a] De Die Sancto Paschae *O*: *om. R.* [b] Die *O*: ie *R.* [c] Paschae *O*: Pasce *R.* [d] in introitu *R*: introitum *O.* [e] ora *ed. Lib.off.*: hora *with* h *partially erased O*: hora *R.* [f] capitis *ed. Lib.off.*: capiti *OR.* [g] admonet *O*: ammonet *R.* [h] quadragesimales *O*: quadragessimales *R.* [i] Responsorius *R Lib.off.*: Responsoriis *O.* [j] eos *ed. Lib.off.*: eas *O*: eos *corr. from* nos *R.* [k] In *O*: I *R.* [l] mandatur *R*: manducatur *O.* [m] primogenita *O*: omnia primogenita *R.* [n] Aegiptiorum *O*: Aegyptiorum *R.* [o] est *R*: *om. O.* [p] morte *O*: mortuis *R.* [q] qua *O*: quia *R.* [r] impium *O*: impios *R.*

[15] [a] Letania Maior *O*: In Letania Maiore *R.* [b] non in ieiunio *R Lib.off.*: *om. O.* [c] Potest *R*: Post *O.* [d] precari *O*: pretari *R.* [e] Alii . . . Romani *O*: *om. R.*

[16] [a] Pentecosten *O*: Pentecostes *R.* [b] prima *O*: a prima *R Lib.off.* [c] ad diem *O*: adiem *R.* [d] quinquagesimum *O*: quinquagessimum *R.* [e] .l. *ed.*: .ł. *? abbrev. for* uel *OR.* [f] quinquagenarius *O*: quinquagenuarius *R.* [g] Ebreos *O*: Hebreos *R.* [h] iubileus *R*: iubeleus *O.* [i] fit *O*: sit *R.* [j] Ebreos *O*: Hebreos *R.* [k] apparueruntque *O*: apperuitque *R.* [l] Exodo *R*: in Exodo *O.* [m] Sinai *O*: Synai *R.* [n] septem *O*: .vii. *R.*

Apparatus fontium

1 Ideo . . . ab angelis: *Lib.off.* III.lx.10.
2 Et ideo . . . celebrabant: *cf. DEC* 1.
3 Missam . . . excelsis: *Lib.off.* III.lxi.1.
4 De missa . . . et Alleluia: *Lib.off.* I.lxi.2.
5 In Theophania . . . occidere: *from Lib.off.* IV.xxxiii.1.
6 Oportet . . . angelorum: *Lib.off.(R1)* IV.xxxiii.18.
7 Suscepimus . . . tuam: Ps. XLVII.10 *(from the Mass introit or gradual for Candlemas).*
8 Et postquam . . . uocabitur: Luke II.22–3 *(from the gospel of the day).*
9 Decretum . . . subiecta: *from Bede, In Lucam* I.ii.22, *lines* 1664–6 *and* 1691–6.
10 In Septuagesima . . . passionem Domini: *from Lib.off.* IV.xxxiii.18.
11 Populus . . . sustineamus: *from Lib.off.* I.i.2 *and* 5; *cf. LME* 26.
12 saltem . . . dies .lxx.: *cf. DEC* 4.
13 Hoc sufficit . . . uenerunt: *from Lib.off.* I.iv.4 *and* 5.
14 Dies Passionis . . . Christi: *from Lib.off.* IV.xx.1 *and* 2.
15 Turba . . . ingressus est: *from Lib.off.* I.x.1 *and* 2.
16 Quinta feria . . . dabat: *from Lib.off.* I.xii.52.
17 Non bibam . . . reliqua: Matt. XXVI.29, *quoted at Lib.off.* I.xii.34 *(this not in R1), but also at Lib.off.* I.xv.2.
18 Romanus ordo . . . fugerunt: *from Lib.off.* I.xii.54.
19 Notandum . . . officio suo: *from Lib.off.* IV.xxi.4, 5 *and* 6.
20 Igitur . . . ecclesiam: *from Lib.off.* IV.xxi.6 *and* 7.
21 Accenduntur . . . sepulchro: *from Lib.off.* IV.xxii.1.
22 Parascheue . . . praeparabant: *from Lib.off.* I.xiii.1.
23 Et discendum . . . celebrari: *Lib.off.* I.xiii.14.

24 Dominus enim . . . resurrectionem suam: *from Lib.off.* I.xv.2 *and* 3.

25 Per omnes . . . Iudaeis: *from Lib.off.* I.xiii.17.

26 Nobis . . . inluminata: *from Lib.off.* I.xviii.1 and 5.

27 Qui cereus . . . testamento: *from Lib.off.* I.xx.1.

28 Post epistulam . . . hic: *from Lib.off.* I.xxxi.7.

29 In commemoratione . . . recordetur: *from Lib.off.* I.xxxii.3.

30 In tempore . . .mulierum: *from Lib.off.* I.xxxi.10.

31 quae ausae . . . tremor: *from Lib.off.* I.xxxi.9.

32 Sanctus . . . mundi: *from Lib.off.* I.xxxi.10 *and* 11.

33 Die sancto . . . Christus: *from Lib.off.* I.xxxiv.1 *and* 2.

34 transitum . . . dignatus est: *Bede, De temp.rat., c.* 61, *lines* 14–16.

35 In Exodo . . . liberans: *from Bede, De temp.rat., c.* 63, *lines* 11–13 *and* 7–9.

36 transitus . . . dignatus est: *Bede, De temp.rat., c.* 63, *lines* 33–4.

37 Romani . . . Domini: *from Lib.off.* I.xxxvii.6.

38 Tempus . . . Pascha: *from Lib.off.* I.xxxvi.1.

39 Illi dies . . . plenus: *from Lib.off.* I.xxxv.3.

40 apparuerunt . . . ignis: Acts II.3.

41 Nam sicut . . . in igne: *Bede, Exp.act.apost.* II.1, *lines* 34–6.

42 Spiritus . . . facit: *Bede, Exp.act.apost.* II.3, *lines* 47–8.

43 Et quia . . . colitur: *from Lib.off.* I.xxxix.1.

A newly-found fragment of an Anglo-Saxon psalter

HELMUT GNEUSS

A notable addition to our knowledge of Anglo-Saxon manuscript fragments with Old English interlinear glosses has been made in a contribution by Professor Herbert Pilch of Freiburg to the recently-published Festschrift for Anatoly Liberman,[1] and I hope to show that the leaf he describes and edits has deserved closer inspection.

Manuscript Br. 1 at the Schlossmuseum of Sondershausen, in northern Thuringia, is a leaf from a psalter with an Old English continuous gloss, written in Anglo-Saxon England and originally containing text and gloss of Ps. VI.9 (*Discedite*) – Ps. VII.9 (*populos*). Unfortunately, at some stage in the history of the leaf, no doubt after the complete psalter manuscript had been dismembered, a strip of vellum amounting to more than a third of the leaf, was cut off on the right-hand side of the recto, with corresponding loss of text and gloss on the left-hand side of the verso.[2]

The present size of the fragment is 300 × 77–100 mm; the original size would have been *c*. 300 × 180–90 mm. The height of the written space is now 210 mm; originally the written space may have covered 210 × *c*. 140 mm. There are seventeen lines of Latin psalm text to the page, and these lines appear to have been spaced for an interlinear gloss. The manuscript may be said to have presented a generous layout, and as for the text-pages it could certainly vie with other eleventh-century glossed Anglo-Saxon psalters like London, British Library, Arundel 60, Cotton Tiberius C. vi, Cotton Vitellius E. xviii and Stowe 2.

Every psalm verse begins with a new line; initials to the verses are in red, green or blue. The rubric to Ps. VII is in red uncials. The script of the Latin text is in Anglo-Caroline minuscule, Style IV, with characteristic **ra**-ligatures.[3] The

---

[1] H. Pilch, 'The Sondershäuser Psalter: a Newly Discovered Old English Interlinear Gloss', *Germanic Studies in Honor of Anatoly Liberman*, ed. K. G. Goblirsch, M. B. Mayou and M. Taylor [= *NOWELE* 31/32] (Odense, 1997), pp. 313–23. Readers who have an opportunity to compare this article with the present paper will have no difficulty in seeing why a further description and edition seemed in order.

[2] For the loss of text and for the following discussion, cf. pls. III and IV.

[3] For Anglo-Caroline minuscule in the eleventh century, see T. A. M. Bishop, *English Caroline Minuscule* (Oxford, 1971), esp. pp. xxiii–xxiv, and D. N. Dumville, *English Caroline Script and Monastic History: Studies in Benedictinism, A.D. 950–1030* (Woodbridge, 1993), esp. ch. 4. For the **ra**-ligature, see *ibid.* p. 147 and n. 38, and N. R. Ker, *English Manuscripts in the Century after the Norman Conquest.* (Oxford, 1960), p. 22, who points out that this particular ligature 'is hardly found after the Conquest'.

Old English gloss is in Anglo-Saxon minuscule[4] and may well have been written by the scribe of the Latin text; as far as I can see, there is no change of scribe in text or gloss of the leaf. As would appear from the fragment, the punctuation is not wholly consistent; in some cases, analysis depends on whether we assume that the modern division into psalm verses must have corresponded to that in Anglo-Saxon manuscripts. In the Sondershausen fragment (=Ns), a major medial pause in a psalm verse is indicated by two types of the *punctus elevatus*, and in one case (Ps. VII.7) by a *punctus versus*. The end of a verse is occasionally marked by a single dot, but normally – as is clear from the verso of the leaf – by a special variant of the *punctus versus* (;·), but always at the *end* of a line.[5]

As can be deduced from the script, the psalms and the gloss were written about the middle of the eleventh century, no doubt in England, but there is no indication of the place of origin or provenance of the manuscript. Nor can we be sure how the fragment came into the collection formerly owned by the Princes of Schwarzburg-Sondershausen; the legend on the earlier of the two stamps on the recto reads 'FÜRSTL. SCHWARZBURG. LANDES-BIBLIOTHEK SONDERSHAUSEN'. It seems likely, or at least possible, that its home until the sixteenth century was the *Stift* (collegiate church) of Jechaburg, less than two miles west of Sondershausen. According to sources that are not now considered wholly reliable, Jechaburg was founded as a Benedictine abbey in 989 by Archbishop Willigis of Mainz. The abbey is said to have been converted into a *Stift* for canons (later Augustinian canons) – a rather unusual development – in the early eleventh century, which by the beginning of the twelfth century (when the earliest documentary evidence becomes available) was combined with the seat of one of the four archdeaconries of Thuringia in the diocese of Mainz. After the spread of Protestantism in Thuringia, Jechaburg was secularized, probably in 1543.[6] But

---

[4] Not, as Pilch ('The Sondershäuser Psalter', p. 314) remarks, 'in the Irish minuscular script'.

[5] For the punctuation system here used, see P. Clemoes, *Liturgical Influence on Punctuation in Late Old English and Early Middle English Manuscripts*, Dept of AS [Univ. of Cambridge] Occasional Papers 1 (Cambridge, 1952), and now M. B. Parkes, *Pause and Effect. An Introduction to the History of Punctuation in the West* (Aldershot, 1992), esp. ch. 4 and pp. 301–7. The type of *punctus versus* employed in the Sondershausen fragment appears to be much less frequent than other types and does not seem to occur in the plates reproduced in Parkes's standard work.

[6] For a survey of the history of Jechaburg, with bibliographical references, see W. Gresky, 'Jechaburg', in *Handbuch der historischen Stätten Deutschlands. IX. Thüringen*, ed. H. Patze and P. Aufgebauer, 2nd ed. (Stuttgart, 1989), pp. 214–15, and cf. *ibid*. pp. 402–8 (W. Hartung and W. Gresky, 'Sondershausen'). For the library and archives of Jechaburg, see W. Gresky, *Der thüringische Archidiakonat Jechaburg. Grundzüge seiner Geschichte und Organisation* (Sondershausen, 1932), p. 2, and S. Krämer, *Handschriftenerbe des deutschen Mittelalters*, Mittelalterliche Bibliothekskataloge Deutschlands und der Schweiz: Ergänzungsband I, 3 vols. (Munich, 1989–90) II, 731. See also Pilch, 'The Sondershäuser Psalter', p. 313.

there is no certain way of proving that the psalter fragment was ever at Jechaburg, or that it had actually reached Thuringia before the end of the Middle Ages. A vertical crease in the middle of what remains of the leaf, ending in two tears at top and bottom, may suggest that it was used as a folder or wrapper at some time.

The Sondershausen leaf is not the only extant fragment of what must once have been a complete glossed psalter, presumably followed by canticles. For it is possible to demonstrate that two further fragments that have been known for some time must almost certainly have come from the same manuscript. These are two strips cut vertically from different leaves, now Cambridge, Pembroke College 312, C nos. 1 and 2. They contain fragments from Ps. LXXIII.17–LXXIV.3 and LXXVII.31–43 and were first described by Neil Ker and later edited by Klaus Dietz.[7] The other fragment comes as a horizontally cut strip from the central bifolium of a quire and is now MS 188 F 53 of the Stadsbibliotheek at Haarlem. Preserved in it are sections from Ps. CXIX, CXX, CXXI and CXXII. This fragment first became known when René Derolez described and edited it in 1972.[8] Both the Pembroke and the Haarlem fragments were removed from the bindings of books; unfortunately it is not known what these books were, so that – as in the case of the Sondershausen leaf – we have no clue as to origin and provenance of the original psalter manuscript or as to the time and place when and where it was taken apart.

The identification of the fragments as coming from one and the same manuscript is based on a number of reliable comparative criteria. All three fragments appear to have been written by the same scribe; they agree in the type and size of handwriting of Latin text, rubric and gloss; in the form and colour of the verse initials; in the system of punctuation used, and especially in the form of the *punctus versus* which they employ, apparently a form not frequently found elsewhere, if at all. In the three fragments, the number of lines of Latin text per page is seventeen, as can be seen on the Sondershausen leaf, and as becomes clear from the space needed to reconstruct complete leaves from the other

[7] N. R. Ker, *Catalogue of Manuscripts Containing Anglo-Saxon* (Oxford, 1957), no. 79; K. Dietz, 'Die ae. Psalterglossen der Hs. Cambridge, Pembroke College 312', *Anglia* 86 (1968), 273–9. See also the description by P. Clemoes, *Manuscripts from Anglo-Saxon England. An Exhibition in the University Library Cambridge* (Cambridge, 1985), pp. 6–7, and *The Salisbury Psalter*, ed. C. and K. Sisam, EETS os 242 (London, 1959), 67, n. 1. The fragments are now kept at Cambridge University Library.

[8] R. Derolez, 'A New Psalter Fragment with O.E. Glosses', *ES* 53 (1972), 401–8; see also N. R. Ker, 'A Supplement to *Catalogue of Manuscripts Containing Anglo-Saxon*', *ASE* 5 (1976), 121–31, at 122. The shelfmark given erroneously for the fragment should be deleted from P. Pulsiano, 'Psalters', *The Liturgical Books of Anglo-Saxon England*, ed. R. W. Pfaff, OEN Subsidia 23 (Kalamazoo, MI, 1995), 61–85, at 69 (no. 36).

fragments;[9] also, the original size of the leaves was no doubt the same. Finally, the fragments agree in the language and textual relationship of their Old English gloss, as I hope to show in what follows.

TEXT AND GLOSS

Anglo-Saxon psalter manuscripts with continuous or partial Old English gloss

Unless otherwise indicated, text and gloss are contemporaneous, and the gloss is continuous. Other contents of the manuscripts (calendars, canticles etc.) are not recorded.[10]

A London, British Library, Cotton Vespasian A. i:
Psalterium Romanum, s. viii$^{2/4}$, Old English gloss s. ix^{med}. Origin Canterbury, St Augustine's?

B Oxford, Bodleian Library, Junius 11 (S.C. 5139):
Psalterium Romanum, s. x^1, from Winchester?

C Cambridge, University Library, Ff. 1. 23:
Psalterium Romanum, s. x/xi or xi^{in} or xi^{med}, from Ramsey or Canterbury?

D London, British Library, Royal 2. B. V:
Psalterium Romanum, s. x^{med}, from Glastonbury or Abingdon?

E Cambridge, Trinity College R. 17. 1 (James 987):
Psalterium triplex, s. xii^{med}, Psalterium Romanum glossed in Old English, with numerous corrections and alterations; from Christ Church, Canterbury.

F London, British Library, Stowe 2:
Psalterium Gallicanum, s. xi^{med} or xi$^{3/4}$, from South West England, probably Winchester, New Minster.

G London, British Library, Cotton Vitellius E. xviii:
Psalterium Gallicanum, s. xi^{med} or xi$^{3/4}$, from Winchester, New Minster.

---

[9] It should be noted that Anglo-Saxon psalters of the tenth and eleventh centuries, glossed or unglossed, mostly of smaller size than the book from which our fragments come, have between twenty and twenty-seven lines of main text to the page. Only Lambeth Palace Library 427 has sixteen, but that is a considerably smaller manuscript (212 x 158 mm). The large Bosworth Psalter (Add. 37517), with twenty-five lines on pages of 390 x 265 mm, remains a special case.

[10] For printed editions of the glossed psalters here briefly listed, see H. Gneuss, 'Liturgical Books in Anglo-Saxon England and their Old English Terminology', *Learning and Literature in Anglo-Saxon England. Studies presented to Peter Clemoes on the Occasion of his Sixty-Fifth Birthday*, ed. M. Lapidge and H. Gneuss (Cambridge, 1985), pp. 91–141, at 115–16, and P. Pulsiano, 'Psalters', pp. 61–70 and 76. Also see both articles for Anglo-Saxon psalter manuscripts without Old English glosses.

H   London, British Library, Cotton Tiberius C.vi:
    Psalterium Gallicanum (incomplete), s. xi$^{3/4}$, from Winchester (Old Minster?).

I   London, Lambeth Palace Library, 427:
    Psalterium Gallicanum, s. xi^1, from South West England.

J   London, British Library, Arundel 60:
    Psalterium Gallicanum, s. xi^2, from Winchester, New Minster.

K   Salisbury, Cathedral Library, 150:
    Psalterium Gallicanum, s. x^2, from South West England; Old English gloss s. xi/xii.

L   London, British Library, Add. 37517:
    Psalterium Romanum, s. x$^{3/4}$, from Canterbury (Christ Church?); Old English continuous gloss to parts of the psalter.

M   New York, Pierpont Morgan Library 776:
    Psalterium Romanum (incomplete), s. viii^{med}; few Old English glosses s. ix, numerous scattered Old English glosses s. x^2 ('M^2').

N   Cambridge, Pembroke College 312, C nos. 1 and 2 + Haarlem, Stadsbibliotheek, 188 F 53 + Sondershausen, Schlossmuseum, Br. 1:
    Fragments from a Psalterium Gallicanum, s. xi^{med}, from Ps. VI–VII, LXXIII, LXXIV, LXXVII and CXIX–CXXII.

Ns The Sondershausen fragment (this siglum for one of the N fragments is only used for the purposes of the present article).

The Latin text

Editions of the Psalterium Romanum and Psalterium Gallicanum that provide a full textual record of all psalter manuscripts written or owned in Anglo-Saxon England are not available. The critical edition of the Romanum records the readings in psalters ACELM and Berlin, Hamilton 553, but not those in manuscripts BD (listed above), British Library, Arundel 155 and Harley 603, and of the 'Paris Psalter', Paris, Bibliothèque Nationale, lat. 8824.[11]

The standard critical edition of the Gallicanum[12] has only variants from the imported Utrecht, Universiteitsbibliotheek, 32 and the Gallicanum version in E.

---

[11] *Le Psautier romain et les autres anciens psautiers latins*, ed. R. Weber, Collectanea Biblica Latina 10 (Rome, 1953). Three early English fragments of Roman Psalters are listed by Pulsiano, 'Psalters', p. 69. For the Latin texts of the psalter, see *The Salisbury Psalter*, ed. Sisam and Sisam, pp. 47–52, and especially for the Romanum, M. Gretsch, *The Intellectual Foundations of the English Benedictine Reform*, CSASE 25 (Cambridge, 1999), 21–5 and n. 46.

[12] *Biblia Sacra iuxta Latinam Vulgatam Versionem. X. Liber Psalmorum* (Rome, 1953).

No English manuscript has been utilized for the Gallicanum text in the Vulgate edition by Robert Weber and Roger Gryson.[13]

As was to be expected in a psalter copy of this date, the Sondershausen fragment exhibits the text of the Gallicanum, that is, the version that from the time of the tenth-century Benedictine reform gradually replaced the Romanum in England. All cases in which readings of our fragment differ from those of the Romanum have been pointed out in the textual notes to the edition below. They are of some interest because the Old English gloss of the so-called D-type ultimately goes back to an exemplar prepared for an Anglo-Saxon copy of the Romanum in the tenth century.

The Old English gloss and its relationship

The Old English interlinear glosses in Anglo-Saxon psalter manuscripts follow three basic text types, whose earliest representatives are manuscripts A, D and I.[14] The D-type gloss first appears about the middle of the tenth century in BL Royal 2. B. V and becomes extremely influential in the late tenth and the eleventh century,[15] as can be seen in a number of manuscripts based on a D-type exemplar: FGHJK (L partly) M²N. The Sondershausen fragment therefore belongs in this group, but as will be seen, no clear stemmatic relationship – as envisaged by Karl Lachmann or Paul Maas – to any of the D-type codices can be established. In what follows, I list all cases of significant variant readings within the D-type group that allow us to link Ns with one or more manuscripts of the group. I include the readings of the A-type group (ABC) and of psalter I. Because of its late date and the complex character of its gloss, no variants from E are given.[16] There are no Old English glosses to Ps. VI and VII in L, while

---

[13] *Biblia Sacra iuxta Vulgatam Versionem*, ed. R. Weber, 4th ed. prepared by R. Gryson (Stuttgart, 1994), pp. 770–954.

[14] There is now a voluminous literature on the textual relationship of the Anglo-Saxon psalter glosses, beginning with the studies of Lindelöf and Wildhagen early in the present century. Most of this work has been briefly discussed, with bibliographical references, by Pulsiano, 'Psalters', pp. 74–7. For the relationship of the manuscripts with D-type glosses, *Salisbury Psalter*, ed. Sisam and Sisam, pp. 52–75, remains important. See also F.-G. Berghaus, *Die Verwandtschaftsverhältnisse der altenglischen Interlinearversionen des Psalters und der Cantica*, Palaestra 272 (Göttingen, 1979), and W. Hofstetter, *Winchester und der spätaltenglische Sprachgebrauch*, Texte und Untersuchungen zur Englischen Philologie 14 (Munich, 1987), esp. 67–88.

[15] For the significance of the Old English gloss in D, see now Gretsch, *The Intellectual Foundations*. The gloss is no doubt a product of the tenth-century Benedictine reform, and the possibility of a ninth-century forerunner can now safely be rejected. See the very cautious note on this question by H. Schabram, *Superbia. Studien zum altenglischen Wortschatz, Teil I: Die dialektale und zeitliche Verbreitung des Wortguts* (Munich, 1965), p. 23.

[16] For this gloss, see now P. P. O'Neill, 'The English Version', *The Eadwine Psalter. Text, Image and Monastic Culture in Twelfth-Century Canterbury*, ed. M. Gibson, T. A. Heslop and R. W. Pfaff (London, 1992), pp. 123–38.

these psalms were part of the portions of M now lost. In the forms recorded below, all spelling variants are given, except variations between ð and þ, æ and ae, where the same reading occurs in more than one manuscript.

1. Ps.VI.10   *assumpsit*: AB genom, C genam, D onfeng
           suscepit: F he underfeng, G onfeng, H (*no gloss*),
                  J onfengc, K anfeng, Ns o[   ], I underfeng

2. Ps.VI.11   *Erubescant* (1): A scomien, B scamigen, C scamigyn, DH ablysi-
                            gen ł scamien, F scamian, G [   ]miað,
                            J scamiaþ, K sceamian, Ns ablysigen ł scamiað,
                            I ablysian hi ł scamian

3. Ps.VI.11   (om.) ABCDH
          uehementer: F ðearle, GJ swiðe, K swyþe, Ns þearle;
                            I swiðlice ł swiðe

4. Ps.VI.11   *erubescant* (2): A scomien, B scamigen, C scomigyn,
                            D aswarnien, F sceamian heom, G scomiað
                            hiora, H aswarnigen, J scamiaþ, K aswarnian,
                            Ns aswarnien ł[   ], I aswarnian hi ł
                            gesceamige heom

5. Ps.VII.2   *libera me*: A gefrea me, B gefreo me, C alys me, D alys me
          saluum me fac: F gehæl me, GJ halne me do, H (*no gloss*), K hal
                            me do, Ns halne me do, I gehæl me

6. Ps. VII.2   *eripe me*: ABC genere me, D genere
           libera me: F alis me, G genere me, HK (*no gloss*), J ales me,
                            Ns genere me, I alys

7. Ps. VII.3   *(Ne) quando*: ABC æfre, DGHJ hwonne, F ahwænne, K (*no
                            gloss*), Ns hwonne, I ahwanne

8. Ps. VII.3   *rapiat*: A geslæcce, *from* geslæ, B gereafige, C reafige,
                            D gegripe ł reafie, FK gegripe, G gerefne,
                            H gegripe ł reafige, J gereafige, Ns gegripe,
                            I gelęcce ł ... gripe

9. Ps. VII.3   *non est*: AB nis, C nys, DFH nis, G ne is, J ne biþ, K na is,
                            Ns ne byð, I nis

10. Ps. VII.3 *qui saluum faciat*: A se ðe hie hale gedoe, B se þe hie hale gedo,
                            C se þe hi hale gedo, DH þe halne do, F se ðe
                            gehalne gedo, G se se hie halne gedeð, J þe þe hi
                            hale gedeþ, K þa hal do, Ns þæ halne do, I se þe
                            gehæle

11. Ps. VII.5   *retribuentibus*: AB ðaem geldendum, C þam gyldendum,
                            DFK gyldendum, H gildendum, G þam æfter-
                            gyldendum; J þam æftergildendum, Ns [g]ylden-
                            dum, I forgyldendum

12. Ps. VII.5   *mala*: AB yfel, C yfyl, DFGH yfelu, J yfele, K yfel, Ns
yfelu, I yfelu
13. Ps. VII.6   *deducat*: AB gelaedeð, C gelædyð, D gelede he,
FGJ gelædeþ, H gelæde he, K lædeð, Ns
gelædeð, I gelæde
14. Ps. VII.7   *in ira*: AB in eorre, C on yrre, DH on eorre, F on
graman, G on . . . yrre, J on irre, K on yrre, Ns
on eorre, I on . . . graman
15. Ps. VII.7 *quod mandasti*: A ðæt ðu bibude, BC ðæt þu bebude, DFH þe
ðu bebude, GJ þæt þu bebude, K þa þu bebude,
Ns ðe þu bebude, I þæt þe þu bebude
16. Ps. VII.8   *regredere*: A gaa eft, B ga eft, C gaa, DK gehwyrf,
F gehwyrfdum, GJ gang þu, H gehwyrfþ, Ns
gehwyrf ðu, I gehwyrf
17. Ps. VII.9 *(domine) iudica*: AB doem, C dem, D dem
   (dominus) iudicat: FGJ dem ðu, HK dem, Ns dem ðu, I demð

For the relationship of the Sondershausen fragment (Ns) with the D-type
psalters, the results of the foregoing comparison can be thus summarized:

1.	Ns = DGJK	Ns ≠ F	
2.	DH	FGJK	
3.	F	GJK	(D Romanum)
4.	DHK	FGJ	
5.	GJ(K)	F	(D Romanum)
6.	(D)G	FJ	
7.	DGHJ	F	
8.	FK (and DH?)	GJ	
9.	J	DFGK	
10.	DH	FGJK	
11.	DFHK	J	
12.	DFGH	JK	
13.	FGJ	DHK	
14	DH	FGJK	
15.	DFH	GJK	
16.	DK (H?)	FGJ	
17.	FGJ	DHK	

From this it will be clear that a stemmatic relationship within the D-group or
between Ns and one or more manuscripts of the group cannot be established.
In any case, because of their dates, FGHJK could not have been the immediate
exemplar or exemplars of Ns. If Ns had only one exemplar, this must have been

III Sondershausen, Schlossmuseum, Br. 1, *recto*

IV Sondershausen, Schlossmuseum, Br. 1, *verso*

remarkably close to D, but the possibility that Ns had more than one exemplar cannot be excluded. That neither the A-group nor a gloss of the same type as that in I can have influenced Ns seems obvious.

More light on the relationship of the gloss in Ns may be thrown by an investigation of the overall usage of D-type psalters. Thus, our comparison of the glosses to *uehementer* in Ps. VI.11 (above, no. 3) would seem to suggest some closer link between F and Ns. But D, being a Psalterium Romanum, omits *uehementer* here. In other passages, D glosses *uehementer* by *swiðe*, yet in Ps. XX.2 by *þearle*,[17] and this might cast doubt on an assumed link between F and Ns.

For the relationship between the Pembroke and Haarlem fragments to psalters DFGHJK, the picture is not much different. Dietz was inclined to consider F closest to the Pembroke gloss, whereas Derolez, on the basis of the Haarlem fragment, suggested that G was the nearest relative of N.[18] But neither F nor G can account for all readings in the two fragments, or in Ns.

LANGUAGE

As is to be expected, the Old English gloss in the Sondershausen leaf, like that of the Pembroke and Haarlem fragments, shows the characteristics of late West Saxon. The only clear exception is the Mercian form *eorre* 'ira' (cf. Campbell, § 154 (3), and Sievers–Brunner 1965, § 107) in Ps. VII.7 which, however, should not be considered as representative of the glossator's or scribe's dialect; it has simply been copied from an exemplar with a D-type gloss. For the form *eorre* is found not only in AB VII.7, but also in DH, and it is well known that occasional Anglian forms occur not only in D, but in all manuscripts of the D-group.[19]

---

[17] See P. Pulsiano, 'Defining the A-Type (*Vespasian*) and D-Type (*Regius*) Psalter-Gloss Traditions', *ES* 72 (1991), 308–27, at 327.

[18] See Dietz, 'Die ae. Psalterglossen', pp. 275–6; Derolez, 'A New Psalter Fragment', p. 408, and Berghaus, *Die Verwandtschaftsverhältnisse*, p. 89. For the Haarlem fragment, H could not be drawn upon because the text after Ps. CXIII B.11 is lost in this manuscript.

[19] Cf. Pilch, 'The Sondershäuser Psalter', p. 316, who considers the form in Ns 'dialectally significant'. For the Anglian elements in D, see K. Wildhagen, 'Studien zum Psalterium Romanum in England und zu seinen Glossierungen', *Festschrift für Lorenz Morsbach*, ed. F. Holthausen and H. Spies, Studien zur englischen Philologie 50 (Halle, 1913), 418–72, at 449–51; for Anglian traits in the vocabulary of the gloss in D, see F. Wenisch, *Spezifisch anglisches Wortgut in den nordhumbrischen Interlinearglossierungen des Lukasevangeliums*, Anglistische Forschungen 132 (Heidelberg, 1979), 66, 327 and *passim*. For psalter glosses and the political background to the linguistic situation in tenth-century England, see now Gretsch, *The Intellectual Foundations*, ch. 8. In the Haarlem fragment, at Ps. CXXII.3, *ancillae* is glossed by the Anglian dialect word *mennene*. Again, forms of this word are not only found in ABC CXXII.3, but also in DGJ; cf. Derolez, 'A New Psalter Fragment', p. 406, and Wenisch, *Spezifisch anglisches Wortgut*, pp. 167, 199 and 303, with notes.

The spelling of short *a* before nasals follows standard late West Saxon practice; it is normally *a*, while *o* occurs only in words with low sentence stress (*forþon, hwonne, þonne*), exactly as described in our historical grammars (Luick, § 112.1; Campbell, § 333; Sievers–Brunner 1965, § 79, n. 3). Apart from this, *o* is not 'more frequent overall' as Pilch (p. 316) claims.[20]

As for the vocabulary, Pilch (p. 315) notes that *gehwyrf* (VII.8), *pearle* (VI.11), *aswar[d]nian*[21] (VI.11) and *ablysigen* (VI.11) are forms of 'relatively rare and (by the standards of late West Saxon) probably archaic words, so they suggest a relatively early date of the present psalter gloss (say ninth century) and a reasonably close relationship between the *Sondershäuser Psalter* and the Lambeth, Stowe, Bosworth and Salisbury psalters'. For the mistaken idea of a possible ninth-century date of the D-type gloss and for the gloss relationship, see above. Of the four Old English words, *ablysian* and *aswarnian* are in fact relatively rare, but this is presumably due to the character of our written transmission, and, in any case, their use is not restricted to psalter glosses. Neither rare, nor archaic by the eleventh century, is *pearle*, an adverb used by Ælfric and Wulfstan, and in late poetry (*The Battle of Maldon*), while *(ge)hweorfan* is at least common in poetry and earlier prose and therefore not unusual in a psalter gloss that originated in the tenth century.[22]

EDITION

The following edition reproduces the lineation, text, gloss and punctuation of the manuscript fragment without any change or emendation, but word-division has been normalized, and letters that are partially lost are placed in round brackets. Square brackets enclose words and letters of the Latin text now lost; these could be restored without doubt or difficulty because the English tenth- and eleventh-century manuscripts of the Psalterium Gallicanum, for the passages here under discussion, not only agree among themselves but also with the text as established in the critical edition of 1953; for one doubtful but insignificant reading, see textual note 19, below. I have made no attempt to restore the lost portion of the Old English gloss except where part of a gloss word remains in the fragment; in these cases I have supplied the word-form that appears the most probable one after consulting psalters DFGHJK. Abbreviations and

---

[20] In stating that the spelling *find* (Ps. VI.11) has been noted for the dative singular only, Pilch seems to have misunderstood E. Sievers and K. Brunner, *Altenglische Grammatik*, 3rd ed. (Tübingen, 1965: Pilch refers to the 1st ed. of 1942), § 286, n. 2. For Brunner, as for Campbell, *Old English Grammar* (Oxford, 1959), § 632, *find* and related spellings are of course the regular forms for nominative and accusative plural, too.

[21] No reason for his emendation, phonological or semantic, is given by Pilch.

[22] For *ablysian* and *aswarnian*, see *Dictionary of Old English*, ed. A. Cameron, A. C. Amos, A. diP. Healey *et al.* (Toronto, 1986–), s.vv. For the employment of poetic words in the tenth-century D-type gloss, see now Gretsch, *The Intellectual Foundations*, ch. 3.

contractions have been indicated by means of italics. Superscript numbers in text or gloss refer to the textual notes below.

Recto

	gewitað	fram	me	ealle
Psalm VI.9.	Discedite	a	me	omnes q[ui operamini]

	unrihtwisnesse	forþon	g[ehyrde]
	iniquitatem⸴	quoniam	e[xaudiuit][1]

	drihten	steefne[2]	wopes	(m)[ines]
	dominus	uocem	fletus	(m)[ei]

	gehyrde	drihten	ben[e]
10.	Exaudiuit	dominus	depr(e)[cationem meam]

	drihten	gebed	min	o[nfeng][3]
	do*minu*s	orationem	meam	s(u)[scepit]

	ablysigen ꝇ scamiað	7	syn gedrefed
11.	Erubescant	*et*	conturbe[ntur]

	þearle	ealle	find
	uehementer[4]	om*ne*s	inim[ici mei]

	syn gecyrred	7	aswarnien ꝇ[6]
	conuertantur[5]	et	erube[scant]

	swiðe	hrædlice	
	ualde	uelociter.	SEPTI(M)[US PSALMUS]

DAUID QUEM CANTAUIT P[   ][7]

	drihten	god	min
Psalm VII.2.	Domine[8]	deus	meus [in te speraui]

	halne	me	do	of
	[9]saluum	me	fac	ex[9] o[mnibus]

	ehtendum	minra
	persequentibus	(m)[e]

283

7	genere	me
et	libera[10]	me.

3.	þilæs	hwonne	gegripe	swaswa leo
	Ne	quando	rapiat	ut	leo (a)[nimam meam]

þon*ne*	ne	byð	se þe	alyse
dum	non	(e)st	qui	redimat (n)[eque]

þæ	halne	do
qui	salu(um)[11]	faciat

Verso

		min	gif	ic dyde	ðys	gif	is
VII.4.	[Domine de]us meus	si	feci	is(t)ud.	si	est

[unrihtwisne]s	on	handum	min(um)
[iniquitas]	in	manibus	meis	;

	[g]yldendum	me	yfelu
5.	[Si reddidi	ret]ribuentibus	michi[12]	mala/

	[b]e gewyrhtum	fram	feondum	minum
[decidam]	(m)erito	ab	inimicis	meis

[inanis][13] ;·

	feond	sawle	mine
6.	[Persequat]ur inimicus	animam	mea*m*

		7	fortredað	on eorðan
[et comp](r)ehendat[14]/ *et*	conculc*et*	in terram

	(m)in	7	wuldor	min
[uitam]	(m)eam[15]	et	gloriam	meam

	gelædeð
[in pulue]rem	deducat	;·

284

		drihten	on	eorre	þinum		upahefe
7.	[Exurge]	domine	in	ira	tua	et[16]	exaltare

	feonda	myra[17]	
[in finib](u)s[18]	inimicorum	meorum[18]	;·

	drihten	god	min
[Exur]ge[19]	domine	deus	meus

	ðe	þu bebude
[in prece]pto	quod	mandastiˊ

		[gesom]nung	folca	ymb
8.	[Et sina](g)oga	populorum	circum	

	þe	
[ ][20]	þe	
[dabit	t](e)	;·

[ðiss]um ł	þas[21]	on	heannesse	gehwyrf ðu
[Et prop]ter	hanc	in	altu(m)	regredere[22].

		dem ðu[23]	folce	
9.	[Domin](u)s	iudicat	popul[os][24]	;·

Textual notes

1 First letter not *e* caudata (as in Pilch); the apparent loop under the *e* belongs to the following *x*.

2 Second *e* smaller; same hand?

3 *onfeng*: This is the reading of DGJK; see above, p. 279. The Gallicanum reading is *suscepit*, as in psalters FGHIJKNs, whereas the Romanum has *assumpsit*, as in ABCDE, but this difference would hardly affect the Old English gloss.

4 *uehementer*: a Gallican reading, omitted in the Romanum and so in psalters ABCDE, but also in H, which confirms the extremely close relationship of H with D or a D-type gloss; *uehementer* is recorded and glossed in Old English in FGIJKNs; for the relationship of these glosses see above, p. 278.

5 *conuertantur*: the Gallican reading, as preserved in psalters GHIJKNs, all glossed *syn gecyrred* (or related forms), which may go back to a D-type gloss. The Romanum reading is *auertantur retrorsum*, preserved in manuscripts

ABCDE and glossed *syn forcyrred onbæc* (or related forms) in ABC, *syn gecerred on hinder* in D, and similarly in E.

6　The alternative gloss, now missing, was very probably a form of *scamian*; see above, p. 279.

7　The rubric to Ps. VII, now faint, particularly *DAUI*, but visible, is in uncials. Pilch's restoration of the end '*quem cantauit d[omino]*', is certainly wrong, as the last clearly legible letter is *P*, not *D*. The available space suggests that some shorter version of the rubric as established in the critical editions of the Gallicanum and the Romanum[23] has to be assumed: 'PSALMUS DAVID QUEM CANTAVIT DOMINO PRO VERBIS CHUSI FILII IEMINI'; psalters FGH have almost exactly corresponding rubrics; literally the same wording is in A. Unfortunately, the editors of some of the Anglo-Saxon psalters have simply ignored and omitted the rubrics.

8　*Domine*: with large red initial *D*, see pl. III.

9　*saluum me fac ex*: the Gallican reading, extant in psalters FGHIJKNs. The Romanum variant is *libera me ab*, preserved, as was to be expected, in ABCDE. For the Old English renderings, see above, p. 279.

10　*libera me*: as in the Gallicanum and the Anglo-Saxon psalters FGHIJK, the Romanum reading being *eripe me*, recorded in England in manuscripts ABCDE. For the Old English glosses, see above, p. 279.

11　*salu(um)*: erroneously restored to *salum* by Pilch; see his note 10.

12　*michi*: *h* partly legible.

13　[*inanis*]: omitted by Pilch, because what remains of this line is blank, except for the *punctus versus*; see pl. IV. All English and continental psalters, Roman and Gallican, have *inanis* here.

14　[*comp*](*r*)*ehendat*: Psalterium Romanum reads *comprehendat eam*. This Latin text and the appropriate Old English pronoun in the gloss are represented in manuscripts ABCDE, and there appears to be an echo in MS. I (which does not have *eam*): '*gehæftnige hi ł gegripe hi*'. The Gallicanum variant, without Latin and Old English pronoun, appears in England in psalters FGHJK, glossed by forms of (*ge*)*gripan*.

15　(*m*)*eam*: final *m* inserted (by corrector?).

16　The Psalterium Romanum and a number of manuscripts of the Gallicanum, including the Anglo-Saxon manuscripts G and J, have *et exaltare*; in MS I *et* has been added, perhaps by the glossator. Ns shares the omission with FHK.

17　*myra*: there is no trace of an abbreviation mark for *n*. For the form, see Campbell, *Old English Grammar*, § 474.

18　*inimicorum meorum*: Psalterium Romanum reads *inimicorum tuorum*, as in the Anglo-Saxon manuscripts ABCDE and their Old English glosses. The

---

[23] See above, p. 277, nn. 11–12.

Gallicanum reading, as in Ns, is represented by manuscripts FGHIJK, together with their Old English glosses. In H, however, *meorum* is not glossed, which again testifies to H's close adherence to a D-type gloss: the glossator of H may have been uncertain whether to follow his Latin lemma or his exemplar, as authority for his work.

19 According to Pilch's edition, this is glossed by *aris*, which was most probably the translation for [*Exur*]*ge*, but has actually been lost in Ns. The critical edition of the Gallicanum has *et exurge*, which, however, is not the common reading of all Gallicanum manuscripts. *Et* is in the Anglo-Saxon psalters FGI, was erased in K, and is omitted in HJ; the reading of Ns must remain uncertain.

20 It is impossible to say definitely for which verb *ymb* served as a prefix; psalters ABCDEHK have forms of *ymbsellan, ymbsyllan*; GJ have forms of *ymbsettan*; cf. also F *ymbtrymdon*, I *ymbtrymð* ł *ymbhwyrfeþ*. A form of *ymbsellan* in Ns seems most likely in view of the close relationship with D and H.

21 [*ðiss*]*um* ł *þas*: The combination does not occur in other Anglo-Saxon psalters. Ns or its exemplar may therefore have been able to draw on two exemplars. Cf. *ðissum* and related forms in ABCFGJ, *þas* in DEHK. As so often, psalter I is independent of both groups: *for þissere intingan*.

22 *regredere*: Pilch reads *ingredere*, which is not in the manuscript.

23 *dominus iudicat* is the Gallicanum reading, as found in psalters FGHIJK, whereas *domine iudica* is that of the Romanum, as exhibited in ABCDE. It seems curious, however, or perhaps it is an indication of the pervasive influence of the D-type gloss, that except for psalter I (*demð*), all glossed Anglo-Saxon Gallican psalters provide an OE gloss that renders the Roman reading: HK *dem* (as D), FGJNs *dem ðu*. For a few Romanum readings in the Haarlem fragment and for a gloss rendering a Romanum variant in the Pembroke fragment, see Derolez, pp. 406–7.

24 *popul*[*os*]: *os* lost in lower tear.[24]

---

[24] I wish to thank all those who very kindly helped me in the preparation of this article: Ms Christa Hirschler, Deputy Director of the Schlossmuseum at Sondershausen, who sent me photographs of the fragment here discussed, patiently replied to all my enquiries and allowed me to go through the numerous manuscript fragments in her care; Ms Jayne Ringrose of the Department of Manuscripts, Cambridge University Library, and Mr Rob Dekkers of the Stadsbibliotheek Haarlem, who supplied me with photographs of the Pembroke and Haarlem fragments; Professor Michael Lapidge, whose advice on palaeographical questions was important; Mechthild Gretsch, who knows more about Anglo-Saxon psalters than I do; and Carolin Schreiber, who produced a perfect computer version from my handwritten exemplar.

Two runic notes

R. I. PAGE

I. A RUNE READ

A runic text that has, as far as I know, attracted little attention lurks at the bottom right-hand corner of Tabella III of part 3 of Hickes's *Thesaurus*.[1] It has thirteen graphs, labelled '*e Cod. Cottoniano*, Otho *C. 5. p. 41*'. The graphs are the Anglo-Saxon runes:

ᚺᛖᚦᛁᚠᚱᚾᛁᛗᛁᚾᛁᚤᛟ

Transliterated: 'c o n s l r u i e i u s', followed by what appears to be the bind-rune 'k̑u, that is, the late additional rune *calc* bound with *ur*. The *sigel*-rune 's' is a comparatively rare form found occasionally in manuscripts, on coins and in inscriptions. The other runes are common English types.

As it stands the sequence makes no sense but it is clarified by the simple emendation of one graph. The fifth rune is 'l', *lagu*; I would amend it to 'e', *eh*. 'l' is, so to speak, the left-hand half of 'e'; and an error of drawing could be either that of the original scribe or of the eighteenth-century draughtsman, apparently Humfrey Wanley himself. Indeed, a sketch of these runes in the same form occurs on 138v of Wanley's manuscript 'Book of Specimens', now Longleat House, MS 345.[2] Thus the error cannot be attributed to Michael Burghers, the engraver who prepared the plate for press and of whose accuracy Wanley had occasional doubts.[3] An original written *eh*-rune may have faded in part and thus resembled 'l'. So I correct the text to 'cons<e>ruieius'.

The meaning becomes plain from the Hickes attribution of the runes to London, British Library, Cotton Otho C. v, a codex badly damaged in the 1731 fire. This formed part of a seventh-/eighth-century gospelbook, divided into two by the sixteenth century. The other bit of it is now Cambridge, Corpus Christi College 197B, a manuscript that is also fragmentary and has lost most of its side

---

[1] George Hickes, *Linguarum Vett. Septentrionalium Thesaurus Grammatico-Criticus et Archæologicus*, III, *Grammaticæ Islandicæ Rudimenta* (Oxford, 1703). I thank Dr S. D. Keynes for drawing these runes to my attention and giving me his expert advice on Wanley's 'Book of Specimens'; also Dr David Parsons and Professor René Derolez for helpful comments on a first draft of this note.

[2] S. Keynes, 'The Reconstruction of a Burnt Cottonian Manuscript: the Case of Cotton MS. Otho A. 1', *Brit. Lib. Jnl* 22 (1996), 113–60, at p. 154, n. 116.

[3] *Letters of Humfrey Wanley, Palaeographer, Anglo-Saxonist, Librarian 1672–1726*, ed. P. L. Heyworth (Oxford, 1989), p. 107.

margins.[4] Otho C. v held the gospels of Matthew and Mark and some extraneous material. Wanley's annotation to Smith's 1696 catalogue of the Cotton Library notes that it had 109 folios.[5] Page 41 would contain part of Matthew's gospel. Sure enough, Matt. XVIII.31 reads, in the Vulgate version, *videntes autem conservi eius quae fiebant contristati sunt valde*, given in the Authorised Version as 'So when his fellowservants saw what was done, they were very sorry.' The Hickes runes represent part of this, with the final graph either 'ku' attempting the Latin *qu*- or, possibly I suppose, the 'pseudo-rune' 'q', *?cweorð*, which occurs in a variety of shapes in manuscripts, though not, as far as I know, in this particular form.

The question then arises, why and when was the phrase *conservi eius* put into runes? I suggest it was an Anglo-Saxon marginal addition to Otho C. v which Wanley observed and recorded. It could then form one of the small group of marginalia that transliterate manuscript material into runes. An obvious parallel is the word 's w i þ o r' standing in the margin of Cambridge, Corpus Christi College 41, p. 448, rendering the first word written on the adjoining line.[6] There is a variant of the practice in the marginal gloss 'm a i o r i' to the text's *grauiori* in Munich, Bayerische Staatsbibliothek, Clm. 3731, 7v, a manuscript in Anglo-Saxon minuscule of the late eighth century.[7] Unfortunately my suggestion cannot be confirmed, for the text passage did not escape the 1731 fire that destroyed so much of Otho C. v. Wanley's 'p. 41' is now fol. 6 of what remains. On each side of it are the centre parts of ten lines. The last readable word on the recto is *dimisit* (Matt. XVIII.27). The first line of the verso is hardly legible because of show-through, but a library hand has identified it as part of verse 32, and certainly verse 33 began two lines lower down. Matt. XVIII.31, together with any related annotation, has vanished altogether.

Why such transliterations were done I do not know, unless it was to celebrate some reader's skill in the runic character. In any case, the Otho C. v runes give another example of the use of that script in the study/scriptorium, within a learned manuscript context. It helps to illustrate the varying relationship between runic and Roman characters.[8]

[4] *Codices Latini Antiquiores. A Palaeographical Guide to Latin Manuscripts prior to the Ninth Century.* II. *Great Britain and Ireland*, ed. E. A. Lowe, 2nd ed. (Oxford, 1972), no. 125; J. J. G. Alexander, *Insular Manuscripts 6th to the 9th Century* (London, 1978), no. 12.

[5] Thomas Smith, *Catalogue of the Manuscripts in the Cottonian Library 1696*, ed. C. G. C. Tite (Cambridge, 1984), p. 72.

[6] R. I. Page, *Runes and Runic Inscriptions. Collected Essays on Anglo-Saxon and Viking Runes*, ed. D. Parsons (Woodbridge, 1995), p. 124.

[7] R. Derolez, 'Epigraphical versus Manuscript English Runes: One or Two Worlds?', *Academiae Analecta*, Mededelingen van de Koninklijke Academie voor Wetenschappen, Letteren en Schone Kunsten van België, Klasse der Letteren 45 (1983), 71–93, at 91.

[8] As adumbrated in R. I. Page, 'Runic Writing, Roman Script and the Scriptorium', *Runor och ABC. Elva föreläsningar från ett symposium i Stockholm våren 1995*, ed. S. Nyström, *Runica et Mediævalia, Opuscula* 4 (Stockholm, 1997), 119–40.

Two runic notes

Rigsarkivet (National Records Office) Copenhagen, Privatarkiv no. 6431 is that of the Icelandic scholar Grímur Jónsson Thorkelin (1752–1829). Within it is a package labelled 'Thorkelinske Noticer fra hans Ænglandsrejse' – Thorkelin's reports on his travels in England, which took place between 1785 and 1791. This contains a group of rough notebooks and some separate sheets. A scrap of loose paper among them records, in a contemporary hand but not perhaps Thorkelin's, the following cryptic text:

ERY.RI.VF.MOL   Found in 1773 at Lynstock
YRI.VRI.NOL   Castle near Carlisle, & not far from
GLES.TE.SOTE.THOL   the Picts Wall in Cumberland.

Written below this entry is the comment: 'At S! Brides near Egremont & Whitehaven is a Curious Font inscribed with the like Runic Characters . . .' with cross-references to Camden's *Britannia* (Edmund Gibson's 1695 edition) and to letters of William Nicolson, archdeacon and then bishop of Carlisle. The allusion here is to the Bridekirk font which has an inscription in early Middle English using a mixture of Norse runes with occasional bookhand supplements.[9] From this it is natural to conclude that, though presented in Roman transcription, the Linstock Castle text also was in runes.

Unfortunately, the writer of the note failed to say what his strange text was preserved on. However, there is a powerful clue. Probably the only people the Linstock Castle text makes any sense at all to are those who know a small group of Anglo-Saxon rings with similar legends cut in runes round their hoops.[10] There are three of them:

1. An electrum ring found in the 1730s in the general neighbourhood of Bramham Moor, Yorkshire, though the exact find-spot is not as clear as might be.[11] It is now Nationalmuseet, Copenhagen, no. 8545. Its text, which is divided into three sections, reads:

'ærkriuf lt‖kriuriþon‖glæstæpontol'.

2. A gold ring turned up in 1817 at Greymoorhill, Kingmoor, Cumbria (NGR NY 395597), now in the British Museum: *Ring Catalogue* no. 184. This has an almost identical legend, the last three runes set within the hoop:

---

[9] R. I. Page, *An Introduction to English Runes* (London, 1973), pp. 195–6 and pl. 14.

[10] D. M. Wilson, 'A Group of Anglo-Saxon Amulet Rings', *The Anglo-Saxons: Studies in some Aspects of their History and Culture presented to Bruce Dickins*, ed. P. Clemoes (London, 1959), pp. 159–70. My thanks to Sir David, to Leslie Webster of the British Museum and to Michael Lerche Nielsen for further scrutiny they gave to this material.

[11] R. I. Page, 'The Finding of the "Bramham Moor" Runic Ring', *N&Q* 9 (1962), 450–2, with additional provenances given as Har(e)wood and Sherburn in Elmet.

'+ærkriufltkriuriþonglæstæpon|tol'.

3. It is, however, the third example that is most significant for the present note. This ring, of agate, is also in the British Museum: reg. no. 73, 2–10, 3; *Ring Catalogue* no. 186. It has no known provenance, for it was first recorded in 1824, by which time it had already passed into a dealer's hands. Its text begins with two curious symbols based upon cross motifs, then continues:

'·ery·ri·uf·dol·yri·uri·þol·*les·te·pote·nol'

A couple of the graphs demand comment. The *y*-rune is of a form found elsewhere in manuscript rather than epigraphical transmission.[12] The *i*-rune has in two cases short sloping twigs at top and base, therefore slightly resembling the rune *eoh/ih*, transliterated 'ï' in my system;[13] but these twigs are probably only decorative. The rune represented above by an asterisk looks like the later Norse dotted **k** (=/g/). Alternatively the dot could be accidental; and the rune would then be a Norse form of k, which also can give /g/ in early Viking Age inscriptions. This would correspond with the 'g' rune at this position in rings 1, 2, but it presents the problem of what a Scandinavian type is doing among Anglo-Saxon runes. The only alternative identifications seem to be as the quite rare epigraphical and manuscript variant 's', ᚴ [14] (but note that elsewhere ring 3 has the more usual 's') or as a badly formed 'w'. Both conflict with the texts of rings 1, 2.

Of the two recensions of this mysterious text that are evidenced by the three rings, that of 1, 2 must be regarded as primary. Dickins pointed out that its opening letters coincide with sequences in an Anglo-Saxon charm for staunching blood – two versions survive, giving *ærcrio/ær crio*;[15] and later scholars have recorded in other charms letter groups and rhyming patterns that approximate to bits of the gibberish of these ring legends.[16] The text divisions into the number 3 and its multiples may be important too, for this figure is prominent in charms[17] – thirty runes in three groups of nine, nine and twelve in ring 1; thirty runes divided twenty-seven and three in ring 2. In consequence these objects are presumably to be identified as 'amulet rings', what the Anglo-Saxons might have called *lyfesne* or in Latin *phylacteria/filacteria* or *ligaturae*.

The text of the agate ring is then a corrupt version of that on rings 1 and 2.

[12] R. Derolez, *Runica Manuscripta: the English Tradition*, Rijksuniversiteit te Gent, Werken Uitgegeven door de Faculteit van de Wijsbegeerte en Letteren, 118° Aflevering (Brugge, 1954), pp. 46 and 48.

[13] R. I. Page, 'On the Transliteration of English Runes', *MA* 28 (1984), 22–45, at 32.

[14] *Ibid.* p. 32.

[15] B. Dickins, 'Runic Rings and Old English Charms', *ASNSL* 167 (1935), 252.

[16] H. Meroney, 'Irish in the Old English Charms', *Speculum* 20 (1945), 172–82; G. Storms, *Anglo-Saxon Magic* (The Hague, 1948), pp. 236, 298, 301–2 and 306.

[17] Storms, *Anglo-Saxon Magic*, pp. 96–100.

The more common 'y' has replaced the regionally diagnostic 'k', *calc*. The rhyming 'd o l', appears instead of the unpronounceable 'l t'; while rhyming 'þ o l' and 'p o t e n o l' replace the partly rhyming 'þ o n', 'p o n t o l'.

The Linstock Castle inscription corresponds closely to that of the agate ring, 3. The two have the same separation into short sequences, and a couple of the distinctive differences from 1, 2: 'e'/E in place of 'æ', 'y'/Y in place of 'k'. Yet the ring 3 and Linstock texts diverge in some places. MOL in place of 'dol' may not be significant, for the runes 'm' and 'd' are similar in form and not infrequently confused, even in Anglo-Saxon times.[18] The positional interchange of 'þ o l'/NOL and 'n o l'/THOL could be a careless error on the part of the Thorkelin transcriber. The variation 'p o t e', SOTE could show misidentification of the *p*-rune as 's'; 'p' is fairly rare epigraphically and has the occasional manuscript variant with no upper twig, which bears some resemblance to 's'.[19] The Linstock division into three lines (corresponding to divisions on ring 1) is worth taking into account, though it may simply be for ease of lay-out in the copy.

There are at least three possible explanations of the Linstock Castle report:

(1) it presents an eighteenth-century scholar's attempt at transliterating the runes of ring 3. This would give a find-spot for the agate ring – Linstock Castle (NGR NY 429585). The question then arises: would an antiquary of that date have access to material that would enable him to achieve such a task? The answer is 'yes', for Hickes had made the evidence available in 1705. His *Thesaurus* reproduces, among many others, the runes of British Library Cotton Domitian, ix and (the lost) Otho B. x and Galba A. ii, and of Oxford, St John's College 17, which would suffice for the transliteration.[20]

(2) it represents the legend of a different runic ring, now lost, which was closely related to that of ring 3 but had certain variations of reading and perhaps format. There is no way of testing this hypothesis, other, I suppose, than finding the ring.

(3) it represents a text in Roman script on an unknown object, now lost. This would be important as providing another example of the two writing systems, runes and Roman, being used for the same, or similar, purposes. Against this is the accompanying reference to the Bridekirk font, which is suggestive but not conclusive.

It might be possible, by working through Thorkelin's surviving correspondence with English antiquaries, to clarify the matter further.[21] Meanwhile, rather than

---

[18] Derolez, *Runica Manuscripta*, pp. 12 and 13.   [19] *Ibid.* pp. 22 and 25.

[20] Hickes, *Thesaurus*, III, Tabellæ II, VI.

[21] Though conversely this might lead to more confusion, since at one time or another Thorkelin seems to have known ring 1; as K. M. Nielsen points out in his 'Rasmus Rask om de Ældre Runer', *Aarbøger for Nordisk Oldkyndighed og Historie* (1971), 120–45, at 138–42.

multiply lost Anglo-Saxon inscriptions *praeter necessitatem* I would plump for explanation (1) above; though with some misgiving. Linstock Castle and Greymoorhill lie close together, perhaps suspiciously so, being only about 4 km apart. Bramham Moor/Sherburn in Elmet/Harewood are some distance away, say 125 km, but still they are in Northumbria. The new provenance, whatever its explanation, supports the evidence for a regional, north-country, practice of inscribing this cryptic text, presumably on amulet rings.[22]

[22] Dr Alzheimer strikes again! Since this paper appeared in proof form I have reconsulted an article of mine of some thirty years ago: 'Runes and Non-Runes', *Medieval Literature and Civilisation. Studies in Memory of G. N. Garmonsway*, ed. D. A. Pearsall and R. A. Waldron (London, 1969), pp. 28–54, at 52–3. There I note, in a sale catalogue of 1778, the item 'An antient Runic ring, found near the Picts Well, 1773'. From its date and provenance this is almost certainly the ring mentioned in Thorkelin's papers. The ring's runic text is then confirmed, and option (3) above deleted. The catalogue has the intriguing addition, '*See the account with it.*' Perhaps Thorkelin's paper is this account, or a copy of it.

Bibliography for 1997

DEBBY BANHAM, CARL T. BERKHOUT, CAROLE P.
BIGGAM, MARK BLACKBURN, SIMON KEYNES and
ALEXANDER RUMBLE

This bibliography is meant to include all books, articles and significant reviews published in any branch of Anglo-Saxon studies during 1997. It excludes reprints unless they contain new material. It will be continued annually. The year of publication of a book or article is 1997 unless otherwise stated. The arrangement and the pages on which the sections begin are as follows:

Carl Berkhout has been mainly responsible for sections 2, 3 and 4, Alexander Rumble for sections 5 and 8, Debby Banham for section 6, Mark Blackburn for section 7 and Carole Biggam for section 9. References to publications in Japan have been supplied by Professor Yoshio Terasawa. Simon Keynes has been responsible for co-ordination.

The following abbreviations occur where relevant (not only in the bibliography but also throughout the volume):

AAe   *Archaeologia Aeliana*
AB   *Analecta Bollandiana*
AC   *Archæologia Cantiana*
AHR   *American Historical Review*

AIUON	*Annali, Istituto Universitario Orientale di Napoli: sezione germanica*
ANQ	*American Notes and Queries*
AntJ	*Antiquaries Journal*
ANS	*Anglo-Norman Studies*
ArchJ	*Archaeological Journal*
ASE	*Anglo-Saxon England*
ASNSL	*Archiv für das Studium der neueren Sprachen und Literaturen*
ASPR	Anglo-Saxon Poetic Records
ASSAH	*Anglo-Saxon Studies in Archaeology and History*
BAR	British Archaeological Reports
BBCS	*Bulletin of the Board of Celtic Studies*
BGDSL	*Beiträge zur Geschichte der deutschen Sprache und Literatur*
BIAL	*Bulletin of the Institute of Archaeology* (London)
BN	*Beiträge zur Namenforschung*
BNJ	*British Numismatic Journal*
CA	*Current Archaeology*
CBA	Council for British Archaeology
CCM	*Cahiers de civilisation médiévale*
CCSL	Corpus Christianorum, Series Latina
CMCS	*Cambrian Medieval Celtic Studies*
CSASE	Cambridge Studies in Anglo-Saxon England
CSEL	Corpus Scriptorum Ecclesiasticorum Latinorum
DAEM	*Deutsches Archiv für Erforschung des Mittelalters*
EA	*Études anglaises*
EconHR	*Economic History Review*
EEMF	Early English Manuscripts in Facsimile
EETS	Early English Text Society
EHR	*English Historical Review*
ELN	*English Language Notes*
EME	*Early Medieval Europe*
EPNS	English Place-Name Society
ES	*English Studies*
FS	*Frühmittelalterliche Studien*
HBS	Henry Bradshaw Society Publications
HS	*Historische Sprachforschung*
HZ	*Historische Zeitschrift*
IF	*Indogermanische Forschungen*
JBAA	*Journal of the British Archaeological Association*
JEGP	*Journal of English and Germanic Philology*
JEH	*Journal of Ecclesiastical History*
JEPNS	*Journal of the English Place-Name Society*
JMH	*Journal of Medieval History*
JTS	*Journal of Theological Studies*
LH	*The Local Historian*

296

MA	*Medieval Archaeology*
MÆ	*Medium Ævum*
MGH	Monumenta Germaniae Historica
MLR	*Modern Language Review*
MP	*Modern Philology*
MS	*Mediaeval Studies*
MScand	*Mediaeval Scandinavia*
N&Q	*Notes and Queries*
NChron	*Numismatic Chronicle*
NCirc	*Numismatic Circular*
NH	*Northern History*
NM	*Neuphilologische Mitteilungen*
OEN	*Old English Newsletter*
PA	*Popular Archaeology*
PBA	*Proceedings of the British Academy*
PL	Patrologia Latina
PMLA	*Publications of the Modern Language Association of America*
PQ	*Philological Quarterly*
RB	*Revue bénédictine*
RES	*Review of English Studies*
RS	Rolls Series
SBVS	*Saga-Book of the Viking Society for Northern Research*
SCBI	Sylloge of Coins of the British Isles
SCMB	*Seaby's Coin and Medal Bulletin*
SettSpol	*Settimane di studio del Centro italiano di studi sull'alto medioevo* (Spoleto)
SM	*Studi Medievali*
SN	*Studia Neophilologica*
SP	*Studies in Philology*
TLS	*Times Literary Supplement*
TPS	*Transactions of the Philological Society*
TRHS	*Transactions of the Royal Historical Society*
YES	*Yearbook of English Studies*
ZAA	*Zeitschrift für Anglistik und Amerikanistik*
ZDA	*Zeitschrift für deutsches Altertum und deutsche Literatur*
ZVS	*Zeitschrift für vergleichende Sprachforschung*

1. GENERAL AND MISCELLANEOUS

Alsop, J. D., 'William Lambarde's Place of Birth', *N&Q* 44, 469

Ausenda, Giorgio, 'Current Issues and Future Directions in the Study of the Early Anglo-Saxon Period', *The Anglo-Saxons*, ed. Hines, pp. 411–50

Ausenda, Giorgio, ed., *After Empire: Towards an Ethnology of Europe's Barbarians* (Woodbridge, 1995)

Banham, Debby, Carl T. Berkhout, Carole P. Biggam, Mark Blackburn, Simon Keynes and Alexander Rumble, 'Bibliography for 1996', *ASE* 26, 265–315

Bankert, Dabney Anderson, Jessica Wegmann and Charles D. Wright, *Ambrose in Anglo-Saxon England, with Pseudo-Ambrose and Ambrosiaster*, OEN Subsidia 25 (Kalamazoo, MI)

Berkhout, Carl T., 'Old English Bibliography 1996', *OEN* 30.4, 3–32

Bernstein, Melissa J., 'An Introduction to the Internet for Anglo-Saxonists, Part 2: Pedagogical and Scholarly Highlights', *OEN* 31.1, 22–7

Birrell, T. A., 'The Circle of John Gage (1786–1842), Director of the Society of Antiquaries, and the Bibliography of Medievalism', *Antiquaries, Book Collectors and the Circles of Learning*, ed. Robin Myers and Michael Harris (Winchester and New Castle, DE, 1996), pp. 71–82

Bjork, Robert E., 'Nineteenth-Century Scandinavia and the Birth of Anglo-Saxon Studies', *Anglo-Saxonism*, ed. Frantzen and Niles, pp. 111–32

Cannon, John, ed., *The Oxford Companion to British History* (Oxford) [includes numerous short entries on Anglo-Saxon subjects]

Carley, James P., and Colin G. C. Tite, ed., *Books and Collectors 1200–1700: Essays presented to Andrew Watson*, Brit. Lib. Stud. in the Hist. of the Book (London)

Carruthers, Leo, *L'Anglais médiéval* (Turnhout, 1996)

Cessford, C., 'Northern England and the Gododdin Poem', *NH* 33, 218–22

Clement, Richard W., 'The Beginnings of Printing in Anglo-Saxon', *Papers of the Bibliographical Soc. of Amer.* 91, 192–244

Damico, Helen, '"My Professor of Anglo-Saxon Was Frederick Klaeber": Minnesota and Beyond', *The Preservation and Transmission of Anglo-Saxon Culture*, ed. Szarmach and Rosenthal, pp. 73–98

Dekker, Kees, 'Jan van Vliet (1620–1666) and the Study of Old English in the Low Countries', *The Middle Ages after the Middle Ages in the English-Speaking World*, ed. Marie-Françoise Alamichel and Derek Brewer (Cambridge), pp. 27–42

Farrant, John H., 'John Collingwood Bruce and the Bayeux Tapestry', *AAe* 5th ser. 25, 109–13

Fleming, Robin, 'Henry Adams and the Anglo-Saxons', *The Preservation and Transmission of Anglo-Saxon Culture*, ed. Szarmach and Rosenthal, pp. 13–36

Frank, Roberta, 'The Unbearable Lightness of Being a Philologist', *JEGP* 96, 486–513

Frantzen, Allen J., 'Bede and Bawdy Bale: Gregory the Great, Angels, and the "Angli"', *Anglo-Saxonism*, ed. Frantzen and Niles, pp. 17–39

Frantzen, Allen J., and John D. Niles, 'Introduction: Anglo-Saxonism and Medievalism', *Anglo-Saxonism*, ed. Frantzen and Niles, pp. 1–14

Frantzen, Allen J., and John D. Niles, ed., *Anglo-Saxonism and the Construction of Social Identity* (Gainesville, FL)

Gameson, Richard, *Saint Augustine of Canterbury* (Canterbury) [exhibition catalogue]

The Study of the Bayeux Tapestry (Woodbridge)

Giménez Bon, Margarita, and Vickie Olsen, ed., *SELIM 1996: Proceedings of the Ninth International Conference of the Spanish Society for Medieval English Language and Literature* (Zaragoza)

Goblirsch, Kurt Gustav, Martha Berryman Mayou and Marvin Taylor, ed., *Germanic Studies in Honor of Anatoly Liberman* (Odense) [=*North-Western European Lang. Evolution* 31–2]

Godden, Malcolm, *et al.*, '*Fontes Anglo-Saxonici*: a Register of Written Sources Used by Authors in Anglo-Saxon England. Twelfth Progress Report', *OEN* 30.3, 11–13

Goffart, Walter, 'The First Venture into "Medieval Geography": Lambarde's Map of the Saxon Heptarchy (1568)', *Alfred the Wise*, ed. Roberts *et al.*, pp. 53–60

Graham, Timothy C., and Paul E. Szarmach, '1997 NEH Summer Seminar at the Parker Library, Corpus Christi College, Cambridge', *OEN* 31.1, 20–1

Grocock, Christopher, '"Squaring the Circle": Bede Meets the Tourists', *Med. Life* 4 (1996), 8–10

Hagedorn, Suzanne C., 'Received Wisdom: the Reception History of Alfred's Preface to the *Pastoral Care*', *Anglo-Saxonism*, ed. Frantzen and Niles, pp. 86–107

Hall, J. R., 'Mid-Nineteenth-Century American Anglo-Saxonism: the Question of Language', *Anglo-Saxonism*, ed. Frantzen and Niles, pp. 133–56

'Nineteenth-Century America and the Study of the Anglo-Saxon Language: an Introduction', *The Preservation and Transmission of Anglo-Saxon Culture*, ed. Szarmach and Rosenthal, pp. 37–71

Hawkes, Jane, 'Symbolic Lives: the Visual Evidence', *The Anglo-Saxons*, ed. Hines, pp. 311–44

Higley, Sarah, 'The Four Questions: the ENGLISC List in Action', *OEN* 30.3, 14–17

Hiltunen, Risto, 'An Aspect of "ESP" in a Historical Perspective: the Case of Anglo-Saxon Law', *To Explain the Present*, ed. Nevalainen and Kahlas-Tarkka, pp. 51–62

'Medieval English Studies in Finland and Japan', *Med. Eng. Stud. Newsletter* 37, 3–5

Hines, John, 'Religion: the Limits of Knowledge', *The Anglo-Saxons*, ed. Hines, pp. 375–410

Hines, John, ed., *The Anglo-Saxons from the Migration Period to the Eighth Century: an Ethnographic Perspective* (Woodbridge)

Howlett, David, *British Books in Biblical Style* (Dublin)

Ito, Eiko, 'Hideo Yamaguchi 1907–1997', *Med. Eng. Stud. Newsletter* 37, 1–3

Jackson, Peter, '*Fontes Anglo-Saxonici*, 1993–97: Prospecting and Retrospecting', *Med. Eng. Stud. Newsletter* 37, 31–7

Jensen, S. R., *Beowulf and the Monsters* (Sydney)

Jin, Koichi, *Aspects of English Syntax and Style* (Tokyo)

Karkov, Catherine, and Robert Farrell, ed., *Studies in Insular Art and Archaeology*, Amer. Early Med. Stud. 1 (Oxford, OH, 1991)

Kelemen, Erick, 'A Reexamination of the Date of *A Testimonie of Antiquitie*, one of the First Books Printed in Anglo-Saxon Types', *ANQ* 10.4, 3–10

Kendrick, Laura, 'The American Middle Ages: Eighteenth-Century Saxonist Myth-Making', *The Middle Ages after the Middle Ages in the English-Speaking World*, ed. Marie-Françoise Alamichel and Derek Brewer (Cambridge), pp. 121–36

Klein, Bernhard, 'Constructing the Space of the Nation: Geography, Maps, and the Discovery of Britain in the Early Modern Period', *Jnl for the Stud. of Brit. Culture* 4, 111–29

Kristensson, Gillis, 'In Memoriam Professor Olof Arngart', *ES* 78, 385

Lendinara, Patrizia, 'ISAS 1997', *Med. Eng. Stud. Newsletter* 37, 44

Looijenga, Tineke, and Quak, Arend, ed., *Frisian Runes and Neighbouring Traditions. Proceedings of the First International Symposium on Frisian Runes at the Fries Museum, Leeuwarden 26–29 January 1994* [=*Amsterdamer Beiträge zur älteren Germanistik* 45 (1996)]

McAllister, Barbara, 'The Jarrow Lectures', *Med. Eng. Stud. Newsletter* 37, 29–30

Mills, A. D., 'John McNeal Dodgson: a Personal Memoir', *Names, Places and People*, ed. Rumble and Mills, pp. xiv–xxv

Nevalainen, Terttu, and Leena Kahlas-Tarkka, ed., *To Explain the Present: Studies in the Changing English Language in Honour of Matti Rissanen*, Mémoires de la Société Néophilologique de Helsinki 52 (Helsinki)

Niles, John D., 'Appropriations: a Concept of Culture', *Anglo-Saxonism*, ed. Frantzen and Niles, pp. 202–28

Ogawa, Hiroshi, 'Tamotsu Matsunami 1924–1995', *Med. Eng. Stud. Newsletter* 36, 3–6

Perrello, Tony, 'Anglo-Saxon Elements of the Gloucester Sub-Plot in *King Lear*', *ELN* 35.1, 10–16

Phillips, Andrew, *The Rebirth of England and English: the Vision of William Barnes* (Hockwold-cum-Wilton, Norf., 1996)

Pollington, Stephen, *First Steps in Old English* (Hockwold-cum-Wilton, Norf.)

Pulsiano, Phillip, 'Research in Progress', *OEN* 30.4, 33–40

Richmond, Velma Bourgeois, 'Historical Novels to Teach Anglo-Saxonism', *Anglo-Saxonism*, ed. Frantzen and Niles, pp. 173–201

Rissanen, Matti, 'Tauno F. Mustanoja: In Memoriam', *NM* 98, 97–8

Roberts, Jane, 'In Memoriam: Lynne Mary Grundy (1957–1997)', *OEN* 31.1, 10

Roberts, Jane, and Janet L. Nelson, with Malcolm Godden, ed., *Alfred the Wise: Studies in Honour of Janet Bately on the Occasion of her Sixty-Fifth Birthday* (Cambridge)

Roberts, Marion E., and Everett U. Crosby, *The Seventeenth-Century Restoration: Sir William Dugdale & his Circle* (Charlottesville, VA, 1993)

Robinson, Fred C, '*In Memoriam*: John Collins Pope (1904–1997)', *OEN* 30.3, 8–9

'Introduction: Transmitting What is Preserved. How Are We Doing?', *The Preservation and Transmission of Anglo-Saxon Culture*, ed. Szarmach and Rosenthal, pp. 1–10

'John Collins Pope 1904–1997', *Med. Eng. Stud. Newsletter* 36, 1–2

Robinson, P. R., and Rivkah Zim, ed., *Of the Making of Books: Medieval Manuscripts, their Scribes and Readers: Essays presented to M. B. Parkes* (Aldershot)

Rumble, Alexander R., 'Bibliography of the Writings of John McNeal Dodgson', *Names, Places and People*, ed. Rumble and Mills, pp. xxvi–xxx

Rumble, Alexander R., and A. D. Mills, ed., *Names, Places and People: an Onomastic Miscellany in Memory of John McNeal Dodgson* (Stamford)

Sato, Suji, ed., *Back to the Manuscripts: Papers from the Symposium 'The Integrated Approach to Manuscript Studies: a New Horizon', Tokyo, December 1992*, Centre for Med. Eng. Stud., Tokyo, Occasional Paper 1 (Tokyo)

Schadla-Hall, Tim, 'Anglo-Saxon Attitudes: Introductory Remarks to the Conference', *Anglo-Saxon Landscapes in the East Midlands*, ed. Bourne, pp. xv–xvi

Schichler, Robert L., ed., 'Abstracts of Papers in Anglo-Saxon Studies', *OEN* 30.3, A1–A73

Schipper, William, 'ANSAXNET Revival', *OEN* 30.3, 10

Shirai, Naoko, 'Traditions of Beheading: a Comparative Study of Classical Irish and Anglo-Saxon Culture', *Medieval Heritage: Essays in Honour of Tadahiro Ikegami*, ed. Masahiko Kanno *et al.* (Tokyo) pp. 315–28

Spinage, Clive Alfred, *King Alfred: Myths and Mysteries* (Felinfach)

Stanley, E. G., 'The Early Middle Ages = The Dark Ages = The Heroic Age of England and in English', *The Middle Ages after the Middle Ages in the English-Speaking World*, ed. Marie-Françoise Alamichel and Derek Brewer (Cambridge), pp. 43–77

Szarmach, Paul E., ed., *Old English Newsletter* 29.1–4 (Kalamazoo, MI, 1995–6)

Szarmach, Paul, and Joel T. Rosenthal, ed., *The Preservation and Transmission of Anglo-Saxon Culture: Selected Papers from the 1991 Meeting of the International Society of Anglo-Saxonists*, Stud. in Med. Culture 40 (Kalamazoo, MI)

Toswell, M. J., 'Auden and Anglo-Saxon', *Med. Eng. Stud. Newsletter* 37, 21–8

Trahern, Joseph B., Jr, ed., 'The Year's Work in Old English Studies 1994', *OEN* 29.2 (1997 for 1996), 3–165

Turville-Petre, Thorlac, 'Medieval English Studies at the University of Nottingham', *Med. Eng. Stud. Newsletter* 36, 15–17

van der Wurff, Wim, 'Old English at Leiden', *OEN* 31.1, 11

VanHoosier-Carey, Gregory A., 'Byrhtnoth in Dixie: the Emergence of Anglo-Saxon Studies in the Postbellum South', *Anglo-Saxonism*, ed. Frantzen and Niles, pp. 157–72

Wilcox, Jonathan, ed., *Old English Newsletter* 30.1 and 3–4 (Kalamazoo, MI, 1996–7)

Wormald, Patrick, 'The Lambarde Problem: Eighty Years On', *Alfred the Wise*, ed. Roberts *et al.*, pp. 237–75

Wright, C. J., ed., *Sir Robert Cotton as Collector: Essays on an Early Stuart Courtier and his Legacy* (London)

Zeeman, Kenneth L., 'Grappling with Grendel, or What We Did When the Censors Came', *Eng. Jnl* 86.2, 46–9

2. OLD ENGLISH LANGUAGE

a. Lexicon and glosses

Bammesberger, Alfred, 'Die Vorform vom altenglisch *hærfest*', *Anglia* 115, 223–30

Biggam, C. P., *Blue in Old English: an Interdisciplinary Semantic Study*, Costerus ns 110 (Amsterdam and Atlanta, GA)

Breeze, Andrew, 'A Celtic Etymology for Hiberno-English *callow* "river meadow"', *Éigse* 30, 158–60

    'A Celtic Etymology for Old English *deor* "brave"', *Alfred the Wise*, ed. Roberts *et al.*, pp. 1–4

    'Old English *wann* "dark; pallid": Welsh *gwann* "weak; sad, gloomy"', *ANQ* 10.4, 10–13

Coates, Richard, see sect. 8

Conde Silvestre, Juan Camilo, 'Anglo-Saxon Monastic Sign Language in a Semiotic Context', *SELIM 1996*, ed. Giménez Bon and Olsen, pp. 49–61

Cooke, Jessica, 'Problems of Method in Early English Lexicography: the Case of the Harley Glossary', *NM* 98, 241–51

Dalton-Puffer, Christiane, 'On the Histories of De-Verbal Adjectives in Middle English', *Studia Anglica Posnaniensia* 31, 41–55

de la Cruz Cabanillas, Isabel, 'Word Loss in Old and Middle English: Some Possible Reasons', *SELIM 1996*, ed. Giménez Bon and Olsen, pp. 62–71

Discenza, Nicole Guenther, see sect. 3c [*cræft*]

Fischer, Andreas, 'Dream Theory and Dream Lexis in the Middle Ages', *Anglistentag 1995 Greifswald: Proceedings*, ed. Jürgen Klein and Dirk Vanderbeke (Tübingen, 1996), pp. 245–57

   'The Hatton MS of the West Saxon Gospels: the Preservation and Transmission of Old English', *The Preservation and Transmission of Anglo-Saxon Culture*, ed. Szarmach and Rosenthal, pp. 353–67

Frank, Roberta, 'Old English *orc* "cup, goblet": a Latin Loanword with Attitude', *Alfred the Wise*, ed. Roberts *et al.*, pp. 15–24

Green, D. H., 'From Germania to Europe: the Evidence of Language and History', *MLR* 92, pp. xxix–xxxviii

Grundy, Lynne, '*Ece*: "eternal" in Ælfric', *Alfred the Wise*, ed. Roberts *et al.*, pp. 61–4

Grundy, Lynne, and Jane Roberts, see sect. 8

Gwara, Scott, see sect. 5

Healey, Antonette diPaolo, 'Dictionary of Old English', *Dictionaries of Medieval Germanic Languages*, ed. K. H. van Dalen-Oskam *et al.* (Turnhout), pp. 55–62

   'Words, Story, History: the Mapping of Meaning and Toronto's *Dictionary of Old English*', *To Explain the Present*, ed. Nevalainen and Kahlas-Tarkka, pp. 35–49

Holland, Joan, 'Dictionary of Old English: 1997 Progress Report', *OEN* 31.1, 12–15

Kay, Christian, and Irené Wotherspoon, 'Historical Thesaurus of English', *Dictionaries of Medieval Germanic Languages*, ed. K. H. van Dalen-Oskam *et al.* (Turnhout), pp. 42–54

Kitson, Peter, 'Old English Bird-Names (1)', *ES* 78, 481–505

   '*Worth(y)*', *Studia Anglica Posnaniensia* 31, 105–15

Kleinman, Scott, 'Iron-Clad Evidence in Early Medieval Dialectology: Old English *isern*, *isen*, and *iren*', *NM* 98, 371–90

Liberman, Anatoly, 'Etymological Studies VII. A Small Animal Farm', *General Ling.* 35 (1997 for 1995), 97–130

   'Ten Scandinavian and North English Etymologies', *Alvíssmál* 6 (1996), 63–98, and 7, 101–4

Lutz, Angelika, see sect. 2b

Mancho-Barés, Guzmán, 'Norse Vocabulary in the *Peterborough Chronicle*. A Case-Study of Historical Sociolinguistics', *SELIM* 1996, ed. Giménez Bon and Olsen, pp. 174–87

Moskowich-Spiegel Fandiño, Isabel, 'Language Contact and Language Change: the Danes in England', *Revista Alicantina de Estudios Ingleses* 8 (1995), 139–53

Mucciante, Luisa, *Contributo allo studio dei latinismi nell'inglese antico*, Quaderni della Sezione di glottologia e linguistica (Chieti), Supplementi 2 (Alessandria, 1995) [repr. of 1989 ed.]

Nagucka, Ruta, 'Glossal Translation in the *Lindisfarne Gospel according to Saint Matthew*', *Studia Anglica Posnaniensia* 31, 179–201

Nevanlinna, Saara, 'Lexical Variation in the Old English Gospel Manuscripts and a Note on Continuation', *To Explain the Present*, ed. Nevalainen and Kahlas-Tarkka, pp. 135–48

Núñez Pertejo, Paloma, 'On the Role of the Auxiliary *weorðan* in O.E.', *SELIM 1996*, ed. Giménez Bon and Olsen, pp. 207–14

Parkes, M. B., '*Rædan, areccan, smeagan*: How the Anglo-Saxons Read', *ASE* 26, 1–22

Platzer, Hans, 'The Temporary Merger of OE *scitan* and *scyttan*, or: a Case of Harmless Homophony', *Studia Anglica Posnaniensia* 30 (1996), 69–82

Polomé, Edgar, 'A Few Notes on the Indo-European Religious Vocabulary', *Germanic Studies*, ed. Goblirsch *et al.*, pp. 331–6

Rissanen, Matti, 'In Search of *happiness*: *felicitas* and *beatitudo* in Early English Boethius Translations', *Studia Anglica Posnaniensia* 31, 237–48

Roberts, Jane, and Christian Kay, 'A Thesaurus of Old English', *Dictionaries of Medieval Germanic Languages*, ed. K. H. van Dalen-Oskam *et al.* (Turnhout), pp. 31–40

Sandred, Karl Inge, see sect. 8

Sauer, Hans, 'On the Analysis and Structure of Old and Middle English Plant Names', *A History of English* (Seoul), pp. 133–62

Smith, J. B., 'Vernacular Names of Plants: Crosswort and Weymouth Pine', *Notes & Queries for Somerset and Dorset* 34 (1996), 69–72

Sonderegger, Stefan, 'Language and Culture in the Germanic-Speaking World: the History of the Written Word', *Kungl. Humanistiska Vetenskaps-Samfundet i Uppsala: Årsbok 1996*, pp. 57–89

Stiles, Patrick V., see sect. 8

Venneman, Theo, 'German *Eisvogel*, Greek *halkyón*, English *alder*. A Study in Old European Etymology', *Interdisciplinary Jnl for Germanic Ling. and Semiotic Analysis* 1 (1996), 113–45

'Zur Etymologie der Sippe von engl. *knife*, franz. *canif*, bask. *kanibet*', *Germanic Studies*, ed. Goblirsch *et al.*, pp. 443–62

Wagner, Norbert, 'Ahd. *leffur*. *lefs*: ae. *lippa*', *Historische Sprachforschung* 110, 161–5

Watts, Victor, 'Middle English *utlete*', *Names, Places and People*, ed. Rumble and Mills, pp. 378–82

b. Syntax, phonology and other aspects

Allen, Cynthia L., 'The Origins of the "Group Genitive" in English', *TPS* 95, 111–31

Anderson, John M., 'On Variability in Old English Syntax, and Some Consequences Thereof', *TPS* 95, 9–40

'Preliminaries to a History of Sentential Subjects in English', *Studia Anglica Posnaniensia* 31, 21–8

Arnold, Mark D., 'Double Object Constructions and Indirect Object Passives:

Problems Posed by History', *The Proceedings of the Fifteenth West Coast Conference on Formal Linguistics*, ed. Brian Agbayani and Sze-Wing Tang (Stanford, CA), pp. 1–15

Bammesberger, Alfred, 'Frisian and Anglo-Saxon Runes: from the Linguistic Angle', *Frisian Runes*, ed. Looijenga and Quak, pp. 15–23

Barrack, Charles M., 'PGmc. *-VC,iV*: a Response to Murray', *Interdisciplinary Jnl for Germanic Ling. and Semiotic Analysis* 2, 117–78

Bredehoft, Thomas A., 'First-Person Inscriptions and Literacy in Anglo-Saxon England', *ASSAH* 9 (1996), 103–10

Colman, Fran, 'Old English <ie>: That Is (,) an Orthographic Problem (*noch einmal*)', *Studia Anglica Posnaniensia* 31, 29–39

d'Alquen, Richard, 'Non-Reduplication in Northwest Germanic: the Problem That Won't Go Away', *Germanic Studies*, ed. Goblirsch *et al.*, pp. 69–91

Díaz Vera, Javier E., 'The Dynamics of Old English Phonemes: a Dependency Approach', *SELIM 1996*, ed. Giménez Bon and Olsen, pp. 72–8

Fischer, Olga, 'On the Status of Grammaticalisation and the Diachronic Dimension in Explanation', *TPS* 95, 149–87

Fontana, Josep M., 'On the Integration of Second Position Phenomena', *Parameters of Morphosyntactic Change*, ed. Ans van Kemenade and Nigel Vincent (Cambridge), pp. 207–49

Hiyama, Susumu, 'Approaches to Word Order in Old English', *Kagoshima Stud. in Eng. Lang. and Lit.* 28, 87–98

'Cross-Tabulation in the Old English Syntactical Database', *Kagoshima Stud. in Eng. Lang. and Lit.* 28, 99–111

Hogg, Richard M., 'Some Remarks on Case Marking in Old English', *TPS* 95, 95–109

Howe, Stephen, *The Personal Pronouns in the Germanic Languages*, Studia Linguistica Germanica 43 (Berlin and New York, 1996)

Howlett, David, see sect. 4 [glossary]

Kastovsky, Dieter, 'Morphological Classification in English Historical Linguistics: the Interplay of Diachrony, Synchrony and Morphological Theory', *To Explain the Present*, ed. Nevalainen and Kahlas-Tarkka, pp. 63–75

'Morphological Reclassification: the Morphological and Morphophonemic Restructuring of the Weak Verbs in Old and Middle English', *Anglistentag 1995 Greifswald: Proceedings*, ed. Jürgen Klein and Dirk Vanderbeke (Tübingen, 1996), pp. 273–84

Kilpiö, Matti, 'Participial Adjectives with Anaphoric Reference of the Type *The Said, The (A)forementioned* from Old to Early Modern English: the Evidence of the Helsinki Corpus', *To Explain the Present*, ed. Nevalainen and Kahlas-Tarkka, pp. 77–100

Kim, Hyeree, 'Subcategorization Inheritance in Old English P–V Compounds', *Jnl of Ling.* 33, 39–66

Kim, Suksan, 'On Nonlocal Compensatory Lengthening', *Theoretical Ling.* 23, 1–19

Kiparsky, Paul, 'The Rise of Positional Licensing', *Parameters of Morphosyntactic Change*, ed. Ans van Kemenade and Nigel Vincent (Cambridge), pp. 460–94

Kishida, Takayuki, 'On the Post-Prepositional Case in *The Parker Chronicle*', *Ann.*

Collection of Essays and Stud. (Faculty of Letters, Gakushuin Univ.) 44, 17–35 [in Japanese]

Kitson, Peter R., 'The Dialect Position of the Old English Orosius', *Studia Anglica Posnaniensia* 30 (1996), 3–35

Koopman, Willem F., 'Another Look at Clitics in Old English', *TPS* 95, 73–93

Kortlandt, Frederik, 'How Old Is the English Glottal Stop?', *Germanic Studies*, ed. Goblirsch *et al.*, pp. 175–9

Kristensson, Gillis, 'The Voicing of Initial Fricatives Revisited', *Names, Places and People*, ed. Rumble and Mills, pp. 186–94

Kroch, Anthony, 'Comments on "Syntax Shindig" Papers', *TPS* 95, 133–47

Kroch, Anthony, and Ann Taylor, 'Verb Movement in Old and Middle English: Dialect Variation and Language Contact', *Parameters of Morphosyntactic Change*, ed. Ans van Kemenade and Nigel Vincent (Cambridge), pp. 297–325

Krygier, Marcin, *The Disintegration of the English Strong Verb System* (Frankfurt am Main, 1994)

'Theory Recycling: the Case of *i*-Umlaut', *Studia Anglica Posnaniensia* 31, 117–21

Kubouchi, Tadao, see sect. 5

Lass, Roger, *Historical Linguistics and Language Change*, Cambridge Stud. in Ling. 81 (Cambridge)

'Why *House* is an Old English "Masculine *A*-stem"', *To Explain the Present*, ed. Nevalainen and Kahlas-Tarkka, pp. 101–9

Looijenga, Tineke, see sect. 9*i* [runes]

Lutz, Angelika, 'Lautwandel bei Wörtern mit imitatorischem oder lautsymbolischem Charakter in den germanischen Sprachen', *Germanic Studies*, ed. Goblirsch *et al.*, pp. 213–28

'Sound Change, Word Formation and the Lexicon: the History of the English Prefix Verbs', *ES* 78, 258–90

Millar, Robert McColl, 'Some Patterns in the Non-Historical Demonstrative Usage of the *Peterborough Chronicle* Annals 1070–1121', *N&Q* 44, 161–4

Mitchell, Bruce, 'Unexpressed Principal Clauses in Old English', *To Explain the Present*, ed. Navalainen and Kahlas-Tarkka, pp. 125–34

see also sect. 5

Nicolaisen, W. F. H., 'Periodization in the History of English', *General Ling.* 35 (1997 for 1995), 157–76

Nielsen, Hans F., 'Developments in Frisian Runology: a Discussion of Düwel & Tempel's Runic Corpus from 1970', *Frisian Runes*, ed. Looijenga and Quak, pp. 123–30

Ogura, Michiko, 'Three Features of Old English Verbs of Motion', *ES* 78, 316–29

'The Variability of OE *Faran* and *Feran*', *To Explain the Present*, ed. Nevalainen and Kahlas-Tarkka, pp. 149–62

Page, R. I., 'On the Baffling Nature of Frisian Runes', *Frisian Runes*, ed. Looijenga and Quak, pp. 131–50

Parsons, David, 'The Origins and Chronology of the "Anglo-Frisian" Additional Runes', *Frisian Runes*, ed. Looijenga and Quak, pp. 151–70

Ritt, Nikolaus, 'Now You See It, Now You Don't: Middle English Lengthening in Closed Syllables', *Studia Anglica Posnaniensia* 31, 249–70

Roberts, Ian, 'Directionality and Word Order Change in the History of English', *Parameters of Morphosyntactic Change*, ed. Ans van Kemenade and Nigel Vincent (Cambridge), pp. 397–426

'Remarks on the Old English C-System and the Diachrony of V2', *Language Change and Generative Grammar*, ed. Ellen Brandner and Gisella Ferraresi (Opladen, 1996), pp. 154–67

Romano Mozo, Manuela, 'Some Examples of English Grammaticalization Processes from a Self-Regulating Point of View', *SELIM 1996*, ed. Giménez Bon and Olsen, pp. 296–303

Sánchez Miret, Fernando, Antonios Koliadis and Wolfgang U. Dressler, 'Connectionism vs. Rules in Diachronic Morphology', *Folia Linguistica Historica* 18, 149–82

Saorin Iborra, Ania, 'On the Personal Pronouns in the Vespasian Psalter: Peculiarities of the Language of the Mercian Gloss', *SELIM 1996*, ed. Giménez Bon and Olsen, pp. 315–25

Seppänen, Aimo, and Gunnar Bergh, 'Subject Extraction in English: Some Problems of Interpretation', *Studia Anglica Posnaniensia* 30 (1996), 45–67

Shields, Kenneth, 'Typological Plausibility and the Deictic Origin of the Germanic Dental Preterite', *Leuvense Bijdragen* 86, 125–9

Stévanovitch, Colette, *Manuel d'histoire de la langue anglaise des origines à nos jours* (Paris)

van Gelderen, Elly, 'Inflection and Movement in Old English', *German: Syntactic Problems–Problematic Syntax*, ed. Werner Abraham and van Gelderen (Tübingen), pp. 71–82

van Kemenade, Ans, 'Negative-Initial Sentences in Old and Middle English', *Studia Anglica Posnaniensia* 31, 91–104

'V2 and Embedded Topicalization in Old and Middle English', *Parameters of Morphosyntactic Change*, ed. Ans van Kemenade and Nigel Vincent (Cambridge), pp. 326–52

Vezzosi, Letizia, 'Il passivo in anglosassone', *Quaderni della Sezione di glottologia e linguistica* (Chieti) 8 (1996), 113–43

Warner, Anthony R., 'Extending the Paradigm: an Interpretation of the Historical Development of Auxiliary Sequences in English', *ES* 78, 162–89

'The Structure of Parametric Change, and V-Movement in the History of English', *Parameters of Morphosyntactic Change*, ed. Ans van Kemenade and Nigel Vincent (Cambridge), pp. 380–93

Wedel, Alfred R., 'Verbal Prefixation and the "Complexive" Aspect in Germanic', *NM* 98, 321–32

Wełna, Jerzy, *English Historical Morphology* (Warsaw, 1996)

Wetzel, Claus-Dieter, 'Philologisch-sprachgeschichtliche Anmerkungen zu altenglisch *frempe* "fremd" und seinen Derivaten', *Fremdheit und Reisen im Mittelalter*, ed. Karl-Heinz Spiess and Irene Hansch (Stuttgart), pp. 7–16

3. OLD ENGLISH LITERATURE

a. General

Anderson, Earl R., 'The Seasons of the Year in Old English', *ASE* 26, 231–63

Baker, Peter S., 'Old English and Computing: a Guided Tour', *Reading Old English Texts*, ed. O'Keeffe, pp. 192–215

Donoghue, Daniel, 'Language Matters', *Reading Old English Texts*, ed. O'Keeffe, pp. 59–78

Dyas, Dee, *Images of Faith in English Literature 700–1500: an Introduction* (London and New York)

Howe, Nicholas, 'Historicist Approaches', *Reading Old English Texts*, ed. O'Keeffe, pp. 79–100

Lapidge, Michael, 'The Comparative Approach', *Reading Old English Texts*, ed. O' Keeffe, pp. 20–38

Lees, Clare A., 'At a Crossroads: Old English and Feminist Criticism', *Reading Old English Texts*, ed. O'Keeffe, pp. 146–69

  'Engendering Religious Desire: Sex, Knowledge, and Christian Identity in Anglo-Saxon England', *Jnl of Med. and Early Mod. Stud.* 27, 17–45

North, Richard, *Heathen Gods in Old English Literature*, CSASE 22 (Cambridge)

O'Keeffe, Katherine O'Brien, ed., *Reading Old English Texts* (Cambridge)

Page, R. I., see sect. 5

Pasternack, Carol Braun, 'Post-Structuralist Theories: the Subject and the Text', *Reading Old English Texts*, ed. O'Keeffe, pp. 170–91

Pearsall, Derek, 'Language and Literature', *The Oxford Illustrated History of Medieval England*, ed. Nigel Saul (Oxford and New York), pp. 245–76

Raw, Barbara C., see sect. 5

Rissanen, Matti, 'Genres, Texts and Corpora in the Study of Medieval English', *Anglistentag 1995 Greifswald: Proceedings*, ed. Jürgen Klein and Dirk Vanderbeke (Tübingen, 1996), pp. 229–42

Scragg, D. G., 'Source Study', *Reading Old English Texts*, ed. O'Keeffe, pp. 39–58

Szarmach, Paul E., 'The Recovery of Texts', *Reading Old English Texts*, ed. O'Keeffe, pp. 124–45

Tilling, Philip, 'The Literature of Pre-Renaissance England', *Introducing Literary Studies*, ed. Richard Bradford (London and New York, 1996), pp. 61–77

Treharne, Elaine M., 'Old English Literature [1994]', *Year's Work in Eng. Stud.* 75, 91–123

b. Poetry

i. General

Faulkes, Anthony, *Poetical Inspiration in Old Norse and Old English Poetry*, Dorothea Coke Memorial Lecture 1997 (London)

Fulk, Robert D., 'Rhetoric, Form, and Linguistic Structure in Early Germanic Verse: Toward a Synthesis', *Interdisciplinary Jnl for Germanic Ling. and Semiotic Analysis* 1 (1996), 63–88

Head, Pauline E., *Representation and Design: Tracing a Hermeneutics of Old English Poetry* (Albany, NY)

Huisman, Rosemary, 'Subjectivity/Orality: How Relevant Are Modern Literary Theories to the Study of Old English Poetry? What Light Can the Study of Old English Poetry Cast on Modern Literary Theory?', *The Preservation and Transmission of Anglo-Saxon Culture*, ed. Szarmach and Rosenthal, pp. 313–31

Magennis, Hugh, 'Food, Drink and Feast in Old English Poetry', *SELIM 1996*, ed. Giménez Bon and Olsen, pp. 154–73

McKie, Michael, 'The Origins and Early Development of Rhyme in English Verse', *MLR* 92, 817–31

Minkova, Donka, 'The Credibility of Pseudo-Alfred: Prosodic Insights in Post-Conquest Mongrel Meter', *MP* 94, 427–54

Momma, H., *The Composition of Old English Poetry*, CSASE 20 (Cambridge)

Orchard, Andy, 'Oral Tradition', *Reading Old English Texts*, ed. O'Keeffe, pp. 101–23

Rodrigues, Louis J., trans., *An Anglo-Saxon Verse Miscellany* (Felinfach)

Schaefer, Ursula, '*Ceteris Imparibus*: Orality/Literacy and the Establishment of Anglo-Saxon Literate Culture', *The Preservation and Transmission of Anglo-Saxon Culture*, ed. Szarmach and Rosenthal, pp. 287–311

Stanley, E. G., 'Old English Poetry: "Out of the People's Warm Mouth"?', *N&Q* 44, 6–21

Thormann, Janet, 'The *Anglo-Saxon Chronicle* Poems and the Making of the English Nation', *Anglo-Saxonism*, ed. Frantzen and Niles, pp. 60–85

Wehlau, Ruth, '*The Riddle of Creation': Metaphor Structures in Old English Poetry*, Stud. in the Humanities 24 (New York)

ii. 'Beowulf'

Aguirre, Manuel, 'The Phasal Structure of *Beowulf*', *SELIM 1996*, ed. Giménez Bon and Olsen, pp. 8–16

Andersson, Theodore M., 'Sources and Analogues', *A Beowulf Handbook*, ed. Bjork and Niles, pp. 125–48

Betancourt, Antonio Luis, trans., *Beowulf, Prince of Geatland* (Colorado Springs, CO)

Bjork, Robert E., 'Digressions and Episodes', *A Beowulf Handbook*, ed. Bjork and Niles, pp. 193–212

Bjork, Robert E., and John D. Niles, ed., *A Beowulf Handbook* (Lincoln, NE)

Bjork, Robert E., and Anita Obermeier, 'Date, Provenance, Author, Audiences', *A Beowulf Handbook*, ed. Bjork and Niles, pp. 13–34

Bridle, Edward, see sect. 3*biii*

Cain, Christopher M., '*Beowulf*, the Old Testament, and the *Regula Fidei*', *Renascence* 49, 227–40

Carroll, Joseph, 'The Prose *Edda*, the *Heimskringla*, and *Beowulf*: Mythical, Legendary, and Historical Dialogues', *In Geardagum* 18, 15–38

Chase, Colin, ed., *The Dating of Beowulf*, Toronto OE Ser. 6 (Toronto, Buffalo and London) [reprint of 1981 edition, with afterword by Nicholas Howe, 'The Uses of Uncertainty: on the Dating of Beowulf', pp. 213–22]

Bibliography for 1997

Clark, George, 'The Hero and the Theme', *A Beowulf Handbook*, ed. Bjork and Niles, pp. 271–90

Cronan, Dennis, 'The Origin of Ancient Strife in *Beowulf*', *Germanic Studies*, ed. Goblirsch *et al.*, pp. 57–68

Evans, Stephen S., *The Heroic Poetry of Dark-Age Britain: an Introduction to its Dating, Composition, and Use as a Historical Source* (Lanham, MD, New York and London) see also sect. 6

Fulk, R. D., 'Textual Criticism', *A Beowulf Handbook*, ed. Bjork and Niles, pp. 35–53

Getty, Michael, 'Was Finite Verb Placement in Germanic Prosodically Conditioned? Evidence from *Beowulf* and *Heliand*', *JEGP* 96, 155–81

Gould, David, 'Euphemistic Renderings of the Word *druncen* in *Beowulf*', *N&Q* 44, 443–50

Heaney, Seamus, 'The Funeral of Beowulf', *TLS* 19 September, p. 4

'The Last Survivor', *TLS* 14 November, p. 13

Hill, John M., 'Social Milieu', *A Beowulf Handbook*, ed. Bjork and Niles, pp. 255–69

Hills, Catherine M., '*Beowulf* and Archaeology', *A Beowulf Handbook*, ed. Bjork and Niles, pp. 291–310

Hodges, Kenneth, 'Beowulf's Shoulder Pin and *wið earm gesæt*', *ELN* 34.3, 4–10

Irving, Edward B., Jr, 'Christian and Pagan Elements', *A Beowulf Handbook*, ed. Bjork and Niles, pp. 175–92

Jack, George, ed., '*Beowulf*: a Student Edition* (Oxford and New York) [corrected reprint of 1994 edition]

Klaeber, Friedrich, *The Christian Elements in 'Beowulf'*, trans. Paul Battles, OEN Subsidia 24 (Kalamazoo, MI)

Lee, Alvin A., 'Symbolism and Allegory', *A Beowulf Handbook*, ed. Bjork and Niles, pp. 233–54

Lerer, Seth, '*Beowulf* and Contemporary Critical Theory', *A Beowulf Handbook*, ed. Bjork and Niles, pp. 325–39

Louden, Bruce, 'A Narrative Technique in *Beowulf* and Homeric Epic', *Oral Tradition* 11 (1996), 346–62

Mitchell, Bruce, and Fred C. Robinson, 'A Preview of *Beowulf*: an Edition with Relevant Shorter Texts', *Med. Eng. Stud. Newsletter* 36, 19–22

Niles, John D., 'Introduction: *Beowulf*, Truth, and Meaning', *A Beowulf Handbook*, ed. Bjork and Niles, pp. 1–12

'Myth and History', *A Beowulf Handbook*, ed. Bjork and Niles, pp. 213–32

Noro, Toshifumi, 'The Word "weallan" in *Beowulf*', *Philologia* (Mie Univ.) 29, 5–57 [in Japanese]

O'Keeffe, Katherine O'Brien, 'Diction, Variation, the Formula', *A Beowulf Handbook*, ed. Bjork and Niles, pp. 85–104

Olsen, Alexandra Hennessey, 'Gender Roles', *A Beowulf Handbook*, ed. Bjork and Niles, pp. 311–24

Orchard, Andy, 'Unrecoverable Magic', *TLS* 20 June, p. 20 [review of Trevor Eaton's *Beowulf* recording]

Osborn, Marijane, 'Translations, Versions, Illustrations', *A Beowulf Handbook*, ed. Bjork and Niles, pp. 341–72

Prescott, Andrew, 'The Electronic Beowulf and Digital Restoration', *Lit. and Ling. Computing* 12, 185–95

Princi Braccini, Giovanna, 'Termini e scenari della giustizia in antichi testi poetici germanici (*Muspilli, Georgslied, Beowulf*)', *La giustizia nell'alto medioevo (secoli IX–XI) = SettSpol* 44, 1105–95

Reading, Peter, 'From *Beowulf*', *Poetry Wales* 32.3, 9

Richardson, Peter, 'Point of View and Identification in *Beowulf*', *Neophilologus* 81, 289–98

Robinson, Fred C., '*Beowulf* in the Twentieth Century', *PBA* 94, 45–62

'Sigemund's *fæhðe ond fyrena: Beowulf* 879a', *To Explain the Present*, ed. Nevalainen and Kahlas-Tarkka, pp. 200–8

Rose, Gregory F., 'Four Minims and a Quandary: *Beowulf*, 1382a', *Peritia* 11, 171–87

'A Look Back at Kevin S. Kiernan's *Beowulf and the Beowulf Manuscript*. The Kiernan Theory Revisited: *Beowulf* at the Court of Cnut?', *Envoi* 6, 135–45

Schaefer, Ursula, 'Rhetoric and Style', *A Beowulf Handbook*, ed. Bjork and Niles, pp. 105–24

Shippey, Thomas A., 'Structure and Unity', *A Beowulf Handbook*, ed. Bjork and Niles, pp. 149–74

Stockwell, Robert P., and Donka Minkova, 'Old English Metrics and the Phonology of Resolution', *Germanic Studies*, ed. Goblirsch *et al.*, pp. 389–406

'Prosody', *A Beowulf Handbook*, ed. Bjork and Niles, pp. 55–83

Swanton, Michael, ed. and trans., *Beowulf*, rev. ed. (Manchester and New York)

Taylor, Paul Beekman, 'The Dragon's Treasure in *Beowulf*', *NM* 98, 229–40

Thormann, Janet, '*Beowulf* and the Enjoyment of Violence', *Lit. and Psychology* 33.1–2, 65–76

Tolley, Clive, '*Beowulf*'s Scyld Scefing Episode: Some Norse and Finnish Analogues', *Arv* 52 (1996), 7–48

Trask, Richard M., trans., *Beowulf and Judith: Two Heroes* (Lanham, MD, New York and Oxford)

Waugh, Robin, 'Literacy, Royal Power, and King-Poet Relations in Old English and Old Norse Compositions', *Comparative Lit.* 49, 289–315

iii. Other poems

Ai, Low Soon, 'Mental Cultivation in *Guthlac B*', *Neophilologus* 81, 625–36

Alexander, Michael, 'Ezra Pound as Translator', *Translation and Lit.* 6, 23–30 [*Seafarer*]

Barkley, Heather, 'Liturgical Influences on the Anglo-Saxon Charms against Cattle Theft', *N&Q* 44, 450–2

Biggs, Frederick M., 'Deor's Threatened "Blame Poem"', *SP* 94, 297–320

Breeze, Andrew, '*Æpplede gold* in *Juliana, Elene*, and *The Phoenix*', *N&Q* 44, 452–3

Bridle, Edward, '*Ecgtheow's Message*? A Possible Link between *The Husband's Message* and *Beowulf*', *Parergon* 15.1, 1–19

Bueno Alonso, Jorge Luis, 'Anthropology and Old English: Linguistic, Symbolic, and Conceptual Bases of *The Wanderer*', *SELIM 1996*, ed. Giménez Bon and Olsen, pp. 32–41

Champion, Margrét Gunnarsdóttir, 'From Plaint to Praise: Language as Cure in "The Wanderer"', *SN* 69, 187–202

Deane, John F., trans., 'The Dream of the Rood', *Christ, with Urban Fox* (Dublin and Fredonia, NY), pp. 17–22

Dendle, Peter, '*Solomon and Saturn* 44a: ðæs deofles dream', *NM* 98, 391–6

Dockray-Miller, Mary, 'The Feminized Cross of *The Dream of the Rood*', *PQ* 76, 1–18

Dyas, Dee, 'Land and Sea in the Pilgrim Life: the *Seafarer* and the Old English *Exodus*', *ELN* 35.2, 1–9

Fee, Christopher, '*Judith* and the Rhetoric of Heroism in Anglo-Saxon England', *ES* 78, 401–6

Griffith, Mark, ed., *Judith* (Exeter)

Haines, Dorothy, 'Vacancies in Heaven: the Doctrine of Replacement and *Genesis A*', *N&Q* 44, 150–4

Halácsy, Katalin, 'Formulaic Composition *vs.* Creative Talent in Two Anglo-Saxon Poems', *HUSSE Papers 1995*, ed. György Novák (Szeged, 1995), pp. 87–96 [*Brunanburh, Maldon*]

Head, Pauline, 'Voices of Stone: the Multifaceted Speech of *The Dream of the Rood* and the Ruthwell Cross', *Assays* 9 (1996), 57–77

Higham, N. J., see sect. 6 [*Brunanburh*]

Hill, Thomas D., 'The *Liber Eliensis* "Historical Selections" and the Old English *Battle of Maldon*', *JEGP* 96, 1–12

Hoek, Michelle C., 'Anglo-Saxon Innovation and the Use of the Senses in the Old English *Physiologus* Poems', *SN* 69, 1–10

Hollis, Stephanie, 'Old English "Cattle Theft Charms": Manuscript Contexts and Social Uses', *Anglia* 115, 139–64

Hough, Carole, see sect. 3c [*Juliana*]

Irvine, Susan, 'Adam or Christ? A Pronominal Pun in *The Dream of the Rood*', *RES* 48, 433–47

Isaac, G. R., 'The Date and Origin of *Cædmon's Hymn*', *NM* 98, 217–28

Ishiguro, Taro, '*Daniel*: the Old English Poem of *Nebuchadnezzar against God*', *Essays in Honour of Shimsuke Ando and Haruo Iwasaki*, ed. Keiko Kawachi and Takami Matsuda (Tokyo), pp. 462–78

Klein, Thomas, 'The Old English Translation of Aldhelm's Riddle *Lorica*', *RES* 48, 345–9

Lucas, Peter J., 'Franciscus Junius and the Versification of *Judith, Francisci Junii in Memoriam*: 1591–1991', *The Preservation and Transmission of Anglo-Saxon Culture*, ed. Szarmach and Rosenthal, pp. 369–404

Matto, Michael, 'The Old English *Soul and Body I* and *Soul and Body II*: Ending the Rivalry', *In Geardagum* 18, 39–58

McKill, Larry N., 'Patterns of the Fall: Adam and Eve in the Old English *Genesis A*', *Florilegium* 14 (1995–6), 25–41

Mintz, Susannah B., 'Words Devilish and Divine: Eve as Speaker in *Genesis B*', *Neophilologus* 81, 609–23

Oka, Fumiko, '*The Wanderer*, ll. 41–44: The Ceremony of Homage in the Feudal Vassalage and in the Troubadours' Love Poetry', Oka, *Investigations on Courtly Words and Others* (Tokyo), pp. 165–93

O'Neill, Patrick P., 'On the Date, Provenance and Relationship of the "Solomon and Saturn" Dialogues', *ASE* 26, 139–68

Phillips, Helen, 'The Order of Words and Patterns of Opposition in the *Battle of Maldon*', *Neophilologus* 81, 117–28

Pulsiano, Phillip, '"Danish Men's Words are Worse than Murder": Viking Guile and *The Battle of Maldon*', *JEGP* 96, 13–25

Stévanovitch, Colette, ed., *La Genèse, du manuscrit Junius XI de la Bodleienne*, Publications de L'Association des médiévistes anglicistes de l'enseignement supérieur, hors série 1, 2 vols. (Paris, 1992).

Toporova, T. V., 'Indoevropeiskie paralleli drevnegermanskikh zagovorov', *Voprosy Iazykoznaniia*, no. 2, pp. 142–9 [*Charms*]

Toswell, M. J., 'The Relationship of the Metrical Psalter to the Old English Glossed Psalters', *ES* 78, 297–315

Trask, Richard M., see sect. 3*bii* [*Judith*]

Waugh, Robin, 'The Characteristic Moment as a Motif in *The Finnsburg Fragment* and *Deor*', *Eng. Stud. in Canada* 23, 249–61

c. Prose

Bremmer, Rolf H., Jr, 'The Germanic Context of "Cynewulf and Cyneheard" Revisited', *Neophilologus* 81, 445–65
see also sect. 4 [Ælfric]

Chapman, Don, 'Pragmatics of Analyzing Compounds in Wulfstan's Sermons', *The Twenty-Third LACUS Forum*, ed. Alan K. Melby (Chapel Hill, NC), pp. 575–84

Clemoes, Peter, ed., *Ælfric's Catholic Homilies. The First Series. Text*, EETS ss 17 (Oxford)

Cross, J. E., and Andrew Hamer, see sect. 5 [Ælfric]

Discenza, Nicole Guenther, 'Power, Skill and Virtue in the Old English *Boethius*', *ASE* 26, 81–108

Frantzen, Allen J., 'Sodom and Gomorrah in Prose Works from Alfred's Reign', *Alfred the Wise*, ed. Roberts *et al.*, pp. 25–33

Godden, Malcolm, 'Wærferth and King Alfred: the Fate of the Old English *Dialogues*', *Alfred the Wise*, ed. Roberts *et al.*, pp. 35–51

Hart, Cyril, 'Some Recent Editions of the Anglo-Saxon Chronicles', *MÆ* 66, 293–301
see also sect. 6

Hill, Joyce, 'Ælfric's Homily on the Holy Innocents: the Sources Reviewed', *Alfred the Wise*, ed. Roberts *et al.*, pp. 89–98
see also sect. 5 [Ælfric]

Hough, Carole, 'Alfred's *domboc* and the Language of Rape: a Reconsideration of Alfred Ch. 11', *MÆ* 66, 1–27

'A New Reading of Alfred, Ch. 26', *Nottingham Med. Stud.* 41, 1–12

'A Reconsideration of Ine, Ch. 23, with a Note on *Juliana*, Line 242a', *NM* 98, 43–51

Kitson, Peter, see sect. 2*b* [OE Orosius]

Knock, Ann, 'Analysis of a Translator: the Old English *Wonders of the East*, *Alfred the Wise*, ed. Roberts *et al.*, pp. 121–6

Kubouchi, Tadao, see sect. 5

Lazzari, Loredana, ed. and trans., *La Versione anglosassone della 'Vita Sancti Nicolai' (Cambridge, Corpus Christi College, MS 303)*, Quaderni della Libera Università 'Maria SS. Assunta' 11 (Rome)

Lenker, Ursula, *Die westsächsische Evangelienversion und die Perikopenordnungen im angelsächsischen England*, Münchener Universitäts-Schriften, Texte und Untersuchungen zur Englischen Philologie 20 (Munich)

McDougall, David, and Ian McDougall, '"Evil Tongues": a Previously Unedited Old English Sermon', *ASE* 26, 209–29

Millar, Robert McColl, and Alex Nicholls, 'Ælfric's *De Initio Creaturae* and London, BL Cotton Vespasian A.XXII: Omission, Addition, Retention, and Innovation', *The Preservation and Transmission of Anglo-Saxon Culture*, ed. Szarmach and Rosenthal, pp. 431–63

Olsen, Alexandra, 'The Homiletic Tradition in Old English', *In Geardagum* 18, 1–13

Page, R. I., 'Old English *winterdūn*', *Names, Places and People*, ed. Rumble and Mills, pp. 301–6 [in *Gerefa*]

Pilch, Herbert, 'The *Sondershäuser Psalter*: a Newly Discovered Old English Interlinear Gloss', *Germanic Studies*, ed. Goblirsch *et al.*, pp. 313–23

Richards, Mary P., 'Anglo-Saxonism in the Old English Laws', *Anglo-Saxonism*, ed. Frantzen and Niles, pp. 40–59

Roberts, Jane, '*Fela martyra* "many martyrs": a Different View of Orosius's City', *Alfred the Wise*, ed. Roberts *et al.*, pp. 155–78

Rodrigues, Louis J., 'Margaret of Antioch – Pseudo-Saint and Martyr', *SELIM 1996*, ed. Giménez Bon and Olsen, pp. 265–71

Rodríguez Redondo, Ana Laura, 'Compositional Strategies of Old English Testaments or Wills', *SELIM 1996*, ed. Giménez Bon and Olsen, pp. 287–95

Rulon-Miller, Nina, '"Cynewulf and Cyneheard": a Woman Screams', *PQ* 76, 113–32

Scragg, D. G., '*Wifcyþþe* and the Morality of the Cynewulf and Cyneheard Episode in the Anglo-Saxon Chronicle', *Alfred the Wise*, ed. Roberts *et al.*, pp. 179–85

Stanley, E. G., 'On the Laws of King Alfred: the End of the Preface and the Beginning of the Laws', *Alfred the Wise*, ed. Roberts *et al.*, pp. 211–21

Stanton, Robert, 'Rhetoric and Translation in Ælfric's Prefaces', *Translation and Lit.* 6, 135–48

Swan, Mary, 'Old English Made New: One Catholic Homily and its Uses', *Leeds Stud. in Eng.* 28, 1–18

Szarmach, Paul E., 'Alfred's *Boethius* and the Four Cardinal Virtues', *Alfred the Wise*, ed. Roberts *et al.*, pp. 223–35

Toswell, M. J., see sect. 3*biii* [glossed psalters]

Treharne, E. M., *The Old English Life of St Nicholas with the Old English Life of St Giles*, Leeds Texts and Monographs ns 15 (Leeds)

Whatley, E. Gordon, 'Lost in Translation: Omission of Episodes in Some Old English Prose Saints' Legends', *ASE* 26, 187–208

Wilcox, Jonathan, see sect. 5 [Vercelli Homily X]

4. ANGLO-LATIN, LITURGY AND OTHER LATIN ECCLESIASTICAL TEXTS

Arngart, O., see sect. 5

Beare, Rhona, 'Earl Godwin's Son as a Barnacle Goose', *N&Q* 44, 4–6

'Gerald of Wales on the Barnacle Goose', *N&Q* 44, 459–62

Bethel, Patricia, and Margaret J. Pullan, 'Theodore's Lark', *ELN* 34.3, 1–4

Biggs, Frederick M., 'Unidentified Citations of Augustine in Anglo-Latin Writers', *N&Q* 44, 154–60

Bliese, John R. E., see sect. 6

Bremmer, Rolf H., Jr, 'The Reception of the Acts of John in Anglo-Saxon England', *The Apocryphal Acts of John*, ed. Jan N. Bremmer (Kampen, 1995), pp. 183–96

Brown, George Hardin, *Bede the Educator*, Jarrow Lecture 1996 ([Jarrow])

'The Preservation and Transmission of Northumbrian Culture on the Continent: Alcuin's Debt to Bede', *The Preservation and Transmission of Anglo-Saxon Culture*, ed. Szarmach and Rosenthal, pp. 159–75

Bruni, Sandra, ed., *Alcuino: De Orthographia*, Millennio Medievale 2, Testi 2 (Florence)

Connolly, Seán, trans., *Bede: on 'Tobit' and on the 'Canticle of Habakkuk'* (Dublin and Portland, OR)

Corrêa, Alicia, 'St Austraberta of Pavilly in the Anglo-Saxon Liturgy', *AB* 115, 77–112

Cubitt, Catherine, 'Unity and Diversity in Anglo-Saxon Liturgy', *Unity and Diversity in the Church: Papers Read at the 1994 Summer Meeting and the 1995 Winter Meeting of the Ecclesiastical History Society*, ed. R. N. Swanson, Stud. in Church Hist. 32 (Oxford, 1996), 45–57

Dales, Douglas, see sect. 6

Delierneux, Nathalie, 'Arculfe, *sanctus episcopus gente Gallus*: une existence historique discutable', *Revue Belge de Philologie et d'Histoire* 75, 911–41

Driscoll, Michael S., 'Penance in Transition: Popular Piety and Practice', *Medieval Liturgy: a Book of Essays*, ed. Lizette Larson-Miller (New York and London), pp. 121–63 [Alcuin]

Eby, John C., 'Bringing the Vita to Life: Bede's Symbolic Structure of the Life of St. Cuthbert', *Amer. Benedictine Rev.* 48, 316–38

Field, P. J. C., see sect. 6 [Nennius]

Gullick, Michael, see sect. 5

Gunn, Victoria A., see sect. 6

Gwara, Scott, '*Doubles entendres* in the Ironic Conclusion to Aldhelm's *Epistola ad Heahfridum*', *Archivum Latinitatis Medii Aevi* 53 (1995), 141–52

Gwara, Scott, ed., and David W. Porter, trans., *Anglo-Saxon Conversations: the Colloquies of Ælfric Bata* (Woodbridge)

Hen, Yitzhak, 'The Liturgy of St Willibrord', *ASE* 26, 41–62

Hen, Yitzhak, ed., *The Sacramentary of Echternach (Paris, Bibliothèque Nationale, Ms. lat. 9433)*, HBS 110 (Woodbridge)

Howlett, David R., 'Aldhelmi Carmen Rhythmicum', *Archivum Latinitatis Medii Aevi* 53 (1995), 119–40

   'Insular Latin Writers' Rhythms', *Peritia* 11, 53–116

   'Israelite Learning in Insular Latin', *Peritia* 11, 117–52

   'A Polyglot Glossary from the Twelfth Century', *De mot en mot: Aspects of Medieval Linguistics. Essays in honour of William Rothwell*, ed. Stewart Gregory and D. A. Trotter (Cardiff), pp. 81–91

   'Rubisca: an Edition, Translation, and Commentary', *Peritia* 10 (1996), 71–90

   'Seven Studies in Seventh-Century Texts', *Peritia* 10 (1996), 1–70

Howlett, David R., ed., *Dictionary of Medieval Latin from British Sources, Fascicule V: I–J–K–L* (Oxford)

Ireland, Colin, 'An Irish Precursor of Cædmon', *N&Q* 44, 2–4

   'Penance and Prayer in Water: an Irish Practice in Northumbrian Hagiography', *CMCS* 34, 51–66

Kelly, Joseph F., 'On the Brink: Bede', *Jnl of Early Christian Stud.* 5, 85–103

Kienzle, Beverly Mayne, 'Exegesis on Luke 10:38 around 1100: Worcester MS F. 94, ff. 1r–2r, A Tribute to James E. Cross', *Med. Sermon Stud.* 40, 22–8

Lapidge, Michael, ed., *Columbanus: Studies on the Latin Writings*, Stud. in Celtic Hist. 17 (Woodbridge)

Lapidge, Michael, and Peter S. Baker, 'More Acrostic Verse by Abbo of Fleury', *Jnl of Med. Latin* 7, 1–27

Law, Vivien, *Grammar and Grammarians in the Early Middle Ages* (London and New York)

Lenker, Ursula, see sect. 3*c*

Mostert, Marco, see sect. 5

Newlands, Carole E., 'Bede and Images of Saint Cuthbert', *Traditio* 52, 73–109

O'Loughlin, Thomas, 'Adomnán and Arculf: the Case of an Expert Witness', *Jnl of Med. Latin* 7, 127–46 [Bede]

Orchard, Andy, 'The Sources and Meaning of the *Liber monstrorum*', *I monstra nell'inferno Dantesco: tradizione e simbologie. Atti del XXXIII Convegno storico internazionale, Todi, 13–16 ottobre 1996*, ed. E. Menestò, Atti dei Convegni del Centro italiano di studi sul basso medioevo – Accademia Tudertina e del Centro di studi sulla spiritualità medievale, ns 10 (Spoleto), 73–105

Otter, Monika, 'The Temptation of St. Æthelthryth', *Exemplaria* 9, 139–63

Porter, David W., 'Anglo-Saxon Colloquies: Ælfric, Ælfric Bata and *De Raris Fabulis Retractata*', *Neophilologus* 81, 467–80

Raw, Barbara, 'Alfredian Piety: the Book of Nunnaminster', *Alfred the Wise*, ed. Roberts *et al.*, pp. 145–53

Rumble, Alexander R., see sect. 6

Sharpe, Richard, *A Handlist of the Latin Writers of Great Britain and Ireland before 1540*, Publications of the Jnl of Med. Latin 1 (Turnhout)

Smith, Julie Ann, see sect. 6

Springer, Carl P. E., see sect. 5

Thomas, Charles, 'Christian Latin Inscriptions from Cornwall in Biblical Style', *Jnl of the R. Inst. of Cornwall* ns 2, 2.4, 42–66

Toswell, M. J., see sect. 5

Van de Weyer, Robert, trans., *Bede: Celtic and Roman Christianity in Britain* (Berkhamsted, Herts)

von Padberg, Lutz E., see sect. 6

Webber, Teresa, 'The Patristic Content of English Book Collections in the Eleventh Century: Towards a Continental Perspective', *Of the Making of Books*, ed. Robinson and Zim, pp. 191–205

Wieland, Gernot, '*Aures lectoris*: Orality and Literacy in Felix's *Vita Sancti Guthlaci*', *Jnl of Med. Latin* 7, 168–77

5. PALAEOGRAPHY, DIPLOMATIC AND ILLUMINATION

Arngart, O., 'Three Notes on the St Petersburg Bede', *Names, Places and People*, ed. Rumble and Mills, pp. 1–7

Broderick, Herbert R., 'The Influence of Anglo-Saxon Genesis Iconography on Later English Medieval Manuscript Art', *The Preservation and Transmission of Anglo-Saxon Culture*, ed. Szarmach and Rosenthal, pp. 211–39

Crick, Julia, 'The Case for a West Saxon Minuscule', *ASE* 26, 63–79

Cross, J. E., and Andrew Hamer, 'Ælfric's *Letters* and the *Excerptiones Ecgberhti*', *Alfred the Wise*, ed. Roberts *et al.*, pp. 5–13

Deshman, Robert, 'Anglo-Saxon Art: So What's New?', *The Preservation and Transmission of Anglo-Saxon Culture*, ed. Szarmach and Rosenthal, pp. 243–69

'The Galba Psalter: Pictures, Texts and Context in an Early Medieval Prayerbook', *ASE* 26, 109–38

Dumville, David, *Three Men in a Boat: Scribe, Language, and Culture in the Church of Viking-Age Europe* (Cambridge) [inaugural lecture]

Farr, Carol, *The Book of Kells: its Function and Audience*, Brit. Lib. Stud. in Med. Culture 4 (London)

'Liturgical Influences on the Decoration of the Book of Kells', *Studies in Insular Art and Archaeology*, ed. Karkov and Farrell, pp. 127–41

Gameson, Richard, 'The Gospels of Margaret of Scotland and the Literacy of an Eleventh-Century Queen', *Women and the Book: Assessing the Visual Evidence*, ed. J. Taylor and L. Smith (London), pp. 149–71

Gneuss, Helmut, 'Origin and Provenance of Anglo-Saxon Manuscripts: the Case of Cotton Tiberius A. III', *Of the Making of Books*, ed. Robinson and Zim, pp. 13–48

Graham, Timothy, 'The Beginnings of Old English Studies: Evidence from the Manuscripts of Matthew Parker', *Back to the Manuscripts*, ed. Sato, pp. 29–50

'Robert Talbot's "Old Saxonice Bede": Cambridge University Library, MS Kk. 3. 18 and the "Alphabeticum Norwagicum" of British Library, Cotton MSS, Domitian A. IX', *Books and Collectors 1200–1700*, ed. Carley and Tite, pp. 295–316

'A Runic Entry in an Anglo-Saxon Manuscript from Abingdon and the Scandinavian Career of Abbot Rodulf (1051–2)', *Nottingham Med. Stud.* 40 (1996), 16–24

Gullick, Michael, 'The Origin and Date of Cambridge, Corpus Christi College MS 163', *Trans. of the Cambridge Bibliographical Soc.* 11.1 (1996), 89–91

Gwara, Scott, 'Newly Identified Eleventh-Century Fragments in a Bagford Album, now London, British Library, MS Harley 5977', *Manuscripta* 38 (1994), 228–36

Hart, Cyril, 'The Canterbury Contribution to the Bayeux Tapestry', *Art and Symbolism in Medieval Europe*, ed. Guy de Boe and Frans Verhaeghe, Papers of the Medieval Europe Brugge Conference 1997, 6 (Zellik), 7–15

Harvey, P. D. A., and Andrew McGuiness, *A Guide to British Medieval Seals* (Toronto, 1996)

Hayashi, Hiroshi, 'A Study of the Charter-Criticism of the Anglo-Saxon Period, its Theory and Practice: a Preliminary Handbook', *Gakushuin-Daigaku-Hogakkai-Zasshi* 31.1 (1995), 77–116; 31.2 (1995), 1–90; 32.1(1996), 107–242; 32.2, 67–106; 33.1, 75–114

Hill, Joyce, 'The Preservation and Transmission of Ælfric's Saints' Lives: Reader-Reception and Reader-Response in the Early Middle Ages', *The Preservation and Transmission of Anglo-Saxon Culture*, ed. Szarmach and Rosenthal, pp. 405–30

Hooke, Della, 'Charter Bounds of the South West of England', *LH* 27, 18–29

John, J. J., 'The Ex-Libris in *Codices Latini Antiquiores*', *Scriptorium* 50 (1996), 239–46

Kubouchi, Tadao, 'The Decline of the S. Noun O. V. Element Order: the Evidence from Punctuation in Some Transition-Period Manuscripts of Ælfric and Wulfstan', *Back to the Manuscripts*, ed. Sato, pp. 51–68

Lapidge, Michael, 'Autographs of Insular Latin Authors of the Early Middle Ages', *Gli autografi medievali: Problemi paleografici e filologici*, ed. Paolo Chiesa and Lucia Pinelli (Spoleto, 1994), 103–36

Lasko, Peter, *Ars Sacra 800–1200*, 2nd ed. (New Haven and London, 1994) ['Anglo-Saxon Art', pp. 67–75]

Lucas, Peter J., 'A Testimonie of Very Ancient Time? Some Manuscript Models for the Parkerian Anglo-Saxon Type-Designs', *Of the Making of Books*, ed. Robinson and Zim, pp. 147–88

Mitchell, Bruce, 'The Sign ₇ in the Annal for 871 in the Parker Chronicle, MS Cambridge, Corpus Christi College 173', *Alfred the Wise*, ed. Roberts *et al.*, pp. 127–33

Mostert, Marco, 'Celtic, Anglo-Saxon or Insular? Some Considerations on "Irish" Manuscript Production and their Implications for Insular Latin Culture, *c.* 500–800', *Cultural Identity and Cultural Integration: Ireland and Europe in the Early Middle Ages*, ed. Doris Edel (Dublin, 1995), pp. 92–115

Noel, William, 'The Utrecht Psalter on CD-Rom', *Gazette du livre médiéval* 30, 37–9

Ogura, Michiko, 'Punctuation Problems on Five Manuscripts of the West Saxon Gospels', *Medieval Heritage: Essays in honour of Tadahiro Ikegami*, ed. Masahiko Kanno *et al.* (Tokyo), pp. 179–87

Page, R. I., 'Back to the Manuscripts: Some Thoughts on Editing Old English Texts', *Back to the Manuscripts*, ed. Sato, pp. 1–27

Parkes, M. B., 'Archaizing Hands in English Manuscripts', *Books and Collectors 1200–1700*, ed. Carley and Tite, pp. 101–41

'Latin Autograph Manuscripts: Orthography and Punctuation', *Gli autografi medievali: Problemi paleografici e filologici*, ed. Paolo Chiesa and Lucia Pinelli (Spoleto, 1994), 23–36

see also sect. 2*a*

Raw, Barbara C., *Trinity and Incarnation in Anglo-Saxon Art and Thought*, CSASE 21 (Cambridge)

Robinson, P. R., 'A Twelfth-Century *Scriptrix* from Nunnaminster', *Of the Making of Books*, ed. Robinson and Zim, pp. 73–93

Sandred, Karl Inge, see sect. 8

Sato, Suji, 'Back to the Manuscripts: Some Problems in the Physical Descriptions of the Parker Chronicle', *Back to the Manuscripts*, ed. Sato, pp. 69–95

'A Note on the *Parker Chronicle* f. 5^v/18–20', *Medieval Heritage: Essays in Honour of Tadahiro Ikegami*, ed. Masahiko Kanno *et al.* (Tokyo), pp. 189–96

Selwyn, David G., 'Thomas Cranmer and the Dispersal of Medieval Libraries: the Provenance of Some of his Medieval Manuscripts and Printed Books', *Books and Collectors 1200–1700*, ed. Carley and Tite, pp. 281–94 [manuscripts from Christ Church, Canterbury, p. 285]

Springer, Carl P. E., 'The Manuscripts of Sedulius: a Provisional Handlist', *Trans. of the Amer. Philosophical Soc.* 85.5 (1995)

Stoneman, William P., '"Writ in Ancient Character and of No Further Use": Anglo-Saxon Manuscripts in American Collections', *The Preservation and Transmission of Anglo-Saxon Culture*, ed. Szarmach and Rosenthal, pp. 99–138

Tite, Colin G. C., 'Sir Robert Cotton, Sir Thomas Tempest and an Anglo-Saxon Gospel Book: A Cottonian Paper in the Harleian Library', *Books and Collectors 1200–1700*, ed. Carley and Tite, pp. 429–39

Toswell, M. J., 'St Martial and the Dating of Late Anglo-Saxon Manuscripts', *Scriptorium* 51, 3–14

Webber, Teresa, see sect. 4

Werner, Martin, 'The Book of Durrow and the Question of Programme', *ASE* 26, 23–39

Wieland, Gernot R., 'The Origin and Development of the Anglo-Saxon *Psychomachia* Illustrations', *ASE* 26, 169–86

'The Prudentius Manuscript CCCC 223', *Manuscripta* 38 (1994), 211–27

Wilcox, Jonathan, 'Variant Texts of an Old English Homily: Vercelli X and Stylistic Readers', *The Preservation and Transmission of Anglo-Saxon Culture*, ed. Szarmach and Rosenthal, pp. 335–51

Woudhuysen, H. R., 'Scraps for Beer' [Sotheby's manuscript sale, including s. x/xi fragment possibly from Christ Church, Canterbury], *TLS* 28 November, p. 21

6. HISTORY

Abels, Richard, 'English Logistics and Military Administration, 871–1066: the Impact of the Viking Wars', *Military Aspects of Scandinavian Society in a European Perspective, AD*

1–1300, ed. Anne Nørgård Jørgensen and Birthe L. Clausen (Copenhagen), pp. 257–65

'Sheriffs, Lord-Seeking and the Norman Settlement of the South-East Midlands', *ANS* 19, 19–49

Ajiro, Atsushi, 'Ælfric's *Lives of Saints*', *Daito-bunka-Daigaku-Kiyo (Jinbun-kagaku)* 34, 349–65; 35, 145–53 [in Japanese]

Alexander, Louis M., 'The Legal Status of the Native Britons in Late Seventh-Century Wessex as Reflected by the Law Code of Ine', *Haskins Soc. Jnl 7*, 31–8

Atkin, M. A., '"The Land between Ribble and Mersey" in the Early Tenth Century', *Names, Places and People*, ed. Rumble and Mills, pp. 8–18

Ausenda, Giorgio, ed., see sect. 1

Bailey, K. A., 'Buckinghamshire Slavery in 1086', *Records of Buckinghamshire* 37, 67–78

Bailey, Richard, 'St Wilfrid, Ripon and Hexham', *Studies in Insular Art and Archaeology*, ed. Karkov and Farrell, pp. 3–25

Banham, Debby, 'The South Cambridgeshire Dykes: Early Medieval Documentary Evidence', in Malim *et al.*, 'New Evidence on the Cambridgeshire Dykes and Worsted Street Roman Road' [sect. 9], pp. 98–100

Barnwell, Paul S., 'War and Peace: Historiography and Seventh-Century Embassies', *EME*, 127–39

Bliese, John R. E., 'St Cuthbert's and St Neot's Help in War: Visions and Exhortations', *Haskins Soc. Jnl 7*, 39–62

Bourne, Jill, 'An Anglo-Saxon Royal Estate "æt Glenne" and the Murder of St Wigstan', *Anglo-Saxon Landscapes in the East Midlands*, ed. Bourne, pp. 147–63

Bourne, Jill, ed., *Anglo-Saxon Landscapes in the East Midlands* (Leicester, 1996)

Breeze, Andrew, 'Worgred, First Abbot of Glastonbury', *Somerset and Dorset Notes and Queries* 34.347, 175–8

Brett, Martin, 'The English Abbeys, their Tenants, and the King (950–1150)', *Chiesa e mondo feudale nei secoli X–XII*, Miscellanea del Centro di studi medievali 14 (Milan, 1995), 277–302

Brooke, Christopher N. L., 'The Diocese of Hereford, 676–1200', *Trans. of the Woolhope Naturalists' Field Club* 48.1 (1994), 23–36

Brooks, Beda, *The World of St Mildred, c. 660–730: a Study of an Anglo-Saxon Nun in the Golden Age of the English Church* (Bath, 1996)

Brooks, Nicholas, 'The Anglo-Saxon Cathedral Community, 597–1070', *A History of Canterbury Cathedral*, ed. Patrick Collinson, Nigel Ramsay and Margaret Sparks (Oxford, 1995), pp. 1–37

'Medieval Bridges: a Window onto Changing Concepts of State Power', *Haskins Soc. Jnl 7*, 11–29

Campbell, James, 'The United Kingdom of England: the Anglo-Saxon Achievement', *Uniting the Kingdom: the Making of British History*, ed. Alexander Grant and Keith J. Stringer (London, 1995), pp. 31–47

Cessford, C[raig], 'Early Medieval Maiden Castle: a Reassessment', *Somerset and Dorset Notes and Queries* 34.344 (1996), 46–9

'Northern England and the Gododdin Poem', *Northern History* 33, 218–22

Chadwick, Henry, 'Not Angles but Angels? St Augustine of Canterbury and the Conversion of the English', *Lambeth Palace Library Ann. Rev. 1997*, 57–64

Cholokian, Rouben C., 'The Bayeux Tapestry: Is There More to Say?', *Annales de Normandie* 47.1, 43–50

Clark, Christine G., 'Women's Rights in Early England', *Brigham Young Univ. Law Rev.* (1995), 207–36

Coates, Simon, 'Perceptions of the Anglo-Saxon Past in the Tenth-Century Monastic Reform Movement', *The Church Retrospective: Papers Read at the 1995 Summer Meeting and the 1996 Winter Meeting of the Ecclesiastical History Society*, ed. R. N. Swanson, Stud. in Church Hist. 33 (Oxford), 61–74

Corcos, Nicholas, 'Glastonbury Abbey and the Acquisition of its Manor of Wrington', *Somerset and Dorset Notes and Queries* 33.344 (1996), 78–82

Corfe, Tom, 'The Battle of Heavenfield', *Before Wilfrid*, ed. Corfe, pp. 65–86

Corfe, Tom, ed., *Before Wilfrid: Britons, Romans and Anglo-Saxons in Tynedale*, Hexham Historian 7 (Hexham)

Corfe, Tom, and Rosemary Cramp, 'Bernicia before Wilfrid', *Before Wilfrid*, ed. Corfe, pp. 57–64

Cownie, Emma, 'Religious Patronage at Post-Conquest Bury St Edmunds', *Haskins Soc. Jnl* 7, 1–9

Cramp, Rosemary, *Whithorn and the Northumbrian Expansion Westward*, 3rd Whithorn Lecture (Whithorn, 1995)

Cubitt, Catherine, 'The Tenth-Century Benedictine Reform in England', *EME* 6, 77–94 see also sect. 4

Dales, Douglas, *Light to the Isles: a Study of Missionary Theology in Celtic and Early Anglo-Saxon Britain* (Cambridge)

Davies, John Reuben, 'Church, Property and Conflict in Wales, AD 600–1100', *Welsh Hist. Rev.* 18.3, 387–406 [includes Bede on battle of Chester, etc.]

Dodgson, John McNeal, see sect. 8

Dumville, David, *The Churches of North Britain in the First Viking-Age*, 5th Whithorn Lecture (Whithorn)

'The Idea of Government in Sub-Roman Britain', *After Empire*, ed. Ausenda, pp. 177–216 [Gildas]

Evans, Stephen S., *The Lords of Battle: Image and Reality of the 'Comitatus' in Dark Age Britain* (Woodbridge)

Faith, Rosamond, *The English Peasantry and the Growth of Lordship* (Leicester)

Fell, Christine, 'A Funeral Monument', *Names, Places and People*, ed. Rumble and Mills, pp. 55–76

Field, P. J. C., 'Nennius and his History', *Studia Celtica* 30, 159–65

Fleming, Robin, 'Christ Church Canterbury's Anglo-Norman Cartulary', *Anglo-Norman Political Culture and the Twelfth-Century Renaissance: Proceedings of the Borchard Conference on Anglo-Norman History 1995*, ed. C. W. Hollister (Woodbridge), pp. 83–155

Fletcher, Richard, *The Conversion of Europe: from Paganism to Christianity 371–1386 AD* (London)

Foss, Peter J., 'Market Bosworth and its Region: Clues to its Early Status and Connections', *Anglo-Saxon Landscapes in the East Midlands*, ed. Bourne, pp. 83–105

Gardner, Rex, 'The Departure of Paulinus from Northumbria: a Reappraisal', *AAe* 5th ser. 24 (1996), 73–7

Garrison, Mary, 'The English and the Irish at the Court of Charlemagne', *Karl der Grosse und sein Nachwirken*, ed. P. L. Butzer *et al.* (Turnhout), pp. 97–123

Graham, Timothy, see sect. 5

Gunn, Victoria A., 'Bede and the Martyrdom of St Oswald', *Martyrs and Martyrologies: Papers Read at the 1992 Summer Meeting and the 1993 Winter Meeting of the Ecclesiastical History Society*, ed. D. Wood, Stud. in Church Hist. 29 (Oxford, 1993), 57–66

Hadley, D. M., '"And they proceeded to plough and to support themselves": the Scandinavian Settlement of England', *ANS* 19, 69–97

Halpin, Patricia A., 'Anglo-Saxon Women and Pilgrimage', *ANS* 19, 99–122

Hare, Michael, 'Kings, Crowns and Festivals: the Origins of Gloucester as a Royal Ceremonial Centre', *Trans. of the Bristol & Gloucestershire Archaeol. Soc.* 115, 41–78

Hart, Cyril, 'The Anglo-Saxon Chronicle at Ramsey', *Alfred the Wise*, ed. Roberts *et al.*, pp. 65–88

  'Some Recent Editions of the Anglo-Saxon Chronicles', *MÆ* 66, 293–301

  'William Malet and his Family', *ANS* 19, 123–65

Hart, Cyril, ed., *The Thorney Annals 963–1412 A.D.* (Lampeter)

Haslam, Jeremy, see sect. 9*b*

Hayward, Paul, 'The Idea of Innocent Martyrdom in Late Tenth-Century and Eleventh-Century English Hagiology', *Martyrs and Martyrologies: Papers Read at the 1992 Summer Meeting and the 1933 Winter Meeting of the Ecclesiastical History Society*, ed. D. Wood, Stud. in Church Hist. 29 (Oxford, 1993), 81–92

Hen, Yitzhak, see sect. 4

Herbert, Kathleen, *Peace-Weavers and Shield-Maidens: Women in Early English Society* (Hockwold-cum-Wilton, Norf.)

Hesse, Mary, 'The Early Parish and Estate of Ickworth, Suffolk', *Proc. of the Suffolk Inst. of Archaeol. and Hist.* 39.1, 6–27

  'The Field called "Augey" in Ickleton: an Anglo-Saxon Enclosure?', *Proc. of the Cambridge Antiquarian Soc.* 85, 159–60

Higham, N. J., 'The Context of *Brunanburh*', *Names, Places and People*, ed. Rumble and Mills, pp. 144–56

  The Convert Kings: Power and Religious Affiliation in Early Anglo-Saxon England (Manchester)

  The Death of Anglo-Saxon England (Stroud)

  'Patterns of Patronage and Power: the Governance of Late Anglo-Saxon Cheshire', *Government, Religion and Society in Northern England, 1000–1700*, ed. John C. Appleby and Paul Dalton (Stroud), pp. 1–13

Hill, David, and Sheila Sharp, 'An Anglo-Saxon Beacon System', *Names, Places and People*, ed. Rumble and Mills, pp. 157–65

Hines, John, see sect. 9*b*

Holmes, Michael, *King Arthur: a Military History* (London, 1996)

Hough, Carole, see sect. 3*c* [three entries]

Hudson, John, 'The Abbey of Abingdon, its *Chronicle* and the Norman Conquest', *ANS* 19, 181–202

Huggins, Peter, 'Nazingbury 20 Years On, or "Where Did the Royal Ladies Go?"', *The London Archaeologist*, 105–11

Keene, Barbara, and Michael Sampson, 'Identifying the Domesday Manors of Nochecote and Loteland', *Devon and Cornwall Notes and Queries* 38.1, 15–16

Kemble, J. V. H., 'A Profile of Boundary Markers', *Essex Jnl* 32.2, 56–9

Keynes, Simon, 'Anglo-Saxon Entries in the "Liber Vitae" of Brescia', *Alfred the Wise*, ed. Roberts *et al.*, pp. 99–119

'Giso, Bishop of Wells (1061–88)', *ANS* 19, 203–71

'Introduction', in Peter Hunter Blair, *Anglo-Saxon England*, new ed. [Folio Soc.] (London), pp. xv–xxix

'The Vikings in England, *c.* 780–1016', *The Oxford Illustrated History of the Vikings*, ed. Sawyer, pp. 48–82

Kleinschmidt, Harald, 'The Geuissae, the West Saxons, the Angles and the English: the Widening Horizon of Bede's Gentile Terminology', *North-Western European Lang. Evolution* 30, 51–91

'Polanyi Revisited. The Reorganization of Trade in Early Medieval Europe. The Case of Hamwih/Southampton', *Comparative Stud. of Urban Hist.* 16, 17–34 [in Japanese]

'Stirps regia und Adel im frühen Wessex: Studien zu Personennamen in der Epistolographie, Historiographie und Urkundenüberlieferung', *Historisches Jahrbuch* 117, 1–37

Lewis, Carenza, Patrick Mitchell-Fox and Christopher Dyer, *Village, Hamlet and Field: Changing Medieval Settlements in Central England* (Manchester)

Lewis, C. P., 'Joining the Dots: a Methodology for Identifying the English in Domesday Book', *Family Trees and the Roots of Politics*, ed. K. S. B. Keats-Rohan (Woodbridge), pp. 69–87

Lund, Niels, 'The Danish Empire and the End of the Viking Age', *The Oxford Illustrated History of the Vikings*, ed. Sawyer, pp. 156–81

Lundgren, Tim, 'The Robin Hood Ballads and the English Outlaw Tradition', *Southern Folklore* 53 (1996), 225–47

MacGregor, Arthur, and Moira Hook, see sect. 9*a*

Maddicott, J. R., 'Plague in Seventh-Century England', *Past and Present* 156, 7–54

Malim, Tim, *et al.*, see sect. 9*a*

Marett-Crosby, Anthony, OSB, 'St Augustine of Canterbury, 597–1997', *Ampleforth Jnl* 102.1, 7–15

Margham, John, 'Saints in an Island Landscape: a Study in Church Dedications' [pre-1200], *Proc. of the Isle of Wight Natural Hist. and Archaeol. Soc.* 13, 91–106

Mason, Emma, *Westminster Abbey and its People, c. 1050–c. 1216* (Woodbridge, 1996)

Meaney, Audrey L., 'Hundred Meeting-Places in the Cambridge Region', *Names, Places and People*, ed. Rumble and Mills, pp. 195–240

Mitchell, Bruce, see sect. 5

Moore, John S., '"Quot homines?" The Population of Domesday England', *ANS* 19, 307–34

Nelson, Janet L., 'Anglo-Saxon England, *c.* 500–1066', *The Oxford Illustrated History of Medieval England*, ed. Nigel Saul (Oxford), pp. 25–60

'The Franks and the English in the Ninth Century Reconsidered', *The Preservation and Transmission of Anglo-Saxon Culture*, ed. Szarmach and Rosenthal, pp. 141–58

'". . . *sicut olim gens Francorum . . . nunc gens Anglorum*": Fulk's Letter to Alfred Revisited', *Alfred the Wise*, ed. Roberts *et al.*, pp. 135–44

Nightingale, Pamela, *A Medieval Mercantile Community: the Grocer's Company and the Politics and Trade of London, 1000–1485* (London, 1995)

Oda, Takuji, 'Alfred "*the Really* Great" – What Happened at the Battle of Ashdown', *Essays in Honour of Shinsuke Ando and Haruo Iwasaki*, ed. Keiko Kawachi and Takami Matsuda (Tokyo), pp. 10–26

'*Passio Sancti Eadmundi* and *Vita Aelfredi Magni* (I)', *Keio-gijuku-Daigaku-Gengo-bunka-Kenkyujo-Kiyo* 28, 87–98 [in Japanese]

Ohashi, Masako, 'Bede and the Paschal Controversy: the Problem of Interpolation and Manipulation in the *Ecclesiastical History*', *Nanzan-Shingaku (Bessatsu)* 13 (1996), 127–254 [in Japanese]

Owen, A. E. B., 'Roads and Romans in South-East Lindsey; the Place-Name Evidence', *Names, Places and People*, ed. Rumble and Mills, pp. 254–68 [Anglo-Saxon fords, pp. 260–5]

Parsons, David, 'Before the Parish: the Church in Anglo-Saxon Leicestershire', *Anglo-Saxon Landscapes in the East Midlands*, ed. Bourne, pp. 11–35

'Introduction: Leicestershire in the Anglo-Saxon Period', *Anglo-Saxon Landscapes in the East Midlands*, ed. Bourne, pp. xix–xxii

Parsons, David, 'British *Caraticos, Old English *Cerdic*', *CMCS* 33, 1–8

Pegg, Valerie, 'Alfred's Footsteps' [mostly posthumous], *Winchester Museums Service Newsletter* 26 (1996), 12

Pelteret, David A. E., 'The Preservation of Anglo-Saxon Culture after 1066: Glastonbury, Wales, and the Normans', *The Preservation and Transmission of Anglo-Saxon Culture*, ed. Szarmach and Rosenthal, pp. 177–209

Princi Braccini, Giovanna, see sect. *3bii*

Rees, Daniel, ed., *Monks of England: the Benedictines in England from Augustine to the Present Day* (Downside)

Reilly, Lisa, 'The Emergence of Anglo-Norman Architecture', *ANS* 19, 335–51

Reuter, Timothy, 'The "Feudal Revolution": Comment 3', *Past and Present* 155, 177–95

Roffe, David, 'Great Bowden and its Soke', *Anglo-Saxon Landscapes in the East Midlands*, ed. Bourne, pp. 107–120

'The Making of Domesday Book Reconsidered', *Haskins Soc. Jnl* 6 (1994), 153–66

Rumble, Alexander R., '*Ad Lapidem* in Bede and a Mercian Martyrdom', *Names, Places and People*, ed. Rumble and Mills, pp. 307–19

Sanchez, Valerie A., 'Towards a History of ADR: the Dispute Processing Continuum in

Anglo-Saxon England and Today', *Ohio State Jnl on Dispute Resolution* 11 (1996), 1–39

Sawyer, Peter, ed., *The Oxford Illustrated History of the Vikings* (Oxford)

Shadrake, Dan, and Susanna Shadrake, *Barbarian Warriors: Saxons, Vikings and Normans*, Brassey's History of Uniforms (London)

Smith, Julie Ann, 'The Earliest Queen-Making Rites', *Church Hist.* 66.1, 18–35

Smyth, A. P., 'The Solar Eclipse of Wednesday 29 October AD 878: Ninth-Century Historical Records and the Findings of Modern Astronomy', *Alfred the Wise*, ed. Roberts *et al.*, pp. 187–210

Stafford, Pauline, *Queen Emma and Queen Edith: Queenship and Women's Power in Eleventh-Century England* (Oxford)

Stanley, E. G., see sect. 3*c*

Strickland, Matthew, 'Military Technology and Conquest: the Anomaly of Anglo-Saxon England', *ANS* 19, 353–82

Suppe, Frederick C., 'Who was Rhys Sais? Some Comments on Anglo-Welsh Relations before 1066', *Haskins Soc. Jnl* 7, 63–73

Tamaki, Atsuko, and Tadahiro Ikegami, 'The Parish Churches and their Priests in Anglo-Saxon England', *Seijo Univ. Arts and Lit. Quarterly* 160, 29–47 [in Japanese]

Thompson, Michael, see sect. 9*a*

Thorn, F. R., '"Another Seaborough", "The Other Dinnaton": Some Manorial Affixes in Domesday Book', *Names, Places and People*, ed. Rumble and Mills, pp. 345–77

Thornton, David E., 'Maredudd ab Owain (d. 999): the Most Famous King of the Welsh', *Welsh Hist. Rev.* 18, 567–91

Toswell, M. J., see sect. 5

Tranter, Marjorie, 'A View from Across the Border', *Anglo-Saxon Landscapes in the East Midlands*, ed. Bourne, pp. 181–90

van Houts, Elisabeth, 'The Memory of 1066 in Written and Oral Traditions', *ANS* 19, 167–79

von Padberg, Lutz E., 'Topos und Realität in der frühmittelalterlichen Missionpredigt', *Hagiographica* 4, 35–70

Walker, Ian W., *Harold: the Last Anglo-Saxon King* (Stroud)

Watkins, Carl, 'The Cult of Earl Waltheof at Crowland', *Hagiographica* 3 (1996) 95–111

Webber, Teresa, see sect. 4

Williams, Ann, *Land, Power and Politics: the Family and Career of Odda of Deerhurst*, Deerhust Lecture 1996 (Deerhurst)

'The Spoliation of Worcester', *ANS* 19, 383–408

'A West Country Magnate of the Eleventh Century: the Family, Estates and Patronage of Beorhtric Son of Ælfgar', *Family Trees and the Roots of Politics*, ed. K. S. B. Keats-Rohan (Woodbridge), pp. 41–68

Wilmott, Tony, 'The Aftermath of Rome', *Before Wilfrid*, ed. Corfe, pp. 29–39

Wormald, Patrick, 'Giving God and King their Due: Conflict and its Regulation in the Early English State', *La giustizia nell'alto medioevo (secoli ix–xi)* = *SettSpol* 44, 549–83

7. NUMISMATICS

Barclay, Craig, 'Coin Finds Reported to the Yorkshire Museum, 1992–96', *Yorkshire Numismatist* 3, 159–73 [includes thirty-one single finds and one hoard of the Anglo-Saxon period]

B[esly], E. M., and N. McQ. H[olmes], ed., 'Coin Register 1996', *BNJ* 66 (1996), 140–72

Blackburn, Mark, 'England, Wales and Scotland: Medieval', *A Survey of Numismatic Research 1990–1995*, ed. C. Morrisson and B. Kluge (Berlin), 323–43

'Hiberno-Norse and Irish Sea Imitations of Cnut's *Quatrefoil* Type', *BNJ* 66 (1996), 1–20

Blackburn, Mark, and Michael Bonser, 'Another Lincoln Mint-Signed Coin of Eadred', *NCirc* 105, 282

Blackburn, Mark, and Ian Carradice, ed., 'Coin Hoards 1997', *NChron* 157, 213–48 [includes six Anglo-Saxon hoards, at 229–32]

Bonser, Mike, 'Fifteen Years of Coin Finds from Productive Sites', *Yorkshire Numismatist* 3, 39–45

Booth, James, *Northern Museums. Ancient British, Anglo-Saxon, Norman and Plantagenet Coins to 1279*, SCBI 48 (Oxford)

'Northumbrian Coinage and the Productive Site at South Newbald', *Yorkshire Numismatist* 3, 15–38

Chick, Derek, 'Towards a Chronology for Offa's Coinage: an Interim Study', *Yorkshire Numismatist* 3, 47–64

Colman, Fran, 'More Meetings of Philology and Linguistics – with a Little Help from their Friends: on a Recently-Discovered Anglo-Saxon Coin', *To Explain the Present*, ed. Nevalainen and Kahlas-Tarkka, pp. 25–33

Dunger, G. T., 'A New Moneyer for a Portrait/Dorob C. Penny of Ecgberht', *NCirc* 105, 322

Hines, John, 'Coins and Runes in England and Frisia in the Seventh Century', *Frisian Runes*, ed. Looijenga and Quak, pp. 47–62

Pedersen, Anne, 'En runesceatta fra Gudme', *Nordisk Numismatisk Unions Medlemsblad*, 21–3

Pirie, E. J. E., 'Eanred's Penny: a Northumbrian Enigma', *Yorkshire Numismatist* 3, 65–8

Sinclair, May, 'A New Moneyer for the Saxon Mint of Winchcombe', *NCirc* 105, 370 [Harthacnut, Arm-and-Sceptre type, Ægelwi]

Smart, Veronica, 'A Problem of Convention: a Belated Reply', *Yorkshire Numismatist* 3, 69–72 [how to normalize Northumbrian moneyers' names]
see also sect. 8

van der Meer, Gay, 'An Early Seventeenth-Century Inventory of Cotton's Anglo-Saxon Coins', *Sir Robert Cotton as Collector*, ed. C. J. Wright (London), pp. 168–82

Weichmann, Ralf, *Edelmetalldepots der Wikingerzeit in Schleswig-Holstein. Vom 'Ringbrecher' zur Münzwirtschaft*, Offa-Bücher 77 (Neumünster, 1996) [includes several hoards with Anglo-Saxon coins]

8. ONOMASTICS

Atkin, M. A., see sect. 6

Cameron, Kenneth, 'The Danish Element in the Minor and Field-Names of

Yarborough Wapentake, Lincolnshire', *Names, Places and People*, ed. Rumble and Mills, pp. 19–25

Cameron, Kenneth, with John Field and John Insley, *The Place-Names of Lincolnshire*, V. *The Wapentake of Bradley*, EPNS 73 (Nottingham)

Coates, Richard, 'The Plural of Singular -*ing*: an Alternative Application of Old English -*ingas*', *Names, Places and People*, ed. Rumble and Mills, pp. 26–49

Cole, Ann, '*Flēot*: Distribution and Use of this OE Place-Name Element', *JEPNS* 29 (1996–7), 79–87

Dodgson, John McNeal, '*Wigingamere*', *Names, Places and People*, ed. Rumble and Mills, Appendix, pp. 383–9

Dodgson, John McNeal, ed. Alexander R. Rumble, *The Place-Names of Cheshire*, V: 2, *Introduction, Linguistic Notes and Indexes, with Appendixes*, EPNS 74 (Nottingham)

Ellerington, Enoch, 'The Derivation of the Place-Name Puckington', *Somerset and Dorset Notes and Queries* 33.344, 75–8

Fellows-Jensen, Gillian, 'Scandinavians in Cheshire: a Reassessment of the Onomastic Evidence', *Names, Places and People*, ed. Rumble and Mills, pp. 77–92

Gelling, Margaret, 'The Hunting of the *Snōr*', *Names, Places and People*, ed. Rumble and Mills, pp. 93–5

Grundy, Lynne, and Jane Roberts, 'Shapes in the Landscape: Some Words', *Names, Places and People*, ed. Rumble and Mills, pp. 96–110

Hill, David, and Sheila Sharp, see sect. 6

Hooke, Della, 'The Survival of Pre-Conquest Place-Names (Mostly Minor) in Worcestershire', *Names, Places and People*, ed. Rumble and Mills, pp. 166–81

Hough, Carole, 'The Ladies of Portinscale', *JEPNS* 29 (1996–7), 71–8 [OE *port-cwēn(e)*]

'The Place-Name Fritwell', *JEPNS* 29 (1996–7), 65–70

Insley, John, 'Ratley and Roothill', *Namn och Bygd* 85, 51–5

'A Scandinavian Personal Name in Wales', *Names, Places and People*, ed. Rumble and Mills, pp. 182–5

Jacobsson, Mattias, *Wells, Meres, and Pools: Hydronymic Terms in the Anglo-Saxon Landscape*, Acta Universitatis Upsaliensis/Studia Anglistica Upsaliensia 98 (Uppsala)

Keats-Rohan, K. S. B., and David E. Thornton, *Domesday Names: an Index of Latin Personal Names in Domesday Book* (Woodbridge)

Meaney, Audrey L., see sect. 6

Mills, A. D., 'Three Difficult Place-Names Reconsidered', *Names, Places and People*, ed. Rumble and Mills, pp. 241–6 [Skilgate, Somerset; Wellesbourne, Warwickshire; Havenstreet, Isle of Wight]

Owen, A. E. B., see sect. 6

Owen, Hywel Wyn, 'Old English Place-Name Elements in Domesday Flintshire', *Names, Places and People*, ed. Rumble and Mills, pp. 269–78

Page, R. I., see sect. 3*c*

Parsons, David, and Tania Styles, with Carole Hough, *The Vocabulary of English Place-Names (á – box)* (Nottingham)

Rumble, Alexander R., see sect. 6

Sandred, Karl Inge, 'Reading a Kentish Charter', *Names, Places and People*, ed. Rumble and Mills, pp. 320–5 [Sawyer 1458]

Smart, Veronica, '*Æle-/Ele-* as a Name-Form on Coins', *Names, Places and People*, ed. Rumble and Mills, pp. 326–9

Stiles, Patrick V., 'Old English *halh*, "Slightly Raised Ground Isolated by Marsh"', *Names, Places and People*, ed. Rumble and Mills, pp. 330–4

Thorn, F. R., see sect. 6

Wagner, Norbert, '*Tulling* und ne. *dull*', *BN* 32, 14–15

9. ARCHAEOLOGY

a. General

[Anon.], 'British Feet', *Discover* June (1996), 20 and 26 [research by Phyllis Jackson]

'Excavation Round-Up', *B.A.A.S. Bull.* 18, 5–6 [includes the discovery of four re-cut ditches at Seabank, Bristol, dating from the mid-eleventh century]

'Excavation Round-Up', *B.A.A.S. Bull.* 20, 5–6 [includes possible Anglo-Saxon structural features at Thornbury, near Bristol]

'The Making of England', *Brit. Archaeol. News* 7.1 (1992), 5 [a British Museum exhibition]

'Reports from Archaeological Units', *Bull. of the Surrey Archaeol. Soc.* 311, 10–13 [includes Anglo-Saxon finds and structural features]

'Reports from Archaeological Units', *Bull. of the Surrey Archaeol. Soc.* 312, 12–14 [includes Anglo-Saxon finds and structural features]

'Reports from Archaeological Units', *Bull. of the Surrey Archaeol. Soc.* 314, 7–13 [includes Late Saxon domestic and industrial features]

'Work Undertaken by Units in the Historic County [of Surrey]', *Bull. of the Surrey Archaeol. Soc.* 310, 16–18 [Anglo-Saxon discoveries include pottery, a pit and ditches]

Archibald, Marion, Michelle Brown and Leslie Webster, 'Heirs of Rome: the Shaping of Britain AD 400–900', *The Transformation of the Roman World AD 400–900*, ed. Webster and Brown, pp. 208–48 [consisting mostly of the catalogue of the 'Heirs of Rome' exhibition, British Museum, in collaboration with the British Library]

Bedwell, Peggy, 'The Re-Burial of Saxon Bones', *Bull. of the Surrey Archaeol. Soc.* 308, 8–9 [concerning the recent re-burial of bones from Tattenham Corner]

Bowman, Paul, 'Contrasting Pays: Anglo-Saxon Settlement and Landscape in Langton Hundred', *Anglo-Saxon Landscapes in the East Midlands*, ed. Bourne, pp. 121–46

Cessford, C[raig], see sect. 6

Cooper, Nicholas J., 'Anglo-Saxon Settlement in the Gwash Valley, Rutland', *Anglo-Saxon Landscapes in the East Midlands*, ed. Bourne, pp. 65–79

Cramp, Rosemary, 'Not Why But How: The Contribution of Archaeological Evidence to the Understanding of Anglo-Saxon England', *The Preservation and Transmission of Anglo-Saxon Culture*, ed. Szarmach and Rosenthal, pp. 271–84

Crawford, Barbara E., 'Are the Dark Ages Still Dark?', *The Worm, the Germ and the Thorn*, ed. Henry, pp. 1–4

Davies, J. L., 'Early Christian and Medieval', *Archaeol. in Wales* 19 (1979), 35–46 [includes reports on Rhuddlan (the probable site of the *burh* of *Cledemutha*), and Offa's Dyke]

'Early Christian and Medieval', *Archaeol. in Wales* 20 (1980), 56–89 [includes reports on the Late Saxon defences at Rhuddlan, and Offa's Dyke]

'Field Surveys', *Archaeol. in Wales* 13 (1973), 11–56 [includes reports on Offa's Dyke, the Saxon defences of Hereford, and a possible Anglo-Saxon spearhead from Lugg Bridge, near Hereford]

Denison, Simon, 'First Tewkesbury, Now Stamford Bridge', *Brit. Archaeol.* 27, 5 [the battle-site is to become a housing estate]

Evison, Martin, 'Lo, the Conquering Hero Comes (or Not)', *Brit. Archaeol.* 23, 8–9 [early medieval migrations considered in the light of genetic, linguistic and cultural studies]

Farley, Michael, 'Archaeological Notes from Buckinghamshire County Museum', *Records of Buckinghamshire* 37 (1997 for 1995), 173–8

Field, Naomi, and Ian George, 'Archaeology in Lincolnshire', *Lincolnshire Hist. and Archaeol.* 31 (1996), 49–68

Flores, Nona, ed., *Animals in the Middle Ages* (New York, 1996)

Glosecki, Stephen O., 'Movable Beasts: the Manifold Implications of Early Germanic Animal Imagery', *Animals in the Middle Ages*, ed. Flores, pp. 4–23

Hall, David, *The Fenland Project, Number 10: Cambridgeshire Survey, the Isle of Ely and Wisbech*, East Anglian Archaeol. Reports 79 (Cambridge, 1996)

Harvey, P. D. A., and Andrew McGuiness, see sect. 5 [seals]

Hedges, R. E. M., P. B. Pettitt, C. Bronk Ramsey and G. J. van Klinken, 'Radiocarbon Dates from the Oxford AMS System: *Archaeometry* Datelist 23', *Archaeometry* 39.1, 247–62 [includes Anglo-Saxon material]

'Radiocarbon Dates from the Oxford AMS System: *Archaeometry* Datelist 24', *Archaeometry* 39.2, 445–71 [includes Anglo-Saxon material, including bones thought to be the remains of St Chad]

Henry, David, ed., *The Worm, the Germ and the Thorn: Pictish and Related Studies presented to Isabel Henderson* (Balgaries)

Hicks, Carola, 'Isabel B. Henderson: a Bibliography of her Published Works', *The Worm, the Germ and the Thorn*, ed. Henry, pp. 188–90 [principally on art and sculpture]

Hills, Catherine, 'Frisia and England: the Archaeological Evidence for Connections', *Frisian Runes*, ed. Looijenga and Quak, pp. 35–46

Hines, John, 'Cultural Change and Social Organisation in Early Anglo-Saxon England', *After Empire*, ed. Ausenda, pp. 75–93

Hirst, Susan, and Philip Rahtz, 'Liddington Castle and the Battle of Badon: Excavations and Research 1976', *Archaeol. Jnl* 153 (1997 for 1996), 1–59 [no evidence was found that suggests this was the site of the siege of Badon]

Holroyd, Isabel, and Jeremy Oetgen, ed., *British and Irish Archaeological Bibliography* 1.1 and 1.2 [formerly the *British Archaeological Bibliography*]

Hooper, Bari, 'A Medieval Depiction of Infant-Feeding in Winchester Cathedral', *MA* 40 (1996), 230–3 [includes a summary of the early medieval evidence]

Karkov, Catherine, 'The Decoration of Early Wooden Architecture in Ireland and Northumbria', *Studies in Insular Art and Archaeology*, ed. Karkov and Farrell, pp. 27–48

Lavell, Cherry, *Handbook for British and Irish Archaeology: Sources and Resources* (Edinburgh)

Liddle, Peter, 'The Archaeology of Anglo-Saxon Leicestershire', *Anglo-Saxon Landscapes in the East Midlands*, ed. Bourne, pp. 1–10

MacGregor, Arthur, and Moira Hook, *Medieval England: from Alfred the Great to Richard III* (Oxford)

Malim, Tim, *et al.*, 'New Evidence on the Cambridgeshire Dykes and Worsted Street Roman Road', *Proc. of the Cambridge Ant. Soc.* 85 (1997 for 1996), 27–122

Margeson, Sue, *The Vikings in Norfolk* (Norwich)

Margeson, Sue, Brian Ayers and Stephen Heywood, ed., *A Festival of Norfolk Archaeology* (Norwich, 1996)

Martin, Edward, Colin Pendleton and Judith Plouviez, 'Archaeology in Suffolk 1996', *Proc. of the Suffolk Inst. of Archaeol. and Hist.* 39.1, 77–103

Meeson, Bob, 'Time and Place: Medieval Carpentry in Staffordshire', *Vernacular Archit.* 27 (1996), 10–24 [includes a brief account of the Anglo-Saxon mill at Tamworth]

Morris, Richard K., 'An English Glossary of Medieval Mouldings c. 1040–1240', *Archit. Hist.* 35 (1992), 1–17

Nenk, Beverely S., Sue Margeson and Maurice Hurley, 'Medieval Britain and Ireland in 1995', *MA* 40 (1996), 234–318 [pre-Conquest index, pp. 235–6]

Newman, Rachel, 'The Dark Ages', *The Archaeology of Lancashire*, ed. Newman, pp. 93–107

Newman, Richard, ed., *The Archaeology of Lancashire: Present State and Future Priorities* (Lancaster, 1996)

Oakey, Niall, *et al.*, 'Excavations at Orchard Lane, Huntingdon, 1994', *Proc. of the Cambridge Ant. Soc.* 85 (1997 for 1996), 123–58

Peacock, D. P. S., 'Charlemagne's Black Stones: the Re-Use of Roman Columns in Early Medieval Europe', *Antiquity* 71, 709–15

Rees, Helen, 'Tail Go Swish and the Wheels Go Round . . .', *Winchester Museums Service Newsletter* 29, 9 [concerning the uses of the horse, especially the eating of horse-meat]

Richards, Julian D., 'An Archaeology of Anglo-Saxon England', *After Empire*, ed. Ausenda, pp. 51–74 [cemeteries]

Snape, Margaret, 'An Anglo-Saxon Watermill at Corbridge', *Before Wilfrid*, ed. Corfe, pp. 40–56

Snyder, Christopher A., *Sub-Roman Britain (AD 400–600): a Gazetteer of Sites*, BAR Brit. ser. 247 (Oxford, 1996)

Taylor, Alison, *Archaeology of Cambridgeshire*, I, *South West Cambridgeshire* (Cambridge)

Thompson, Michael, *The Medieval Hall: the Basis of Secular Life, 600–1600 AD* (Aldershot, 1995)

Tyers, I., 'Tree-Ring Analysis of Claydon House, Middle Claydon, Buckinghamshire', *Ancient Monuments Laboratory Reports* 18 (1995) [some of the timbers used in the house were felled in the mid-eighth century]

[various authors], 'Bedfordshire', *South Midlands Archaeol.* 27, 1–15
  'Buckinghamshire', *South Midlands Archaeol.* 27, 15–35
  'Northamptonshire', *South Midlands Archaeol.* 27, 35–45
  'Oxfordshire', *South Midlands Archaeol.* 27, 45–77
Webster, C. J., and R. A. Croft, ed., 'Somerset Archaeology 1995', *Somerset Archaeol. and Nat. Hist.* 139 (1996), 151–77
Webster, Leslie, and Michelle Brown, ed., *The Transformation of the Roman World AD 400–900* (London)
Wilkinson, Ian P., 'Geological Controls Governing Anglo-Saxon Settlement in Framland Wapentake', *Anglo-Saxon Landscapes in the East Midlands*, ed. Bourne, pp. 53–82
Williams, Howard, 'Ancient Attitudes to Ancient Monuments', *Brit. Archaeol.* 29, 6 [the attitude of the Anglo-Saxons to earlier structures]
Wood, Ian, 'The Transmission of Ideas', *The Transformation of the Roman World AD 400–900*, ed. Webster and Brown, pp. 111–27 [includes consideration of Anglo-Saxon artifacts, especially the Ruthwell and Bewcastle crosses]
Young, Andrew, ed., 'Summary of Avon Archaeological Unit Fieldwork Projects, 1994–1995', *Bristol and Avon Archaeol.* 12 (1994–5), 68–9 [includes reports on West Wansdyke and a settlement at Keynsham]

b. Towns and other major settlements

Albarella, U., M. Beech and J. Mulville, 'The Saxon, Medieval and Post-Medieval Mammal and Bird Bones Excavated 1989–91 from Castle Mall, Norwich, Norfolk', *Ancient Monuments Laboratory Reports* 22
[Anon.], 'The Banister Fletcher Lecture: History of the Street Plan of the City', *Jnl of the London Soc.* 433, 23–4 [includes a brief summary of the Anglo-Saxon evidence]
Ayers, Brian, 'The Archaeology of Towns in Norfolk', *A Festival of Norfolk Archaeology*, ed. Margeson *et al.*, pp. 65–71
Christie, N., and S. T. Loseby, ed., *Towns in Transition* (Aldershot, 1996)
Cowie, Robert, and Deyman Eastmond, 'An Archaeological Survey of the Foreshore in the Borough of Richmond upon Thames: Part 1, Time and Tide', *The London Archaeologist* 8.4, 87–93
  'An Archaeological Survey of the Foreshore in the Borough of Richmond upon Thames, Part 2, Down by the Riverside', *The London Archaeologist* 8.5, 115–21 [includes Anglo-Saxon fish-traps]
Cracknell, Stephen, and M. W. Bishop, 'Excavations at 25–33 Brook Street, Warwick, 1973', *Birmingham and Warwickshire Archaeol. Soc. Trans.* 97 (1991–2), 1–40 [includes Anglo-Saxon]
Crummy, Phillip, *City of Victory: the Story of Colchester – Britain's First Roman Town* (Colchester) [includes a post-Roman chapter]
Davies, J. L., 'Early Christian and Medieval', *Archaeol. in Wales* 14 (1974), 27–43 [includes report on Hereford]
  'Early Christian and Medieval', *Archaeol. in Wales* 15 (1975), 53–67 [includes report on Hereford]

'Early Christian and Medieval', *Archaeol. in Wales* 21 (1981), 56–65 [includes report on *burh* site at Rhuddlan]

Denison, Simon, 'Waterfront "Used at Synod of Chelsea"', *Brit. Archaeol.* 27, 5 [waterfront would have been used by those attending the synod of 787]

Dobney, Keith, Deborah Jaques and Brian Irving, *Of Butchers and Breeds: Report on Vertebrate Remains from Various Sites in the City of Lincoln*, Lincoln Archaeol. Stud. 5 (Lincoln)

Dodgson, John McNeal, see sect. 8

Dunn, Gillian, 'Chester Archaeological Service: Recent Work', *Archaeol. North West* 4 (1992), 3–6

Farid, Shahina, and Gary Brown, 'A Butchery Site in *Lundenwic*', *The London Archaeologist* 8.6, 147–52

Falkner, Neil, 'Verulamium: Interpreting Decline', *Archaeol. Jnl* 153 (1997 for 1996), 79–103

Gurney, David, 'The "Saxon Shore" in Norfolk', *A Festival of Norfolk Archaeology*, ed. Margeson *et al.*, pp. 30–9

Haslam, Jeremy, 'The Location of the *Burh* of *Wigingamere*: a Reappraisal', *Names, Places and People*, ed. Rumble and Mills, pp. 111–30

Lebecq, Stéphane, 'Routes of Change: Production and Distribution in the West (5th–8th Century)', *The Transformation of the Roman World AD 400–900*, ed. Webster and Brown, pp. 67–78

Medlycott, Maria, 'Historic Towns in Essex', *Essex Jnl* 32.1, 10–13

Moffett, L., 'Botanical Remains from Worcester Deansway', *Ancient Monuments Laboratory Reports* 19 (1995), 39/95 [includes the Anglo-Saxon period]

'Plant Remains from an 11th Century Cesspit at Lincoln, Danes Terrace (DT 1 74)', *Ancient Monuments Laboratory Reports* 18 (1995)

'Plant Remains from Flaxengate, Lincoln', *Ancient Monuments Laboratory Reports* 21 (1996)

Murphy, P., 'Orchard Lane, Huntingdon, Cambridgeshire: Plant Macrofossils and Invertebrates from Late Saxon Contexts', *Ancient Monuments Laboratory Reports* 20 (1996)

Palliser, David, 'On the Earlier Origins of English Towns', *Brit. Archaeol.* 24, 8–9

Rogers, Penelope Walton, *Textile Production at 16–22 Coppergate*, Archaeol. of York 17.11 (York)

Roskams, Steve, 'Urban Transition in Early Medieval Britain: the Case of York', *Towns in Transition*, ed. Christie and Loseby, pp. 262–88

Sankey, David, and Malcolm McKenzie, '7–11 Bishopsgate: a Hole in the Heart of London's Business District', *The London Archaeologist* 8.7, 171–9 [includes a dark earth layer with Anglo-Saxon artifacts]

Shaw, Mike, Andy Chapman and Iain Soden, 'Northampton', *CA* 155, 408–15

Shoesmith, R., 'Reports of the Sectional Recorders: Archaeology 1994', *Trans. of the Woolhope Naturalists' Field Club* 48.1 (1994), 140–3 [includes a brief account of evidence from Hereford]

Starley, D., 'The Assessment of Slag and Other Metalworking Debris from Franciscan Way, Ipswich, 1990', *Ancient Monuments Laboratory Reports* 19 (1995)

Teague, Steve, 'Excavations at 12–15 High Street', *Winchester Museums Service Newsletter* 28, 4–5

Wilson, P. R., *et al.*, 'Early Anglian Catterick and *Catraeth*', *MA* 40 (1996), 1–61

Woodger, Aidan, 'The Archaeological Reinvestigation of Bolsa House (76–80 Cheapside) in the City of London', *The London Archaeologist* 8.6, 143–6

c. Rural settlements, agriculture and the countryside

[Anon.], 'Fieldwork and Excavation in 1996', *Med. Settlement Research Group Ann. Report* 11 (1996), 37–54

'The Shapwick Project', *CA* 151, 244–54 [a project to investigate the origins of a Somerset village]

Arrowsmith, Peter, and Mark Fletcher, "Nico Ditch" and "Carr Ditch": a Case of Mistaken Identity?', *Archaeol. North West* 5 (1993), 26–32 [it seems likely that re-cuttings of the ditch have destroyed pre-Conquest evidence]

Bick, David, 'Earthworks in or near Hay Wood, Oxenhall', *New Regard* 11 (1996), 35–7

Blue, L., 'Maritime Archaeology in Britain and Northern Ireland, 1996', *International Jnl of Nautical Archaeol.* 26.3, 252–62 [includes a brief note on the water-chute of an Anglo-Saxon mill at Corbridge]

Bruce-Mitford, Rupert, ed. Robin J. Taylor, *Mawgan Porth: a Settlement of the Late Saxon Period on the North Cornish Coast: Excavations 1949–52, 1954 and 1974*, Eng. Heritage Archaeol. Reports 13 (London)

Cole, M., 'Report on the Geophysical Survey at Mornington House Farm, Gosberton, Lincolnshire', *Ancient Monuments Laboratory Reports* 19 (1995) [presents limited evidence for Anglo-Saxon occupation]

Connor, Aileen, Luke Fagan and Mark Fletcher, 'Nico Ditch: Excavations at Kenwood Road, Reddish, Stockport', *Archaeol. North West* 1 (1991), 3–7 [a linear earthwork which may be early medieval]

Davies, J. L., 'Early Christian and Medieval', *Archaeol. in Wales* 16 (1976), 38–45 [includes report on Offa's Dyke]

Denison, Simon, 'Rare Early Saxon Village in Midlands', *Brit. Archaeol.* 26, 5 [Eye Kettleby, near Melton Mowbray]

Harbottle, Barbara, 'Medieval Settlements in Tyne and Wear: Excavations, Mostly in 1992', *Archaeol. North* 5 (1993), 12–13 [brief account included of an attempt to locate the pre-Conquest village of Bishopswearmouth]

Lilley, Keith D., 'MSRG Annual Conference 1996: Villages and their Territories', *Med. Settlement Research Group Ann. Report* 11 (1996), 9–10

Margeson, Sue, 'Viking Settlement in Norfolk: a Study of New Evidence', *A Festival of Norfolk Archaeology*, ed. Margeson *et al.*, pp. 47–57

Meaney, Audrey L., see sect. 6

Medieval Settlement Research Group, 'Medieval Rural Settlements – a Policy on their Research, Survey, Conservation and Excavation', *Med. Settlement Research Group Ann. Report* 11 (1996), 5–8

Palmer-Brown, Colin, 'Two Middle Saxon Grubenhäuser at St Nicholas School, Church Road, Boston', *Lincolnshire Hist. and Archaeol.* 31 (1996), 10–19

Parfitt, Keith, 'Whitfield Churchyard Evaluation', *Kent Archaeol. Rev.* 128, 181–3 [no new Anglo-Saxon evidence, but includes a brief account of the settlement excavated in 1995]

Rees-Jones, J., and M. S. Tite, 'Optical Dating Results for British Archaeological Sediments', *Archaeometry* 39.1, 177–87 [includes material from Anglo-Saxon water mills at West Cotton, Northants.]

Rogerson, Andrew, 'Rural Settlement *c.* 400–1200', *A Festival of Norfolk Archaeology*, ed. Margeson *et al.*, pp. 58–64

Sirot-Smith, Martin, 'Sulgrave – 1: the Early Centuries', *Cake and Cockhorse* 14.1, 8–16

d. Pagan cemeteries and Sutton Hoo

[Anon.], 'Anglo-Saxon Cemetery at Bottledump Corner: a Correction', *Records of Buckinghamshire* 37 (1997 for 1995), 1–2 [this corrects an erroneous caption to fig. 1 in the article by Parkhouse and Smith in the previous volume]

Baker, Evelyn, 'Dying for a Pint or Bedford's Oldest Residents', *Bedfordshire Mag.* 203, 122–3 [?sixth-seventh-century cemetery]

Fell, Vanessa, 'The Anglo-Saxon Cemetery at Snape, Suffolk: Scientific Analyses of the Artefacts and Other Materials', *Ancient Monuments Laboratory Reports* 20 (1996)

Finney, T., 'Investigation of a Skull Fragment from Cremation 704, Mucking, Essex', *Ancient Monuments Laboratory Reports* 20 (1996)

Greatorex, Christopher, 'Eastbourne's Oldest Cemetery', *Sussex Past and Present* 83, 6–7

Härke, Heinrich, 'Finding Britons in Anglo-Saxon Graves', *Brit. Archaeol.* 10 (1995), 7

Meadows, Ian, 'Wollaston: the "Pioneer" Burial', *CA* 154, 391–5

Parfitt, Keith, and Birte Brugmann, *The Anglo-Saxon Cemetery on Mill Hill, Deal, Kent*, Soc. for Med. Archaeol. Monograph Ser. 14 (London)

Rahtz, Philip, 'Sutton Hoo, 1987', *Brit. Archaeol. News* 2.3 (1987), 35

Turner, Dennis, 'Croydon Anglo-Saxon Cemetery', *Bull. of the Surrey Archaeol. Soc.* 302 (1996), 6–7 [concerning a proposed development of the site]

Watson, J., 'Mineral Preserved Organic Material Associated with Metalwork from Excavations on the Westhampnett Bypass, West Sussex', *Ancient Monuments Laboratory Reports* 18 (1995), [includes material from an Anglo-Saxon grave]

Welch, Martin, 'The Anglo-Saxon Cemetery at 82–90 Park Lane, Croydon, Surrey: Excavation or Preservation?', *The London Archaeologist* 8.4, 94–7

Wymer, J. J., 'The Excavation of a Ring-Ditch at South Acre', *Barrow Excavations in Norfolk, 1984–88*, by Wymer, with contributions by Alison Cameron *et al.*, East Anglian Archaeol. Reports 77 (Dereham, 1996)

e. Churches, monastic sites and Christian cemeteries

Adams, Max, 'Excavation of a Pre-Conquest Cemetery at Addingham, West Yorkshire', *MA* 40 (1996), 151–91

Anderson, S., 'The Human Skeletal Remains from Farmer's Avenue, Castle Mall, Norwich (Excavated 1989–91)', *Ancient Monuments Laboratory Reports* 21 (1996)

[Anon.], 'Saxon Site at Flixborough', *Brit. Archaeol. News* 6.5 (1991), 59

Bennet, Paul, and John Williams, 'Monkton', *CA* 151, 258–64 [includes a small Anglo-Saxon cemetery]

Boyleston, A., and C. Roberts, 'Lincoln Excavations 1972–87: Report on the Human Skeletal Remains', *Ancient Monuments Laboratory Reports* 22 [includes four Anglo-Saxon burials]

Crawford, Sally, and Chris Guy, 'As Normans Tore Down Saxon Cathedrals', *Brit. Archaeol.* 29, 7 [the relation of the Norman Worcester Cathedral to its predecessor]

Denison, Simon, 'New 7th Century Remains Found at Ripon', *Brit. Archaeol.* 24, 5

Geake, Helen, *Use of Grave Goods in Conversion Period England, c. 600–c. 850*, BAR Brit. ser. 261 (Oxford)

Gem, Richard, and Malcolm Thurlby, 'The Early Monastic Church of Lastingham', *Yorkshire Monasticism*, ed. Hoey, pp. 31–9

Hall, R. A., and Mark Whyman, 'Settlement and Monasticism at Ripon, North Yorkshire, from the 7th to 11th Centuries A.D.', *MA* 40 (1996), 62–150

Hall, Richard, 'Antiquaries and Archaeology in and around Ripon Minster', *Yorkshire Monasticism*, ed. Hoey, pp. 12–30

Hill, Peter, *Whithorn and St Ninian: the Excavation of a Monastic Town, 1984–91* (Stroud)

Hoey, Lawrence R., ed., *Yorkshire Monasticism: Archaeology, Art and Architecture from the 7th to 16th Centuries* (London, 1995)

Loveluck, Chris, 'Uncovering an Anglo-Saxon "Royal" Manor', *Brit. Archaeol.* 28, 8–9 [Flixborough]

MacAulay, Stephen, *Late Saxon and Medieval Archaeology at Ramsey Abbey, Cambridgeshire: an Archaeological Evaluation*, Cambridgeshire County Council Archaeol. Report 129 (Cambridge, 1996)

Mills, Peter, 'Excavations at the Dorter Undercroft, Westminster Abbey', *Trans. of the London and Middlesex Archaeol. Soc.* 46 (1997 for 1995), 69–124 [includes structural evidence from the mid-eleventh-century monastic settlement]

Mortimer, C., 'Non-Ferrous Metalworking Debris from Barking Abbey (Site Number BAAH95), London', *Ancient Monuments Laboratory Reports* 20 (1996)

Penn, Kenneth, 'The Early Church in Norfolk: Some Aspects', *A Festival of Norfolk Archaeology*, ed. Margeson *et al.*, pp. 40–6

Rahtz, Philip, and Lorna Watts, 'Kirkdale Anglo-Saxon Minster', *CA* 155, 419–22

Rahtz, Philip, and Lorna Watts, with Harold Taylor and Lawrence Butler, *St Mary's Church, Deerhurst, Gloucestershire: Fieldwork, Excavations and Structural Analysis 1971–1984*, Reports of the Research Committee of the Soc. of Antiquaries of London 55 (Woodbridge)

Roberts, Marion, 'Thomas Gray's Contribution to the Study of Medieval Architecture', *Archit. Hist.* 36 (1993), 49–68 [an eighteenth-century view of Saxon and Norman churches]

Ryder, Peter F., 'Some Medieval Churches in County Durham', *Durham Archaeol. Jnl* 12 (1996), 61–87 [includes Anglo-Saxon]

Schofield, John, 'Saxon and Medieval Parish Churches in the City of London: a Review', *Trans. of the London and Middlesex Archaeol. Soc.* 45 (1996 for 1994), 23–145

Scobie, Graham, 'The Nunnaminster', *Winchester Museums Service Newsletter* 28, 2–3

Tyers, I., 'Tree-Ring Analysis of Timbers from the Stave Church at Greensted, Essex', *Ancient Monuments Laboratory Reports* 20 (1996)

f. Ships and seafaring

Geake, Elisabeth, 'Saxon Boat Builders on the Right Tack', *New Scientist* 29 August 1992, 11

Gifford, Edwin, and Joyce Gifford, 'The Sailing Performance of Anglo-Saxon Ships as Derived from the Building and Trials of Half-Scale Models of the Sutton Hoo and Graveney Ship Finds', *Mariner's Mirror* 82 (1996), 131–53

Goodburn, D. M., with contributions from C. Thomas, 'Reused Medieval Ship Planks from Westminster, England, Possibly Derived from a Vessel Built in the Cog Style', *International Jnl of Nautical Archaeol.* 26.1, 26–38 [includes a brief account of Frisian boat fragments from London of the tenth to eleventh century]

g. Sculpture on bone, stone and wood

Bailey, Richard N., *Ambiguous Birds and Beasts: Three Sculptural Puzzles in South-West Scotland*, Fourth Whithorn Lecture (Whithorn, 1996)

England's Earliest Sculptors, Publ. of the Dictionary of OE 5 (Toronto, 1996)

Dornier, Ann, 'The Breedon Lion and its Associates: a Comparative Study of Anglo-Saxon and Frankish Architectural Animal Panels', *Anglo-Saxon Landscapes in the East Midlands*, ed. Bourne, pp. 37–52

Hawkes, Jane, 'Old Testament Heroes: Iconographies of Insular Sculpture', *The Worm, the Germ and the Thorn*, ed. Henry, pp. 149–58

Sidebottom, Phil, 'Monuments that Mark Out Viking Land', *Brit. Archaeol.* 23, 7

Turner, Dennis, 'Anglo-Saxon Sculpture in Surrey', *Bull. of the Surrey Archaeol. Soc.* 305 (1996), 7

Weatherhead, Rennie, 'Anglian Cross Fragments Found in East Lothian', *Trans. of the East Lothian Ant. and Field Naturalists' Soc.* 22 (1993), 53–61

h. Metal-work and other minor objects

Ager, Barry, 'A Late Roman Buckle- or Belt-Plate in the British Museum, Said to be from Northern France', *MA* 40 (1996), 206–11 [the plate has close connections with the early Anglo-Saxon Quoit Brooch Style]

Anheuser, K., and C. Mortimer, 'Analysis of Non-Ferrous Metal Artefacts from Barrington (Edix Hill) Anglo-Saxon Cemetery, Cambridgeshire', *Ancient Monuments Laboratory Reports* 21 (1996)

[Anon.], 'AS Treasure Saved for Warwickshire', *Brit. Archaeol. News* 5.1 (1990), 4 [Wasperton Collection]

Coatsworth, Elizabeth, Maria Fitzgerald, Kevin Leahy, and Gale Owen-Crocker, 'Anglo-Saxon Textiles from Cleatham, Humberside', *Textile Hist.* 27.1 (1996), 5–41

Denford, Geoffrey, 'Stolen Anglo-Saxon Buckle and Plate Recovered', *Winchester Museums Service Newsletter* 26 (1996), 8 [concerning a buckle from Droxford]

Farley, Michael, and John Hines, 'A Great Square-Headed Brooch Fragment from Buckinghamshire', *MA* 40 (1996), 211–14

Henry, Philippa, 'A Culture-Historical Approach to Late Saxon Textile Studies', *Archaeol. Textiles Newsletter* 22 (1996), 7–11

Hines, John, *A New Corpus of Anglo-Saxon Great Square-Headed Brooches*, Reports of the Research Committee of the Soc. of Ant. of London 51 (Woodbridge)

Hinton, David A., 'A "Winchester-Style" Mount from near Winchester', *MA* 40 (1996), 214–17

Hutchinson, M. E., 'A Technical Examination of the Non-Glass Beads from Two Anglo-Saxon Cemeteries at Mucking, Essex', *Ancient Monuments Laboratory Reports* 19 (1995)

Iles, Robin, 'A Stirrup-Mount from Headbourne Worthy', *Winchester Museums Service Newsletter* 26 (1996), 7

Jessop, Oliver, 'A New Artefact Typology for the Study of Medieval Arrowheads', *MA* 40 (1996), 192–205

Magnus, Bente, 'The Firebed of the Serpent: Myth and Religion in the Migration Period Mirrored Through Some Golden Objects', *The Transformation of the Roman World AD 400–900*, ed. Webster and Brown, pp. 194–207 [dealing with bracteates and relief brooches, mainly Scandinavian]

McCarthy, Mike, 'The Work of Carlisle Archaeological Unit 1990–94', *Archaeol. North* 8 (1994), 8–15 [includes an illustration of a tenth-century belt-set]

McCulloch, Paul, 'Excavations at Monk Sherborne', *Winchester Museums Service Newsletter* 26 (1996), 5–6 [a hoard of ironwork includes a sixth- to seventh-century buckle]

Mortimer, C., 'Analysis of Non-Ferrous Metalworking Waste from Castle Mall, Norwich, Norfolk', *Ancient Monuments Laboratory Reports* 21 (1996)

'Analysis of Two Anglo-Saxon Gold Pendants from Barrington Edix Hill, Cambridgeshire', *Ancient Monuments Laboratory Reports* 20 (1996)

'Technical Analysis of the Belt Set from Grave 117, Mucking Anglo-Saxon Cemetery, Essex', *Ancient Monuments Laboratory Reports* 18 (1995)

'Technical Analysis of the Ripon Jewel', *Ancient Monuments Laboratory Reports* 20 (1996), 3/96

Mortimer, C., and M. Stoney, 'Decorative Punchmarks on Non-Ferrous Artefacts from Barrington Edix Hill Anglo-Saxon Cemetery 1989–91, Cambridgeshire, in their Regional Context', *Ancient Monuments Laboratory Reports* 21 (1996)

Murphy, P., 'Anglo-Saxon Hurdles and Basketry, Collins Creek, Blackwater Estuary, Essex', *Ancient Monuments Laboratory Reports* 18 (1995)

Rahtz, Philip, 'St Cuthbert A.D. 687–1987', *Brit. Archaeol. News* 2.7 (1987), 67 [St Cuthbert relics]

Ryan, Michael, 'Links between Anglo-Saxon and Irish Early Medieval Art: Some Evidence of Metalwork', *Studies in Insular Art and Archaeology*, ed. Karkov and Farrell, pp. 117–26

Starley, D., 'Assessment of Metalworking Debris from No. 1 Poultry, City of London, 1994–6', *Ancient Monuments Laboratory Reports* 22

'A Technological Study of Knives and Spearheads from the Excavations at Mucking, Essex', *Ancient Monuments Laboratory Reports* 20 (1996)

Watson, J., 'Iron Coffin Fittings from Ailey Hill, Ripon, North Yorkshire', *Ancient Monuments Laboratory Reports* 21 (1996)

Williams, David, 'Metal Detector Finds: Recent Recording Work', *Bull. of the Survey Archaeol. Soc.* 310, 8–10 [includes Anglo-Saxon metalwork]

i. Inscriptions

Brooke, Christopher J., 'Ground-Based Remote Sensing of Buildings and Archaeological Sites: Ten Years Research to Operation', *Archaeol. Prospection* 1.2 (1994), 105–19 [includes laser surface profiling of the runic inscription on the Bewcastle Cross]

Graham, Timothy, see sect. 5

Higgitt, John, 'Early Medieval Inscriptions in Britain and Ireland and their Audiences', *The Worm, the Germ and the Thorn*, ed. Henry, pp. 67–78

Looijenga, Tineke, 'On the Origin of the Anglo-Frisian Runic Innovations', *Frisian Runes*, ed. Looijenga and Quak, pp. 109–22

Okasha, Elisabeth, 'Anglo-Saxon Architectural Inscriptions', *The Worm, the Germ and the Thorn*, ed. Henry, pp. 79–84

j. Pottery and glass

Bayley, J., and S. Rye, 'Glassworking Crucibles from Excavations at Buckden, Hunts, 1961–64', *Ancient Monuments Laboratory Reports* 21 (1996)

Mortimer, C., 'Analysis of a Fragment of Decorated Saxon Vessel Glass from Westminster Abbey, London', *Ancient Monuments Laboratory Reports* 19 (1995)

'Compositional and Structural Analysis of Glass Beads from Barrington Anglo-Saxon Cemetery, Cambridgeshire', *Ancient Monuments Laboratory Reports* 21 (1996)

'Compositional and Structural Analysis of Glass Beads from Mucking Anglo-Saxon Cemeteries, Essex', *Ancient Monuments Laboratory Reports* 21 (1996)

'Glass Linen Smoothers from 16–22 Coppergate, York', *Ancient Monuments Laboratory Reports* 18 (1995)

Williams, D., 'A Petrological Examination of Middle Saxon Ipswich Ware Pottery (English Heritage Ipswich Ware Project)', *Ancient Monuments Laboratory Reports* 21 (1996)

k. Musical instruments

10. REVIEWS

Abrams, Lesley, *Anglo-Saxon Glastonbury* (Woodbridge, 1996): M. Chibnall, *EconHR* 50, 556; A. D. Frankforter, *Church Hist.* 66, 894; L. Marston, *Somerset Archaeol. and Nat. Hist.* 139, 188–9

Aertsen, Henk, and Rolf H. Bremmer, Jr, ed., *Companion to Old English Poetry* (Amsterdam, 1994): A. Liberman, *ES* 78, 190–3

Andrews, Phil, *Excavations at Redcastle Furze, Thetford, 1988–9* (Gressenhall, 1995): J. Newman, *MA* 40, 336–7

Aston, Michael, and Carenza Lewis, ed., *The Medieval Landscape of Wessex* (Oxford, 1994): N. J. Higham, *Med. Life* 6, 35; C. C. Thornton, *Somerset Archaeol. and Nat. Hist.* 139, 190–1

Bailey, Richard N., *England's Earliest Sculptors* (Toronto, 1996): J. Hines, *N&Q* 44, 539–40

Baker, Peter S., and Michael Lapidge, ed., *Byrhtferth's 'Enchiridion'* (Oxford, 1995): J. Hill, *EME* 6, 97–8; J. D. Pheifer, *N&Q* 44, 247–9; C. Ruff, *Envoi* 6, 92–5

Bede and his World, with a preface by Michael Lapidge ([Aldershot], 1994): J. W. Houghton, *Libraries & Culture* 32, 132–3

Bischoff, Bernhard, and Michael Lapidge, *Biblical Commentaries from the Canterbury School of Theodore and Hadrian* (Cambridge, 1994); J.-M. Auwers, *Revue d'Histoire Ecclésiastique* 92, 1052–3; H. Gneuss, *Anglia* 115, 251–5; A. Härdelin, *Kyrkohistorisk Årsskrift* 1997, 197–8; E. A. Matter, *Speculum* 72, 435–7; R. W. Pfaff, *Church Hist.* 66, 893; B. Ward, *JEH* 48, 145–8

Bjork, Robert E., and John D. Niles, ed., *A Beowulf Handbook* (Lincoln, NE): S. J. Harris, *Envoi* 6, 155–61

Blair, John, *Anglo-Saxon Oxfordshire* (Stroud, 1994): S. Youngs, *Minerva* 7.1, 57

Britton, Derek, ed., *English Historical Linguistics 1994* (Amsterdam 1996): L. Wright, *N&Q* 44, 536–7

Broderick, George, *Placenames of the Isle of Man*, 1, *Sheading of Glenfaba (Kirk Patrick, Kirk German, and Peel)* (Tübingen, 1994): J. Insley, *BN* 32, 239–43

Brown, Michelle P., *The Book of Cerne* (Toronto, Buffalo, and London, 1996): T. H. Bestul, *Envoi* 6, 33–9: W. Noel, *EME* 6, 230–2

Brown, T. Julian, *A Palaeographer's View*, ed. Janet Bately *et al.* (London, 1993): M. Kauffmann, *RES* 48, 367–9

Cameron, Kenneth, *English Place Names*, rev. ed. (London, 1996): A. Everitt, *JEPNS* 29, 89–94

Cameron, Kenneth, with John Field and John Insley, *The Place-Names of Lincolnshire*, III (Nottingham, 1992 for 1988–9): K. I. Sandred, *Anglia* 115, 97–100

Cameron, M. L., *Anglo-Saxon Medicine* (Cambridge, 1993): J. M. Riddle, *Speculum* 72, 121–2; W. O. Schalick III, *Bull. of the Hist. of Medicine* 71, 142–4

Carruthers, Leo, *L'Anglais médiéval* (Turnhout, 1996): M. Windross, *AB* 115, 453–4

Clark, Cecily, *Words, Names and History*, ed. Peter Jackson (Cambridge, 1995): G. T. Beech, *Med. Prosopography* 18, 243–4; P. Cavill, *Nottingham Med. Stud.* 41, 186–91; P. McClure, *JEPNS* 29, 94–9; K. I. Sandred, *Namn och Bygd* 85, 152–5

Clarke, Peter A., *The English Nobility under Edward the Confessor* (Oxford, 1994): S. Morillo, *Speculum* 72, 804–6

Clayton, Mary, and Hugh Magennis, ed. and trans., *The Old English Lives of St Margaret* (Cambridge, 1994): B. Millett, *MLR* 92, 162–4; K. O'Brien O'Keeffe, *Speculum* 72, 451–3; E. G. Whatley, *Peritia* 10, 415–19

Clemoes, Peter, *Interactions of Thought and Language in Old English Poetry* (Cambridge, 1995): R. S. Allen, *MLR* 92, 682–5; J. Hill, *MÆ* 66, 314–16; H. Magennis, *ES* 78, 78–83; D. G. Scragg, *RES* 48, 76–7

Conner, Patrick W., ed., *The Abingdon Chronicle* (Cambridge, 1996): C. Hart, see sect. 3c; A. R. Rumble, *History* 83, 124–5; E. G. Stanley, *N&Q* 44, 374–7

Bibliography for 1997

Connolly, Seán, trans., *Bede: on the Temple* (Liverpool, 1995): W. A. Chaney, *Church Hist.* 66, 324; T. McIntyre, *Downside Rev.* 399, 155–6; L. E. von Padberg, *Francia* 24.1, 198–200

Costen, Michael, *The Origins of Somerset* (Manchester, 1993): D. A. Carpenter, *Southern Hist.* 16, 186–7

Crawford, Barbara, E., ed., *Scandinavian Settlement in Northern Britain* (London, 1995): C. Batey, *EME* 6, 232–4; K. Cameron, *JEPNS* 29, 99–100

Cubbin, G. P., ed., *MS D* (Cambridge, 1996): C. Hart, see sect. 3c; E. G. Stanley, *N&Q* 44, 374–7

Cubitt, Catherine, *Anglo-Saxon Church Councils c. 650–c. 850* (Leicester, 1995): L. J. Abrams, *JTS* 48, 721–4: S. Coates, *History* 82, 286–7; R. Meens, *Tijdschrift voor Gescheidenis* 110, 63–4

Damico, Helen, and John Leyerle, ed., *Heroic Poetry in the Anglo-Saxon Period* (Kalamazoo, MI, 1993): H. Magennis, *ES* 78, 83–6

Dark, K. R., *Civitas to Kingdom* (Leicester, 1994): I. N. Wood, *NH* 33, 278–9

Darlington, R. R., and P. McGurk, ed., *The Chronicle of John of Worcester*, II (Oxford, 1995): S. Keynes, *Speculum* 72, 177–9

Davis, Craig R., *'Beowulf' and the Demise of Germanic Legend in England* (New York, 1996): R. E. Bjork, *Scandinavian Stud.* 69, 388–9; M. Swan, *MÆ* 66, 317–18

Derolez, R., ed., *Anglo-Saxon Glossography* (Brussels, 1992): P. A. Thompson, *Jnl of Med. Latin* 7, 255–8

Doane, A. N., *Anglo-Saxon Manuscripts in Microfiche Facsimile*, 1 (Binghamton, NY, 1994): A. Mentzel-Reuters, *DAEM* 53, 302; N. Speirs, *RES* 48, 369–71

Düwel, Klaus, ed., *Runische Schriftkultur in kontinental-skandinavischer und -angelsächsischer Wechselbeziehung* (Berlin, 1994): R. Nedoma, *Die Sprache* 37, 105–15

Dumville, David N., *English Caroline Script and Monastic History* (Woodbridge, 1993): M. J. Franklin, *Southern Hist.* 16, 185–6; F. Gasparri, *Le Moyen Âge* 103, 371–3; G. H. Martin, *The Library* 6th ser., 19, 363–4

Liturgy and the Ecclesiastical History of Late Anglo-Saxon England (Woodbridge, 1992): M. McC. Gatch, *Church Hist.* 66, 328–9

Dumville, David N., ed., *Facsimile of MS F: the Domitian Bilingual* (Cambridge, 1995): D. Donoghue, *Speculum* 72, 463–4; C. Hart, see sect. 3c; C. Insley, *EHR* 112, 1232–3; E. G. Stanley, *N&Q* 44, 374–7

Eales, Richard, and Richard Sharpe, ed., *Canterbury and the Norman Conquest* (London, 1995): F. Barlow, *Southern Hist.* 18, 155–6; H. E. J. Cowdrey, *EHR* 112, 960–1; F. Rexroth, *DAEM* 53, 378–9

Earl, James W., *Thinking about 'Beowulf'* (Stanford, CA, 1994): D. C. Baker, *ELN* 35.1, 49–50; H. Barkley, *Speculum* 72, 464–6; J. Hill, *MLR* 92, 160–2; T. A. Shippey, *JEGP* 96, 248–51

Ferrari, Michele Camillo, *Sancti Willibrordi venerantes memoriam* (Luxembourg, 1994): L. Wankenne, *RB* 107, 185

Fichte, Jörg O., and Fritz Kemmler, *Alt- und mittelenglische Literatur*, 2nd ed. (Tübingen, 1994): M. Markus, *ZAA* 45, 79–81

Foley, John Miles, *The Singer of Tales in Performance* (Bloomington, IN, 1995): K. Reichl, *Anglia* 115, 532–5; G. Russom, *Speculum* 72, 468–9

Frantzen, Allen J., and Douglas Moffat, ed., *The Work of Work* (Glasgow, 1994): W. Steurs, *Le Moyen Âge* 103, 416–18

Fulk, R. D., *A History of Old English Meter* (Philadelphia, PA, 1992): H. Momma, *ELN* 35.1, 79–83

Gameson, Richard, *The Role of Art in the Late Anglo-Saxon Church* (Oxford, 1995): F. Barlow, *EHR* 112, 698–9; S. A. Brown, *AHR* 102, 433; L. Brownrigg, *EME* 6, 104–6; R. McKitterick, *TLS* 20 June, p. 20

Gameson, Richard, ed., *The Early Medieval Bible* (Cambridge, 1994): L. W. Countryman, *Church Hist.* 66, 98–9; C. De Hamel, *EHR* 112, 427–8; T. O'Loughlin, *Peritia* 11, 413–15; M. J. Swanton, *MLR* 92, 408–9

Godden, Malcolm, Douglas Gray and Terry Hoad, ed., *From Anglo-Saxon to Early Middle English* (Oxford, 1994): J. Hill, *Anglia* 115, 380–3; T. A. Shippey, *MLR* 92, 165; H. L. C. Tristram, *ASNSL* 234, 133–6

Griffiths, Bill, *An Introduction to Early English Law* (Hockwold-cum-Wilton, Norf., 1995): H. Sauer, *DAEM* 53, 260

Grinda, Klaus R., and Claus-Dieter Wetzel, ed., *Anglo-Saxonica* (Munich, 1993): U. Schaefer, *ASNSL* 234, 128–33

Günzel, Beate, ed., *Ælfwine's Prayerbook* (Woodbridge, 1993): P. E. Szarmach, *Speculum* 72, 100–1

Hall, David, *The Open Fields of Northamptonshire* (Northampton, 1995): A. R. Dewindt, *Albion* 29, 86–8

Harvey, P. D. A., and Andrew McGuiness, *A Guide to British Medieval Seals* (Toronto, 1996): D. Heissen, *Albion* 29, 80–1

Healey, Antonette diPaolo, *et al.*, ed., *Dictionary of Old English: A* (Toronto, 1996): J. Bately, *N&Q* 44, 373–4

Higham, N. J., *The English Conquest* (Manchester, 1994): D. P. Kirby, *EHR* 112, 155; R. C. Stacey, *Speculum* 72, 167–9; I. N. Wood, *NH* 33, 273–7

    An English Empire (Manchester, 1995): R. Abels, *Albion* 28, 658–60; H. Vollrath, *DAEM* 52, 718; I. N. Wood, *NH* 33, 273–7; B. Yorke, *EHR* 112, 957–8

    The Kingdom of Northumbria (Dover, 1993): I. N. Wood, *NH* 33, 273–7

    The Origins of Cheshire (Manchester, 1993): I. N. Wood, *NH* 33, 273–7

Hill, John M., *The Cultural World in 'Beowulf'* (Toronto, Buffalo, and London, 1995): G. Clark, *Speculum* 72, 483–5; R. Marsden, *RES* 48, 373–4; E. G. Stanley, *N&Q* 44, 433–4

Hill, Joyce, ed., *Old English Minor Heroic Poems* (Durham, 1994): D. Donoghue, *Speculum* 72, 169

Hollis, Stephanie, *Anglo-Saxon Women and the Church* (Woodbridge, 1992): J. Verdon, *CCM* 40, 284–5

Hollis, Stephanie, and Michael J. Wright, *Old English Prose of Secular Learning* (Woodbridge, 1992): F. Wenisch, *Anglia* 115, 243–7

Hooke, Della, *Pre-Conquest Charter-Bounds of Devon and Cornwall* (Woodbridge, 1994): L. Olson, *EME* 6, 236–7

Hutcheson, B. R., *Old English Poetic Metre* (Cambridge, 1995): A. H. Feulner, *Interdisciplinary Jnl for Germanic Ling. and Semiotic Analysis* 2, 347–50; R. D. Fulk, *Language* 73, 866–9; M. Griffith, *MÆ* 66, 313–14

Irvine, Martin, *The Making of Textual Culture* (Cambridge, 1994): M. Camargo, *MP* 94, 500–3; J. Hines, *MLR* 92, 405–6

Jack, George, ed., *'Beowulf': a Student Edition* (Oxford, 1994): H. Gneuss, *Anglia* 115, 388–9; J. D. Niles, *Speculum* 72, 176–7

Jolly, Karen Louise, *Popular Religion in Late Saxon England* (Chapel Hill, NC, 1996): J. Blair, *Albion* 29, 271–2; R. W. Pfaff, *AHR* 102, 797–8

Jones, Michael E., *The End of Roman Britain* (Ithaca, NY, and London, 1996): N. W. Nolte, *Albion* 29, 269–71

Kastovsky, Dieter, ed., *Historical English Syntax* (Berlin and New York, 1991): I. Milfull, *Word* 48, 296–303

Keynes, Simon, ed., *The Liber Vitae of the New Minster and Hyde Abbey Winchester* (Copenhagen, 1996): J. Bately, *N&Q* 44, 370–1; P. A. Hayward, *MÆ* 66, 129–30; H. R. Loyn, *JEH* 48, 542–3

Kiernan, Kevin S., *'Beowulf' and the 'Beowulf' Manuscript*, rev. ed. (Ann Arbor, MI, 1996): G. F. Rose, see sect. 3*bii*

Kornexl, Lucia, *Die Regularis Concordia und ihre altenglische Interlinearversion* (Munich, 1993): U. Schaefer, *ASNSL* 234, 138–40

Krygier, Marcin, *The Disintegration of the English Strong Verb System* (Frankfurt am Main, 1994): H. F. Nielsen, *Jnl of Eng. Ling.* 25, 266–9

Laing, Lloyd, and Jennifer Laing, *Early English Art and Architecture* (Stroud, 1996): C. S. Drake, *Med. Life* 7, 37

Lapidge, Michael, *Anglo-Saxon Litanies of the Saints* (London, 1991): H. Gneuss, *Anglia* 115, 251–5

Lapidge, Michael, ed., *Archbishop Theodore* (Cambridge, 1995): N. Brooks, *EHR* 112, 1227–9; H. Gneuss, *Anglia* 115, 251–5; A. Härdelin, *Kyrkohistorisk Årsskrift* 1997, 197–8; R. W. Pfaff, *Speculum* 72, 852–4; A. P. Smyth, *Albion* 28, 459–60; B. Ward, *JEH* 48, 145–8; P. Wormald, *N&Q* 44, 242–4

Lapidge, Michael, Malcolm Godden and Simon Keynes, ed., *Anglo-Saxon England* 24 (Cambridge, 1995): A. J. Kabir, *N&Q* 44, 108–9

Anglo-Saxon England 25 (Cambridge, 1996): R. Derolez, *ES* 78, 478–9

Lenker, Ursula, *Die westsächsische Evangelienversion und die Perikopenordnungen im angelsächsischen England* (Munich): P.-M. Bogaert, *RB* 107, 392–4

Lewis, Carenza, Patrick Mitchell-Fox and Christopher Dyer, *Village, Hamlet and Field* (Manchester, 1997): K. Troup, *EconHR* 50, 833–4

Leyser, Henrietta, *Medieval Women. A Social History of Women in England 450–1500* (London, 1995): Y. Wada, *Stud. in Engl. Lit.* (Tokyo) 74, 61–4 [in Japanese]

Lindsay, W. M., *Studies in Early Medieval Latin Glossaries*, ed. Michael Lapidge (Aldershot, 1996): P. Rusche, *Jnl of Med. Latin* 7, 263–6

Love, Rosalind C., ed. and trans., *Three Eleventh-Century Anglo-Latin Saints' Lives* (Oxford, 1996): J. F. Kelly, *Church Hist.* 66, 560–1; D. Rollason, *History* 83, 125–6

Magennis, Hugh, *Images of Community in Old English Poetry* (Cambridge, 1996): J. Neville, *Envoi* 6, 200–1

Magennis, Hugh, ed., *The Anonymous Old English Legend of the Seven Sleepers* (Durham, 1994): G. Waite, *Parergon* 14.2, 213–16

Marsden, Richard, *The Text of the Old Testament in Anglo-Saxon England* (Cambridge, 1995):
A. N. Doane, *Envoi* 6, 103–13; K. Madigan, *Church Hist.* 66, 792–3

McCully, C. B., and J. J. Anderson, ed., *English Historical Metrics* (Cambridge, 1996): M.
Griffith, *N&Q* 44, 537–8

McReady, William D., *Miracles and the Venerable Bede* (Toronto, 1994): G. H. Brown, *Peritia*
11, 406–9; J. T. Rosenthal, *Speculum* 72, 861–3

Mitchell, Bruce, *An Invitation to Old English and Anglo-Saxon England* (Oxford, 1995): J.
Bately, *Reading Med. Stud.* 22, 110–11; K. Leffel, *Language* 73, 663–4; F. Le Saux, *Le
Moyen Âge* 103, 155–6; Russell Poole, *RES* 48, 75–6; B. Yorke, *Southern Hist.* 17, 115

Morillo, Stephen, ed., *The Battle of Hastings* (Woodbridge, 1996): G. Cronin, *Parergon*
15.1, 241–4

Muir, Bernard, J., ed., *The Exeter Anthology of Old English Poetry* (Exeter, 1994): S. E.
Deskis, *Speculum* 72, 535–7

Newton, Sam, *The Origins of 'Beowulf' and the Pre-Viking Kingdom of East Anglia*
(Woodbridge, 1993): M. J. Franklin, *Southern Hist.* 16, 185–6; T. D. Hill, *Speculum* 72,
541–3; J. S. Ryan, *Parergon* 14.2, 223–4

Nightingale, Pamela, *A Medieval Mercantile Community* (New Haven, CT, 1995): E. Clark,
Albion 29, 79–80; P. Spufford, *AHR* 102, 798–800

Noel, William, *The Harley Psalter* (Cambridge, 1995): J. Backhouse, *AntJ* 77, 423; R.
Gameson, *JEH* 48, 540–2; R. W. Pfaff, *EME* 6, 109–10

North, J. J., *English Hammered Coinage*, 1: *Early Anglo-Saxon to Henry III c. 600–1272*, 3rd
ed. (London, 1994): H. Pagan, *BNJ* 66, 178–9

Orchard, Andy, *The Poetic Art of Aldhelm* (Cambridge, 1994): K. Bate, *MLR* 92, 164; S.
Gwara, *N&Q* 44, 244; M. W. Herren, *Peritia* 11, 403–6; R. Poole, *Parergon* 14.2,
229–31; J. Stevenson, *MÆ* 66, 130–1

Pride and Prodigies (Cambridge, 1995): R. D. Fulk, *RES* 48, 372–3; D. McDougall,
N&Q 44, 245–7; H. Wirtjes, *MÆ* 66, 316–17

Page, R. I., *Runes and Runic Inscriptions* (Woodbridge, 1995): J. E. Cathey, *Speculum* 72,
872–3; P. Cavill, *EME* 6, 110–11; E. G. Stanley, *N&Q* 44, 431

Pasternack, Carol Braun, *The Textuality of Old English Poetry* (Cambridge, 1995): R. S.
Allen, *MLR* 92, 682–5; J. Hill, *MÆ* 66, 314–16; S. Horner, *Envoi* 6, 115–22; H.
Magennis, *ES* 78, 78–83

Pelteret, David A. E., *Slavery in Early Mediaeval England* (Woodbridge, 1995): A. J.
Frantzen, *Albion* 28, 664–6; P. Freedman, *AHR* 102, 435–6; E. Klingelhöfer,
Speculum 72, 208–9; P. Stafford, *History* 82, 125; A. Woolf, *Æstel* 4, 154–60, and
EME 6, 244–5

Pfaff, Richard, W., ed., *The Liturgical Books of Anglo-Saxon England* (Kalamazoo, MI,
1995): E. G. Stanley, *N&Q* 44, 431

Phillips, Derek, and Brenda Heywood, *Excavations at York Minster*, I, ed. M. O. H. Carver
(London, 1995): P. Rahtz, *MA* 40, 319–25

Pirie, E. J. E., *Coins of the Kingdom of Northumbria, c. 700–867 in Yorkshire Collections*
(Llanfyllin, 1996): S. Lyon, *BNJ* 66, 173–6; H. Pagan, *NC* 157, 274–82

Pulsiano, Phillip, *Anglo-Saxon Manuscripts in Microfiche Facsimile*, 2 (Binghamton, NY,
1994): A. Mentzel-Reuters, *DAEM* 53, 302; N. Speirs, *RES* 48, 369–71

Raffel, Burton, and Alexandra Olsen, *Poems and Prose from the Old English* (New Haven, CT, 1998): R. P. Tripp, Jr, *In Geardagum* 18, 67–8

Ramsay, Nigel, Margaret Sparks, and Tim Tatton-Brown, ed., *St Dunstan: his Life, Times and Cult* (Woodbridge, 1992): L. Kornexl, *Anglia* 115, 247–51

Rees, Daniel, ed., *Monks of England: the Benedictines in England from Augustine to the Present Day* (Downside): M. Murphy, *Downside Rev.* 115, 309–12

Remley, Paul G., *Old English Biblical Verse* (Cambridge, 1996): A. Härdelin, *Kyrkohistorisk Årsskrift* 1997, 202–5

Rickett, Robert, *The Anglo-Saxon Cemetery at Spong Hill, North Elmham, Part VII* (Dereham, 1995): C. Scull, *Britannia* 28, 509–10

Roberts, Jane, and Christian Kay, with Lynne Grundy, *A Thesaurus of Old English* (London, 1995): P. Cavill, *Nottingham Med. Stud.* 41, 186–91; R. Dance, *MÆ* 66, 312–13

Robinson, Fred C., *The Editing of Old English* (Oxford, 1994): F. Le Saux, *Le Moyen Âge* 103, 369–71; T. W. Machan, *MLR* 92, 157–9; E. G. Stanley, *N&Q* 44, 431–3; R. P. Tripp, *Reading Med. Stud.* 22, 129–31

The Tomb of Beowulf and Other Essays on Old English (Oxford, 1993): A. Crépin, *EA* 50, 344–5; F. Le Saux, *Le Moyen Âge* 103, 156–8

Robinson, Fred C., and E. G. Stanley, ed., *Old English Verse Texts from Many Sources* (Copenhagen, 1991): P. E. Szarmach, *Peritia* 11, 409–11

Schaefer, Ursula, *Vokalität* (Tübingen, 1992): K. Reichl, *Anglia* 115, 529–32

Schmidt, Gary D., *The Iconography of the Mouth of Hell* (Selinsgrove, PA, Cranbury, NJ, and London, 1995): T. H. Ohlgren, *JEGP* 96, 434–7

Schwyter, J. R., *Old English Legal Language* (Odense, 1996): S. van Romburgh, *Amsterdamer Beiträge zur älteren Germanistik* 48, 247–51

Scragg, D. G., and Paul E. Szarmach, ed., *The Editing of Old English* (Woodbridge, 1994): J. Harris, *Speculum* 72, 1215–16

Smyth, Alfred P., *King Alfred the Great* (Oxford, 1995): M. Altschul, *AHR* 102, 1463–4; B. S. Bachrach, *Jnl of Military Hist.* 61, 363–4; D. R. Howlett, *EHR* 112, 942–4; T. Johnson-South, *Albion* 29, 78–9; T. Shippey, *London Rev. of Books* 22 February, pp. 21–2

Stafford, Pauline, *Queen Emma and Queen Edith: Queenship and Women's Power in Eleventh-Century England* (Oxford): L. Abrams, *TLS* 17 October, p. 33

Stancliffe, Clare, and Eric Cambridge, ed., *Oswald: Northumbrian King to European Saint* (Stamford, 1995): S. Ashley, *EHR* 112, 1226–7; J. Barrow, *DAEM* 53, 278–9; J.-C. Poulin, *Francia* 24, 200–1; S. Trafford, *Med. Life* 6, 36

Stanley, E. G., *In the Foreground: 'Beowulf'* (Woodbridge, 1994): J. Bately, *MLR* 92, 159–60

Stevenson, Jane, *The 'Laterculus Malalianus' and the School of Archbishop Theodore* (Cambridge, 1995): N. Brooks, *EHR* 112, 1227–9; H. Gneuss, *Anglia* 115, 251–5; B. Nassif, *Church Hist.* 66, 790–2; B. Ward, *JEH* 48, 145–8

Stevick, Robert D., *The Earliest Irish and English Bookarts* (Philadelphia, PA, 1994): C. A. Farr, *Albion* 28, 657–8

Sturdy, David, *Alfred the Great* (London, 1995): T. Shippey, *London Rev. of Books* 22 February, pp. 21–2

Sullivan, David, *The Westminster Corridor* (London, 1994): J. Blair, *EHR* 112, 158–9

Surber-Meyer, Nida, *Gift and Exchange in the Anglo-Saxon Poetic Corpus* (Geneva, 1994): E. Tyler, *EME* 6, 248

Swanton, M. J., ed. and trans., *The Anglo-Saxon Chronicle* (London, 1996): T. Shippey, *London Rev. of Books* 20 March, pp. 18–19

Terasawa, Jun, *Nominal Compounds in Old English* (Copenhagen, 1994): D. Donoghue, *Speculum* 72, 571–2

Thompson, Michael, *The Medieval Hall* (Aldershot, 1995): R. Gilchrist, *Albion* 28, 461–2; B. Meeson, *Vernacular Archit.* 27, 116–17

Toswell, M. J., ed., *Prosody and Poetics in the Early Middle Ages* (Toronto, Buffalo and London, 1995): R. S. Allen, *MLR* 92, 938–40; A. L. Klinck, *Eng. Stud. in Canada* 23, 223–5; R. Poole, *RES* 48, 375–6

Trask, Richard M., trans., *Beowulf and Judith* (Lanham, MD): R. P. Tripp, Jr, *In Geardagum* 18, 65–7

Tristram, Hildegard L. C., *Early Insular Preaching* (Vienna, 1995): A. O'Leary, *Peritia* 11, 412; C. D. Wright, *CMCS* 33, 110

Tweddle, Dominic, *et al.*, *Corpus of Anglo-Saxon Stone Sculpture*, 4: *South-East England* (Oxford, 1995): B. C. Raw, *EME* 6, 113–14

von Padberg, Lutz E., *Mission und Christianisierung* (Stuttgart, 1995): R. Meens, *EME* 6, 114–15; H. Rosenberg, *Church Hist.* 66, 325–6

Warner, Peter, *The Origins of Suffolk* (Manchester, 1996): M. Todd, *Albion* 29, 459–60

Webster, Leslie, and Michelle Brown, ed., *The Transformation of the Roman World* (London, 1997): H. Chadwick, *Hist. Today* 47, 53

Welch, Martin, *Discovering Anglo-Saxon England* (University Park, PA, 1992): M. Jones, *Speculum* 72, 576–7

Welna, Jerzy, *English Historical Morphology* (Warsaw, 1996): M. Voss, *Arbeiten aus Anglistik und Amerikanistik* 22, 278–82

Wilcox, Jonathan, ed., *Ælfric's Prefaces* (Durham, 1994): C. Larrington, *RES* 48, 374–5; U. Lenker, *Anglia* 115, 526–8; G. Waite, *Parergon* 14.2, 213–16

Williams, Ann, *The English and the Norman Conquest* (Woodbridge, 1995): F. Barlow, *Southern Hist.* 18, 153–5; G. Garnett, *EHR* 112, 1236–7; J. J. N. Palmer, *History* 82, 291; M. F. Smith, *Albion* 28, 462–3; R. V. Turner, *AHR* 102, 798

Wilson, David, *Anglo-Saxon Paganism* (London, 1992): E. James, *Med. Life* 2 (1995), 34

Wright, Charles D., *The Irish Tradition in Old English Literature* (Cambridge, 1993): D. F. Melia, *Speculum* 72, 584–5; H. L. C. Tristram, *ASNSL* 234, 136–8

Yorke, Barbara, *Wessex in the Early Middle Ages* (Leicester 1995): H. R. Loyn, *Southern Hist.* 18, 152–3